AN UNEXPECTED CODDIWOMPLE

THE STORY OF A FATHER'S SUDDEN DEATH,
A BOX OF WWII LETTERS,
AND A DAUGHTER'S LIFE TRANSFORMED

LORETTO M. THOMPSON

W. Brand Publishing
NASHVILLE, TENNESSEE

j.brand@wbrandpub.com
W. Brand Publishing
www.wbrandpub.com

Cover Painting: The Ditching ©2000 Gil Cohen. All Rights Reserved.
Cover Design: Kevin Opp Design

An Unexpected Coddiwomple / Loretto M. Thompson. —1st ed.
Available in Hardcover, Paperback, Kindle, and eBook formats.
Hardcover ISBN: 978-1-950385-12-6
Paperback ISBN: 978-1-950385-10-2
eBook ISBN: 978-1-950385-11-9
Library of Congress Control Number: 2019943865

Dedication

To my mother and my fathers,

Frank and Paul

"Letters are among the most significant memorial

a person can leave behind them."

– Johann Wolfgang von Goethe

TABLE OF CONTENTS

AUTHOR'S NOTE

Before you join me on my coddiwomple, there are a few things I would like you to bear in mind as you read my father's letters. They are as follows:

At the time the letters were written, my father was twenty-two years old, although, to me he seems older.

These letters were written in the 1940s, at the height of a worldwide conflict, and at a time where individuals were frequently referenced by their nationality. In most instances, these references are not, nor are they meant to be, derogatory in nature, with the possible exception of the enemy. Even so, I found myself a bit uncomfortable with these references as they are no longer used. His letters were written almost 80 years ago. We've come a long way since then. I mention this so you are not surprised when you come upon them. I hope when you encounter them you bear this in mind and attribute them to a sign of the times—possibly the influence of immigrant grandparents, as most immigrants were referred to by their nationality—and grateful that times have changed. I truly believe he meant no harm, since many of the men he refers to by their nationality were also his best pals.

In an effort to keep the letters in their purest form, very little editing was done. As a result, you may encounter unique spelling and grammar, turns of phrase, punctuation, and language that appears incorrect. Some seem to be his attempt at humor, some are old English spellings—both sets of grandparents emigrated from the UK (England and Ireland), which may have influenced his choice of words and phrases—and some are simply slang used in the 1940s. I felt adding *sic* next to each one would become distracting; therefore, I have left most of them in their original state. You will encounter words such as to-morrow, tho, youse, altho, week-end, till, asparagrass, and numerous incorrectly spelled words used in rhyming. There are also many abbreviations; therefore I have added a glossary in the back of the book for your reference.

Finally, remember that practically every letter was written to his mother, brother, and dog. The things he shares with them surprised me; they may surprise you as well. I believe this is a testimony to how close they were as a family.

With these things in mind, I hope you enjoy our stories.

PROLOGUE

The death of a parent inevitably changes the way we view our lives. I was quite young when my father died. I'm undecided as to whether having known a parent for years and then losing them is more or less heartbreaking than losing a parent when you're too young to remember them, when you've had no chance to develop a relationship with them. Whenever I consider this, I usually conclude that they are equally devastating.

To say I've missed my father my entire life begs the question: How do you miss someone you've never known? I have a few memories of him, each precious to me for a different reason. One is of sitting on the sink in the bathroom while he was shaving using a brush and cup with soapy foam, him stirring it, putting it on his face and then placing a dollop of foam on my nose. Another is of getting the dreaded brush for pushing my two-year old brother off the chair and then lying about it. The punishment was more about the lie than the actual pushing, I learned much later from my mother. I also remember he had this little rhyme he made up for me: Loretto Marie is the girl for me. These few random memories are not much to hang onto for a lifetime, but they are truly all I have. These, and the memory of the last time I saw my father.

It was on Christmas Eve 2003, after decades with no significant recollection of my father ever being alive, that my mom surprised all of us with a gift set of four VHS tapes. Apparently while my older brother was recuperating at her house from an injury earlier that year, she'd given him a "project" to keep him occupied. He was given boxes of 8 mm film reels and his job was to splice them together in chronological order, so they could be taken to the video place and transferred to VHS. It was the most remarkable gift. The movies had been filmed from as far back as 1956 up to the 1970s when my mom gave up movie-making. The reels totaled 5,000 feet.

Watching those movies was the first time I remember seeing my father alive. He was laughing, dancing, eating, drinking, smoking, walking, talking, cooking . . . he was living. There was no sound on the movies of course, so I never heard his voice, but I certainly saw him and he was very much alive. As exciting as it was to see, it was also sad because I had no feelings toward him whatsoever. He was just someone I knew about, but not someone I knew. He was quite entertaining though: dancing at parties; cooking at picnics; he was at their wedding; on their honeymoon; at the christenings of most of us; on vacations; and then, just as suddenly as he left us that sunny day in June 1965, he was gone from the movies too.

2

It was only natural to be curious about him, to wonder what he was like in general, his personality, his disposition, and if I'd inherited any of his traits. I wondered about his feelings toward things going on in the world, family, faith, friendship; what he dreamt of for his life and whether or not his dreams had been fulfilled in his short forty-four years. He was so young when he died, yet he had contributed so much in his brief life. This was how I conditioned myself to cope with losing him. I told myself he must have gotten all his work done on earth early in his life, and the Lord took him back home because his work was finished. Though I did not like His decision, who was I to argue with God?

In the years following his death, I'd occasionally meet people who had known my father; I can remember listening to them tell of all these wonderful things about him. What a caring and thoughtful person he was. How his generosity knew no limits. How much he loved all of us. What a great doctor he was, and how he cared for so many people. The praise was endless. I also remember becoming very angry internally that those strangers had known him when I never did. I was angry that they had been able to spend time with him when he hadn't been able to spend any time with me. They knew all these things about him that I never knew, and he was my father. It seemed very unfair to me.

It was 1997 when I finally came to terms with my anger, right around the time personal-development courses were starting to peak. I had attended a seminar hoping to better understand why I never seemed to form lasting relationships with the men I dated. The seminar walked us through different ages in our lives, specific ages at which any sort of traumatic occurrence could potentially derail certain aspects of personal development in our adult lives. One of those ages was four years old. Throughout the seminar, I uncovered a pattern I had never seen before. From my perspective, all the men I'd ever loved had left me. It may have been my own doing, or theirs, or out of anyone's control, but for whatever reason, my relationships never seemed to endure for long. During the exercises I traced back all my loves—first through my adult relationships, including the soon-to-end relationship with Pop Ott, who would die at age ninety six the following month; then further back to my Grandpa; and eventually ending, or beginning, with my father—and I realized that for almost fifty years I had never truly grieved his death.

After the seminar, I decided to visit the cemetery and have it out with him. It was a rainy, cold, and gray Saturday; ideal weather for a cemetery visit. I'm not sure how I managed it; after all, I'd only been there occasionally since his death and never really paid much attention to where he was located since my mother had always led the way. Somehow, I managed to find his headstone. I still cannot explain what happened to me that day. All I remember is that I succumbed to the deepest sorrow I'd ever felt in my life, sorrow that erupted from so deep within me that it frightened me as it poured out and was peppered with a form of uncontrollable anger. There I was, alone in a cemetery, on a rainy Saturday, yelling at my father for dying and leaving me, crying inconsolably. All the anger I had buried for almost five decades came pouring out. Then, just as quickly as it had begun, it ended. Like a switch was turned off.

Altogether it lasted no more than ten minutes. I felt exhausted but oddly much lighter in spirit too. Later that day as I tried to sort out the whole experience in my mind, it occurred to me that most likely the feelings that had erupted represented the grieving of a four-year-old girl who had lost her father; short in duration yet dramatic in expression. My anger with him disappeared that day, in much the same way the encounters with people who had known him had disappeared many years earlier. Once again I was back to wondering about him, until one spring afternoon in 2014 when everything changed forever.

THE CATCHER

1965

It was late in the afternoon when the expectant mother met the two men in suits at the front door. One of the men instinctively positioned himself behind her. The man in front of her avoided making eye contact. He cleared his throat, swallowed, raised his red, swollen eyes to meet hers and said, "He's gone." The woman collapsed into the arms of the man standing behind her. The woman was my mother. The man who caught her was my Uncle Harry. The date was Friday, June 25, 1965.

———

The day was superb for springtime, with the temperatures approaching 80 degrees, a gentle wind, plenty of sunshine, and no clouds in sight; definitely not a day for six children under the age of eight to learn about death. As the northerly breeze blew with just enough strength to send the delicate scents of spring frolicking between yards and into the open windows of our home, nestled on the quaint residential island hugging the shores of the Straits of Niagara, that perfect day may have been described as unforgettable. For all of us, it was.

The day before had been Friday, report-card day for my older sister; her first. As we sat around the breakfast table I remember my father telling her that he was "going to see that report card today, no matter what." In the afternoon Missy Buhr, our babysitter, had come over to watch us so my mother could take the boys for haircuts. It had seemed like an ordinary day, but there was nothing about it that would ever be remembered as ordinary. Before my mom returned home with the boys, all this company started coming to our house. Once she got home, there was a lot of talking, and then we saw two men coming up the front walk. We were shuffled into the playroom and the door was closed. My older brother was supposed to be with us, but for some reason he was in the living room just off the front foyer. What he saw that day has stayed with him his entire life.

———

The headline in Saturday's paper read: "Physician Collapses, Dies at 44." The article went on to explain that our father, Dr. Frank G. Thompson, 44, a leading internist in Niagara Falls and a member of the staff of both Mount St. Mary's Hospital and Memorial Hospital had died Friday afternoon after being stricken in Memorial Hospital with an apparent heart attack.

Included in the article was a brief timeline of his life. He was born in Buffalo, but lived in Niagara Falls most of his life and graduated from Niagara Falls High School in 1939. From there he had attended Niagara University from 1941—1943, and that during World War II he served with the Army Air Corps as a radio operator in Europe. Upon his discharge from the military in 1946, he attended the University of Buffalo Medical School, where he received his medical degree in June 1950. He served his internship for several years at E.J. Meyer Memorial Hospital, in Buffalo (currently Erie County Medical Center), and eventually took up residency there as an internist. In 1956 he joined a medical partnership in Niagara Falls.

The article then listed all of us who had been left behind; our mom; three daughters; three sons; and a brother, Harry T. Thompson of Niagara Falls. The details of the funeral services were provided as well; Monday at St. John de LaSalle Church. Finally, friends were told they may call at the family residence. The burial would be in Riverdale Cemetery.

Later Saturday afternoon we found ourselves in the playroom once again with Missy Buhr. All the curtains were closed. I remember being told not to look out the window. However, like most mildly disobedient children would, I wanted to see what was outside those windows that we weren't supposed to see. That's when I saw them. All the people lined up outside our house. The line went down our long sidewalk, across the front of the house, and down the street. They were all dressed up, like we were, in "good" clothes, not "play" clothes. We only wore these clothes on special days and to church. Something special had to be happening. Many years later I realized what was going on that day.

Suddenly, the door opened and our mother came into the playroom. We were told to come with her. Missy Buhr kept hold of the two youngest and we followed her into the living room. Grandma and Grandpa were there, and Maimie Ott and Pop Ott, Uncle Harry and Aunt Mary Ellen, Aunt Alice and Uncle Art, and some other people I didn't know. There were flowers everywhere. We followed our mother to a big box with shiny material that was in the place where the couch used to be.

"Daddy has gone to heaven. If you want to, you can say goodbye to him," my mother told us.

I remember getting up on a little step that was sitting next to the big box. When I looked inside, there was Daddy! But he was sleeping.

"Can I touch him?" I asked.

"Yes," my mother answered. For some reason I decided not to. I wish I had.

After that day, we didn't have a Daddy anymore. Our new baby was born a few weeks later. We had another little brother. That made seven of us and our mom. In those early years, I always wondered if my baby brother and my father had passed each other when he was on his way to heaven and my brother was on his way to our house. Funny the things you think of when you're young and unknowing, but if it had been possible, it would have been great because the two never met.

Growing up, I don't remember ever questioning why he was gone. He was just gone. I do remember thinking he was watching us though, especially when we were at church. There was this canopy above the crucifix at the front of the church and I used to think he was up there, on that canopy, invisible, watching us. I suppose I thought that's where heaven was. Several years ago they remodeled our church and removed the canopy. I'm glad they didn't do it when I was young. Where would my father have hidden to watch us? All those years and I never really asked about his dying; it was just understood by all of us -we didn't have a father; he had died when we were young. We knew he was a doctor and was loved by many, and that he had loved all of us. Other than what we'd been told about him, the memories our mother shared with us, and very few memories of our own, we had no connection to him whatsoever.

At some point growing up I remember being told by our mother that our father had been a radio operator on a B-17 in WWII. When we'd asked about the crew photo that hung in the boys' bedroom, we'd often hear the story about how he'd written his mother every day when he was in the war. It was a story that clearly illustrated his love of family and one that my older sister took to heart when she wrote our younger brother every day when he was serving in Iraq. In today's world, we communicate so easily. Send someone a text, or shoot them an email. We take it for granted, how easy it is to connect with each other. To sit down and write an actual letter today is a rarity. Just the concept of writing your family a letter every day at age twenty-two, let alone while training to go to war, shows a level of dedication and effort we're no longer accustomed to. Yet, in 1944, it was the only affordable way to stay connected with family and friends, it was a soldier's lifeline to home, and it served as a reminder to them of what it was they were fighting for. Returning home to their loved ones was their reward for making it through the world's most deadly conflict in history.

THE BOX

Present Day

Courageous and faithful are the two words that best describe my mom. The times both of these qualities were evident in my lifetime are too many to count. I think about it sometimes, how in 1965 she was widowed at age thirty-five. To lose the love of her life so suddenly, to be left with six children and eight months pregnant with her seventh, I cannot imagine how she managed to keep it all together. Single moms were not common in 1965, and it's possible the relatives were subconsciously divvying up the children as was the norm in the day, assuming she would never tackle raising seven children alone. But that's precisely what she did.

As an adult, I came to realize the enormity of her loss, and I would ask her how she managed to cope. She would just say, "I had all of you to keep me busy, and by the end of the day I was just too exhausted to think about it." Of course, with none of us really having any recollection of our father, any memories she shared with us were cherished. All told, she had eleven years with him; we all had less of course, but the youngest, had zero.

"Your father wrote his mother every day when he was in the war," my mother told me. The number of times I'd heard this story escapes me, but I never tired of hearing it. We were at lunch and somehow had gotten onto the topic of World War II.

"I have all the letters in the basement," she said, "I always thought I would read them someday, but now I could never read them." The resignation in her voice was painful to hear. My mom suffered from a visual double whammy: macular degeneration and glaucoma.

"I'll read them to you," I offered. "We'll read them after church on Sundays, when we're alone and it's quiet." Her face lit up.

"Oh, that would be perfect," she said. "They're in a box in the basement. I'm not sure what condition they're in." I told her it didn't matter; we'd take a look and see how it went. That was May 3, 2014.

Of all the times I had heard that story, I never knew the letters still existed. At eighty-five years old, my mother continues to surprise me. Sure, her memory repeats itself but the reruns of her stories always summon welcome imagery in my mind, no matter how many times I hear them. Apparently my grandmother had saved all the letters he'd written to her, and when my mother and father moved into our family home fifty-five years ago, the letters were among the treasures they brought with them from their first flat in his childhood home on 9th Street in Niagara Falls. Having lived in our home my entire life, I thought I had a pretty good idea of its contents, but to my surprise an unknown treasure had been unearthed.

After church on the Sunday following the revelation about the existence of the war letters, I ventured into the basement to find the box. I brought it upstairs, dusted it off, opened it, and caught my breath—but not because of the dust. There, lovingly preserved for over seventy years, were hundreds of letters, in perfect condition. I had no idea. Of course my mother did say he wrote every day, but I thought it was an exaggeration. I was wrong.

What started off as a loving gesture to read to my visually impaired mother ultimately became the impetus behind my next five years of coddiwompling. As we read the letters, the story might have been that of any soldier at the time, but in reading them, I experienced the unexpected gift of getting to know my father, to finally hear his voice through his written words. Though he was in his early twenties, his writing answered many of my questions. He wrote about family, faith, and friends. He shared his feelings about the war, society, what he wished for his life, and because the letters were written to his mother, they were intentionally light and entertaining so as not to cause worry at home. Added to this unimaginable opportunity to finally get to know my father was the unexpected gift of watching my mother fall in love with him all over again.

In time, as I read his letters, I found I was growing to love him too. That's when I decided I needed to type his letters so my siblings could experience the same connection to him I was experiencing, and that is precisely what happened. In the fifty years that had passed since his death, we never really talked about him among ourselves. This, I now realize, was an absolute shame. Sadly, since he was a stranger to us, we somehow managed to unintentionally minimize his life. That is no longer the case. These days we talk about him frequently. We laugh, and speak of him as though we've known him all our lives. How amazing it is that someone who's been dead for over fifty years could be so alive through letters written twenty years before his death . . . letters that led me to people and places and a past I had given up on knowing.

FRANK'S PEOPLE

It's reasonable to accept I would know little about my father's family and friends, or even his life, having never known him. So, in reading his letters, many questions about his past came up, which further fed my hunger to know more about him. Of course, the most obvious person to ask was my mother; however, these letters were written ten years before they met, so like me, she also knew very little about this part of his life. Couple that with the fact that there was an eight year age difference between them, and she would have been fourteen years old when he wrote his first letter, and the likelihood of them being aware of each other would have been low.

When I'd ask her about some of the people he mentioned in his letters, she would tell me what she knew, but in truth, that was very little. She had been brought up in an era where women did not pry into the lives of men. Her position was, "If he wanted me to know, he would have told me." In today's environment of "too much information," this did not make sense to me, but that was her stance in the 1950s and with no other living relatives who knew my father, I was left on my own to uncover what I could of the people who had been central to his early life.

I'd like you to meet some of them now as they will pop in and out of his letters; it would have been helpful to me if I had I known a bit about them as I read the letters. You may choose to read these descriptions now, or you may simply come back to them as they crop up in the letters; either will work. However, I've chosen to share them with you now to provide you with a familiarity I would have been grateful to have beforehand, instead of having to track them down as his story unfolded. Allow me to introduce you to Frank's "people."

THE TENTH-STREET THOMPSONS. Frank and Harry's father, Harry Theophilus, was the first son of Alan William (Gramps) and Ada Thompson born in the United States. Both Alan and Ada were born in England though they married in Australia. The family emigrated to the U.S.in 1890 with their second and third children, the first having died shortly after his birth. Upon arrival, they settled in Jersey City, New Jersey where two years later they welcomed their first child born in America, Frank's father Harry Theophilus. In 1904, Alan and Ada, and their now seven children moved into a single family home on Tenth Street in Niagara Falls, New York

Harry Theophilus, Frank's father, attended Niagara Falls High School, from where he graduated in 1909. His whereabouts are unknown until the birth of his first son, Harry Thomas, in Buffalo where, like his father, he had a successful career in the insurance business. Marriage records indicate he married

Barbara Agnes Thompson on November 15, 1916. In 1924, he left his position as deputy superintendent at Metropolitan Life in Buffalo to accept a promotion to Niagara Falls District Manager. He and Barbara, together with their two boys Harry and Frank (born in Buffalo in 1921), returned to Niagara Falls and moved into a double family home on Chilton Avenue. Harry flourished in his role as manager of the Niagara Falls district. All seemed to be going well for Harry and his little family until May of 1928. Young Harry was nine and a half years old and Frank had just turned seven two months prior when, at age thirty-six, their father succumbed to pneumonia after being ill for only one week.

Barbara, referred to by names in my father's letters such as Mother, Little Babry, Contessa, Tessa, the Mater, and other terms of endearment, was born in 1892 in New Philadelphia, Ohio, to immigrant parents from Ireland and England. She was the eldest of her siblings, which included one sister, Mary Ellen (Maime) and one brother, Frank George. City directories indicate the family had moved to Niagara Falls, New York, sometime before 1918, with all three children eventually marrying and calling Niagara Falls their home. After her husband's death, Barbara moved into the two-family home owned by her parents on Ninth Street, where she would remain until her death in 1955, the year my mother and father met.

Harry Thomas, Frank's brother, graduated from Niagara Falls High School in 1937, and continued his education at Niagara University, which he later graduated from with a degree in accounting. After working his way through school as a clerk in accounts payable for the Carborundum Company, Harry left "Carbo" after over ten years of service to pursue a lifelong career in hospital accounting and finance. In 1941 Harry's number came up on the draft list in the Niagara Falls Gazette. Prone to epileptic seizures, Harry did not pass the Army physical, and therefore did not serve—at least not in the military, though he certainly served at home. In September, 1958 he married Mary Ellen Fritz from Niagara Falls. His brother Frank was married and practicing medicine in Niagara Falls by then, treating patients at both Niagara Falls Memorial Hospital and Mt. St. Mary's Hospital, where Harry was employed as business office manager and accountant. I often wonder if my father stopped to see his brother after completing his rounds at St. Mary's on the day he died.

Mike. An integral part of the family, Mike was a spry, black cocker spaniel, so loved by Frank that he was included in practically every letter he wrote home from the war. Often lovingly referred to as "de la Spuzier," Mike had a tight grasp on Frank's heart, so much so that he would name his second son Michael.

Barbara's sister Mary Ellen, **Aunt Maime** to Harry and Frank, married John Robert Perry, two years before Barbara's marriage to Harry. Mary Ellen and J. Robert, as he was known, had five children, two of whom also served in the Army Air Corps, Richard (Dick) and Bobby (J. Robert, Jr.). One of five children,

Dick Perry was the same age as Harry, born in 1918. He presumably enlisted shortly after the attack on Pearl Harbor and trained as a pilot in the Army Air Corps. He was assigned to the European Theatre of Operation in 1944, where he flew a converted B-24 called a C-109, which he believed was "nothing more or less than a big gas tanker. Treacherous as hell." Bobby, eight years younger than Dick, would also enlist to be a pilot upon turning eighteen years old in 1944, but would never see combat as the war was winding down by that time, and the need for pilots was waning.

Franklin E. Ott, known to me my whole life as Pop Ott, and to my father as Coach, was born in 1901 and, grew up in Greigsville, New York. Upon graduation, he pursued his education in physical sciences in Geneseo. In 1924, he accepted a position in Dansville as the high school physical director. By December of 1927 he announced his engagement to Dorothy Fedder, also from Greigsville. Six months later, on July 16, 1928 they were married at St. Patrick's church in their hometown, with Franklin's only sibling, Alonzo, arriving from New York City to be his best man. That same year, the board of education in Niagara Falls hired eight new teachers, including Franklin Ott (Coach), who would serve the city as physical training instructors in their grade schools. Franklin and Dorothy moved to Niagara Falls, and rented a flat on Seventh Street. At the end of the 1929—1930 school year, in which he was a teacher at South Junior High School, Franklin was appointed staff of Niagara Falls playgrounds, and responsible for teaching swimming at the boys pools located at the junior high school and Niagara Street. That summer he and Dorothy moved to 454-9th Street, next door to Harry and Frank. Both teachers and with no children of their own, it is conceivable that Franklin and Dorothy took a special interest in the two young boys living next door, especially upon learning they had lost their father less than two years prior. Franklin's relationship with two generations of Thompson's would last until his death almost seventy years later.

Dr. Arthur Muldoon. Art Muldoon was a lifelong resident of Niagara Falls, New York. His family originated in London, Ontario, Canada but they moved to Niagara Falls around the turn of the century. Art was the sixth of seven children and would ultimately marry and settle down in Niagara Falls where he enjoyed a successful medical practice. Art's older sister Loretto Gertrude would also remain in Niagara Falls, eventually marrying Wallace Assema, a Dutch immigrant. Loretto and Wallace had two children, a daughter, Mary Augusta and a son, Thomas. Art was not only family to Loretto and Wallace; he was also their family doctor. Among his many patients was the Harry Theophilous Thompson family. The importance of this connection would not be known for many decades, but it would prove pivotal in Frank's and Mary A.'s lives.

THE MIX-UP

1943

Immediately following the events of December 7, 1941, the city of Niagara Falls mobilized its defenses. As a dominant source of power in the country, as well as a center for chemical manufacturing, the city had been preparing for the possibility of war long before the attacks on Pearl Harbor. Once the U.S. was no longer a neutral bystander of WWII, the relationship with their sister city across the Niagara River grew even stronger as Canada had entered the war in 1939, two years prior to the U.S.

Bell Aerospace was hard at work producing the P-39 Airacobra and eventually the P-63 Kingcobra, which were ultimately sent to the USSR. The chemical warfare plant, while creating harmful gases to be used in warfare, simultaneously created harmful gases affecting the environment, and the lives of Niagara Falls residents. Over the next few years, like many cities across the U.S., Niagara Falls adopted a war-time lifestyle. Rationing, food stamps, Victory Gardens, War Bonds, and black outs became a way of life. Residents saw many of their men off to war, including their mayor, and even many women would join the WACs, driven by a need to contribute more directly to the war effort.

In 1940, a little over a year preceding the events that hurled the U.S. into a war its citizens mostly wanted to avoid, Congress enacted the first peacetime draft in the history of the nation and the Selective Service was instated. At nineteen, my father would have been just under the minimum draft age of twenty-one. However, in November 1942, with the U.S. fully engaged in the war, the draft ages were expanded and the minimum age was dropped to eighteen. In anticipation of the upcoming age change, on September 3, 1942, a now twenty-one-year-old Frank walked out of the headquarters of the Reserve Officers' Training Corps (ROTC) Infantry Unit in Niagara Falls as a member of the Enlisted Reserve Corps of the United States Army. Having enlisted prior to December 5, 1942, ensured that he would not be drafted, therefore removing the uncertainty of the draft board assigning him to wherever they saw a need. Instead of taking a chance waiting out the draft, he joined those who enlisted or "volunteered for induction" before the deadline and therefore was offered the benefit of having some voice as to which branch of service he would enter and in some cases what specialty within his preferred branch.

Military marketing was relentless prior to my father receiving the letter informing him that he was now eligible for shipment with the Army Air Corps. The recruitment for pilots and air crew was unyielding. Posters claiming,

"THERE'S A PLACE FOR YOU ON THIS TEAM," "THE ARMY AIR FORCES WANT YOU," and "A CAREER IN THE AIR AWAITS YOU" were some of the tactics used to entice young men to enlist. U.S. Army Air Corps recruiting trailers played in all the movie houses, tempting young men by telling them "a seat on a B-17 was waiting" for them, and that they could pick up complete information at the box office on their way out of the theatre for their "chance of a lifetime."

—

On January 27, 1944, with an unusually balmy temperature hovering around 45 degrees, my father boarded a train bound for Fort Dix, NJ. The emotions he felt leaving his family and heading off to war will remain a mystery. He was certainly patriotic, as he obviously anticipated serving his country and knew he would be called eventually, especially after joining the ROTC two years prior. Though prepared to serve in some capacity, it appears he wanted to serve his country his way, which was very different from how things ended up.

His original intent upon enlisting was to serve as an Air Corps cadet in the Army Air Forces or AAF; however, at some point he must have learned about the need for men in the Weather Service. No doubt hopeful the schooling required for this specialized role would delay his being shipped overseas, he completed the application. This would have been the perfect strategy had the military not grossly overestimated their need for meteorologists. By the time all the miscommunications took place, the Army had made the decision to cut off applicants. This is where my father's plan fell apart. What follows is my best estimation of how my father ended up reporting for duty on that balmy January afternoon.

As a member of the ROTC, and a student, my father's status was Private, Enlisted Reserve Corps (ERC) unassigned as of January 9, 1943. On that date, he wrote the University of Chicago requesting acceptance into the "B" or Premeteorology course that started on March 1, 1943. In the months preceding his letter, all implications by the military were that there was an overwhelming need for men to fill these positions. Given the demand from other branches and the specific qualifications required for the AAF Weather Service, which my father possessed, men to fill these positions were diminishing quickly and therefore it was reasonable for him to believe there was a pretty good chance his application would be accepted. Accompanying his application was a letter of recommendation from one of his professors stating, "He has a splendid character. He is honest and reliable. I think he is loyal to the United States of America."

War news in January of 1943 signaled a change in the British approach to their efforts against Germany following the Casablanca Conference between President Roosevelt and Prime Minister Churchill. The outcome of this conference was the decision to commence 24/7 destruction on Nazi Germany with the Brits continuing their night bombings and the Yanks commencing the controversial daylight bombings. That January the first B-17 Flying Fortresses and B-24 Liberators began arriving in England as part of the U.S. Eighth Air Force. As my father awaited a response to his letter of the ninth, the RAF was in the throes of night raids that wreaked havoc on German factories and surrounding towns, including the Friedrich Krupp Germaniawerft A.G., which, unknown to my father at the time, would be one of the targets he and his crew would bomb two years later.

It wasn't until April 24 that my father finally received a response from War Department Headquarters of the Army Air Forces Meteorology Procurement Office in Chicago, Illinois; it was not the response he had hoped for. The letter explained that indeed the Meteorology Procurement Office had requested the Adjutant General to call him to duty on January 19, 1943, and assigned him to Hamilton College; however, for some unknown reason the office had never issued the order.

Unable to provide a definitive explanation as to why this never happened, the general indicated that perhaps my father had expressed a Signal Corps or other branch preference upon enlistment, which would have made the meteorology assignment impossible. Further, the general went on to explain that as of January 28, his office was no longer permitted to assign men from the Enlisted Reserve Corps to Meteorology, that all quotas had been met, and that no additional courses were planned. He closed his letter with, "In view of this situation, it is very unlikely that any action will be forthcoming in your case."

Most likely frustrated, my father sent a quick response to this letter inquiring about his chances since he had written prior to the cutoff date. On July 14 he received another correspondence from Chicago. This time he was told that he had been found educationally qualified for pre-meteorology training, and that the voluntary induction authorization papers had actually been issued to him. For whatever reason, this induction was not accomplished or if he was a member of the ERC, the subsequent assignment would not be forthcoming. The general once again explained that since the courses had already commenced, and no additional assignments could be made, his application was being returned.

By now it was late July, 1943, and the British military had reluctantly shifted from their previously moral position of dropping only leaflets on German civilians to relentless bombing raids targeted at the German workforce itself. While this was something Churchill had claimed he would never do, they were forced to acknowledge that if the number of factory workers was reduced in addition to damaging or demolishing the factories, production would be severely crippled or eliminated. Two of Germany's cities suffered the worst consequences of this decision. The first city was Hamburg, where half of the city was destroyed leaving almost half a million people homeless and over 40,000 dead as a result of non-stop day-night-day raids that created the first firestorm of WWII. However, in the second city, the Battle of Berlin would take much more effort, result in many more casualties, and endure much longer.

My father may have had a sense of foreboding upon receipt of the July 14 letter. Clearly the Weather Service was no longer an option, and though he had enlisted to become a pilot, an eventuality of many in the Weather Service, he did not receive any further correspondence from the military about his status until December 11. The letter was from the Army Service Forces in New York City regarding Air Forces Enlisted Reserve. Though as an enlistee he did not receive the standard draftee "Greetings" letter, my father's letter advised him that he had been transferred from the Air Forces Enlisted Reserve for Pre-Meteorology Training to the Air Forces Enlisted Reserve (Air Crew) Training, and that he was now available for shipment to an Air Corps installation for Pre-Aviation Cadet Training. He left Niagara Falls in late January to report for duty at Fort Dix, New Jersey.

FORT DIX, NEW JERSEY

1944

Return Address:
Pvt. F.G. Thompson
A.S.N. 12,107,602
1229 R.C.
Company "C"
Bks. 8
Ft. Dix, N.J.

January 27th, 1:00 PM

Dear Mother and Harry,

Just arrived Trenton. Was delayed when I got off at Quakertown instead of Jenkintown but it proved worthwhile as they grow Grade "A" Red-heads there. Layover for 3 hours. This is a great way to get here and people are still more fun than anybody. All's well and will start for Dix in a few moments.

Love to all, Frank

January 27th

Company C Barracks #8

(But God only knows where we really are at Ft. Dix N.J.)

Dear Mother, Harry and Mike,

Well, here we go again. I am in the barracks at Ft. Dix. Don't send anything to me as yet because I am not completely sure as to where you should send it.

The trip wasn't bad with the exception of my 3 hour "layover" at Jenkintown. My timetable gave Jenkintown as the first stop after I changed at Bethlehem. So when I heard the conductor mutter something with a "town" on the end I assumed I was at my destination. I got on the next train to Jenkintown at 10:56 ~ arrived in Jenkintown at about 12:00. I then took an express to East Trenton and from East Trenton a gasoline car into Trenton. I walked about 3 blocks to the Greyhound terminal and the trip here took about 30-45 minutes into Ft. Dix.

When I arrived the M.P. at the gate asked me if I was just reporting. When I answered in the affirmative he said, "Well, you don't look happy about it."

Thus far all that has happened to me is: I have been checked in; not classified or taken aptitude test. I have received 2 duffle bags and a rain coat but as yet no uniform ~ I guess that comes to-morrow. I have been assigned to a barracks and received my bedding—3 blankets and 2 sheets.

As I see it now, I will remain here at the reception center until I am assigned to Air Cadet training. I may not even receive basic training here. How long I will be here I cannot tell but when I have been here 21 days I get a 3 day pass–I probably won't be here long enough to get the pass.

The only reason I can get time to write you now is that since we have not (all 7 of us E.R.C.s) received any uniforms, we are regarded as civilians and get all privileges before those in uniform. This won't last long believe me. But at any rate we went into the mess first.

We had beef stew, with carrots and white potatoes–sweet potato on the side–2 pats of butter–biscuit–apple and celery salad–pumpkin pie–boiled cabbage and hot chocolate.

It is served in a tin pan with 6 divisions and you get a knife, fork, table spoon to manipulate with. We didn't march far to the barracks but boy was I sorry I lugged all that stuff with me. Oh well–live and learn. Thus far I haven't taken the shaft too much but this is the calm before the storm. To-morrow we will probably slide into some of those nice details.

The place is large enough to have 3 or 4 separate bus lines–that is bus routes.

Looks great so far but I think that now I better get someone to show me how to make my bed.

Tell the Otts I already have my money belt on–be good!

Love, Frank

10:45P

Since I wrote above I have been completely outfitted G.I. - what I mean. I am going to have a terrible time keeping track of clothes because you just hang them up in the barracks bag at the foot of bed and have to trust the honor of the other fellows. You can write me at the address on the envelope but don't send anything but letters until I try to get some idea of how long I'll be here from the classification officer to-morrow.

I also got my shots in arm and since lights are out at 10 bells, I'd better close, Frank

January 28th, 2:20 PM

Dear Mother,

I well realize anything I have written so far has been poorly written. I am afraid most what I will write will be the same because up to now and throughout my "processing" I think that I will have very little time to sit down and do a good job.

Please tell those whom you see who expect to hear from me that time now is very precious and damn well taken up.

I guess I can bore you with the G.I. routine. I think you will be interested and I have really nothing else to talk about although when I write to other people I guess I will have to forget about it because most of them have gone through that song before.

Last night we went to bed at 10 bells only to arise at 5:45 this morning. Formation in the company street is at 6:00, then we have a half an hour to straighten things up in the barracks and then breakfast.

The meals are O.K.–good wholesome food and you can go back for more only you MUST eat all you take.

As you know, here we rub shoulders with everything and anything but my first impression is that most of them seem to be a damn good lot. We're all in the same boat. Few of the fellows here have been here longer than a month. The vast majority have been here from 1-3 days or a week. Everyone helps the other guy and the administration is tempered so that although you get pushed and there is no coddling–not too much is expected of you if you have any initiative and use your head.

I can hardly pass judgment upon how well I like it. Of course I have the Air Corps (of course I can't be absolutely sure until I am interviewed tomorrow). There seem to be a lot of married men here. I would say that the morale among these is not too good. After they get classified and assigned to some type of unit, they get about 13 weeks basic training–I think they get some special (little) training and then are available for shipment. These fellows have little to look forward to.

Our regular uniforms around here are "fatigues." What a sloppy outfit. You never saw a bunch so sloppy and dirty looking. The only thing I can do is to bathe and shave daily and wash up underwear and socks daily. The fatigues will not dry overnight in the barracks and though you washed them out at night they would not be dry in the morning. You cannot leave them out later than morning because of inspection.

This morning I took a physical. This afternoon I thought we would take our I.Q. test but no, we were sent back to our barracks.

I sat down with the idea that I had a lot of time and could write a long letter. I no sooner got started when it seems that there is to be an inspection to-morrow and we had to pitch in and get the barracks in shape. We wiped down all the posts and rafters–shelves–window sills. We swept and mopped the floor–learned how and then made our beds G.I. style. After that I sat down and started to write when some joker yells attention and a second Looy breezes up the stairs. He caught a couple fellows sleeping and then gave me and another fellow hell for writing letters when we should have been cleaning the barracks for inspection to-morrow. We then had a fire drill and formation. I didn't know that we were supposed to be busy until chow at 4:15 (or at least look busy).

Sacrilegiously I took pleasure in eating meat today–I don't think I would have but we were late for chow at 11:15 and meat was about all that was left.

Up to this point I have been having a good time and can honestly say I am enjoying myself but wait till I start to get the dirty end of the stick–then I'll probably change my tune. It's really an experience if you have a sense of humor and something to look forward to, but if anything should happen and I don't get to the Air Corps you will have one sad son on your hands. Don't pray I don't get in the Air Corps because if I don't—ASTP is practically closed and O.C.S. is closed so if I miss I will probably be out of the country in 6 or 8 months.

I sure hope my two pals are keeping in good shape—and that you are not tight on funds until we can get that cheque cashed.

If I put you down as a dependent you would get immediately a $50 gift from the government but I'm afraid if I do, it would jeopardize my chances in the A.C.

Well, be good you two and I wish I was having that beer with you tonight but I must get down and get my shower and shave now so, so long till tomorrow.
Love, Frank

January 29th , 8:45 PM

Dear Mother, Harry and Mike,

I guess youse are the only guys I have written so far so I may have to forget you when I write to-morrow and send out some cards to all the people who have been so nice to me.

One of the most important items today was that I finally crapped. I was getting worried but when I was on the john at last, I got a call over the P.A. system and didn't really get started. Later though I finished and then once again so I guess I'm O.K.

I took my I.Q. test today but don't know the results. I won't know till my interview on Monday. I also took out 10 Gs worth of insurance. Enclosed please find duplicate of contract.

So far it has been a cinch but I dread the day (probably Monday) when I finish my processing and then unless I am assigned to special detail I will get the "shit" jobs. I have already got my eye open for a soft job—I'm learning fast.

I got my traveling pay today—$21.90 so send me that registered letter in a hurry so I can register the endorsed cheques and return a 20 buck bill with it.

How is the money situation? I kind of worry about it.

I haven't received anything from you yet, but I suppose that is to be expected because I understand that the mail is slow getting out of here.

Tonight two other fellows and I went to the PX and had a few beers—great stuff! Pabst on draught even if it is only 3.2.

I wish I could describe some of the fellows I am with but I'm afraid it would take too long. Three or four or five of us have stuck together pretty well and have been having a good time. One I think is Jewish—35—school teacher. One is an expert on ball bearings, another "Harwick" is a Catholic—we go to Kirk together to-morrow. These guys are more mature, married, but I find they like to do what soldiering we have to do first and "Goldbrick" afterwards. The younger squirts just gripe and fart around.

Well, I guess I'd better get going now. I have a hot Pinochle game coming up for about 20 minutes before lights out. I love and miss you two, so take good care of youse and Mike.
Love Frank

January 30th, 3:00 PM

Dear Mother, Harry and Mike,

Well, how are things at old 450 ½ these days? Today being Sunday we went to church at 7 bells. You never saw a place so jammed in all your life. The middle aisle was completely jammed. The altar itself was packed with men and small rooms on both sides of the altar were packed. The Chaplain told us that they have Novenas on Tuesdays so I guess perhaps I can make it.

Also because today was Sunday we had particularly good chow—celery, quarter of a chicken, dressing, sweet potato, bread and butter, creamed lima beans and corn, ice cream and coffee. I'm afraid I didn't get enough chicken but I'm learning to give the cook that "come hither" look and I won't walk away without being completely "gutted" again.

This afternoon they took us out to drill. Of course the secret to the whole situation is to keep us busy. If we are not busy we are writing for something or are restricted to quarters and most of us have found that when restricted, if we clean up the place, we accomplish our responsibility and pass the time. None of us get weepy if we keep busy. I did O.K. at drill. They took out the fellows who had had it before and drilled us separately.

About keeping the place clean. This is the way they work it. Six of the fellows are orderlies and it is their particular responsibility to see that all beds are made up to the crease and the barracks itself, including latrine, are spotless. After a fellow has been here 21 days he gets a pass from Sat. noon to Monday morning at 5 bells. If the barracks does not pass inspection we are "Gigged"—that means restricted to barracks and have a "G.I." party. This comprises the whole personnel of the barracks with scrub brushes on their knees. Also all fellows who are eligible for "passes" do not get them. So—the fellows who have been here longest boot the rest of us in the tail and we try to make everyone pitch in and do his share.

Incidentally, when I was signing up for insurance yesterday I had an opportunity to look at my Army record. There was recorded there, in the record, of my transfer, so I guess I'll get in the Air Corps although I won't be absolutely sure until I interview a classification officer. I think I'll get this interview to-morrow.

Lew Harwick, one of my buddies, and I just finished the 2 plain Nestles bars. We have been smoking quite a bit. Cigarettes are a soldiers best friend and the carton of Camels Dorshel gave me sure have been a Godsend.

I'll admit I was completely all wet about some things you thought I should get before I left. Please try to send me before next Thursday if possible (insure it):

One of those aprons with a plastic soap dish in it. Room for razor, toothbrush, tooth paste, and shaving cream only—as small and simple as possible.

The cheapest and flimsiest slippers you can find.

I think I have everything else I'll need for a while. Please believe when I say I want compact and small things I mean just that because I have no room for anything else.

I am going to try to send packing box home as soon as possible because if they see it during inspection I'll get the business. Did you get the Army package with my clothes in it? I've been trying to wear my own underwear and use my own handkerchiefs and towels because then I'll have all Army issue clean and intact when clothes inspection comes around.

I'm afraid I won't be able to wear the wing-tipped shoes but I'm going to keep them and try to get away with it.

8:50

This evening we went out and had a few beers—had a shower and shave (and the washing). Before we came back we saw part of a stage show through the Recreation Hall window. Don't let anyone kid you about these service shows. You line up 2 hours before showing time if you want to get in. Frankly, it's not worth it. I think I'd rather use my time keeping clean because it's such an essential to your health.

Well, I squeezed a letter in to youse guys today but to-morrow I have to write to Granddad and the Otts to say nothing of wee Ann—please be good and keep well. Yours with love, Frank

February 2nd, 1:20 PM

Dear Mother, Harry and Mike,

I got your letter this morning. It came just in time to save me making a phone call to the Falls sometime this afternoon. I was beginning to think that someone was ill or something.

I didn't write at all yesterday because I worked like a beaver. I got up at 4:00 AM to report for K.P. I was assigned a job of keeping 8 coal stoves going. It was one of the dirtiest jobs I have ever done and now my one and only fatigue uniform is filthy and I dare not wash it for fear it won't get dry in time for the next formation. I worked like hell to finish my job in K.P. by 5:30. We had to take all stoves apart and clean them before we could leave. Immediately after, I got to the barracks to wash and then reported for a Fireman's job. In order to get the job I had to work from 6-12 last night—so "my day" from 4 AM until 12 the following night was well taken up.

I got this Fireman's job on the night shift so that I can be on the alert in the day time if anything should or can be done about getting me back in the Air Corps.

Harry will never believe this but another fellow and I fire 5 furnaces of five barracks. We also have to keep hot water furnaces going and water temperature up.

This job is known as a "Goldbricking" job however on these cold nights you really shovel the coal, but the big feature of it is that, although I have to report for all formations, I am practically excused from other details and probably no more K.P.

I told you before that 3 or 4 of us had been paling around together. You'd be surprised how each has his little tale of woe—how quickly men cleave to one another and how we all look out for one another. One of the fellows has left already. It's too bad, he had more pep and life than the rest of us put together but now the 3 remaining are all Firemen and we are waiting to be shipped out.

A little more about my chances for the Air Corps. It was exceedingly unfortunate that Major Campbell transferred me back to the E.R.C. from the Air Corps. This place is gutted with men trying, and most of them merely waiting, to get in the A.C. Although the Sergeant in charge told me he would write Sergeant Cuff in Buffalo to get my record, I sort of feel that only an act of God will get me in now.

About an hour after I read your letter I saw Jerry O'Hara in a formation. He was still in his civvies. I couldn't talk to him—just yelled at him. He looks fine. I'm sure he and Bob (haven't seen him yet) will get in the A.C. easily and probably long before I do if I'm that lucky.

It looks as though I'll be here some time—the Sergeant in charge of the A.C. recruiting told me to sit tight and I would hear from him when he gets my records from Buffalo. This is the 1st chance I've had to write since I wrote Major Campbell in New York so I think I'll write Sergeant Cuff immediately and get copies of my record myself.

Please tell all those grand people that I will write as soon as I get time to but I'm trying to get myself straightened out now. I'm including a little booklet which I feel Harry will be needing—maybe Mike too!
Love, Frank

February 3rd, 5:30 PM

Dear Mother, Harry and Mike,

Just time to write a little. I thought I'd better let you know that all's well.

Felt like a Hot Rock today when I got mail in both mail calls. One letter from Harry—his second note and John's letter.

Have to report for formation now so be good.
Hurriedly with love, Frank

February 4th, 12:15 PM

Dear Harry, Mother and Mike,

Sorry I could only drop you a short line yesterday but I had to go to the hospital to get another shot in the arm—that makes the third one. We had to march down in formation and wait for some time and that consumed the time I usually reserve for writing. I worked the fires from 6-12 last night. That's the best shift because then I have the morning to sleep—the afternoon to write and can do some washing and take a shower in the evening and still get some sleep before I tend the fires 12 midnight until 6 the following day.

Since we are firemen, although we must be at all formations, we still have an excellent chance of missing all special details.

Today was a good mail day. I got a card from Coach—I must write the Otts this afternoon. I also got a card from the fellow I told you about who came in here with us. He is in Aberdeen, Md. I got a letter from Ann too. Tell Harry that I think she wants him to help her set up a set of books for her sorority so tell him to get in shape.

I am holding my breath about the Air Corps—as long as I can stay here until I can get some word from New York or Buffalo I may stand some chance of making the grade. If I can survive the shipping lists until maybe Wednesday of next week I may stand a chance. There are so many transfer men here from other units to the Air Corps that I think Major Campbell transferred me back to E.R.C. with just that in mind.

I saw Jerry O'Hara at chow today but still haven't had a good chance to talk to him.

The life here is a lazy one. In peace time the Army must be a terrible thing. I honestly believe I am getting the best rest here I have had in 4-5 years. True you are kept busy with getting all the things done and yet your life is ordered. I am sleeping like a log. Even when I have to sleep before everyone else hits the hay the boys marvel at how I knock off.

I am eating more than I ever did at home. The company has filled up tremendously since I came in and at each mess they feed over a thousand men. With this number to feed and even with 50-80 KPs per shift, they can hardly do a Cracker Jack job of preparing the meals. Meals have been growing slightly worse ever since I came here. Even with all of this, I eat everything in sight. I'm even eating a couple slices of bread at all meals now. As a rule I eat three full meals but when I fire 12 midnight to 6 AM I get in an extra one just before starting work. This is another special privilege for firemen.

It is easy to see where Ned Maloney spent so much money. Quite a few of the fellows fall out of the chow line and go into the Service Club to eat. They have to pay for meals there but a lot of them do it anyway. I don't think I've spent a lot of money but even so we drank beer two or three nights—I've bought shoe shining equipment—soap—ice cream, candy—milk—aspirins—all these little things count up but I've been husbanding my money.

I haven't yet heard from you as to whether, after consulting time out of here to the Falls and back (you will have to do this at your end because I cannot do it here), you want me to try to come home. Since I am a fireman I become eligible for a pass a week from tomorrow. As much as I'd like to come home it may not be feasible. However, check the time closely on all lines and if you think I can make it—I'll be more than willing to try. Of course I may be shipped before then but when I do get shipped it may be some distance away. The pass will be of the 36 hour variety. Starts 12:00 Saturday afternoon and I must report back by 5 o'clock Monday.

How are you guys making out on the meals?

Too bad we ain't got the capital to get the pictures—little Babry had better get hers taken in a hurry.

Ann wants a picture. I kind of thought she would and I don't like the idea—I guess I'd better kill this thing damn soon but I don't seem to have the guts.

It's bad for the barracks that we have so many "kids" in here. They do a lot of gambling—that's how you can tell they're such kids. They have been losing from 10-20 bucks a night—it's a shame but I guess they'll have to learn the hard way.

Do you know if Bealys got the card I sent them? If they didn't please find out what amount of postage I must put on the letter to get it to them–tell Harry to give them all a little squeeze in just the right place for me. Well, I guess I'd better get going. I have more letters to write–shine my shoes and break up and remake my bed yet sooo...
Love, Frank

February 5th, Saturday 11:05 AM

Dear Mother, Harry and Mike,

Got Harry's letter today. Thanks so much for the things you are sending. There really is no rush about them now I guess. Although they haven't arrived as yet they probably will be here Monday. They have been shipping Air Cadets out of here by the hundreds but I guess I'll be here some time before I can get my situation in order.

I received a grand letter from Fran Bealy with Harry's. Tell little old fat ass that he has been doing grand by me and I sure appreciate it. I can understand how busy you must be Mother–you always are. Well, I can't write much because, in addition to owing (sic) a couple of letters and I still haven't written the boys at the plant, I have been all screwed up in my fireman's shift. For three straight nights now I have been stuck with the 6-12 midnight shift. This is so much better for sleep but they have an order here that you can't shower and shave from 5:45 in the morning until 6:00 at night. You cannot get to do it until after inspection. That leaves me in a fix and although I have been sneaking in for a shave I feel I should shower every day. My washing is behind too.

I got John Dick's letter. I should do a lot more writing but time simply won't permit.
1:20 PM

I just got back from formation. I saw Jerry O'Hara. He wanted to know if I was go-ing to stay here forever. The story is that the processing of the Cadets has proceeded very rapidly. There must be a lot of schools ready to take them now. A lot of them have been getting out in 3 days without getting any K.P.

Incidentally, John Dick just passed his 40 hour check in primary flying. He said he was scared stiff because he was the third man to go up and the first two washed out.

I managed to write the Otts yesterday. I'll have to get one off to Grandpa and the Beals soon but the Lord only knows when. Well, be good youse guys.
Love, Frank

February 7th, 3:10 PM

Dear Mother, Harry and Mike,

I couldn't write yesterday because I have been working like a beaver. Because the fellows were on pass, the firemen left had to work extra hours and I'm about dead but I must let you know the good (?) tidings.

I was "boarded" by the [sentence was never finished]
3:40

Just answered "mail call"–O BOY! O BOY! O BOY! Received your package and registered letter–also Harry's letter–also got a letter from Mother and Ed Greely in the morning mail. The donations were made to order and I will try to send check with this letter tonight registered per instructions. I am keeping green slippers–gave white away. Should have kept white for lightness of weight & ease in packing but fell in love with green ones at 1st sight.

Right here and now I want to thank you two for your swell "meaty" letters. The news, humor, general reports - general make up and contingent continuity has been Grade A.

Today has been about the best day I've had in the Army.

Well, I guess I've kept you in suspense long enough. I was boarded and accepted by Aviation Cadet Examining Board this afternoon so I hope I shall be leaving by next shipment. I am enclosing the instructions I received–please comply and also package my two Griffon's Mathematical Analysis books. Please try to make sure that answer books are with them. I am certain answer books are in the text next to 1st page. Please keep letters & credentials, and books in readiness for immediate shipment when I send you the address of my basic training camp.

At least I have some purpose–some goal. I have observed that men become stupid, sullen and without character when they lose purpose.

I think I shall be able to get Communion tomorrow and at the same time make the Novena. Much is contingent upon the shift I fire.

Just getting called out for formal retreat–will have to finish after chow.

Well, I guess I have summarized all the dirt at this end–will probably elaborate later.

Thanks many times but send nothing more to me as yet. I've got to hurry to 5:30 formation so lots of love, Frank

Tuesday

Could not get this registered last night so will try this morning. Incidentally, tell Mrs. O'Hara that she probably won't hear from Jerry for a while.

When a man ships he is restricted, cannot call home or write so in case you miss three or four letters at a crack from me you'll know that I'm on my way to Basic. Love again, Frank

February 8th, 1:15 PM

Dear Harry,

Thought I'd better drop you a special line, primarily because you've been so decent about seeing that my name is mentioned in mail call and secondarily because I wanted to send a slight donation to help you get us a valentine for little Babry.

I am expecting to be shipped out soon and when I am shipped I will be restricted and unable to let you folks at home know about it till I reach destination. The reason for secrecy is obvious and I would not dream of violating it.

I'm afraid I can't get a suitable valentine for the Mater here and I can't even suggest what you should get unless it would be underwear–something in the personal line anyway.

What a hell of a mess down here. As I have written before I fire the furnaces. We work an alternating shift of 6 hours at night 6-12 and 12-6. Since we had worked extra hours over the weekend I insisted upon working 6-12 Monday. I figured that would leave me time on Tuesday (since I wouldn't start till 12 bells at night) to do some washing–get some extra sleep and maybe do some letter writing. Well, our room orderlies weren't on the job and we are Gigged tonight–having a G.I. party. That means everyone has to scrub from 6-9 tonight and get the barracks in shape.

I'm going to try to sneak to church and get to Communion and Novena but that means I'll miss chow–oh boy they kind of keep you hopping. On top of this I'll have to go to work at 12 midnight till 6 this morning. What a life!

Thanks so much for the trouble you went to over my classification. I have been made an A/C and they can't ship me too soon. Incidentally, the Mr. House you spoke of is Colonel House. I understand he's very nice and more than glad to help anyone in trouble. Well, be a good boy–that's all for now.
Love, Frank

February 9th, 1:10 PM

Dear Mother, Harry and Mike,

Well, I guess I'll have to snap off a "quickie." I planned on having extra time yesterday but since the barracks had a G.I. party I was delayed again. Oh people, I've never felt so dirty. It's a crime to have facilities to wash right here and not be able to utilize them when you feel it is so necessary.

I don't particularly dislike the Army, but the inertia around here is beginning to get to me. I don't mean that I am not kept busy but there is no purpose in what I do here so I'd just as soon get going.

All my little boys around here either shipped out yesterday or are leaving today. We looked after them closely while they were here. They're still in the formative stage and we slightly older ones tried to steer them on the right track. We took care of them because they all had colds and really didn't know how to take care of themselves. We ran the Vicks line crazy–cough drops, nose drops–and VapoRub with aspirins. One even checked up on their BMs–they were so young and to feel sick when you're so completely away from the ones who have taken care of you all your life is a pretty lonely experience I guess. They were so grateful and such fine kids that it broke your heart to see them split up into different units and shipped with older men.

Lew Harwick left yesterday also. That leaves only Abraham Aaron, a Jewish fellow and myself of the bunch I entered with. Abe is 36 years old–he is a linguist and has taught in New York for some years. And has written a modern text in Hebrew which he hopes will be accepted for study in Jewish Sems. He is an individual acquaintance of whom I am proud, fine character although delicate in the sense that the Army adjustment and the low moral character of some of the fellows is a hard blow to him at times. This last is merely guessing on my part for he is putting his all into it and you would never really know how hard it is for him unless you watched him closely. I have no doubt that he will be placed in the intelligence corps for he has a fluent knowledge of the Ukrainian and Baltic languages–Slavic tongues too.

Meeting men like him is perhaps the very best in the Army for me. It makes the Army worthwhile for you know that, unless you were in this exact position, you should never come in contact with men like Abe.

I think I have learned a lot in two weeks. The Army can breed years of tolerance and understanding into you in a very short time. It is also an essential, if you would pass what little spare time you have pleasantly, that you develop a sense of judgment of men which is accurate and can function almost immediately. You have no time to delve into the characters of some of these morons—loud mouths and a few men who must be an asset to the Army only in that they can carry a gun.

By the way, I went to Mass, Communion, and Novena between 5–5:20 yesterday—made me feel swell—most innocent Confession in years—I couldn't make it last week because I had K.P.

I hope you are saving my letters. They should make an interesting chronicle for me one day—especially these early ones. Please give my best to all for I won't get time to write anyone.

Yours with love, Frank

February 10th, 2:45 PM

Dear Mother, Harry and Mike,

I got both of your letters today in this morning's mail. You should have the endorsed cheque by today or tomorrow at the latest. I would not advise sending other one along just yet unless it is absolutely necessary. The amount of it sounded good—I only hope it will hold things down for a while.

I am considering going into New York for the weekend—it seems a shame to miss going there when I'm so near but I may decide not to go after all—I hate to spend my capital reserve. I have still in the neighborhood of 45 "stibokes" on hand and am going to try to hold on to most of it although I'm spending some every day for cigarettes and milk. Maybe I'll get a few beers tonight—I shall have time I hope to shower and shave. You never can be absolutely sure of what shift you will be working because each shipping list takes some of the firemen. I hope I am called tonight or tomorrow.

I got a haircut today. Not a G.I. but if I had seen the whole business in a movie I probably would have laughed myself silly.

The barber shop, today, had about six barbers working. Three Negros, one Italian, one Indian, and the other I failed to classify into any category. Three sides of a large room are outfitted for the barbers—I'd say to accommodate at least four on a side. On the fourth side of the room there are two long rows of benches and seats and all those who would be mangled sit in these, moving up a seat each time one of the shearers calls "next."

I drew, at my turn, one of the Negros. He was short. My guess is that he may have been a marihuana boy but the only damage he did was to relieve me of a small part of my right ear. This boy moved in jerking snappy movements and he seemed to be everywhere at once. They don't give you a good haircut and they don't waste any time doing it. According to my timing they average 12-14 minutes per man.

I had talked with the other boys before I went over and when he started the routine about a shampoo I was ready with a brash "no thank you." Here, of course, is where I made a grave error. Maybe I was a little too abrupt. The lad started to strop the razor with that glint in his eye. Let me tell you that the shave on the back of the neck and around the ears was quite an experience–I held my breath and was relieved when he drew blood near the end. He nicked my ear but it wasn't as severe a casualty as my mind had conjured up. It was quite an experience.

I had my 4th shot today. I don't mind getting them and as yet I have not had much of a kick back from any of them but the part I don't like is seeing the 12 or 14 ahead of you get jabbed with that needle.

The stock joke to all newcomers here is when they march in everyone yells "Look out for the hook!"–This is with reference to the shots, two of them; you get almost as soon as you arrive. We then get them aside and glibly describe that the first shot is called the Torpedo and the second one the Umbrella and that both are administered up the rectum.

Well, nothing of any importance has happened today except that the chow at noon was quite good. We had roast pork, sweet potatoes, apple sauce, cabbage slaw with carrots and celery, bread and butter, coffee and tangerines.

Well, I guess I'd better get this off to youse guys–If I hurry I can get it in the 3:30 outgoing mail. Be good.

Love, Frank

February 11th, 1:50

Dear Mother, Harry and Mike,

Well, it looks like I'm going to get a pass this weekend. I'm afraid I'm not quite as fortunate as the majority of the fellows are since they live in N.Y.C. but for me it's too long a chance to take to get home. I spoke for the pass and committed myself so I guess I'll have to take it or get a couple follows in wrong and spoil it in the future weeks for other firemen.

It will be nice in the respect that I won't have to answer to Army routine for a couple of days and I won't have to work a lot of extra hours on the fires. This in itself is worth it. Also I'd like to drop in on the Fellemen's and maybe get in touch with Keaty and his sister. I'll also get a chance to get my uniform pressed–I've managed to snag a couple of coat hangers from fellows who were leaving so once I get it pressed I can keep it decently.

I don't like to spend the money but I'll go as cheaply as possible–I understand there are places where you can sleep for free but the fellows recommend the YMCA @ 50¢ per night so maybe I'll do that.

Of course I'm still not absolutely sure that I'll survive tonight's shipping list. I think I would be just as well off if I didn't but we shall see.

I'm glad you got my letter and I think perhaps that I can explain the delay in mail leaving here. There are fellows leaving in large groups every day or so. Although Non-Coms caution men not to write home and the men know that all telephone wires are tapped, still they invariably try to let the folks back home know about it. For this reason mail going out on the day of a shipment is held up a day or so until the fellows are well on the way. The reason for this is obvious.

I shall be extremely glad, if I get away, to put on my civilian shoes. The ones I have were O.K. until about 5 days ago. At that time the right one started to hurt above the heel. Last night I got in bed early since I had to work the 12-6. I lay in bed and my right side ached clear up to the groin. When I started to work last night, mindful of the way I had been hobbling about, I took 5 envelopes with me and packed the bottom and sides of the heel with them.

This certainly did the trick and I have been absolutely O.K. since. In town I should be able to buy some heel lifts which will eliminate the expenditure of envelopes.

Tell Harry that you just don't "get in there and fight" in the Army. You're damn lucky if you can get anyone at all to listen to you. Everyone has a tale of woe and I figure I was just very lucky. I'm very grateful for the trouble he went to for the news of it sustained me but unless they had decided to act on it here I would have been up shit creek.

I'm going to sneak out in a few minutes and change my bed linens. Last night we had chow at 12 midnight and as it so happened the Lieutenant was in the kitchen having coffee. I put the question to him and he told me I could go over today and I'm going to stop in the PX and try to get a valentine to send to Ann in the hospital. You don't tell which hospital she is in so I guess I'll airmail it to St. Mary's and hope for the best.

Well, I have no further news. I'm waiting to be shipped and it can't come too soon. I'll write you from N.Y.C. tomorrow providing I get out of here, so till then, be good youse guys.
Love, Frank

February 13th, Rex Hotel, N.Y.C.
Dear Mother, Harry and Mike,

Well, here I am in the Big City. Suppose I really shouldn't have come but I hated to tick around the camp when I could get out and since I'd never been here, the place sort of offered a challenge.

Practically one-third of the barracks came to New York. I could have probably stayed with some of them if I had worked on them but then the bunch that has stayed is not the type I would pick as friends with the exception of Abraham Aaron. I believe I have written to you about him before. He wanted me to come with him but I couldn't see it when I discovered he and his wife have only a two room apartment. He has taken my fatigue uniform and is going to have his wife put it in the washing machine with his. Thank heavens at least I'll have a clean uniform to start this week with at camp.

The trip from camp to Trenton and Trenton to N.Y.C. was uneventful except that it was terribly crowded. We had to stand from Trenton in.

When I got here I left the boys at Penn Station and was completely alone in the big city. This didn't bother me much. Walked around a while and then went to the "Clinton" to get a room. I hadn't bargained with the crowded conditions here and the hotels I tried were unable to fix me up. At this point I returned to Penn Station to the U.S.O. Travelers Aid and inquired about a room, single, with bath. There were none to be had. About this time a sailor came up to the window. Apparently he had been there before and was ready to take a double room so then and there we made a deal. The Travelers Aid could not highly recommend the Rex Hotel but at least it was a place to park the carcass.

The sailor was a Southerner—Carey Higdon. He was fairly well acquainted with N.Y.C. since he has been at St. Albans Hospital recovering from an appendectomy. He was a fine chap—wants to be a minister when he gets out of the Navy. Doesn't smoke or drink, chew or "dip" (that's snuff).

We walked from the station to the hotel. The room is not much, believe me, but we were lucky to get it.

Well, when I got to the room I shaved and washed again. We then went out to get our uniforms pressed (while you wait) and both got shines. After scouting around a bit we found a place to eat and had a chicken dinner.

It was at least 8 or 8:30 by this time.

After eating we went to a Service Man's Center run by Pepsi-Cola in Times Square. By the way the hotel is on 47th Street just off Times Square. There, after a little fooling around, I got in touch with the Fellemen's. Elizabeth gave me instructions as to how to get to E 78th Street but I was awfully confused.

Then Carey and I came back to the hotel and I picked up a couple of those clean handkerchiefs I have been husbanding. (At camp I got me some Kleenex). Carey then took me as far as the Subway. I picked up some people from Syracuse who "took care of the Army" and saw that I got well on my way. It's really very simple, but when at first you're so unfamiliar with the place the proposition looms in gigantic proportions. Elizabeth had told me to come right up so I left Times Square as soon as possible.

When I arrived at the apartment house I got the number of the apartment and went up. When I got there no one answered the buzzer. This certainly stumped me and I went down stairs to check. The clerk said that was the right apartment and that the girls and old lady had left a short time before—probably for a movie and should be back by 10 o'clock. Well, I was certainly surprised but decided that since I assured Elizabeth that it probably would take me some time to get there that maybe they had stepped out for a while.

Well, I left the apartment house and found me a bar that wasn't crowded and had a Rupert beer on draught.

I had three very slowly and called the apartment again. I got a rise out of them and when the thing was finally washed out it seems that the clerk had given me the number of the Feltmann apartment and the Fellemen's had been there all the time. Elizabeth was having a foursome for bridge but she made such a fuss that I didn't feel like I was imposing too much. Fortunately Agnes was there too and God love Mrs. Fellemen–she almost cried. Such kissing etc.–and me not having seen a women for 17 days.

Well, the party settled down and we had a drink. I answered Mrs. F's queries and talked with Agnes–when Elizabeth was dummy she would shoot over and get in on the session.

The guests (I'm afraid I broke things up slightly) were quite distinguished in a way. One–Ralph Leopold is a concert pianist and ripped off a few selections. I didn't feel too bad about coming up because Elizabeth assured me this was a duty gathering and the folks bored her stiff. She oiled them well in a manner I'm sure you're well acquainted.

Mrs. Fellemen says she was quite ill at Christmas time and didn't get to cards but is going to write you now. She certainly is grand.

I tried to get hold of Kitty Keaty but I have only her address and there are a number of phones at that address–so guess I'll miss the Keatys this time.

I've got to call up a couple of the fellows and make arrangements to meet them at Penn Station tonight. We are going back a little early–we want to have a margin of time in case the unforeseen occurs.

I've got to shave now and get going.

Went to get some things. Church 8:00 this morning. Actors Chapel on 49th Street. Carey left for N.J. to visit his sister. He wanted me to come along but I didn't think it wise so he left for the train when I left for church.

Well, guess I'd better sound off.

Lots of love, Frank

February 14th, 1:05 PM

Dear Mother, Harry and Mike,

Well, here I am back at Ft. Dix again. We got back about 12:20 this morning. Although we had till 5 AM we thought it wise to get back early just in case we were to be shipped but no such luck.

I got a grand bunch of mail today. Valentines from Ellis and Simcoe Streets. I received your valentine on Saturday just before I left for N.Y.C. also got one from Ann. I got Harry's letter and also a card from Lew Harwick. They have put him in the Infantry in Camp Wheeler, GA.

I guess I'd better tell you about the tail end of the trip to N.Y.C. After I finished my last letter to you from the hotel and mailed it and went back upstairs, shaved again and checked out and went down to Penn Station and checked my bag. I walked back to Times Square and took the subway to Fellemen's as I had told them the night

before. I arrived between 1 and 1:30. We had dinner. Ham, pineapple, sweet pota-
toes, carrots and pears, sour beets, chocolate pudding and coffee. Not too bad for
the facilities they have. I don't like the way Elizabeth handles her mother or the way
she does some other things but did my best to oil her all the way. I felt, all the time,
conscious of the uniform. You know it was really funny. After being here at Ft. Dix
for 2 ½ weeks in fatigues we thought we were pretty Hot Rocks when we put on the
O.D. uniform. Ho Ho—then we get into town. Well, I think most people understand
that you are issued a uniform not measured for one.

Agnes had skipped a house party on Long Island to be present—darn white of her
I'd say. Agnes and Mrs. Fellemen got the dinner—with all due respect and credit
I think that Elizabeth made the Manhattans—period. Elizabeth really is a charac-
ter—one of these days you and I shall take her over the coals just for fun. During the
course of the meal they wanted to know where I worked, etc. Somehow I got on Miss
Walton at the plant and described her as the professional type who was neither ac-
cepted by the women or the men. I'm sure Elizabeth winced—I just barely caught it
out of the corner of my eye.

After dinner we talked a while and since Elizabeth apparently had some sort of en-
gagement she suggested that Agnes and I go over to Radio City. Agnes really made
quite an impression on me. She has a very sallow complexion and not too good skin—
quite dark hair—a nose just a little too large—plain figure but she knows how to dress,
is very good company and in all quite a classy, although far from, lovely dish. I say
she impressed me—after being at Dix away from "soft and sweet smellin" it wouldn't
probably taken a million dollars' worth of woman to impress me but I don't think I'm
so far gone yet that I wasn't truly "conscious of her quality."

For my money, though even just from a picture, Mary is lovely in the truest sense of
the word. Well, Agnes and I went to Radio City to see "Jane Eyre" with a stage show.
I guess I'm not too appreciative of N.Y.C.—on the way to Radio City we stopped
at Rockefeller Center—you know—where they have the ice skating. The thing that
impressed me most was when we stopped for about 10 minutes in St. Patrick's
Cathedral.

Solemn Benediction was going on and the choir was wonderful. The church itself is
tremendous and the interior was magnificently decorated without being too ornate.

When we arrived at Radio City we (incidentally it is supposed to be the largest
movie house in the world) we had to wait about an hour to get in.

The show was long and pretty good even though I almost fell asleep during it. But
here comes the payoff. I knew we were supposed to meet Elizabeth at the Savoy
for cocktails but she had stated no definite time—I'm sure she left it that we would
meet her when we got out of the show. Anyway when we met her at the Savoy Plaza
she had been waiting 1 ½ hours. All hell broke loose. Poor Agnes—she was blamed
although I tried to assume the responsibility. The tirade was terrific—not at all the
thing I expected from a sophisticated woman of the world. It did me good—I could

hardly keep from laughing for smooth Miss New York had vanished and in her place Mrs. Murphy was bawling hell out of the kids.

It was too late by that time to get cocktails in the Savoy Plaza so we got a bite to eat and they took me to Penn Station. In all Mother, your friends done dandy by me. My stay would have been dull had I not had some place to go. Mrs. Fellemen is a wonderful person; she made me feel so welcome. She is going to write you. They all very much want to have you come to N.Y.C. particularly now since I am here and they figure I could get in to see you in N.Y. whereas home is too far to go.

They want me to come in next week—want me to go to Scarsdale, etc. I think they are sincere about it too but unless you were there I don't believe I would try to make it again. I had a grand time and they were lovely to me but I took that little jaunt, although I couldn't afford it, for a purpose. I learned what I wanted to know—I have a good deal more confidence in my ability to get any place I want to go—and a good deal less confidence in my appearance as a soldier. Unless there is something very special in N.Y.C. (you for instance, Mother) I don't think I'll go as a private to N.Y.C. again.

Elizabeth has had a good deal of experience traveling by plane and says that I would be taking a terrific chance, not only on the weather, but also there is the stipulation that my reservation might be canceled at the last moment due to priorities. As a result I don't think I'll make it home or anywhere else next week even though I can get a pass. Well, I've got to write three bread and butter notes—one to the Fellemen's, one to Agnes, and one to Mrs. Aaron for washing my fatigues. Why the hell don't you write me a long letter like this one and the one before it? I'm not complaining cause youse two guys have done excellently by me but I'm just more or less remonstrating myself because when I sit down to write you I don't seem to be able to stop abruptly—don't get time to write the others I should be writing too. I got another letter from Fran. Guess I'll have to write her again soon. She is a swell cookie to bother with me. Guess I'd better get to my other missives so be good!

Love, Frank

THE GOLDFISH CLUB

Present Day

Until mid-January 2015, I had only been reading the letters to my mother. The idea that I should type them hadn't come to me yet. It was during one of our reading sessions that my mother started to tell me about the Goldfish.

"Your father was so proud of that fish," she said. "His crew would tease him about how he fussed so much with his radio equipment, and he told them he 'wanted to be prepared in case something happened and he needed to get the equipment out of the plane quickly . . . he wanted to be sure they could radio back to the base in case of an emergency,' and thank God he did, because when their plane went down in the ocean, he was able to radio back and they were all saved."

Once again, this was a story I had been told a number of times, but until the letters, it had never seemed real. "I have more of your father's Army things in a box in my cedar chest . . . maybe there is something in there about the fish." More treasures unearthed in my family home, so upstairs to the cedar chest we went.

The items in this box ranged from his medals, honorable-discharge papers, a letter from President Truman thanking him for his service, and more. Among this second treasure trove was a little booklet called The Goldfish Club. We knew it had something to do with his plane going down, but nothing more. I made a copy of the booklet and took it with me to do some searching on the Web.

I learned that membership in The Goldfish Club was an unofficial recognition given to WWII soldiers by the PB Cow & Co. rubber company, an English manufacturer of the "Mae West" life jackets and dinghies, which were standard equipment on WWII aircraft. If a soldier survived a crash, water landing, or ditching as a result of their life jacket or dinghy, he was awarded membership into The Goldfish Club and received a membership card and badge upon which a winged goldfish was embroidered. While this was not an official military badge of the U.S. Army Air Corps, soldiers who received the badge were allowed to sew it on their uniforms in a designated location. Of course, research begets more research, and knowing his plane had ditched, the entire crew survived, and he received membership into The Goldfish Club, I now wanted to know what had happened—when did they ditch? Why did they ditch? I began my research by emailing The Goldfish Club contact listed on the group's website.

Within twenty-four hours of sending my inquiry, I received a response from Art Stacey in the UK, the current membership secretary of The Goldfish Club.

Unfortunately, I can find no trace of him or his ditching in my existing records. This, I'm afraid is all too common. At the end of WW2 there were well over 9000 members, of which your father would have been one. However around 1953 most if not all of those records were lost, believed destroyed, An appeal went out for members to reapply but the majority did not, I suspect for many and varied reasons. More than likely your father, having returned to the States did not even hear about the loss and the subsequent request to rejoin.

You say that you have very little further information. Are you in possession of his membership card or perhaps his flying logbooks? Did he ever mention the type of aircraft he flew during the war? Any old wartime buddies he mentioned or kept in touch with? Any bits of information, no matter how trivial might help me to locate the date, aircraft and the ditching record of someone on his crew who did rejoin and whose details I still hold. If anything comes to light please do not hesitate to contact me again.

However, without any further information I am afraid I can be of little further assistance but I wish you well in your search.

Based on Art's request, the following Sunday at my mother's we returned to the documents from both boxes. Explaining what I needed, my brother mentioned that he had the crew photo in his room and retrieved it for us. As though from the heavens my stepfather was trying to help us, there on the reverse side of the crew photo, in my stepfather's familiar printing, were all the names and positions of the entire crew. We were in business . . . or so I thought. I emailed Art with the newfound information, some photos, and a little background as to what had ignited our search for answers.

Thank you for all that extra information. That is an amazing story and how sad that your father died at such a young age after surviving against all the odds his wartime service. The photos are incredible and the Goldfish Club emblem can be clearly seen displayed proudly on your father's flying jacket.

Unfortunately I still cannot find any trace of any of his fellow crew members. 336 Bomber Sqn was part of the 95th Bombardment Group stationed at Horham airfield in Suffolk in south east England. It was the only unit in the 'Mighty Eighth' Air Force to receive three Distinguished Unit Citations. There are lots of internet sites devoted to the 95th and I have just spent an hour going through their actual combat records but once again without success. I shall return to it again when I have an hour or two to pass on a wet winter afternoon . . .

If you do manage to locate your father's original membership card that will have the date of his ditching on it. If it has been lost then I can supply a replacement based on the original design, with the club's compliments. For your information, the club offers associate member-ship to direct blood relatives of former Goldfish such as yourself and your brother. It is a nice way to keep in contact with what is quite a unique association. If you require any more details just let me know.

To say I was disappointed would be an understatement. I appreciated all that Art was doing to help. He even sent me the link to the 95th Bomb Group Heritage Museum in Horham, England, suggesting I contact them to see if they had any information. I was feeling a bit low that morning after receiving his email, but when I returned to my computer after lunch, everything changed.

It's me again. Your father ditched on 26th May 1945 in the North Sea. The aircraft was a B17G 338333 'Heavy date' No enemy action was involved in the ditching as the war in Europe finished on May 8th. The captain was Lt Roger W Sundin. Your father flew with him on April 4, 5, 7, 8, 9, 10, 15, 20 and May 1, 3, 10,1945 all on ops against Germany in the final few weeks of the war,

The other guys on your photo are: 2nd Lt Robert B Turner (Co-Plt) 2nd Lt Shackelford (Navigator) 2nd Lt Herb Robinson (Bombardier) S/Sgt Sterling Shaffer (Ball turret Gunner) S/Sgt J H Kimpel (Waist gunner) S/Sgt Joe Ferniza (Top Turret Gunner/Engineer) S/Sgt Daniel H Spencer (Tail Gunner) and your father as Radio Operator.

Well, that passed a wet afternoon....!

Best wishes, Art

—

Hi Art,

WOW! You are incredible...I'm glad it was raining or you may have been out enjoying the nice weather..haha!

You are AMAZING! I'm guessing you've told me all you were able to uncover and I cannot tell you how much I appreciate your efforts.

It's too bad so many years have passed before I learned of all this or I may have been able to find out what exactly happened to cause them to ditch. All these men are probably long gone. My father would be 94 this year. I'm reading a book now called The Goldfish Club. Are you familiar with it - I can't imagine you wouldn't be...anyway, it got me wondering what may have happened to cause his plane to ditch. Of course I'm grateful for his surviving it or the seven of us would not be here . . . he actually went on to become a medical doctor after he returned from the war.

Art, thank you again. My mother will be thrilled to learn what you've uncovered for us.

Have a great day and stay dry!
Warmest personal regards, Loretto

—

Dear Loretto

Delighted to have been of help. Is your Goldfish Club book by Danny Danziger? If it is, I know the book and Danny well. My entry to the Club is the second story.

Just bear in mind what I said earlier about your father's membership card and if I can be of any further help just ask. If I find out any more details about your father's ditching I will let you know and if Jas Phillips does include it in a future Newsletter I will send you a copy.
Best Wishes, Art

Our final emails were about the book I had mentioned. I had not yet cracked it open when I learned that Art had his own chapter. At that, I made it a point to read his story. Art wrote of an incredibly harrowing experience and I congratulated him on his excellent life-saving piloting skills. Of course more congratulations were in order when I learned that he had also been recognized by Her Majesty, and I felt there was no harm in congratulating myself for having solved part of the mystery. Though pleased with what I'd uncovered, I still wanted to know what actually happened on "Heavy Date" that caused it to ditch in the North Sea over seventy years ago. True to form, my research had begotten more research and armed with Art's information, the answers awaited me in the soon-to-be- discovered accident report.

GREENSBORO, NORTH CAROLINA - PART 1

1944

Return Address:
Pvt. F.G. Thompson
A.S.N. 12,107,602
304th Wing
1183 Tr. Gr. Bks #382
B.T.C 10
Greensboro, N.C.

February 16th, 4:40 PM

Dear Mother, Harry and Mike,

Well, here I am at Basic as you wished in your last letter. Incidentally, I just barely had time to scan the letter before we left for chow prior to shipping Tuesday. We started at about 5 PM Tuesday and arrived in Greensboro at about 6:30 or 7:00 this morning. The trip was not good as we were crowded and it was all you could do to get any sleep. We have been kept going all day up to this point. (I just drew night guard duty 3:30-5:30 this morn so it looks like I won't get an abundance of sleep tonight unless I hit the hay early.) Up to this point we have heard only a little about the classification tests we are to take. This is really not Basic but P.A.C. (Pre Aviation Cadet) training we are to receive.

Let me tell you just a bit about this camp and the group I am with. They have a laundry and dry cleaners here. The cost is deducted from your pay. The camp is much more crudely set up than Dix. There are fewer conveniences and although we thought Dix was a mud hole this place is a thousand times worse but lady this is a camp. They treat you like a white man here. We have a Sergeant who is a prince. We met our officers this afternoon and they're Grade A. They have special times for complaints but the Captain said he'd rather that we "bitch" to him first. He said he'd be available at any time of any day to listen to our troubles and problems.

I'm going to have a tough time competing with the group I'm with. Of 150-160 about 60% are transfer men. They have spent at least a year in the Army—many of them have just transferred from A.S.T.P. where they have been studying precisely what they will be quizzed on here. Most of them, due to their year's experience, are in fine physical shape. The only way I'd stand a chance competitively speaking is that I may be gifted with coordination etc. which I understand plays a larger part in you examination here.

On top of this these fellows have been treated like "shit" in other units—here the story is completely different and believe you me even from just this first day it has become obvious that these boys won't be flunked without one helluva struggle. Nor will I!!! Right now I'm ready to give all I've got and please God I hope it will suffice.

Any advantage I might have over 17 year olds as far as drill and stability is nullified in my present company. They operate like the veterans they are and because they know our Sergeant is O.K. they are treating him with kid gloves.

You tell me not to be backward in coming forward with the gimmes. Well, now I'm in a position to ask and I'm gonna. My last letter should have given you a rough idea of what I mean.

On second thought don't send the Matrix shoes. They won't do here. I must have absolutely plain toes so anything I own is out. Please get me four new ties. I will be wearing them here. Don't forget the socks—to me they're vital. I'd prefer it if you would wrap books—credentials and articles of clothing in packages if it is not too much trouble. I don't want an extra box around here just now. Please insure packages for just a little anyway so that I'll be absolutely sure to get it. Don't send check until you get an answer from your first letter—I'd rather be sure that things are getting through before we take a chance.

With the math books please try to scare up my high school physics review book—I'm sure this would be a terrific help if it only gets here in time.

At any rate, whatever comes or goes, at least I have some goal again—we'll have a darn good whack at it.

About a picture for Ann. Please have Harry send it to 17 Tudor Place, Buffalo 9 NY. I can't see much sense in sending it here and then having to ship it all the way back.

You speak about a sore throat—boy did you strike it on the button. After 5 days at Dix I had a whopper—and cold on head and chest to boot. The cold in both places I got rid of but the sore throat hung on. I went to sick call. What they gave me there alleviated it for short periods but I don't lose the damn thing until I was about 2 hours outside of Dix yesterday. Everything is O.K. now. They examined our throats here today and gave us all Sulfadiazine tablets against cold. We may be relatively south but that doesn't mean much as far as weather is concerned. We wore overcoats here today and were damn glad to have them. I haven't seen Jerry as yet—he'll probably make out fine—he would.

Could get some laundry in today but I cleaned everything before I left Dix so I'll get things set for the week. Ford is far better than Dix—facilities for entertainment are far better but I don't think I'll be doing much playing around just yet.

Well, guess that's about all for now—be good!
Love, Frank
P.S. You might include a simple but complete sewing kit—got a pair of socks that's on the way.
F.G.T.

February 17th, 10:40 AM

Dear Mother, Harry and Mike,

Second day at Greensboro. Processing has not begun as yet so we are staying in the barracks putting serial numbers on all clothing and dubbing (waterproofing) shoes. I heard more about classification tests. What Jerry said is certainly true, the "casualty" rate is 85-90%, the reason being that they just don't need Pilots. Probably we will start taking initial tests tomorrow. You see these tests were never given before to men until after Primary Flying had been completed but now due to the excess of men, the tests are given before you even get a crack at flying or school. It doesn't look like I've got much chance but we'll see. If I flunk out they'll probably use me somewhere - it's a cinch they won't let me resign.

While these series of tests are going on don't expect to hear from me because I think I'll be very busy. Sorry I haven't written some of the folks you mentioned. If I write to them I consume the time I'd be writing to you so I haven't thought it worthwhile yet - haven't sent a word to the boys at the plant yet or John Dick or a hundred others I should be writing. I should get going but I'm afraid they'll just have to wait.

Nothing of particular interest here today. Got a mask yesterday - we have to carry them all day on Wednesday. It has rained steadily today although it's not too cold. The boys are griping about the sunny South Land - we haven't seen much of it yet.

Well, guess I may as well close - no news, no nothing. Be good.

Love, Frank

February 18th 7:00 PM

Dear Mother, Harry and Mike,

Well, here we are again. This evening, as last evening I have hid myself away to the library. Primarily I have found a good "Math Refresher" book written for the R. A. F., and I want to review some of it and secondly it is much easier to write here than in the barracks since the ones we have now are very small in a way and the guys are always raising Hell.

We spent the best part of the day hearing lectures on Venereal Diseases, keeping mumm on military information, etc. Most of the fellows have seen so much of this stuff that it bores them completely but about 2/3s of it was new to me.

Now comes the payoff. Tell Bobby Perry to hit his books as hard as he can. Tell him to start keeping very regular hours - even stop smoking and drinking. Tell him to live a model life until he gets where I am now anyway if he wants to make Air Cadet. We have been told by at least 4 officers today from a Lieutenant Colonel down that most of us will not make the grade. There are just too many who can qualify so (although they tell us all would have made it a year or 6 months ago) the limits for qualification have been drastically lifted. Only the absolute cream will be taken now and damn few of these.

The effect of this story was pathetic. A bunch started out singing this morn. But by noon all was very quiet and by 4:30 the griping was everywhere. They really should stop that high class advertising campaign if the A.C. doesn't want the men.

I don't think this hit me as hard as most of the others. I got mine yesterday and that's why I came to the Library last night. I had a feeling that that was the way it was to be.

Maybe I won't make it but it seems to me I've got the stuff and I'll make it if it can be made by yours truly. (Better not let anyone else read this because I sound too much like a shrinking violet but I feel more mature and I have more common sense than a lot of these guys but then maybe I'm only trying to lift my own morale). I don't think I'll be broken if I don't make the grade. You see the Army has done a lot for me already because now I live from day to day. Anyway a new Engineering course is opening up and I think I may be able to talk my way into that.

I have received no mail from you here as yet. Just found out today where I could get it and I found out too late. Should be able to get it by noon tomorrow.

The food is great here and I mean great. The cooks just keep piling it on until you say stop. They don't fool with wasters though. There are signs about the mess hall that "If you accept it - Eat it!" This is a regulation rigidly adhered to by the cooks. If a man tries to throw too much in the waste can a man who is stationed there stops him and makes him stand there till he has eaten all he tried to throw away. You have to give the cooks a dirty look to keep them from giving you too much.

You know you haven't given me any dope on my "baby." Is he being a good boy? If he were down here today I'm sure he would be singing for a little lass to play with. In sharp contrast to yesterday, today was mild and sunny - truly invigorating weather - makes you feel grand to be alive.

I managed to get in a shower today. We will take a physical tomorrow I think. It's a real effort to shower here since the latrines are in separate buildings from barracks. You have to walk maybe half a block and then the place is so crowded you're not sure you can get in. You're never sure of hot H2O.

Well, I've burned up a half hour writing this - can afford it - the time I mean - should be studying and still writing letters to you three is one of the best parts of the day for me. I feel almost with you cause while writing it seems like I'm almost talking to youse. Other letters are a chore in a way because one must repeat what one has already told to the dear ones.

Tell all the lovely people not to expect to hear from me in near future because I don't' like to take time in this crucial period. If they don't like it I'm afraid that's too bad cause I'm determined to give my all to this the next couple of weeks.

Has Harry been a bum lately and how was the party - bet he told me ill about it in a letter that's stalled somewhere because I shipped. Tell that young man to love 'em for me too - be a little patriotic about it.

Guess I'll have to add another page to tell you the best joke I've heard since I donned Olive Drab.

It seems a messenger boy went to a hotel room with a message. When the party answered door it was a lovely, shapely, sweet smellin', pulsating blonde - completely in the nude. The poor boy took in the sight in obvious admiration even when the gal turned her back to him to read message.

Then she quickly turned around and said, - "Get in here - I hear someone coming."

When she had closed the door behind the lad she noticed his wide eyed admiration as he eyed her from stem to stern.

"Well," she said, "which part of my body do you admire most?"

"Well," said the boy, "I'd say your ears."

"My ears?" she gasped. "Heavens why my ears?"

"You see," replied the lad, "you said you heard someone coming?"

"Yes," was the answer.

"Well, ma'am, that was me."

End of joke.

Pretty dirty but one of the officers told it today and it's one of the few I've heard in some time that I got a bang out of.

With that lovely little thought in the mind I'll say adieu for today. Be good.

Love, Frank

February 21st, 6:55 PM

Dear Folks,

Just a hurried note to tell you I received Harry's letter today. Not a God damn thing from Dix yet. No package yet either. Keeping us busy but I'm going to try to make my 1st movie tonight.

Thanks for sending package anyway. Hope we don't start tests till next week - looks that way now.

Send on check but be sure you register it. (Demand return card.) I'm not getting anything down here. 4 wings mail is together and I think there are at least 20 Thompsons.

Forgive me for asking for things - didn't realize you were so tight. Don't bother with socks or ties. Haven't heard if you rec'd laundry box yet but sure would appreciate towels back again. I can get stuff here I guess or in town. Maybe I can send dough if I get paid this month. Send check on and I'll return it as soon as possible.

Love, Frank

February 22nd, 8:55 PM

Dear Mother, Harry and Mike,

Wished to hell you'd sent underwear as I asked - please rush old stuff to me as quickly as possible. I'll try to give you an idea of the situation. You are issued 3 pairs. One I've tried not to wear - am keeping it to wear at physical. If you send others to G.I. Laundry you have to wait a whole week before you get it back. It's next to impossible to launder it because hot water is at a premium and no wash boards. The

Army sets up standards - you have to try to meet them - they don't help you. They expect you to keep clean - God sometimes I don't know what the hell to do. When you ain't got hot water you hate to shower because of damp weather you would catch cold - latrines are poorly if heated at all. Please, please get that old underwear with shirts down here.

Guess I won't get much writing done in next few days - got to try to wash somehow - keep shoes in shape. Incidentally I'm rotating my 2 pairs now and it's not too bad. You might send me 3-4 good wooden clothes hangers if you can spare them. Fraid I'll have to close - lights out at 9:30. We're restricted to barracks for next 48 hours so can't get to library at all damn it - be good.
Love, Frank

February 23rd, 8:45 PM, Wednesday
Dear Mother, Harry and Mike,

Boy did I have a good mail this evening. Nine letters no less. Two from you, two from Harry, two from Mrs. Ott, one from Agnes with invitation to Scarsdale, one from Elizabeth and one from Mrs. Powers. I just spent a grand 40 minutes reading or rather devouring them.

(I'm being constantly interrupted by the fellows hot sexy stories - their experiences - this is real competition believe me.)

I got the biggest kick out of your letters and Harry's. Harry certainly crams the news in. I knew you'd like the way the Fellemen's treated me. Someday I'll get me another crack at Agnes - purely platonic of course.

The trouble is that we are restricted to our barracks - I feel that anything I write is besmirched with the tall tales that are going on about me.

We really started a rigorous phase of our Basic today - a little PT, which blew my ears off - the best part of it is that you know that they're doing it to build you up not tear you down. Much of what we are doing I suppose I shouldn't tell you in detail but most of it so far is not much more that I got in R.O.T.C. at school. We are still getting screwed about the mail. This noon they wouldn't let us go at all. This evening I had to take my choice of getting mail or making Laundry Call. Chow, laundry and mail are all at 6 bells - figure it out. You have to stand in line at all places so you're lucky to make two of them let alone all three.

I still think we start our exams Thursday. We have been working with rifles - they call them "Pieces" here. We will have work with Springfield 1903s, Carbines, 45 pistol and Thompson submachine guns when we finish. Tell Mrs. Ott and Coach that since I've been down here I am issued a Piece in the morning and they let me work with it all day.

I've got to try to get in some studying. I must write folks you tell me of. Sunday I hope I can get to it. I want so much to write but it's so damn hard to arrange my time. You see, as I told you, we have a lot of Pre-service men with our group. These guys are all very wise about "screwing off" for formations. Our Sergeant is still a

Prince but they don't realize, yet anyway, that he's too damn smart for them. So we are constantly being penalized because these 'wise guys' are too wise.

Like this evening I didn't finish chow and getting the mail (I have to walk at least a half mile to get it) till 7:00. I read my mail till 7:45 and then started to write youse. I just can't do it cause I have to get my shoes in shape - leggings - and uniforms hung up in proper order and sequence on rod. I have to shower (if any hot H2O) and shave, check bulletin boards for announcements, and walk to mailbox 4-5 blocks to mail this. I have to wash up underwear and socks too. Not a lot of things but they must be done if you're going to keep healthy and clean and take care of yourself. I'll do my best to try to get letters off on Sunday but even then I may get Guard Duty or K.P. all day so I can't say for sure.

I don't think I've mentioned the fine bunch of fellows I'm associated with. Majority are white men. Most of others haven't even gotten this far. They are an extremely interesting contrast to a lot of us "Jeeps." These guys are completely self sufficient for their entertainment. They have been, during the course of their year or so in the Army, completely weaned from home. Their mail does not come in quantities but is steady and frequent. In an impersonal manner I have been with older (in Army experience) fellows mostly because they know most of tricks and their suggestions and helping hands are welcome in many occasions. I haven't tried to drum up pals in the Army as yet. Just now I prefer, till exams are over, to try to sit back, be quiet, and take in the personalities. I can choose later I think when I have more time. I can choose better because I'll know a good bit of most of them in a week or so more. Well, be good youse guys.

Lots of love, Frank

P.S. Helen's Tie O.K. - Please send couple more of same. 1st package not arrived as yet.

February 24th, 7:35 PM Thursday

Dear Mother, Harry and Mike,

At last here I am over in my little spot in the Library. Boy is it a relief to have some peace and quiet when writing. Restrictions were lifted this evening. Previous service men got passes to go to town. We "Jeeps" will have to wait till next week this time before we can leave [the] Post. Guess maybe when I can I'll go because there are a few things I want to get.

Don't worry about the shoes because I have one pair broken in fine. The other pair is killing me now but they should be O.K. soon. The Army is very particular about your feet. They're (feet) inspected before and after any long marches. Get this - they won't let you darn socks - when you get big holes you salvage them for new ones.

One piece of good news I've been keeping to myself is that I've found a latrine that is only slightly used - I found a wash board and hot H2O there last night and did a good sized washing. Don't think I'll have so much of a problem now. You know it takes a little while to get on to all the ins and outs.

Send my washing home? People I'd love to but it can't be done. You're just not issued that much clothing. Of course you can buy extra clothes in civilian stores but the price is high and the quality low compared to what you are issued so thanks so much just the same.

No package as yet and I made mail call both times today. Got a letter from Ann and one from Fran Bealy - see what swell people they are - nothing from my loved ones today. Wished I had that physics review book last night or a week ago - took Air Cadet Mental today - I didn't do good or bad - maybe on the better side but I can't rely much on that because I think they grade these groups on a sliding scale. Just hope I did well enough.

Biggest news of the day was seeing Jerry O'Hara. I suppose you know by now that he flunked out. Hopes to go to Gunnery School. It doesn't have a very optimistic outlook cause he was a lad that was supposed to have plenty on the ball. Even if he was built up overly he was just fresh from school - everything but the trig should have been hot in his hand but evidently they just don't need him - tell Mrs. O'Hara not to feel bad - I may flunk too, but most of us will lose out just because they don't need us, not because we're not A1 material.

We also took various tests today to classify us in Trade etc. in case we don't pass. The group I'm with have not taken real important exams yet - we'll probably get them very soon.

The weather here today was truly of the summer variety - believe me I don't envy you your snow and wind. It's beautiful here - if you only had time to appreciate it. We will get that time when our Basic is complete. We, after another 7 days, will be eligible for passes every night. I'm a gonna try to hook myself one of these college women after exams and get myself an in - then I should be all set.

Of course after Basic, while you're waiting for shipment, you are stuck with dirty details as latrines - K.P. - guard duty etc. but with the exception of K.P. you have your evenings to yourself and are all set. I hope I'll not forget to keep good and clean though. Honest I've seen so many dirty necks since I've come down here. Next time you see a sloppy or dirty soldier don't condemn him as I have so often done. Just remember that 95% of his fault can be attributed to the unavailability of proper facilities and supplies. The soldier has to be a good man - damn good if he's really spotless all the time. I'm speaking of course of the enlisted men not officers.

Well, I can't dig up much more dirt here I guess - getting so I like the fellows a lot more but most of em don't seem to have enough punch. They know they will be up against it this and next week but they don't seem to care much. One fellow wanted to take my blouse (one with brass buttons) tonight but I sheepishly told him no. Hated to do it but I only have one and I want it filled only with my own sweat. Well, guess that's all. Keep good and well.

Love, Frank

February 25th, 7:30 PM Friday

Dear Mother, Harry and Mike,

Well, another day in Uncle Sam's Army. I made both mail calls today - have been on the alert for registered letter but no dice as yet. As long as it's registered, I'm sure I'll get it.

At last I got issued extra Fatigue uniform. Am going to put it out for tomorrow. I'll turn original model in for laundry Wednesday next. I got another brand new one - thank goodness. I was also issued U.S. and Air Corp insignia so when I get some braid for my cap and shoulder patches I won't feel so much like a Jeep.

We just had a large group of planes go over towing gliders - I swear it's propaganda to get us worked up about gliders.

Package arrived today. I was glad to get books. I'm not studying tonight - decided in favor of writing because our schedule doesn't call for exams tomorrow. I expect to have Sunday to myself so I should get a chance to do most of the catching up I am going to do then. Also must try to do a lot of writing.

Got a swell mail today. One from the Mother, two from Harry, one from Ann, one from Keaty. I got these at noon - almost didn't go to mail call tonight because I got so much at noon but I'm on the look-out for the check.

Tell Harry if he is going to take a picture up to Ann he'll have to wait a while cause she has the mumps in Buffalo and they won't let her come home.

We got more shots today. Third dose of Tetanus and vaccination so probably will have to sleep on my back tonight. I hope I'm not going in too much for the braggadocio, but I don't seem to have all the ill effects the other guys seem to feel - not as yet anyway.

We got another "Preparedness Talk" today. The Top Sergeant came up to give us a lecture. When he came on the field (we were in the bleachers) he was joined by the Captain. They chatted for a while and then the Sergeant almost completely abandoned the scheduled subject in favor of carefully telling us that he thought we deserved some explanation. He went thru the same old story we have heard so many times since we came here - that most of us would not make it. We're getting kind of sick of that Bullshit. We're all gonna make it anyway.

I wrote to the Otts and Bealys last night. They've been so good to me. Mrs. Ott asked me my opinion (in her last letter) of Coach going to Niagara Falls High School. Boy I told 'em. Never would have said a damn thing if I'd been home. Guess I think I have special privileges since I'm away. I let them know how much I think Coach can do at High School, but I also let them know that I, for one, didn't want them to let too much work spoil them. I think I handled it O.K. but you can never tell how people will take these things - hope they're not too sore at me - perhaps I should have minded my own business but then they asked me. It was a golden opportunity anyway and you know me when it comes to spouting off.

Well, guess I can't say much more 'cause I ain't got much more to report. Too bad about J. O'Hara but may be too bad about me soon too.

Pay day is Tuesday I think - I'm kind of anxious to see how much I get. I'm going to try to get shoes here - gonna need 'em to dance in whether I get to be A.C. or not. If I don't make it, as soon as I find out, I'll settle an allotment on you immediately - but I wouldn't depend on getting it cause the Air Corps doesn't know what they've got to deal with since I came down here.

I'm in the barracks tonight - wasn't too bad earlier but now all the Hell is breaking loose. The majority of pre-service men are gone on pass. Only those who are broke have remained. To these veterans the strain is beginning to show cause they haven't been off for some time. They're on edge and at swords points with each other - arguing and raising Hell - couple of fights have been near coming off. I'll be glad when they get some dough and get it off their chests. Well, guess that's all for now.
Love, Frank

P.S. Guess I've spoiled you big by writing everyday - well, you deserve some spoiling, hope I can keep it up
F.

February 26th, 8:25 PM Saturday
Dear Mother, Harry and Mike,

Well, I just got back from Post Office and general scouting mission. You see I had to find where Mass will be tomorrow. At this moment you must have guessed that I didn't go last Sunday. They woke us up for K.P. at 4:30 and we weren't released 'til 7 that night. I had planned to go to a chapel just around corner but I found out there is no Mass there any time. You must have guessed too that I completely missed Ash Wednesday - ate meat 2 or 3 times and all. Fine one I am! Just when I need the Lord - I forget all the training I ever had. It has stunned me to discover just how much in the minority R.C.s are down here. At Dix an Irish Sergeant got us all out - we were informed completely of the hours of Mass and Confessions. Here you have to dig up most of your information. I walked a good hour - covered about 2/3rds of this camp in dark drizzle to find all chapels. At last found one, which had Mass. All chapels at Dix I think, had at least 1 Mass. Have only been able to find 1 Mass at 7 bells tomorrow morning. Next week we will be taking exams. I hope by the time you get this I'll be in a state of grace again. I knew from postings around camp that Mass was at 5:30 weekdays, but we have been in the Field at that time all week with the exception of tonight. I think I'll be able to get information about Confessions at Mass tomorrow and if we have exams we'll get off early so I'll be able to get to Confession - Monday maybe.

Well, we were interviewed today by examiners - this is in case we don't get Cadet. Everyone is interviewed for this - they assume that you won't make it and take your second choice. A lot of fellows get no choice, but from the results of mental I'd taken the day before, I had a choice of only four schools open. I chose Radio - 5 months training in theory and practical side - training for Radio Gunner. This amounts to my third choice really. Primarily I am assigned Cadet. (They don't know it but I'm gonna qualify [I hope]). If I don't I have discovered that, with my two years of college, I can apply for Engineering Cadet. As I understand it this embraces aeronautical engineering. I can't apply or get more dope on it until I find out if I qualify for Cadet or not. Boy am I glad we got me two years of college in a technical course. The way I feel right now I will probably refuse Air Crew if I flunk out for Pilot. In other words, if I am offered Bombardier or Navigator I'll probably refuse in favor of an Engineering course. This plan is in the embryo stage, so I'll have to think more and find out more about it. At any rate in all three, Air Cadet, Engineering Cadet, or even Radio Gunner I'll get some good training. It will be time consuming too. That's the best part of it.

Some of the fellows got word today that they were accepted for Air Crew but would have to take their second choice. We're all glad for them - Pilots haven't been announced as yet. These fellows are the pre-service men who have already taken the exams we will take next week.

I hope to finish up my studying tomorrow. I have discovered the particular type of problem they ask you on the math anyway so I'll be able to hit these anyway. I can't do a hell of a lot but it makes me feel better to think I'm preparing myself.

Well, I haven't got much more to say so be good and night night.

Love, Frank

P.S. I'm going to try to write Bob Perry a long letter - Scare the crap out of him 'cause he'll have to be plenty on the ball to get thru now.

February 27th, 10:25 AM Sunday

Dear Mother, Harry and Mike,

Sunday has well arrived. Last night was the 1st night in the Army that I didn't go to sleep immediately. Guess I just wasn't tired enough. I must be getting a little harder because I didn't mind getting up this morning in spite of the fact that I didn't start to sleep till well after one in the morning.

This church business presented quite a problem because, even though I was up to give very specific instructions to last night's guard - he fell asleep and I wasn't awakened till 5 or 10 minutes till seven.

I then hustled out, 'cause I knew I couldn't make the 7 o'clock number, and got a Post news paper. Here at last I got a schedule of the Masses on the Post. Felt kind of stupid for not thinking of that before, but I just didn't. I went to 9 o'clock - J. O'Hara was just behind me - he's going to get Mechanics Gunner I guess.

Perhaps you don't realize it, but this is the first "Day Off" I've had since I got in the Army. It sure is a relief. I've got my books, but was disappointed when I found I couldn't get in the Library today. I'm at the Service Club. Hereto it's disturbing. In the only room I could get an easy chair, there is a movie going on at one end and a radio blaring at the other. I shall appreciate these things later after exams but I don't too much right now.

I'm going to try to get that letter off to Bobby today - if I can't find (in one of your early letters) his address I shall have to send the letter to you - please have Harry see that he gets it at his earliest opportunity.

Don't misunderstand me. These exams are not of the post college graduate level but you have so little time to devote to each one (problem) that the material must be right at your fingertips. In this connection on the Air Cadet Exam, I think with time to reason by analogy, and think it would have been duck soup for me to get every problem. You don't have the time. Some problems are put in to stall you - some are tricky. A high school man with math up to intermediate algebra and physics can make the grade in my opinion but only if the material is completely at his fingertips. Snap answers are required.

Monday night I'll have to check all my clothing for proper markings. Tuesday night learn 14 General Orders. These are required on Guard Duty to which I shall be assigned after I finish processing here. They also require them to get a pass. I want that pass to get civvy shoes in town Wednesday or Thursday. I also get paid Tuesday. Be glad of that because I'm getting low on cash. Don't get the wrong idea. I have held on to a comfortable margin. Enough and to spare, I think, for a round trip home in case I ever get a chance to take it. I want to leave this money strictly alone - aside from it, I have enough - 33 cents I think but that's plenty. A show is only 15 and cigarettes 12.

Did I tell you I got another haircut? They really chopped me here. When I get into town I'll try to get cheap pictures. Biggest compliment I received here as yet was when the boys at T382 asked me if my blouse was tailor made. They thought it fit like a custom built job. Maybe it's not so bad after all. I'm going to have to exchange all shirts. They gave me 15s with 33 sleeve. Sleeve is O.K. and shirt fits well in body but neck is very sloppy. Felt terrible about it in N.Y.C. but I couldn't do anything about it at Dix. I hate to exchange shirts because they are all brand new ones - I'll probably get second hand ones if I exchange them. Oh well, the Army is a great teacher and one of the biggest lessons is that here, as in life, generally you can't have all you want.

Guess I owe a general apology. Sorry if I sounded "cross" in letter of last Monday but all our morale was low at that time because of the Air Corps Deception, which we all feel we are victims of. I'm afraid all my emotions will creep into letters as much as I try to avoid it. When you live a thing like this Army - to others you get dull and narrow because you're concerned with it only. But what's the big idea? Wasn't I always the "Bitcher?" Things were serene till I arrived and I always raised hell about something. I guess I'm still trying to do it by remote control - got no one to pet and pamper me here (yet anyway).

About the O'Hara boys - yes I think the feeling is general in the Army. I haven't felt it yet - don't expect to. I've told you about the veteran and pre-service men in our barracks. It is a staggering thing to see how rapidly the Army hastens maturity. Most of these guys are not more than 21. The vast majority are in the 19-20 stage. Many of them are married - many are hoping to get married. Too bad in my opinion, although I try, and in a way, I think I can understand it. These guys were not fortunate enough to be in a close home as I was. When young - 18 or 17, they quit school - never got to college - got in industry and big money. These men don't realize what is happening to them. The worst is that they have no conception or just don't give a damn about the future and how a crumbling Economic system will raise a greater havoc in their lives than any war ever could. These men think that they are at the very bottom level of their abilities. They believe that all else in civilian life will be a step up in their earning power.

What they don't realize is that here they are fed, housed, treated medically, and kept in condition and in addition given clothing and spending money. None of them have really had to cope with life really. Boys in the putty stage of life were easily molded into mature soldiers - oh pray for their adjustment back to civilian life because when they are returned - habits and characters will be formed which will leave an indelible imprint on them. In spite of the griping about the Army they don't realize that you get a fairly square deal here - at any rate a man is treated generally as he deserves - given as square a deal as possible. These young men don't know how a depression ridden society can discriminate against them. How circumstances completely beyond their control can push and drive them to a point they never thought possible. These men haven't tasted the losing of one's self-respect yet - the corruption and diplomacy which is an unfortunate characteristic of the capitalistic system for which we are fighting.

I hope not, but I fear, that the same chaotic conditions that were attendant in the wake of the last war will manifest themselves here after this one. What then? American youth will find a new "Enemy" in civilian life - one they can't see and have not been educated to understand. An enemy that will come close to home and affect all of them. How will they cope with it? The Army is teaching them to fight dirty - with no principle. It's teaching them to be completely ruthless. If you could see a couple of the movies I've seen about methods of close combat, you'd understand just how close men are getting to savagery in the South Pacific. Let us hope these men will not try - even as a last effort, to apply these principles to civilian life when they return to it. What can we do about it? I don't know - it is the only way to fight the enemy we have at hand - I hope we won't see repercussions of this "no quarter" training in civilian life in the next 10 years.

Well, I guess I've shot enough bull - I've burned up the morning. Chow in about 15 minutes so be good.

Love, Frank

February 28th, 4:30 PM Monday

Dear Mother, Harry and Mike,

Well, I've been in Army a month now. A month to get a crack at what I did today. Today we took exams to qualify for Air Crew. I fear I didn't do too well. Some of the fellows even feel confident - I have no such feeling - perhaps I've been away from concentrated mental endeavor too long - I don't know but I'm not going to worry about it.

What I did fail to see is how a man who has had nothing of planes can be expected to qualify. You see these exams were designed originally to be given men after they had taken Pre-flight at least. I don't know if they compensate for this - they probably don't because they don't need the men now. I was at a terrific disadvantage because I never owned and wasn't familiar with an auto-mobile or motorcycle.

Tomorrow we take Part I of the Physical and the Psycomotive Apparatus test. Some of these guys claim they did so well and seem so damn stupid - it's hard to understand. Even comprehension tests on this thing dealt with aero dynamic principles - how the hell are you to know anything about this? If this thing indicates your true relative intelligence etc. I think I have as good a chance as any of these babies, well, we'll see in about two weeks. It takes that long to rate papers.

I'm kind of anxious to see how I make out on these apparatus tests. These are the screwy things that Dick described - like Coney Island I guess.

I saw Phillip Gellman here yesterday - you know the kid (Jewish) who was so peppy and used to run around with Schelly Kirtzman. Saw him while waiting to get into the show last night - splurged 15 of my 33 cents. Incidentally - don't miss the picture "Broadway Rhythm." More entertainment per minute than I've seen in any picture for some time - weak plot but lots of music, dancing etc. It was good to see all those women.

As I had figured, I'm going to have a little time - I'm going to try to shave and get to Confession. The situation has changed because Mass this week is at 6:45 and the way the Priest announced it yesterday - I still don't understand in which of the chapels Mass will be.

The Priest yesterday told us in no uncertain terms that we were forbidden to go to town and attend any other religious service. It seems that Greensboro, be-ing a good soldier town - the people in various religious groups have been giving Sunday evening dinners gratis to soldiers. According to the Priest this is just a "come on" for some type of religious service after the dinner. He told us even if it consisted merely of a couple of hymns after dinner it was still a religious ser-vice and we were absolutely forbidden to attend any of these. Novena is held at 7:30 Sunday Eve at St. Benedict's church in town. Rector is Fr. Jordan. I'll try to make it next Sunday - am interested also in Fr. Jordan - it couldn't be the one we know could it? Oh about the other religious service or dinners on Sun Eve, I just pointed it out to illustrate the strained religious feeling down here.

Yesterday was certainly a day of rest. Studied some - some of it helped too. Haven't written Bobby yet - maybe, if you think he wouldn't pay too much heed, I'm kind of wasting my time. He'll have to learn the hard way like young O'Hara.

Well, can't write much more if I'm going to get to church.

As you can see I just refilled pen - got India ink by mistake - probably ruin pen - oh well, be good.

Love, Frank

Dear Mother, Harry and Mike,

Today has been a tense one so far and I'm glad it's over. I took Psycomotive Apparatus tests today and Part I of the Physical. In the former, I feel quite sure I was not much better than average if that and they don't need average men for Pilots. I take Pt. II of the Physical at 2:30 tomorrow - wait about 10 days and then we shall see.

I was too tense, and although I was more calm about it than I think I have ever been about any test, I wasn't quite calm enough.

I waited in line about 1-2 hours easily after physical to get paid - $36.87 - more dough on me now than I have ever had to carry about and I don't like it.

Dearest people your packages arrived last night. Yesterday, as today, my schedule with exams does not permit me to go for mail at noon. Bealy's package arrived at the same time. You should have seen me walking that 1/2 mile back to the barracks with 3 packages - especially that large one. Every G.I. I passed looked with wonder and the majority of them razzed me. I of course - beaming inside had to look like I'd been imposed upon - was carrying home some other fellow' stuff. Oh joy! Oh Bliss and Happy day. Socks and ties were grand - underwear arrived just in time for me to report for physical in glaring white. String bag swell - holds all shining stuff. But the food stuffs - totally unlooked for, certainly hit the spot - the lads and I are just about finishing up now - been trying to find out which ones are liked best but the vote seems about even for the brownies and ones with pecans right now.

The cookies really lead me astray cause I planned on going to Communion tonight but when I got back from being paid I was hungry and for the cookies - so I fell. I didn't make church last night, cause, due to the changes and lack of priests - Mass was again changed and after walking all over camp I found I'd arrived at the wrong place and would be too late to get to the other side of camp for Confession. I'd better make it tomorrow night or else.

Towels are dandy - will be able to have others I have here in laundry tomorrow.

The Bealy's package was grand. Did you know what they sent? Combination shoe shining kit and sewing kit - they buy best quality as usual. They also sent a lovely pair of gloves. They're beauties. It was unnecessary for them to bother, but such thoughtfulness is so like them. Don't tell them, but I can't wear gloves here - maybe I can get away with them off the Post - am not sure cause they're certainly not a G.I. color.

Please, please you people keep this in mind, and try to steer anyone else who is grand enough to send things to me. Somehow I sneaked into barracks - the fellows just missed me coming in, but so many nice things, like those gloves in particular, offers too great a temptation to some people. Aside from "T" shirts and a little soap please don't just send things - I suspect you might have such ideas in mind with my coming birthday.

Please don't send cake - or food cause I'm going out to the Rifle Range soon - don't know exactly when but I hate to take the chance and miss things. Please don't let anyone send me anything of much value unless I ask for it. I didn't show a soul the gloves, but without even trying on, hid them in the very bottom of my foot locker. It's so grand to get things and I felt like a king getting 3 packages but I'd hate to lose things here and it could happen so easily. It's damn hard to write this, but I know you can get it across to the Otts and Bealys, Aunt Maime or anyone else. I want one of those chocolate cakes, if you can manage, one of these days but don't make one for me till I write you about it especially. I've got to write Bealys - it's 6:00 now - got to eat and get my mail - since I can't think of anything more just now.
Love, Frank

THE TURNING POINT

Present Day

While my father worked his way through his big week of exams, the Eighth Air Force worked their way through a "Big Week" of their own. In February 1944, the B-17 Flying Fortresses were joined by their "little friends," the P-51 Mustangs. With the help of these long range American fighters, the focus of the air operation shifted to destroying the Luftwaffe. From February 19 through February 26 the exclusive targets were the aircraft factories and oil refineries. Charged with defending these facilities, the Luftwaffe would take the bait resulting in their anticipated obliteration. In the eight days that comprised "Big Week," the Germans lost over 600 fighters to the Americans 226 bombers.

Back in Niagara Falls, New York, Mother, Harry, and Mike were unaware of another war that was being waged right in their neighborhood. Just up the road from "the little piano box" that was their home stood the Hooker Electrochemical Company, a veiled contributor to the top-secret Manhattan Project. Much of the damage to the city and its citizens as a result of this contribution would not be known to the fullest extent for decades. In 1944 those too young to actively serve in the military were asked to help the war effort in other roles, though some were equally deadly. Countless young men, eager to perform some type of patriotic duty to serve their country, became victims of exposure to a variety of harmful chemicals. These unknowing young men jumped at the chance to help and with the oversight of Army representatives, found themselves directly exposed to uranium.

On other fronts, U.S. forces began the assault on the Mariana Islands, and in Burma the ground forces advanced in the north while the long-range air forces were starting to land behind Japanese lines in central Burma. With his future still unknown, my father was not only settling into Army life, but was also learning to cope the limited information granted to him and his fellow soldiers, forced to approach each day anew and accepting that his destiny was in the hands of others, at least until he survived his tour of duty and returned home.

As I read his letters I learned that my father was quite fastidious and a bit of a control freak. This made me laugh out loud because it made some things crystal clear to me. On countless interactions with my siblings over our lifetime, we were keenly aware of how differently some of us would approach a particular situation from others. Some of my siblings had a more easy-going nature while others, I among them, would be extremely particular to the point of being a bit obsessive. We would tease one another about how these opposing characteristics existed within the same family, and wondered how it was possible. The letters solved this mystery. Some of us had obviously inherited our mother's easy-going personality, and the rest had inherited our father's mildly controlling temperament and meticulous nature. Recognizing this single characteristic that I possessed, which I'd clearly inherited from my father, was a turning point for me. He was no longer a stranger, someone I would always wonder about. Through his written word, I was accomplishing something I had never dreamed possible. I was getting to know my father.

GREENSBORO, NORTH CAROLINA - PART 2

1944

Dear Mother, Harry and Mike,

  I have definite plans today to get to church - I've gotten a recruit - fellow from Buffalo - Rudy Knitter - he's going with me. Two of us should be able to make it.

  Right now I'm anxiously awaiting chow. I get as hungry as a dog down here. Should have mentioned that Knitter and I are quitting smoking starting tomorrow. We're doing it for Lent - we certainly are getting a slow start but we decided to allow ourselves a little extra privilege while taking exams.

  Oh one more thing. You recall my buddy at Camp Dix - Abe Aroni. He is taking Signal Corps. The description of place he's at (Monmouth, N.J.) is terrible and the condition he describes there makes me very thankful that I'm in the Air Corps. Lew Harwick - my beer drinking pal at Dix is at Aberdeen Proving Grounds in the Infantry - the cold he had at Dix developed into pneumonia and he is in the hospital. I guess he is getting on O.K. though. About Abe - to me it is a crime that a man of his ability and special training (as a linguist) should be shunned into Signal Corps. What a waste of intelligence! His whole attitude is optimistic, but I know he's trying so hard to be a good soldier and make the best of his lot that he's having a hell of a time.

  He is very fortunate in that he is still close enough to home to be able to get there weekends. He didn't state as much in his letter, but I think after his first two week's restriction - he will be able to make it. I think the most pathetic thing in the Army is when a married man looks at that empty bunk at night.

  I guess I didn't tell you the cycle of man:

1. Tri - weekly
2. Try weekly
3. Try weakly

Another one that struck me as funny:

  Said the big bell to the little bell

  I've got more dong than you

  Said the little bell to the big bell

  I know but I get more dinging than you

  Mother, you're not supposed to read these or try to understand these - these are for Harry and his boys. We've been getting a big kick out of what he's been sending - appreciate more of the same.

  Well, guess I can't stretch it much more.

Love, Frank

Return Address:
Pvt. F.G. Thompson
A.S.N. 12,107,602
304th Wing
1183 Tr. Gr. Bks #370
B.T.C 10
Greensboro, N.C.

March 3rd, 4:30 PM Friday

Dear Mother, Harry and Mike,

Well, I must confess that I didn't write yesterday. With the exception of days I've had K.P.; I think it's the 1st day I've missed. I went to see Ida Lupino in "Our Times" or something. Anyway I was going to stay in the barracks and write - am I glad I didn't. It seems the Sergeant came in just after four of us left for the show and took all the fellows who were left for night K.P.

In addition to the movie there was a stage show or rather a radio broadcast. They have a splendid Post band. Except for the size, I'd say they compare favorably if are not better than the outfit they have at Shea's Buffalo. The whole orchestra - about 40 pieces and all musicians are Air Corps Men. They have a good glee club & quartet which broadcast with orchestra. Soloists I imagine have had professional experience - one of them is of the opera variety - did a selection from "Aida" and "Old Man River" over the radio last night. These two selections will give you an idea of the scope of the orchestra - it's a grade A outfit.

Wednesday afternoon we had part II of our physical. This was the most rugged part of it. I felt quite fortunate because most of fellows had to go back for pre-check of some sort but I apparently was O.K. the first time round - eyes 20-20 and all. That evening I went to the PX and absorbed a few 3.2 beers - I'm telling you the heat is off now - what a relief after all testing and examining is over - maybe I won't make it but it's a relief anyway to have it all over with.

This morning was cold - I was shivering in my overcoat but in spite of it we had 3 hours of instruction in the field - (in bleachers in the field) in the Carbine. Then we had an hour of PT. If only they'd give you PT every day you'd soon get on the beam, but the way it's organized all you get is wrenched muscles and pain.

This afternoon, of all things, I had a dentist's appointment. Of course it was not with "The Dr. Kay" but a Major examined me. Thank heavens - none to be pulled and I think only 3 to be filled. They only cleaned them today - the fillings will come later.
6:50

Just went for chow and mail - I have never received any mail from the 10th Street Thompsons - have written once but I've received no answer. Funny that I got everything else that was sent to Dix.

Maybe I'll take myself to town tomorrow night - maybe not - got to get myself a ration coupon so I can get some shoes. This will be my first formal step in a concentrated drive on the women of the South - I can't get going with these clod hoppers on. You understand - they're too heavy going out of 2nd story windows, crawling out from under cars etc.

Well, guess that will be about all for now.

Love, Frank

P.S. Second whole day without cigarettes and not sure whether I missed em more as a civilian - or now - but I do miss em.

F.

March 4th, 8:00 PM, Saturday (Night)

Dear Mother, Harry and Mike,

Well, as the paper indicates I've hit Greensboro in a very mild manner but before I become too involved in this evening, I guess I'd better hit today's happenings.

We were kept quite busy all day - in the morning we had three solid hours of "Dry-Fire" with the Carbine. This is damn boring - you simulate actual firing on the range - go through all positions but have no ammunition. Today was wet and cold but we were on the ground doing it anyway. You sure get hardened to these things after a while.

This afternoon and noon were something entirely new. Because this is the 1st anniversary of the B.T.C. #10 we had a big Southern fried chicken dinner with all the trimmings. The Mess Sergeant had table cloths - white - on all tables and to top it off a jazz band, which played while we ate. Where else in the Army would you get a deal like that? It's not heaven on earth here but people when you hear from transfer men how you are treated in other outfits you are certainly glad you are in the Air Corps even if you don't make Air Cadet.

They're not fooling around with men who don't make A.C. either. Some of the fellows who came in with us but who had taken tests before us were shipped back to old outfits or POE tonight.

After our record lunch we had a record parade. We all got into class "A" uniforms and drew rifles and cartridge belts. Then we had a review - Some joker had a citation read about him but I still didn't get who or what it was all about. I'm afraid I was too taken with the spectacle itself - over 2,000 men in review - and I was a part of it. Don't misunderstand me - not much of a "part" but I was there anyway.

Really people the competition in writing this letter is terrific. I'm at the side of a large dance hall. The U.S.O. has a large place here. Bowling Alleys underneath and dancing with good band covers whole upstairs. There are oodles of women - a lot of cuties too. You can imagine what a good boy I am to sit down and write when this is the first time I've been this close to a women in almost a month. I was so busy all day (we had a medical & personal inspection before parade) that I didn't write - so thought cuties or no I'd better get going.

Some of fellows are downstairs bowling. Seven of us who have never been in before came in tonight in a group. This is sure a soldier town - you see them everywhere but there seem to be plenty of women - the catch being you have to be very careful - ones that look 25 are only 14 or 15 and that is true. We're all taking it damned easy and careful - you see "Fornication" is a crime here and with that pleasant thought in mind. Love, Frank

P.S. I think we're going to smoke Sunday - tonight at 12M.

March 5th, 1:40, Sunday

Dear Mother, Harry and Mike,

It's a beautiful day and Sunday to boot. Haven't yet figured out why it's so good— because it's Sunday or because it's beautiful anyhow. The weather here is terribly changeable. We've had all kinds but I think we're in for more of the better variety in the near future.

I wrote you from U.S.O. last night. Hope you get that one—it was written under plenty of strain and temptation. I only had a couple of dances—I'm kind of leery of these affairs— you never know what you will get hooked up with—think I'll wait till I get my shoes and get me a college gal. They at least should be able to keep up an intelligent conversation. The only reason I express doubts as to your getting letter is because we gave letters to a chaperone at the U.S.O. to mail. We were going out to mail them and she said that she would if we wouldn't leave. That's the way it is down here. Where they get all the unattached women from I don't know but there certainly are plenty of them.

I'm still of the opinion that except in only very rare cases, anything you pick up is a slut - maybe I'll get the same at the college but at least she'll have a little education to adorn her physical charms.

I just got back from mail call—finally got a line from Grandpa T. It was a nice note— first I've heard from him. Too bad that it had to have money in it. Would rather have had him just write me. Of course I'll use the two bucks birthday money—think I'll go to town tonight and get a steak dinner. Going to try to make Novena at 7:30 anyway. Maybe we'll stop at the YMCA for a swim first. The town is wide open for soldiers—it's nice but too many soldiers.

I didn't do much in town last night, I had one beer. All beer is sold in Dumps in the true sense of the word. I think it's sold in one hotel but that's all. Didn't get to that hotel last night. We went to U.S.O. and since I hadn't written I wanted to. When I got there I had a couple dances. Nice gals—one lovely in particular but with that damn Southern drawl I can't even get their names. I want to get my shoes and patches (shoulder) and Air Corps braid for my hat before I do much dabbling with the women. I applied for ration stamp last night—it should come along soon. I'm going to buy best town has. I was going to get one badly looking pair of G.I. shoes all shined up this afternoon but the whole squadron has been assigned K.P. for tomorrow. Another 4:30 AM till 7:30 PM session—so I'll wear shabby shoes—a session like that softens them up swell so it will serve a good end.

I got 4 envelopes, contained birthday card from Ann. She couldn't get out so she made one—no use trying to describe it so I'll enclose it. Darn nice of her but I'll have to send her a nasty note and tell her to forget this damn nonsense.

I bowled last night—96 and 98 respectively. Pretty lousy but I had ball trouble—Harry knows what that is only its worse here—there are so damn few balls. With a light one I got strikes and spares but with the heavy one I had no control. I've got the knack again I think—we'll see when I get down to it seriously again.

I'm going to try to keep away from that town. You're happy here and have plenty to do and don't spend money. There is everything here for you on the Post.

It felt so darn good to get in town though—a renewal of that feeling of freedom. I'm going to try to nurse that feeling because it will be old stuff if I make it too often.

Went to 9 o'clock Mass. I've been having quite a contest with myself trying to keep up in the missal. It's tough at Low Mass and that's all you get in the Army—maybe I can hit a good High Mass in town one of these Sundays. I take pride in saying that I shepherd our little flock together and get them all to 9 o'clock Mass all 4 of us. I got them up and "chewed their asses" so we all got there on time anyway.

At chow again today we had a band while we ate. We had baked ham with pineapple-squash—tomatoes with dressing, buttered carrots, chicken noodle soup with cubes of toast thrown in—ice cream, pie, coffee and bread and butter. They certainly do well by us.

I was kind of startled to hear about taxes. I so wanted youse guys to have a little on the side but I guess it can't be just now anyway. Will Harry get his new duds for Easter?—How about that new overcoat? Has Barb got a new dress lately? I've notice no mention of these things in letters—just reassurances that things are alright. What's the straight dope? I've got some dough and if 20 or 30 will help let's hear about it. I don't need it and it doesn't make me feel too good to carry it about. The only reason I hang on to it is that when I ship I may get a 10 day delay in route. Don't get on your ear about this—I won't get shipped till Basic is over and I probably won't get a "delay on route" if I should make Cadet. Still there is a possibility. If I'm kept here long I may be able to get home from here but don't hold your breath waiting. You never know what the hell there is next—therein lies the charm of the Army. I'll close with the Ft. Dix Creed:

TB or not T.B.

That is congestion

Consumption be done about it?

Why of cough! Of cough!

Thank goodness I'm out of that Hole!

Love, Frank

March 7th, 7:20, Tuesday

Dear Mother, Harry and Mike

Since I had K.P. yesterday I didn't get a chance to write. We got up at 4:15 and didn't get back till 8 or 8:45 that night. I was pretty tired. I had P and P - that's pots and pans - OH people was I busy! They had roast pork for 2,000 men, cake, pie, and God only knows what that dirtied a million pots and pans - there were four of us to do it. When we finished a Mess Sergeant and Lieutenant checked up and brought back the greasy ones so we started again. I didn't get any mail at noon but sneaked over at night. I got the package with T shirts and sweater. Gee that certainly is a swell sweater - I've tucked it away and will wear it as soon as I get a chance to display it to advantage. I'm going to try to write Aunt Maime tonight. I got no mail tonight or at noon. At noon they wouldn't let us go and this evening we were assigned to different barracks so with the moving, although I walked all the way up, I arrived too late.

Things are pretty low around here tonight. You see this morning they read off a list of P.A.C.s who qualified. Yours truly was not among those mentioned. I don't feel too badly about it - I won't, I don't think, even if I find out for sure that I have flunked out. In all former cases men who make the grade for Air Crew but fail to qualify for first choice have been called first. They have to sign a release that they are voluntarily taking their second choice. The men who were called are ordered to bring fountain pens tomorrow. This looks like I still may have a chance but this group is larger than it really should be so in that respect it doesn't look too good. They have been rushing things through at a surprisingly rapid rate here so I'll probably know for sure what goes in a day or two.

The rush around here is generally accepted as the end of the B.T.C. #10. I doubt that many, if any, additional Air Cadets will come here. The camp, I hear, is to be changed and adapted to an entirely different set up. Evidently the Air Corps no longer needs men to the extent that they must keep this camp going as an A.C. classification center.

I just left this letter to look up one I got from you yesterday. I'm sorry I don't do better about answering them directly - that is the questions you put. It is a hard thing to do. I just burned all the mail I've received because they took up too much room. You see I've been in upper bunks since I've been here. When I write I sit in bunk but have to slouch because my head scrapes the ceiling. I just never get last letter out and answer it as I should. As to clothes, I have plenty of underwear and socks. Too much is too much of a burden to keep track of now. I can wash out little things now. I have enough handkerchiefs. I still have about eight of the "done up" ones I took from home. I keep these for special occasions and as I get going I'll use them up and then have them done at the laundry.

I feel terrible about Ann. Will try to offer up Communion tomorrow for her if I can make it.

About J. O'Hara. I went to town Sunday. I'd made up my mind to go to Novena. They have a very small church but it's very nice. I saw a gal there that I'm going to meet if it's humanly possible. She was lovely - no kidding. Before I went to church I took Thompson's 2 bucks and treated myself to a steak dinner - steak not so hot. After church I went to U.S. O. There I met Pearly's young hopeful. We left, looked around for some beer but all was sold out at that time - about 9: PM Sunday night. He has been here just long enough to know all the ropes. The time I spent studying has put me way behind in this respect. We got shoe shine, and came back to camp about 10. He had a cold - said he was going on sick call next day. I really don't think it was worse than an ordinary cold though. He'll be O.K. in a couple days I think. About my own health. thank goodness I've been O.K. up to this point, Yesterday was the greatest trial. After we got through K.P. we walked back and were all drenched in a down pour. I fully expected to have a lu lu of a cold today but I hope I've become hardened a little to these things - I felt fine today - you get used to it you know dear. After all, what they give us here is peanuts compared to what you would get in, say, the Infantry. Never fear - if I get sick - I'll get taken care of - I'm no damn good even to the Army if I'm sick. The set up here is much better than at Dix in this respect.

In a way we were lucky to have K.P. when we did yesterday. You see, I discovered in the mess hall one of these very large brooms they used to follow horses with. These are ideal for G.I. barracks so we stole one for our barracks. The G.I. Parties shouldn't be so tough with a broom like that.

Today I got my ration slip for shoes - I'll have to wait till Saturday I'm afraid to get them. I don't think stores are open in evening.

Today also I held, carried and fieldstripped a "Thompson Submachine gun." It was the realization of a childhood dream - I was tickled pink. We will shoot these things on the range next week.

I'm quite sure we will go to range next week so don't send any food till after that. I'll give the green light, and how, when I get back. It is 8 1/2 miles out there and we have to hike both ways. That is going to be just ducky. Just a forewarning not to expect to hear from me much, if any, next week.

Be good youse guys.

Love, Frank

March 8th, 12 Midnight, Wednesday

Dear Mother, Harry and Mike,

Here I am again. It's kind of late tonight because we had another busy day. I've got fire guard from 11:30 till 1:30 so am doing my writing now. The early part of the evening was occupied with getting shoes in shape, checking and arranging laundry and getting generally set in new barracks. I also cleaned out this pen. I hope it holds out because I still haven't written Aunt Maime or Grandpa and I must do so. If I start in pencil again you'll know that the pen is clogged up again.

Well, news as far as classification as a Cadet grows worse merely by the fact that there was none. I'm afraid I'm going to have to disappoint youse guys and the other people at home who expected better things of me. As for myself I won't believe I didn't make it till I actually see the list stating that I was disqualified but frankly, the aspect is extremely dull as to my success at this writing. We know anyway that I was A1 physically and I know that I knew a lot more about physics & math than the rest of these guys. The place I must have gone off is the aptitude and psycomotive tests.

I just got a glimpse of J. O'Hara in a formation today. He signaled me that he is going to the range so tell his mom that he must be O.K. or he never would be going - his cold must be OK.

As to Harry's queries about the fellows getting home. J. Malcomb was on a 10 day delay en route going to a school - gunnery. Bill Edwards is permanent party here and is on a furlough. Jerry O'Hara tells me that Bill is going to try to get some stuff from O'Hara's store and sell it to officers here at 7-10 bucks a package. Still the same old Bill Edwards. From what I judge he hasn't changed much.

One more thing - the fellows from this squadron who qualified were not told in what they qualified, that is Pilot, Bombardier, or Navigator so that will give you a rough idea of how they're taking them now. I still can't understand why they push them in here if they don't need or want them.

We finished our 17th day of Basic training today. That leaves us 13 more. Next week, early in the week, we will go to the range and Bivouac. Here we probably have tactical night problems and extended order drill. I think I'll get quite a kick out of it but I hope the weather warms up cause its turned cold and windy and this would be hell on the range.

We were introduced to 45 cal. automatics today. I guess all P.A.C.s have to qualify with it. It's the "hottest" weapon we are given here because it's the most difficult to do a good job with.

I got stuff back from G.I. Laundry today. If you think city laundries ruin clothes you should see the job the G.I. does on them. I half suspected this and sent only things that didn't matter much so wasn't too startled when things were returned.

As I've told you before I have no shirts that fit me. I have borrowed one but I can't go on that forever. Harry will have to understand that even Errol Flynn tactics won't work if you stink - got to have the old spotless look and smell you know!

As you can see pen is still shot. I'll have to write other folks tomorrow night - I have to get a haircut then anyway so will go from there to library and do a better job. Guess that's all for now so be good youse guys.
Love, Frank

P.S. If the Otts should happen to ask about Gazette I haven't received it yet - but don't say anything unless they ask - they may not have ordered it yet.
F.

March 10th, 3:50 PM, Friday
Dear Mother, Harry and Mike,

Well, I certainly owe this one since I didn't write yesterday. I had a good reason. Then I had a good idea of my status but wasn't sure. Today we were called in and informed as a group. I didn't make it. That's right your little darling was disqualified on the psycomotive tests. Apparently I just haven't the stuff to make a member of the air crew. If that's the way the Army feels about it there is not much I can do about it.

I can't honestly say that I feel brokenhearted because I really don't. The only thing that I don't like is that Harry won't be able to say that we have a gentleman "by appointment of Congress" in the family. Mom won't be able to glow just a little at the bridge club and the Bealys will never see that Forest Green on me. I believe that they are going to make a Radio Gunner out of me. I'm not too keen about this but it is a good deal in that I shall be in school in the country for at least five months. I have no idea of where they will send me but I'm thankful that I shall be in the country for a while. You see, a lot of the boys, particularly pre-service men who flunk out, are sent directly to POE (Port of Embarkation).

We were told today by a captain of the Aviation Cadet that the Age of Education by the Army ended about five months ago. No longer are they going to send men to school because they have built up a backlog of trained men. This is evidenced by the closing of A.S.T.P. In the consideration of all things one of the main reasons that transfers are so hard to get is that too many played the game of transferring from place to place and the Army will no longer tolerate this since men across are having to play the game for the life stake.

Don't let this kid you about little Francis George though. Please don't ever quote me on this but I'm going to play this game as much as I can. Right now, in answer to my query, Engineering Cadet is closed. This closed a few days after I came here but I was told to keep applying at whatever station I am at because it is always opening and closing, the A.S.T.P. anyway. Of course I have no biology but this does not stop me for I made inquiries at classification prepared to bluff my way on the biology. I have all other academic qualifications. I'm leery of med school because frequently when you apply through the Army you are made a medic and sent right over (Bob Mitchell's case). I'm going to look into it further after I get shipped out of here - if I think it's a good deal at any time I'll take a crack at it.

Of course I'm sorry in a way, but the going is pretty tough here as far as qualifying is concerned. I'm glad I didn't write Bobby and get him worked up because as far as I can see the mental means next to nothing (of course let Bobby take bag). I certainly wish him the very best of luck.

Don't make any alibis for me - just say I flunked out in the psycomotive aptitude tests. I think Mother will probably be glad in a way - so am I. In the first place I stated on the psycomotive that I didn't want Air Crew unless the Army thought I was qualified and in the second place I think it does you good not to be on the "top" of the heap all the time. I've been mighty fortunate for years and a little "putting in your place" does you good once in a while. The opportunities in the radio are not too bad if you are good. If you rate at the top of your class many times you get an opportunity for advance training.

The impression they tried to give us is that nothing is certain! You'd laugh to see the confusion of some (not all) of the classification officers. They, themselves, really never know just what is coming off. They are never sure of things and no one will commit himself. Thank heavens I'm in the Air Corps anyway. Whatever happens you have a much better chance here. I'm quite sure if I hadn't been sent here from Dix that I would have been slapped in the Infantry. In Don O'Hara's situation I wouldn't be surprised to see him sent to a POE. If he is, in view of the fact that he has had no particular training, he may be assigned to perpetual K.P. or "general duty." The situation as it exists now is that whatever is needed, wherever is needed by the Army now is being sent. They don't care now about your civilian training unless it is of a very special nature. There is the situation. In a way I wish I could feel sorry for myself but it just isn't there. I feel more or less relieved - you see I have been praying - "If it is God's will that I make it" apparently it isn't and that's fine since that's the way He wants it. Some of the "kids" here are hurt pretty deeply - too many feel that they were roped in - they're stunned to a certain extent at the rapidity at which they were eliminated. You know I always doubted that I was qualified. If ever a fellow had any training to pass "apparatus tests" I had it in the Lab and if I had been qualified it would be something else to look forward to. As it is I'm not sorry I'm here. Of course I miss you three to an extent that there is not much sense in talking about it. The main point is that this is an experience I'm glad I am having and would have hated to miss. Let us hope that I will stay here long enough to merit a 10 day delay or that circumstances will arrange it so that I can get home because you know I never do as well on paper as I do in the flesh.

The way the boys are talking we may go into town tonight. I said last night that I wouldn't because I knew I would have to write this letter but I came back just in time to miss a dress parade and I had time to write so guess maybe I'll accompany the lads.

I think there is dancing tonight - there is dancing for the soldiers somewhere every night in the week so guess I'll take advantage of it even if my shirt (the one I borrowed) is not in best of shape. I don't like the way you keep thinking I'm getting sick. If I do you'll be able to tell by the long long letters I'll write - seems to me time never permits me to say all I want to.

Yes Emily sent me a dollar. The Otts sent me some Fanny Farmers. They were swell and we have eaten most of them. It would have been just too bad though if they had come and I'd been at the range as I will next week. They would have been mashed to hell.

Perhaps Harry can do a little undercover work for me in the shoe shining business. I'd like to get hold of a couple of those cloths they use. At present I think I can do as good a job as any boot bloke here but I can't get that shine that you can see your face in yet. What I really need is some of that "white stuff" they use on Third Street - maybe he can get me some. I'll try to get some pictures taken tonight but won't promise anything because sometimes there is a terrific line and since you wait in line all day I am not too well disposed to do it during off-duty hours.

Well, guess I'd better get going if I don't want to stand in the chow line too long. So sorry didn't make it for your sake but it is undoubtedly better this way.
Love, Frank

March 11th, 7:50 PM, Saturday

Dear Mother, Harry and Mike,

Here I am at the same place as last Saturday Eve. My emotions, however, are entirely different this evening. I really came in to get shoes but it seems the certificate I've got has to be acted upon by the Rationing Board at Camp so I came into town all alone to no avail. (You're going to have a hell of a time reading this - these pens are lousy). I came in alone because none of the fellows wanted to come. We've been assigned to K.P. again tomorrow and since it's a long day they want to get plenty of sleep tonight. My intention was to get my shoes and return directly to camp. I went into the Florsheim shoe store and got the sad story. Then, since I was already in town I decided to write you. I haven't done the writing I should yet. I counted on having tomorrow all day to do it in but I'm out of luck. I won't even be able to make Novena tomorrow night unless I'm lucky enough to get off K.P. darn early.

Last night I came into town. I had patches sewn on and braid put on my cap. If I'd got the shoes I'd have been all set - now I'll have to wait till next Saturday night. I got me some beer last night - first time I've really had my fill since I left home. It really did me good although I had to get out of a warm bed to go to the latrine in the middle of the night. It was mighty cold let me tell you.

We got in late last night so I'm kind of tired tonight. I thought I'd write here though because I can sit in a chair - look at the dollies and I know if I go back to camp before 9 bells, the guys will be working on me to go to the 9 o'clock show.

The big news of the day was one filling in my face. They started out on that one in front. You remember I complained that I would have to have it fixed. They did a grand job on it. You'd hardly know it was filled. Don't think you'd notice it unless you were particularly looking for it.

By the way, I don't think I'll be doing much writing during next week. We are going to the range. I guess conditions are pretty rugged up there so I may not get a chance to write at all next week. Don't you guys stop though - I think they'll try to get some mail to us.

When I got out of dentist's today, I went down to sign form "32" "Statement of Charges." It seems that when I moved from old barracks that someone made off with my canteen, canteen cup - etc. I figured I'd have to buy a new one but when I asked for one, the guys there gave it to me and told me to get the hell out. At any other place I would have had to sign away the cost of it from my next pay but I was pretty lucky.

I went to Confession and Communion this evening before dinner. The only way I can sneak it in is when I have an appointment as I did today. It was a good thing too because I'll miss Mass tomorrow because of K.P.

Really I'm getting quite a kick out of merely watching this dance here tonight - the reactions of the fellows and gals is really something to behold. I guess maybe I'll grab a dance or two - grab a beer or two and hit the bus back to camp.

Be good youse guys.

Love, Frank

March 13th, 12 Midnight, Monday

Dear Mother, Harry and Mike,

Just a line or so to let you know that all is OK. These are hurried days - we seem to be being rushed through our Basic - maybe I'm just slow to follow though.

We have not been worked too hard but well occupied. We start out to march to the range tomorrow - 8 1/2 miles. I've been told that the pack amounts to about 30 lbs. This is small time compared to the 60 that the infantry carries but then we don't get the warm up training that other outfits get.

It's been a great day learning to make packs and generally getting ready. I should have been in bed at 9:30 but guess I won't get much sleep tonight.

I had to clean up mess kit and prepare pack with harness. Some of these jokers will have a hell of a time getting ready because I've had two fellows helping me for about 45 minutes to get straightened out.

I'm not sure how mail will come through but continue to write anyway if you can. I'm worried again about youse guys 'cause I've had nothing from home since Saturday noon.

You've probably written but the mail system is undergoing some more changes. I hope things don't get too tangled up.

Well, be good and I'll try to do better when I'm at the range but I think we'll have "night problems" so we may be working day and night sometimes.

Love, Frank

March 14th, 6:05 PM, Tuesday "At The Rifle Range"

Dear Mother, Harry and de la Spuzier,

A shootin' we will go - a shootin' we will go. We arose at the delightful hour of five o'clock. Preparations were lengthy and time consuming. You never witnessed such buckling, tying, sweating and blue atmosphere in general.

We left the camp gate at 7:50 and arrived on foot (standing up) at 10:20. Really not a bad hike - they had an ambulance with us all the way - more like boy scouts than soldiers. I really shouldn't complain because most of us were slightly dished - not in bad shape at all, but you felt kind of like a "dressed" soldier only. We walked unusually slow - the record for the trip is 1 hour and 35 minutes but we had a 1st Looy with us all the way and the setting of the pace was his doing.

There are 5 of us to a tent here. Leave it to our Sergeant - we were slipped into tents with wooden floors. These are reserved for "permanent party" but somehow we got some of them. In our tent are Knitter (laugh at that one again) Ben Baker (Jew), Bill Rollo (Scotch) and a fellow named Bollard. We had to do some dickering to get in same tent together but we managed. We were first ones to get tent scrubbed and in shape. (This after we had been issued cots - mattresses - all this you carry to your tent). For our promptness in getting situation in hand the Sergeant promised us, if we keep it up, that we will get week end passes next week. Rollo wants us to go to Portsmouth, VA with him to his aunts next week end - we shall see - if we get passes - if we get back to [the] Post in time to use them and if I think I can afford it. Knitter and I feel much the same in that we just don't want to have dough enough to get home, but we want to have enough to raise hell when and if we get there.

I don't know as I made it clear formerly - it really is not clear to me. You asked how long I would be in Greensboro. We should finish Basic 5-8 days after we return from Range. Then we will have a pleasant time. We will be given K.P. one day and Guard Duty the next. This goes on indefinitely until shipment.

It is hard to tell when you will be leaving but if all goes well we should be on the move again within 2-3 weeks. By the time this reaches you please feel free to send me a chocolate cake - you well know what kind. NO rush about it and if you haven't got the makins don't worry about it. We all kind of scorn civilian life now with regard to food because we know how hard it is to get things. Here we have everything.

While at the range here if it rains we will be SOL. When we got here this morning it was a beautiful day - ideal weather. The country here at the range is beautiful - I have never seen such a panorama of color - of the clay colors and foliage on the range itself. This morning - coming in it resembled a huge luscious oriental rug with live colors.

But the clay is the rub. Mud and clay - if it rains here in the next four days we shall be up to our knees in mud - it rained all day Sunday and there are still (evidences of) the hell rain raises here. With rain our schedule will be completely disrupted and we may have to stay here over the weekend - God forbid! Water here is out of Lister Bags. Latrines are of the "camp" variety. Our tent is heated by a small pot belly stove - it's kind of rough but not nearly as rugged as it could be. Our last day here we will go on actual Bivouac - but then it's only one day.

Right after lunch we got a detail. This was really a riot. We went from tent to tent in the "permanent party" section of camp. We picked up barracks bags, cots, bed lockers and equipment of men gone AWOL. It's murder - there really are a lot of them. Well, guess that is darn near all the dope - we will be firing guns tomorrow - it's getting dark and though we sniped a few candles I don't think I'll write much more in this or candle light.

OH - one more thing - I shall get particulars about applying of an allotment as soon as possible - you will have to get affidavits that I contributed to your support. Let you know more as soon as I find out.
Love, Frank

March 15th, 5:05 PM, Wednesday "At The Range"

Dear Mother, Harry and Mike,

I just received your letters of last Saturday and Income Tax Statement. I'll put it in the mail box here immediately but it won't be post-marked till 16th since mail won't leave her till 7:30 AM tomorrow.

How now - what's this about the "back" acting up? Better get to the doctor immediately. If you don't go - I'll call him up from here! That's no horseshit either - so save me the money!

In passing I think youse guys show wisdom in not sending in return with cash. I think you have the right idea - I was going to write same to you this letter because I found out that some of the fellows were doing the same thing.

We fired Carbines and Thompson sub machine guns today. I like the former - will feel much more secure with it than the latter. I guess we won't fire 45 automatics since we didn't qualify as Cadets. This Carbine is really a gun for my money and what's more I can shoot it. Even though I never fired a 30 cal. gun before I think I can manage this baby with pleasure. I'll enclose my scores - these don't count but 5 is a bull's eye and I got a couple - got nothing below a 3. The scores at 200 yds. are more accurate since the fellow marking me was way off the ball at 100 yards.

We decided to have a party up here tomorrow night. Ben Baker and I got stuck with the arrangements so I've got a little extra on my hands. We're going to have 3.2 beer maybe hot dogs, potato chips, etc. - cost 75 cents a throw.

The weather is holding fine so far - let's hope it stays that way. It was actually hot up here today and me with my "longies" on but it gets damn cold at night so I'm leaving them on.

I have the patches all done up in an envelope ready to send but haven't sent as yet. Rollo, Knitter and I had a picture taken - I don't think I sent it but I don't' remember. I wanted to send all together. The works is back in my barracks bag at the Post so I fear I'll have to wait to send it on tomorrow. I think we pull targets for other fellows to shoot - shouldn't be too bad but after that we'll probably draw some "sweet" details and believe me there are plenty of them around here. Well, guess I'd better close - going to try to get a shower in this primitive place - I surely need one.

Love, Frank

March 16th, 4:30 PM, Thursday, "Still at the Range"

Dear Mother, Harry and Mike,

A shootin' we did go! It's all over now. Tomorrow we go on Bivouac - that will mean our overnight in "shelter halves" and "k" rations to eat - night problems to work out etc. It won't be too bad I don't think.

I qualified with the Carbine but by the skin of my teeth. I needed 135 and got 139 out of 200. It was a tough day to fire for most of us who have never done much shooting. There was an intermittent wind which was hard to allow for. Some of the fellows didn't even qualify.

This morning we pulled targets for other fellows' shooting - not a bad job - you get a better understanding of the whole situation when you work in the "pits."

We have been having a really good time up here although I certainly wouldn't want to be stuck here for a long time. We all hit the hay at 8:00-8:15. It gets dark then. We then light up one of our sparse supply of candles - rip up the fire. Ben Baker plays the mouth organ and plays anything so we sing till the other tents start to squawk. The sleeping is good but its mighty cold in the morning.

We have the best bunch foragers in the camp so, although we are not supposed to eat in tents, we have rifled the mess of everything we can carry out and we eat and sing by candlelight in warm cots to our hearts content. The repertoire is certainly of the Smoker variety but some of it is not too bad. We sing all the songs we can get our tongues on and improvise what we can't remember.

The five of us have just been put on a detail to prepare the Bivouac area tomorrow. This ought to be good! We'll probably have a hell of a time out there tomorrow. Our party is coming off tonight - anything that is left over we will grab and take with us.

Well, guess that will have to be all because I must make my pack - and take a shower before chow at 6:00 and the shindig is after that. We've got a small band together and a couple semi-pro fighters to put on a bout.

I also have to go to supply and get my bally ass painted green for tomorrow
Love, Frank

March 19th, 2:25 Sunday

Dear Mother, Harry and Mike,

Rain! Rain! Rain! It's coming down in torrents here and now is turning to hail. The mud is deep everywhere and you can't step over to latrine without getting soaked. Mine is a selfish outlook for I don't care now. We arrived back at the Post at about 6 bells last night. We had a great deal to do upon arrival. I won't attempt to recount it here because it was merely routine and not doubt would bore you as much as it did me. We had to get entirely situated in new barracks again. I then, with a great deal of gusto indulged in the G.I. 5 "Ss" Shower, shave, shampoo, shave and a SH--.

Believe it or not I got ready and went into town. I guess it's that "free" feeling that gets me in there for heaven knows I don't do much when I get there. I stopped in at the U.S.O. They were running a formal St. Pat's dance. Boy did the dolls look luscious. I didn't do much about it because I still don't own a shirt that fits me. I have only one which I borrowed and it's getting rather soiled now. Believe me I'll find a way in the next two days to get my shirts exchanged - I shall also see about that allotment as soon as possible. Also, I still have to see Ration Board about that shoe coupon.

I haven't told you about last two days at the Range so here goes. I told you about the detail our whole tent volunteered for. They told us we were to prepare Bivouac area. Oh were we misled, deceived and generally pineappled counter clockwise. We were told to make packs to carry - we did this the night of the party. These particular packs were to include an extra blanket and overcoat which were not included in the packs we carried out. We started out at 8 o'clock (AM) - walked, carrying these bastards about a mile. Then we set down packs. The true detail was building a bridge! For a while I thought we were in the Engineers not the Air Corps. The bridge had been started, all we had to do was to cut down trees 10" - 12" in diameter, cut them up into 8' lengths, carry these logs 1/2 - a mile and lay them in place on bridgework already put in place by some of the boys on our detail. These last mentioned had by far the worst of the bargain for they had to work in the swamp which we were bridging

They wore hip boots but were drenched by the end of the morning. Of course we thought when we started that we would be given the afternoon off so fellows cutting trees cut big ones indiscriminately - most of them red oak - heavy - oh joy! oh bliss! About ten o'clock we started cutting bass wood - that gave us some relief. The purpose of the bridge is to cut off a 6 mile hike around the swamp to Bivouac area. We worked like beavers all morning and completed about 60-80 feet of it. That's really going when you figure each log across measures only 8-10 inches. My shoulders still ache but more was still to come for we had to shoulder same packs we brought out and march back to range for chow. After chow the "detail" was given ten minutes to draw rifles and put on packs and get ready to march right back out again with our whole outfit. We were a bunch of sad sacs by this time. When we arrived at the Bivouac area we had to pitch pup tents (each man carries a "shelter half" tent, pegs and pole with him). We rehearsed scouting and infiltrating in the afternoon and were prepared for sham battle which came that night. About 8 bells when it was almost dark we started out in groups of 2s and 3s to attack the camp of the 1181st Tr. Gr. Let me elucidate. The woods in which we Bivouac are very thick - very few clearings and in some places trees are so close you can't get your body through. We were attacking a force that outnumbered us 2-1. The woods' ground was covered with leaves and twigs the treading of which can be heard at night in the woods for a great distance. Our problem then was a complex one for we had to advance from all directions while defending force had only to post guards and wait for us to come. They could hear us easily if they were on the alert - but that does not tell the whole story - these poor defenders had the 1183rd to deal with. Most of the defenders were pre-service men (all ours have been shipped) - some of the defenders were men who had already seen action but even they were out of luck.

We were a determined bunch - we crept about a mile on our bellies. It was not much more than this to their camp. We had a distinct advantage. There was a R.R. nearby. The noise of the frequent trains passing covered our movements so when a train went through we would run like hell for about 25 yards and then flop. By this time it was so dark that you couldn't see more that three feet ahead of you. But we infiltrated in the dark. Our C.O. with a couple fellows captured the enemy C.O. and when the whistle blew about half of our 85 men were within the camp of the 1181st. The battle was called early - bet we would have wiped them out if they had let us go ahead. We picked off most of guards and had control of situation even though they called it off 1 1/2 hours before it was scheduled to finish. Needless to say the lads who were in that morning detail were right in there! We captured opposing sergeants - some of our boys had trouble because the veterans of the opposing force didn't capture easy. A broken nose and ankle were about all we suffered when the lads started swinging rifle butts. We were particularly commended by Lt. Jenkenson our C.O. for the job - also by our sergeant.

We returned to camp that night and slept in tents - oh were my feet cold - I slept but not without discomfort. To tell the truth though - anything we did out there was like "cops and robbers" or boy scouts. Don't let anyone in the Air Corps tell you that what we get is tough because it's child's play - a vacation. In spite of the hard work we did on the bridge, we didn't mind it (except that they roped us in with a phony story) and none of us felt any ill effects after it. It was a good work out and the training was fun. The morning following the "battle" we went through a gas attack - actual tear gas but this is anti climax to me because I worked with things more dangerous than I'll ever meet in any kind of actual chemical warfare. You see, most of the most deadly gases are impractical for use on the battle field.

When we came back to range (incidentally we ate "k" rations in the Bivouac area for lunch and they're OK) we had a class on hygiene in the field, ate chow and then they piled us on trucks and brought us back to the Post. That is really the only way to go places - in a truck.

I'll try to write you tomorrow about some of the fellows but I must catch up on letters today - I owe so many. I got another grand letter from Fran while on the range and one from Ann. The Beals sent me St. Pat's day cards. They come near approaching the concern for me and the thoughtfulness that you fellows demonstrate.

I have the patches here and will send them on. I have two dummy 45 cal. shells here for the Powers boys - If I ever get caught with them I'll get court marshaled and that's no kidding so I'll have to be careful about shipping them.

Well, that's all for now (How's the back Barb?) Please be careful

Love, Frank

P.S. Please send Laundry Box. What I don't need I can ship home - maybe some dirty stuff to be laundered again. Also I'm going to try to snag an extra field jacked via statement of charges.

F.

How the hell do you like this paper?

P.P.S. Started getting Gazette. Received three today. After I wear them out I give them to boys from Buffalo.

Return Address:
Pvt. F.G. Thompson
A.S.N. 12,107,602
304th Wing
1183 Tr. Gr. Bks #338
B.T.C 10
Greensboro, N.C.

March 20th, 6:50 PM, Monday

Dear Mother, Harry and Mike,

Well, I received no letters today but I certainly got the next best thing. Lands! $.83 to mail the son of a gun - well, I certainly was glad to get it - I'll be more careful with my requests in the future - I'll be breaking youse guys.

As you have probably noticed from address we changed barracks again and our mess hall is closed down (that's right, not enough men to keep it open) so we have to go almost as far for chow as we do for mail but when I got that package I started right back to barracks. I opened it before I went back for chow. To tell the truth I haven't really passed it out yet - that is cake and cookies because all my buddies have pulled 24 hour guard duty. It's not much fun if you have no one to share it with. Before I got the bundle I was all dressed to go into town - I intended writing from U.S.O. but I'm not going in now - I can't see the point. I still ain't got the clothes I want and to top it off I spilt salad dressing on my O.D. blouse.

Some of the fellows here have already been alerted for shipping - we expect it soon. I pulled K.P. for tomorrow all day so you may not hear from me. I've also got fire guard tomorrow night so I'll be pretty well shot. It goes on and on after you finish Basic - guard duty one day and K.P. the next with plenty of details thrown in. At least on guard duty you have some time to write.

I don't think I'll be here long now because they're closing this wing entirely. I'll certainly be glad of candy bars on the trip which I believe will be farther south or west.

The follows already alerted for shipping in this group have been given no 10 day delay so I don't believe I'll be getting one - all three of us can bitch together on that one.

I'm going to try to take in a show on the Post this evening "The Uninvited" did you see it?

About Jerry O'Hara's coat - they only cost in the neighborhood of 14-16 bucks. Jerry told me yesterday that his C.O. said he'd fix it so that he'd get another coat without paying for it. Jerry will ship darn soon I think. Don't say anything to his mother about above because I think she puts a little color on his letters. The kid is perfectly above board. He doesn't bull around and he must know I write home so take things with a grain of salt.

I spent all day yesterday writing. I'm all caught up with the exception of the Beals and Aunt Emily - I'll try to make these soon but "my work" is going to tie me up.

I'm getting the Gazette now - guess I told you - but I read it now like I never did before - those dear old Otts are certainly on the beam - they haven't written me since that last epic note of mine - I guess I'd better not play the "sage" any more with my elders.

Well, I guess that's all for now - I am going to sneak a piece of cake before I go to show though. The cheese is the berries but next time don't send peanut butter or the candy - I can get these things cheaper (the peanut butter we steal from mess) than you can and we can get them any time. (But you can't get Ritz crackers for love nor money). You fellows have enough trouble getting these things so it's selfish for me to take them when they are so easily at hand.

Guess that's all for now so be good and keep well.

Love, Frank

March 21st, 7:45 PM, Tuesday

Dear Mother, Harry and Mike,

I just got off K.P. since about 4-4:30 this morning. I got another easy job in the supply room but you notice the long hours - particularly on the easy jobs when the "K.P. Pushers" must be dodged continually if you want to keep it an easy job. I have fire guard from 11:30 - 1:30 tonight so I guess I'll hit the hay early tonight. I also have the delightful prospect of guard duty tomorrow for 24 hours so you can obviously see that we are no longer trainees. We are merely waiting for shipment. I really should wash this evening but I can't see it cause I'm too tired. I must get laundry together and I think I'll have to have a couple shirts cleaned even though they don't fit me. I haven't had much appetite today for the cake - there is not much left of it now anyway - they fed us today on stuff that was much too greasy and it hasn't settled well on my stomach. This is the first complaint of this type I have made but we have changed mess halls and the new one is not what the old one was.

The fellows are getting pretty well fed up now. Now is the time when you can tell just how well a guy can take it - the going is rough when you get all the dirty assignments.

I went AWOL long enough to get Harry's Saturday letter. That reception must have been a lulu. With the liquor flowing like that I'd say the thing had been on the fire for a long time. Glad you're taking Ann out and you're a darn fool if you do it just for me - I know you've always kinda liked her and you know as well as she and I do that I've never had any claim on her. Good luck and good hunting.

Love, Frank

P.S. Too dished to make it any longer. Tired, Happy and Well

F.

March 22nd, 6:45 PM, Wednesday

Dear Mother, Harry and Mike,

You'll probably cuss me but I didn't mail the one I wrote yesterday so I'll have to send it along with this one.

For some unknown reason we went to the "field" today - saw movies, chemical warfare (went in cl 2 and gas chamber) and did different things this afternoon. I hope we get more of the same while we're here but the axe is bound to fall soon. We have a record check tomorrow afternoon.

I got Harry's, Mother's, and a letter from Ann in this noon's mail so I didn't even bother to go this eve. I got the Gazette also. You can't expect much more than that.

Nothing in particular happened today - nothing decent that I can get my pen on anyway. I felt a cold coming on last night after K.P. so I took a couple of emperin compounds and went to bed early. I've felt fine all day so I guess all I needed was some rest out of the drafts. I got the pills about 2-3 weeks ago in town thinking of just such a situation - darn glad I got them. I also picked up a darn sturdy pair of scissors at Liggett's here. They must be pre-war cause they're chrome plated. They're really darn nice. They set me back a couple bucks but when I want to cut the old toenails I have to have something sturdy and these sure answer the purpose. I also have had to pick up another pen because in spite of cleaning I couldn't get the other one clear. I didn't know you can spend more damn dough just on little things like that - and you don't know where the hell it goes. Same old story I and youse guys have always had.

This is the payoff. I have to take one pair of shoes to repair. Yes I've finished one pair of these heavy bastards already. That will give you a rough idea of the walking we do. And we don't even pick up a foot compared to the Infantry. The soles are gone. I have on the shoes the same rubber soles I had put on some of my shoes at home - you know what they are - I never wore those out but I've gone through these in less than 2 months.

Flash: Tell Bobby P. if he's still around that all shipments of P.A.C. (cadets) have been canceled - that is shipments here have been scratched. Rumors are fast and heavy around here. Better still - don't tell Bob till I get something more definite on the subject. Rumor has it that they are taking no more cadets but I fear this isn't even feasible.

Well, guess that will have to be all for now
Love, Frank

P.S. If you think anyone else wants patches or even insignia buttons - write me and I'll send them when I ship with Laundry Box. I'll also include dummy shells. They sell all sorts of things at PX but they seem a little gaudy to me - mostly in the line of embroidered handkerchiefs and jewelry.
F.

March 23rd, 6:45 PM Thursday
Dear Mother, Harry and Mike,

Well, here I am again. Under slightly different circumstances today however. I was alerted for shipment. My guess is that they are losing no time in clearing out this particular wing. Jerry O'Hara was alerted with the same outfit but he is going to be an armourer while I believe they will send me to school for radio. Perhaps we will go to same school for gunnery - you never know. I don't know which course I take first but we shall see.

I have no idea where I am bound for and probably won't leave for a day or two. They have taken most of my clothing but that's the way they do things here.

One constructive thing I did manage today was to make application for allotments for you. I've received no word from you as to whether you want said allotment so am assuming that silence gives consent so I am enclosing 3 forms. The 1st I have filled out.

The two blank forms you will have to have some of the family friends fill out and they will have to be notarized. I suggest F.E. Ott and maybe Fran Bealy.

When these two forms are completed and notarized send them with the 1st form to the address indicated on the heading of the 1st form. You'd better look forms over and have whoever fills them out do so uniformly - in the application I claimed 51% of your support. My reason for not claiming before was that I got 2 1/2 months military pay from DuPont and it was not necessary until now.

I guess that takes care of that. Send out forms as soon as possible. You will have to wait 1-3 months for checks - then you should receive all back ones together. It takes machinery that long to go into effect properly so don't be too impatient at first. They will start deducting from my April pay.

I got no mail from you fellows today but since I got two yesterday I really have no right to complain. I got my Gazette which I haven't had time to read yet and of all things I got a birthday card from the Otts. It was mailed on the 7th and I get it on the 23rd. The system here I believe is to blame so I'd advise you fellows to stop writing till you hear from me at the next place. I'll be here another couple of days I think but I rather not have things all screwed up at this end because the mail system here is lousy.

Well, I guess that is all for now.

Be good - I should get time to write a long one tomorrow.

Love, Frank

March 24th, 1:45 Friday

Dear Mother, Harry and Mike,

This may be the last from Greensboro. I can't say for sure because I don't know when we leave yet—couldn't even say if I knew. We had another clothing check today. I did manage to get another Field Jacket. This is the best piece of equipment the Army issues you—I'm going to try to send one home. It is darn dirty since it's the one I wore all through my Basic Training. The one they issued me was a second hand one and not in too good shape. If and when I send it home please have it cleaned. If that won't take out all dirt then try to wash it very carefully. Water will take out water resistant dope in it if it is very hot.

I don't think I'll ever try a job like that again. I almost dropped a purple turd when I had clothes checked and signed a statement of charges for a new one ($6.50). I just ain't the dishonest type (even though I am paying for it).

Harry can wear the thing if he wants to only tell him to be careful where he wears it. Tell him to say he found it on a bus or something if anyone asks him. I really will be worked on if I'm caught so let's hope no one gets wise to me—they can really make *it tough for you—especially with a jacket because they're the most prized piece of equipment of any guy in the Army.*

We will find out time of shipment sometime this afternoon. Just my luck—all PXs are closed for inventories till 5 this afternoon so I can't get what I wanted there.

There is darn little new to tell. They really get you going in a hurry and then keep you hanging on. I had only about 45 minutes to 1 hour to get all things in a barracks bag and report yesterday. I put on clean underwear and clean shirt (still haven't got shirts my neck size) yesterday. You can imagine how I'll feel when I get off that train. I have worn stuff 2 days now—sleeping in underwear. The shirt has a little blood on collar from where I cut myself shaving. It is a "sun tan" shirt and starting to soil at collar too and I don't even know when I ship and all other clothing is in warehouse waiting till I do ship.

I received Mother's and Harry's letters this noon. I guess I'll keep check all right if I can get it cashed. Thanks—I can use the dough. Just a word on that line. They will start taking out of my pay for allotment in April. I don't know full particulars but you should get between 35-50 bucks/month when checks start coming through. In a month or so I may start needing some dough because having signed "statement of charges" and allotment will make it a little tight. I'll be sure to let you know if and when I need it. Don't put too much aside—maybe 5 or 6 bucks. I'll let you know when I get tight if I do.

What bothers me is when the hell do we get paid for this month? We signed payroll here and then they ship us—Big Deal.

You speak of being more like myself in letters from range. Well, we did have a good time there—Sorry if I get a cynical twist on my letters—I really don't feel that way— I'm having a good time and that's no kidding.

The biggest part of Army for me is wondering what the hell is coming next and it has been a revelation to me at how well I get along with the other fellows—

I think I have gained a lot even in just 2 months. That rabid worry trait I had has left me. You just can't worry or speculate about the future in the Army—you'd go bats. I feel both surprised and elated when I find myself ready to ship and not all hopped up about it. This has been one of the biggest holes in my living in my opinion—in our living as a family at home too. It is true that I have that day to day outlook - you'd be surprised how much happier you can be with it. This is easily noticed in the men who have not developed that attitude because they are putting themselves in misery all the time.

If I get unhappy in the Army—don't worry you'll hear about it—in fact you'll see me darn soon after I start to feel that way cause I'll go AWOL in damn short order.

Well, guess that will have to be all for now—Be good—
Love, Frank

March 24th, 2:30 PM Friday

Dear Harry,

I certainly have been meaning to write this for some time partly because I want to set down the facts to read another day and partly because I feel I owe to you a little better explanation of what will follow, I know you had high hopes for me. I write the following, not as a gripe but purely as a statement of the facts as I have tried unbiasedly to observe them down here.

I didn't make Cadet nor did a great many of us here. We were subject to the worst kind of screwing I have ever known of. You see, some of us know that we passed everything - we saw (although we were not supposed to) on our records during a record check that we qualified - this was scratched and we were made A.C.U. or Air Corps Unassigned. It is hard to generalize about a thing of this nature - hard to pick out of the individuals who were chosen some characteristic which you do not possess yourself. We know of cases, in our group of men with as many as 1700 flying hours who did not make it. One fellow who had been a Cadet - was grounded and came here to try again - was not allowed to take psycomotive test over again. He was flunked out on the basis of his psycomotive test results and he had not taken it the second time and had qualified the first time. How they were chosen is a guess - I can't tell - Bill Edwards who marks these tests tells me that it is fair but the number of raw deals here are terrible.

One chap, who is now at an office job working with a Lt. Colonel, had said officer look up his record. The results showed that the kid had passed but someone somewhere had screwed him but good. This is one reason I never felt bad about missing. If I told this to anyone else they would certainly say that it was a case of sour grapes but it really isn't and I know I can write this to you and you will take it for what it is. Don't tell Mother although I think the smell from here is even getting up there and she might think I am unhappy about the whole thing. The cases I cited are ones I know of and my case I know of - they just don't need us, so we took the skids. The men who did qualify are plenty worried because they have just assigned 65,000 Cadets to ground forces. Thank God I ship to some school sometime in the immediate future. This is just one case of the type of screwing you learn to expect in the Army - it's just one of those things - you don't rationalize about it - you accept it.

Now one more thing - about Easter. How are chances of Mother getting her coat? How about your new coat and stuff? I'm leaving here so I won't get paid here but I should get it soon. I should be able to send 20-30 Samoans. You'll have to do the work as far as persuading Barb but I'm telling you that if that coat is not bought or something gotten for you fellows with the money I will send when I get it I'll do the buying at my end hereafter - then you'll have to take what I send and probably won't like it and it won't fit.

I see no reason to let the honorable Tess even know of this notable missive. I'd feel much better if you don't show it to anyone. Try to keep it if you can. I'll want to read it to my Grandchildren and don't betray me with that subtle smirk when you go home for dinner.

Love, Frank

HEAVY DATE

Present Day

It was now the end of March 2015 and I had just finished typing my fifty-third letter. I'd already learned so much about my father that I never knew. Things like he had brown hair, blue eyes, and that at only 5' 10" he was not a tall man. In the videos my mother had given us, the 1956 quality made it difficult determine his specific physical characteristics, and all the photos I had of him were black and white or early color. I also got the sense that he was truly committed to doing his duty, but it seemed that he was always looking for an alternate path to the one the Army was figuring out for him. I'd since looked into the role of a radio operator gunner in the Army Air Corps and I knew he'd eventually be part of a B-17 crew, though at this point he did not know this himself. Knowing that brought me back to wanting to know what had happened to make his pilot ditch their ship in the North Sea. I returned to my earlier emails with the hope of learning more.

Thanks to Art, I was armed with the ship number, the pilot's name, and the date of the accident. I connected with one of Art's referrals, James Muttons, from the Horham, Suffolk sister of the U.S.-based 95th Bomb Group Memorials Foundation. James put me in touch with their group's historian, Phil Samponaro. I had sent James a photo of my father's "blouse," which proudly displayed his Goldfish, to which he responded, "Thank you for sending through the photos, if you ever consider having your father's jacket displayed in our totally pure 95th Bomb Group museum we would be honoured to do so."

James invited me to visit what remained of the old base anytime, offering to provide me with a tour. This offer never left me, and when I eventually did take him up on it, the encounter ignited further discoveries on my coddiwomple.

Phil proved to be quite helpful, as James had indicated. Though he could not add much to what James had already shared, he did provide me with the entire history of the missions flown by Heavy Date, though he was unable to find any record of its ditching on May 26, 1945. One of over 12,000 production Flying Fortresses built to equip more than thirty-three combat groups during the war, Heavy Date flew her first mission on September 9, 1944. She made her home in Horham, England as part of the 336th Bombardment Squadron within the 95th Bomb Group, part of the Eighth Air Force. Against all odds, she survived a total of seventy-three missions until her ditching in the North Sea, where she sank to her final resting place.

In the early years of the war, crews flew the same planes for all their missions; however, toward the end of the war most B-17s were relegated to a "pool," and flown by many different crews. In total, twenty-seven different crews flew Heavy Date. I would later learn two interesting facts about Heavy Date. First, its place of honor in the 95th Bomb Group Heritage Museum in Horham, and second that one of those twenty-seven crews included a tail gunner by the name of Joseph "Ray" Perry, who died in 2017 at age 92 and whose son was the current United States Secretary of Energy. Records indicate that Ray's crew flew Heavy Date a total of thirteen missions compared to my father's crew flying her only three.

In addition to sending me the ship's mission history, Phil included a black and white photo of Heavy Date's nose art. This was the first time I had seen it. Seeing the actual plane only amplified my desire to find out exactly what happened that day in the North Sea.

SIOUX FALLS, SOUTH DAKOTA - PART 1

1944

Return Address:
Pvt. F.G. Thompson
A.S.N. 12,107,602
804 T.S.S. Receiving Bks # 142
Sioux Falls Army Air Field
Sioux Falls, S.D.

March 27th, 11:30, Monday - On a Pullman

Dear Mother, Harry and Mike,

I suppose you are nearing the frantic stage by now. Well, I am still in transit. I am writing on the train - that is why my scrawl is worse than usual. It really is an effort to write against the movement of the train.

We started the shipping movement at 7:00 AM Saturday from Greensboro and I will send you a map of how we came. My suspicion was that we were not going far because it would necessitate travel on Sunday - but we certainly are having some trip. I've known destination since about 4 hours after we started but of course I could not communicate it to you. I write now only because I wanted to have this ready the moment I found out the exact address so you will know that all is well.

I have enjoyed the trip immensely. We have ridden in an old dirty Pullman but have considered ourselves very fortunate not to have to travel in "troopers" or coaches.

We stopped to eat at Cincinnati, Chicago, and St. Paul - eating on diners otherwise. I'm darn glad I saved the Hershey bars for they have carried us through since meal times are indefinite. The junk we have eaten on this trip, you'd think we were worse than kids at a circus.

I'm well and in great spirits because I've really had a swell time on this trip - I never traveled much and the Army is certainly broadening my outlook.

Sadly enough only three of my former buddies from Greensboro are with me. These three I was never closely associated with - they are foreigners. Knitter was supposed to ship with us, but he was scratched at the last minute, damn it anyhow!

I have certainly caught up on my reading - I've read four or five books - no fatigue or tedium has affected me as yet for I've been reading and watching the good old U.S.A. pass by (more than 48 hours traveling now).

It is going to be some contrast in weather - here at St. Peter, Minn. (just passed it) snow is everywhere. Our car is shrouded in ice.

Well, there is not much more to say right now - expect to arrive at destination by 6:30 this eve.

Please get in communication with me immediately and when I get to permanent address I shall let you know more.

Much more love (to cover greater distance)
Frank

March 28th, 3:25 PM, Tuesday

Dear Mother, Harry and Mike,

If you don't get around in the Army you never will! Oh my yas! We arrived late yesterday afternoon. I cannot say that we were all chipper because the surrounding area as we approached destination was indeed desolate. As far as the eye can reach there are barren fields - few houses and few trees - almost no roads and as we came in we saw almost no cars on the roads.

The camp itself offered a desolate appearance for right in the middle of these vast plains you could see only barracks as far as the eye could reach. No trees to break the monotony - not a hill in sight. To the eye there is nothing here but barracks and almost as much mud here as at Greensboro.

I believe that the severity of the winter here has spent itself - it is below freezing of course but you do not feel the cold because it is dry. In the mornings in N.C. we would romp out on the drill field in the morning with wool underwear, fatigues, field jacket and overcoat and still freeze for the cold there bit right through you - here they locked up our clothes when we arrived and we could not get them till about ten this morning. It was cold without overcoats but your clothing was all you needed - for my money it is a healthy cold - a healthy climate.

It is hard to say much about the trip beyond the fact that I had a swell time. I'm with a pretty snappy outfit; most of them have had some college. At all large stations we would get out to eat in the restaurants in the stations. Then when we got through - while waiting - we would get in a formation and sing our bloody lungs out - we collected more than one crowd - but no pennies.

In a way it was even expensive to travel on the Army for it seemed someone was always passing thru the car with something to eat and as I said before we ate everything in sight. Also, someone was always passing a plate to collect for waiters, porters, etc. - big racket. At the stations you wanted to buy things but they were so obviously set out and the prices jacked up to snare the soldiers - most of us didn't fall. They soaked you 30¢/bottle of beer on the train. Most of us have discovered that, though the soldier only gets $50/month, the public is damned determined to take it off him as soon as possible.

The place for my money is O.K. I can't say I like it as well as Greensboro as far as the scenery is concerned but for all other things I can't complain. Maybe when I told you, before I came in, that the glamour and social end in the Army didn't appeal to me, you didn't believe me. My general conduct at N.C. must have convinced you of this. Here as far as I'm concerned is the ideal place to learn, and although they tell me the town of 40,000 is nice, I don't believe I'll be going there much.

We are in a "Receiving" period here which will probably last for 7-10 days. During this period, as I understand it, you do little for you are waiting for a training schedule to be drawn up. I hope to catch up on my writing during this time and do some more reading. I read four or five complete novels while on the train - at all U.S.O.s you can pick up those 25¢ books free so we all read them and traded. I really enjoyed reading more than anything else.

They are not fooling about teaching here - they run courses in 2 shifts - day and evening.

About writing - of course I want to hear from youse but tell the other folks not to write because, as you can see from address, I am in receiving barracks - I will be moved to a more permanent set up in 7-10 days.

I'm going to want my pen - bedroom slippers, etc. but don't send anything till you see I am no longer in "Receiving," when I get with a permanent Sqd. I hope everyone will write. Unless the Army decides differently, I should be squatting here for 5 months anyway and I'm going to settle down to enjoy myself and learn radio.

I don't think I'll lack for things to do but if I do I can always run into St. Paul and see Barb Webb and at extremes - Ames Iowa is only 100-200 miles away.

Pen is running out so

Love, Frank

March 28th, 8:20, Tuesday

Dear Mother, Harry and Mike,

Big night so far! On the way back from chow I heard Fred Waring for the first time since I've been in the Army–he was playing "Stardust"–of all things. That put me right back in a red mohair easy chair with an armchair Zenith and a good meal under my belt smoking a Camel instead of a Chesterfield. We are darn fortunate here because there is music everywhere–every time of the day. All over the Post on telegraph posts there are amplifiers even in the mess halls there's more music.

Another darn nice thing here is the Snack Bar. This is the nicest idea I've seen yet on an Army Post. You get your beer there–they have hot sandwiches, milkshakes, ice cream–anything to eat and it's open till 10 bells at night.

A couple of the boys and I have just returned from there. We listened to the Juke Box there–tell Harry they are still working on Wayne King's "Josephine" hard out here.

I suppose Harry is having a swell time at Liggett's–I'm certainly glad he is getting a chance at a thing like that–I know he thinks he missed something when he quit there so soon after starting before. I'm certain that meeting people in that capacity (even in the Trojan Trade) will not only bring him pleasure but enrich and develop his personality. There is also the convenient outlook that he can always tell the Liggett's to go to hell when he wants to. Don't let them "press" you Harry into doing things. But don't ever give your word that you'll be there and don't show!

Don't know just why I started this. A little spare time I guess.

Well, be good–I'll try to get at it again tomorrow.

Love, Frank

March 29th, 10:30 AM, Wednesday

Dear Mother, Harry and Mike,

I have just finished a letter to the Bealy Clan. I have great plans for my letter writing this day so I thought I'd better sit down and get the most important one off.

At present we are enjoying the period of inactivity that a lot of soldiers dream of. We have no training schedule and no definite assignment so that we are sitting around writing and reading. It is really cold up here and windswept but as I said before it is invigorating rather than the damp penetrating cold of the south.

The arrangement now almost compares favorably with civilian life cause we don't get up till about 7:30 - amble over to chow and return to barracks. We have to stay in barracks from 8-5 but this is a pleasure since it's warm and I for one am having a nice lazy time of it.

I guess I spoke too soon for a lad just stepped in and tells us we have to have identification pictures taken this noon at 1:30 - maybe we'll get stuck with details the rest of the afternoon.

I just interrupted this writing and went to mail call - nothing has been forwarded as yet anyway from Greensboro - nothing of mine at any rate.

Looking about I think I really am going to enjoy it here. I've heard some of the boys going over the code and I've glanced at a couple of books on the subject. It looks pretty rugged to me and I bet I don't do much writing anywhere during the course. They tell me it is a distinct advantage to be able to type when "Receiving." There is another one I missed on but we shall see.

As far as I can find out there are plenty of opportunities here with the exception of furloughs - Incidentally you'd better let me know about the family bankroll. If I apply for Engineering Cadet I must have a college transcript but don't worry about it because I'll have about 5 months here to apply - I'll inquire about the situation when they send us to "Classification", which is part of our processing here.

One thing I heard yesterday is so typical of the Army that I'm sure you'll get a kick out of it.

In the Radio course, they teach you theory and sending and receiving. I imagine you are schooled in all the parts - you have to be able to identify them all but here is the payoff. Under no circumstances can you take the set apart. I don't care if you're on a desert island with a plane shot all to hell, the set is put together with painted screws and these tell the tale immediately if the set is tampered with. You're subject to court martial if you fool with a set under any circumstances.

Well, guess I should close this one. It's really 11:30 almost time for chow. It is really a shame that it takes me so long to write - I often wish I could do the job much more rapidly so be good!

Love, Frank

March 29th, 9:20 PM, Wednesday

Dear Mother Harry and Mike,

Well, I'm starting another one. Just came back from a movie - "Harvest Moon" - it was a good deal better entertainment than I expected. Had my picture taken this afternoon. No kidding it may be only for a permanent pass, but you felt like it was for the Rogues Gallery - you know - they had heights marked in the horizontal lines behind your head.

Maybe I'm writing too much but I like to take advantage of the opportunity. Our respite may be briefer than we expected but it can go on for another week or so as far as I'm concerned. The thing that gets me is how most of the fellows are restless already. They're bitching and worrying about the future after only 2 days of nothing to do. For me I'm having a grand time and I hope it lasts a while longer anyway. A lot of these guys don't seem to know how to amuse themselves. I've finished books by Bromfield, Coward, Hilton's "Without Armor" and now in my second Rex Stout "Nero Wolfe Mystery." I took in the movie this evening - have my beer and a cup of coffee when I want it. I go to chow and belong to the Sioux Falls Air Base Country Club in general. I don't feel any pangs of conscience either. If the Army wants me to fight the war like this it's O.K. with me.

I've written a few letters - hope I get time to write a long one to the boys at the plant tomorrow but it seems they want us in a formation tomorrow at 8 AM - tough life.

By the way there has been a 27 mi/hr wind velocity here today - I still haven't minded the cold here yet - maybe if they dig me out of my burrow I'll begin to notice it.

12:40 March 30

I started this last night after the movie. Guess I'd better pick it up right now or I may be interrupted this afternoon.

This morning we were part of a formation which went to the theatre building and listened to orientation lectures - the best crack was made by the medical officer when in closing his lecture on venereal diseases he said "and when you want to make a water hose into a fountain of delight, be sure to use a rubber connection!" It wasn't a bad morning but it kind of brought me out of the semi-coma state.

Right after the lectures we went to chow and then to the main PX. A couple of the boys and I ran over to the Service Club - went to the library and drew a couple books. These should help while away the hours here in the barracks.

I figure my next move will be to the dentist. I sure want to get those two more teeth filled - of course they don't take many pains with you. You don't get anything to kill the nerve while they are drilling - you just sit there and grit your teeth - that is, wish to hell you could grit them.

A great many of the fellows here are washed out Cadets. In fact I believe that our group is unique in that we never even had a crack at the thing. Most of the ones I have talked to seem to have washed out on physical defects which showed up in the frequent checks the Cadets are getting now.

The way it has been explained to me was that there will be no more transfers from other branches of the service to the Air Corps. The only source upon which the Army will draw for Cadets now is the 17-18 yr. olders who are just coming in. Under these circumstances Bobby should have a darn good chance.

Of course I haven't heard from youse guys yet and they haven't forwarded anything from Greensboro but this is all to be expected. My guess is that you are just about getting my first letter from here now.

By the way did you fill out the forms I sent? They will deduct 22 bucks from my pay and you should probably get about $37/month. I hope this helps. I asked time and again about how you guys are getting along. I hope since my tax was not paid that you may have a little "buffer" that you wanted so much. They should pay us up here soon although the date is obscure. I'm going to try to see the Catholic Chaplain this afternoon. I want to get that check you sent me cashed - I don't really need the dough but I figure I should cash it as soon as possible. You see, any check you get must be endorsed by a Chaplain or some officer so I'll try to get out and do the job this afternoon if headquarters will let me.

Well, guess that's all for now

Love, Frank

April 1944

April 2nd, 12 M, Sunday

Dear Mother, Harry and Mike,

I'm afraid I missed writing yesterday–it was for the usual reason. I wrote Friday that I suspected we were moving and we certainly did. We had to return all bedding (mattresses, quilted comforter, 2 blankets, mattress cover, pillow and cover) to supply in "shipping and receiving." We were then marched about ¾ mile to 804th Sqd. where we again drew all the same bedding and again carried it all to our barracks. We suspect that this is only temporary and we will be moved still another time–oh my aching back!

Of course we got as settled as soon as possible in our new barracks. We were told right away that until we got definite assignment to school we were to have Permanent Party status. We would get details and K.P.–they needed 16 men from 2 barracks of about 80, that's right–go no further–I drew it for yesterday–typical Irish luck. The payoff was if I hadn't been such an "Eager Beaver" cooperating up to the hilt and signed barracks roster among very first I wouldn't have been taken so-oo! To tell the truth I really felt I had it coming to me–I felt guilty–you see I've done nothing but travel and sit around for almost two weeks and that kind of inertia doesn't agree with me too well, although that period was a great relief.

K.P. here is quite a deal! They don't fool–you are awakened at 4:00 AM sharp and you have to report at mess hall at 4:30 because they begin serving at 5:00 AM. At Greensboro they almost always stretched a point, lagged and got you up later. Here there is no foolin! I drew the "China Clipper" or dish washer. At B.T.C. #10–10 men were assigned to the job–here there were 2 of us to do it–I worked my petite ars off. I felt good on the job and healthily tired after. Four or five times the machine broke down but after the first couple of times I got so I could fix it myself. My buddy on the job bitched all day–but to tell the truth–I eat their 3 meals a day and I feel I should "pay my share of the check." Here, while you're in school you don't pull K.P. unless you're a bad boy–permanent party does all the dirty work–it's not really fair.

At about noon we found out that notices have been posted that we start school tomorrow at 7:00 AM so we won't be pulling details–Yo–we start on the morrow. I guess we will be on the Day shift–that gets you up at 5:00 AM in the morning and on the go till 3 in the afternoon with Bed Check from 8:30-9:30 in the eve.

A new policy has been adopted in our class and we'll all have Sunday off. Another new policy is the examing of your work in school–they've eliminated first tests–now you don't get exams till after 1st 9 weeks. All these new items have me smelling a great big Rat. I bet we're lucky if we finish course. I believe we will, if we get a sufficient start, so keep the home fire fingers well crossed.

It is probably in order that I tell you my reactions to the course itself. Here too I fear we have arrived at school well past the opportune stage. I said to you before that there are opportunities here and there certainly are, but the kind of competition you're up against here is terrific. For the most part men who are specialists in radio as civilians have been sent here. In our group there are a great many W.T.S. men (War Training Service). These men are fellows who were civilian Pilots–they were in a special program to make them service or liaison Pilots for the Army. Two weeks before program was to be completed it folded up and after going through Cadet exams (most of men too old to make Cadets) they were shifted here. At school here, as far as I can see, a good deal of emphasis is put on sending and receiving Morse code. These men have it down pat already. We also have a few amateur radio men with us who have civil licenses to send and receive. Don't ask me how I got sent here–me and a few of the rest of us. But you can bet your last "chemise" that little Francis George (Bow!!!!) will be in there pitching. Here at last is something I can get my teeth in in the Army. I'm in perfect physical shape and more than a mere hankering to do a good job so we'll see.

One advantage of K.P. here is that they evidently feel it's so strenuous that you get next day off–it feels fine.

We got up and went to church at 9:00. To tell the truth I'd forgotten it was Palm Sunday but I did get some Palm. Of course we missed chow since at our mess hall (known as the "Biltmore") they serve at 5:00 AM. We went to Snack Bar and had coffee–got back 11:15 just in time to have lunch and from there to Service Club Library. That is where I am now. It's O.K. here–I think there is a former Concert Pianist down stairs for he's been playing everything from "Moonlight Sonata" on. When I say he's good that's no joke.

I received letters from Mother and Harry the day before yesterday. After about 11 days of no word it did me good to just look at that "distinct vertical hand" and that equally (or almost) distinguished accountant's scrawl. I expect I should be getting something from you soon now. I'm being patient and I chuckle to myself every time I think of the look that must have crossed your face when you saw I was in Sioux Falls S.D.

I'm quite sure Jerry O'H. was right about his Texas deal. Almost all Armorer schools are there. I really expected Madison, Wisconsin but it doesn't make a great deal of difference.

Last night after K.P. I took a shower, put on clean underclothes and socks and went out looking for something to eat–that's right! I was still hungry–they fed K.P.s at 4:00 and at 7:00 PM I was hungry again. The climate up here gets you that way every couple of hours. I'll probably go broke just feeding my face up here. It's not that I don't eat at the mess hall because I always have. I've missed only 2 meals in the Army so far but I'm not used to denying my stomach and if I do go broke eating I don't care. I think I'll have to give up the beer here because I piddle when I get near barracks and then every time–just as I get in bed I have to run again. Here, a situation like that is most inconvenient because we are a distance of about a city block or more from the latrine and you run too much chance of catching cold.

Guess I'd better stop–have more to say but won't get this in the envelope if I continue. Have you had to pay extra postage on anything yet? Some of fellows' folks have had to, that's why I ask. Be good you guys.

Love, Frank

P.S. Thanks Harrola for the last mess of jokes–we had a good time with them–I'll leave you with the Army's advice though–"If you can't say no, take a PRO!"

F.

P.P.S. Writing time exactly one hour–have to do better

F.

Pvt. F.G. Thompson
A.S.N. 12,107,602
804 T.S.S. Bks 1221
Sioux Falls Army Air Field
Sioux Falls, S.D.

April 2nd, 4:05, Sunday

Dear Harry,

I am writing this back at the barracks. I've already written home but even so this may arrive before the letter home does.

I feel like a sad sac as far as Easter is concerned–I can't do what I wanted to about it. You see I was expecting to get paid when we arrived here but I guess we won't be paid till the 10th and that will be too late to do much about it.

My situation has been the following. I could get no pass in Greensboro to get in town to buy things except Saturday night. I thought youse guys would want something in the clothes line and I hesitated to buy for you especially in Greensboro because I knew that they saw the G.I.s coming. Also it seemed a little early to get going on the thing—now it's almost too late!

Here I haven't been able to get out. I might be able to get out tomorrow but I would only have 3 hours to get to a new town—snoop around for what I wanted and send it out—even then I couldn't be sure that you'd get it by Easter. I had hoped to send you more money than I am enclosing ($20)–but as I said we haven't been paid.

I don't like the idea of sending money. It's too damn much like the Thompsons but I figured it's about the best I can do under the circumstances. I'll try very hard to do better next time.

I wrote you but I haven't heard. It certainly isn't your fault–I should have had more of an eye to what was going to happen but the shipment caught me flatfooted for although I knew it would come I hardly expected it as soon as it did come.

Anyway please take enclosed $20 and do the best you can.

I won't get a chance to mail this registered until tomorrow. Not even sure I'll get off to send it then so I realize you won't be able to do much with it even when it arrives. Love, Frank

April 3rd, 4:30 PM, Monday

Dear Mother, Harry and Mike,

Well, finished first day of school today. More about that later. Yesterday when I got back to barracks there was mail call and I got Mother's first letter to S.D. It did me good to get it–just to know we were in direct contact again you might say. I must have read the letter 3-4 times anyway but I had to sneak it cause some of the fellows haven't heard direct from home as yet and we don't like to get them too worked up–especially the married ones–a couple have wives who are expecting and it's darn hard on them–darn hard on us too cause we have to live with them. I'm just getting a good idea of what I must have been like for the past 2 years. I have the letter here and will try to answer some of questions you asked in this and former letters.

The picture we had taken in Greensboro is lost–that's why I asked if I sent it home–I haven't been able to find it.

Only 3 men from 1183rd came with me–none of my buddies–so as so often happens in the Army–you find new friends.

I was going to send night letter when I arrived but couldn't see dramatizing the thing and maybe getting youse guys worked up by telegram etc.

Don't feel bad about allotment–I have lots of company and we're all pinching the pennies. Just as long as I can keep enough on hand to get home if I get the chance it will be fine. Anyhow–wait till you start getting it–Uncle Sam takes his time about these things and they won't deduct anything from my pay till the April one.

I hope to hell that Mrs. Ott didn't have mailing address of Gazette changed to Receiving Barracks cause, if it is that way, it will go to Receiving first instead of directly here.

Please send on my Physics book to this address. I thought I might be able to use Matrix shoes but no go I'll still have to buy some.

Cake and cookies arrived in wonderful shape. Just opened cheese yesterday. Don't send too much cheese only 1 lb. at a time—it's awfully nice to have on hand when you get hungry.

With book, please send pen and that black handled knife with long blade to address on this envelope.

No—I guess I'll never get tired of your telling me what to do!

I haven't sent more patches because I haven't found any flannel ones yet—only rayon—the latter will wash but flannel are nicer I think.

I hope that clears up most things for a while. OH—it will be fine if you can send pictures here too when you get them.

School, of course, wasn't tough the first day. I feel sure I'll like it. Hope I don't go screwy with the code. The "di's" and "dah's" drive most the fellows a little nuts after awhile.

I just left this letter to get my mail. This incident has burned me up more than anything yet in the Army. They are Holding Up our mail till the windows in barracks are cleaned. We just finished shining them as best we could—we can't get cloths—we've wiped toilet paper and done the best we could but you know it's hard even when you have clean cloths.

Little later. He gave us mail after inspecting individual windows—also we threatened to go to the C.O. We could have the damned Sergeant broken for that job. He is the kind of lad that wants to pray that he never goes overseas—he'll catch a slug right between his shoulder blades pronto.

With the mail I was returned two letters I sent on 28, and 29—the wonder—you get discouraged—the Bastards in Sioux Falls won't even let a poor Pvt's mail through. Of course the Army told us of change in postal regulations but not till after I had sent these. I'll try to get them out right away if I can get to Post Office.

It looks like they're getting to be pretty rough on us here about regulations so I guess I'd better close now—got a lot of little odd jobs to do before I hit the hey and we have to get up real early.

I just got a couple Gazettes from Greensboro—hope I get a chance to look them over before "bed check."

Love, Frank

P.S. don't send slippers

April 4th, 4:30, Tuesday

Dear Mother, Harry and Mike,

Well, these are busy days—let me give you an idea. 5:15 we are awakened. 5:30 Roll Call 5:30-6:00 chow (incidentally all latrines close at 6:00 so if you don't get your piddle in in a hurry you're out of luck). Lines are long at chow so you have to wait some time. You must go to chow in a formation. All this takes time. When you get back after chow you have to get everything ready for inspection–here that means very very apple pie and G.I. order. The big trouble being that each Post has its own conception of order. At 7:00 AM we have to be at classes ready to work–you have to arrive in a formation. Then we have 1 ½ hours Code and 1 ½ hours Theory. Then chow again. Here the line is almost endless and as always happens to me, I generally wind up on the tail end. You have 1 ¼ hours for chow but it is everything you can do to get back to class after noon chow. Then we have 1 ½ hours Theory and after that 1 ½ hours of Code which is the end of school. We march back to the barracks then and have, or are supposed to have, a full hour of PT. It hasn't lasted this long yet but you certainly work up a sweat. After that you have an hour of squadron detail which embraces getting the barracks in good shape–you know windows, etc. We have chow at 5 PM and that is our day. We have pass privilege from 5-8:30 with bed check at 8:30. I guess that sums up our day.

School is not hard and you have no school work to do after 3 PM. The instructors are of the High School variety–but I'm paying particular attention to the work because it's the simple things that you slip up on. Code is a matter of catching on. I've almost decided to "wash back" the 1st week of Code in order to get a firm foundation. Maybe I'll go in for evening classes at night–haven't decided yet–to me it is very important to get the code well at first because it's just like learning a new language.

One thing is very apparent here. The chow here can in no way compare with Greensboro. I had a meal at noon today that is the worst slop I have ever set down to. There better not be any more like that! One thing–we get all the milk we can drink here.

They are sticklers on regulations here but I feel that most of it will do me good. I think–at least I tried to convey the idea or thought I did–that we had it quite easy at Greensboro.

Haven't got the Easter package as yet but will sure be looking for it. I hope youse guys haven't done too much. I fear I'm a little on the shy side of doing my part–I really feel bad about it but maybe I'll be able to do better next time. That's a threat as well as a promise.

Yes Haroola, that is Mr. King's arrangement of "Josephine!" They really buy it by the nickel at the Snack Bar.

I have written Greensboro to try to find out what happened to Rudy but as yet have received no answer–I was so sure he was coming with me that I didn't get his serial no. so I'll have to wait to find out where he went.

We didn't get any brew in Milwaukee but got some good stuff in Chicago. They wouldn't let some of the fellows buy anything in the bar there because they didn't look 21 years old. Were they roaring.

I'm going to try to get some of my stuff in shape now because it looks like we'll stay here a while so be good you dear, dear people.

Love, Frank

April 6th, 4:45 PM, Holy Thursday

Dear Mother, Harry and Mike,

Well, how the hell are youse anyhow. I'm not in such good touch with youse cause I was the recipient of nothing yesterday but am anxiously waiting the mail now—it is already 15 min. overdue.

I just ran up and got a haircut and Confession and laundry are scheduled for to-morrow—I want to be in good shape for Pastor—well, as good as possible under the circumstances.

School ran along smoothly—not doing too well with the code but it's only the 4th day. I should get along O.K.—here's hoping anyhow. There is darn little new here—PT is still a bit of a strain but I'm getting there.

I think perhaps I'll take in a movie tonight—sorta take the curse of the routine off things.
5:50 PM

Well, they broke routine for me! Just told us to move out to–10 barracks down the street—Oh my aching ass! It's a riot around here—we had to move everything (iron bunks too)—while moving got my mail and then since we missed chow formation—had to sneak into another formation into chow. I ate—read mail—and am now trying to finish this one. Got a letter from Beals and from Mother and Harroola.

I had some trouble about cards (also the PX has no cards) and you know I hope youse guys have a Real Happy Easter—Hope Mother finds a coat she likes and Har-roola knocks em dead in his new chapeau. Have to cut it short if I'm going to make show and the lads are waiting.
Love, Frank

Return Address:
Pvt. F.G. Thompson
A.S.N. 12,107,602
804 T.S.S. Bks 1241
Sioux Falls Army Air Field
Sioux Falls, S.D.

April 7th, 6:00, Good Friday

Dear Mother, Harry and Mike,

Well, it is Good Friday (Guess I'd better go back to the pencil - damn pen is no good). It hasn't seemed at all like the "Holy Season" so I'm going to go to "Tenebrae Devotions" and Confession tonight. It's at 7:30 and I still have to shave but I thought I'd get this off now. One thing about which they were very considerate was the fact that fish was served at both meals today and they omitted meat from the breakfast menu.

I have made no special plans for Easter (this is a subtle hint for an invitation to your Easter dinner) and I think I'll write a few letters. Try to get up for early Mass - (High) at 7:45 and they're also having a Solemn High Military Mass in the theatre at

4:30 PM. The Bishop Brady of Sioux Falls will be the celebrant and since I've never been to one of those it should be an experience - maybe I'll make this one too - just for good measure. Please toss off an extra High Ball or two for me at about 3 o'clock for I have a feeling my tonsils will be particularly dry and rasped about that time.

A week from now I plan to go to town. I found me a lad here who is an agent for a photograph studio in town and I can get a $3.50 photo (4 proofs) for $1.00. This is a special deal for soldiers so I think I'll have the old puss taken again with G.I. hat on

Since it's getting late and I have to shave I guess I'd better be on the move so so long till to-morrow.
Love, Frank

April 9th, 11:30, Easter Sunday
Dear Mother, Harry and Mike,

Here it is Easter Sunday. Boy oh boy did I do well! Right now I'm sitting in the barracks at a desk they have here for us. Fortunately it is right next to my bunk. I have what is left of the first box of candy in front of me and it's not going to last many minutes more. I have a big Ceegar in my face and I feel good and content and at peace with the world.

It certainly was a grand box. You fellows must be just a bit psychic cause what you sent sure fit the bill. You shouldn't do so much - after all I guess I'm getting the cream of this thing. I don't suppose that Harry told Barb of my rather have-arsed attempt to do the right thing for Easter for you people. I'm not sore at Harry but here after if you won't play ball with me I guess I'll have to send flowers or send something I know darn well you don't want or need. Something that doesn't fit, etc. I thought what I sent might help with the new glad rags if nothing else - and when I got Mother's letter telling the higher cost of coats I felt good about the whole thing. Then I read Harry's little note. Oh I can understand how you look at it Haroola but I wish you'd have tried to see it my way a little more.

Now about that "Super Box." The Sox - someday I'll tell you the whole story about the sock situation and how the reinforcements arrived at the critical moment. It was indeed a crucial moment. The shirt - you'll never know how the old vanity and self assurance was lifted at the sight of that - just to know I have a shirt that fits. Of course my issued ones are in laundry - they must be cleaned before they can be exchanged. Here I have (just as in Greensboro) no free time when exchange is open. Also the laundry shrinks the shirts and the fellows all think that they will fit when I get them back. Why didn't I send them in BTC #10? The laundry there murdered shirts - you had to take them to a civilian laundry there also. The Sergeant kept assuring me he'd get me an appointment for exchange which he never did. Now even if they don't fit I'll have one that does fit and that will be great. The color is quite close to G.I. but I'll have to wait and see if I can get out of the Post in it so keep your fingers crossed - they're pretty touchy here. It is great to have an extra one - I'm afraid it set you back quite a bit. In fact the whole business probably damaged the budget plenty. I'm not afraid of sending even that shirt to the laundry here because I've seen the work they do on them and it compares very very favorably with any laundry work I have ever seen.

You should get a good laugh out of the packing case here. No I haven't sent it out yet but when I do I plan to put in it some of the odds and ends I've collected along the line. When it got here it was flatter than a pancake and on top of that I had no place to put it. I couldn't get it in a barracks bag, so I was stuck with it. For inspection it had to be hidden away, but where? You'd never realize how skimpy and clean cut Army barracks are till you try to hide a dusting rag or "packing case." Finally I put it under the mattress and there it stays every day. I can't sleep on it so I have to put it out at night. I'll get rid of it as soon as possible because its presence jeopardizes my weekends (gigs) and I want to get rid of that field jacket too.

I meant to go to Communion yesterday at 5 PM but when I got to barracks from school a fellow came around with mints (after dinner variety) so I took one and hence broke my fast. It's always something. I did go this morning though and it made me feel a good deal better.

I've been passing out my candy. You really don't need to go to chow here these days cause everyone got something for Easter and candy and cookies are everywhere. It is an unwritten law in the barracks that when a man brings around food from home - you have to take some whether it looks good or not. You run the risk of a frigid exterior of a man whose stuff from home you refuse - I had to learn that the hard way. In the barracks you share anything to eat - the guy that doesn't is black. Then too you know you can't eat it all yourself - I'm saving extra candy and nuts for a less abundant time when we'll all enjoy them more.

Of course, being moved about so much, you don't get much chance to get real chummy with anyone but three of us have more or less stuck together - Polish lad named Kostishack and a fellow from Syracuse - Bill Hughes - the former had 3 years of Journalism at Columbus Ohio. We are all split up as far as classes are concerned. A lad from Middle West works with me in Lab - his name is Terry, nicest guy you'd ever want to meet. We have Blaze, a minister's son, who holds up Protestation here - biggest boast is that Congregational and Unitarians are going to merge. Dave, next bunk, turned down a contract in Metropolitan Opera Chorus to enlist in Air Corps. No kidding you'd die to hear these guys - everywhere you go - no matter what the situation someone yells - "you too can have silver wings" - it's the biggest laugh in the Air Corps now. That is a quote from the Air Corps big posters they have everywhere. The biggest laugh I've had here was the third day we got here. Still in "Reception" and the snow had reached blizzard proportions. It was the coldest day we had here. A 3 stripe General was lining us up in a formation and some wise G.I. yells out "God dammit! Get these men out of the hot sun" - that phrase is a by word here - I think I laugh every time I hear it.

Thanks so much again for the grand box - going to try my shoe polish now - that sure is the McCoy. I have a small stock of ties now and should be all set for a big week end next week - I'll have to raise hell so I'll have a lot to write you on next Sunday.

Love, Frank

P.S. Fanny's all gone now!

April 9th, 2:45 PM, Still Easter Sunday

Dear Mother, Harry and Mike,

Since I didn't write yesterday I suppose I'd better dash off another one. I didn't include enough in the 1st one anyway.

I got the letter with the two semolians - this time it sure came in handy - don't know exactly why cause I haven't spent it yet but I keep roaming about with the lads and when we're not in the barracks eating we're in the Snack Bar or the PX or the Service Club eating - on our day off all we do is eat. Every time hereafter you feel like sending me money, put it under the mattress and then if I ever should have to write home for some - you'll have a little on hand.

To tell the truth I'm glad you got the light tan coat. I always liked the other one you had. I hope that "light" refers to color and not the weight. I never felt that the black one was heavy enough to keep you warm.

I did get the pictures. The fellows comments were, quote 1st "Is that your mother?"(Amazed tone) 2nd "You sure look a lot like her", 3rd "Gee I bet she's a lot of fun"! Although the picture can be professed to bear a likeness to you I can heartily agree with your first impression of the picture. I would say it was a distortion due to the angle at which it was taken - oh it's like you but the lines in your face are not that soft - a little sharper I'd say - and you're a lot lovelier looking than that anyway. Just as in my pass picture - they murdered me. I don't often get what I'd call a good picture - I'm too self conscious while the taking is going on.

The Gazette got here yesterday. It came late to Sioux Falls while I was at chow. When I came in it was only half there. There is a fellow from Niagara Falls in the same barracks. He was asleep when I got in so I didn't awaken him. I'll have to find out just what McCarthy he is.

The physics book is text by "Duff" and knife - the pocket knife.

I was going to write the Otts but I've sent two now unanswered and I suppose they keep pretty well in touch with my goings and comings anyhow. I should write the Beals because they're so grand, but don't feel much like it right now.

The best part of the pictures is that the leather folder fits into my O.D. shirts pocket and I can carry it with me all the time. Awful nice thing to have cause when you're alone or doing a little "Bunk Fatigue" you merely open it up and there youse are. Just like one of the comments last night - one of the fellows opened a box from home (a suit box) full of cookies and as he lay in his upper bunk his buddy said - look at him! Eatin' cookies and dreamin' of where they came from. Well, guess that says it all for now.

Love, Frank

P.S. Second letter because they clamp down on Air Mail wt. here and since I had a lot to say thought I'd stretch it a bit.

F.

April 10th, 5:00 PM, Monday

Dear Mother, Harry and Mike,

I put the salutation on this and just then "chow call." So here I am at 6:00 back at it again. We were supposed to have a "short arm" inspection before chow and get paid at the same time and on top of that I had to take shoes in for repair. All this from 4-5. Well, I got shoes in and we all went and got paid but we did miss the inspection. They should have known we would be O.K. because most of the fellows didn't have any dough as of when we arrived.

I got your registered letter and what I sent for Easter - I didn't send your Easter present back did I? I did the best I could - I didn't want it that way - money is kind of repulsive to me too when it comes as a gift but since I didn't see where I could get you fellows something up to your standard I thought that the money might help with your coat etc. Oh well, I guess there's not much sense in sending it back and forth at 40-50 cents a throw. Well, I made a fine showing for Easter anyhow didn't I? First Easter away and nothing at home for my loved ones. Leave us forget the whole business - I'm ashamed but I'll do better I promise you!

I'm going to try my best to get that jacket out of here tomorrow - my luck with the packing case has held so far - no use stretching it till it gives out. I'll include an Air Corps "T" shirt and a couple other odds and ends - hope all arrives in tact cause that case is a mess.

By the way I go to dentist at 3 PM on the morrow - they'll probably drill me to hell and back.

The way you talk in your letter I must have given you the impression that I'm going hungry - I'm sorry! for they do feed us here, you know, it's only the climate I guess and the fact that we seem to get so little free time that you can either go to show or eat during your off duty time and that's about all. I'd have more time but I climb into bed early - I find too much foolin around leaves you just a little dull the next day and you have to really be on the ball if you want to make a good grade in an intensive course like this one.

I delayed this letter again. Now I'm several blocks from barracks. Leave it to little Francis George (bow) - I found me a little frequented PX and I'm a sittin here with a couple buddies - drinking 3.2 listening to a Juke box an finishing my letter on the table - lots of room - good company and music - even a G.I. couldn't ask for more. As for my doing without here - never fear - I never would have sent dough if I couldn't have afforded it. I have everything I need and want. I haven't gotten shoes yet - couldn't make it at the right time when stores were open. I've always had the dough but didn't get *proper ration card till my last day at B.T.C. #10. I wanted to wait here till I found out if I could wear my Matrix. I could but I'd always be dodging M.P.s so I've decided to get me another pair. That's first on Saturday night's mission.*

I must tell you this before I forget it. It's a good illustration of the fact that here - up North - people still have a heart under their ribs for a soldier. This is true - heard it in the latrine last night.

A G.I. Joe went up to Hotel Carpenter desk last night and wanted a double room. The desk clerk looked at his name and asked if he wanted a bathroom. He said he did but couldn't afford it. When the clerk surrendered the key to him she said that she would like to have his buddy sign register too when they came in that night. The soldier replied that the other person was his wife - he was to be married that after-noon - he was bringing his wife! He was calm and unabashed but the clerk blushed and said "Then you will want a bath? The G.I. answered "yes but I just haven't the money." The clerk replied "What you want is the Bridal suite - $21.00 please." The lad got the suite and was tickled pink. God Bless that clerk!

One more item - you must remember Churchill's tribute to the RAF when they defeated the Nazis in the Battle for Britain in the air - Never have so many owed so much to so few. On the wall of the mess hall where we wait in line is an appropriate parody - Never have so many waited so long for so little! Not bad - what? Well, it's 7:15 now - I really started this at 5 PM - you can see where my time goes. Am includ-ing a little tidbit I picked up for Harry. Maybe his buddies will get a little kick out of it. Of course Mother is not supposed to read it - Be good and please keep well.
Love, Frank

April 11th, 8:20, Tuesday
Dear Mother, Harry and Mike,

How the hell are you guys anyhow? Today was a busy one too. Right after school I went to dental clinic - had 2 filled including that molar that had a hole the size of a dime. In the Army they don't deaden anything - they just drill. Of course when they drill & the tooth gets hot, the nerve starts to act up but they drill anyhow till the job is done. I have another appointment for Thursday - I think that will finish things up. Hope so

I guess that about sums up most everything. I should make some comment about the barracks I guess. We have a swell bunch of fellows in here - they're great! Ev-eryone works for and on everyone else to see that we all get through inspections etc. They're a great bunch. A great many of them are from West and Middle West and they're the cream of the crop.

By the way all PACs who were selected in Greensboro in my group have been transferred to ground combat forces - or the infantry of the Air Corps. I guess I'm a pretty lucky lad - those guys haven't enough training to lick postage stamps let alone Japs. God help them if they get shipped to a POE.

Oh boy oh boy do I keep busy - going all the time and getting plenty of sleep just about fills up my 24 hours.

I have to shave yet and read my Gazette so nite nite.

Love, Frank

April 12th, 4:00, Wednesday

Dear Mother, Harry and Mike,

Well, I just finished PT. The weather is grand here today and hence they ran us the equivalent of around a city block 3-4 times. I'm still sweaty and am sitting in barracks cooling off. I have plenty of time to get packing case off before 3 bells but the order of the day is stay in barracks till "pill call." I guess we get more Sulfadiazine and by that time it will be too late - maybe tomorrow. The pills are darn good I think - they certainly did the trick for me against colds in Greensboro.

I haven't passed my 4 WPM check in Code yet. I'll have to get going and pass as soon as possible.

To-morrow I have another session with the dentist - hope they clean them (teeth) again when they finish. When I got at Dix - of course - I used tooth paste. I soon found that I didn't clean teeth right with paste for I started to get a black deposit on lowers that the paste wouldn't remove. I've been using powder but I have a little starting again so I hope they clean my teeth.

I'm groping for something to write but nothing out of the ordinary has happened - even here with all the boys around I haven't seen a thing that is worthy to mention. I guess maybe I'll get me a couple of beers this evening and get to bed early again so that I'll be on the ball on the morrow. The lads didn't arise promptly enough this morning so we will have to stand Reveille in the morning - early - rumored at 4:30 AM.

No mail as yet - won't get it till 4:30 and it's 4:20 so - o - o Be good till tomorrow.

Love, Frank

April 13th, 4:25, Thursday

Dear Mother, Harry and Mike,

While I'm waiting for mail call I guess I better dash off the latest to you fellows. I had a double filling and a single one done this afternoon. I still have to go back and get another double filling done. Guess the old teeth weren't in as good shape as I thought. Let's see. One in Greensboro, a double and single last Tuesday and three today and two more next Tuesday that makes about 9 in all - It's almost worth be-ing in the Army just to get the work done. It will sure be a relief to get it finished up.

Today I passed my 4 WPM check and am working on 6 WMP. I'll have to keep on the ball - it's a pleasure to see even that little progress - makes you feel like you're getting someplace. I went into supply and they will let me know as soon as possible when I can exchange Suntan shirts. Maybe to-morrow or Saturday. I also took more pills today - I wonder how long they'll keep that up?

Guess I'll go to show again tonight. Going to make it the last one for a while but it's Paul Lukas and Errol Flynn in something about - oh it's "Uncertain Glory" - and I'd like to see it. As long as it doesn't interfere with my writing youse I guess it's OK. I wrote Gramp and Bealys last night. Stayed in and that's about all I did.

I just rec'd my mail. I got your letter with Lavery's letter in it. It was peculiar for I also rec'd a letter from Abe Aaron. I had lost track of him and I wrote to his wife thanking her for washing my fatigues last time and asking her to forward the letter to him. He seemed pleased as pie to hear from me and of course I laid on the old oil to his wife - that went over big I guess cause he claims his wife carries the letter with her.

I never (Chow call interrupted me here and now I can't remember what "I never.")

It is 8:00 PM - I just came back from show. It wasn't as good as I had expected - story weak and casting indiscriminate in my opinion. But I don't suppose you're interested in my "Picture Reviews."

Your comment on T Davis - I've been hoping that he'd get out of it - not so much for Tom but for his family. I know now a little of the Army - It might finish him for his family. About his running around - well, you've just heard - Haroola and I know more about it - you can't condemn a man for the conquest attitude - they all get it you know, Mother. Even you said yourself that you knew he was crazy about Lois. To me that seems enough. I only hope the Army doesn't take him and really take him away.

I have found out that there is a Technical Library in school building and I believe I will be spending more of my 2 1/2 - 3 hours free time there. Of course as far as the Theory is concerned I always felt I never knew quite enough about it and if I plug here I'll get an opportunity to pick it all up. Just think if I got going I might be able to repair the Zenith one of these fine days.

I also understand that we go on the night shift the 30th of this month. That won't give us but one day to raise hell but it will give you more time to study.

About Saturday - we may get a room in town over night. I bet we go to Hotel Carpenter where that "Patriotic" clerk is.

They claim there is a beautiful Cathedral in town and I want to see that. I guess there are a couple dances going in town so after I get my shoes we may make a night of it. If we get a room we're going to get a bath - oh do I want to get in and soak.

Well, I guess that will have to do for tonight. Be good youse guys.
Love, Frank

April 14th, 5:00, Friday

Dear Mother, Harry and Mike

I just got Harry's letter written Wednesday. I'm afraid the vacation comes a little late - let's see - I started school about April 4th so we should finish middle to last part of August. I don't think we'll get "delays" and I think furloughs are out of the question. I guess they are even cutting them out after Gunnery School. But then you never know what circumstances will prevail at the time. General Fichte inspected the Post yesterday. Never can tell what will happen now. Right after he came to Greensboro the PACs were transferred to Ground Combat. We will take up the situation when the opportune occasion arrives. If we have to, we may go into collusion with Dr. Muldoon - we'll dream up some-

thing anyhow. I could really go for one of those "up one side of the street and down the other" sessions.

Oh Boy Oh Boy Oh Boy!!! Some of the lads wanted me to take in a show but I can't see it. I've been spending too much time in movies. Think I'll investigate Technical Library this evening if I can work it in. I have to pick up my clothes at the cleaners this evening too so you can see I'm not exactly loafing all the time.

I got two Gazettes this evening so I guess I'll have to try to look them over pronto. Be good fellows -
Love, Frank

April 16th, 11:45, Sunday

Dear Mother, Harry and Mike,

I'm down to my letter again today - wasn't sure I'd get to it. We went to town last night sans the blouses. We wore overcoats and the M.P.s didn't' get us at the gate. I wore my sweater for the first time and felt all dressed up. Of course it handicapped me for I couldn't go any place and dance but I did get my shoes. I had an awful time getting what I wanted. Florsheim didn't have a shoe in the place to fit me so they recommended a couple places, since they told me there was no Matrix Shoe Store in town, I went to the Nettleton Store. I couldn't get Nettletons - they were all out of them but I did get Edgertons to fit (these are Nettletons second quality) they're not bad at all although I wanted a little better shoe. I think they will serve the purpose. I never bought a plain toe before because you know how I twist a shoe, so to eliminate this as much as possible I got me some wooden shoe trees. So now, at last, I'm all set in the shoe department.

We didn't do an awful lot - I kept leading the lads around looking for and in shoe stores. After I got them we looked the Main drag over. It's a nice clean town - they've got some darn nice small stores here - swell tweeds and beautiful sweaters.

We soon got tired of walking so we found a place to sit down - by peculiar coincidence it happened to be a bar. We had a few and by that time we had worked up an appetite so we were off to get a meal. I had Flank Steak - it was really good - French fries, cabbage salad, scotch barley broth, crackers and bread and butter, coffee but I didn't even attempt dessert because I had really eaten at chow and couldn't eat any more. It was too bad we didn't have our blouses because we couldn't go anyplace to dance for fear of getting caught so we went to see "Gung Ho" and then hopped the bus home.

We stopped in a darn nice book store here - they have a darn good selection. I was almost tempted to buy a "Radio" text but then decided not to because we do have the library here and it's hard to do any serious studying in the barracks anyway.

Our mail was late yesterday but I did get it just before I went to town. I couldn't wait to read it so did so while I ate. I got a grand mail - 4 letters. Mother's,

Harry's, Norma's and one from Ann. I had a swell half hour eating steak and reading news from the home circle. About the 3.2 - I don't think I ever drink as much as I had at home or as you fellows have so don't worry about it.

They have scheduled a Malaria lecture for us on our day off - some nerve but I have to get going so I'll have to close. Be good and keep well.

Love, Frank

P.S. Don't worry - just because I didn't mention it I went to 10 o'clock.

F.

April 17th, 6:00 PM, Monday

Dear Mother, Harry and Mike,

I must tell you about yesterday. At about 3:30 we got our blouses from cleaners so, although we had to be in by 8:30, we streaked for town again. Bill Hughes and I went in alone because most of the other guys were in town already. First we went to U.S.O. It's better here than in Greensboro. For hospitality give me the North any day. The women in this town are grand. You walk down the street and look them over and they don't look right nor left, they look darn hard to get. They really dress here too - and they have lovely legs - that is a generalization. In the South there are too many women with spindles. The women here are healthy looking and have just a little muscle in just the right places. Their stand offish attitude makes you want to get acquainted whereas in Greensboro you were afraid if you started to talk to one and didn't lead her to a bed in the next 20 minutes she'd spit in your eye. At the U.S.O. we got free coffee and sandwiches (they charged us in Greensboro). They have a swell place to dance and believe me that's where next Saturday might well find me.

When we left the U.S.O. we got shoe shines (my new boots are a glistening - have them under my bunk with shoe trees in them - already 2 guys are going to get the same). After that we went to a combination bowling alley and arcade. Here I spent nickels and more nickels. They had a lot of machine gun and rifle games there and we met up with some of the "live wires" we came on the train with. Then preceded quite a contest. We shot darn near everything in the place - and this is not vanity when I say I outshot the best of them - rifle "experts" and all. It did me good. Of course when I shot for record I was nervous - I had a poor gun and the magazine fell out 3 times. At the arcade I was in rare form and a lot of fellows spent a few nickels tryin' to wap me. I feel I can tell you this because you know I never shined at anything like that. We had dinner at a very nice place - breaded pork loin - new potatoes with parsley - corn - salad - bread & butter - pie and coffee for 80¢. Really was O.K. and a nice atmosphere too. The name is the "Chocolate Shop" - it's laid out completely with booths and there were probably more people eating than Louie's' could accommodate. The thing that gets me is how a town of 40,000 can have so much and Niagara Falls have so little by comparison. It's a dandy place all right.

There is the embryo of an idea in my head. I've been thinking that maybe we could arrange for dear Mother to come out here for a couple weeks. I think I could get a bedroom and kitchenette reasonably - I was thinking of the idea out loud and two fellows here offered to pay your way out here if you'd cook them a meal. Oh, I know you won't get all lit up about this but still keep it in mind - it might be feasible one of these fine days.

Tell Harry I expect a play by play description of his date!

I got a box of cookies - fudge candy - pinochle deck - mints and mixed nuts from the Nut House today. Of course you can't guess who it was from. Yes - 917 Walnut have really put time and I suspect ration points in that box. Toll House and Brownie cookies with nuts - nuts in the fudge - each cookie wrapped individually - the fudge in a separate box and mints and nuts in individual packages. Wish to hell Ann wouldn't do that stuff although it was grand as well as opportune to receive it. Chow was good at noon but in addition to PT we had extra drill this PM - we had to clean storm windows and replace them with clean screens and of course clean the windows. This made us ravenous cause we ate lunch at about 10:15 so just imagine us at a "piss-poor" chow tonight. So I've really been filling up as have the rest of the fellows. Guess that will be all for now.

Love, Frank

P.S. Can't even avoid windows in Army I know you must be getting a kick out of that.

April 19th, 6:35 PM, Wednesday

Dear Mother, Harry and Mike,

Yes I'm using my pen. It sure is a satisfaction - It feels good in my hand. I have many things to do so I'd better dash this off in a hurry. I didn't write yesterday - just plain didn't feel like it. I went to dentist yesterday afternoon for last fillings and they were beauts. Oh, it hurt a little in the filling, but the after affects have been a might bad. You see, he put a silver filling right next to the gold crown. This is the fundamental of a wet electrical cell. Two metals of different potential - then put them in an acid solution and an electric current flows. The saliva in my mouth is both the moisture and the acid and last night every time I touched the crown with my tongue I got ionization and the resultant electrical current played Hell with the nerves of both teeth. I complained of it before I got out of the chair for I knew darn well what was going on but the Lt. (Dr.) assured me it would be OK. It isn't an ache, but every time I got saliva or touched my tongue to the metal, the nerves hollered bloody murder for an instant. I went to the show when I got out. My appointment had been for 5 o'clock and I missed chow. I thought the show would take my mind off the thing and it helped. I did get sleep - slept fine and in the morning it was O.K. but started again about 9:30 or 10 AM. It feels fine again now but if it hurts again to-morrow I'll go back.

The box arrived in grand shape. The tooth powder was fine. I have a full box but the ends are cardboard and the powder leaks out and gets all over everything, so I'm glad to have these neat little containers. We draw foot lockers to-morrow so the lock came just in time. I'm glad to have the Physics book. I am familiar with it and it will help fill in gaps in the Theory end of the course. The soap is fine - I sure will stink purty when I step out. I'm putting the soap in with my O.D.s so they'll smell nice. Cigarettes also came in handy - I was just going to PX for some.

I sure had a busy day today. After school PT and drill. Then I got my laundry and shoes from repair. Then I went to mail room and got my package - returned to barracks and then stood in line to sign payroll. When I returned, the barracks had marched off to chow so I had to sneak into another formation to get my meal.

When I finished chow I returned to barracks and opened my package. I rearranged laundry and at last all my socks, underwear and towels are clean. I really feel good about that. The sock situation was certainly critical there for a while for there is no place or no way to wash out your worn socks here. It all has to go to the laundry. My how the days go by here! The days are whipping past and it's hard to see where it's gone until you look at the work we have covered in the radio here. About the laundry - I'm allowed 30 pieces a week for $1.50/month so get the neighbors and your own laundry together and send it down! I never have 30 pieces a week - oh yeah!

How about Tom Daroy - does this 26 year old regulation save him? I hope so. I received Fran's letter today - but got none from home. Let's go fellows - a little better coordination if at all possible. You see I raise hell with the mail man. Time and again I get him up out of a sound sleep to go over and get the mail - then I don't get any letter - get two the day before or the next day so the mail man is just about ready to tell me to "Blow it out my Barracks bag." Don't get sore now - I just filling up this page and I guess that's about it so be good.
Love, Frank

April 23rd, 11:10 AM, Sunday
Dear Mother, Harry and Mike,

Back at the barracks. Noon chow is well over and I'm settled down to writing and studying. Planned sojourn into town looks like it may have to be postponed because the weather here is miserable. We have had a steady downpour all morning and apparently we can expect no respite today.

It was really fun at the dance last night. The girls were so wholesome and sweet and well built and charming and well built and attractively dressed and well built! One of them told me of the session this afternoon. It would really be a good idea I suppose to go to town this afternoon because not many of the fellows will be there due to the terrific rain but I can't see getting O.D.s all drenched and out of press.

When I got in, home or barracks, last night I took the citrate and it worked for me as soon as I got up so I'm cleared there. I went to Mass this morning. It's getting more satisfying at Mass now - not so much like a competition. I start in the missal with the priest and end up with him too.

One thing I didn't mention about that dance last night was that they raffled off a telephone call home to any service man there - of course I didn't win it - my Irish luck - but it was pleasant speculating about it.

I wrote last night from U.S.O. Don't know whether you will have that one by now or not - that is by the time this one gets there. I'm going to stay here till mail call - haven't heard from you in two, well, almost three days now. I haven't rec'd package as yet - all this is no doubt due to some discrepancy in the mail.

I got my shirts from exchange yesterday. In a way it was a disappointment. I took in 3 brand new ones and I got back one pretty good one but the others are well worn. Well, I'll wear them as often as possible to wear them out - then maybe I'll get some new ones. I wore my "Easter" shirt to town last night and felt all dressed up with my "Civvy" shoes and freshly cleaned & pressed blouse and pants - clean socks, underwear and new tie. I must get me a haircut soon it's well grown in now from the "slicing" I took in Greensboro. Maybe I'll get it cut in town.

Boy I bet this is dead reading but unless I write the incidentals I have nothing to say. I should really write the Beals but I know I won't get to it today. Haven't thanked them for the socks yet but I should get it done to-morrow night. By the way it would be a good idea if you would send me a list of things you need. Don't laugh - I was in a drug store last night and they have all manner of things that have ceased to be seen on the counters at home. Rubber hot water bags and all stuff like that there.

I just opened a can of pineapple one of the boys got from home - I did it with my knife. Experience gained at the cafeteria has done me good here too. We were all wondering how to open the darn thing and since I'd seen it done before I was not to be caught with my pants down. The pineapple was warm but darn good.

Well, guess I'd better dry up so be good.

Love, Frank

April 24th, 3:50, Monday

Dear Mother, Harry and Mike,

PT is just over and I'm all sweaty and a settin on my bunk. We had a scare in school today - we almost got the "Quiz Kids." I call it a scare because there were a couple things I wanted to check up on and had left it for tonight - you see I haven't changed much - I still let things go.

I must tell you about yesterday. After I wrote you I hit the books for a while. I couldn't get any of the guys interested in discussing the stuff - they all seem to feel that they get enough 6 days a week. It stayed miserable and so I studied on. Finally I got a bit tired and restless so Bill Hughes and I jumped into our O.D.s rain or no rain and jumped on the bus to town. We arrived at the U.S.O. with only a few drops of rain on us for the bus passes about 20 ft. from the barracks and stops in town about the same distance from the U.S. O. We got there just in time to play 6-8 games of ping pong and then on to the Free lunch. This we demolished in short order. After reading the Sunday papers including "Terry and the Pirates" we got our coats and proceeded to the Masonic Temple. Here we found a place to shine our shoes - shot a couple games of pool and at 5 o'clock no - it was 6 PM we went for the Free Masonic lunch and then there was dancing there sponsored by the "Pleiades." O joy, oh bliss

- They'll be shoving me thru the 16th or 18th chair (degree) soon. It's a good place to go though - the girls are grand and everyone in uniform is welcome so I can't see not taking advantage of it. And did I meet a sweet little brown eyed baby - soooo.

She goes to (I think it's) Augustana, a girls Arts College about two miles outside of town. She comes from Minn. - pretty nice!

I left early though. We had to be back by 8:30 and we must have been back by7:45. I wanted my mail and sure enough I had two letters - one from Haroola and one from Mother, but still no box. Don't get the wrong idea - maybe I've been expecting it for too long now - it will probably get here by 4:30 before I'm even finished writing. I've had the boys drooling since I first heard of the box and believe me we are looking for it with a good deal of anticipation.

Well, I'm surprised that the Tessa would be ready and willing to come out here. Really I think the change would do you good Mom. It's good country out here just as it is anywhere in the good old U.S.A. Here is the way I've looked at it. It would be kind of hard on Mother because I couldn't spend a lot of time with you but I think I could get permission to stay out overnight week nights while you're here. I've been inquiring around and I heard that I could get maybe a three room apartment for about $25/month. Bill Hughes and I thought that maybe if we rented one you could have it for two weeks and his wife the other two weeks or maybe something like that. Oh well, that of course is in the future and I still have to find out the train fare. The deal I would really like is - if they give delays in route here after graduation maybe Mom could make it that week and then I could take her back to the Falls again. That would be O.K. but you know the Army - we'll have to see about it.

Gee hasn't Aunt Maime got enough to do with her brood without knitting for me - don't get me wrong - I love it. Just to prove to you that I think about her often I already bought her a Mother's Day card for the 12th - thought it would be a nice idea to send her one - don't you tell her now. The sweater I have fits swell around the neck but if she could, without pulling it out, make the neck just about 1 1/2 inches deeper - then it wouldn't show above my blouse. If the thing is well on the way please don't say anything because it will be perfect for me as is. They are swell - at all these dances the fellows wear sleeveless sweaters - the blouses are too hot and with a sweater you don't have that "bare shirt" look - they all wear them here only I haven't seen one that can compare with my cable stitch.

I wish you'd write and tell me just what is wrong with Bobby that he has to see a doctor. You must keep vigilant watch on our Haroola Mother. It might be a good idea to investigate these Sulphadiazene tablets - I think they have had a great deal to do with keeping most of us in shape and right at this changeable season we're really open to a lot. Interruption - mail call - then chow.

I see by the latest that I'm not getting a box. Well, I have a letter here that says something was coming and Harry wrote me about it too. It didn't come again today - somebody is going to catch hell in another day or so!

Seriously I hate to ask for things unless I really need them. The same goes for food when I know how hard and expensive it is to get for you PFCs (Poor Fouled Civilians - that's what the boys call it here). I know it's extra work and that you get awfully tired the way you insist on keeping things at home. I hate to pester and it really isn't neces sary for you know that the old "bitcher" would be sounding off if things weren't OK.

About the mail - I have written every day since I've been in the Army with the exception of days I had K.P. and the dentist the other night. I mail mine about the same time every night so, at least, I figure you should get one every day. Don't expect this to last - as this course gets tougher and as the place becomes so familiar that I can think of nothing to write I probably won't get to it.

No I don't need more sox or underwear just yet. I have enough to change sox everyday and underwear every two so I'm pretty well off in that respect.

I didn't know about Ann's situation although I did know that after a couple of disappointments she did say she was going to try for a Falls School.

About the Air Mail Stamps - I've often meant to say why don't you just try 3 centers. I got a letter mailed by Ann Friday night 2:30 with the one you mailed Air Mail Saturday morning so maybe they don't give the 8¢ stamp the classification it deserves. In Ann's letter she says nothing about her new position so I really had no idea of it till I got your letter. I also have a letter from the Beals - I must get to that now - I'll have to write and thank them for the sox so be good you fellows.
Love, Frank

April 25th, 6:45 PM, Tuesday

Dear Mother, Harry and Mike,

Today was a long day. In fact I am just back in the barracks on my own time. As soon as we got out of school we were sent to a lecture on the Automatic Pistol. We had had all this at B.T.C. #10 and when I got out at about 6 PM I was tired as well as bored. In this particular subject I think the repetition has a point because we will soon fire pistols on the range and it is a complex and dangerous weapon - I was glad to be refreshed on it. At any rate I just got out of chow and I'm' kind of tired. Not even my Gazette came via the mail today so I'm glad in a way that I'm back a couple - I'll catch up to-night.

Another thing that made the day trying was that I went up before the "Quiz Kids" today. The entire oral examination lasted about a half an hour. There were three sections - Direct Current - Alternating Current and Vacuum Tubes. I feel quite satisfied that I passed but I wasn't the ball of fire I'd have wished for - just a little too nervous at the outset. I won't know the grade till next Saturday so I'll pass it on to you when I find out. I hope to get off 8 WPM in Code in a couple days and I have been working hard at it. I guess that almost covers all the developments at school. I don't know when we go to the range but it won't be a session like Greensboro. We will go out there and fire and right back again.

Bill Hughes laughed at me when I'd come in with cuts from shaving till he shaved beside me one afternoon. He then promptly sent home for his electric razor and said that it was the only thing for a beard and skin texture like mine so I now have an electric razor in my foot locker - haven't tried it yet but it should simplify the shaving situation.

We have a squadron dance coming Thursday night so I'm going to rest up to be in tip top shape for it. The boys who have been say that they are wicked affairs so we have that to look forward to. Well, I guess I haven't enough to fill another page so be good and keep well.

Love, Frank

April 26th, Wednesday

Dear Mother, Harry and Mike,

I just received Mother's letter of Sunday and Monday. I think I answered most of the questions in previous letters.

No, I don't want the ration book - the thought just occurred to me at the time. Just be careful and be sure and cover yourself. I took my exams and didn't make honor roll. I found that out today - won't know my exact grade till Saturday. Even my instructor told me he was disappointed - he called me for it and I certainly did but I guess I messed up on being just a little too nervous to make a good impression on the examiner - that is the first one, so he probably fixed me right there. I've felt damn disgusted all day but there is no sense in that so I'll just have to try to do much better - don't know how because I've been almost teaching three or four guys in my spare time - well, just the fortunes of war I guess.

I shall write a special letter to Fran - I do hope it's nothing of a serious nature. She's kinda my strong front at the Beals I think.

So the pin is growing on you - well, I'm glad. I didn't think it made too good an impression at first - maybe it looks cheesy at home but it didn't look too bad here. Please get the jacket in good clean condition for me - I'll be wanting it ready when I get home.

They really worked us out today with drill and PT. 1/2 hour solid exercises 1/2 hour solid running on the double - that's no stretching either and 1/2 hour drill. Then I got a haircut and then chow so you can see how much we are booked solid here.

I did sneak out to the show tonight. I saw a lad from the Falls - Benny something - Harry had him calling at 4:40 for him in the mornings before school a few years back - hope maybe you can place him from that - I didn't get a chance to talk to him.

Nothing else very new I guess except that the place is flooded with more washed out Cadets and that the whole place is undergoing a complete reorganization - we get a new C.O. to-morrow. Well, be good and keep well.

Love, Frank

April 27th, 6:55 PM Thursday
(Army and Navy Masonic Service Center Letterhead)

Dear Mother, Harry and Mike,

You can see from the stationary just where I am - no, I'm not going APO but the set up here is nice and the fellows I'm with wanted to shoot a little pool so I came along and am getting out my letter for the day. We came into town because the

804th Sqd. dance is at the Coliseum tonight. There are going to be free refreshments and our pass privilege has been extended so we are all on hand.

We came in early hoping to find stores open but they were mostly all closed soooo since we had missed chow we hunted up a place the fellows at the barracks recommended to eat. It's a hole in the wall - run by three women. The tables are scoured till there is no paint left on them. It would compare favorably, in appearance (outside only) to one of the very small "joints" at home. It certainly isn't pretentious but did we get a steak - one of the best I've ever had out or in the Army. Not a lot of trimmings but not a lot of price and we're used to going without the atmosphere. It certainly was a good deal.

I guess maybe I should tell you a little about camp - yes things are due for a change. It is a pity but we have a new C.O. and he is formerly C.O. of a Cadet school so everything is about to be changed. This is independent of a complete shapeup as far as organization is concerned - we will have to wait and see what materializes as regards the latter. We have to march to chow now and march back - at mess today there was more brass than you could shake a stick at. And were the officers burned about it too. From Majors right down we were well corralled and made to march back to school from chow. It is easy to see that there is a terrific overage of officers and they are trying to give them something to do.

So Haroola is going to skip the light fantastic Saturday night - good hunting old man. Mother shouldn't be too critical of your women, old man, but I would suggest getting out of your cocoon and interesting yourself in some sport or art or some damn thing where you will meet some of the nicer dolls. That's one thing that is definitely impressed on you as you walk around the streets of any town when you're in the Army. There is a dearth of men everywhere of course but you can't meet a nice girl just anywhere so you find some place or something when you are going to come in contact with them. Of course this is easier said than done but it should be easier for you than the boys in the Army. You know we are all leery of these babes in the U.S.O.s, in fact leery of them all period. Thanks for the jokes Harry - I'll have to try them when all the lights are out in the barracks just before we go to sleep - that's the universal time for tellin' them you know.

Harry speaks of the stink (political) at home. Send me some of the dope, I mean the inside, on the story will you. Of course I've been following it in the Gazette but I have about four fellows asking me about it each night (yes they are interested too) so I like to get something to tell the boys - they all read my Gazette and it's like a continued story - we are all wondering which way things are going for I have explained to them that the Gazette is G.O.P. and is telling only their side of the story.

About precautions with the jacket - those were only if Harry wore it and was questioned - I don't think he would be, but if he is, tell him to say he found it on a bus or even that I sent it home. I had the jitters when I was making off with it - don't know why I should but I did - I paid for it so it wasn't stolen. They wouldn't let me take it home I know if I got a furlough, so I wanted to have one there when I arrived. The blouse is O.K. but too heavy and fancy for a lot of things I'd want to do when I get home so don't worry about the darn thing. Harry - just don't let anyone take it off you - that's all. I really feel if you'd like to wear it that you'd be perfectly all right so go ahead with my blessing.

By the way, I hope you wear the grey pinstripe Saturday night. I always find it helped any conquest and it's seen a lot of things and will bend easily in the right places in the clinches.

I guess I'd better dry up and I must write Fran a note so be good and keep well. Love, Frank

April 27th, 10:30 PM, Saturday

Dear Mother, Harry and Mike,

As you can see I'm at the U.S.O. again. I didn't write previously because I didn't really have the time. We went to school - PT and then to a medical lecture and that booked us solid up to 5:15 - then chow and rush to get shaved and dressed and into town on very urgent business. We hoofed around town quite a bit and went several places - among the most satisfying was a dance at the Masonic Temple. No kidding the girls there were luscious to look at and darn hard to get to. Of course that made me feel quite good but I had a couple severe blows to my ego and vanity.

Somehow at home I've been riding on the crest of something that I never quite appreciated. Of course as a G.I. you are all alike and dressed identically - if you want to make an impression on a girl you have to do it in the few minutes you can dance with her before you're cut. Oh boy oh boy - a young chick really put me in my place when she asked me, "Do you talk?" I was quite abashed - over a period of years my line has really deteriorated and log of "small talk" is just about nil.

Well, here looks like a problem worthy of my attention - Guess I was cooped up too long and I well knew that I hadn't been meeting the quota of new girls I should, but if I'm going to get hold of anything here it will take some real concentrated effort on my part let me tell you.

I'm all set for the campaign. I may come in to-morrow for a couple "Tea Dances" and see what I can do. I may as well get into the swing of things. I plan to study a good deal to-morrow - won't make town if I don't get done what I want to.

I'll have to make this a quickie for this place closes at 11:00 and it's getting near that now.

I passed 6 WPM today and am working on 8 - got to get going there too. We have exams next week and change instructors the week after as we go into our "second phase" of the course.

Right now I'm drinking a coke but I'd like a little something not so sweet so I think I'll hit the road back to camp and get a couple beers on the way.

I'll go to 7:45 Mass in morning. I've got a bottle of "citrate." Maybe you'll get a laugh out of this - I never did go to a dance before with citrate in my pocket.

I got it before I went to the dance and of course everyone who has checked the coat tonight figures I have a 1/5th of something. I got the stuff to clean me out good while I'll be at camp to-morrow - haven't done that in some time and I've tried to think of it as standard practice every once in a while.

Guess that includes most of biological, social, and mental news of the day. Be good. Love, Frank

April 28th, 6:05 PM, Friday

Dear Mother, Harry and Mike,

Well, we had two swell meals today. Tonight I was given almost more than I could eat and consequently I'm stuffed - had my two cups of coffee (incidentally these cups hold exactly 1/3 of a quart) and of all things we finally have a radio in the barracks. Right now it's Fred Waring. "Time On My Hands" and "The Time Is Now" and "G.I. Jive." I am, in my mind's eye, in an awfully easy red mohair chair beside an armchair Zenith with a big black spot in my lap - I can hear Tessa starting the dishes and maybe I'll wake Haroola and make him help tonight - it's a damn pleasant thought isn't it? God has certainly been good to us - we have had so much of one another.

Enough of this sentimental slop - I'm on my bunk, propped up by my barracks bag and it sure is good to hear a radio again.

Well, I went to the Sqd. dance last night. It wasn't' bad at all. The place was extremely nice for a G.I. dance and there were a good deal more women than I expected. I had quite a few dances and was particularly impressed with a willing blonde whose accent, voice, and facial features reminded me of Mrs. Pedrick of all people. She was well spoken and could she dance! She works in a law office and her name is Ann Fredricks. She is nice people.

There was plenty of beer if you wanted to stand vigil at the bar but I was more interested in dancing. Best news of all today is that we don't lose our Major Jeff after all so everyone feels much better today.

I'm going into town to-morrow night to see if I can get the things you want. You might send along a couple of the biggest needs each week and then maybe I can shop for them - give me a good excuse to poke around the stores and I've kinda missed my pokin around. No - I didn't know Dick was in England - looks like he'll be flying paratroopers over for the big invasion doesn't it - well he'll be in on the biggest show on earth - in a way I envy him - in a way I don't.

I don't know when we go on the night shift but probably in a week or two so about then I'll be pestering you for things to eat. I can see me just out of school at 11:00 PM - hankering for something to eat. We're thinking of buying a Silex and electric unit for the barracks - you know - coffee before you go to bed. We're going to shop around for one of these too.

Yes, I know it's three months - didn't think I could stay away that long. The time has been passing so rapidly I hate to see it go here. I have been happy in the Army I think - the secret is never to set still. If you keep well on the go you don't have the time or energy to be blue. This radio is fascinating to me. I'm very glad I'm getting that. My last letter should let you know about the Gazette. Harry tells me of the O'Hares of Tenth Street. I certainly would like to do or write something but I don't know exactly how to make the expression. I'm asking for constructive criticism - I suppose I certainly deserve a bawling out but I hope it's never too late to say or do something nice.

Tell Haroola I'm still on 8 WPM. Wish I could pass the check to-morrow, - I hope I hope I hope.

Well, I guess I'd better toddle along now. I have a couple things yet to do and I want to get to bed early so I'll be as fresh as possible for school to-morrow. I've been shaving with an electric razor lately - it certainly is a rest for the old "Puss" and although you don't feel as clean, it serves the purpose well enough for school.

The fellows are going to take our pictures soon - I must get one in my fatigues - I'm the sloppiest looking soldier in them that you've ever seen. The cameras are arriving from home now so it shouldn't be long.

Be good and keep well.

Love, Frank

April 29th, 8:30 PM, Saturday (Nite!) -

(Letterhead Army and Navy Masonic Service Center)

Dear Mother, Harry and Mike,

Here I am back at that den of iniquity again. I like to write here because they have individual writing desks and I can take my own sweet time.

I just finished doing the town with Bill Hughes - we were shopping. No electric irons for love nor money - I expected this - I could get the kind you heat on the stove though - interested? Don't worry about the clothes pins - I think they can be procured - how many do you need at the moment and how soon? We even tried second hand stores for irons - best I could do was a new one at a hardware store in about July. Keep looking at home - really I think yours could be fixed easily. Just where does the cord burn out? If the wires themselves go I'd say you had worn out insulation in between resistance plates. By taking iron down these could be easily renewed by anyone who knew anything about it. What you're probably doing is shorting out resistance plates because of worn out insulation - with reduction of resistance, the current is being boosted to a point where cords are going. I'd get it fixed as soon as possible because you have a fire hazard on your hands - throw a gentle hint to Mr. Shepard - he probably knows just what I mean.

By the way I never heard if you got the hat and what color those new pants of Haroola's?

I found out my mark today - 3 points shy of Honor Roll - 87%. I think I got reamed counter clock wise but I won't be again. I'll be glad when I get on night shift because I'll have a better deal on the studying. I was told that the use of too technical terms in your exams works against you. Of course you are responsible for no math

- well, formulas, which are purely a matter mathematical substitution I didn't learn by heart - I guess this was one fault of mine. I handed one examiner terms that are not dealt out till almost the end of the course - he was very nice though for he asked me to explain them which I promptly did. He took some time with me and I find he asked me questions which none of the other fellows had - he told me I did very well. This was on Vacuum Tubes and I knew it cold.

Questions I ask in class are often met by - "you don't have to know that - that's a radio engineer's job." You see the G.I. instructors aren't well versed in their subject and I certainly don't blame them. They didn't ask to be instructors - most of them hate it. So it looks like I'm going to do a lot of digging on my own. It's hard under the present set up because you have to dodge a bed check if you go to the library and studying in the barracks or dayroom is impossible. I'm still on 8 WPM but feel I'm almost ready to pass it and get on to 10 and with that, enough of school.

I don't know if they will raffle off a phone call tonight but I'm here anyway. It's a darn shame that all classes now get Sunday off. This town even now is jammed with G.I.s - it's very noticeable right here - there are so many more fellows here tonight than there have been previously. Well, when it gets too bad we are going to start and take little shoe string trips on the weekends and maybe do some horseback riding. Might as well see some of this part of country while I'm here.

This evening was fun for we went in a lot of places and found a couple good places to eat. Cheap and clean in a part of town where there are almost no G.I.s - purely civilians - mostly men on the business of outlying farmers from surrounding country. People are grand here - aloof enough till you show them you want to be friendly and then they're grand.

I was going to have snaps taken this evening but it is raining again (as ever on my week-end off) so I'll get them soon. If I find out the type of film the fellows use may- be Harry could get some at the store eh - then I could have a roll of eight or so taken.

Harry - I'd be glad to tell of any little intimate situations I become involved in but I'm doing my best not to become involved. (That's too damned easy too). Honestly I never thought too much of a girl who picked up the "temporal" Army and I suppose I'm leery even now. Don't' want the easy ones but we'll see - I should have four more months here.

I even went to station here tonight - Fare round trip for civilian about 45 dollars - furlough rate for me about 30 - that's round trip.

Well, I must get on to the dance. The dollies are in Formals tonight in here - you must picture me drooling. The competition will be darn keen though - honest, wom- en don't appreciate what they have here - I never saw so many fine looking fellows. Well, be good.

Love, Frank

NICE TO MEET YOU

Present Day

May 1944 began the Allies' preparation for D-Day. Eisenhower had taken over as Supreme Allied Commander of the air forces. The barrage of day-night bombings had all but destroyed the Luftwaffe. With the exception of Germany's flak batteries, the Germans were practically defenseless by air. Bomb targets were shifted to focus on all modes of transportation, destroying rail yards, roads, and bridges; anything that allowed the Germans to move about on the ground was wiped out. In the Pacific, April saw the activation of the U.S. Twentieth Air Force under General Henry H. Arnold; his job was to execute strategic bombing operations against Japan. While Allied troops landed in New Guinea, the Soviets took Yalta in mid-April, and by early May, had secured the port city of Sevastopol in the Crimea. The Allies were making progress on all fronts, and my father was still busy learning radio.

By now I had been typing for a solid four months. On average, my father wrote twenty-six letters per month his first year of service. It hadn't been an exaggeration at all when my mother told me he had written his mother every day when he was in the war. I wondered why and found it unusual that a now twenty-three-year-old soldier would be writing his mother every day. His comments about getting off his daily letter seemed as though the three of them had made some sort of promise to write one another daily. The more I read, the more I realized this was indeed the case.

His level of commitment to his family struck a chord with me, as did some of his sentimental comments to his family. I loved that about him. He seemed so close with them and always worried about them, especially about their money situation. The rationing was clearly evident wherever he was stationed and though I was aware of the limits on foods and such, reading his letters made it more real for me. I gained a much better understanding of what our relatives endured during a war that followed so closely the hardships of the Great Depression. We live in an age where everything is available all the time. I'm not sure how we would fare if we were asked to live under the same limitations and circumstances.

Some other things about my father were gradually becoming clear to me. I never knew he was so deeply religious. My mother has always had a strong faith, so it seemed only natural that their shared devotion to God would have drawn them to each other. I also got a big kick early on when he mentioned that there were "Grade A redheads" at the station where he had his "layover" on his way to Dix, because my mother was a redhead. Other mentions in his letters such as how he preferred college girls—my mother has her masters degree in early childhood education—coupled with all the comments about how he was so particular about keeping himself clean and healthy—the socks, the underwear, the showers—all seemed to foreshadow his decision to become a doctor. He was even doctoring the young fellows in his barracks, helping them with their colds.

I remember my mother commenting on my father's affinity for neckties. He had told her that he liked to wear a different tie daily for his patients, that they were a great conversation starter. I knew that he had hundreds of ties and based on the letters, it appears that his penchant for ties started long before he was a doctor. After his death, his ties were among the things my mother had hung onto. I never knew this until one Christmas, during my mother's quilting phase, when my sisters and I each received an evening bag she had made for us patterned after a "crazy quilt" design. For those not familiar with crazy quilts, these are quilts with no distinct pattern; the pieces are random in size, shape, and placement. Each of our bags had pieces sewn together that had been cut from our father's ties. The bags were beautiful. Attached to each one, she had chosen charms that reflected our individual personalities. My charms were a ballerina, a sewing machine, a G clef, a ballet slipper, and a cameo. It was such a personal gift, thoughtful, and sewn together with love.

My mother had also told me how much he loved to shop. Well, that fondness was reinforced on multiple levels in these letters. He seemed to enjoy the hunt, but she told me he would only buy quality or not buy at all. She told me of how when they were married, he would go shopping for her Christmas gifts at L.L. Berger's on Main Street in downtown Buffalo. She said he would walk in the store and ask to have a "salesgirl" help him. Little did his helper know what lay ahead. Together they would go from floor to floor, department to department, stopping in lingerie, shoes, handbags, coats, and dresses. In each department, he would select precisely what he'd like to see my mother wearing, and at the end, would pay for it, have it wrapped, and then delivered to the house.

On one shopping occasion they'd gone on together before they were married, she needed a dress for a special occasion they were going to attend. She had tried on a few dresses and modeled them for him. Of course, she was always a size six, except when she was pregnant, and would have looked gorgeous in anything she wore. After she had tried on a few dresses, she told him which one she liked the best with the understanding that if he was in agreement, it would be the one they would purchase. However, he must have liked them all on her and, to her surprise, he'd bought them all. To this day she still has lingerie and handbags he purchased for her at L.L. Berger's all in like-new condition. Years later the humor in this love of shopping was not lost on my mother whose second husband, my step-father, loathed shopping. As fate would have it, in the mid-eighties I actually worked at L.L. Berger's, downtown on Main Street, in the shoe department. To think that my father had shopped at that very store, walked the same floors I had, and I never knew it.

I was so excited to be learning about him, and not just about the obvious things; I was learning some intimate things about him too. The more I read, and the more I learned, the more I realized that this gift had truly been brought about by divine providence. First his mother had to save the letters, then they had to be safely brought to our family home, then my mother had to save them safely, and then they had to fall into my hands.

You may recall my telling you I have very few memories of my father, one of which being of him shaving. Each time he wrote about shaving in his letters, I found myself sitting on the sink watching him with the brush in the cup making a foamy lather, and waiting for him to place that dollop of shaving cream on my nose. Whatever was happening was happening for a reason, and I was determined to work my way through his letters, in order, and see what else was in store for me at the end of my coddiwomple.

SIOUX FALLS, SOUTH DAKOTA - PART 2

1944

May 1st, 2:45, Monday

Dear Mother, Harry and Mike,

I was about to extol the improvement in chow and then the boys tell me that 65 men reported to sick call with Tomean poisoning from Sunday evening chow. Thank heavens I didn't eat there Sunday night—it being pay day we splurged and ate at the Snack Bar before going to see Betty Grable in "Pin Up Girl." This was a poor—very poor movie. The only thing that saved it was some precision drill by a chorus team at the end. This saved the picture for the fellows here. They almost went nuts because those girls certainly did a splendid job—better than most of us could do. Oh—I didn't mention that I got a letter from Norma.

Things here haven't changed too much yet but I almost died when they started marching us back from chow in formations. Exaggerating Army regulations and carrying them to a degree that is darn disagreeable is referred to by the men in the concise phrase "chicken shit." Not at all a nice thing to write, but in order to get the full significance of what follows, I have to mention it. The first day of chow line was extremely long and the men in line, seeing their buddies being lined up to march back to school there arose from the mess hall the loudest and most determined ring of chicken and rooster calls I've ever heard. It was a riot because as I told you before there was enough brass around to dazzle you. The outcome of this was (apparently the officers felt cheap) that a captain interviewed a number of classes during school and honestly asked why all the complaining. He was met by a few souls, supported by all, who told him that they couldn't stomach the meals and what was more having to stand in such a line for such a mess of slop got them down. Result—we are getting much better meals and it's a great relief. Maybe I can save some money now.

What I started to say about the change in school was that it is very agreeable—there is only one civilian woman instructor in the bunch and we drew her. She is very attractive and knows radio cold. Her very proximity—perfume she wears too—and does she know radio. I'd sure like to tune her frequency to my circuit. I'm going to do a lot of studying now—keep my shoes shined too.

Johnson didn't get a furlough, he got a delay in route. He had applied for a transfer to photography and got it. His work here he apparently never considered seriously—I met him on the bus coming in a week ago Sunday—he told me of his "delay" then 12 days and the fellows told me he left a week ago today for home. Kind of a nice chap—a little blowy though.

117

Guess that will have to be all for now. I have to write Ann. I certainly beat her to the punch on her new job—I shouldn't have stolen her thunder but I did—I wrote and congratulated her before she had even written me about it. She seems quite happy about it and I'm glad for her folks too.

Well, be good and keep well!

Love, Frank

May 2nd, 3:50 PM, Tuesday

Dear Mother, Harry and Mike,

It has rained here all day. It was a surprise to me for last night was really beautiful—the nicest evening we've had here I'd say. The good thing about it is that if it rains all week it may be nice on the week-end.

Our lovely little instructor is having her hands full because the G.I. instructor who is supposed to help got himself a furlough. Don't know whether they will replace him or not but there are entirely too many in the class to do a good job with. That is the principle reason I'm going to try to do a little "boning" on my own. We're working on the Superhetrodyne type receiver now—that is the type used in most commercial jobs. It keeps you humping in class to get it all and I feel that I'm not getting all I should —hence I'm an "Eager Beaver."

I'm waiting now for the mail. It should be in about 4:30. They've started another new wrinkle here. We have to wear a class A uniform to evening chow. In other words—O. Ds and not fatigues. I'm sure I fail to see just what they hope to accomplish by this. You run a hell of a risk in getting everything spotted at that mess hall. Maybe the C.O. has stock in the local drycleaners. I know the Post C.O. has a good deal of stock in the town laundries and made himself a real pile before they put up a Quartermaster laundry. They used to charge the fellows $3.50 instead of $1.50 for a month's laundry.

Code under the new setup (change in phase) is not so good. Here too the class is too large, the room is too small and the instructor personnel in addition to being less efficient than our others are fewer in number.

I'm not off 8 WPM yet or maybe I'll croak with it. I feel I'm ready to pass it but I haven't made it as yet—here's hopin for a good to-morrow.

Have the Keoughs arrived home yet? I'm glad Tom won't see the Army for a while anyway. Honest, we laugh like hell when we see 1 ½ million more men to be taken this year—what are they going to do with them? I shouldn't be too critical because we certainly have the easiest branch of the Army but Goodness—they give the Infantry the highest priority—Air Corps is no longer important—then the Infantry say they have plenty of men so where do we go from here?

We really had a lot of fun around here last night. I must have been crying half the evening I was laughing so hard. The way these guys horse around and then Kostishack started a parody on the High Command that would have laid anyone in the aisles. I'd write most of it to you but I can see that its humor lies only here where all the associations of his subject are. Unless you were in the Army you wouldn't appreciate it. It wasn't dirty—just darn foolishness—entirely extemporaneous but everyone added their two cents and we all laughed ourselves sick. On top of that about 9 PM one of the fellows came in—peculiar situation—he was almost dead drunk but could walk a straight line and talk quite normally—the only way you could tell was the half casts to his eyes—we all knew he was almost out cold. Some of his better pals took the opportunity to get the inside information on his girl—Oh he'll be sorry—he's sorry right now.

Well, guess I'd better jump into the O.D.s if I expect to eat tonight so, be good. Love, Frank

May 3rd, 3:15 PM, Wednesday

Dear Mother, Harry and Mike,

You see I am reduced to the paper they gave me at school. I've run out and am too lazy, in addition to it being too miserable out, to go the PX so I've started on this. The paper they buy here comes in a convenient portfolio so I like to buy the whole works—it's a lot easier than the stuff I had from home.

It is still raining. I've never seen it rain so long and so much. There is a high velocity wind too, which doesn't help matters. It has rained almost continually since last Saturday with the exception of Monday night. With this new deal on "dressing for dinner" none of us are too happy about the weather. We just get things pressed and cleaned and then we are required to wear them in the rain. Oh well, there are a lot worse things, but it eats into your budget because cleaning is undoubtedly your biggest single expenditure. This is especially so of most of us newer fellows because you have to send pants and blouse continually until you get a real firm press in not often worn O.D.s. Once you get a permanent press established it's OK.

Well, let's see what more can I tell you? I came mighty close to passing 8 WPM today but not quite. In theory we put together a Superheterodyne receiver on "bread boards." Yes it worked—a little bit anyway. There are still too many fellows at each bench. Oh that instructor—Kaa runch! And can she dress. Blue tweed suit Monday—black suit yesterday—brown Gabardine today. She's good at radio but maybe I'd learn more from a less informed less attractive teacher.

I felt fairly well satisfied today. Some of my studying last night paid off and it was good to see it.

I received Mother's letter just after I mailed mine. Boy that one was filled with news wasn't it? It is peculiar because most of us picture home as inert in our minds I guess. Things stopped dead there the moment we walked out the door only the truth is that things do roll on.

I saw Ann's picture in the Gazette—it (the Gazette) got here with the letter—good timing eh? I didn't think too much of the picture either. No. I don't have a picture of Ann—have never asked for one. Why should I have one? Just like most things my mind's eye can take anywhere and I can visualize all the things I used to know. Even with your pictures—I only look at them occasionally but I can see you as often as I please and you are with me frequently.

I'm anxiously awaiting "mail call" tonight and looking for that much mentioned "honey of a box." I should get a letter from Haroola tonight with his report on Saturday's activities–hope he has included all the lurid details.

Well, I guess I have just about milked all the sources of information dry. I have to get dressed in O.Ds to eat tonight–I'm thinking seriously of going to the library tonight in spite of the miserable weather. So, be good and keep well you three.
Love, Frank

P.S. Keep look-out for change in address–we will get new designation soon as result of reorganization–don't know just when.

May 4th, 4:45 PM, Thursday
Dear Mother, Harry and Mike,

Well, the box finally did arrive. I almost got brained because the "mail man" had to carry it all the way here from head of the Squadron Street. The wind had reached proportions that fellows from Florida called hurricane proportions. It was darn heavy and I guess he almost toppled over with it a couple of times.

What a box! You weren't kidding when you said it was a honey. I have the cheese tucked away in my locker–I'm waiting for some more beer to come to the PX (it's been out lately). The oranges come in fine. Just before I go to sleep I have one.

Generally by the time you get in bed you find that what you want more than anything is a drink. But once you're in bed you'll be damned if you'll get out on the cold cement floor and then hike to the latrine to get one. I always save my oranges from chow just for this. Now I'm way ahead of the game. All the cookies were gone before I went to sleep last night. It did me good and would have you too. I've listened to superlatives about your baking from women and men at the house. I always knew how good it was but it's hard sometimes not to make a compliment about cooking a repetition or use a worn phrase.

You should have seen the fellows here. Now they (the cookies) didn't look too good when they arrived. Unfortunately they had taken quite a beating. One corner of the box was broken out and some of the cookies were broken and mashed–particularly the top ones. But did these guys enjoy them. They all wanted to know if you made em and they certainly did make em vanish. There were quite a few in the barracks last night and they all had some cookies.

I didn't get to the bottom layer till this afternoon after school–mmmmm cupcakes. Guess there won't be much sense in going to chow tonight. I'm pretty well full now. I have the candy bars in my locker too. That is going to save me some dough. I've eaten more sweets since I've been in the Army than I have before in all my life. You get hungry and all you can buy are sweets so you eat em.

The weather has certainly taken a drastic turn. We have right now what you would call a blizzard at home. But of course nobody takes it as anything exceptional. Last Monday night our fatigues were more than enough–it was so hot you could smell Morell's packing plant. We've had overcoats on today. The bad weather brings PT

inside and only ½ hour of it and no drill so there lies the advantages of bad weather–
and that is why I've been able to write so early in the day.

I received Harry's letter. Sounds like he had a grand time. Guess you are matur-
ing?? Hell you just have never given yourself a chance. I'd like to see the picture but
as you say–certain risks are involved so if you think they're too great (and I certainly
don't blame you) don't send it. Just give her a little squeeze extra for me next time.

I've put that trick key chain away. I'm saving it for a time when I feel like going
slightly batty–then I'll take a whirl at it.

I've added the gum to my dwindling stock. I've started chewing it a bit in Code class.
Surprise! They took my paper to "checkers" for 8 WPM. I'm not sure I've got it and
won't be sure till to-morrow but my instructor seems to think I made it. Three cheers–
now on to 10 WPM. You see all the time after last Saturday I was on 8 I was delinquent according to the schedule. Oh I'm not behind so much–some haven't got 4 yet!

Miss Wise heart wasn't at our class today. Maybe that's good. All I do is drool
when she is teaching anyway.

Interruption–I just changed into O.D.s for chow and mail call–no mail today but I
could hardly expect it after yesterday.

I got a pamphlet from Grandpa yesterday too–its direct from England–concerns a
completely Allied outlook on the Air Power of the war–not bad either. I also received
the two latest El'Chems. Did you give them my address? I can't understand why but
those damn things made me feel worse than I ever have in the Army. Not home-sick
but just brown inside. Haven't analyzed why yet–but you'll know when I figure it out.

Last night I really bloated myself. I felt so jubilant I took in a movie. Big night! We
had Sulfa Pills again and it seems to me that every time I take them I feel like I'm
catching cold so I got in bed. Felt fine again today. I really believe that those pills help
us a lot more than any of us realize–that's why I always take mine.

Guess I can't think of any more just now–that box should hold me for some time
now–I still have some peanut butter (brought it from Greensboro) for the crackers.
Gosh–thanks so much.

Love, Frank

P.S. The boys keep asking about that cheese but I'm holding out for beer with it.
F.

May 5th, 6:20 PM, Friday

Dear Mother, Harry and Mike,

I received the two letters today. I had intended going to Communion this afternoon
but they pulled "Retreat Parade" on us so I was out of luck. Maybe I'll make it over
the week-end.

I'm very sorry to hear about Fran. I must write soon.

Well, the axe fell on me this morning. According to the "checkers" I didn't pass my
8 WPM. I'll try to find paper and enclose it. I had only 2 mistakes in 132 characters.
They allow three. I was passed at first, then someone else checked it and decided

from the "width of the pencil marks" that I had filled in two characters after the check was over so it was disqualified. Gee was I sore!

I'm all dressed up now. We had retreat and I'm all ready for anything. I'm going to "Tech Library" now and study for a while. Then I'm going over to the Service Club to a dance. I've signed out so I won't be caught by bed check. We go on night shift next Monday. And to think it took me all this time to learn how to beat that bed check. Now that I've found out–I go on nights and can't use it. It has really been a temptation to go to St. Paul over the week-end but I really don't feel as though I can stand the pressure. It is nice to know anyway that if I want to beat the "Schedule" some time that it can be done.

Radio has been moving along at a rapid rate. That's why I'm going to hied myself off and study a bit. This two weeks is of great importance to me. I'm making a stab at understanding it all. It's so much easier to reason it out when you need it than to memorize the whole works. About 9 or 9:30 I'm going to meet the fellows and go to the dance for a while. Maybe we'll even commit mayhem on that cheese to-night. You can never tell. More pills (Sulfa) today and yesterday. They have had too many colds I guess–either that or are conducting something of an experiment of a biological nature. Hope to devote a large part of Sunday to writing Aunt Retta and the Lads of 105–Guess that includes most of it.

Love, Frank

P.S. Guess I should write the Otts and Grandpa too eh?

May 6th, 7:50 PM, Saturday

Dear Mother, Harry and Mike,

How is every little thing? I'm at the U.S.O. tonight–just a brief stop-over till I meet some of the fellows. I had to take care of a couple little details on my own and then came up here. I passed another 8 WPM check today but no doubt they'll disqualify it as they did the last one.

They certainly kept us on the hop today. We got out of school at 2:30, at 2:45 we started PT at 3:45 we had a "personal inspection" and at 4 bells we marched off to a medical lecture in Class "A"s (O.D.s) with gas masks. Then of course chow and then I rushed like hell to get a shower (very very cold)–change sox underwear and shirt and get into town.

Aside from that I guess there is not much more to tell. The phase I'm in in theory is said to be the most difficult–very few get good marks. It's easy to see why–there is certainly a lot crammed into it. I've been doing a bit of boning–Hope I get it all. It means a lot to me to do a good job–even as a G.I.

I didn't receive any mail from home to-day but got a nice letter from Lavery. He tells me that I'm lucky I got into any Tech school at all. He is at Twin Engine (Secondary) School. He says that 3-400 Cadets (imagine getting that far) were shipped direct to the Infantry when he got there.

Well, I must rush off with the boys–they have arrived–we're going to get in on the ground floor on the "telephone call" at the Masons. May go horseback riding tomorrow–wish me luck.

Love, Frank

May 7th, 10:50 AM, Sunday

Dear Mother, Harry and Mike,

Well, I just got off a "quickie" last night. I can see I'll have to do better than that. Last night after I left the U.S.O. I joined some of the lads and first we went to the Arcade and tried our hand at some fancy shooting. I wasn't so good last night. We had a couple hot dogs and coffee and thence to the Masons to dance. I really enjoyed myself there last night. Thursday, no Friday night at the Service Club was a fizzle–really no manner to get to know a girl. You get to dance about 30 sec. and then are cut–most unsatisfactory. But last night I must have danced with 8 or 10 different ones. I'm losing some of my shyness and am trying desperately to develop a line of chatter that will meet the competition. What once was second nature to me certainly deteriorated when I was in the "Hermitage" for the last couple years. Oh I'll get there yet!

We left the dance at about 11:30–had a couple quick beers and just made the midnight show. It was "9 Girls." Not too good (I had the culprit discovered in the first 10 minutes of the picture). They also had a March of Time. In the last two reels of this I have seen–it has certainly deteriorated–one of Island and this one about "Music for the Armed Forces." They prove no point as I can see–maybe I'm all wet because that probably isn't their purpose. We got in last night about 2:30–hot rocks–we don't really do much but we have a good time anyhow.

Today loomed with our usual luck regarding the weather. The sky is very overcast and rain is eminent in my opinion. Bill Hughes wants me to go horseback riding with him this afternoon and I'm all for it but I'll be darned if I'm going to get drenched in the bargain. Guess maybe I haven't said much about Bill–he is a pretty ordinary guy but darn good company. We like to do mostly the same things–little to a moderate amt. of drinking–not too many movies and we hope to see a little of the surrounding territory before we leave here.

As a civilian he was a Foreman in one of the larger Syracuse Laundries. Oh he has had no education beyond High School but has a good background in literature, apparently picked up on his own as a civilian. We both like to bowl–play pool, ping pong and we've had some good (cheap) week-ends in town. Bill goes to all the dances with me–he rarely dances but he loves to go and watch. He feels a little inferior about his dancing, so he says. We're going to the Post dancing class if we can get in soon. Bill is married and has a little girl about 5 years old. I suppose I could team up with someone younger (he is 26) but the Army has done things to a lot of the youth of America. I honestly don't enjoy getting tight a couple or more times a month and I can't see picking up the local sluts–as yet I haven't found such an outlet necessary. My schooling here, I figure, requires regular hours and if I get too tied up in town I'd never do justice to anything. I really have a good time doing the simple things in my time off–I never had the chance to devote a lot of time to shooting pool or swimming or a lot of other things–soo on I go–still being a good boy and trying to do the best job I can of what I have to do no matter how insignificant it may be.

I just came back from chow–it certainly has improved. Celery soup–chicken a la king–mashed potatoes–corn (niblets)–quartered tomatoes–milk and bread pudding with a liberal amount of fruit salad mixed in and topped with chocolate sauce.

I made 8:45 Mass this morning and afterward went to the Service Club and read the funnies and had coffee and sweet rolls. I really lag around and lazily take my own sweet time in the morning and the afternoon just worry about having a good time.

There is a dance at the local K of C tonight so I think I'll make my way there and see what the Right Handers have to offer. The place we plan to go riding is right near a girls' college so maybe we'll see some of the local bells there too.

Well, I have to shave and get ready to go to town. Mail call is due in about 10 minutes so I won't seal this till I see what is forthcoming.
Love, Frank

P.S. You shouldn't have sent the dough but oh thanks anyhow.

May 7th, 6 PM, Sunday
Dear Mother, Harry and Mike,

Well, this is the second one today. Somehow I thought I'd get this right off while the smell was still fragrant and the feeling still fresh in my pants. Oh my y(ass) we did go a horseback riding. I did it once in the Falls if you remember but I had a dilly of a horse there–out here the horses are Western, the saddles are Western and the horse has a lot of life in him. A lot for me anyway. You would have died laughing and Bill Hughes almost did. You see I didn't know how to steer the blasted beast and most crucial of all I didn't know where the brake was (or break if you like).

Let me begin at the beginning. Right after chow we started out. We wore our oldest (out of press pants) and carried best ones with us in Bill's furlough bag. I also took my now famous (in barracks 1241) sweater as I didn't want to wear my blouse. We nosed around at the U.S.O. till we found out where the Academy was and boarded a bus. We got off at the end of the line and walked to the Academy. Once there we had to wait for horses. We (Hughes being a rider of some repute) took the $1.50 numbers in preference to the $1.00 jobs. I had a hell of a lot of courage didn't I? After asking Bill on the side how to board the bloody beast I got on without too much ado and with practically no trouble at all walked the son of Satan out away from the farm. I was a little nervous at first and just as Bill was telling me some of the fundamentals the fiery creature took off toward a small rural gas station. I managed to stop him between a gas tank (pump) and a car and then we started out fairly rationally again. Oh I cantered a little, posted the beast a little and had a slight gallop. By this time Hughes was a slight distance behind me and he picked up the gait to catch up.

My horse (this speeding up was contagious) when he heard the other one gaining started off at a terrific rate (terrific for me). Being imperfect in the art of bridling the bastard I wound up at a gallop up a driveway. Long–fortunately and hedged (high bushes) on either side. By the grace of God I managed to stop him just before I ran all over the yard of the place. Then I turned him about, walked him to the road and began again. Courage and ambition spewed over within me as I trotted on so we started to gallop again. I still didn't get the steering right–this time at a full gallop straight through a carefully planted victory garden and half way across a farm. I couldn't turn him because by the time I got to the field I was hemmed in by fences and towards the road there was a big ditch. My hat was brushed off by the nearby tree branches–lovely time indeed!

Oh yes I finally stopped the S.O.B. and got him out of there only after the lady of the farm gave me hell about the garden and told me if I couldn't ride I shouldn't be on a horse. I apologized profusely at the top of my lungs (she must have been a ¼ mile away). Hughes recovered the fallen chapeau and we continued. By this time I had learned by grim experience about how to handle him and we bounded over the hill and vale at various speeds till my upholstery was well torn and packed. Then we came back, with and on the horses believe it or not. Oh it was great fun–poor horse I really pitied him. These horses are well worth the charge for riding them–they have plenty of life and it's kind of a thrill to try to manage one. The ones I rode at home just walked–stopped to eat grass and you had to boot them to even get them to get going at a walk again. But here they have plenty of pep and if you loosen that bridle ¼ of an inch you're off at about 25 per. It took considerable holding and talking to hold the animal down on the way home for he knew he was well on the way home and wanted to make it in the least possible time. I guess I'll try that as often as I can afford it and I should be able to make it often.

From the stables we went back to the YMCA–There we showered and did a little swimming. Hughes is a pretty good diver. We also changed pants and felt in fine fettle. From the "Y" we went to the U.S.O. and had the free lunch. From there to here of course we had to rush to make the free lunch here too but our schedule is rigid and we adhere to it very closely.

We did some community singing and then went upstairs where we beat Hughes 2 out of 3 games of straight pool. Then I sat down to let you in on the latest. Bill and I both agree this has been the best time yet.

Now we are off to the K of C dance. You see we have extra time off due to the change to the night shift.

Well, after 2 today I can't promise much more or any tomorrow unless I make a killing at the dance.

See here now–no more of this money stuff please. You fellows need it and the Army gives me everything I need. I hope I didn't poor mouth it in a letter to you–If I did honest I didn't mean to. If and when that allotment comes through if you want to send me a couple of bucks a month or so that's O.K. but I won't stand for any more of such stuff—understand!

Glad you got your bonnet—Tess. I'll try to answer a little better next time. I should write the Beals, got another one from them today—God bless 'em—

Be good and keep well—your loving (weary ass) son.

Frank

May 8th, 9:15 AM, Monday

Dear Mother, Harry and Mike,

Oh my, oh my—this sure is the life! I'm at it earlier than usual this morning—we change shift today—really since we have Sunday off we got the best deal of all from it. Saturday from about 6 PM till this afternoon at about 3 bells. I said I wouldn't write unless I made a killing and Oh Joy, Oh Bliss, Harry would have been proud of me. Evidently all I needed was to get with the "right handers" again—yes this week-end was the very best I've had since I left home and you can take N.Y.C. and burn it.

After I wrote you from the Masons, Bill and I took off for the K of C. We had a little trouble finding it and the rain was just coming down slightly. In our tour to find the place we passed the Cathedral. Since I had not as yet seen it and Hughes had apparently always wanted to see a large Catholic church, particularly the Stations, we stopped and made a visit. It's a beautiful church—compares favorably with Fr. Baker's although it is on no-where near the scale nor as ornate.

After we left the church we found the dance. First we had a beer at the bar taking care to avoid the "one arm bandits." From there we went upstairs to look over the field. The girls were not of a dazzling variety except one or two. Then I spied this luscious job in a black and white (dog-tooth like my sport coat only a smaller figure) suit. Well, Harry knows me and how shy I am. He knows that I never try for the best looking doll on the floor. Primarily they have too shallow personalities and secondly you can never dance with them for more than a couple quick phrases so I had a couple dances and then finally I was tugged and I spy her talking with one of the chaperones. That was just too much so I ambled over and before I knew it there I was going stronger than I had thought possible. Little Francis George (Hubba, Hubba) had resurrected the line of banter from away back and was pouring it on (subtlety of course) so thick that you could cut it with a knife—and what's more, I wasn't half tight doing it and drool-ing from B.U. like I did on some of those classic beer nights with the genial Harroola. The fact that she helped a good deal with a sharp sense of humor carried me on—my vocabulary reached new heights—strictly Hubba, Hubba all the way through.

She is about 5'6"—big brown eyes and a figure that Petty dreams about. A little too much make-up but she knows how to put it on—definitely not the sweet type—but the type that you notice first in a room of dolls and wish you could see her on a beach with or without.

Her name is Hazel Oswald and come to find out from a Mrs. Murphy she was the local candidate for Mardi Gras Queen.

Don't misconstrue me—I had plenty of competition—some of the lads were determined as I was but as I was really cookin' on the front burner and I agree with Harry Copelin in this case that who cares who dances with her—it's the guy who takes her home—yep I done it.

Well, anyway she was swell company and a good dancer and she's a Cadillac and I was a complete gentleman all evening. I asked if I could call her for a date some evening—got the green light so one of these fine Sundays off I'll have to get going again. Thought I'd wait a couple weeks—if I can hold out that long. We'll have to see what it brings. She probably has a G.I. on the string for every night in the week but that's O.K. with me but it's grand to know that if need be you can get hold of something kind of dazzling to walk into the Sqd. dance with.

The way I feel today they could drag me out in Class "A" with bunk and footlocker on my back and mattress cover optional and I wouldn't get sore. Oh I'm not consumed with "l'amour toujour"—but honest I really believed that things like that had ceased to happen and really complacently adjusted myself to it.

It was an invigorating experience—my ego was boosted 100% - you see a couple pretty smooth cookies were right on my tail—covered with campaign ribbons—Non-Coms—one lad from the RAF so I felt very happy about the whole thing.

Well, I guess that about sums up the week-end. It was swell through and through and cost me about $2.50 in all (sugar cookies included). Hazel didn't want to eat or drink afterward—wouldn't even have a beer at the K of C—wouldn't ride home in a cab either—insisted upon walking home. Too good to repeat soon again—anyway this peak of elation should last me for some time and primarily I'm here to learn radio.

I hope by the time you get this clothes pins will have arrived—I shall get more as soon as possible and try to get them off to you—is there anything else?

Right now I'm in Service Club—may go to movie at 11:45. It's great here. We are in the recording room listening to Kastilonets (spelling?) recordings—some long haired stuff too. Only thing lacking is you and you and de la Spusier too. Well, be good and keep those over coats buttoned up.

Love, Frank

P.S. Just read your letter again Mother—Chapeau sounds knobby—almost right enough to do you justice.

Return Address:
Pvt. F.G. Thompson
A.S.N. 12,107,602
3507 A.B.U. (T.S.)
Section "M" Bks 1241
Sioux Falls Army Air Field
Sioux Falls, S.D.

May 12th, 11:30, Friday

Dear Mother, Harry and Mike,

Well, since we are tired of getting dressed for dinner and since I have a couple dirty jobs to do this afternoon we decided not to go to chow. I'm at the PX now completely equipped with Swiss cheese, sardines and crackers. We were sabotaged on the beer–a new regulation states that it cannot be sold until 5 o'clock but that's O.K. since I'm not too keen about drinking much before school. We're going to settle for milkshakes and make a meal of what we have. I got a letter from Aunt Maime yesterday. She must have shipped it out just as soon as she got the card–afraid I sent it prematurely but I wanted to get it off. When you want things to arrive in a hurry they never do and vice versa.

Change of scene–the fellows came up with the milkshakes we killed the sardines and Swiss cheese and most of the crackers. We came right back to barracks–we wanted to be here for mail call. We arrived early so I went to the latrine and scrubbed my G.I. shoes with G.I. soap and brush. You have to do this every time now and then for you get too much polish on and you can't get a shine. I had just finished covering them with saddle soap (this softens leather and prevents cracking) when mail call came. It was a good thing I got a couple letters. I won't say anything more. Mother the old cry about too much at once is coming again. I am trying my best to keep well and healthy and bring you back a better if possible, piece of carcass than the one I took away. I deny myself a lot of pleasure and stuff because I must be in the best possible condition to meet any test which may be in store for me. My part has been relegated to insignificant, that's true, but I don't care too much for myself–I'm doing it for you. I do not think it is too much to ask the same of you. Home won't mean much if you two don't keep in shape–I'd say you're letting me down if you're going to extend yourself to such a degree. I hear from my directions that Harry has certainly become the head of the house and is doing a splendid job. Well, he better put his foot down and I mean it.

More about horses and the inherent smell. Mother you don't think I'd wear those anywhere after the horse do you? We took newly cleaned ones in with us and checked them at the U.S.O. Upon return we got them and went to the "Y" and showered and got sweet and clean and pure and nice. The horse pants are in cleaners now–I get them to-morrow.

Let me know, I know you will, as soon as you get allotment. You just have to keep pushing the Army you know. If you haven't gotten it by the end of this month I'll refuse to sign payroll for following month. That seems to bring results–main trouble being that you have to get nasty before you get much action.

We had drill and PT today. I still have to work up a good shine on my shoes–shave and get my laundry before school. All things in box. Thanks again. Once again I wouldn't blame J. O'Hara for the line. I think his mother is the one who is putting it on. Innocent enough if she enjoys it. Oh–I still have in reserve two pairs of last sox you sent—keep 'em for special—you know. We will soon go into Suntans which reminds me that I'll have to send my pants—have never worn them but they are creased.

Guess that includes most of all of it and I have lots to do before school so, be good and careful (this is extra this time).

Love, Frank

May 13th, 12:30, Saturday

Dear Mother, Harry and Mike.

Mail call just got over and no letter from home. I did get a note from Grandpa T. Not a lot in it but I appreciate getting a letter from him. He says "will try to write a better letter next time"—I think he does splendidly.

This place is getting rougher all the time—a whole new list of additional regulations out last night. Soon I expect "Piss Call" 40 men in formation to the latrines. Truthfully it doesn't bother me much—hasn't as yet anyway.

Oh—the fellow (Otto J. Taylor) with whom I have been working on the receiver and I have been working on our attractive little instructor. She finally broke down and started giving us tips and then sent our set down to be tuned by maintenance. This really isn't cricket on her part but we've been kidding her that ours was going to be the "kit of the week." I guess she is taking us seriously. Taylor told her, on one of her inspections of our set, that I thought she was getting quite a kick out of watching us. She said she really did. Then I told her we really enjoyed coming to her class and she promptly replied, Oh Thompson—I bet you tell that to all your instructors. It's a good thing that students can't date instructors—otherwise her telephone wire would be red hot.

Well, guess that better be all. I must get to Confession and try to get a haircut and get my pants from cleaners. Be good.

Love, Frank

May 14th, Mother's Day, Sunday

Dear Mother, Harry and Mike,

Well, Happy Mother's Day to you precious! Went to church at 7:45 this morning and had breakfast at the Service Club. By the time I returned to the squadron it was almost time for PT. Being still in need of a haircut I goofed off PT and went to the barber's and got my ears lowered. I really didn't need a haircut in the true sense of the word but we had our personal inspection just 15 minutes after PT yesterday—my hair being damp from perspiration it curled, regardless of curling around my ears and where it was too short to curl it stood straight up so as I was caught.

I was lucky to get off PT. The boys covered me—I didn't know the penalty is a week's restriction—3 days K.P. and 3 days drill. I'll think twice before I try it again. As things go the fellow who is always there and misses one day always gets caught and the constant "goof offs" never catch it. You can bet your knobby new turban I won't take a chance again. I can't see stretching the luck too far.

As soon as I got back from barber's I took a shower and shave—boys weren't finished with PT yet so I had plenty of room and did a good job. By that time it was time for lunch. Not bad—pork, string beans, mashed potatoes, milk, lettuce and dressing and the ever present Jell-O. I then returned to the barracks to await mail call. Still no letter from home—I suppose I'll get three or four to-morrow—dammit—it really pisses me off.

I did get a swell package though. I must write Aunt Maime about the sweater. They are both so lovely I'm the complete envy of barracks 1241. That blessed donation of baked goods is really going to help. I think I'll save the bread—it's so moist and nice. The cake won't last long. No we didn't rip into them immediately. We had just eaten so I couldn't really do justice to the cake as yet. I figure on waiting till tonight when all the lads return from school—then we will really kill it. Honest, sometimes when you get out of school you're so hungry you wake up chewing the comforter.

I must tell you about the weather. Today is a beautiful day. It is so hot that just coming into town I have sweated right through my shirt. Yesterday was a beauty—the camp would lighten the hearts of all women. There is an awful lot of beautiful hunks of man lying about all over the company area—just toasting. Believe me that is where I'll be the next few days too. It is beautiful in town right now. So many little white houses with dripping green lawns—so white and so green.

Guess we feel lazy this Sunday—we had planned on going to Sioux City or somewhere but decided to postpone the adventure. It will keep. Also I hear there is a lake within 20 miles so I can see myself lighting out for there one of these coming week-ends.

No continuity of thought in this little note—let's get back to the box. The stamp is the berries—Bill Hughes wants me to ask Harry to order one for him but I see where there is an office supply place in town here—we will try there in the morning. That is what I should have done and saved the genial Haroola the trouble. You can imagine how convenient it is to have a stamp when all clothing must be marked. They are getting darn tough about it too. To-morrow I shall get to work and put my name all over everything. That should boost my ego too. The cigars are just the thing for coming afternoons in the sun. I must stop writing for things—honest I'm going to hate to move—I've really acquired a lot of things. I have been going to get some powder. Right now we use it on our feet you know—I never did get it—I'll really need it if I go on any big eagles too.

Have I covered everything? I was being waited upon when the box arrived but I held up the parade—I just had to. Wish I'd brought that cake with me today, right now my mouth is watering at an awful rate.

Don't plan on doing much this afternoon—of course we will hit the free lunches—maybe a show and a few beers. Also there is a big park near where we went riding last week—we may go there.

Hughes and I are going to bring our Suntans in with us in the morning and press them at the U.S.O. They will be optional after to-morrow and if the weather holds anything similar to the past two days O.D.s will be unbearable. Anyway, we will have to wear them after the 1st of the month so we want to get set. Pressing pants is one of the domestic arts I have never acquired but I will (should use "I shall" to express determination).

This evening I feel quite sure will find us in the K of C. No there is not a dance there this week but the quiet, the lack of G.I.s, the cold bottled beer, the pool tables, the lovely big overstuffed chairs, and the friendly atmosphere of the place has quite affected Hughes. He has that "Hell with any place else" attitude right now. Bill didn't do much dancing last Sat. night but he did get on darn friendly terms with Mr. Murphy–the (what will we call him) the proprietor or bar keep or general caretaker.

The whole situation makes me laugh. Bill an APO. gets the keys to the city for us so to speak. Guess he liked the way the right handers do things.

Well, I guess I've really stretched this one. I do much better sitting at a desk anyway.

I am enclosing a little card - guess the box arrived too early but that's me you know–too early or too late. The revision on the printing I felt was necessary–would have sent it sooner but the Army has taught me the practical lesson of not planning and I wasn't sure but what they'd have me doing, signing the payroll (just missed that today) or mending the Colonel's girdle, so I waited to send it.

Be good youse guys.

Love, Frank

May 15th, 12 M, Monday

Dear Mother, Harry and Mike,

Back with the Masons again. Today, thus far, has been as busy as we manage to make most of our free time busy.

Last night after I wrote you we took advantage of the Free lunch and entertainment put on here by some of the nearly high school girls. The place was mobbed with G.I.s so we went up to the K of C. The setup there is the berries. Murphy took us to the pool table in the cellar. It was so nice and cool in sharp contrast to the rest of the city. We had some good cold beer while we played–we're just not used to the alcohol I guess–three bottles a piece over a 2-3 hour period had us feeling Rosy. We had a darn good time anyway. The pool table is brand new and there are two ping pong tables too–almost no one there too. We played 2 out of 3 game serves for the beers. I didn't do too well but then I'm just really learning.

We got back to camp at about 11:15 and killed the cake. When I say killed it I'm not kidding. It didn't last longer than about 20 minutes. All the fellows were just out of school and I didn't have the heart to sneak the cake to the dayroom. Soooo it vanished as in thin air. You've never seen one cake more appreciated. I thought maybe I could get away with saving part of it but the fellows hung around my bunk until it was all gone. I got about three very large pieces but I had to eat like hell to salvage that much.

The bread is going to catch hell when I get back now–we have to be in school at 3 bells so we'll have to start back soon I'm afraid.

This morning was profitably spent. When we got in on the bus the U.S.O. wasn't open so we came here. We shot some more pool–I beat Hughes 3 out of 5 this time.

One game I ran six balls–pretty good for a beginner. I beat the pants off Bill. Then at 10 bells we went to the U.S.O. to the G.I.s room–drew the large electric iron and proceeded to press our Suntans. Oh I'm getting there too. We hated to send em to the laundry because they are so new looking just now. We could have had them pressed, that is really all they needed for they are not dirty just wrinkled from being in the foot locker. If we'd had em pressed it would have meant waiting for them about a week so we did it ourselves. Not too bad a job either. The material is not easy to handle because it's so new but now they are set for a while.

Upon completion we checked the pants and came here for more pool. Hughes just can't believe I beat him so badly. We would have much rather go to the K of C but I don't think we'll have time.

Did I tell you yesterday that the box arrived in wonderful condition–it sure was a good packing job.

Well, guess that's all for today–hope the boys get my mail for me.
Love, Frank

May 16th, 12:55, Tuesday

Dear Mother, Harry and Mike,

I was exceedingly gratified to hear that the allotment will come through. I had a Hell of a row with the man who takes care of that stuff at Headquarters. When that slip you filled out came he said you filled it out all wrong–I then proceeded to make a complete fool out of him by reading the instructions in a loud and steady voice. I then chewed his ass purple–It did my heart good–first time I've told anyone off in the Army. We compromised and he didn't send in the slip–they are so screwed up up there–he actually didn't know why he had given it to me in the first place. You can see why I've been somewhat worried about it.

Bravo about the picture of Mike. I am particularly sentimental about him. You see, you two know I'm away and where. He doesn't–wonder if he still remembers me?

About the picture for Grandpa. I may as well tell you that I had one taken and hoped to have it for Mother's Day but couldn't get it till the 20th. I'll ship it on as soon as it is ready. The proofs were very poor and though I didn't pay much for it, even so it won't be worth the money.

Well, I have lots of letters to write but I'm not going to write anymore today. The heat has really bushed me. I'm going to try to get some sleep.
Love, Frank

May 17th, 11:30, Wednesday

Dear Mother, Harry and Mike,

Another very hot day! Once I get acclimate to it I'm sure I'll like it. Hope to lay in the sun and hour or so today.

I guess I'm supposed to state a preference in box contents. Please don't do too much. Anything that will keep for a few days is really the object. The nut bread is really the cat's meow. I have some when I feel like it and it keeps grand and moist. I wonder if you could get me a small sausage of some description? Some Sergeant goes through nights now with sandwiches @ 10 cents/throw but I hate to take a chance on some of the meat especially before going to sleep.

Please send me as soon as possible those old blue swim trunks (please pull holes together) and also the gym trunks that I was issued at N.U. I'd certainly appreciate these as quickly as possible. I'll be wanting to swim as soon as I can get the trunks and I need the gym pants for PT to save fatigues from sweat and attendant smell. I fervently hope this will be the last I'll write home for because soon I'll have more than I can carry when I move.

School is still rolling along. I think I passed 10 WPM last night. Can't say for sure till the paper comes back from the checking section. I shouldn't be long on 12 WPM because I took a check last night and only had 1 too many errors.

Did I tell you that the Receiver we built was exceptional. It brought in 9-10 stations—hell our Zenith won't do that. I know I didn't tell you that the fellow I built it with is down with the mumps. I think that is why I haven't felt too fit the past couple days—I think my system has licked the thing now as I feel a good deal better now.

Afraid this will have to be a shortie cause I have to get dressed for chow now and later I must write Aunt Maime and Grandpa.

Lots of love people—be good.

Frank

May 18th, Thursday

Dear Mother, Harry and Mike,

Another Thursday—Gee how the days roll by! Before I know it another day off will be here and that is never hard to take.

Nothing much new to report—felt better this morning getting up than I have in a week. I must be getting used to this shift and the hot weather. I was told yesterday that having this shift for only six weeks is not a rumor now but factual—that sounds like a good deal to me.

One of the advantages of this shift is being able to get into the sun. Otherwise it is a very lazy set-up -Too much bother to go into town on any day except the one you have off. You take lots of showers, write letters and that is about all. I must get into the sun today. My face is tanned a little already. I'm going to take it gradually for the sun shines here with an intensity that I have never before witnessed. Some of the boys are in extremely sad shape from over exposure and I'm sure I don't want to feel like that. The burn sneaks up on you for there always seems to be enough wind so that you don't notice it while the actual burning is going on.

I absolutely must write the Beals. Norma, Dave and Bobbie sent me a Spiritual Bouquet. Great relief to know that people are trying to help you spiritually at home. Somehow I don't think I have led any worse life in the Army—better if anything, but your environment is just not conducive to piety.

I was quite worked up for a while when I got Harry's letter about the Otts, then I didn't know what to think—he closed it very casually so I thought then that maybe things were probably not so bad. I'll probably get more on it today if I get a letter.

Well, the 1st check on 10 Words per Minute didn't go through. I took another last night. I'm quite sure I got this one. I left one character out but copied the rest solid. 10 WPM is a rather tough one for it is 4 min in length. That means you have to copy 200 characters in 4 minutes and are allowed only 4 mistakes. Also if 2 mistakes are made on the same character the check is disqualified. I expect to be going on to 12 this evening. This I don't expect to be very bad for it has a rather good rhythm. The next one "14" is the stinker—many a good man has been stopped cold on that one and I suppose I will be too.

I'm using this paper because I wanted to get this written while, or that is before PT. I have an extra free hour this morning because I drilled yesterday. Can't get more paper till PX opens at 9 bells.

Don't really know as yet what we will do for the week-end. I expect it to be rather quiet. Three or four of us are considering going up to the K of C with our books and tearing down the subject. I think we hit the "Quiz Kids" sometime next week and I for one want to be on the ball.

Well, guess that is all for today.

Love, Frank

May 19th, 12:30, Friday

Dear Mother, Harry and Mike,

Chow is over—not bad either. It was good last night too. You'd die to see me eat spinach and ask for more. Anything that's green I hang around for a second portion—must be the Irish in me.

Bill Hughes would really appreciate a stamp like mine.

Pvt. William A. Hughes

A.S.N. 42,092,055

How much are they? He will send the money as soon as payday arrives.

I just got a letter from John Dick. He is just five weeks from graduation and is getting his uniforms fit—not bad, what? I still don't know whether he and Mary Jane are busted up for good—he will probably be with her when he gets his leave after graduation.

I am so glad you are helping the Otts. I haven't had a line from them since two or three weeks after I arrived at Greensboro. But they are the ones I would go to if I were in a jam.

I just absolutely have to write the Beals 'cause I didn't make it yesterday. I'll never get any sun 'cause all I do is sit inside and write. I don't write a lot of people but it takes me so damned long to write anything.

Be good youse guys.

Love, Frank

May 20th, 11:15, Saturday

Dear Mother, Harry and Mike,

Up to this point we have had our medical lecture, PT and personal inspection. It is raining to-day so the curse has been taken off most of this since PT and inspection were inside.

I am going to try to send this Airmail in hopes I catch you in time to stop the sending of shorts—both pairs. I found out that a place in town will sell a pair for a little more than one Berry and I can use these for both purposes.

Please, maybe this will be too much, but I would like 2 more shirts. I will send some patches along to-morrow. If possible I would like them taken in to 31" at the waist. Even if they won't let me wear them past the guard at the gate I'll keep them in town and change to them when I get there. Maybe we can impose on Aunt Maime—I hope I hope that is to sew the patches on and take the shirts in.

When you buy the shirts—I know you'll go to Kleinhans but I might suggest that you take a look at the real G.I. thing in an Army Navy store first—then by comparison buy the thing nearest to it. I prefer civilian cut but I can't be sure how the color will hold after a couple trips to the G.I. Laundry.

School rolls along as per usual. All hell is going to break one of these fine days. You see the boys are "washing back" voluntarily. Some of them like it here and want to stay on and others want to be just Radio Mechanics. A lot want to get out of the Air Corps because most opportunities are gone here now. A great majority don't want to go to gunnery. I personally can't feel that way about it.

Mail call is over now and so is chow—meals have been very good for the past 2 or three days. I got a letter from Norma—Thank heavens I wrote yesterday. Say I completely missed Ascension Thursday—Big deal—didn't even think about it at night time although it was announced last Sunday. I'm always in hot water somewhere. I didn't even realize it till I got Norma's letter. They are good at writing—guess I'll have to ask someone to start mentioning these Holy Days in letters a couple days ahead of time. I don't think a Right Hander in the barracks made it—we all completely forgot.

Just found out they have a boating lake on the Post and soon will open a roller skating rink. These are in addition to a newly completed swimming pool. Maybe that doesn't sound good. I'm going to have to investigate but good.

Well, there is not much more to say I guess. Anticipate a quiet weekend—have lots of letters to write and some serious studying to do. Don't know where I'll write from but I'll probably get to it.

Love, Frank

May 22nd, 10 AM, Monday

Dear Mother, Harry and Mike,

I'm at the Service Club again this morning. Somehow I just couldn't roll out of that "Sac" in time for chow so I've brought my books over here and am going to try to brush up a little on Radio. We get the "Quiz Kids" again this week. It should be to-morrow but they may spring it today. Bob Miller, a former W.T.S. man is going to meet me here in a few minutes so we should develop a lot of good points.

We came back to camp last night at about 1:30, maybe a little earlier. After we ate at the Masons (they even had Hot Dogs yesterday) we went back to the U.S.O. and saw the Sunday night movie. It was "The Fighting Chetnicks." Philip Dorn played the lead and I enjoyed it more than any movie I've seen in some time.

After that Bill Hughes and I walked all over quite a bit of the residential district. There are some lovely homes here and the lawns are splendidly cared for. It was good to see kids on bicycles, kids playing ball and wiener roasts in backyard fireplaces. We walked around till about 9:30 and wound up at the K of C.

This should get you. There we met one of the local parish assistants, a Father Miller. We had quite a good time with him. He darn near gave me a sound dubbing in ping pong but we licked the pants off him at pool. He is a swell scout and we enjoyed talking with him. Boy am I getting in solid–Parish priest and all.

I even saw Hazel–the girl I met at the dance at the K of C - yesterday. Of course she had some Corporal in tow but she went out of her way to be nice all of which was very gratifying and rounded out the day completely. I'm pretty sure I could play in that league so I'll have to get on my horse.

Can't do much about it for a couple weeks though. Bill Hughes thinks his wife is coming out for three or four days next weekend. She is bringing her sister and of course I have been appointed 4th wheel on the wagon. Oh why do I get in on these things? It's the least I can do I guess but I do kinda hate to be dragged in. It will probably mean at least some small expenditure that I would rather put elsewhere.

Did I tell you that in addition to passing 10, I passed 12 (code speed) last week and am now on 14? This one is a stinker and my guess is that I shall be on it at least a week and probably a good deal longer. Well, I guess that about sums up all of the "Day Off" activities.

Just one more thing–I still can't get over how grand everyone in town has been to us. It is a truly wonderful thing they are doing. You just don't need money to do so many things. This thing, the attitude of the people here im-presses me to such an extent that I can't help repeating it. Nothing is done on the half-assed basis we are so familiar with at home. These folks are the salt of the earth and believe me; before I leave I'm going to find some way to thank them. When you see men (civilians) at the Masons, serving cake and washing dishes and running around in aprons–you know that they're giving up their day off or their golf or what have you. It is a great spirit–we could use a lot of it all over the country.

Guess that's all for today–won't get mail till 12:30.

Love, Frank

May 23rd, 12:40, Tuesday

Dear Mother, Harry and Mike,

I somewhat revised the plan yesterday and wound up out in the sun doing my studying. I got a start—didn't stay longer than 35-40 minutes so just got a start, darned if I want to get burnt to a crisp—nice even job is my hope.

Say, I just got your letter of Saturday and two—no less—boxes. My Goodness I'll bet there never was a G.I. in the Army who was quite so well boxed. And am I going to eat—Kaarunch. In spite of my canceling order for trunks they are quite acceptable.

The canned goods are certainly the number and the sausage—Oh baby. I can see myself getting well gutted tonight The cigars too are a quantity of more than ordinary value here. I can see myself worming my way into "Murphy's" good graces with a couple of them—of course they are hard to get here.

Both boxes arrived in splendid shape—Poor Ward—he had to carry them to the barracks—mine and about 6 others so I don't envy him.

May 24th, 8:45, Wednesday

Well, I guess I did it—yep I missed yesterday but you can see from the aforementioned that I started out with the best intentions.

The big trouble all started with the coming Memorial Day Parade. Since we are on the "night shift" of course we have to be there with bells on and this entails a lot of extra "mass" drill. They worked us so hard yesterday that no one has drill today so I should be able to finish in good time today. We had received special commendation from Colonel Rogers, C.O. of the Post when we stood retreat one night as "the best marching outfit on the field" sooo we are first in the parade on the 30th. The Governor of S.D. will review the outfit and it promises to be quite an affair—all taking place during our time off of course.

We have three more weeks of this night shift—I think it will be quite a relief to get on days again. I had to take a "Sending" check last night—fortunately did quite well. Had to send only 8 W.P.M. but got credit for 11. Had a "Readability" of 4 which is O.K. since 5 is perfect. I am still on 14 in Receiving and will probably be there for a while. The "Quiz Kids" are still hanging over me—we get them sometime this week and in Theory I am wiring a Transmitter.

Well, Mom, your cake has been a memory now for about 8 or 9 hours. Gee was it good! They had a vegetable plate for dinner last night—I think this is the only thing they serve that I just can't eat. I have tried before. So I ate what else there was there and then went back to the barracks and started on the cake. We finished it after school—it just (the cake) doesn't last long enough.

I have all the other things well tucked away and as a final snack, before going to bed I had some of the sausage. It sure hit the spot. I'm not going to give much of it away for it should keep well enough and is just the thing before going to bed.

I shall take the jacket in as soon as possible but don't want to go into town until after my examination is done. I get a little review done each day and that may be the thing to pull me through. I guess the Honor Roll is out of the question in this phase–the boys who have taken it say that it–the exam–is awfully rough so I just hope to keep on my toes.

Bill Hughes got word from his wife that she will arrive here late Friday night. Too bad she had to come over the Holiday–we almost went nuts getting a room but finally did manage to find one. His sister-in-law is coming too so I hope the four of us will be able to find some place to swim on Sunday–I could really go for that. Since I am to be the "fourth" I hope this dolly is nice but even if she is I'll be darned if I want to spend much on her–if they don't like it they can lump it.

Glad to hear that the Otts are fine and not glad to hear of O'Sheas. Just what did happen, I'm completely in the dark in that respect–all I know is–there was an accident.

Poor Ann–I must write and thank her. Her attitude sounds just like her–she just never will get down on things. Wish more men in the Army had that attitude–it would make it a lot easier for all of us.

Guess I'll have to close here PT calls–and I have to get going.
Love, Frank

May 25th , 12:30, Thursday

Dear Mother, Harry and Mike,

Mail just came. Two letters from home. Be Gory I wish it would rain more often on Mondays. That was the best letter I had received in some time–to hell with the house cleaning!!! Oh I don't mean because of the money. It certainly comes in handy for I was about at rock bottom. But it was informative. Lots of dope and that is what I like to hear.

It is good to see the progress they are making in Italy isn't it?

Poor Mr. Burns. My heart has gone out to him for years now and this last seems terrible even though it must have relieved him of a terrible burden and worry. Do you see what I mean when I say that I cannot bitch about the Army or most anything–there is so much torment and sorrow in the world today that petty discomforts are rendered insignificant.

Certainly was nice of Dick to send so much home. Someday I'll tell you the story of how he managed to send so much home on what he was making. Wish I could do the same–especially I have seen some swell grey checked slacks and lovely sweaters–but fraid I just can't make it.

I wrote Ann that I counted on her as my "Friend at Court." I will go to Communion for her Sunday–Hell and High water. I'll try to write again very soon. Tell her, if she mentions my letter, that I don't expect any answer–just the news that she is on the mend.

No Harry I haven't taken Hazel out as yet. Would make a stab at it this week-end but have to play the genial host to Bill Hughes' Sister-in law. It is the least I can do because I feel he would give me the shirt off his back. Three of us are always covering up for one another and we have about five more in the "outer circle" so guess it won't hurt me.

To you and Tessa—Thanks a million for the Fiver. I realize that you both could certainly do with it right now especially near the end of the month. When I was around we never had 5 to spare so close to pay day so you can hardly expect me to feel that you are not sacrificing plenty to send it. You say you are not but I kinda smell a rat. I know how Harry earned it cause I drew that trick myself for a while and I know how Tessa scrimped to hang on to it. For the love of God—please don't go without! I absolutely don't need it for anything other than pleasure and believe me I didn't anticipate much pleasure when I left home. We enjoy the simple things—make a lot of them—talk em up and really have a good time on a little. One thing I will do is get my fill of beer this weekend. Don't get me wrong. I have always had at least 20-25 on the side since I came into the Army and still have. I'm going to put it in the bank here soon for it proves too much of a temptation near the end of the month.

Yes I still get the Gazette. I take it to school with me and read it during the breaks and while waiting in chow line. Rarely get beyond the headlines, funnies and society page and sports but then I never did. So please mention anything that comes up for chances are I may have missed it.

I'll write Dorshel as soon as exams are over—no haven't had them yet and expect them today—have to go and study now.
Love, Frank

May 26th, 1:00, Friday

Dear Mother, Harry and Mike,

It was a temptation to take in a show this afternoon but I had too many little items to take care of. I got a haircut—have to get out to-morrow—and turned in the laundry—with this hot weather I just have to have clean underwear and towels and socks. And then that little item of writing home—I never would have made it if I'd have gone. Anyway I just can't see spending such a beautiful afternoon in the movie. A lot of the fellows go but unless I especially want to see something I rarely go anymore. Would much rather lie around—get some more sun today I hope.

I definitely have the "Quiz Kids" the second period this afternoon. I certainly hope I do well. If they treat me like a man I'll get by fine but their general attitude is enough to get anyone down. Don't know as you have noticed or not but the big story around here is a bill in Congress to make all R.O.M.s Flight Officers. Afraid I don't take too much stock in it. The story goes that it has passed the House and is now going to the Senate. I would appreciate some straight dope on it if you can get it for me—Harry might manage to get hold of a Congressional Record. No hurry as it doesn't bother me much to tell you the truth.

I found out that another possibility is no go here. I thought I might stand a chance to get in Radar but I would have to wash out in Code to make it. I guess I just wasn't brought up that way for something rebels in me when I think of deliberately failing in anything. Think it over—it is a 22 weeks course and I think I would very much like to have the technical knowledge but I wouldn't care much for the job I would be preparing myself for even though I am not looking forward to gunnery. Also there is a Biological concern in question–short X-rays which are used in Radar tend to make a man sterile. I think I'd rather be shot than impotent. After all a family is the height of my ambition and I'd hate like hell to have saved it for years only to find that I had lost it in this scuffle.

We had a dress rehearsal for Tuesday's parade this morning. All kidding aside it really is an impressive sight. N.Y.s ROTC was boy scouts compared to the scale on which this thing is being done. Thousands of men on that cement apron even though you are only one in a million it makes you stop to think. When the write up of the thing appears in the Post paper I'll be sure to send a copy home.

Well, guess I'd better get a going if I'm going to get any sun. I feel it essential to get this for in a cap in uniform you just don't get enough of it. It is essential to your health you know. Have to take good care of little Francis George (let's all bow to-gether). So I'm off–have to shave and shower before school too so I'll be lucky to get 45 minutes to an hour's worth.

Love, Frank

May 28th, 5:30, Sunday

Dear Mother, Harry and Mike,

Well, how are you all? Here I am in the Albert Hotel. Bill Hughes and family are "quartered" here. We spent the afternoon in Sherman Park–1st opportunity I'd had to see it–lovely place but the ins and outs of it still puzzle me.

Can't write much–Bill is right here–guess we'll go bowling now. We came up to rooms, Sid Blaze, Bill and myself and the women. We just washed up and the three of us G.I.s are waiting for the women to get dressed.

Went to 7:45 Mass as per usual–and breakfast at the Service Club. Back to Sqd. street for PT then chow and then Blaze and I came right in and met Hughes and his folks at one of the social restaurants.

Guess that sums up the day up to the present.

Yesterday was a good one in school. I did make Honor Roll by skin of my teeth–bare 90% also my check on 14 was sent to the checking section–maybe that will get through–I hope so.

Leaving the attractive instructor behind will hurt but progress must continue you know.

About this deal–I plainly got caught with the "other" one. Mrs. H. is very attractive but sister nicht so good–well, at any rate–just not my type. Darned if I'll spend much–just rolling along with the crowd you know.

I have the picture and tomorrow I will get to town early and try to get it packed someway. I was going to get a frame for it but think it is hardly worth even that much embellishment so will just send it on.

Payday is next week so I have a nice clean shirt and pants tucked away–maybe I'll get me a date next Sunday who is to my particular liking–Here's hoping.

Be good–I'll have to cut out these hurried ones eh?

Love, Frank

May 29th, 1:00, Monday

Dear Mother, Harry and Mike,

Well, I'm back in the comparative quiet and comfort of the barracks. Can't say truthfully that I enjoyed myself much but it was something different anyway. Yesterday we bowled, had a bite to eat and took in a show—that was after I wrote you from the Hotel.

Hughes' sister-in-law was all set for me to stay in late last night but I fooled 'em. I was in bed at about 12 and I'm still tired. Maybe I'll sleep a little in the sun before school.

I got up for chow this morning and went right into town. I changed the bed jacket—had to get a little different color—it's rose I guess, in order to get it in the large size. Hope you like it and hope it fits—was tempted to get a silk quilted one but decided that you wouldn't wear the darn thing so had to settle for what is on the way. Also put picture in the box. I'll have to get Bill to get a couple snaps of me in my Suntans. The fellow who took other snaps is shipping to-morrow and does not have negatives back as yet but he has promised to send me a bunch of them when he gets them so just have to wait I guess.

We start a whole new phase of school today. Not sure what it is but I think from here on in all we do is tune transmitters and receivers and familiarize ourselves with the various and complex details involved in air communication.

I have loads of letters to write but just won't get to it today.

To-morrow is big parade—just hope I don't pass out on that plane apron. That sun really beats down and even in G.I. shoes your feet bake.

Try to write a longer one to-morrow hope parade doesn't interfere with my writing at all.

Love, Frank

May 30th

Dear Mother, Harry and Mike,

Well, at last I find myself with the time to do a little better than the last two.

In the first place I did pass 14 WPM last Saturday and am now on 16. Just this one and 18 to go in order to get what is required for graduating as an R.O.M. from here. Of course I would like to make 30 but this will probably prove impossible for me, however, if I hit the ball I should have plenty of time in which to try it.

Yesterday we started a new phase in Theory. As I said before we will be tuning sets from here in. It is a great satisfaction just to handle these special Signal Corps and Air Corps sets for they are truly engineering masterpieces. We have Technical sets at their best. Big disadvantage is there are too many in the class. We have 17 men and one instructor. The casualties in the last "Quiz Kids" were staggering and a lot of fellows "washed back" a week in Code. This means they are back a class in Theory and must take 7 hours a day of Code till they catch up. This next is not in the order of bragging but I wanted you to know—maybe you will get a little satisfaction from it as I did. Our class "46" is divided into 4 sections. I am in D. Of my section only about

10% had marks higher than 85 and of my section of 150 the three highest marks were one 92 and two 90s of which of the latter little F.G. was one. Of course I'm not particularly "starring" but it does me good to do this well.

I must tell you of the parade! We arose at 6:00 AM and were shaved and shined in Suntans at 6:20 for Reveille. We had chow—barely enough time to get "Sac" and clothes in order and then were called for Parade Formation. Now comes the pay off—we are last barracks on the street soooo we lined up and marched off at the tail end. About 1/3 of way to Air Field we were turned off out of Parade. Yes they had too many and they marched us back so we had a free morning. I went with some of the fellows over to the field and we watched for a little. Big Soldiers now—we held some of the little children on our shoulder so they could see over heads of adults who packed the area. The Governor spoke and it was really a splendid spectacle—only two of the men from our barracks got stuck with marching so the day has proved to be somewhat of a holiday. After the Governor spoke (shoulders starting to hurt) we broke through line and got kids a front row view and then went to Service Club to write. That is where I started this letter.

Now to get to something that really bothers me. I actually feel guilty because I fear I have treated Hughes rather shabbily. I can't help it—I want to do better but it is not in me. I can't go with his sister-in-law. He is not having the time he anticipated because he has two women on his hands—I know that the idea was for me to take over but I just can't see my way clear. I spent 6 bucks over the week-end which is more than I should have. Oh she'd pay my way but I never did that and I won't start now. So the past couple times I have bowed out. Bill knows I have money—he has offered to even lend me some but it's no go! It is the well-known story—two sisters completely different—his wife is delicate and feminine and nice—any of the fellows would envy him her but this sister for my money quite the opposite. I could really go for his wife but this deal is more than I agreed to. If Bill parts company with me soon I won't blame him—I suppose I am directly to blame but that's tough—I'm sorry, feel cheap, and ashamed to let a pal down. Guess I shouldn't write you my troubles but it hurts me to let anyone down and Hughes and I have gone through the fat and lean here—sharing what we had even Steven but as much as I want to I just can't help here.

The biggest contrast you've ever seen is—this gal and Bill's wife—I don't know, I don't think I'll try to explain it to him, so I'll just let it ride.

Am I'm glad you got G.I. Shirts—one would be enough if you still want to take the other back—you see the laundry just sent back the first one you sent and practically ruined it. I have to take it in to town and have it done over. Just taper seams—perhaps you'd better make waist 32" on second thought you see much to my surprise I weighed myself Sunday—152 lbs. so if this goes on I may need a little more room. On alteration—Aunt Maime can estimate waist—open seams and straight taper to estimated waist line which should measure 32" all around—I'd tell you which button to call waist but even on my issued shirts buttons are spread differently on each shirt. After waist leave remainder of width below waist at its original width—still have that lil old rear end you know. I'll try to send patches in another envelope along with this letter.

Yes you're right about having plenty of folks to write to. I guess I'll take Barracks Guard sometime this week and really catch up. Spend best part of day just writing letters.

Guess I'd better close this thing and get it off. And send patches too. And please don't go Pearl O'Hara on me about the mark—I know I haven't given you much to tell about me and I know you so want to—my Army career sort of petered out before I even got started but I am not exceptional here—so far from it—just a lucky day and couldn't help letting you in on the actual statistics.

Got to go now. School calls and I have much to do before then so be good.

Love, Frank

May 31st, 8:40, Wednesday

Dear Mother, Harry and Mike,

Well, the end of the month has arrived. I can hear them calling roll for the payroll from here. I'm taking this time to write for I am way on the end of the line and will have to sweat out a long one when I do go over.

We will get passes and be allowed in town right after being paid but don't think I'll go in. I have a lot of writing to catch up on and had better get to it.

Right now I think I'll run over and get in line. I figure I'll have a long wait but the trouble is that you never know when they might start two lines so guess I'll finish this right after being paid.

11:40

It took a while to get paid and then I decided in favor of a shower and shave before getting back to letter. I also got my shoes out of repair. I am now done up in Suntans awaiting the call to chow—then after that I'll be waiting for mail call. Oh the simple joys and tribulations of this G.I. I do have a hell of a time don't I?

I was in a melancholy mood yesterday—I advanced but I am alone. Of the 8-10 fellows who started with me from this barracks I am the only one still in class 46. Even the fellows who were in my Theory class—the ones I chummed with are gone now. The only ones left I wouldn't be bothered with. Hughes, Cofrances washed back in Code. Kostishack back in Theory—Daher, Whitman and Miller all had sessions in the hospital. Taylor was in with mumps and Terry washed back in Code so that now I'm all alone.

This is what is wrong with the Air Corps. The rest of the services hate us because they envy us the best food and no one can blame them for disliking the attitude of most men in the Air Corps. The big trouble is that you work or fight or what have you in such small units. A man really never has a buddy long in the Air Corps because small units are always on the move somewhere—it is a constant of motion—a situation which is unavoidable and one that once you get caught in it, it develops a type *of independence in a man that is totally untypical of the spirit of comradeship and teamwork that is so characteristic of the other branches of the service.*

About 25% of the barracks graduates in the next few weeks and we will have to start all over. It is a shame for we have such a swell bunch here now. You start over making friends and pals till you get damn tired of it and then you just go on your own—too much effort after awhile.

But that is the way it goes—and it is valuable as an experience and in adjusting yourself to anything.

Chow is over now and a fruitless mail call (can't expect much—got 4 yesterday). I bought Harry's matches and plan on going into town to-morrow to send them out but on second thought I may not make it till the next day—I always seem to have so darn much to do and so little time to do it in.

Guess I'd better roll on—have a couple more to write.

Enjoyed letters I got yesterday a great deal—by the way just what does Francis Patrick do at Carbo?

Be good, people.

Love, Frank

POP OTT

Present Day

With all the mentions of the Otts in my father's letters, Mrs. Ott and Coach, I thought you may like to know a little more about them and how they fit into the story. After our father's death, Pop Ott, assumed a similar role with us as he had with our father and Uncle Harry. He was a sort of surrogate father, uncle, or grandfather, although he was too young to truly be a grandfather to us. He and his wife Dorothy, Maimie Ott as we referred to her, became two of the central "relatives" upon whose enduring presence our earliest memories were built.

Each night before bedtime when my father was alive and continuing after his death for many years, we would kneel in front of the collection of children's rocking chairs in our living room, one for each of us, lined up in front of the fireplace where above the mantel hung a wood carving of the Madonna and child. I learned when I was much older that when my parents had purchased the house, the wood carving was the first thing my father had hung on the day they moved in - it was a gift from a patient. It remains there to this day. While kneeling before the Madonna each night we would say our bedtime prayers. One Our Father, one Hail Mary, and then we would recite our intentions: "God bless Mommy, Daddy, Grandmama, Grandpapa, Mamie Ott, Pop Ott, Barbara, Frank, Loretto, Michael, Therese, Christopher," and until Peter was a few months old and we realized what we were saying, we would end with, "and God bless our new baby." Of course we adjusted our intentions as our family members were called home, but like our prayers, Pop Ott was a constant in our lives until his death at age ninety-six in 1998.

Throughout our lives we never knew very much about Pop Ott; just that he had been a long-time friend of our father's as well as a coach and teacher at several schools in Niagara Falls. We knew Maimie Ott had been a teacher in Niagara Falls as well, but just as we didn't really inquire much about our father's absence, we didn't inquire much about Pop Ott's presence. While I was growing up, he and Maimie Ott had been in attendance at every special occasion I can remember. With the exception of the times they'd travel to Lakeland, Fla. to visit his sisters, they were present at every Baptism, serving as godparents to my younger sister, all of our weekly Sunday dinners, they were there for all our birthdays, First Communions, and every holiday—including many Christmas and Easter eve's when they would spend the night at our house and be there when we awoke in the morning for Christmas presents from Santa or Easter baskets from the Easter Bunny. Pop Ott, being a physical education teacher, taught all of us how to swim, and he had the most gorgeous garden at his house, which he tended with patience and care, as he did all of us. He would explain all the different flowers when we'd visit and was a permanent fixture in our lives as he must have in our father's and our Uncle Harry's.

As a rule, we had never been allowed to sleep over at anyone's house. This, I learned, was our father's rule, which my mother continued after his death. The two times in my lifetime that I can recall breaking this policy were on that heartbreaking June day our father died, when we'd all been shipped off to various relatives as she came to terms with our loss, and when we were individually allowed to spend the night with Mamie and Pop Ott. As with everything, we took turns, starting with the oldest, Barbara, and then Frank had his turn, and finally it was my turn, forever third in line.

As you can imagine, sleeping over was a big deal, but what made it an even bigger deal was that we got to go by ourselves, without any other siblings. This made the sleepover even more special. The fact that Mamie and Pop Ott had no children added to the excitement as they doted on us in general, but to have the undivided attention of two adults was practically unheard of in our family. We also got to wear our best pajamas, mine a nightgown reserved for special occasions such as Christmas and Easter, most likely so we looked presentable in the photos and movies taken on those holiday mornings. That day I was filled with anticipation as I packed my ballerina suitcase and brought it with us when we went to visit. That evening, as my mom and siblings returned home, I stayed with Mamie and Pop Ott for my big adventure. I've never forgotten that night, it was 1967 and I had just celebrated my seventh birthday.

Mamie and Pop Ott lived in Lewiston, New York. It was August, and so it stayed light for a long time. They had a walk-in closet at their house, and whenever we'd visit, they'd ceremoniously take us into that closet where they had a few children's games, including one that had fishing poles with magnets on the end of the line, and fish with metal discs so we could catch them with our poles. They had Tiddlywinks, Jacks, Checkers, and the card game Old Maid. In the garage was our favorite game, croquet. I can't recall what else, but to a child with six siblings, to be given the chance to be an only child with all these toys and games was truly rare and one to enjoy to the fullest.

After everyone had left, I was allowed to play with some toys for a bit before heading to bed. It was a strange room of course and it took me a while to fall asleep. There was a little light in the plug to help me find my way to the bathroom if I had to go during the night. Eventually I fell asleep, for how long I am unsure, but the next thing I remember was that I was being awakened by my mother, who walked me half asleep out into the living room where the ambulance men were rolling Mamie Ott out of the house on a table with wheels.

There were all these lights flashing, and people I didn't know. I went home with my mother that night, and she told me that Mamie Ott had died and gone to heaven. In the morning, when I woke up in my own bed, I remember my sister asking me why I was home. I told her that Mamie Ott had died and mom had brought me home. She became very mad at me and told me it wasn't funny to lie about something like that. I told her I wasn't lying and shortly afterwards, my mother told her and my other siblings the sad news. Once again, the intentions included in our prayers at the end of the day were adjusted.

A widower now, Pop Ott continued to be a constant in our lives, continuing to attend family functions, celebrations, and Sunday dinners. Even as he aged and moved into an adult care facility, and eventually a nursing home after an amputation due to diabetes, we would pick him up and bring him to our house. When it became too difficult to do so on our own, we'd have him transported by a professional service. Eventually we could not bring him to us any longer, but that didn't stop us from seeing him. For years my mom and stepfather would visit weekly, and my sister and I would visit him every Sunday after church. Toward the end of his life, he just didn't want to be here anymore. He would ask us why he couldn't go, and we tried to comfort him. It was on a cold January day in 1998 that with mixed emotions I said my goodbye to him. I was thirty-seven years old and he had been with me my entire life. He still is.

SIOUX FALLS, SOUTH DAKOTA - PART 3

1944

As my father moved forward with his training, the war was moving forward on all fronts. Early in the month the B-29s completed their first combat mission in Japan while the U.S. and British airborne troops, with many losses, managed to land behind German lines in preparation for the "Allied Campaign in Europe." Meanwhile, back in Niagara Falls, the first German prisoners of war (POWs) began arriving at Fort Niagara. By the end of the war, their ranks had grown to just under two-thousand. Through the terms of the Geneva Convention, these POWs were not permitted to undertake any military tasks, and therefore they were put to work on local farms. This was the ideal solution as there was a shortage of men to work the farms, and later harvest the crops. The alliance proved beneficial for my father's loved ones at home; while on the other side of the ocean the invasion that had been planned for the past two years was being set in motion.

—

June 1st, 11:20, Thursday

Dear Mother, Harry and Mike,

Just got back from PT. It was really rugged but expect it to get worse soon. They have about 7-8 pretty rough obstacle courses here and we're going to see plenty of them but soon.

We were due for drill this morning but rather fortunate circumstances sent us over to hear a lecture. I say fortunate for the talk was given by the original Father Flannigan of Boy's Town. He is an exceptionally fine speaker as are most priests who achieve much success in any line. He told us some of Boy's Town - his main example was of an 8 1/2 year old Bank Robber. His main theme was a plea for the "Back to Religion" idea - a country that is stupid in the love of God cannot hope to lead the world in war, and more important, in peace. It was well put - made good listening - I for one could have stood more.

I should go into town today or to-morrow but just can't "see my way clear." Maybe I'll get in Saturday. I have to get those matches out and buy me a Suntan hat, get me some oranges - oh I'll be a real busy boy when I get there.

Nothing more new I guess. I'm going to take a shower now and spend the afternoon in the sun. I'll leave this letter open for now so in case I get some questions in mail call, I hope, I hope.

Later: No mail as yet - things are FUBAR again but the boys are working on it. Intend spending afternoon in the sun with my old pal Otto Taylor. He is over in the next squadron. He has been coming over here the past two afternoons so it's my turn to go over there.

He is now two weeks behind so we're going to talk radio - maybe I can help him a little. He took my notes yesterday - I still maintain that discussion is the best way to learn. Taylor has a darn good head on his shoulders so we both learn and reestablish facts once we get going.

Guess I'll close this now - got to get going if I'm going to see Taylor.
Love, love, love, Frank

June 2nd, 12:40, Friday

Dear Mother, Harry and Mike,

We were supposed to drill today but it was abandoned in favor of a G.I. Party. We scrubbed barracks and windows. Then we had PT. You would have laughed at the G.I. Party. We took all the beds and foot lockers out and had most of the floor cleaned. We were sweeping last of water out when it started to rain - of course all the beds started to get wet. We all laughed our heads off because all of us tried to get our bunks in the narrow door at once. Rain inside, water inside, bed on your shoulders, someone pushing you and no place to go because there are four or five guys with their bunks ahead of you. Oh we had quite a time believe me.

I have finished chow and mail call, which produced but one letter from the Bealys, namely Norma. I think I'll enclose it for I'm sure you will get a kick out of it and remember "mums" the word.

Things were pretty well worked up here last night. The boys heard that this Flight Officer deal went through - passed Congress and now requires only the President's signature. I can't get too worked up about it myself. Maybe that is why things have taken such a turn toward the more rugged side here. However this is the way I think it is destined to run. You have to be qualified for combat crew to get the rating and as near as I can find out only about 20% of the fellows who graduate from here do qualify for combat crew. If all this is true it will certainly put a new complexion on things.

Oh another thing - I also hear from a supposedly good source that class 69, one that just started, is the last one that will go through here. The big point being that all candidates for this school are washed out Cadets. But - there are no more washed out Cadets hence it looks like an end to R.O.M. School at Sioux Falls before the next winter breaks its back.

Oh yes, I suppose if this thing really does go through, Francis George might be an officer yet but there are far too many slips and red tape in this man's Army so I'm not thinking much about it till the whole thing is formally broken to us at school. As far as I'm concerned the thing is not law yet so let's not talk it around - the bulk of this information takes the form of rumor and cannot be relied upon but I have to let the steam off to someone and I guess you guys are the goats.

To-morrow I'll go to town. Get those matches sent out - get me half a dozen nice oranges, take civvies shirt to a decent laundry and get information about going to

Garrison - 20 miles from Sioux Falls for a swim Sunday - like to lay in the sun all day and then get me a good steak dinner.

I have to write the Beals now. Should write Gramp too so, be good.

Love, Frank

June 4th, 11:20, Sunday

Dear Mother, Harry and Mike,

Well, I'm afraid I missed yesterday but you can understand why. I took that excursion into town. By the time chow was over and we were waiting for the bus we had but 2 hours to go in and get back. On top of this, I forgot my Day Tags and was turned back at the gate so Bill went in alone with our laundry and I met him as soon as I could get back which was almost an hour later.

As I told you the G.I. Laundry murdered the first shirt you sent me so I was bringing it in to a civilian laundry but Bill tried around and no civilian laundry in town would take it. No G.I. clothes would be taken anywhere. So we had to settle for taking the things to the dry cleaners - they said they could get the many creases out of it but I won't believe it till I see it. I'll do the thing myself at the U.S.O. if this doesn't bring results.

I had planned on going swimming to-day but clouds are everywhere and no sun (as per usual on my day off). So we are in town at the Masonic Temple. I feel good - nice to have time to yourself - no plans - got up early this morning - John Kostishack and I went to Mass at 7:45 and then breakfast at the Service Club. PT - shower and shave - into Suntans and then into town. I bought me a new bonnet yesterday - now I know how women feel with a new hat - just feel good all over. Got money in my pocket - may take in show - maybe have a bit of dinner at an expensive place and on top of that there is a dance at the K of C tonight and maybe I'll see Hazel so it looks like a full day however I decide to spend it.

I guess maybe it's one of those quiet days like you fellows have when Harry just wants to stay home. We brought our rain coats - we carry on weather or no.

No new developments in school except that we continue. First week of Aircraft Radio Fundamentals now over and I go on alone. From now on it is going to be cutthroat on my part in class. It will be for me a competition to beat the other fellow out. I helped Bill Hughes on his material for the last "Quiz Kids" and he feels confident he got through OK. I may spend some time with Taylor in the next squadron, but as far as the guys in my class are concerned - don't ask me what I'm bucking for - but I hope to do the best I can.

This is a long stretch - 10 weeks before we are quizzed again so you just have to keep on the ball.

I'm still on 16 WPM in Code but feel I am improving and hope to knock it off next week some time.

Mail was delayed today so we didn't wait for it.

Guess I'll sound off for I can't think of anything else at the moment so

Lot of love, Frank

June 5th, 11 Am, Monday

Dear Mother, Harry and Mike,

Well, I'm not still here–no, but I'm back again. Yesterday, after I wrote you, Hughes and I went over to the U.S.O. Of course we took advantage of the lunch here and entertainment first.

Then at the U.S.O. we took in a movie, "Trade Winds." It was really an oldie. After that, a bite to eat and then we went up to the K of C to the dance. All this time the weather was turning, of all things, colder. At the K of C I had a few beers and a few dances. Hazel was not there, suppose she was running around with that damn Corporal again–Ah well, she just doesn't know what she's missing. Of all women I pick to fool around with, I pick the one my instructor at school is sweet on. I think I pulled anchor in time–I hope so for marks this session depend on the instructor–he is a pretty good egg–a little too effeminate for my money but he does know his radio and I am fortunate in that.

After the dance wound up we started back to the Post. By this time it was really cold but no bus was in sight and we started to walk and walked all the way before a bus passed us. My shoulders were a little chilly all night but I slept well. Didn't bother to get up for breakfast, instead, when we got up, we turned laundry in and went to town for a double order of wheat cakes. A double order–bacon–all the syrup you wanted–four pats of butter–all the coffee you wanted for 51¢ not bad eh? After that we went up to the Masons again and that is where I originally started this letter but a pool table became vacant so I left the letter. We shot pool for a while and mangled the ping pong table and then stopped for something more to eat and I had 2 beers before coming back to camp. This morning when I got up it was so cold in the barracks that you could see your breath. I started into town with my heavy underwear top on and also a sweater under my raincoat. No kidding, it is really cold here again.

You haven't commented about my extra 6 lbs.–am not sure just where it is - probably it's in the usual place but I've noticed since I've been in the Army that I have more trouble keeping my ring on my finger–yes even my fingers have grown thinner.

Guess that will have to be all for now–I'm darn glad I didn't try to go swimming. *Love, Frank*

June 6th, 9:00 AM, Tuesday

Dear Mother, Harry and Mike,

I am at it early this morning–the boys are busy G.I.-ing the barracks. No I'm not goofing off in particular because I swept and mopped my own area and my conscience is at rest.

Say I haven't had a letter in the past couple days–I suppose that two or three are up at the mail room just waiting for some generous soul to sort them so I can get them.

Of course the big news of the day is invasion. Oh God may it only be a speedy success. Reports we have had up to this point are of course too general as it is much too early to ascertain any success or failure. I fear this is the answer to Aunt Maime's mail problem too. Dick has probably been a busy boy.

One item I have been meaning to mention is your getting allotment. It certainly is gratifying to know that you are getting any. No I have not had it taken out except for two months so far. You should have received a double check but as far as I can find out here you are lucky to be getting it so soon–truly I was surprised. The next one should be double but may not be. It will just ride along till they discover the discrepancy and then it will be taken care of. I hope you don't experience what a lot of other fellows have–that is their people getting the first one or two and now being back a month or two. If the amount is not made up in a couple months I'll put a chaser on it but for now I feel we are fortunate.

They took it out starting in the April pay, if I mentioned that it was a short pay that was because they took the Field Jacket out on the one before or the March pay.

About the invasion–they were supposed to blow sirens and wake us all up when it started but we rolled out this morning only to have the Sgt. tell us it was underway. Of course we turned on a radio–you'd be surprised at the effect on the men. Oh, they were excited–lots of jabbering–lots of hoping and darn little speculating. Greatest surprise was stated at the point of attack. Guess we were all hoping that old "Yankee Ingenuity" would pull a surprise punch at some totally vulnerable point. You almost would have expected the boys to cheer but in a way–that is the beauty of the Army philosophy–the feeling Army life inbreeds into you. As long as no one is sticking a knife in YOUR ribs–all hell can break loose and it doesn't bother you.

Beyond this there is little new to report. School now, that is the thing, is definitely tied up with the sets that are used on the planes. They are beautiful things but–suppose I shouldn't mention much about them. In Code I'm coming along closer to passing "16"–should get it sometime this week–I hope, I hope.

Guess that will be all for right now.
Love, Frank

June 7th, 10:30, Wednesday
Dear Mother, Harry and Mike,

Well, today is equivalent to another day off as far as loafing around is concerned. It is my turn to take Barracks Guard today so I just finished mopping the floor and tidying up a bit and am now awaiting the Lieut. or non-com who will go through for the inspection. I expect to get a lot of writing done today–hope I don't disappoint myself. It is still on the chilly side–we are still wearing Field Jackets–we all say we enjoyed Sioux Falls' summer–both days. But I think we will be cussing the heat around here when summer really comes.

I am still surprised at the serenity at which we are all taking the invasion but then I guess there is no real point in getting too het up about it for we are like you in the respect that none of us know much about it as yet.

I rec'd 2 letters yesterday–Harry's and Mother's. Gosh it is good to hear from home–
it had been two days. Do you really like the bed jacket–can't say as I was too well
pleased about the final thing. I bought it a full month before Mother's Day so to be
sure and have it but the longer I had it on hand the less I seemed to like it and then
the color of the one (larger size) I finally sent looked a little cheesy to me but I figured
the silk quilted ones too darn impractical and when I came to change it there was just
nothing else.

About the picture–I thought twice before I had it taken with hat on but then I figured
you wanted to see the whole works–thus the hat. "Hats" will be worn on the right side
one fingers width above the right eye and the same above the right ear–thus no curls–
still have a couple but since part is on the left we have to sacrifice the old ace in the hole
but when I get them in the telephone booth I take the hat off–that does it every time.

You know the element of surprise. That artistic masterpiece of Harry's has gone
the rounds of the barracks. Mother I hope you didn't see it–it was darn clever anyhow and we all got a good laugh out of it.

Bill and I are still going together. When Harry and I get together I shall have to
tell him some of the real treatment of that week-end with Bill's sister-in-law. Yes it's
even better than the "screen door episode." I was the complete butt of the joke and
the great amount of laughing Hughes and Kostishack and I have had over it. Bill has
said nothing about the week-end and I am well content to let it ride.

I suppose now would be a good time to write Bobby–maybe I'll try that today.

That was some lining in mother's last letter–don't start splurging now that you
are getting all that money from the Govt. It seems like such a puny stab or attempt
to help even a little so you shouldn't be sending it off to me like that. Anyway on the
strength of it I tried to get a date last night but the line was busy every time I tried
but today I'm Barracks Guard–no school so I will camp on the phone till I get some
sort of satisfaction.

About the shirts–if it isn't too much I wish you would have them taken care of.
Here I won't get them for a month and on top of that they refuse to sew the patches
on so that is why I wanted it done at home in the first place. The tailor shops are really busy here and you have to wait too long and they soak you too much.

Well, guess we'll have to make that all for right now–have a lot of writing to do but
if I catch up I may write you another so–so be good.
Love, Frank

June 7th

Dear Mother, Harry and Mike,

Just a hurried note. We came into town just to get laundry but when the rest of
the bunch heard we were coming, we were imposed upon to a terrific extent. Yes, we
have a whole list of things to get for the boys and are barely going to have time to
get all of it.

We did blow ourselves to a grand meal. Got it in a department store here, I should say the department store. It was a great meal–chicken, biscuits, darn good salad, swell coffee and "Fresh Strawberry" shortcake–Huba Huba. The place had been recommended to me by one of my old instructors. The service was swell and sweet rolls like the ones mother never did get around to making.

Have to scoot off now to do a thousand errands. Won't be able to see if I got any mail till I get back–probably have to read it in school cause we are playing it awfully close to the margin.

Be good.

Lots of love, Frank

June 8th, 12:30, Thursday

Dear Mother, Harry and Mike,

Not much new to report. Weather still on the chilly side and a continued drizzle. I built a fire last night and we have a couple going this afternoon. I spent an enjoyable evening at home? (in barracks) last night. I had me a radio, Time Magazine, Esquire, couple candy bars and I listened to all the programs. I have to go back to school to-day and must catch up on what I missed which shouldn't be too bad. In a way I hated to take Barracks Guard yesterday but it was my turn so I figured I'd better step in.

PT was inside today and I have done very little. Being slightly flush I allowed my-self to lose ½ rock in a crap game. It put in the morning fine but when we gathered about 6 fellows and they started to get going steep I shot my 50¢ and got out.

I intend getting a haircut this afternoon–have to work that item in before the rush gets there for Saturday's inspection. Am now awaiting mail call–don't expect much for I have done so well the past two days.

Should have mentioned "patches" in yesterday's opus–they should be centered–½ inch from shoulder.

Guess this just about sums up all the local malarkey which totals just about noth-ing sooo be good.

Love, Frank

June 10th, 12:20, Saturday

Dear Mother, Harry and Mike,

Well, that hurried little ditty yesterday was hardly adequate was it? As soon as mail call is over I'm going to the telegraph office and send you a night letter–didn't find out till yesterday after I got back from town just when Ann was graduating so I figured I really should come forth. Please let me know the price and I will send money on immediately–let's not forget or get around this item. This is one thing which I feel I want to pay for myself so please see it my way.

I will realize the imposition but I am in kind of a tied up position. I could not be sure that money Air Mailed would reach you in time and since I didn't sign pass master yesterday I can't get out today to telegraph flowers and I'm not too keen about doing it that way anyhow. Ann certainly has her hands more than full. Her mother is in the hospital. Taken rather suddenly—she is at clinic on N. Oak St. (?). All this happened while Ann was taking exams and of course she is Chairman of their Class Day Program so I imagine she has been really busy. Sooo—under the circumstances I should do something and I guess flowers are the best way.

What I sent was surely suggestion and I realize that this is certainly short notice so I know that you will do the best you can.

Now I have plenty of cash so don't forget to let me know. I do hope you do it up brown anyway.

I did a surprising thing yesterday. Yep—opened an account with the Postal Savings at the Post Office.

Since I have been here I have carried my "little extra" on me at all times and it's a damn nuisance and temptation. With that money I financed, crap games, seduction of WACs, 3 or 4 Mother's Day gifts, the sending for of wives and the shipping of them home, the return of pawned jewelry, binges and a thousand other things. No I didn't lose a penny of it and I was glad to let the fellows use it because times arose which were of the emergency nature. Now my credit is darn well established and I can borrow from almost anyone in the barracks.

Stopped to send night letter—got my laundry and went to Confession.

Don't send any oranges—I can get good ones here—also have arranged to get extra ones from mess hall so we can dismiss that.

Have to get to school now so be good—

Lots of love, Frank

June 10th—Western Union
(referred to as Night Letter)

DEAR FOLKS. ANN GRADUATES TUESDAY MORNING. PLEASE SEND CORSAGE TO HER HOME MONDAY EVENING SUGGEST GARDENIAS. SOMETHING SPECIAL LEAVE IT TO YOUR DISCRETION. LOVE FRANK

June 11th, 2:10, Sunday

Dear Mother, Harry and Mike,

Here I am again today—almost same time and same place. Another one of those passive Sundays with nothing planned and kind of a relief not to have your time scheduled for you. We wait all week for this day and when it comes we really don't do much but we sure have a grand time doing it.

Guess I'd better start with this morning. My alarm clock buddy awoke at 10 till 7 but since rain was coming down in buckets he decided not to wake me. When I did get up it was too late to go to 7:45 Mass but I did make it to 8:45. I still had breakfast at the Service Club—of course this involved goofing off PT but my luck held and they didn't catch up with me. I went to Communion—I must do this more often for the Sacraments are right under my nose and I am such a fool not to take advantage of it. I have so much to be thankful for. We had a very good dinner. I waited for mail call and was glad I did for I got Tess's letter. Now look—I don't blame you a bit for getting sore at me. You are at home (too far away) trying to do everything to make things comfortable for me. I change my mind and horse around and keep you in suspense and wasn't it ever thus? Honest I'll try to do better. I think I did Airmail a couple letters and that "night letter" you should have by now must keep you at your wits end. Please bear with me—It's awful nice to have guys like you at home!

Guess I'd better answer some of today's questions (in letter I just rec'd). Thanks a million for the Sawbuck—I think I wrote about it before—mail here doesn't get the treatment it should and I didn't get it till Tuesday and I had written in the morning and so didn't mention it till Wednesday's letter. No—Beyond the ever welcome Gazette I have heard no word from the Otts.

In Thursday's excursion into town I bought Father's Day cards for the whole barracks and myself included—also a couple sympathy cards—the fellows are sending more and more of them—hard job to shop for one of those for someone else.

The bunch I am studying with—well, most of them are just mediocre. I do much better if the competition is keener. Beyond this—the course is really getting stiff and I'm going to have to do plenty of studying from here in believe me. We have to familiarize ourselves with a great many sets—the timing procedures are detailed and examinations rough in that they include a time limit.

Don't take chances please. I don't—I button up my overcoat and dress for the weather and take preventative measures, and be mighty careful see, so you better do the same.

Well, we are a little too early for chow here as yet so I guess we will shoot some pool and play some king pony—Good clean fun you know. Please, be good and careful. Love, Frank

June 12th, 2:00, Monday

Dear Harry,

Where to start—I hardly know. It certainly sounds like a splendid opportunity to me. Let's try to look at it from all angles. My particular viewpoint is your C.P.A. and what this would mean to you later in life. Things like this are not apt to be thrown your way often, particularly after this fracas is over. If only both you and Mother could manage somehow in N.Y.C. Did you tell them you are making much more than they offer and if the salary were upped to the point where you could keep you and Tess in N.Y.C. you might consider it? Please do not forget You are in demand—they want you—they need you—at present you are set. Tell them it is a matter of sound business principle that you can hardly be expected to release a position and sacrifice security and established seniority for less than a 33 1/3% increase. You have to show these babies that you are a good business man—once you prove that, they will want you even more. Don't be pushed around—not with conditions as they are.

Your big advantage, in my opinion, would be getting your C.P.A.—of course I imagine they threw that in your face aplenty. With what you make now plus Liggett's what they offer is peanuts.

There should be some way you could safeguard your position at Carbo by getting some type of extended leave of absence–tell them you will be working for your C.P.A. and have all intentions of returning to your home once you have achieved it.

You couldn't profitably touch the thing for less than 200 or 200 and a quarter–the thing is ridiculous now at their price.

If you could work it out somehow–for a while the two of you would have to live in N.Y.C.–if you went on the road it would be not so good for Tess.

In closing this side of it–it is the chance you have wanted and deserved–give it plenty of consideration.

Now on the other side of the book.

You won't like N.Y.–You won't like the people–You won't like traveling and eating out, a lot if it should come to that. You would have to give up a lot to make the grade–close the Tavern and both of you move to N.Y.C. It is a great place to visit–maybe you'd like it there–that's the chance you take. One thing I'm sure of is that it would do you a world of good. Nothing bolsters a man's confidence more than proving his self-sufficiency to himself. I believe that!

Once again, the final decision rests with our one and only. Oh I don't mean out of gratitude but just the way we have always felt. We'll do it her way because that is the way we want it. Remember that no matter what you do, you will at times regret your decision no matter how things go or what you decide. You'd have to get rid of Spusie too you know, but that is an insignificant detail.

My final advice is to take it 1. If you get more money, 2. If Mother is not just willing but enthusiastic about it, 3. If you yourself want it enough to give up much of what you've known as Home all your life.

If only I were home to help now, just when you need me most, but I guess I never have quite made the grade in that respect.

Whatever you do–do it clean and complete and to hell with what follows. Let's not hear any "if onlys" a few years hence.

Do not forget to work it at the Carbo if you should decide not to take it–after all you can say you gave up a big opportunity to retain your seniority. If it seems feasible, ask your office manager advice–hold it under his nose–I don't give a damn who he is–such loyalty and ability so recognized by an outside source should be worth something extra. Get what you can now in any event.

Myself–I will always feel, in a way, responsible in a way–but never mind–we'll set this world slightly on fire again with our little team once the lights go on again.

Finally–don't forget the most important–Ask God! Go to Communion and light a candle–he will set you right for you have lived too good a life for him to let you down.

Maybe you can get a postponement of the offer. Sit down with pencil and paper and systematically write out every possibility. Finally–congratulations–Give Mother a big kiss and a love for me—above all she is our first consideration. I knew you had it in you.

Love, Frank

June 12th, Monday

Dear Mother, Harry and Mike,

Yesterday after I wrote we took in the Free lunch here. Afterwards a group from Madison put on a little entertainment which wasn't too bad. After that we had one of the best community sings yet. By the time we got through, all the "fair weather lads" had left so that if the fellow who was directing (he was extremely good) could have worked with the bunch a half an hour he could have had a first class glee club.

We saw the show at the U.S.O. later and then went to the K of C, shot a lot of pool and had some beer.

Then we had some hamburgers before we came back to camp. That was our big day. Pretty simple but we seem to enjoy it more that way. This morning we passed up chow and went back to town and got some swell hot cakes—did some reading at the U.S.O., more ping pong and pool at the Masons, then a swell bacon and tomato sandwich and back to camp.

Fraid this is a skimpy letter but you can see I'm becoming acclimated to the Army— just a lazy loafer at heart—and it's all manifesting itself now.

Just be good will you?

Lots of love, Frank

June 13th, 11:25. Tuesday

Dear Mother, Harry and Mike,

Another very wet rainy day. However, the weather in general has warmed some and I believe we will be in for a very hot spell once it has rained itself out.

It is peculiar that we have had rain every Sunday but one since I came here. Of course it doesn't bother us much anymore. It is a distinct advantage in a way for not so many fellows are out on pass when it rains and hence things are not so crowded.

I meant to say something before. J. O'Hara has been quite fortunate in getting B-29 school. I think he will get Flight Officer out of it. The way the story goes here— Everyone on the ship—those big babies—has an officer's rating. Hope he gets it—it will kind of take the curse off things for him. Most of us don't mind having every-thing in the book thrown at us if there is something at the end of it.

Say, how are the Keoughs? I never hear you speak of them—evidently everyone is still going together.

Has Mary Hogan completely recovered and is her engagement still in the broken up stage? I see by the paper where they are still getting married with a vengeance— nice idea—I admire their courage.

How are the Otts coming along with their settlement? After all 500 semolians shouldn't have been sneezed at eh? It is nice that Coach got himself fixed for the summer—don't tell me that Mrs. has not picked up something?

By the way what does Dorothy O'Hara plan on doing? I suppose she will grab an office job somewhere and that will terminate any of the advantages she might have gained from four years of college. That is one reason I definitely disapprove of women taking Business—at least if they take Arts they have a splendid cultural background with which to rear a family. But in business they don't even get this.

Started a new Phase in school yesterday. No more of the 3 hours of Code—now we get just an hour. Big thing now is the Tactical Procedure. The learning of the special procedure which must characterize military communications.

I have a Tuning check coming up this week on our most important set so all in all— study is going to have to take up a good deal of my time. As you continue in school you realize more and more the importance of the Radio Operator. All communications and orders etc. go through him and he must be extremely accurate and well on the ball. Navigation too is a part of the course so that someone can be the goat if the Navigator gets out of kilter. some potential glossary or background info

Sooo I mean to hit the ball. I'd hate to let someone down merely because I wasn't awake in class one day. Sooo I must be off—try to do a good job—don't ask me why.
Love, Frank

June 14th, 11:20, Wednesday
Dear Mother, Harry and Mike,

Got Harry's letter today. Yesterday was a record mail, Mother's letter, one from the Biels, J. Dick and one from "Mildred's little Julie." I must write answers but lately have just not been in the mood.

The story on the film sounds great—I should be able to get some pictures now. Please no more allusions about steaks—I drooled yesterday till I almost went through the fence.

Tell me just what is the story on J. O'Hara? First he is at B-29 school then he's home—what goes?

Harry tells me Mother's cold is breaking. That sounds much better. Julie's letter was really a riot—got a great deal of pleasure from it—just damned nonsense by it's good to get one like that once in a while. Still no word from the Otts - 804 T.T.S. should make no difference—anyhow if it wasn't enough they would send it back to the sender.

Yesterday I turned in a check for 16 WPM. Don't know yet how it will come out— will have to see this afternoon.

This morning they tossed us a little surprise. We were told to fall out in fatigues for PT. Only 5 barracks in the squadron fell out in uniforms—the rest in shorts. First they told us we were going to a lecture but the word got out that we were going to the swimming pool. This pool has been built entirely by the G.I.s and it is a beauty—almost on a scale with Hyde Park but—here's the rub—it was leaking 6" of H2O an hour so they dug out all around it to find the leak. We were taken over—not to swim but to put the dirt back around the base of the pool—O Joy, Oh Bliss! It wasn't bad—I didn't mind it a bit because they didn't keep us at it long. Hope that pool will be in shape soon. Although it would never be finished if they left it up to our bunch–goofing off is an art with us. The Captain in Charge raised Hell–said he could have done more with a table spoon–Oh we didn't kill ourselves!

The weather is distinctly hot and very sunny here at last today–I imagine will be getting plenty of the same from now until the end of August.

Guess that will have to be all for right now.

Love, Frank

June 17th, 1:10, Saturday

Dear Mother, Harry and Mike,

I am a bad boy! Didn't write yesterday. I did get a letter from Gramp - he makes such a splendid effort because sadly enough he has nothing whatsoever in common with me. I also got a U.S. News from him. I really do appreciate this and I must write him to that effect. Here I have lost practically any connection with business or political trends - this magazine, though republican, is about the best in its line in my opinion and I must write and thank Gramp for it.

Thanks ever so much for taking care of the flowers. I believe she would be home right after graduation - maybe not - but I think she would be looking after her Dad - in any case all I could do was try. Still feel guilty about the money - hope you can understand my situation - you didn't comment as I expected but it doesn't make much difference I guess. The occasion certainly demanded a great deal more but I could hardly do that without committing myself and that would never do.

Today they pulled us out to see the "Battle of China." These are morale films. I hope one day that some of the civilians get to see them. It was one of a series of 7 such films. "Battle of France," "Battle of Britain," Russia, etc. Pretty gory spectacle in spots. What they did (the Japs) to women and children. I hope you never hear of. This was propaganda of course, but actual pictures don't lie. If anything would make a man transfer to ground forces just to get his hands on those bastards - this was it. Incidentally today being "Gas" day we wore gas masks throughout the entire production - my head just about came off.

Just signed the payroll before I got my mail - a letter from Mother and Harry. I'm so glad to hear colds are breaking a little - certainly glad I haven't had one with the exception of one I had soon after I got here.

By the way I passed 16 WPM day before yesterday and came so close to passing 18 last night that it was a heart breaker. Have had half of my tuning check - get the rest of it this afternoon. Of all things - last two days they sock us with a new instructor who is doing the examining - Big Deal!

Jerry O'Hara is mighty lucky! Good deal on the furlough and the pay. You see, he gets $4 extra for his P.F.C. Stripe and then 50% of his pay as "Flying Pay," I think Lincoln, Nebraska is an overseas training center. If he goes to no tech school he will go over as a "Career Gunner." Frankly, I'm just as well pleased to be set as I am. Of course at this stage of the game I will probably be put in the same position but only about 20% of the men from here ever become R.O.M.G. (Radio Operator Mechanic Gunner). Yes, I may not - and quite probably will never - use this training for as I understand it now what they want are gunners and more gunners. Boys who have left here and written back tell us that now they are giving Corporal's stripe and a new wrist watch and a 17 day delay in route out of gunnery*. Aside from this I don't look forward to gunnery. They tell me it's a 16 hour day there.

Well, I guess this winds up most of the news for today. Be good and please be careful with those colds.

Love, Frank

*This is far too good to last till I get there.

June 18th, 2:10, Sunday

Dear Mother, Harry and Mike,

Here I am same time, same place, same position on the dial with my antenna at resonance and my oscillator pushing up around the high frequencies. Thank God for Sundays in more ways than one!

Went to church in the theatre and went to Communion. Then we went to the Service Club but the Colonel put out a new order that no men would be served in fatigues so that topped off a little of the usual enjoyment. We had quite a crew this morning. John and I got three other fellows out and 5 of us went together. For a while it looked like we would get nothing for breakfast and 5 men started back to the barracks with empty stomachs and bitching at the Post C.O. like blazes. But on the way back we noticed that one mess hall was still serving so out of the 5 we made a formation and brazened it right in to a full meal. God must have had his eye on us for we returned full.

Our squadron headquarters has had a lot of trouble because fellows are continually asking to get out of PT and go into town to church Sunday morning. The result of this is that the squadron Chaplain apparently was asked to conduct a "Field" service (for all faiths) in the company street. We got notice of this yesterday but of course this is no good for a Catholic. Well, when we got back the service was just about to start. It is really a nice idea for the Protestants so I took me a look in the company street to see how it was coming along. I felt pretty badly when I saw the showing that was made so I rounded up our 5 right handers (2 already back in bed) and we started out. Before we left we said just enough apparently to shame the guys lying in bed and by the time we got through old 1241 had a good showing. We sang our heads off, lifted hats for Benediction, bowed heads, etc. We did our best any way to help out the cause. According to the Chaplain in Greensboro we did the wrong thing but it served a good purpose I think. It was a shame. That street is crowded for PT, but they just don't come out for God.

I just got soundly trimmed in Ping Pong. Am not ashamed because this guy has beat everyone in the place and yours truly came closer to beating him than anyone here. I was playing way above my average game and had him worried at times. You can expect a semi -pool and -ping pong shark when you see me again. Anyway it's an excuse to get out. Sometimes I wonder if you don't wonder what I'm doing with the time I put in on these pure and simple parlor games. Ah well, I had to mature some time you know.

I did get a letter from Ann today. I'm afraid things are going to be a little trying for the little gal. They were to bring her mother home last Sunday but feeling weak she said she'd stay the extra day. It was a good thing for she hemorrhaged and had to have transfusions all that night. Looks like Mrs. McGuth won't get well in a hurry and poor little Ann is going to have to be the strong right arm. She doesn't say so of course but that is what I surmise. She got the posies at an opportune time - the neighbors had taken them and she got them after coming home from Buffalo and seeing her mother. I think she liked them.

A little about conditions at the Post - not crying mind you - just reporting. Under this new schedule we will be on the go from light in the morning till midnight. They have cut our pass time (from what I hear at the request of some of the local merchants) and from now on we will have little time to ourselves. Two hours in the afternoon and during that time you are ever at something - shoes need shining, or brass - personal sox have to be mended and buttons and a million and one other things. I did very poorly last week - 82 in Tactical Procedure so I see where I shall have to study some. It all adds up to the fact that I shall be left little time for writing so please understand; tell all the nice people at home that I shall do my best.

Regulations are now coming out at an almost staggering rate and they are no sooner posted than someone is at a typewriter drafting a new change. In addition to all this, I start Air Craft Recognition on squadron detail hour so I lose more time. A lot of the older Army men have been in a lot of Dutch because they won't take this crap at first but things get continually rougher - to an extent now that even Officers cannot leave post except under prescribed conditions. In a way it keeps you on the ball but gets terribly tiresome. The town has put on a curfew Saturday night and whether it will be extended the entire week remains to be seen.

So it goes. I'm getting a big laugh out of most of it - till they catch me. My bunk buddy has written me a few communiqués on this subject. Tell Haroola to expect them and to keep them for they are really priceless. Guess I'll see the usual show today - free eats and maybe K of C.
Lots of love, Frank

June 20th, 2:00, Tuesday

Dear Mother, Harry and Mike,

Using this paper and pencil to facilitate speed. Many and stringent are the changes. The crux of the whole affair is that our Major "God Bless Him" is at odds with the Colonel - the latter having threatened to break the former but major. Jefferys is too damn smart for him so we carry on. Keeping on the move is the only solution and that is one reason why my writing has been thin lately.

Lawdy did I get a box today or did I get a box? Gee it was grand people! On this new schedule (till midnight) a fellow gets awfully hungry. We have been robbing the mess hall for our snacks but that is merely chance "takes" so I feel swell that my personal food situation has been stabilized at such an opportune time. The sox are the herrys.

I had been wearing the ribbed forest green ones you sent me on Sundays but of course they are off color for Suntans.

The G.I. Laundry has ruined my issued summer sox so the sent ones are just what was needed.

Ties are always welcome although I get them cleaned and now have four I have never worn. This is good cause if you put on anything brand new you feel all dressed up. Maybe it looks just like the old one but you know it's new anyway. I am way behind in writing letters so please excuse the haste. Will try to write a long one to-morrow and tell you some of the latest trials & tribulations - Just now I must write Fran and Jean - it was so good of Jean - Mom your friends just never tire of being good to you and yours do they?

Lots of love (this line at least was written deliberately)
Frank

June 21st, 2:05, Wednesday

Dear Mother, Harry and Mike,

Well, people I am on the rush again. This new schedule gives you so little time and in addition to that we have Aircraft Recognition so we are kept quite busy.

Thanks again for the box. Sausage was murdered last night but have enough for tonight too so am well set. Nothing is new in school except it gets more complicated and additional things to remember when you are hardly in a receptive mood.

Great are the trials of our particular squadron. Our C.O. does not get along so well with the Post C.O. and things are tightening rapidly. So I sit here on my bunk and watch the world roll by smoking a juicy big cigar. Thanks for those too. Spam particularly welcome, as well was the cheese.

Got Harry's letter today. Expected mirror to go thus long ago. Thank heavens no one got hit or cut by it. Mother must be more careful - now the neck business. How is the cold coming? I do hope you two are taking good care of one another!

Harry - my admiration and envy for latest feminine contact - have long drooled slightly over that myself. This is one I can see - if you don't want it, keep it on the string for me. Is she the tall or short one - as I remember they traveled as a team!

Picnics sound like a lot of fun. It does me a lot of good to hear what you guys are doing. Mom seems to get out a lot more than she did when I was around and that makes me feel good.

This is the last thing I'll say about that job at New Imperial - Be careful of Wafer - He is a wiley bastard I think. He has kept prostitutes in that place ever since I could recognize them - and I don't believe he has any scruples such as pinning a rap on a young part time bookkeeper.

Have to close I guess - Time grows short and still plenty to do. Hope when I've come adjusted to this I'll be able to do better.
Love, Frank
   P.S. Bill is extremely grateful and elated over the stamp. Thanks.
F.

                                     June 22nd, 1:30, Thursday
Dear Mother, Harry and Mike,
   Well, I'm at it a little earlier today. Don't know why I even sit down to write unless it is just to let you know that I am well, ragged, fat and sassy and getting along fine (so little new happens). Aircraft Recognition takes a large portion out of the morning and we missed about half of PT. We arrived just in time to run the obstacle course. This morning the Captain gave a little speech urging fellows to get behind the Major as much as possible. We have a good record - guess that's what gets the Colonel's goat.
   Maybe this is premature but I don't think so. Mom, if you plan on coming out here you had better start planning now. Can't tell you exactly when would be best to come. Apartments are out I have found upon inquiry. Haven't been able to find anywhere near a good deal as yet and Sunday is a bad day to look. Watching papers here and hasn't done much good - I had hoped to sub-let a place but have no line on anything as yet. Rooms are hard as Hell to get at Hotels but I think we could manage one. Best week to come would probably be the 18th - that is my 18th week of school. I am now completing my 12th. Of course I can't even guarantee how much time I would have to spend with you. The 18th week I would be on rifle range (yes again here). But that means I would be on duty from only 8 AM till 5 PM here. I would have a pass every night till 2 AM. That is the set-up now. Fraid it is all terribly uncertain but it ever is in the Army. Then too how about money - can you afford it? I would like to have you here for graduation but last two classes have been shipped to gunnery before they graduated and I understand that our flying time has been eliminated from the course. It's a hell of a set up right now for the present situation has no precedent on the field. I had hoped I would be able to spend almost a whole week here with you but a situation like that has passed into "The Good Old Days" on the Post. What you would do with yourself from morning till I am off I don't know. It is all a chance and Mom, I shall leave it entirely up to you. If I'd had the week as I planned before shipping we could have picnics and drink lotsa beer and have some good meals but now we are holding our breath waiting for what is next. Sooo it is entirely up to you mom! Talk it over with your big Boy and see what he says.
   Right now your little one is going to have to write another letter so, be good and more careful - Darned if I approve of this chiropractor business.
Love, Frank

June 23rd, 2:00, Friday

Dear Mother, Harry and Mike,

How is that neck today? I can see Mrs. Keough's influence in this chiropractor deal. Please see a Medico - my guess is that your teeth are the cause of it all Mom. Cash in bonds, sell the Homestead - whatever you have to do please get this thing taken care of.

I got Mother's letter in today's "Take" and the darn thing worries me. I also got a letter from D. A. Brown today - Good old Brownie - might have known that he would be the only one to answer me. I must write him but I have soo many I must write that I don't know just where to start to tell the truth.

Lots of news in Gazette today - Ruth Hammond - Glad to see that reach an inevitable conclusion but Mimi - that strikes a little close to home - why it should don't ask me now but even then I am glad for her. I'm sure her folks will be pleased. She has been a good little girl and deserves a good break. Maybe I'll write her too but I better wait till to-morrow. Somehow watching this "Passing-Parade" in the Gazette over a period of 4-5 months the effects are varied and become more vague. First you hate to see them all being knocked off and you feel that you as an individual are missing out to a certain extent and then an increasing feeling of relief falls over you and it seems like you are shaking off some sort of boundary that limited your thoughts and activities for some time. There are so many lovely young girls and I am approaching the age where for a few years hence - age, one way or another, won't matter. So you take a final glance at those pictures - pat the paper a little - remember how you held that or those bundles of charms once when you weren't quite sure what to try next. Those days when you were pioneering in women - those exhilarating first times. And then you laugh when you think of how many followed them. Those were good days but there should be a lot more of them and you close the Daily Blot and Blurr - feel pretty good all over about something so intangible you can't describe it. Then you finish that letter to Mother cause you still have to shower and shave. So, be good.

Love, Frank

June 25th, 6:10, Sunday

Dear Mother, Harry and Mike,

How is every little thing? I'll get right down to Brass tacks cause as usual not much time. First I'd better mention I passed 18 WPM and am working on 20 now. Got a grade of 88 for last week's work in 274N Command Set but - and a big but - 60 in Tactical Procedure - I'm really going to have to work in that. They don't fool grading papers if you don't write a 1 or 0 with extra lines in it you lose 10 points right there, well you know I never was too precise and I am paying dearly for it now.

This morning we meant to make church at 7:45 but all 5 of us overslept. So I finally got to 12 noon but couldn't make Communion that late. Our one and only day off is being cut up with lectures now - this is a little present from the Colonel and some Section had to take these lectures on Sunday and since the Colonel apparently resents terribly our Major who is completely behind the men, the Post C.O. stuck our squadron with these lectures on our Monday morning off. Not just one Monday but the next 4 of them. This is just a sample - one fellow got Hell for crossing Squadron Street to mail letters in Fatigues during our 2 hour off duty period in the afternoon. So many have signed 104th Article of War for things like no patches or Dog Tags and such that it ceases to be funny or out of the ordinary.

So many Non-Coms have been broken that they all are trembling now.

It is really funny - so long as we can laugh at it they can't hurt us physically or psychologically. More of our pass time cut for Air Craft Recognition and after church and chow we all went swimming in the municipal pool here - finally got in town about 2:30 or 3 bells. Nice swim - plenty of dolls to look at and lots of lovin goin on around the pool on the grass. It's so hot here that we are perspiring through our shirts but everyone is that way so none of us feel too bad about it.

Guess we shall go over to the U.S.O. for the movie now - "Foreign Correspondent." These oldies are good - not one as yet that I have seen before. Last night we had a grand feast with Spam some "Homemade" bread - pickles, chocolate and all the trimmings - oh thos the berries.

I should be doing so much writing that it hurts but I'll just have to "goof off" one of these days and catch up. I expect to get Hell but if next Sunday is as nice I'm going out of town and to Hell with being back on Monday.

Hughes as yet does not have his camera and if it is not here by Sunday next I imagine we will rent one.

Any way we are having one Hell (good) of a time - this oppression of late makes life much more complicated but much more interesting - you really have to out think 'em now - Huba Huba
Love, Frank

June 27th, 1:45, Tuesday

Dear Mother, Harry and Mike,

Here I am ready to write something and can't think of a thing to say. We had an almost unbearable heat spell Sunday and Monday but were grateful when a high wind broke just before going to bed last night. And Boy did we sleep - just like a bunch of dead men at Reveille this morning.

The longer schedule is beginning to tell its toll - most of us darn tired. Not that we are worked so hard but just that you have to be on the alert so much that even when you can relax it is difficult to do so completely.

It is good training anyway but it is too bad that they had to invade our one day off. Really the psychological effect is worse than actually being here. The one day's respite helped a great deal but this has been taken and when you do get into town the place is mobbed with G.I. So we plan getting out of here next week end. Probably go to a small town where there is swimming 40-50 miles from here - get a bottle and really have a good rest and get the Khaki out of our eyes for a few hours. We're sticking our necks out of course but 1st offense is only 2 days on the Goon squadron and we figure it is well worth the risk. I'll be a hell of a soldier if I don't get me ars chewed out proper soon.

I got a graduation announcement from John Dick - Harry he will be home soon - maybe is now - if you see him tell him to write me from his next stop otherwise I won't be able to contact him at all.

Gee the War news sure sounds good doesn't it? Hope to goodness they can push on successfully and rapidly.

Got no mail from home today - probably get a record take to-morrow. I have not been doing right by Fran but the one letter I do write is home where I am bound first and where my whole being is when I fall asleep at night. I must write to so many, Gramp and Fran and Dorshel, and Brownie and Ann and a dozen more but I just can't make it lately, but never fear I'm scheming to beat this too. Please make my apologies - most important is to let you guys know that I am disgustingly healthy - getting lazy (ever more) from the Army - I am happy and getting along fine.
Love, Frank

June 30th, 8:35, Friday

Dear Mother, Harry and Mike,

Well, I'm at it real early today - we will get paid this morning so I don't know as I could get to it later as I plan going into town wit da swag.

Didn't write yesterday. They pulled a big surprise on us yesterday - told us to fall out for PT in Fatigues. To tell the truth we expected to dig another swimming pool but we were very pleasantly surprised. Our bunch went to Aircraft Rec. but after it we went on what was to be an exceptionally long "cross country" run. But we didn't run - after a hell of a long walk to what used to be the old Bivouac area we discovered we were guests of the squadron at a combination picnic and beer party. Gee did that old beer taste good under the hot sun.

The ham for sandwiches was still hot when we got to it and even the potato salad was good. On top of that they had one enormous cake. Only cake I've ever seen that size and it was actually good to eat. I had quite a streak of luck - had to sweat out hardly any lines to get plenty of what I wanted including beer. We had footballs and softballs and bats and I for one had a good time. They didn't even try to sell bonds which made the afternoon complete. As the afternoon wore on after 6-7 beers we came back, mainly to avoid being stuck with cleaning up the area. I hit my old sac then and snoozed a bit. It was peculiar to me the effect that little beer had on me but then I'm not used to it anymore and on top of that it's a little different drinking (for me) under the hot sun.

So we had a good time! I was glad for the squadron footed the bill and they really didn't have to do anything like that. Guess they feel that they should try to keep us happy once in a while. But that is our C.O. for you - he is a real soldier - haven't heard a bad word about him since I've been here.

We have had a couple AWOL cases here lately. With all this malarkey from the Post Headquarters we fully expected court martials for some of the boys, but in one case he asked the fellow what his name was again. When the guy repeated it the Major asked him if his dad had been in the last war. When the fellow replied in the affirmative Major Jefferys said he was sure he knew him during the last war, then told the boy to go to his barracks and not let it happen again.

This is one reason why in this squadron where the Chicken Sh-- is the worst cause the Colonel is at odds with our Major that we don't mind it so much. We know that the C.O. is completely behind his boys and if he puts out an order we know there is a good reason for it or he wouldn't issue it.

In school now we are using the Radio Compass. Most interesting course yet. Last night we took bearings along a hypothetical course from N.Y.C. to Syracuse to Toronto to London to Detroit to Toledo and ended up at St. Louis. This is supposed to be the Navigators job but the radio man gets it in the end.

Well, guess I'd better get in that pay line - no doubt we have a long wait - going to eat dinner in town today - big celebration so, be good youse guys -
Love, Frank

July 1944

July 1st, 1:50

Dear Mother, Harry & Mike,

Just a brief line to let you know that all is well.

Ran into town this afternoon for a lark - had decided to come but they changed passes (issued new ones) and it took so long to get mine that other fellows decided not to come. But I came in anyway but it certainly is not worth it. But you know me - I had an idea I was coming in so here I am.

I got Mother's letter today - it is terribly hot here again today - hope good weather holds for day off to-morrow or that is what is left of the old day off.

Going to get me a couple long cool beers now - I can just taste them - then I'll have to run back to camp.

Be good youse guys.
Love, Frank

July 2nd, 9:10 AM, Sunday

Dear Mother, Harry and Mike,

How are my pals this morning. I am often with you on Sunday mornings. This Sunday morning has turned ideal. We did get up this morning and went to church and Communion. We put on Class "A"s and so had breakfast here at the Service Club. We have just taken out Kostelanetz Records and are in the recording room just a listening. I'm writing on Ferde Grofe's "Grand Canyon Suite" - the album.

Many and varied are the implications which arose concerning our out of town trip so I am just as well pleased that we have decided not to go. There is to be a big picnic in town today and a dance at the K of C so it looks like a full day if we decide to make it thus.

One thing that came up last night that kind of knocked things in the head was the fact that they didn't wait till my 18th week to put me on the Range. I have to start Monday morning at 6:30 - it would have been tough if we were depending on this for Mother's coming here. And that is the way it goes in the Army.

Here is another angle - I'm not asking for money now so don't get me wrong - that is the straight dope but - if I am lucky and do my firing next Wednesday I may be able to get me a three day pass. So I'm going to be a very good boy. What I want to say is this - if you were going to send me any money early this month I wish you'd telegraph it this time so that I might get it maybe by Wednesday.

This is the whole story - I have plenty of money in Post Office but if I get a three day pass I would kind of like to go to Chicago or St. Paul - see a little bit of what it is all about. I have on hand enough to see me well through the month but didn't plan on the pass if I should get it. I am an old miser - I hate to take the money right out again. Now don't get sore - I honestly don't need the money - I have banked enough to take care of me but good, more than enough to even come home from here if I should get the chance, I just thought that if you might possibly be going to send me some it might not be too much of an inconvenience to telegraph it in time for me to go to St. Paul on some of it. If you haven't planned on it or it is in any way inconvenient just forget it because I can draw the stuff in a couple minutes.

So you can see why I'm going to be a good boy and meet all formations - want to get the old pass if I can. Might even decide to go up to the Badlands here in S.D. - that is where they have sculptured those huge busts of Americans or did you know?

I am so glad that Fran is improving - what matters a slight delay as long as she does come along fine?

I was terribly sorry to hear of Harry's big date falling through - darn the luck any way but better days are coming Kiddo just be patient a little longer - that's a threat not a promise.

Well, beyond the aforementioned I guess that I have little new - Oh got a 100 in last Tactical Procedure test - this going on the range washes me back a week to class 47.

It ought to be pleasant in a way - this next week - actual duty from 6:20 till 5 PM is hell but you get your pass every night. I'll be able to do a few things maybe. At any rate it will be a welcome change.

Well, be good youse guys.

Love, Frank

July 3rd, 7:20, Monday

Dear Mother, Harry and Mike,

Well, how are we all today? I can speak well for this 1/3 of the family (or should I say 1/4). Today has been a swell one up to this point. I am late writing, you see we were awakened at 6:30 and were on "Dry Firing" range until 4:50 this evening. So up we jumped when we returned from range and came in town for a bite to eat.

First thing we did was get a drink of Brandy - True Thompson Tradition - it just gave you the right touch before eating - you know almost like Sunday at home.

We then started to look up a place to eat - John, my bunk mate wanted some Chop Suey so we went to the Chinese place here in town. We got in and I started to order Roast Beef but then we both spotted Broiled Salmon Steaks and decided to settle for that. Gee was it good! We had Fried potatoes, soup, peas, fish, two coffees, lots of bread and butter and prunes for dessert (we like to get these for they are good for what oils us.). Everything was so hot and good tasting it really was an event. And the check - that was an event too $1.12 - nope that was for the two of us. Almost felt ashamed to pay for it but it made the last nibbles go down even better.

So here we are at the Masons writing home. This range is really a good deal we are off and can have our passes every night until one o'clock. It is great on the spirit but may prove a little depressing on the pocket book but this is the best week (most free) week we will have here and if I can't have you here Mom, I'm going to try to do the best I can, although anything I do do will be dwarfed by comparison. Mom - just say a little prayer that I fire this darn gun as early as possible - now do as I say, you don't know what it will mean to me to get it out the way as early as possible. Then I'll get the rest of the week off.

I am glad in a way that we are getting some extra training in this particular piece because in my opinion it is the poorest and most dangerous weapon in the service. Its efficiency is too damn low and besides I think I'm going to make a terrible mark with it. Honest I can't even hold it steady long enough to shoot a Bull.

Well, I guess that is all for just now not much new - the range itself is hell in a way - it's so dry and monotonous - but the good part is getting off every night and coming to town when there are practically no G.I.s anywhere.

Be good youse guys.

Love, Frank

July 4th, Tuesday

Dear Mother, Harry and Mike,

Well, how goes it today? I should tell you a bit about the finish of last night I guess. Well, we left the Masons and hunted up a bar where a lot of the lads from the barracks hang out. We did some serious ale drinking. There were plenty of women there sho nuff but we didn't even take a stab at it, all for which leads me to Mother's latest words in today's letters. So you have wondered too about my being with the older (in experience anyway) fellows. I have often wondered myself and figured you must too. But I came into the services at a peculiar time - then they were taking men with families and boys of 18 - my kind had gone long since and now have their commissions and are doing their bit - but then too I haven't stopped any slugs as yet either.

Oh girls are easy to find Mom, and my dear someday we'll get together an see just what you mean by a little good clean hell raising. At present I just can't see it. This is a G.I. town - women have had plenty of men around for more than a year here now and they get used to picking and choosing. I'm certainly no prize package (except to you maybe) and I don't have the dough to spend on gals and moreover I won't let them pay our way like so many of the fellows do - I haven't brought myself to that yet - but maybe I'll come around. Mom, in the Army when you are in uniform with at least 20 more like you within 10 feet in every direction subtlety just doesn't exist. I always felt when I saw a somewhat parallel situation at home that if she picked him up or vice versa they both knew what they wanted. Just because I have on the Khaki now hasn't changed my opinion on that score. Sure there are a lot of them that can't be picked up and you do meet them at places like the K of C and Service Club dances (where I am now) so you get to know them so what.It is all so terribly dissatisfying - to me at any rate - sure the gal is taking a chance - a Hell of a big one but so am I? Don't believe too much of this Stage Door Canteen Horse Crap! Then there is the case of the boy who does date one gal steady and she is left with a broken heart when he leaves - and maybe he isn't too happy about it either.

You wonder why I get pissed off when I keep moving ahead and most of the fellows I started with have washed back some. There it is in a nutshell. There is nothing stable! The only ones you really get to know are the lads in your barracks and those in your classes - don't think much of most of the guys in my class at school at present and this new Range schedule changes them most every week now anyway. So for any companionship that leaves the barracks, I don't enjoy drinking a lot - and "shacking up" as we call it here doesn't much appeal to me. Oh physically I'm just as bad as anyone - worse I fear but spiritually I fear it and mentally to me it's like a bottle of old preserves I'm saving to sit down at my leisure and enjoy that relaxation to its fullest extent.

Seems to me you would have looked a little further - why does Jerry O'Hara's little gal at home mean so much to him - and John Dick's whole life centered around home and Mary Jane after he left - I don't think I'm any more holy than they are but I do think they probably see things the way I do. In order to get much pleasure out of even a conversational acquaintance with a girl, I have to stand as an individual - not be judged as one of a group which is inevitable in the Army.

I hope I am blessed with some of your personality Mother, but you know yourself, it's a little hard to live with at times isn't it? Why did you lead such a model life since Dad has been gone and why did you hate being called a widow - being put in a class.

Well, I want a lot from life and I'm not afraid to work for it but I wouldn't like champagne out of a tin cup - I feel I am missing a hell of a lot but until I can enjoy life's sweetest under the conditions I want, then I'll just do without if I never experience them.

And so I have no sweetheart at home. I think Ann would like to be, but marrying her would be the dirtiest trick I could ever play on her. But what I have got at home is you - at least 20 men in my barracks look for that distinctive handwriting on the letter envelopes with me - and I'm sure they're a little low when it doesn't show in the bundle - just think of that when you start house cleaning first!

Well, this has turned out to be of some length and some intensity too I guess but pretty well sums up the situation. Mustn't get the wrong idea from all this, I'm happy here and having a good time. I wouldn't be anywhere else if I could I guess, not until this thing is over anyway.

Married men make fairly good companions and, contrary to reports, they talk an awful lot about their wives and kids. The barracks itself now has only about six fellows left who were there when we came in and they are scheduled to leave in the next 2 or 3 weeks, and so goes life at a Tech School. It lacks a lot of things but you get an awful lot of pleasure out of the little things and a big kick out of individual personalities.

Well, got to go now guys. Be good and take it easel [sic].

Love, Frank

July 7th, Friday

Dear Mother, Harry and Mike,

All goes well at Sioux Falls. I have been taking it so easy the past few days that I'm afraid I won't be easily able to get back into the school routine. We start back this afternoon. Whether they will review our last week's work or start us on advanced stuff and automatically wash us back is purely a matter of conjecture at present. A final try at a three day pass today proved futile. Personally, at this point, I wasn't as interested in getting the pass as I was going through the necessary channels and red tape to find out about it. It is necessary I think to know just where to go at the right time with the right story so that should other opportunities arise you can act rapidly.

We fired yesterday. As expected I didn't do exceptionally well but I feel sure I qualified. We had far from ideal conditions while firing yesterday - a very high wind and with a small weapon it is difficult to use Kentucky Windage unless you are very familiar with the actual firing of the piece. While we were firing, it started to pour rain which didn't make it any easier. I was completely drenched when I came back sooo that left nothing better to do than to change into O.D.s and off for town - dinner and a show a couple brews and back to the sac before the guys got in from school - Oh I've had plenty of good old sleep these past few days - really going to be a hardship to get back to school.

We got in early last night - that is early into the show and when we came out there was a queue about two blocks long waiting to get in. The picture was "[The Story of] Dr. Wassell." I guess the word got around from the fellows who had seen it in the past when it was here and piles of people were waiting to get in last night.

Say - did you see Red Skelton's latest? Now you know I don't like him too well but I really enjoyed that picture - "Bathing Beauty" is the name I think. Tell Mrs. Ott to see it too for her Bamboo glasses are in it in one scene.

We have been laughing like fools all morning - we have assumed that we are still on "holdover" status from the range and are now in the Service Club. I believe we have a perfect right to be here but the parade of guys in here who have no right to be here is really funny. About four of us from the range sit here on the balcony and have been counting off the fellows as they have been seeping in. Pretty soon we'll get a sign 1241 and hang it out over the Service Club door and take roll here instead of at the squadron.

Well, guess that is all for right now, be good youse guys.

Love, Frank

July 9th, 11:00 AM

Dear Mother, Harry and Mike,

Well your letter arrived yesterday and was much more than thankfully received. I suppose you were in conniptions when my Air Mail arrived. I sent the thing, never figuring on the day's delay in mail service over the 4th. It didn't make any difference anyway as the things all turned out. A little sad though cause all other squadrons, well some of them anyway, gave out passes but the powers that be were inexorable in our orderly room.

The Ten Spot, as ever, is certainly a boon to Francis George and has been well mauled in my pocket and believe me will be parting from me soon. To tell the truth the past week off - eating in town - the few beers and movies put a considerable drain on my "hold outs" and it probably is just as well that I didn't take off on a lark somewhere. This morning John and I arose an hour ahead of Reveille and shaved and got haircuts for we had a personal inspection today - with gas masks on. We like to get out ahead of the rush - always gives me an invigorating feeling to get in ahead of the rush and I spend a much better day that way.

Now about that letter - it was a good one - somehow when you send me money you always seem to write such a grand long one. I feel a little guilty about the shirts and Norma too she wrote me "a tailor would do a better job than I" which pissed me off. Why the hell did she offer in the first place? Ah well, they have certainly had their hands full of late and just from her letters I know how Norma plans on getting to Dorset for a while. Another thing - I wouldn't berate Mrs. K too much for the "emergency" call to the Richardson's. You know how Norma gets with a piece of vital information. Mrs. K certainly gets in places at times and noses in, but since I have been a kid I can always remember her being right on deck when there was any kind of trouble. I will never forget all those little desserts she sent in for Grandma just on days when you had worked so hard that you didn't feel like fixing something special for her.

Incidentally I was sort of surprised to hear that John had written you. He is a little guy in stature but he has certainly brightened a lot of hours for all of us in the barracks since I have known him. Met him on the train coming up and we have slept upper and lower ever since. He is the alarm clock type - always the first one up in the morning and he roots me out next. He is married and is hopelessly in love with his wife. Although she is a good deal younger than he is, he is forever getting himself in wrong and I think he rides her and takes advantage of her unmercifully but apparently she thinks enough of him to absorb it all and I guess they have a lot of fun making up all the time.

John had 3 years of Journalism and is as well acquainted with modern literature as anyone I have known as yet. He was picked up by the Draft in his last year at school and has had 26 months service. That experience has helped me a lot because generally he knows just what to do and when. When I told or rather read him what you wrote he laughed about the alleged coming box and said "you wrote your Mother that that was the ulterior motive!"

For the past month the two of us have been going to collaborate on some sort of play - there are innumerable awards being given all over the country right now for just such a thing. I think he writes quite well and if we do come upon a good idea I imagine we will take a crack at it. John has that dry type of humor - usually pretty subtle but the whole thing is would it be appealing anywhere else but the Army? Things of particular interest to us and funny to us; things which anyone out of the service would never understand much less get a kick out of.

I'm goofing off PT again today only today I have no legitimate excuse. Felt pretty confident till I got over here at the Service Club Library and when I looked around I see at least 50% of the barracks here too - ah well, we will march in the "Goon Squad" together.

To-morrow should be OK. John and I plan on wheat cakes in town prior to going to High Mass in the Cathedral. How are we going to get out? That is a question but "Usury" one of the lads from Good Old Gerry's ships out Monday and will be working the Pass Deck to-morrow so all should go well.

What will go in the afternoon I can't quite say for sure but probably some swimming and a show or some pool at night.

Well, be good youse guys.

Love, Frank

THE CONUNDRUM

Present Day

The July 1944 letters marked seven months of typing, throughout which time I was naturally telling people about discovering the letters and the story that was unfolding. Every person I told had the same comment, "You should write a book." The thought had crossed my mind months before when, during one of our reading sessions, my mother commented, "These letters read like a book. They're more like a story than letters." She was right of course and the comment had stayed with me, gnawing at my heart and my mind all the while I was typing. Much like Oliver Wendell Holmes had written, "A person's mind, once stretched by a new idea, never regains its original dimensions." How true I was finding this to be. I could not let go of the idea of sharing this story.

There was no denying it was a fascinating tale, and I was finding my father to be a likeable, smart, and funny man, but was it my place to write the story? I went round and round with this in my mind. If I didn't tell it, who would? If I did tell it, it would be an ideal way to honor his life. I couldn't get beyond the fact that these were his letters, intended for his family, therefore somewhat personal; I felt that I needed someone's permission to share them with the world, but whose? I mentioned I was thinking of writing a book to a few of my siblings, and to my mother, and no one threw out any objections, but I still felt the nagging need for some sort of permission. Then, in the summer of 2015, I resolved my conundrum.

While typing the Sioux Falls letters, I was entertained by the antics of my father and his pals, but it was when he wrote about his bunkmate, Johnny Kostishack, that I got the permission I had been seeking. In the July letters, he mentioned that he and his friend Johnny were considering writing a play about their life in the Army, citing awards that were being offered for "just such a thing." He explained to his mother and brother that the two of them planned to collaborate, and he too questioned the level of interest in such a story. After reading that he and Johnny were contemplating writing a play about the very things he was writing home about, I thought perhaps he wouldn't mind so much if I wrote about them on his behalf. Still wavering a little, I looked at the date he wrote that letter. It was my birthday. I no longer wondered if he would mind. I took that non-coincidence as his giving me permission to tell his story.

175

SIOUX FALLS, SOUTH DAKOTA - PART 4

1944

Dear Mother, Harry and Mike,

I had quite a struggle with myself getting at this one. I'm in that lazy mood and have been out napping for the past hour. Not really able to doze soundly because my conscience keeps telling me that I must write so here I am.

First time in a long time I have had something definite to write. Had my first ride in a jeep yesterday, but then that is ahead of the story. It all started when I got going on those pictures I wanted to send you. Hughes camera is definitely on the wry now but I made a deal with the barracks leader. I traded him one of my films for a 616 which would fit his camera and he let me take his camera.

Yesterday we went to Mass at the Cathedral but returned for mail and decided to stay for chow. The sun showed itself after chow so I ushered the lads out and was busy taking pictures when up buzzes an M.P. and takes my name & serial number. He started admonishing me for taking pictures at the Post. But I must have looked honest and innocent for when I pleaded ignorance of the regulation he softened up but took the camera and said he would take it to the Gate House, register it and I could pick it up right there as soon as I went to town.

So, since we were all going into town, I told Cpl. Arri, who owned the thing of the situation and started in for the Post gate. Almost got there when the same M.P. pulled up in a Jeep and said that I was wanted for further questioning, so after saying adieu to the lads, he carted me over to the Provost Marshal's office. There, a Tech Sergeant in charge started to ream my ars. I took full responsibility for the camera of course but I had to pull Arri in on it later when the Sergeant demanded that I open the camera and take out the film. Arri had put film in for me and I didn't know how to open the damn thing. So I had to tell him it was not my camera. This is an unpardonable sin in the Army. If you get in a jam you sweat it out yourself and you damn sure don't turn anyone else in, but they had me cornered and I could do nothing else. Since Arri is a non-com I was afraid they might break him and I was almost sure they would when they brought Arri in and the Sergeant wanted to know where he had got Arri before. It seems that the Cpl. had been in Mitchell, small town about 70 miles from here, the last week end and been picked up out of uniform. I was afraid it would go hard with him but the Sergeant let us off without even reporting it to our C.O. so that was that, but I have been kidded to death about my "Pals" the M.P.s and the ride in that Jeep.

Thanks a million for the extra fiver Mom. Now I think we better make that all for this month, eh? I feel so guilty about you sending me so much in so short a time when you fellows have a lot better places to put it than I have. Right now I am on the crest of a financial wave so let's not do any scrimping to send me more.

Yesterday afternoon and evening included movies, a bite to eat and later in the evening Hughes and I started out on a round of a lot of the local so called "hot spots." We hit eight or ten if we hit one. Hardly enough women in town to go around all the G.I.s but had no trouble getting dances here, there and the next place. Now, in this line, Niagara Falls has nothing but you should see this place. We finally wound up at one place about 4-5 miles out of town. This one is typical of several they have here. The prohibition practice of bringing your own bottle is very much in Vogue so they charge you a small cover charge and 15¢ for chasers and 25¢ for beer. From there we really went to a dump - The Chicken Inn. Here they sold no beer wanted 75¢ for hard liquor per drink but what they really tried to do was sell you a pint for 5 bucks. High price was because it is illegal to sell whiskey on Sundays here. So I grabbed one of the few babes there had a few dances and then we got out.

It was an educational evening if nothing else. Got to go now folks so take it easel (sic) and be good.

Love, Frank

July 11th, 11:45, Tuesday

Dear Mother, Harry and Mike,

Another day another Dollar, eh? I wrote youse guys a fairly long letter yesterday but had to leave in such a hurry I'm not sure it was mailed. Someone is ever going to mail box and picks up everything in sight so I'll just assume that someone stuck it in the box and not repeat the story about the M.P.s unless I hear from you to the contrary.

In school I am in entirely new surroundings. All new fellows and it is the same old story of getting used to things again. I have a new instructor in Tactical Procedure. I have already asked to be moved to some other B.D. but the Room Chief can't do it because this class has them practically hanging from the ceiling. Now I know what Dad meant about Miss Curth at Ashland Ave. School. Maybe I'll get under her skin in a while but I doubt it. Instinctively I sorta disliked her at first and then when I heard that Southern drawl and such smacking of gum (while she lectures) and contorting of facial muscles for emphasis. She is married and to top it all first name is Edna - that was the last straw. She will never see 35 again for my money but I don't think the blood has started to cool as yet. She wears no brassiere or girdle - it's hot here but not that bad. So she irks me but I simply shall have to apply the old oil and hope for some sort of progress.

Just got Mother's letter and Harry's too. One of those good days. Harry I think I like the one about Dr. Hodge best. I was so sorry to hear about Ann. Being away and not in close touch with things I almost believed that she would come through this siege too. May God Bless her, she has always been sort of a symbol to me and the memory of her I suppose I shall always carry with me as sort of a Talisman - probably the only true personification of faith and piety and complete happiness I have ever seen.

Mail call is over and chow will come up soon so I'll just be off - Have so many letters to write - I haven't written a soul but you guys in over a week now so, be good. Love, Frank

July 12th, 1:45, Wednesday

Dear Folksies,

Well, your box arrived this noon with a vengeance. I have just been gloating since it arrived and am finally down to writing about it.

It certainly was a beaut. I skipped chow completely and have finished a good third of the cookies single handed. It was a good time to open the thing cause most of the fellows went or were just coming back from chow and they weren't hungry at all. I suppose we shall finish up the box after school tonight. At present I am smoking a Dutch Master, I generally have a cigar, when I have them, after noon chow and these are dandy. The Yardleys certainly took my eye (Gee will I stink pretty) and the nuts are safely tucked away against those between meal snack hunger craves.

Now regarding the main item - the shirts. Boy that one, well both, are beauties, but I sure do like the one in particular. I certainly must have sent exact instructions or Norm put in a few ideas of her own or she followed that explicitly for they are form fitting to a Tee. The heavier shirt is ideal - just the way I want it but the other one - well, I think I'll have to have those little strips removed completely or lowered for they show at the sides. At first sight this practical touch annoyed me - when I put the heavier job on with pants I found it was completely O.K. and the strips did not show at all but the lighter one did show. I talked the situation over with Bob Miller - he is probably best dressed G.I. on the Post - he said that strips were just the thing for he has had to have his fitted shirts retailored repeatedly because they rip out. Now I am well set - you'll never know what a relief it is.

They couldn't have arrived at a more opportune time for my G.I. shirts, two were supposed to go to laundry this week and I have only one clean one. I say supposed to go for I found this morning that I hadn't turned them in - put them in wrong barracks bag so it will be a week and a half before I get them clean again. That would have left me with one clean one over the week end and this happens to be the only one I have now that is not tailored.

You probably don't know it but it is an awful lot of fun to get boxes from you guys. Do you remember those small straw suit cases that Dad brought us from one of the conventions? As I remember it was still [when we were living] in Buffalo and I must have been all of 4 or 5 - well, the feeling I get is only comparable to that I got as a child. So many neat little mysterious packages - oh lotsa fun.

The cookies and bread arrived in wonderful shape and will certainly be duly punished. I ate some slop last night at chow that was terrible but I was so hungry I almost had to eat it. Now I can turn up me nose knowing that I have something to tide me over - well over the hump.

About school - I have passed 20 WPM. Now working on 25. This is a big jump and you can't print it - you have to write it. The conversion from printing to writing is really very difficult for me and I probably will never pass it here at Sioux Falls but we are going to have a good stab at it anyhow. It is just like starting all over again.

Well, guess I'd better close this epic so, be good guys - thanks a million - I appreciate youse so much.

Love, Frank

July 14th, 11:45, Friday

Dear Mother, Harry and Mike,

How is every little thing today? Fraid I missed yesterday. We went into town to get a few things and that consumed the time I usually reserve for writing. I wore ma new shirt and felt swell with it on. And when I got back - low and behold I had another, yes another package. Well, time didn't permit eating anything just then but I took stock thoroughly. Last night right after chow I jumped the formation with a couple of the lads and we killed the last of the cookies. Boy I'm really set in the evenings now. I got me some oranges in town and John got some cherries so we have fruit - you can imagine where the Hell we are putting all the stuff - I think I have stuff farmed out in three or 4 other fellows' footlockers. That lobster looks good. The cheese and bread were certainly punished [last] night. I must get the cheese and sausage eaten quickly before it spoils. We don't need a lot, but sardines and stuff, just something before going to bed sets you up fine. Peanuts before school yesterday oh I'm getting myself in fine style all this should hold me for some time now. Don't know just how we'll manage the shrimp but we'll find a way.

Not going to chow today - at noon that is. I have plenty to eat and besides I wanted to be sure and write since I missed yesterday. We are just back from PT. Today we did a lot of double time - too fast to walk and too slow to run comfortably but I did work up a good sweat. Right now am on the old sac still in gym trunks writing and listening to St. Louis Blues over one of the radios. Have to take a shower soon.

Yesterday in town we got what came out of "Forbidden fruit" snapshots. They are rather poor - to be expected since I was unfamiliar with the camera or any camera for that matter. I'll enclose a couple of them - these are definitely the poorest, but cheer up the better ones I want to have enlarged and get the fellows to autograph them and put their home addresses on the back just so I can keep track. When I get these I'll send em home too. About me in these things, I scowl much too much, and don't think all my uniforms look like that one I have on. I generally take a clean one all pressed etc. to wear Sunday - then I wear it to chow all week while the other is getting cleaned - a week worn one is what I have on and I admit it's pretty bad. Most of us won't wear a clean one to chow cause when you have to wash your tray, if you don't spatter it yourself - some else does.

Harry mentions Barb Lacy - Just how did he get to know who she was. She is B.S. Lacey's daughter - they live at the Heights and I presume she is now working at the plant - that at least covers her being with Kay Delaney. At DuPont B.S. Lacey is one of the few staunch holdovers from old R&H. He owns enough DuPont Stock so that he works only when he damn well feels like coming in. He is known as a consultant chemist and is generally engaged in reading journals or calculating thermodynamic energy changes in chemical reactions to see if they are thermodynamically possible. Then if he finds they are thermodynamically impossible they send the reactions into Lab 105 where Cass and his Hungry Hord make em work anyway.

Yup I know his daughter - did once anyway - met her at Helen Hanes' place and they went to that dance in Ransomville with us that night. She couldn't dance then so we toured the High School a little - she was a little too young then - why don't you take a crack at her Harry?

Well, people I still have to study for a Tactical Procedure examination this afternoon so, be good.

Love, Frank

July 16th, 11:40, Sunday

Dear Mother, Harry and Mike,

How are we all today, eh? I have been up and at em for some time now. I should be able to write a decent letter today - that is if I can think of something to write about. All things this week-end are limited by the change in schedules - that is - our going on the day shift again to-morrow. We are getting less than 12 hours free time of the 27 we are supposed to ge,t which does not set so well. Also, no mail today - none until 5 PM tomorrow. Didn't hear from you yesterday but did get special carton of 5 pkgs. of Old Golds from the Plant. Have to write and thank them for that now I suppose.

I left a call with the C.L. last night and we got up at 6:45 washed and shaved and got all spruced up. Then we got our passes and off to town by 8:30. John and I always have the first cup of coffee at a small cafe then we go on to the Hotel and get the Sunday paper (I still have to read "Terry and the Pirates" on Sunday you know) then we go to the Eat Shoppe. This morning we really splurged - to such an extent that chow call just went by board for me completely. First we have a large bowl of oatmeal with plenty of butter and pure cream almost so thick you could cut it. Then we had sausage and pancakes with lots of syrup and butter and coffee. Stuffed and with the paper well read we waddled across half the town to church at the Cathedral. It was grand just taking your own sweet time and arriving enough ahead to have another cigarette in front of church.

After church we walked back to camp. The main purpose was to get the mail but none till 5 to-morrow so I thought I'd better get this out.

This afternoon, at last, I'm going to see "The Desert Song" - I missed it in Greensboro for some unknown reason and have been sorry ever since. So, I imagine we will start in shortly. I think we will walk - I must have a pocket full of bus tokens in my pocket but everything is so crowded, there is not much pleasure in riding. Then too we almost always get a ride into town if we start walking. The walk is almost too pleasant to take the offered rides but you hate to offend the good people.

Next week end looks like something different. We have been requested to (thru the Post paper) help with the local harvest and we will probably do that next week-end. We will get a good home cooked meal out of it and 60¢/hour to boot. Best part of it is that 6 to 8 of us should have a Hell of a good time together. We expect it to be darn hard work but figure we should manage one day of it. Out in good old sun all day - how does it sound? The only reason I haven't signed up yet is that it looks, from the schedule as it has been posted, that we may have to miss church on Sunday - don't know yet just what provisions have been made - will probably have to see the Chaplain about it first however it looks like a good deal - help with the labor short-age - help ourselves a little - get a good meal on the farm and see a little of South Dakota - the real S.D.

School is not going along as I would like it. Drew a 96 in the final quiz in this week's theory but don't seem at all able to catch on to this Tactical Procedure. Drew a fat 50% on this week's final. Am not sure whether to ask to wash back a week or not - and this instructor gets on my nerves - you know, in a cold sweat from the time I go in till I get out, and you just can't send accurately on a telegraph key when you feel like that. As I see it the fault definitely lies with me alone for a lot of the rest seem to be getting on well.

Later 5:30

Well, I didn't close this, thought there might be more to add. Saw "The Desert Song" and, while it was fair entertainment, they certainly murdered the story to an extent where I couldn't enjoy it. We came back to camp because there is not much you can do when you have to be in so early - may write a few more letters before hitting the hay this evening. I am a little tired and want to be awake in the morning for school which will roll around early in the morning again for a change. I'm anxious to see if things change on this shift. When you are in the squadron during the day, the Big Wigs hate to see you idle I guess, for they dream up all sorts of little things for you to do, but now since our free time comes when all these routine experts want to get home too, I expect to see a sharp decline in all this hooey - around here at any rate. I hope so.

Well, guess that is all for now, be good people.

Love, Frank

July 18th

Dear Mother, Harry and Mike,

Say, I've been a bad boy the past few days haven't I? Well, I'm staying in tonight for the specific purpose of writing - am I forgiven - I hope so! Last night we reveled in our first night on the new schedule. Nothing very serious but we did have a swell time here in the barracks. Bill Hughes went over to the mess hall and talked them out of a loaf of rye so we had Spam and cheese on rye and cakes. The night before we had peanut butter and tea and coffee from Thompson's adequate store. We have been partying a bit lately cause our W.T.S. men are getting discharges and Bob Miller got his today on a dependency claim. A couple more have been eliminated here and so the old gang is slowly dribbling out - our barracks is practically wholly repopulated.

Today was a busy one - right after school we had the inevitable PT. I had to eat, sign the payroll and get my laundry in - had to take John's too because he is off at the show.

By the way if you get a chance to see the Ghost, no it's the "Canterville Ghost," by all means do so. It's got Charles Laughton but it really is different and I'm sure you'll enjoy it. And if you're not completely in love with the feminine lead in the picture when you come out, I miss my guess. Oh, I forgot to mention that after PT we also had Peter Parade, first time I've stood it since I got here. Down at Greensboro it seems like we were forever at it.

Gee I don't really know what the hell to write about. Nothing of particular interest has happened here lately. This week in Theory at school is really boring. Maintenance and Inspections and we have a couple very putrid instructors. Hope I'm doing a little better in Tact. Pro. I hope I hope.

Got no mail today but got two yesterday so I certainly can't complain. The boys are all pretty sore - they have been screwing us out of our 1st turn at chow and boy it really is not setting well. It's a peculiar thing how you can feel the grumblings of discontent like distant thunder and I certainly hope it never, that is the storm, breaks.

Well, I can't think of much more - main point is to let you know I am fine and in there pitching. You guys be good and keep well.

Love, Frank

July 19th, 9:15, Wednesday

Dear Mother, Harry and Mike,

Don't know how far I'll get with this - lights have to go out very soon but I thought I'd try to sneak this one in.

Got mail from Mom, Harry and Ann today - Good day, eh! Just saw Sinatra and G. Murphy and oh Gloria DeHaven in "Step Lively." Really went just to see how the boys reacted to "Frankie." It was a riot at first such moans & groans but honest, by the time the thing ended, he had soothed to quiet the savage beast and most of us then got a chance to really enjoy the picture. It was OK. Really just the thing for the G.I.s, maybe the civilians will even enjoy it too,

Thanks so much for the newsy letters, also the dough Haroola - Gee guy you shouldn't. Does my heart good (guess I'm really terrible) to hear that or to hear about Quen. Also livens other parts of the old anatomy. She is still about the most satisfactory gal I ever knew - how doesn't much matter now - them were the days!

A little surprised to hear that the Beals took off for Dorset without you - I wrote em and kinda thought you'd go but you know best Mom.

Harry tells me that he had an epidemic of forgetfulness. That must bring back memories of me and my particular little struggle. I can fully understand it old man cause I did some of that two job stuff myself. It just isn't possible to keep track of everything when you're working so hard.

Really it's a joke - here am I on the "Gravy Train" and Haroola who might not be able to pass a 64 Physical works his head off to keep me in the Army and the bonds of debt away from the old homestead. Well, I'm really getting a rest and a regular life out of this Army and believe me I'll be back to add my own personal bitches again as soon as Uncle Sam will let me - moreover I still have my all important destiny to fulfill although God only knows just what it may be. Well I'm afraid I'll have to close this guys. All lights are out in the barracks and I'm writing sitting on the cement out front on Gramps' New York Times. There is a small Firelight here and all the guys going by must think I'm nuts. Yes we're supposed to be in bed now.

Bob Miller left today with his discharge in hand. Created a peculiar feeling throughout the barracks. Most of us wouldn't take a discharge although we all say - as the stock G.I. phrase goes "there is nothing wrong with me that a good furlough won't cure."

Well, here is hopin' anyway

Love, Frank

P.S. Please excuse form etc. mosquitoes are eating me up and light is terrible more of the same.

F

July 20th, 5:15, Thursday

Dear Mother, Harry and Mike,

Well, I guess that was a rather hurried little mess I sent off last night. But those were adverse conditions you know. Seems I do much better when I rush it a bit - I keep thinking of things to tell you and when I loll around I just don't have many good brain storms.

We are all now patiently awaiting chow. School is over, as well as PT, and a good shower. School moves along and you get a little shaky when you think how close the final "Quiz Kids" are. Oh Lordy, I hope they don't wash me back - it would be at least 5 more weeks and I don't think I'd want that. The big academic problem here is as follows: It seems that as soon as we report to gunnery we are tested again. This includes code sending, and taking at least 18 WPM, Tactical Procedure, as well as Tuning the various sets and Radio Theory. Scott Field (don't know just where it is) has always been in competition with this, what should I call it, institution camp or confinement. Sioux Falls has always had a better record but the rub is that in this test they give at gunnery they have washed out 39% of our boys - only 3% from Scott Field. The rub is that the examiners are from Scott Field! So the school has been in turmoil - standards have been changed, asses have been duly chewed and names taken - in ink. Oh you have never been acquainted with Real Organized Confusion until you have seen some of the Air Corps.

I still have to study Tactical Procedure for a Weekly Quiz to-morrow. Don't know why I am lingering here.

The democratic convention is on a radio so you can understand the lack of continuity and coherence. As soon as I finish here we are going to get a couple beers - ah it's great to be on the day shift.

We are pretty well decided on the Farm for the week - and - maybe that will give me a good subject for a letter. Of course we still have to be released by the Provost Marshall. We will probably go in fatigues and to tell the truth we are kinda looking forward to the change.

Well, fraid I must be off to a couple 3.2s and then a couple of us are going to have a bull session on the Tact. Pro. Should be writing a lot more to Folks but that's just tough - just you fellows be good and keep well.
Lotsa love, Frank

July 21st, 6:20, Friday

Dear Mother, Harry and Mike,

Well, of all things I finally hit a Tactical Procedure Weekly Quiz - drew a 90 and was so close to getting 100 it wasn't even funny, but as I have told you, 10 points are slashed at even the slightest error so I guess I can't cry too much.

Today the prospects for the Farm do not look good at all - 1st Sergeant told me that the PT Officer would not excuse us from PT and he didn't see how we would make it for the trucks leave at 3 o'clock but we shall see to-morrow.

Thanks Mom for the little dissertation on the "Vanity of Man." John is writing it home to his wife and it has met with a good deal of acclaim here - it's clean too!

We are now listening to Democratic Convention - wouldn't be Sarah Tidelys Grandson if I didn't guess.

We had retreat tonight so that took a good deal of time from the before chow period - I goofed off PT today - spent my time in the orderly room talking with the "Rank."

Yup Mom, I found they pulled the first trick on me yesterday that really hurt. Didn't know of it when I wrote last night, but did soon after. Well, you see someone swiped my brand new tailored, sent from home shirt. I have been able to take everything with a laugh or a slight grumble so far but your little G.I. damn near sat down and bawled. Maybe I haven't seemed to you to be agreeably adjusted but I have tried darn hard to get to the point where they couldn't do anything to me, but I felt so swell and all dolled up and what for? You try to look smart and be a credit to your outfit and what for? Must have been taken while I was at school and now the Section has no Barracks Guard so we are all at the mercy of any would-be thieves. It looks to me like the joint had been well cased. Didn't take em long to get my shirt eh? I had it on my back twice. Well, anyway it was a tribute to your selection and Norm's tailoring.

I have done everything possible to get it back or get some satisfaction but to no avail. It just can be done under this kind of a set-up. I went up to the Captain, he started with a belligerent attitude and wound up meekly, cause lady if I ever told anyone off it was him. Of course the Army assumes no responsibility for clothing other than G.I. so I put in my bitch over a set - a full outfit of Suntans - yes they took the pants too.

Well, the only way - so I am told - that I can get more is to sign statement of charges and have cost taken from my pay. This I have flatly refused to do. My claim is that the government issued me clothing which I am required to maintain and keep. However when I am on Duty at school - as I told the Captain - I cannot be responsible unless I carry the barracks bag with me.

Well, I told him plenty and I'm not through yet - there is the Post Inspector I'll go to and then the I.G.s (Inspector General), moreover when I leave here I will have to have a clothing check and there they will try to make me sign statement of charges for the pants and shirt. They will not let me ship without all my clothes and if I'm here till Hell freezes over I won't sign for those clothes.

Well, I have that off my chest anyway - I've been sick about it since last night. What probably happened was that some of the fellows shipping who knew I had the thing just slipped in and grabbed it. Ah well, so it goes - I suppose I'll get over it. Got to close now - Be good.

Love, Frank

July 23rd, Sunday

Dear Mother, Harry and Mike,

And how is every little thing today on this beautiful Sunday morning? Well, it's a lovely little morning here anyway. Right here and now I want to apologize for that rather downcast letter - the last one. Doesn't take me long to recuperate and you just have to take these things in stride.

They called off the Farm work - that is why I'm writing now - probably would be a haying or what not by now but they called it off from Post Headquarters and that was that. Just another event in which proves you cannot really plan on anything in the Army.

Just came back from Mass here on the Post. Last night I did very little. I had tried to buy Jockey shorts here last Friday (a week ago). Only got a couple pairs because I actually didn't need them but thought I'd get a couple pairs just in case - also had to get a larger size. Well, when I returned to the barracks I found they had given me the wrong thing - shirts instead of shorts so I returned them last night. I had a few beers and came back to the Post to meet some of the fellows from the barracks and went to see "Summer Storm" - George Sanders and Linda Darnell. It was different and both the leads were well done, but the plot itself was one with little satisfaction, but in spite of this I enjoyed it.

We had a little excitement in the barracks yesterday. One of our boys played in Charlie Barnett's Orchestra - well it seems that he called his girl from the orderly room yesterday but while doing so he left his wallet there in the phone booth. When he went back to get it a few minutes later he found that the 1st Sergeant had picked up the wallet. Naturally the Sergeant looked for identification in the wallet and he came upon the fellows pass. Well, passes hadn't been issued for the day so the 1st Sergeant started to put it in the file. There came the rub for he found another pass in the file. Just then the fellow returned for his wallet and he was immediately ushered into the Major. The charge was forgery - there was a different officer's name signed to the duplicate pass than the Major's. He stood a chance of getting 93rd Article of War, which is 5 years in prison or 2 years hard labor and no pay, but as things turned out he only got 6 days restriction and has to sign in at the orderly room every hour on the hour of his free time - good thing the Major is a good egg - anyone else and our asst. barracks leader would have been in one hell of a jam.

Mom asked me how long I would be here. I think I answered that but of course it is subject to change and any statement I make is mere conjecture. As things are set up here now I start my 16th week Monday. Three or four more weeks should see me out or graduated if I am lucky. The big catch is this last "Quiz Kids" - they will wash you back at the slightest provocation and that would be just my luck. Another thing, which has come up here lately, is another change in the general curriculum. The course, apparently, will be increased to 26 weeks. This will include an extra week on each radio set and two weeks of flying. They then will give a Corporal's rating at the end of the course. We are not sure yet whether or not this will take in our class - frankly, I doubt it. I hope at any rate to get out around the last of August or the 1st of Sept. and probably on to gunnery at Yuma, Arizona. Baby just look at that place on the map - S.D. is comparatively unpopulated but Yuma looks to me like the original "God's Country."

Don't know - haven't decided what I will do with today - probably some swimming - then there is a picnic in McKinnon Park - movies this evening and maybe a little dancing at the Masonic Temple - Oh well, we shall see.

No mail till 5 this afternoon so I won't know latest reports till then. Well, guess that is it for today.

Love, Frank

July 24th, 6:20, Monday

Dear Mother, Harry and Mike,

Monday again and the start of a new week. Getting my week of Review in now. Next week we get "Voice Procedure" or how to use a microphone intelligently and then the Final "Quiz Kids." The following week I get a course in the Elements of Navigation and after that a week during which I should get my first experience as an operator in the Air.

Many are the rumors here about the course for they are, I believe, replacing our most important set with a newer and better one. Whether or not we will be given instruction in this new set is of course a mystery to me.

Yesterday we browsed around quite a bit - ate in a couple places (lordy, we are always eating) took in a show and arrived back at the Post about 40 minutes late.

I haven't been called down about it yet so looks like the right guy was C.O. last night anyway.

We could get in no mail yesterday so I faired rather well today. Got Mother's letter, Haroola's and one from Fran. If she is feeling anywhere near as well as she sounds she must be in pretty good shape.

We just got a letter from Bob Miller - you know the fellow I told you about who got the discharge. He started off to think he'd get a ride to Sioux City - he thought he might have enough luck to get a plane that was going somewhere near Miami which is his home. And did he have luck- got on a C47 at the Airfield in Sioux City and went straight to Miami - one stop at Tennessee for gas - and arrived at home at 11:15 the same night - the co-pilot of the plane drove him right to the door of his home - pretty sweet, eh. Gosh it did all of us good just to listen to his letter - how the wife & kids almost knocked him down at the door. Of course, that none of us were in the least envious, goes without saying.

I must be doing something with my Code and Tact. Pro. instructor - yet I squeezed out an 88% average this week. Gosh something should happen - it is healthy to know that shaving every morning and turning on the old charm (subtly of course) is not completely in vain.

Haroola - you just wait till I climb those iron stairs - fear not we shall rip that damn town out by the roots I promise you. And these flighty dames we shall scorn and tacitly spit upon. We shall devote our time and energies exclusively to the younger - the newer - the uninitiated range of 10-14 or maybe 14 1/2. I have been storing up a lot of sensual desires - and reluctant to satisfy them here - don't know the back doors to most of the joints and husbands turn up here at the damnedest times. I am saving my money and a few other things so do'est thou likewise and leave us prepare ourselves.

Well, enough of this Malarkey - above all - Be good - Mom see the dentist - Harry go down and see Quen - and take Mike out for something too.
Love, Frank

July 25th, 8:40, Tuesday

Dear Mother, Harry and Mike,

I am trying to sneak at least the start of this one in Code class. The speed - 25 - I am on now necessitates writing instead of printing so I may get away with it. Thought I'd try to write this one cause I should write Gramp and maybe Fran this evening. Nothing of particular significance has occurred except I suppose I had some chance of getting Instructor here but I didn't bother to try for it. The extension of 6 weeks is being made apparently and they will need more Instructors. I really actually stand very little chance no matter how good my marks might be for physically I am eligible for Air Crew or Gunner and as long as I am qualified, there is where I will be sent I believe.

Say I'll bet you wonder about a couple of the latest letters coming so close together. Well, to tell the truth, I have started to pull a new one. I get the letters written and then I put them in my folder and don't find 'em again for a couple days. Oh well, even though they be a little late, you know I am thinking of you any how when they do get there. Looks very much like impending showers but the way it always works out is that it doesn't start until after PT and then we don't get out of a thing. We also have an Orientation Lecture this evening before chow - that should be good too.

Well, I only have a couple more minutes that I can sit here and get away with this - we will have to "send" for 20 minutes then school will be over for the day.

Blue Baron is going to be playing on the Post tonight so maybe I'll drop over to see that. Got to sign off for now. Be good.

Lots of love, Frank

July 25th, 6:15, Wednesday

Dear Mother, Harry and Mike,

Well, things have been rather rough today. Plenty of PT and drill on top of that. We had "token" spot checks on attendance at both for too many guys have been goofing off lately. I am really tired tonight.

Thought I'd scratch this off as soon as possible. I have some studying to do and maybe I'll read just a little before retiring (just get that word). Well, anyway 5 AM rolls around all too soon and I just have to be on the ball these days.

Final Theory exam in about 1 1/2 weeks and as I don't look forward to spending any part of the winter here we'll just have to get through the first time.

Thanks a lot for those delicate little verses Harry - we all really enjoyed them. I lent em out for the boys to enjoy. Didn't get any mail today - just a second - I'll try to dig out yesterday's - as I remember I was supposed to answer a lot of questions.

1st the coffee. We tried it one night, also the tea. We can get the water almost hot enough but can't keep it that way long enough. We are working on a method now - think we will try Sterno but until we meet with a little more success you'd better not bother with any more just yet. Soap is a little hard to get here and you can get only one bar at a time when they have it at the PX.

When I first came here I got two or three cartons of cigarettes the first of the month but now we can only get two pkgs. at a time however, for the difference in price, I hardly deem it worthwhile for you guys to bother with them and send em all the way out here. They only cost us 12¢/pkg. here.

Hankies always come in good and I have a pretty good stock now. Pretty well set - thanks youse just the same.

Just one little thing that bothers me. I still worry about you fellows and the money proposition. I read a little between the lines too and I wish you would cut me off your financial donation list. Really, there is no reason under the sun why I should be getting it and I certainly hope you are not depriving yourselves for me. It's not worth it fellows - no kidding!

Say, one more thing. If you see another pair of shower slippers around town, pick them up please. I really think I have gotten more pleasure and satisfaction and good use out of the ones you sent me at Ft. Dix than almost anything I have. You see I do all my lounging in those and my gym or swim trunks. Of course they are not much good in the winter but I expect Yuma next and the pair I have is getting pretty well shot.

Guess that will have to be all for now folks - still have to shower and intend to climb in early - so, be good.

Love, Frank

July 28th, 6:30, Friday

Dear Mother, Harry and Mike,

The weather really cools here in the mornings and evenings now. Hit the cement in the Field Jacket this morning for Reveille although mid-morning till sundown is still very warm.

I got Harry's letter yesterday and one from Mother today, also a good one from Norma from Dorset. Mother, you say that "what is fair for one is fair for another" when you wrote me in this one. I bet you were tired and pretty well disgusted with the Otts and a number of other things. I'm sorry when I disappoint you like that, although I never promised to write every day - I did try while I could think of things I thought were interesting and different, but after the routine of 6 months it is hard to dig up anything of even an amusing nature. On the other hand, I know very well that when I was home you kept so busy that you made an event of writing anyone - and with Harry so busy and working so hard I well realize that it has been rather selfish of me to keep on complaining as I suppose I have. Well, all this adds up just that you mustn't feel too bad when you miss a day or so - I imagine it's pretty hard to keep thinking of things to say for you just as it is for me. This is the last I'll ever mention this.

Last night I missed writing - went to see "Mr. Skeffington" - Bette Davis and Claude Reine. The latter stole the picture, can't say as I enjoyed it to a great extent for she kind of pisses me off anyway.

Today was indeed a busy one. Pulled 100 in Tact. Pro. weekly quiz. In the squadron we had a speedy PT and then right back and dressed in class A's for standing retreat. We weren't even allowed to take a shower (guards at the latrine). So, grimy underneath and clean outside, we stood retreat. I had to sweat out a line for laundry and another long one to get a haircut for inspection tomorrow and sandwich chow in between.

The squadron has a big dance to-morrow night so I expect to make that. Free beer and dancing with the old section "M" pass being the ticket of admission.

Am looking forward to Sunday. Plan to play tennis best part of the day and go swimming. We will be right at the U.S.O. picnic at the tennis courts. Probably take in a show and maybe a little dancing afterwards.

Last Saturday they took us over the roughest obstacle course on the field. Hope we don't have to take it again to-morrow because I'm just getting over an 8 inch brush burn on my shin from crawling a rope. Don't want to rip that scab off now I hope I hope.

Well, guess that will be all for today -

Be good.

Love, Frank

July 30th, 11:20, Sunday

Dear Mother, Harry and Mike,

   Kept well on the go again yesterday. We took our PT in the new Post swimming pool. They really have done a fine job on that pool. It is only about 3/4 as long as the Hyde Park, but it is as wide and has been finished along very similar lines. Six diving boards of various heights make it superior to the Home Town in that respect.

   After we returned we stood inspection and then off to chow. Shower and shave and stuff and then off to town. A crowded G.I. town on a lovely night. Hughes and I went to the K of C where we had the pool table all to ourselves for a couple hours and had a pretty good game. From there we went to the Masonic dance for a couple hours. There are really some lovely gals there - long dresses last night - had a few dances and then we took off for the Section "M' dance. What we went through there to get some beer is too long a story to tell here but after while it just got to be more of a contest more than wanting beer, but Hughes and I did finally get some - 2 large G.I. pitchers worth, which we shared with no one - believe me we were in a mean mood but this rapidly improved after we finished the beer.

   After the dance we came back to the barracks and were soon sound asleep, but our peace and sleep we found were to be interrupted. I was awakened by someone yelling - Everybody up - let's go with comforters - at the first instant I noted a fire about a foot high near one of the fellows bunks - about 3 bunks from me. By the time I got up and grabbed my comforter the flame was about seven feet high - way out of the comforter class. Believe me it was a real blaze. All of one man's clothes went up in a flash. Some of the lads who had originally sensed the fire already had extinguishers and soon put it out but not before the roof was badly charred and a good section of the walls and all one fellow's clothes on the hangers were completely shot. Of course, usual G.I. style, none of us know how it started in fact we don't know a damn thing - and if we keep up the silent campaign we hope the guy will get his clothes without having to sign a statement of charges. It is always something in 1241.

   Of all things - a letter from the Otts - Mrs. talks as though she had been writing me right along - funny, this one got here and the others didn't. She asks me if I saw Coach's picture in the Gazette - I haven't received the Gazette for the past 3 or four weeks - after all, I don't know how they paid for it - maybe in the 3 month installment plan. Frankly, all this doesn't matter anymore - I have written them at least four or five times and rec'd no answer. They are the only ones aside from Grandpa that I have written and got now answer. I did get their box when I came here - wrote and thanked them for it - I haven't had a line from either of them since Greensboro. Yup, it hurt a bit at the time but as I say, it just doesn't matter anymore. Please tell her when you talk with her that I shall write soon and don't mention the Gazette. I'll write a letter and this one she won't want to keep.

Ah, tis a great life. Well, I'm supposed to meet Duttine (Northwestern Med Student) and Hughes in town soon so will have to take off -

Be good.

Love, Frank

July 31st

Dear Mother, Harry and Mike,

Well, I'm all curled up on my bunk with a couple letters beside me. Yup, I got Mother's Saturday and Friday opuses today. So, will try to do my best by answering them.

Payday today so I'm in the bucks and also a whole tenner from home so I am very well-heeled at present. Thanks a million folks! The obvious thing after payday is to go into town and spend it but I had already decided to stay in and catch up on some letters. I hope you guys don't mind this paper too much but it is in a pad and easiest to write on in the bunk. It is a good thing I didn't plan on going into town this evening because they restricted the whole barracks to the Post. It seems that our housekeeping hasn't been quite up to par lately. I believe that a large part is due to the oily carbon that got tracked all over from the late arson (?) attempt. 1241 is not alone however—only 5 barracks were not restricted. We get so we half expect these things—particularly when the guys want out most.

Well, I'd better get to answering the latest. Yup 6 months is a long time isn't it. Would certainly like to come home for a couple weeks but honestly can say that if I had a discharge offered me to-morrow like Bob Miller I would turn it down flat. But when this thing is over they'd better not try to hold this boy too long.

I rather guessed you would like to have me take Instructor—I guess it is not too late as yet—if I could have you both out here I suppose I would take it but someone would have to give me an awfully good sales talk on it right now before I would even think of it twice.

When I think of that shirt even now I get sore but I'm going to see this thing through. Just wait till they try to make me sign statement for those things at a clothing check before I leave. I'll sweat it out and raise all the stink I can—I figure it will be good experience anyway. It is so rare that you get an opportunity to tell an officer what you think of some of the regulations he guards with such scrutiny. If they order me to sign the thing I'll ask for an interview from the Post Judge Advocates Division or the law arm of the Army. You see someone has to (ran out of ink) be the goat and I know they will try to stick the Buck ass private but we'll see. No, don't even try to get another shirt. I plan to get a complete new outfit in town soon. I need the clothes and will need em worse at Yuma for there, I understand, they don't wear fatigues to school as we do here but they wear Suntans so I'll be wanting extras anyway.

I wouldn't worry too much, Mom, about my being in the country for a while. As it is now I get an extra week here and may request an additional one to familiarize myself with this new "Collins" transmitter. I have also heard that gunnery has been increased from 6 weeks to 13, so I shall be at gunnery for some time I guess. On top of that the worst part of it is that if I am lucky enough to get a delay out of gunnery, us they have been doing, it still probably will be after Christmas before I get home. Fraid it looks like we'll have to sweat out another 6 months anyway.

Of course this is (in the overall outlooks) a very good indication—there apparently is no rush for the men so they are going to freeze us in Tech Schools—the whole of which could be a good deal worse.

Say—if you didn't see "Home in Indiana" I recommend it highly. Introduces some new talent, which, in addition to being a great relief, is really good. It is a very good "Horse" picture.

The meal at Loren's certainly sounds good. Don't like the being sick business—have, as you know, suspected the teeth for a long time. Will the pulled ones be bridged or are you going to have em all pulled.

I well know you hate even the thought of the latter but please don't bargain a little vanity for your health. Besides you and I know folks (you'd be surprised about the large no. here in the Air Corps) who have had splendid work done and really look extremely well. These new plastics have taken the artificial look out of teeth and there is a good chance that your whole digestive system would profit by doing some honest to goodness chewing for a change.

Yes, if Don is a "pass and furlough" clerk—with a little pull he could write himself anything. I know of cases where these guys, when not able to get a furlough, have been allowed to write themselves 4 or 5 consecutive 3 day passes which works out better than a furlough. Also, maybe and probably this has nothing to do with the situation, but right now with liquor so short it is an excellent bargaining agent. Don is a fool not to take advantage of it if he can—the stuff can be shipped by R.R. express you know.

Harry should be considering women seriously now. It pays to be choosey and the time will come when he can even be choosier than he is now.

I hope so much that Harry will be able to get a new coat—He's gotta look sharp if he wants to be seen with me in my snazzy Olive Drab when I get home.

Well, I guess I'd better close this one—won't be able to think of a thing to-morrow. Love, Frank

August 1944

August 3rd

Dear Mother, Harry and Mike,

Didn't write last night—took my pass into town on big shopping excursion—got me a pair of pants. Don't like much spending the dough but really needed the pants and it feels good to have em on hand.

This evening I went down to the chapel. Thought I'd go to Confession but the Chaplain had some sort of catechism class so after a while I got tired and left—decided in favor of a beer. Have to be heard before Mass or during to-morrow afternoon I guess. Really don't like the idea but it is the only way I guess. Somehow I don't think you live long enough with your penance that way but fraid that is the way it will have to be. I also had to study a little for a Q Signal quiz last night—drew a 100% today so guess it was worthwhile.

We have another Tact. Pro. quiz to-morrow so I should be getting at that now but gosh if I study I don't write at all. I should write Gramp & Mrs. Ott and Ann but here I am—undoubtedly won't get beyond my own little twosome tonight.

I will undoubtedly stay in this weekend and try to brush up for my "Quiz Kids" session which comes next week. Boy I sure hope they don't wash me back.

As soon as I can find out the postage rate I will send you an illustrated letter about the school here—it will give you a slight idea of the classes here and the Post itself. Of course like the photos in the N.U. yearbook they are definitely propaganda for the institution.

Honestly folks, it is so hot here right now it's terrific. I'm lying on the old sac propped up by my comforter and the old perspiration is just pouring off. I soaked clean through a G.I. issue shirt tonight—it is wringing wet. You know—so hot that when you don't have to move it just isn't worth the effort. That is what got me kind of sore when I made the effort to go to Confession tonight and couldn't get heard. The real trouble is that we now have only 2 Catholic Chaplains on the Post, which makes it tough all around.

Thanks Haroola for the letters of the past couple days—I have to hand it to you two—you sure keep on the go—no lack of the old energy in the family unless perhaps it's the G.I. of the family!

Honest, every once in a while I'm tempted to gripe but when I look back on the past 6 months and truthfully consider the Boy Scout existence I've lead—well, you just can't complain.

Think I have something big cooking for week-end after next—won't say anything till it actually materializes cause seems to me I've planned so many little things and they just never seem to pan out.

I think they have decided to cut out drill for a while—I hope so—it is such a farce around here anyway.

We had an orientation lecture here this afternoon after PT. Took a shower before chow and you can bet your neck I'm going to take another before I hit the hay which will be soon. These particular weeks are so dry they really do tire a fellow—oh it's awful rough!

Say isn't the war news splendid. I eat it up every day—have even taken to reading some of the news in the newspapers for a change. Do manage to hear H.V. Cal. every now and then. That does me a lot of good too.

Well, guess this is all for now.

Love, Frank

August 4th

Dear Mother, Harry and Mike,

Thought I would start this early so maybe I can get a couple more off tonight. We have already had PT and retreat parade and are now awaiting chow. Retreat kinda screwed up my plans to go to church today but that is just one of those things I guess.

Got Mother's letter just a moment ago. It is still plenty hot here too. We have had rain the past two nights but it doesn't seem to cool it off much. School rolls along as per usual pulled a 98 in Tact. Pro. quiz today. Still it really doesn't make much difference what you make on these weekly examinations for they only count them 30% of your grade. Well, our W.T.S. men (fellows who were originally pulled into Army and were to be trained as flying instructors) were pulled out of school today. They will all be sent to places like Ft. Dix to "Separation Center" detachments and from there they will be discharged. It is really good in a way to see them go for they have taken a bigger screwing than any other group I know of. It created a minor panic when they pulled em out though—most of Field knew that they were expecting news of discharges and when it came everyone went crazy. Well, we wish them our best, try to forget what they will be going home to and carry on. Well, guess that is about all for now except the following table which is to me of more interest than anything I have seen yet.

	Churchill	Hitler	Roosevelt	Il Duce	Stalin	Tojo
Year born	*1874*	*1889*	*1882*	*1883*	*1879*	*1884*
Age	*70*	*55*	*62*	*61*	*65*	*60*
Took office	*1940*	*1933*	*1933*	*1922*	*1924*	*1941*
In office	*4*	*11*	*11*	*22*	*20*	*3*
	3888	*3888*	*3888*	*3888*	*3888*	*3888*

Half of 3888 = 1944 End of War
Half of 1944 = 9th month Sept. 7 HR. 2 PM
For Supreme Being or Ruler—First Letter of Each Name—CHRIST
Not bad eh—Let's hope these statistics don't lie.
Love, Frank

August 6th

Dear Mother, Harry and Mike,

Well, I have just oodles of letters to answer today. I am loafing in my bunk just taking it easy. Had a rather late session last night and arose early this morning. Went into town for the usual Big Sunday morning breakfast and Mass at the Cathedral.

Missed yesterday but I'm sure you'll understand. Right after school the usual PT and then you have to fight to get a shower before personal inspection. After inspection instead of going to chow I shaved (shaved only with electric razor for inspection) and three of us went to Snack Bar for a hamburger and beer and then off to town. We did a little shopping and then saw Jack Carson's latest vehicle—not exceptional but fairly good entertainment. After the show Al Daher and I went to the dance at the Arboda. This is a large dance hall—very similar to Glen Park (what it used to be). It is a swell place to go I think and in spite of contrary verdicts by some of the cats in the barracks I enjoyed dancing to the band very much. I was so busy dancing that I got in only one beer before they closed down the bar—that's pretty bad for me. After we left this dance we went to the Carpenter Hotel for a snack.

Oh I enjoyed eating in class for a change—generally the fellows seek out the cheaper places but for me—I would rather pay more cause I certainly have a taste for the most refined atmosphere. We started to look for a cab to get back to base in and ran into a couple more of the lads from the barracks—a few minutes later four dollies come down the main drag—well, ourselves being then 4 in number swore a pledge of solidarity for the evening (you know—that we would not accept a separate Peace [or piece]). Then ensued the best talked rat race I have ever been a party to. I usually don't go in for just plain grabbing them off the street but there wasn't an "other one" among the whole 4 so we were pretty lucky. And so you can understand why I came in a little tired and almost completely untainted with alcohol last night. So I was not to readily awakened at 7:30 this morning by friend Kostishack who had returned to barracks after only going to the show last night—2 hours snoozing isn't much when you're used to your 7 or 8.

We woke Daher up and the 3 of us bounced into town got our breakfast and went through the ritual of the Sunday papers and then, well gutted, we slowly ambled to church for the 10 o'clock number nodding to all the sprightly dressed sweet young things as if we'd lived here all our lives.

Church was rapid and to my dismay I had forgotten my missal but maybe because of it I spotted a gal I'd met here when I first came. Left the boys and walked her home and met her folks (not particularly my idea of a good time). I took my leave shortly— she asked me to call her—maybe a good idea. Have to see how the old bank roll holds because I'm coming near shipping time and am getting all wardrobe cleaned and pressed and picking up various things I figure I'll need. Oh its 3-4 weeks away but I don't want to be running around on the last few nights looking for stuff. Also I want to keep a little on hand for the last two weeks I should be flying and should have most evenings off so I can't play all the time can I? Should get another pay just before shipping so I will be all set. By the way, if what Mrs. Ott says is so—if you are going to send any jack down here or any place else I go I'd recommend it be registered. Funny thing—I got Mom's letter last night about the difficulty and today I get another letter from Mrs. Ott (second in space of 8 days) and also 1st copy of Gazette in 4-5 weeks. Have to write Mrs. Ott this afternoon also I want to get some final studying done for my session with the "Quiz Kids" is sometime next week—maybe to-morrow, and I just have to pass that one. Big trouble is—for past 2 weeks no classes have started here. First time they have missed at least one class per week in 2 years. Hence the civilian instructors are already a little worried about their jobs —and the "Quiz Kids" are all civilians. Last week they washed back 90% of a class so you can see my worrying is not without cause.

Say—my watch—I think is on the blink—rapid temperature changes here may have caused snapping of mainspring just as happened at home once—may have to send it home—will be lost without it—

Be good youse guys.

Love, Frank

August 8th, 5:05, Tuesday

Dear Mother, Harry and Mike,

First—ma watch is O.K.–just a little stiff for a couple days I guess. I'm taking this time between PT and mail call and chow to write cause I have the old books tonight. Certainly don't feel like it but then I have been lucky–didn't get em yesterday or to-day so the old axe has got to fall to-morrow or the next day. Really feel like raising a large load of Hell tonight for some reason but rationality tells me to stay inside and gather up the loose ends.

For the past two days we have been in "mock ups." Small compartments built to resemble a radio operator's cabin on a plane have been built and you and another fellow get in and are completely isolated from the rest of the group. Each pair has a receiver and a transmitter–you have a net control station, A.A.C.S. station and a D.F. station. The control station opens the net and you proceed on a hypothetical flight problem, going through all transmissions necessary to take a plane off–land it and all the intervening communications such as frequency checks, navigational checks, direction finding, official messages, new orders, and a host of other things.

Really is very interesting although today I drew the net control station and I really sweated it out till I got going and became accustomed to it. If you get the jitters at all let me tell you it really shows up on that key when you are sending.

Hope to goodness I hit the "Old Kids" O.K. cause if I do I should have a rather pleasant 2-4 weeks flying and school only from 7 AM till 1 PM which is a dream, maybe then I can get a little more of old S.D sunshine. Right now I am stalling. I expect mail. Oh Ho Here tis.

Later

Well, I read the mail and had chow which was P-Poor. I read Harry's letter and enjoyed the pictures very much. I've been showing the fellows and boy, oh boy Mom, would you be surprised–as far as they are concerned you are his girlfriend or wife–nope they won't believe you're my Mom. Oh I've been having lots of fun with them.

Harry seems to be having a very full time and seems to be making the most of everything. Well, I'm afraid I'll have to get a goin.

Got plenty to do. Be good.

Love, Frank

August 11th, 8:00, Thursday

Dear Mother, Harry and Mike,

I'm late getting started tonight. The perspiration is pouring off of me in buckets full. It is very hot here now and to me it is perfect weather for the evenings cool off so that you need a blanket to sleep under. This would be the place for me to spend a vacation–up around some of these lakes–it is perfect vacationland for my money–sun is so hot when it is shining.

Well, gee thanks a million for the fin. I guess that is why I'm a little late this eve-ning. Took care of the hair cut situation–really scalped me this time–bought up odds and ends, couple beers and returned–shirt completely soaked with sweat–then folded and put away all my laundry. All sounds insignificant enough I admit but it all takes time. Lucky tonight because only about 20 ahead of me at the barbers. Pants cost me $4.95–have been husbanding my money cause I want to splurge a few nights before I leave here–of course I will be paid before leaving but every little bit means so much especially when you are going to a new camp and you can never tell what things will be there.

Received two letters today–Mother's and Harry's. Harry's date sounds swell and of course Mom, I can sympathize with you in your standing and waiting and crowding–after 6 months I've learned to suffer it with complacency but I shall never get used to it.

I have been reading of the murder in town since I've been getting the Gazette again–certainly don't like it and it worries me with the Big Boy out so much. Thank Heavens we still have de la Shpusie–he is darn good protection as an adequate warning. To say that the infantile worries all of us is an understatement–reports are coming in from homes of most–you can fight Japs and Fascists but a thing like that, the bravest of us fear–the worry of it we carry with us subconsciously–Please don't go to movies–go to early Masses where there are few people and ventilation is best–tell Harry to go to Novena at St. Mary's if he must–God will forgive him if he has to miss but be careful–keep him out of water–if he wants to swim let him go to the Y Pool or better not at all. OH you can say piss on him–he is in Sioux Falls S.D. but I'd be just broken if either of you took sick–please give me this–that you won't take any chances either of you.

I'm still showing off my snaps–typical of the Army even we boy scouts–don't give that "drop in sometime" business. People you will never know when I get a furlough–I'll just "drop in" as you put it. 80% of getting home will be coming in unannounced but I'm afraid it will be a long time hence.

Did you get illustrated letter–gave it to a Corporal to mail and gave him a stamp for one like it of his own–maybe the bastard didn't mail it. Well, if you don't get it soon I'll buy another.

Still no "Quiz Kids"–the axe must fall to-morrow. Reason I didn't write last night was I spent evening in new tuning lab on my own time. Had Sergeant there ask me questions and check my procedure–sort of a wind-up taper-off review. Feel fairly confident but am still the old worrier.

I have to take no more spot checks or checks of any type in Code–I am through–first crack out of the bag I was fortunate enough to pass my 5 minute exemption check in Code and so in that respect at least I am finished with all that is required of me here.

Otto Taylor came in and interrupted me–old bull session for about half an hour. Now writing by fire light and the bugs are having dinner for fair. Have to close now–just haven't enough red corpuscles for em all.

Love, Frank

August 12th, Friday, 8:25

Dear Mother, Harry and Mike,

Late again tonight. Reason this time is that I took in a show. We had to stand retreat tonight and it was quite a maneuver. After retreat we returned to the squadron. Fumigating of individual mess halls has reached ours so that for the next 8 days we have to march across half the field to eat morning and evening meals. So Hughes and I took off and sneaked into another Squadron mess hall and just made the 6 PM show. Not very good but created the required diversion. Just had a couple beers - they taste so good when it's so warm.

Well, I still haven't seen "Quiz Kids." I go to assembly room each day like a cat on a tin roof and then they miss me - just barely today - I have to get them to-morrow - it is the last day of our class. As far as I can find out they have been giving the boys the jitters - wish they had taken me today - well, I'll get it soon enough. 1st 3 days this week we had Mock Ups which was really fun but the past two days they have kept us just sitting listening to some joker beating his gums.

Well, I got me no mail today but I now am stuck with the responsibility of getting it for the barracks. It all came to this: Breckenridge, Hughes, Daher, Kostishack and myself are the only ones of the "Old Guard" still remaining. Our model barracks leader, Corporal Ani and his assistant "Ward" (played bass with Charlie Burnett) have left. I do so much yelling about the mail that the new barracks leader "Murphy" has stuck me with the job. At least I shall always get my mail as soon as possible and maybe from there I can bitch more effectively about not getting some of mine.

Things have taken a turn here that none of us quite understand. For the past 3 weeks no new classes have started. Also class 46 (the one I was in before I washed back a week to go on the range) washed ahead 2 weeks and graduated with class 44. They got no flying at all. Maybe they are going to close the old institution up soon - can't say - just have to wait and see.

Also we get another shift change again. Yup, after only 6 weeks we go back on nights - that will be August 28th. Hope I will be just about through here by then. Going to start working now on a pass to St. Paul for when the change in shift comes we get a little extra time from Saturday at 5:30 till Monday at 3-3:30. Not enough time to make it home - dammit, but maybe I can get to St. Paul anyway.

Well, guess that is all the dirt from here for now.

Be good!

Love, Frank

August 13th, Sunday, 2:30

Dear Mother, Harry and Mike,

As per usual I missed on good old Saturday—yesterday—so will try in some manner to make up for it now. At present I'm lying on my comforter in the blazing sun—not best posture in the world for turning out a letter but thought I'd have a try at it.

Last night proved to be one I won't readily forget. Stowed away more beer than I have in ages—maybe than I ever have, I lost count after a while. We had hamburgers and beer at the Snack Bar last night and walked into town. Stopped in the K of C for another couple quick ones and there we met a fellow by the name of Olsen. I have seen him at the K of C a number of times. So after the preliminaries we took off with him and his car—real class and hit a number of places. Finally wound up at the Elks. They have a swell place here and some swell bottled beer. We cheered Olsen on till he took about seven dollars out of the quarter machine and then forcibly dragged him away. We were set for the rest of the evening. We stayed there a couple hours talking with some officers who, if anything, were a good deal farther gone than we were. No kidding for about 20 minutes there one time I was almost asleep but my stomach was doing so many nip ups I thought all that good beer might take a round trip. However I soon got my second wind and my interest and outlook rapidly improved. We wound up with steak sandwiches and "Red" Olsen drove us back to camp. Gee did I sleep. Got up a little later than usual this morning. Couldn't quite make 10 o'clock Mass so we took in the 11 o'clock number. Honest it makes you feel sad at the number of fellows in this barracks now who profess to be Catholics and just lay in the old sac on Sunday morning. They claim it is a lot easier to stay in bed and think of church than to go to church and think of bed.

Of course we had the usual large breakfast but not at the same place—didn't quite measure up but our "Eat Shoppe" was closed. I did have some orange juice and gee was it ever good. A large glass with some ice in it. First I have had since I left home and I didn't realize how much I wanted some till I saw someone else drinking it this morning.

Sunday, on this shift is my "Lazy Day." Laying in the sun proved too much for me—was drawing the life right out of me so as you can determine from "a little better writing" I am now on ma bunk. After I came in from church I did quite a few odds and ends. Get laundry ready, straighten locker, G.I.'d my civilian shoes and treated them to two coats of saddle soap and polish. Just a lot of little things I like to do at my leisure—wouldn't be my grandmother's grandson if I didn't like to putter a bit. Too damn hot to be in a mobbed town so I stayed in this afternoon. I said the beer last night was good—we all woke up this morning with no hangover so it must have been good.

I got Haroola's letter—I sent an illustrated letter home a little better than a week ago. My big mistake was apparently getting one of the boys to mail it. He's probably in Yuma now. My guess is that he didn't mail it so he probably will mail it from there soon. If you don't get it in a few days let me know and I'll get another.

Well, I had the "Quiz Kids" Saturday. I was no ball of fire but I will be terribly surprised if I fail. Next week I am due for Towers—simulated operations in Mock Radio Control towers. Should be interesting. Yesterday also I went to the Flight Surgeon for my physical for gunnery. Correction on the weight—only 149 stripped. Guess I had reached a fairly level weight at home. So you can see I was a busy boy Saturday and on top of that it has been so hot here of late that you don't feel like much beyond lopping.

I still have a Tactical Procedure Quiz to pass next week and spot checks in sending and blinkers, but I shouldn't have too much trouble there. If I don't get blinkers right away I'll get someone to take it for me. There is a great deal more of that going on than I ever suspected. Even one of the instructors came up to me the other day and asked me to take the 5 minute receiving check for one of the fellows. Don't know why he picked on me unless it was that when my check came back there was not a mark on it. Five minutes solid at 18 WPM is not bad in any man's language, but my guess is that when the testing section found the 1st minute O.K. they didn't bother correcting the rest of it.

So it looks like Yuma Arizona from here. Snakes and heat and black widow spiders–Oh home was never like this but still I am a little anxious to be on the move again. Although Yuma will never be anything like Sioux Falls has been.

Well, guess there is not much more to tell from here so, be good!

Love, Frank

August 14th, 7:00, Monday

Dear Mother, Harry and Mike,

Am waiting for the laundry line to thin out so I guess I'd better do my dashing off of this one right now.

They really ripped it to us today. Took my final sending check and passed. We also had two blinker checks. Hope I passed one of these–will know to-morrow–if they don't jerk me out to take a third and last one during class to-morrow I will know that I passed it. If I am called out, I get one more chance and if I don't make it then they will wash me back–how far I don't know.

Also to-morrow I get my final Tact. Pro. test. Apparently I passed Theory for they pulled out all "Wash backs" and I wasn't among them. We were supposed to have Towers today but there were entirely too many in the class to be accommodated by the (I think there are only 8) Towers. So they put us in a code room- gee you get bored stiff–today. I learned to play a new battle ship game–played that for at least two hours–it put in the afternoon admirably. Guess I'll just have to sweat it out till it comes my turn. Of course it is a denial of all we have had here–I mean the inactivity of these last few weeks. It seems to me that there is so much we could still learn and then they stalemate us completely but that is the old Army game over and over again.

Apparently the powers that be here want more spirit, so some Non-Coms came to the section area today with a jeep equipped with an amplifying system. All it amounted to was a sing fest. This is a great idea but they certainly picked a poor time and did a poor job. We had just "double-timed" in from the PT field and were sorely in need of a shower. On top of that we had to get our laundry in to night and we all wanted mail so you can see that any inch of enthusiasm was non-existent. That is the whole trouble–you cannot make men sing; singing is about an emotion *like fear or joy or love—you cannot order a man to be afraid or to laugh and expect a genuine result. So they piddle around aimlessly and fool around and accomplish nothing.*

The biggest crime is that there they have in a lump a generous slice of the cream of America and they let it rot for want of any incentive whatsoever—sometimes I think I'll drop a little constructive criticism in the suggestion box that they are always hollering about. Might get me court marshaled but then it might give me a lot of satisfaction too.

Well, guess that will have to be all for tonight—Be good, people.
Love, Frank

August 16th, 1:15 PM, Wednesday
Dear Mother, Harry and Mike,

As you can see from the stationary I am at present holding down a chair at the Service Club. By rights I should be in school but things have taken an unusual turn and I haven't quite decided whether it is for the better or not.

This morning about half an hour after we had been seated in our 1st class - Code - 35 of us were pulled out and herded to another section of the school. It seems that we are "washing ahead" of all things and will be graduated next Saturday. I had an inkling that we might be shoved ahead a week but was hardly prepared for this two week boost. Originally I was in class 46 and washed back to 47 because of a week on the range. Now I find myself getting ready to go out with class 45. What does it mean? I hardly know myself nor does anyone else seem have any of the inside dope. Why 35 of us were picked I don't know either - certainly wasn't marks - one reason given was that we had finished all exams but then the order in which we took exams had no rhyme or reason - not alphabetically nor by classes.

Anyway apparently we are in our final week of training here. The part I am not at all keen about is that most of our practical "operational" training has to be sacrificed which for my money is no good at all.

With graduation coming Saturday we will undoubtedly be shipped early next week although there is no sure way of telling what the hell will actually happen.

The reason I am off now is because the last week or rather two weeks is made up of lectures only lasting from 7 AM till 12:05 which lines up a beautiful day. That is the reason I was looking forward to these next two to three weeks. Of course the Section Command tries to get you on "work call" during that off time but that, with a little sneaking, can be avoided and coped with in some manner when they catch up to you as inevitably happens.

I am going to wrap my books - maybe to-morrow and send them home as soon as possible. I also still have a couple odds and ends to take care of in town before I leave. I have been hanging on to a ten spot for dear life which should more than adequately take care of all things and I also think they will give us a partial pay before we ship so I'll be all set financially.

I have to get me, among other things, some Radio Operator Mechanic patches - we call them B.T.O. patches (Big Time Operator) patches and I will try to send a couple home. They are worn on the right sleeve 4 inches above the cuff at the crease in the middle of the sleeve so if you can prevail on some kind of soul to sew one on that field jacket if it is still around I would appreciate it.

The weather here has taken a crazy turn. This morning at reveille it was so cold you needed a field jacket for comfort and all day there has been a heavy mist like we have at the Falls everywhere. I started to carry my rain coat over here but put it on before I was half way here. I notice that just now the rain has started to come down. Here's hoping it holds till after PT and then we can take it inside.

By the way I hope this letter isn't too disconnected. About four feet from me is a WAC who is throwing her old pins around in a most disconcerting manner.
Later

No the WAC didn't get me but I ran out of ink, of all times, and when I got back to the barracks there was PT and some mail and then chow and then I read the Gazette. Gramp sent me the Times so looks like I'll spend a busy evening just writing. Started a letter to Gramp Sunday - have to finish it tonight.

Just read about the Cassidy wedding - never did hear of the groom. From Mom's letter I think you're kinda busy baking and cleaning and what not - don't overdo, remember what happened in the heat of one summer? Glad you liked the illustrated letter - have Haroola show Gramp will you - I think he'd be interested. Communication Cadets ceased to be an opportunity from here the week I started school here - it closed leaving about 200 men here on a waiting list who are either stuck here now as instructors or have been sent POE. That was what Chuck Donahue was trying to make.

About the mail - please keep it coming. I should get at least one letter from you in answer to this one. I expect to ship next Monday or Wednesday although I cannot be sure when it will come. If you were going to send me something you had better hold it, but if it is on the way that's fine too.

So it looks like a rather enjoyable sojourn at Sioux Falls S.D. is almost at an end. It's a shame in a way because this has been a good Post, but I sure don't want to be here for winter and it is time I move on anyway. Be Good.
Love, Frank

August 17th, 2:15, Thursday
Dear Mother, Harry and Mike,

Well, today, as far as it has gone, proved to be of a great deal more interest than I had originally anticipated. They do things in the Army at such a rapid pace that at first it floors you but then you are glad of it for in many cases you don't have too much time to sweat things out.

We no sooner had roll called this morning when the Tech Sergeant in charge called off twenty names, mine among them, and shortly thereafter we were herded into a truck and driven over to the Air Field. There we were given our S.O.I.s (special operating instructions) in a briefing room and at 8:15 we drew parachutes. Shortly after that we went out in groups of 4 with an instructor and took our places in the training planes. They are twin motored A.T. 18s–low wing, monoplanes which have been obsolete for combat service for some time now I guess. We did not have to wait long for the pilot, a Lieutenant, and the co-pilot was a Lieut. Colonel, and apparently they wanted to get in some flying time. Well, there we were and off we went. We were in the air about two hours and the 4 of us rotated on the equipment. I was on the Liaison set the first hour and the second hour I doubled up with another fellow and we took bearings and shot fixes with the radio compass.

It was really a good experience. When we came down our logs were taken from us immediately and we had a little "fatigue" session as it is called, where we went over our logs as a group and with the man who had been in charge of the Net Control Station on the ground.

I really enjoyed myself. We had a peach of an instructor who went with us and I found what little I did was a great deal easier and with much more satisfaction than the one day I had in the Towers.

Here I was expecting not to see the inside of a plane until gunnery due to being washed ahead but we are getting a few surprises. We may be lucky enough to go again–I certainly hope so. It gives you a much better idea of what you are really responsible for and I'm telling you that the transition from school to a plane is a plenty big one. It is O.K. to talk about it but, like so many other things, you just have to do it before it means much to you.

It was an experience too from the scenic viewpoint. This is such a beautiful farm country and because this is the wettest summer they have had here in ten years the farms were very green and the newly plowed earth was a very black contrast to it. Also the people would come out of the houses to look and wave as we passed over.

You soon begin to see why those who have flown to any extent say that it gets in their blood. I believe that the fact that it is three dimensional, something most of us have never experienced, is one of the main reasons. I did get plenty of chance to look around when I was on the compass but when on the Liaison I was a busy boy every minute believe me.

To-night I'm going into town for a while. Don't expect to make a late session of main reason–I want to get my books wrapped to send off. Any shopping I do will have to come after that–probably wait till Saturday night.

Guess that's all for today. Be good.

Love, Frank

August 18th, 5:50, Friday

Dear Mother, Harry and Mike,

Yes things rush on here! This morning I took off for school for although I expected I would be on shipping orders, I had received no notification. Frankly, I was a little disappointed for after writing you that I would probably ship I found myself still on the school rosters. So I flew again—did a much better job this time all of which goes to prove that you can do almost anything if you make up your mind to or are given the training and put in the situation where you have to use it. Had a pretty good time but we had to wait till 1 o'clock before we ate and from 5:45 till 1 is a long drag. After chow I returned to section area only to find Buck Ship on my bed that I was on shipping orders and was supposed to report at 11 this morning. Immediately went to the Sergeant in charge of shipping and he told me to have all my clothes in barracks bags up in front of section with all G.I. clothing except 1 uniform, helmet liner and gas mask. I thought I had little enough time in Greensboro but here I really had to get going. It certainly was not my fault that I missed the first call but what the Hell, I had no notification, but everyone treats you as though you were goofing off when it is really not your fault.

I have to have a physical "short arm" to-morrow at 7:30 in the morning and close out of here with the administrative section. I saw the Major today and I must sign statement for the Suntans. I am quite sure that I could have raised quite a stink but when it came to a show down I didn't have much stomach for it—looks to me like I'd be getting yours truly into a mess of trouble to say nothing of killing any chances I might have in the future for getting home for a few days.

After I reported with my clothes they let me go—I have a check on them to-morrow I think. I don't believe there will be any formal graduation for us. We will probably just get our "laundry slip" and that will be the end of it.

The crux of it is that I ship Monday from where God only knows although Yuma Arizona is a mighty good guess. Went to town about 4 o'clock and sent out books so expect them. Shopped around a bit and drew my little wad from the Post Office. God knows I hate to carry it around with me but from what I understand of the schedule at these Gunnery Schools I would have no opportunity to get it transferred or to get it once it was transferred. Have to dream up some way of keeping it I guess. Also we get a partial pay of 10 bucks before shipping so I will be well set.

Next couple of days will no doubt be busy ones—also and being stuck with this uniform till the time I arrive at destination, which won't be before Tuesday or Wednesday at best. But I fooled em there. I have the shirt you sent me and the pants I bought in the cleaners and will get them out before I ship so I'll be able to change if the going gets too bad. I really expect it to be hot on the way down and Lord only knows what it will be when I get there. I certainly have accumulated a lot of stuff—bought a laundry bag a few months ago and that and my hand bag will be full by the time I leave with just my personal stuff. Extra towels, underwear, clothes hangers, sweaters, and a hell of a lot of whatnots.

Guess that completes the dirt for now. Be good—
Love, Frank

August 19th, 2:45, Saturday

Dear Mother, Harry and Mike,

This is going to have to be a shortie because at 3:30 I have to meet a formation to get my partial pay of ten stibokes. As usual prior to shipping I have been running my little ars ragged trying to sandwich in everything.

Had my clothing check and record check, which consumed all morning. I was last one through before permanent party shut down to go to lunch. I returned to barracks and got my own Suntans from cleaners after I had my chow. I then took my personal things all the way back again to put them in barracks bags which we will even see very little of until we arrive a destination.

Still no exact idea of where we will go—still think it's Yuma—will send night letter when I get there. I also got my certificate of graduation, checked with shipping clerk about physical & dental check—just finished shower and shave and am sitting here now for the first time today not on the run. They fill out so many forms which don't mean a damn, it is little wonder the Army is so screwed up all the time. I got all new woolen sox in exchange for mine—all of which were shot. If you have had a chance to get me those slippers please ship them as soon as you find out my new address. The ones I have I won't even bother to take with me as they are shot on the bottom and safety pins holding tops together.

I am going to try to buy up some candy and something to eat of some description in town tonight. I have already got stuff to read. My guess is that this will be one of those cattle car shipments with about 350 going. It is a far cry from the last trip with 30 or 32 and I do not expect it to be anywhere near as pleasant as the last trip.

I do expect to take time enough to sit down to-morrow and write a "historical last" from Sioux Falls. We have to be on deck ready to leave at 7:30 Monday morning but probably won't be on our way before noon and so Sunday will probably be the last.

Think I'll hit the sac now for a few minutes. Be good.

Love Frank

August 20th, 12:20, Sunday

Dear Mother, Harry and Mike,

Well, this will be the last one from Sioux Falls. Your reminder about the Holy day did come late. Three of us made mental notes of it but you become so ingrained in the routine that it just goes over your head. I haven't gone to church as yet today. It is not as bad as it sounds. What I really want to do is go to Communion and I snacked before coming in last night and so of course couldn't go this morning but I am fasting from 12-4 this afternoon and will be able to go at 4:30.

Last night I went into town with Al Daher and it proved to be quite an evening. We both had a couple little items to go and after that I had some pictures taken. Bill Hughes had some taken and they turned out so well that I got some too. They are only of the cheap variety—you get 4 poses and 3 of each picture for a buck. Hughes' pictures turned out so well that I thought I'd better get some. What we are doing is *trading them and putting our addresses on the back so that we will always be able to keep track and in touch with one another. I won't be here to get them on Wednesday but the boys will send em along to me when I write from the next place. We had a hell of a time getting them taken –two rather attractive girls taking the pictures and a middle aged woman supervising the job. Well, first it rained heavily last night–of course my raincoat is with my barracks bag in shipping and receiving so I borrowed John's to go to town. It leaked slightly at the shoulders and that left the shirt damp in spots that would show up in photo so Al and the two girls and I decided a change was necessary–so Daher and I changed shirts on the spot with the girls scurrying to the next room–they then decided I should take his tie too (-spot of rain on mine)– finally all set to go–but no–another conference dictated a little powder. Finally after lots of horsing around we got four pictures taken. The payoff came when we had to re-change the shirts to leave–the girls made no effort to move out so I just turned my back while I unbuttoned my fly and tucked in the shirt but this was too much for Al–he fled to a small back room muttering bewilderedly–"I'm just not used to it." We razzed the dickens out of him for by this time we were fairly well acquainted. Where we slipped up was we should have dated em right there and then. The older woman was there all the time which made everything on the "legit" but we weren't sure of where we were bound for so like fools we let it go–opportunities like that don't come every day but then we have skipped a lot of em here.*

From there we went to see Red Skelton in "Bathing Beauty" again–would see it 12 times more just to see Ethel Smith play that organ. We originally planned to go to the Arkoda to the dance later but upon getting out of the movie, we decided on the strength of a good, cold ale to go down and look in at the Coliseum where the instructors were holding a dance.

When we got there a staff Sergeant wouldn't let us in because we weren't from section "B" or instructors–he said there were no extra girls and that the thing was so exclusive that the Colonel himself was there and had even ordered M.P.s to keep out. Well, after that we should have been discouraged but that Sergeant laid it on too thick–we took it as a challenge and reasoned that a place as big as that could not be guarded completely, but after we cased the joint we found it was completely covered. Then the thing became (John just decided that the flies around here are the German's new secret weapon–they are eating us alive–cool weather is driving em into the barracks) a contest. We almost developed into second story men but worked an old Army routine and before we could stop to think we were inside. We made it in time for the entertainment which included a Glee Club which was directed by a boy who used to be with F. Waring–it was extremely well done. Then we danced with what proved to be a most delightful excess of girls. We wound up with bacon tomato and lettuce sandwiches and French fries and coffee and back to camp.

Hughes, Kostishack and I went in for breakfast this morning–stopped at U.S.O. for more free coffee and rolls and returned for our mail. I got Mother's Thursday letter. It has been a good last week-end—probably see "Dragon Seed" after I go to church and chow this evening and then may hit another dance in town tonight. We'll have to see. Be good youse guys—trip I understand is 3 ¼ days at least but I will ship off a night letter as soon as I arrive and find out my new address—here goes nothing again people.

Love, Frank

THE DITCHING

Present Day

Month after month, I typed, and each letter immersed me deeper in my father's life. I was touched when he mentioned his destiny, for I knew what it was and was unable to tell him. I laughed when he told Harry that they would have to pursue the younger girls, age fourteen and a half. How did he know my mother, his future wife was fourteen years old at that time? I was surprised that, at the age of twenty-three, he knew without a doubt he wanted a family when he wrote, "family is the height of my ambition." Knowing his destiny, his short life, that he would indeed father seven children before his death, I wanted to somehow tell him what I knew of his life seventy years later. He was no longer a stranger to me. He was someone I was getting to know, someone who was easy to love, and someone I was learning to miss.

As for the Goldfish, my curiosity was getting the best of me. I still hadn't learned what exactly had happened to cause his pilot to ditch Heavy Date, and so once again I revisited all the information that had been sent to me previously by Phil and James, and I also tapped Art once more. It was actually one of the links Art had sent me early on that ultimately solved the mystery—or at least part of it. The website was Aviation Archeological Investigation & Research. It was there that I met Craig Fuller.

The website offered copies of U.S.A.F. aircraft accidents. I provided the ship number, the date of the accident, the approximate location, and Craig got back to me that he had located the report. For a nominal fee, I purchased the file. Within twenty-four hours a link to the file was in my Inbox. I downloaded it, printed it out and sat down to learn the truth about the ditching.

Like many of these types of reports, the information was concise. No emotion. Only statements from the pilot and co-pilot; but there were enough details to get a visual of what had happened that day.

The accident occurred after the war had ended, as Art had indicated, and the crew was on a practice navigation mission, which was most likely why it wasn't recorded on the Heavy Date mission log. Sundin wrote in his report:

> I was pilot of aircraft No. 8333 on a routine navigational flight over the North Sea on 26 May 1945. I took off from base at 0800 and proceeded on course at 2,000 feet toward our turning point in the North Sea. At about 0900, I encountered low clouds and let down

to about 800 feet to stay below them as briefed. At
this time, I checked my engine instruments and found
everything normal except the carburetor air temperatures. At approximately 0916 my co-pilot shouted for me
to look at the No. 4 engine. I looked just in time to
see it vibrate violently for about 10 seconds and then
explode. I immediately closed the fuel shut-off valve
and pushed the feathering button. My co-pilot cut the
mixture control. The prop failed to feather. When the
engine exploded it was immediately enveloped in flames.
My co-pilot pulled one CO_2 charge, which reduced the
flames, but only momentarily. I told him to pull the
second charge and it did no good whatsoever. I was at
600 feet by this time with the fire back through the
nacelle going rapidly toward the wing. I told the co-
pilot we were going to ditch and to inform the crew. He
did so while I tried unsuccessfully to contact Air Sea
Rescue on VHF. As soon as the crew was in position we
made a water landing at about 0922. During pre-flight
inspection all instruments had been checked and found
normal.

The co-pilot's statement was virtually identical, but when I read the pilot's Difficulties in Ditching statement, a clearer picture formed of what was happening
back in the radio room where my father and the rest of the crew were positioned for the ditching.

. . . another unnecessary trouble came about as a result
of having the camera doors open. This allowed a tremendous stream of water to shoot into the radio room, on
impact, practically drowning the crew in the radio room.

There was no further explanation about what had happened afterwards. The
letters I was currently typing were from Sioux Falls, S.Dak. I knew I had many
letters to go before I found one explaining what happened, if in fact it existed.
Rather than skip ahead to the late May, early June letters, I stayed the course
and made the decision to find out about the ditching if and when he wrote his
family. Like my father, Mother, Harry, and Mike, my next stop was Yuma, Ariz.

YUMA, ARIZONA - PART 1

1944

August 24th–Telegram
DEAR FOLKS. ARRIVED 4 O'CLOCK THIS AFTERNOON. ADDRESS NAME ASN FLEXIBLE GUNNERY POOL YAAF YUMA ARIZONA. GOOD TRIP. GET THE MAIL STARTED. LOVE FRANK

August 25th, 8:55 A.M., Friday, OH Lord at Yuma
Dear Mother, Harry and Mike,

If this isn't Hell I'm going to reform! Arrived here yesterday at 4 in the afternoon after an interesting but uneventful and rather dirty trip. Consider for yourself–we put on clean Suntans last Friday prior to shipping and took them off last night. Hadn't had a shower since last Monday morning and the water gurgling over me last night certainly felt grand.

No doubt I should start at the beginning. Said my farewells to all my buddies as they left for school in Sioux Falls about 6:45 last Monday morning. Took a shower– put on clean sox and underwear and was ready to meet my shipping formation at 7:30. Our section had drawn baggage detail. That meant that we had to load into a box car barracks bags for the whole shipping order. Consider about 450 some odd men and 2 bags per man–it amounted to 5 truckloads or one well packed boxcar full of G.I. clothing. Little F.G. did not however kill himself since of late I have been trying to develop a modified "goofing off" technique. I soon was off to the commissary and PX where I purchased some large juicy oranges and a little additional reading matter to carry me on the trip. After we had loaded bags they took us for a second breakfast which I ate stubbornly but none the less effectively for I little knew when the hell we would see food again. After that we reformed and marched to the loading area where we waited in the hot sun till we were finally loaded on the train. It was made up "cattle cars" or "troopers" and some Pullmans. Luckily I drew a Pullman and settled myself down with some fairly good books–plenty of cigarettes–candy and my oranges. Since I've been in the Army oranges to me are a gift of the Gods–easy to carry and have lots of juice as well as food value. I shall scout around this evening and get me some for I find they are just the thing before going to bed.

I will enclose another map with which I followed our journey–as you can see from it, we covered a good bit of the Good Old U.S.A. It was indeed an experience to see it all roll by–If I have gained nothing else from the Army–at least I have done a little traveling.

Of course we had to go three men to a compartment–Al Harrison from Texas–a Corporal Demianovitch (Russian I guess) and myself. The former was a likable chap from Texas who is bunking with me now—the latter, Corporal, is from Erie—has a very contagious personality and seems extremely well liked—fraid I could develop no affinity for him whatsoever.

They were a very agreeable pair and we switched each night on the single upper berth so that each of us got to sleep one night alone.

Kansas City was the first big stop and it was there that we got the biggest break of the trip. It was very warm coming to there from Sioux Falls. Would have been unbearable if we hadn't had all windows open and there was the rub. We were all filthy with soot from the train. In Kansas City we found that Yard inspectors condemned our Pullman and we had to layover 4 hours while they got us a new one. It was far from new but it was a honey in that it was air conditioned. In order for the air conditioning to operate all windows had to be closed and so we were kept nice and cool in addition to not getting too much dirtier than we already were. The Major in charge of the troop train, who was a peach of an egg, then took over "drawing room" on our car with the conductor as their headquarters so that we were well and promptly informed of what was going on throughout the rest of the trip.

The chow all the way was terrible! We were fed at ungodly hours and what we got we kept alive on and that says it all. At various stops we did get off long enough to race like hell into station lunch rooms and get cupcakes and jelly rolls, ice cream, and candy. All in all I enjoyed the trip a great deal—wish I was an expert on long vivid panoramic descriptions but I fear I am not. We did get a good glimpse of the Foothills of the Rockies as well as the Corn Belt. Long level stretches as far as the eye could reach and also saw oil country in Kansas where you could see nothing but orderly planted derricks right into the horizon.

At El Paso a lot of the lads left the train for some beer, but I was already in bed and could not see getting out considering that we never knew when the train stopped how long it would stay. I think at least 60% of the train was in town but all managed to make it back except 2 Staff Sergeants and a Private; we had been told that it would be our own responsibility if we missed the train. The Major was so decent about it—I for one didn't want to cause him any trouble but let me tell you—when we hit a station of any size it was as though the locusts had arrived and we scurried and rushed to get things bought and get back on that train before it pulled out. Frankly, I'm amazed that we lost only 3 on the way.

Better say a bit about Yuma I guess. It is a very small town—at least judging from what we saw coming in yesterday. There would be little to do there even if you did get a pass, which I hear are not to numerous here. My guess is that we are about 6 miles from there anyway. Desolation is the word for the place at first sight—there is not a tree in sight (only those few palms etc. which have to be watered daily) and any vegetation is scrubby and offers little relief from just rock and sand everywhere. In the distance all about us are large rock hills—maybe they're mountains—can't say for sure just yet. From about 9 in the morning till 7 at night you are principally conscious of the hot sun beating down on you and you are glad of your plastic helmet liner (referred to as "piss pots" in the Army).

We were brought to the camp in buses and trucks yesterday. We are in a Student Pool for Flexible Gunnery Students and from what I judge we won't start school until probably a week from Sunday. When we got here we were issued silver painted helmet liners which we have to wear at all times. This enables us to be spotted in an instant and believe me there are no bushes to beat around here and [it's] plain to see the S.D. methods will not work here. We are quartered in tents at present which are not bad at all, having wooden floors and sides halfway up and screened the rest of the way–also electric lights. When we are assigned to school we will be moved to more tents or barracks, some of which are air conditioned and some not–tents are said to be better than barracks not air conditioned.

Chow here is reminiscent of Greensboro and it looks like I may be living to eat again instead of eating to live as we did in Sioux Falls. I managed to get off with just policing the area this morning and have spent the best part of it in the bunk with just my shorts on writing to youse guys. We have another work call at 1 o'clock this afternoon–hope to dodge that one too. Expect to pull K.P. any time now.

Just came back from chow–really very good no kidding–ate enough to hold a horse. Correction–I find we have to stand another clothing check this afternoon instead of work call. We will soon be through processing I believe.

All in all I'd say it is not a half bad place. Heat is really terrific but suppose I shall get used to that in due time.

Mess hall is air conditioned - Gravy is best I've tasted since I left home - French Fries for breakfast - this makes up for an awful lot in my case anyway.

Say, I hope you won't mind reading a few "wants." I'd like those shower slippers as soon as possible. Would also like a small can of olive oil for my hair - it is getting terribly dry and this climate is not going to help it much. If it is at all possible I'd like some Sun goggles - not the glasses type but the large goggles if you can get them. Don't get the glasses type for I think I can get those here, I mean this kind [hand drawn image of goggles was drawn here in the original letter].

Think they come in leather cases I think. They certainly would come in handy around here otherwise you go about squinting 90% of the day. Get that old mail down here pa leese. I imagine it will take some time before it gets here. 4 to 5 days is my guess.

Latest rumor is that we may go to our school squadrons Sunday - well, we'll have to wait and see about that. Be good youse guys.

Lot of love from God's Country Yuma

Frank

Enclosure: Map from Bell System Service

Text on map: Good Luck! Here's a map of the United States to help you keep track of your travels. Also, there's information to assist you in making long distance calls.

Telephone wires are loaded with war calls - but we'll do our best to get your calls through. If there's a delay, it will help if you will remain nearby so we can tell you when your call is ready.
Northwestern Bell Telephone Company

Return Address:
Pvt. F.G. Thompson
A.S.N. 12,107,602
Flexible Gunnery Pool
YAAF
Yuma, A.Z.

August 26th, 11:50 AM, Saturday

Dear Mother, Harry and Mike,

Chow is just over and was indeed a good one. Of all things green olives and apple pie - not square Army pie either - came in little round tins and we each got a good sized wedge.

Later 2:00 PM

I just finished goofing off work call and procured myself a supply of ice water. Anything cold to drink is at a premium here and while the sun is up all you do is drink and you just can't satisfy your thirst no matter how you try. Finally met with some success after wrapping myself around 5 bottles of beer last night. Of course I'll have to cut out that nonsense cause my budget just won't stand it but it sure hit the spot before going to bed. I'm writing on my bunk again today. To-morrow should tell the tale whether we start school next week or have to stick here an additional week. It is really a chore to even write and if you note any splotches on the paper it is from sweat.

Finished up all processing this morning and I do hope I don't draw K.P. on Sunday - to-morrow - really t'would spoil my whole day. Was quite sure I was getting used to the heat till about an hour ago and now I wonder again.

Took a bit of a look around the Post last night after chow. They have a fine PX and one building strictly devoted to selling soft drinks and beer. There was a large line outside the theatre last night so I don't expect I'll be going there much. Can't see sweating out any line I don't have to. The Service Club is small - it is air conditioned and very nicely furnished although I would call it wholly inadequate for a Post of this size. Tried to get some decent stationary last night but they are all out of it - did manage to get a carton of Camels last night so am well set in that direction.

How goes all things in dear old Niagara Falls? It is just a week now since I've had any word, having rec'd a letter last Sunday afternoon. They are going to have a mail call at 4 this afternoon - hope I'll be lucky but am not too hopeful for I imagine it takes a long time for mail to get here. Some of the fellows got some yesterday forwarded from Sioux so we shall see.

I certainly have quite a few letters to write but guess I'll leave em till maybe this evening. Have to write the boys and then reestablish communications with what few people I do write to. Don't know what the hell I'll do when I start school - ah well, will take care of that when the time comes.

I really think if you are doing something definite you don't mind the heat so much - it is this sitting around in it that tends to get you on your ear. I read a good bit on the train and during all the waiting during processing I have finished up most of the books I had on hand.

Well, I may take a shower now or may try to sleep - haven't quite decided - above all be good and if it is even slightly hot there now please toss down at least 2 (two). Rye and Ginger Ales for me right now!
Love, Frank

August 27th, 9:00 AM, Sunday

Dear Mother, Harry and Mike,

Well, today is the dear old Sabbath. Haven't been to Mass yet - thought I'd at least start this before the real heat of the day started. Will have to go to church at 6 or 7 this evening for there are only 3 Masses on the Post and we had a formation at 8 o'clock when the 1st Mass was scheduled. They called off men who will go to school next week. We of Section M were not called so we stay here another week. This means lots of 18 hour K.P. and plenty of details in the hot sun for next week. Oh we'll bear up O.K. under the work, but the thing that makes you wonder is why the hell did they rush us so at Sioux Falls if we were certainly not needed here. But that is just the way it goes and I for one am not going to rush my Army training to an abrupt finish even if it does mean more time in dear old Yuma.

Say - how do you like this stationary eh? Pretty snappy, what? The emblem at the top is the same one on our silver helmet liners. I found me a slightly air condi-tioned dayroom last night and did manage to get off a few letters - one to the Beals and Gramp and the lads at Sioux Falls. Chances are some of the boys will be com-ing down next week and I'll see some of them before I am transferred to a school squadron.

All the lads are "pissin and moaning" about the fact that most of us only missed being called for transfer by a few names on the shipping list - we are now at the top of the list and K.P. to-morrow or at best on Tuesday is a virtual certainty.

I spent a heller of a Saturday night last night. Had me three beers but was grate-ful for an opportunity to get some writing done. Yesterday you would have roared if you could have seen us. After I wrote you guys, we spent the heat of the afternoon in our Sacs. You didn't dare squirm cause if you did you were bound to hit some of the iron on the bunk and that was only inviting a burn. I know it sounds farfetched but its true - wouldn't believe it myself unless I was experiencing it. We then proceeded to spend the afternoon in a sort of scuttle - from the bunks to the latrine for a cold shower - we didn't bother to dry ourselves but just put the damp towel on the bed and lay down until the heat consumed the refreshing effect of that shower and then we went off for another one.

We are hardly children of the sun as yet but we all hope we'll become acclimated soon. Coming in on the train the porter put it rather well when he described the place. "Yuma is 200 miles from anywhere and in the middle of nowhere - A'hm glad I live in Little Rock, Arkansas where the sun shines cool."

Or did I write that one to you before. Incidentally there is no disciplinary problem here. If you are not playing the game they wash you back a week and you spend that week doing K.P. Nothing like Sioux Falls; where the boys were always full of Hell and matching wits with the "Quiz Kids" - hoping to be washed back a few weeks.

From what I can find out you get Corporal stripes, wrist watches, and wings out of here and so coupled with the heat - the incentive boosts the fellows along. Also I believe we will be taking at least an hour of Code and an hour of Radio Mechanics each day along with your gunnery, which totals up to an 8 hour school day - and if you are delinquent in anything they fix you up with more classes in the evening.

Any flying we do here will be done in B-17s or Boeing Flying Fortresses of which there are a great number here. Sometimes, they tell me, the runways get so hot that the tires of the planes stick and they can't get them off.

I guess I'd better close this baby. I want to scout around and try to scare up a Sunday paper - heard something about capitulation of Balkan Satellites but have no news of the war itself since last Sunday. Also if I write too much I won't have anything to say the next time. If I miss a day soon - to-morrow or Tuesday you'll know I drew K.P.

Got a letter from Harry. Forwarded from Sioux Falls yesterday. It was good to hear from home. Hope his date with Mary proved an immense social success - Harry size up the 17 year old sister for me - if she is anything like Mary maybe you can fix me up when I get home within the next year or so.

Be good, people - I am off to mail this and scout the Post a bit again.
Lots of love, Frank

August 27th, 3:00 PM, Sunday

Dear Harry (old boy old boy)

No doubt it is high time I addressed one to you at the office. One of the main reasons is the enclosed poster - I felt you would get the same kick out of it that I did. It was one of the last things I did at Sioux Falls - tearing it down from the latrine wall. Some darn fool has embellished it. Must have been done the night before I got it for I had had my eye on it for some time figuring on doing with it just what I am doing now. At any rate it needs some cleaning up before you can show it in mixed company. I had in mind that the Porter Road Clan might particularly enjoy it.

By the way how do you like our little mascot on the letterhead - the YAAF stands for You Are Absolutely FU--. AH many are the attributes of Arizona - it's a pity that you miss many of em for the sun and heat obscure a good many things.

They really feed us well here as I have mentioned before. Today I had a couple steaks and this morning's breakfast featured eggs sunny side up. In another hour and a half we eat again and then I have to hear Mass at 5 or 6 o'clock. Today I have found a new cooling agent. Beer doesn't go on sale till 4 in the afternoon so I have been drinking milkshakes between meals. They really give you a shake here too for 15 cents.

Say how do things go with this Keenan gal. Have you started to Storm her as yet. Knowing myself - if I were in your boots I know I would have started that by now anyway - couldn't help myself don't y'know.

Boy kid, if and when I get home, we shall do some tall stepping so save your nickels and lick our chops. By the way how is Chum Gwen coming along and what does neighbor Mal do with her spare time these days?

Well, guess I'll toddle along - Be good and behave yourself and if "you can't say NO take a Pro."

Love, Frank

August 29th, 12 M, Tuesday

Dear Harry,

I'm writing at high noon. Have to report in about 50 minutes for Work Call. I write specifically in reply to some information Mother wrote of in her 1st letter to reach here - Got it thank heavens yesterday after coming off K.P.

What I have to say I kinda hope you will keep to yourself if it is at all possible. The subject is your vacation. It would mean a lot to me if you could be off when I or if I get a chance to come home. I didn't want to mention it and cause a lot of hopes, there and here, that the Army in a minutes' notice can end, may knock into a cocked hat. If you didn't have to work at the office maybe I could help you nights at Liggett's - that would be a lot of fun anyway.

Here is the dope. Our course here will be 7 weeks. That would leave me out of here graduating on October 22. It would take me 3-4 days to clear here and get home. You see they are granting "Delays" to every graduate. Of course the time I'd have is arbitrary - best conditions would be assignment to Westover Field in Mass. Fellows who are going there this week got 18 days including traveling time. What I hope for is this but of course I have no idea as to what my assignment for overseas training will be. What I want to ask is could you possibly rearrange or leave at an indefinite status your exact vacation date? Maybe you could explain to Steve - tell him otherwise I'll have to come up there if he doesn't fix it and put a few through each day just so we can bat the breeze. I really don't want you to tell Mother that the way it looks now is very definitely that I will get some time anyway - I'd love to surprise her. You can explain to her any juggling you may have to do by telling her the real reason but don't let her know that it is a pretty sure thing. Be casual about it you know!

If you had planned something definite to do or you think this may jeopardize any possible advancement you may get - forget the whole thing. We'll have plenty of time together anyhow but if you can do something we can at least sleep late - the whole Thompson Tribe that is.

Be good - I hope to be seeing you in 8-9 weeks.

Love, Frank

August 29th, 2:40 PM, Tuesday

Dear Mother, Harry and Mike,

Greetings from the Sunny Southwest. Ah yes, my children, there is a sun down hyar. Yesterday morning I was rudely awakened and noted the time to be 3:15 AM. Yes my dears it was the call to K.P. and I was it! Our whole section from Sioux Falls drew it and all fellows in my tent had to go but goodness such a time to pull a man from his sac. There is little purpose in going through the wailing which must accompany any description of such a detail but we made it and were released at 8 PM last night. I did drink me lots of milk and many cold fresh juicy peaches from the icebox. Also met a couple of the lads who were in 1241 at S.D. The best part of the day was when I got off and went directly to the mail window, which was slammed in my face, but shortly opened and I got a letter from home - addressed direct to Yuma yet! Apparently the air mail stamp made some difference in this case - in this part of the country. Sorry Mom that you were disappointed - I had very faint hopes of getting home from Sioux Falls - hope I didn't lead astray in my letters. Have not as yet got the pictures of Mike - do hope they forward them here soon. T'was indeed a newsy letter and just what the M.D. ordered particularly after a 17-18 hour detail. Today I had to take pot luck on work call and luckily pulled an easy one which I drew again this afternoon. This morning we rode around in a truck all morning - this noon they dismissed us as soon as we got there so I had me some milk and got a haircut and came back to the pool where I am writing this on my sac, which by the way is almost steaming. Didn't notice the heat once yesterday on K.P. - it is just when you are doing nothing that it bothers you to any degree.

Say, just in passing, how would you like my hair combed back? It is growing in that direction since I've been wearing this helmet liner.

Ho. Ho so the Thompsons were glad of my out for Alan. Although there is plenty of excuse for the lad. I think a lot of that will occur after this thing is over. Fellows think you can "goof off" in the world the way you can in the Army and it can't be done - particularly the younger G.I.s who never did work before coming into the Army. Also the point must be considered that the freedom we talk about plays strange tricks on a fellow when he realizes that it really is his - especially when he has traveled some with the Army. The Army kills the inherent reticence in a man as far as fear of unknown places and new associations are concerned - generally we stay home believing that initiating ourselves into a new community and environment and meeting a new society of people will not only be difficult at the outset but is hardly worthwhile to compensate for the loss of the prestige we may have built up at home. These things coupled with love for family generally keeps us near the home of our parents. If the Army does not make a lie of these things it certainly minimizes their restraint on the individual. I also think a lot of boys will find that, after this war, the social barriers that they may have experienced as civilians and saw crumble as servicemen will again be erected overnight, for peace in America has no use for a soldier and the camaraderie that is the Army will have outlived its usefulness.

However, I cannot say even in the light of what I believe above that Don O'Hara is right and I am wrong or Alan is right - the coming years will tell the story. See I do ramble on when I get going don't I?

Well, the mail list has been posted so I must be off to see if I drew any today I hope I hope! Be good.

Love, Frank

August 30th, 3:15, Wednesday

Dear Mother, Harry and Mike,

Well, I went over and got my mail yesterday and got the Beal's letter - I also got letter back I had written them - have to put a stamp on it I guess. Apparently some in Yuma aren't up on their mail regulations - always has gone through before.

I didn't do so well today on the detail. Today I dug holes in the nice dry sandy desert. Not little holes - nay large - big - deep holes 4'x3' and specifications called for 14 feet deep - we were helping build a new Familiarization Range for 50 cal. machine guns. And as you threw out a shovel full (the level of the ground at this point above your head) two shovelfuls would fall back in or the sides would cave in - yea I ama yee sandy G.I. this day.

At the present moment I hold my breath - K.P. list for the morrow has been posted! 6:05

Well, this is some time later eh! Well, you see I had to check the above mentioned list - not on it - that means I'll get it for sure on Friday so no letter then youse guys. Also a very big event - 3 letters from home. The ones with pictures of De la Shpusier from Sioux Falls and 2 mailed directly here. One from Harry mailed 2 PM on 27th and another from the Mater mailed 7 PM on the 27th.

Oh t'was great - lotsa news and I love those pictures of my pup - I like the one where he is lying on the chair with his big ears and long tongue stickin out. Did you bathe him prior to proving him photogenic? He looks it. Had forgotten his ears were that long. I think he makes me homesick more than anything cause you see I can't write him and maybe he doesn't understand why I'm away. Don't let him forget me will you.

I am worried too about Gramp. Guess I'll have to write him soon and more often. If he gets any kick out of my poor efforts it is the least I can do. And Harry I fear I never did get enlargements but I found a guy here with a good camera and we took some pictures this afternoon and will finish up roll soon as we can think of enough ways to take the pictures. I also expect some from Sioux Falls - ones I had taken last Sat. night there but I wrote and asked Bill Hughes not to send them until I sent him a squadron address - that was really not necessary but I had hopes of being assigned last week. This kid who is taking em this time is going to have jumbo prints made so I hope they come out well. When Kostishack gets here (John has fellow's address) I have to write N.C. cause a guy who shipped this owes me some prints that we took when we first got there - they are not bad at all.

Nope - none of my buddies are with me but I'm used (now) to starting from scratch and am with a bunch, 6 of us, in the tent now that I'd like to stay with. Half of us are Mics and they are an exceedingly fine group I'd say, but when we move to the squadron no doubt this will be broken up too. Expect most of Gang from Sioux Falls here in 2-4 weeks.

I got mom's letter Monday and Beal's letter - God love and Bless them all - Tuesday. Am quite let down to hear that that "Handsome Puss" salutation is routine - stock as it were - here all this time I thought it was just for me.

And I think I'll keep all the snaps of my old lover - just wait till I get hold of all of you. Well, I guess that is about all for right now. It is really fun to sit down and write when you have things to answer and stuff about home to write about.

Well, I must rush along now I guess. My boys are holding a place for me in the queue at the show so I'd better get down there - utter a prayer that I don't get killed when I try to cut the line. Dirty trick but necessary if I am to get this off to you and see the show too tonight.

Be good, people.

Love, Frank

August 31st, 5:30, Thursday

Dear Mother, Harry and Mike,

How goes it today? I received Harry's letter an hour ago. Congratulations old boy - maybe I shouldn't say that because you have been given more work, but more responsibility means that you well merit it in the office and no doubt you will get more dough - although your advancement would be quite enough for me to hear of yet it makes me sad often when I think of how youse guys must be scrimping to get everything done - let alone send me money.

Today was a rather dull one here and this morning I managed to avoid any detail but this afternoon I drew a session in the Quartermasters Supply which was not bad at all. I have been reading "Wuthering Heights" in my spare moments and beyond a doubt it is the most sullen and morose book I have ever encountered and yet for some reason I am drawn to it and am always ready to pick it up again.

I fear at present there is little new to report except that I will be quite glad to be assigned next Sunday. If you will remember at the Reception Center at Ft. Dix I had ants in my pants - this existence in the "pool" is quite as pointless as [that], though the hours seem to me quite long, I yearn to get on with it and quit the piddling around.

Be good, people.

Love, Frank

September 1944

September, 2nd, 6:25, Saturday

Dear Mother, Harry and Mike,

At present I am settled in the dayroom and intend to spend at least till 11 bells writing. Sorry I didn't make it yesterday but K.P. puts you in that "what the hell" frame of mind. I pulled the old often illustrated and referred to vegetable detail and peeled potatoes for 16-18 hours running. Thank heavens I received three (no less) letters yesterday. One from Mother, Harry's and one from Gramp. Since I got the two (from 450 1/2) yesterday I didn't expect any today but Ann wrote, which helped a good deal. I also want to write Norm Dorshel this evening so you can see I have a lot to do.

This morning's detail encompassed construction and carpenter work. We were out in the desert helping to build a track around which movable targets will be pulled for a new 50 cal. machine gun range. This afternoon we (inspected for repairs first) loaded over 400 Army cots on trucks and unloaded them again at a different warehouse - did it via the chain line method and after having that many cots thrown at me and tossing em on to the next guy my shoulders are a little tired this evening. All good stuff though. It certainly conditions you mentally, as well as physically. I find almost all the work you do in the Army doesn't hurt you a damn bit - it's just that your buddies are back in the sac taking it easy and they sure do razz you about it when you come back dirty and tired - but that is good for you too so all's well and a good healthy physical tired is a thing I missed for a long time at home. Anyway I'm too lazy to take much voluntary exercise - guess they invented PT for Joes like me.

Ann tells me that John Dick is going to marry Mary Jane - my guess is that that set up will be a competition from the word go but apparently it was meant to be - I must write the lad and give him the jolly "Ha Ha - so you're going to get it with your shoes off routine."

To-morrow we should move to our squadron and start gunnery - the first week of which is made up of more processing and immeasurable checks on what we learned at Sioux Falls. We will be checked on swimming ability and will be issued oxygen masks which we will keep while on the field. Most important will be physical tests in a pressure chamber. If there is anything wrong with you it shows up there. The main purpose being to check your bodily reaction to the changes in pressure you experience in high altitude flying. Watch for change in address on to-morrow's letter. We should move out of this section of camp at about 8 or nine o'clock in the morning. Here's hoping anyway. I know the Beals will scold but haven't been able as yet to get to Post Office to get a stamp on letter I first wrote them - I'd better get one soon!

I just wonder how it is going to be hitting the old Code again after an absence of 2 weeks. I don't suppose you knew that the Radio man on a Bomber Crew is the most continually schooled man of the group. That code speed is a delicate thing and must be kept up. In O.T.U. (overseas training unit), which is the next step after gunnery, we have to go to school and even when assigned to a Theatre of War we will still be going. Also at any mistakes Radio men are grounded and go to school at their Operations Base. The Radio man is the only one on the crew who never does get out of school. I am kinda looking forward to tooting those 50 cal. machine guns - going to try to learn that baby from A. to Z - just as I tried to hit Radio at Sioux Falls for in either line I want to be absolutely certain in my heart that I know how to do my bit so that there is no chance of my letting men who are depending on me down.

I shall let you know to-morrow of the change - it better come cause another week of hard work will drive me to eating what little grass they have here.

Right now I feel very dirty and have a lot of washing to do. I have the Rinso but not the mood to be sudzing. I see myself doing a lot of my own stuff here for everything that is washed or dry cleaned must be sent to Phoenix and returned - 10 day service is record time and it is generally 2-3 weeks I guess.

Well, I must be on my horse I guess - Be good, people.
Love, Frank

September 3rd, Sunday, 4 PM

Dear Mother, Harry and Mike,

Well, we have moved into our school squadron and start processing to-morrow. These movings are tiresome and get me down a bit. All my O.D.s were cleaned and pressed at Sioux Falls when I stopped wearing them and they certainly are a mess now. So I'll have to get em all done again I can see that. Aside from that, the situation looks all right. I am in a barracks, which is air conditioned and it certainly is a relief to sit here on my bunk in comfort. Sand is not blowing in all the time—we have a good concrete floor under us and some joker right next to me has his radio on now. I do miss music of any kind and the news too. Aside from buying the papers I heard nothing of the news while in the pool.

I undoubtedly won't finish this at this sitting for we must be off to chow at 4:30 in order to get to the 5 o'clock Mass so that we will be out early enough to get a couple cold beers from the PX which closes at 6 (of all things) on Sunday.

I spent a very quiet Saturday night last night. I started by writing a letter to youse guys and wrote Ann and Gramp and Mr. Dorshel and it took me until 10:30 to complete the job.

Monday, 11:50 AM

Well, I'm a bad boy! Didn't get to finish last night as I expected to, so I'll try to finish up before mail call, which is at 12:30. Fellow next to me has radio with news on—sure sounds good.

We went right to chow after I left this letter yesterday but there was a long line and we found we couldn't make the 5 o'clock number so we had a couple beers and then went to 6 o'clock Mass. After that I was prevailed upon to go to see "Janie." It was good but I wouldn't say exceptional. The most interesting part was the reaction of the G.I.s to the various parts of the show which pertain to the Army. Facilities for seeing a show here are far too limited for the number of men who want to get in. Almost mob conditions resulted shortly before the show opened the doors and M.P.s had to be called out before things reassumed any order. Me–I was right in the middle of it–boy it was rough–for 5 minutes I never stepped on the ground–just on the other guys.

This morning we never had a chance to do much beyond make up the sac and straighten up a little. We were rushed out to chow and very soon after we fell out and went to theatre where we have listened to 1st aid lectures and movies all morning. As I understand it this is characteristic of gunnery–they keep you humping all the time–not hard work but you have rarely a spare moment.

Just had mail call a little earlier than expected. I received Mom's Thursday letter, which was good as I got none yesterday. Please note new address on this letter and notify any concerned. Hate like hell to take glasses from Coach and will return them when I leave this stretch of Arizona. Sorry you fellows couldn't make it away for the Holiday, I'm sure it would have done you both good. Ah well, one of these fine days when we have a car we shall piss on them all. Ann told me about possible delay in opening public schools–I'm afraid she is a little edgy about starting but that is to be expected especially since she doesn't know what grade she'll have until the day she starts.

Please do not send any food but thanks a million for the thought. Nothing but canned goods would be of much good by the time it got here and stood much of the heat and with rather rigid inspections I don't know where I'd keep even that.

The meals continue to be the best I've had since leaving home. They have a quality and quantity of beef here which is wonderful. I often wondered where the hell it was going after I got into the Army with so much talk of the best going to the Army–well we are getting the very best here.

At yesterday's dinner we had turkey no less, plenty of green vegetables and what surprised me was that their corn and lima beans here (don't know what else) are frozen stuff. Lots of fresh peas and string beans.

Heat in intensity is with us again today and the barracks is sure an oasis in it all. However you'd be surprised how you get used to dripping all the time–it'll be bearable I guess for 7 weeks anyhow.

Pictures we had this morning were quite vivid in the First Aid line. Sets you to thinking a little of just what those poor devils are actually going through. Lord they must be a splendid bunch–sure have a big responsibility to uphold if we are to follow them.

Hope I feel like washing this evening but I probably won't. I must get hold of something to read too for since I've been here I've established even more firmly the habit of readin while I'm waitin and people we sure do a lot of waitin here. This is the largest group (about 400) that I have ever been in, which apparently they plan to work with as a unit. It is going to be interesting to see just how they handle it. Well, be good now.

Love, Frank

September 5th, 6:55 PM, Tuesday

Dear Folksies,

Have to hustle this one off for we have to fall out in an hour or less. Yup we started falling out before 6 bells this morning and we are still at it. One thing thus far I will dare to generalize about—I am completely bewildered—you don't get ready for things—they just happen—sort of out of the clouds. We listened to lectures and observed movies all day today. Most important of instruction involved high altitude lectures—we will be issued oxygen masks soon now and will take 2 trips in a pressure chamber within the next 4 days.

Yesterday afternoon was really good! We fell out and started what I thought was to be the Mormon pilgrimage to Salt Lake City—but no we stopped dead in the middle of the desert and witnessed a demonstration of incendiary bombs used by the allies. More than 100 lbs. of them were set off—it was quite impressive, quite instructional, and quite hot. One lad who has been here some time estimated temperature to be 130-140. Don't believe he actually knew, but we were all drenched when we finally came in. In that heat 2 or 3 miles of marching in sand is really some chore. Oh wilderness—Ah the heat. It has been warmer the first of this week than last week but don't let all my bellowing get you down—it really is quite an experience and like everywhere else a sense of humor about the whole thing is absolutely necessary.

I received a grand letter from Norma today and one from Harry. Please let Beals know my new address on this envelope—wasn't quite complete yesterday. They are swell to bother with me. I finally chided a 3¢ stamp to get off the first one I wrote to them. Had to burn it cause going to school I can't get to the Post Office and last week we weren't allowed out of the pool Area until 5:30 PM—don't really know why the hell they bother with a Post Office—at least as far as gunnery students are concerned.

To-morrow begins rigid inspections I spoke of yesterday—foot lockers included—third camp I've been in and this is the first place they have ever pulled that. Another thing is that they call roll at the damnedest times and places. I have never been the type to goof off a legitimate regulation formation but boy it is going to be hell on those babies who have made a habit of it. Oh, they won't do much to them if caught—wash em back a week or so and/or give em a little K.P. to boot.

This formation tonight I hear by grapevine is to be a lecture by the Commandant of Students. This evening before chow we had 16-17 minutes to fall out in Class As for retreat with shoes and brass shining. And then they didn't take the majority of us to retreat—ah such a system.

School here I believe will be almost entirely of the "do it" nature. Not much lecture I don't believe. Just as well with this type of thing I think–you just have to learn by doing. Hope we get enough of it although I'm not looking forward to cleaning a 50 cal. machine gun–that ought to be good. They aren't kidding here and to me that's good. I don't believe in being lax about training men for the Big Sho–you just can't take pride in doing anything if they don't make it tough.

Another thing, I told you about the helmets–well, there is a color code here. All helmets have emblem (same as letterhead) on them only they are different colors–while we were in the pool we had orange but 1st formation here we were all issued ones with red emblems on. Each class has its own color and gunnery students have to wear silver helmet liners. Sooo, no matter where you are they can spot you a mile away in the desert and they know where you should be and if you ain't that is just tough.

Oh I forgot to tell you–last night they pulled us out at 7 bells and took us all to the swimming pool to check our swimming ability. It was very fundamental and I passed it O.K. but they sure do keep you going as this hurried missive will attest.

Well, I must hustle off now. It's a great life and this is sure no time to weaken–Huba Huba–it's still fun so never fear and don't worry Francis George is due to be booted around plenty here but we shall survive with the best of them or else. Be good–OH OH Sergeant is now about to pass on more regulations to us so must get going.
Love, Frank

September 6th, 9:00 AM, Wednesday

Dear Mother, Harry and Mike,

I am at it early this morning. We have to have pictures taken, oxygen masks fit and issued and pressure chamber flight this afternoon but this morning we are free (?). I'm sitting on the edge of my foot locker fully believing it is too good to last. This morning was a laugh–they have the fellows so on edge that one whole end of the barracks was up an hour early yet. Such shining of shoes and meticulous making of beds–Huba Huba. Having just about done everything last night I stayed in the sac. I seem to get only a restless nervous sleep in these barracks for some reason and they don't stir this baby until the last minute. Also this morning, feeling a rather demanding call of nature I waltzed to the latrine only to find Orderlies were cleaning it up and no pleading and even explaining that I didn't crap by appointment would get me in. I finally trounced over to next squadron area to relieve myself. This, going into another area, is quite verboten but I was ready to risk all. I just read the "Demerit" list– listing reasons and offenses for which demerits are given. I can see myself on K.P. from here on in each Sunday.

However, I write this only to give you an idea of the prevailing atmosphere not complaining. This is the kind of discipline that we should get and it has been long in coming. It is not too welcome for I have carried on in a rather lax fashion ever since induction and have gotten away with it rather well but I can see that that nonsense must cease here or else my Sundays will be well filled.

Yesterday proved to be a rather long one for we fell out and were marched to PT area at 7 o'clock just after I finished my yesterday's letter. We then listened to Major McCormick welcome us and explain what we were responsible for. We heard a talk from a Tech Sergeant who just got back from Italian Theatre—he was shot down twice and escaped from Italians after being held prisoner for 6 months. Then the Chaplains talked and by then 8:30 had rolled around and after a couple hurried beers I returned to my dear old sac. I guess that covers just about everything to date.

When we came to the squadron—just as I feared we were all split up into separate sections and flights. In the pool, in the tent we had Harrison, Texas—1 year Texas A.M., Hamernik, PA—couple years of General Motors engineering school, Kelly—right off farm from West VA, Moals from Conn. and Johnson from Washington besides Francis George. They were a swell crew and I think we all hated parting company but when the move was finally accomplished I find that Hamernik and Harrison are still with me—we all went to church together Sunday.

Something I haven't mentioned before—I find there is a fellow from home here—permanent party with the Dental Clinic. I often saw him at home—he knows my name but I'll be darned if I know who the hell he is—anyway he tells me I have 4 more fillings to be done—Yee Gads—my mouth must have been as holy as a piece of Swiss cheese. At any rate I'm going up to shoot the proverbial bull with him some night next week as he will be on duty in the Dental Clinic then.

By the way please give the Gazette this address. I haven't received one copy since I left Sioux Falls—I imagine they are holding them up there—someone pinching em or they are just not forwarding them. I got a copy of the Times Magazine from Gramp yesterday—it was thoughtful of him to whip it off to me.

I want to try to write John Dick today but that is a letter I'll have to sit down and write somewhere with lots of room and time. At present I think I shall hit my sac again, read the Times and maybe grab a little shut eye.

Be good, people.

Love, Frank

September 7th, 7:30 AM, Thursday,

Dear Mother, Harry and Mike,

I am at it exceptionally early this morning since I don't expect to be called out before 9:45. They have finally posted the Processing schedule so we have a vague idea now of when we are supposed to be on deck. I have to stand retreat among other things this evening so no doubt I will be late in returning to the barracks.

Yesterday we had pictures taken, Oxygen masks issued and made our first flight in the pressure chamber at 28,000 feet or reduced pressure in the chamber was equivalent to that. These flights are essentially of an instructional and testing nature. Primarily we have to make certain of no leaks in the mask and secondarily we *are introduced to acclimating ourselves to high altitude conditions. The effects of anoxia, or lack of oxygen, were made apparent to us as we were shown methods of regulating our individual oxygen supplies. All interesting, slightly uncomfortable, and extremely important.*

Today I believe we will get our checks in Code and Mechanics. To-morrow I don't know what it will be. Oh yes today we also get a night vision test. Don't know what the hell that is but no doubt I'll know before the day is out.

Last night I took it quite easy. Went to the PX and got myself some more butts and thence to the Snack Bar for a large milk shake. Upon returning to the barracks I took a good shower and hit the sac with a book which I had previously picked up at the library—Title "The Curious Quest" by Oppenheim—you know author of "The Great Impersonation" so I can see me burning a bit of my spare time on that now.

And so it narrows down—as ever, after having been in a new place a few days, it grows hard to think of new things to talk about. I believe I got a better sleep last night as I feel ragged, fat, and sassy today. I think changing pillow to other end of bunk and sleeping in reverse helped because then the lights from orderly room were not shining in my eyes so I am making out better in that respect.

Got no mail yesterday so I cannot discuss much of home with you—hope to hear from youse today. If anything important turns up (you know, good letter material) I'll write another tonight but right now guess that's all.

Lots of Love, Frank

P.S. Be good!

September 8th, 12 M, Friday

Dear Mother, Harry and Mike,

I started, sat down, to write—found the good old pen dry—filled it and then mail call interrupted me again but it was a darn nice interruption. I received three letters from 450 ½ (having been left drooling past 2 days—Labor Day I expect) and a package no less. Everything is perfect—glasses fine—have already written the Otts and thanked for them. The oil I shall try to use week-ends and cigars and butts are fine—well stocked for the remainder of the month concerning the latter.

Well, let's see—we have lots to discuss don't we? Hope Harry is keeping well with all the work—we mustn't let him get run down and shot the way I did. In the Army probably most of us would jump at a chance to squire a gal of the physical attractions of Frieda but after all Harry you are in a position to pick and choose—however the gal has lots of character and also plenty of punch to have so stubbornly acquired her college work as she has—certainly is not on saloon level and yet who are we to look down on the saloon level. I was glad to hear that you had had Labor Day to yourselves at least—we hardly knew it passed here. I suppose I should write Lois Redans—hard job though—but it would be the nice thing to do.

As to a tan in Yuma—little likelihood of it although forearms are nice and brown. We have to wear shirts at all times and don't move without our helmet liners. And when I think of you two topers knocking off for a cold beer in the afternoon—let me hear no more of this telling me to take it easy—you can get little of it and when you do you sweat out a line only to find the prize is lukewarm.

Nope—K.P. is no joke here—am I ever glad the fellows persuaded me to go to the show last night! It took some pushing but I went (picture—Abbott & Costello)—while gone the whistle blew at 9 bells for lights out—the lads in the barracks didn't comply in a split second so, they will all report for K.P. Sunday. Even if a man was asleep and his own light was off he was awakened and his name added to the list. Hope I can have the rest of today and to-morrow for I want Sunday to wash on.

No Mother, I'm not sadly in need of money. They haven't as yet given us all our pay for August (we got only partial pay at Sioux Falls) but that should come along soon. It will be short for me for I have to pay for Suntans but even so I still have a "couple bucks" and will want for nothing.

Yesterday, after I wrote you, I took a night vision test. I didn't pass it on my own but the instructor added a few points on his own and passed me. You see a lot of this in the Army and sometimes it sure makes you wonder. Last night as I told you I went to the show, PX for ice cream later and while waiting in line at show I managed to scoot to library and get me another book. I had finished first one I got although I doubt that I'll have much time to read after this week.

Right now me ars hurts for I am sitting on footlocker to write. Took precaution to snag upper bunk here because we have had reports of so many crawling things in Arizona. In these barracks there is no cause for alarm and sometimes I regret my choice for I can't sit in the old sac and write as I used to.

This morning we took checks on all our radio work—have no doubts that I pass all but blinkers, and if I did pass that it will surprise me no end. I do hope they won't wash me back for it or make me go to night school but the deed is done and I shall have to await developments. This afternoon we are scheduled for another trip in the pressure chamber and this evening on our own time we have to G.I. the barracks so I shall be busy after 2 o'clock.

You'll never know what a relief it is to get those slippers—didn't realize how convenient they were till I left the others behind. Also the soap was very welcome. We can buy it here (not scarce as in Sioux Falls) but it seems to me that I hate to put money in soap—why—don't ask me—I can't reason it out and yet I hate to go to PX and buy it. Maybe because I always had so much of it about me.

Thanks a million again—guess that takes in it all for today—must write Fran—the days I miss letters from you fellows I seem to get one from 440 Ellis St. which couldn't be improved upon.

Must go now—going to try to catch a little shut eye before pressure chamber session.

Be good!

Lots of love, Frank

September 9th, 12:15, Saturday

Dear Mother, Harry and Mike,

Well, how goes it at the homestead today? Just got a letter from Harry and he says things are dead there and I might add a bit of the same tone here. All this morning (and this afternoon I hope) has been spent in the sac. I have been reading W.D. Edmund's "Rome Haul" and it's not bad. Other sections still have parts of their processing to finish up and are doing so and that leaves us free, and any free time in the Army comes in fine as long as you don't stand still too long - says I!

By the way I guess I haven't told you about our celebrities down here. It is natural to expect, this field being only 6 hours from Los Angeles, that any of the big-wigs from there would angle to be stationed here if they could work it. Well, Gene Raymond is lecturing here I understand and Don Budge is a 2nd Looy here in Administration - saw him in the mess hall last Tuesday and has he ever got a car down here too - it looks like one of those custom built jobs.

Also, our squadron mascot is the purest whitest duck you have ever seen. They have a small pool for him and he never strays away. Poor thing - I don't suppose he'd dare take a chance straying from that water. When you see him in the heat of the afternoon with his head under his wing it makes you feel cool cause you can tell that the heat is sure affecting him. He stays up at night, the old rounder, our barracks being right next to orderly room you awake for a moment at night and you can hear him quacking away. His very being is a tribute to the good food here. If we weren't being well fed his old neck would have been wrung some dark night long ago.

Well, I'm afraid that will have to be all for just now - at present there is nothing to tell. We have to stand retreat this evening and that is [the] only formation all day. To-morrow is Sunday and if all goes well I should have it free so be good youse guys. Love, Frank

September 9th, 12:50, Saturday

Dear Harry,

Received your letter regarding your vacation this noon. I'm sorry that I can't say to the hour and minute when I shall arrive next at Niagara Falls but you must know by now that such a thing is impossible. I can only ask you to go ahead and make your plans as best you can and as you see fit.

I repeat—should graduate from here on October 22nd—a day at very least for processing to get out—Record check, physical etc. Tuesday 24th is probably very earliest I could make it out of here. And at that God only knows whether I'll have a week, two weeks, or three or four days. As I said before assignment to Westover Mass. is best deal for me for there I think I would get 18 days including traveling time.

But, and a very big but—flying weather will be closing in there about that time and the odds of such an assignment are certainly not in my favor.

Too many guys in this class from New England States, NY and PA so quota may very well be filled before they reach the Ts, as in Thompson.

There are not assignments to Westover every week—just once in a while.

If I get assigned to Lincoln Neb. or Columbia N.C. with only 9 or 10 days you can see my time home would be very limited. If I am sent to California I probably couldn't make it home at all. So there is the story. I hope for Westover of course but it lies in the balance. Also if I don't make it all the way through it might be a week or two later than I previously planned. Perhaps it was too indefinite to write you in the first place but it would be swell if we could all be free together.

At any rate—go to it old man and whatever you think is best will be O.K. I'm sure. Be sure and be good and set aside a little Jack if you can. Hope to see you about 6 ½ - 7 weeks from now.

Love, Frank

September 10th, 6:45 PM, Sunday

Dear Mother, Harry and Mike,

Well, various and sundry are the changes I have experienced since I wrote you yesterday. I did not draw K.P. but alas to my dismay I found myself on Ammunition detail last night at 6:30. Of course through no fault of my own but apparently our section was stuck and I happened unfortunately to be among the 50 man detail required. This detail I have heard is reputed worse than K.P. and I certainly did not look forward to it but report I did and discovered that the substance of it was preparing live shells (cartridges 50 cal.) in belts for the machine guns on the range. These little cuties come in 110 lb. boxes which inside are broken down into 25 lb. boxes of cartridges. These must be unpacked after being brought to assembly room and prepared in belts. I was fortunate in that I did not draw the heaviest work, carting around the 110 lb. boxes but I did break these open and put them on roller line to assembly room. After I had unpacked and loaded a ton of the things in less than 1 ½ hours I lost count. I was exceedingly fortunate to draw the job on Saturday night for we only worked till 10 o'clock—usually the job lasts till 1 A.M. Also they took us to a mess hall afterwards for meatloaf, beans, Jell-O and coffee. In spite of the fact that I didn't draw heaviest work or longest hours my back has honestly ached with a vengeance since.

On top of that, this morning we were not called for chow and in the Army I have always been one who hates to miss my breakfast. Then to add insult to injury the whole squadron was called out at 9:30 and we were reassigned (dammit) to a new and permanent quarters. I was separated from my pals Hamernik and Harrison and moved to a tent—after that air conditioned barracks folks I protest that it just ain't cricket. I felt bad of course but there is just no help for it and it did me good to see the way these two guys hated to see me go—they helped me get ready and helped me transport all my stuff and many were the sighs and bitches on the part of all three of us. Such is the Air Corps—its biggest and yet an almost necessary fault.

I had previously dedicated Sunday to wash day and if I wanted clean clothes I had to stand by my plan. So wash I did. Did I tell you before that 4,000 gunners here are using latrine facilities designed for 400 cadets? It was not good in the barracks but *it is almost impossible here. I finally (having stolen a bucket from supply last night) sneaked to another area's latrine (strictly verboten) and there on the floor of the shower room did my washing. There are no tubs anywhere much less a wash board, with Rinso I had bought and one of the large bars of Ivory you sent, I finally after about 2 ½ - 3 hours acquitted myself reasonably well. Clothes dry here almost as soon as you put them out but OH my aching back (literally) it was some job! I had previously made arrangements with my boys aforementioned to go to 5 o'clock Mass and after hanging out my wash was getting ready to go when in pops Al Daher who arrived from Sioux Falls Thursday.*

We had a good gab fest and then when the other lads showed up we all went to chow and thence to church—had a couple beers and then some of em went to show—some to Service Club but I thought I'd better get this letter off to youse guys. Before I left Al, I told him of a deal he could get while still in the pool so that he would not draw K.P. as I did. So I walked up here with him and got him fixed up in the mail room at the pool. Now he'll freeze the job and be ready to fix Bill Hughes and John Kostishack up with the same good thing when they come which should be next Thursday. I took precaution to bring paper and am now writing in the Pool dayroom. Not too keen about writing in the tent, my home now. I shouldn't be giving you two the impression I must be giving you about the tents—really in lots of respects it is better than the barracks. For one thing inspections are not nearly so rigorous and I also hear that since we are in tents we will not be assigned Sunday K.P. Also I was not sleeping well in the barracks due to direct cool draughts and I imagine this tent business will be much more healthy for me.

Well, so it goes at dear old Yuma—am very glad I had at least this day to get my washing cleaned up and all things considered the prospect is not too bad. Only 6 weeks to go which I imagine will wing rapidly by once school starts. I believe we start school right off with our guns to-morrow morning.

I am enclosing some of what you two have been crying for. I won't say they are good but with such a subject what the Hell can we expect? There are not as many of the best ones as I wanted but the deal was that most of the old guard of 1241 was to have these made and the other guys got one each—thus the deficiency. Hope to have some others from here as soon as we can get them taken and developed which takes too long here.

I also must take all my O.D.s to the cleaners Tuesday night, as I hear; it takes almost a month to get em back.

Well, turned out longer than I expected. Hope you like the pictures—please save em for me any how—keep one of each pose any how—with my special Sunday Blessing to all three of you and a warning to be good.
Love, Frank

September 11th, 7:40, Monday

Dear Mother, Harry and Mike,

This will have to be a shortie for I have only 20 minutes to get done in. We have sure been kept on the go today. We started right off with 4 hours Weapons, lecture 2 hours and actual field and detail stripping 2 hours, then 2 hours Sighting, 1 hour Radio Mechanix and 1 hour Code and then 1 hour parachute training, 20-25 minutes for chow and then the 1st Sergeant took an hour to tell squadron how to clean up for Inspector General goes through to-morrow. It sure has been a busy day and how.

Truthfully I have done little cleaning or arranging having done most of it yesterday when I moved in. Foot locker is in good shape and after that I don't care much.

As things shape up it sure is a rugged schedule and on top of that 106 of the boys (out of 400) who proved deficient in Code and Mechanix had to go to more school this evening. I was quite fortunate at having missed that session.

No mail again today so I guess I cannot discuss much of mutual interest to all of us. I did get a much better night's sleep in the tent last night and I can tell you I won't be long out of the sac right now. It is a long day. We were actually on duty from 5:45 this morning till 8:30 this evening. Because of Brass Hat inspection we have to get up at 4:15 in the morning for more cleaning—Oh home was never like this but it is good training and I'm sure I shall adapt myself to it—perhaps a little painfully but willingly for I never as yet had that kick in the tail the Army gives most Privates so it has been owing to me for a long time.

Leave us keep our chins up and our noses clean—Huba Huba

Be good.

Love, Frank

September 12th, 6:45, Tuesday

Dear Mother, Harry and Mike,

Finally got a letter today—said once before that I'd say nothing more about these things so I won't but just a post card or something to let me know everything is all right cause I kinda worry sometimes.

Mail call finished up rigors of today's schedule. Can't say as I am too much pleased with the methods or instruction here but then that is the Army and we must accept it. One thing good is that they have issued us all "A Gunner's Handbook," which is a peach, and if I can manage, I'll steal it or something for in spite of its technical subject matter, I feel sure any civilian would get a kick out of it—as a guide to teaching if nothing else.

That I feel bad about young Wilson goes without saying. Honestly don't believe I'll ever see European Theatre. Sure is great to hear about Dick—makes you feel real pride in that end of the family—good to have at least one soldier in the family, maybe I'll get there one of these fine days but I'm not one to rush these things.

You ask me a good many questions—most of these I have answered. About going to school—to be sure it is an experience—these Army Tech Schools, as is to be expected, *are mere products of expediency. Even at this late stage the instructors staffs leave too much to be desired however, war is indeed like the parachute jumping (our last class), you get only one mistake and so we all try to stay on the ball.*

Yes as I have told you before I moved and how. Sleeping is much better in the tents believe it or not so I am glad of the change in that respect. I really took a rooking on the buddy situation though, for I don't give a damn about any of the guys in my tent as yet anyhow.

No dear, I'm not peeved about this alleged money that was supposed to be coming. I honestly don't need anything and have a pay coming up (remainder of August due me) very soon now. If there is any pinching whatsoever—please don't bother—I make out quite handily and heaven knows there is no place to spend money here except on your stomach and thirst both of which are entirely unnecessary.

To tell the truth I have heard from youse, Beals, Gramp, and Ann since I've been here which is pretty good for me. Feel bad about the Beals but there is just no help for it. Wanting stamps just isn't excuse enough to get out of squadron to Post Office and buy stamps. That is one reason I have looked for registered from you so I could get over there at Post Office during the day so please tell them that as soon as I can get some stamps I shall write. They are certainly too, too grand for me to neglect but we are all here at camp in the same boat so there is little we can do about it.

Must be off now—have to get laundry ready to-night, try to study a bit, and stand in line to shower and shave.

And so it goes—we are getting quizzed to-morrow already and also Code checks again. So I'll have to buzz off. Be good, people.

Love, Frank

September 14th, 9:15 A.M., Thursday

Dear Mother, Harry and Mike,

Well, of all things, a breakdown in the schedule. A slight one to be sure but nevertheless a 2 hour respite from the designated course. Two hours of parachute lectures were not forthcoming so I guess I'd better take advantage of the time to write youse.

Yesterday we were well on the go as per usual, had our quiz in Sighting in which you had to make at least 100% or you go back at night for lectures. We also had Code checks to determine whether we go nights for Code next week. Hope I don't get stuck with this night business along the line. It only amounts to an hour but nevertheless is confining.

Last night there was a long laundry line to sweat out. Took better than an hour to get through that one. Turning in laundry here is really the height of laziness—you have to do a lot of bookkeeping (even sizes must be on laundry slips) then sweat out a line to turn stuff in, then wait 2 weeks to get it—another line to get it back—all this just to have someone else do your laundry and you pay for it yet. Oh well, about all I turned in was shirts and fatigues and the large towels. I was disgusted, having worked so hard Sunday most of my stuff was clean, so there was little point in turning it in. After laundry line I joined the lads in a couple beers and by that time it was too late to do anything but hit the old sac.

This morning, already, we practiced for one part of our final phase checks, which come in the fifth week. We had to fieldstrip our cal. 50 machine guns with blindfolds and gloves on in an 8 minute time limit. Fieldstripping is not hard but it will just give you an idea of the rapidity and intensity of the training here after all, today marked beginning of our 4th day's training so you can see that we're not fooling around. No mail yesterday but everything is so completely screwed up here it is not hard to understand why.

War news, what we get of it, is great—sure doesn't look like a much longer pull in Europe at any rate.

Not much more to tell. Aside from school this past week I have done nothing else and I fear I cannot dig up much of interest to write about. Just that all's well, when not bubbling over with sweat, it's with rigour, and gunnery is fast becoming a reality to us all. We should fly Saturday—merely a familiarization hop but maybe it will give me something to tell you about then. Be good.

Love, Frank

P.S. Am enclosing outline of what yee old radio operator is responsible for so you'll have an idea.

F

September 15th, 9:45 AM, Friday

Dear Mother, Harry and Mike,

Well, it happened again today—2 hours free time. Don't know of what they are thinking lately but I hope it lasts. I felt real smug last night when I got three (3) letters. One from Mother, Norm and Ann. I carried em back to tent and had myself a real reading fest—just like a dog with a bone you know. Say haven't I been the jerk; I forgot that I could send Beals mail to Box 52 Bridge St P.O. so I must write Beals tonight.

Can't really understand why you're not getting mail for, with exception of 2 days K.P. and last Wednesday, I have managed a line or so every day. Let us hope that Don O'H and Earl Richardson go to Europe. They may be there a long time but there is little doubt in my mind but what they would be a good deal safer there. Just what line are they in? My last impression was that they are both in the Infantry. Not a too delightful prospect if they see much action but I hope things will be over in Europe soon.

Things roll along here in an uneventful pattern, a pattern for which I'm grateful, for if it changes too much it will only mean that lil old Francis George will probably be in difficulties and that I don't want.

I believe we fly to-morrow—hope we go in the morning for the sand reflects the heat here. This sends up hot air currents which bounce hell out of the planes. Gunners who graduate from here don't talk about who got sick but how many times they got that way. These air currents cause some type of rolling as on a ship and I hear a lot of the boys wind up slamming in the bomb bay.

Yesterday we started getting our actual Parachute Training. Simple tumbling, jumping from 6-8 feet platforms and buckling on and fitting parachute harnesses. You'd have died if you could have heard us doing this last. Two of the harness straps go around your legs and between and there was an awful lot of talk about safeguarding the "Family Jewel"–such readjusting of straps to keep it from peril.

Found out yesterday that I passed my Code so I don't have a night session in that anyway. The fellows from Scott Field seem to have a little more trouble than we are having.

Right now some Looy is making an inspection so I expect him any minute now. Half of the guys have cleared out but I'll be darned if he can scare me away–like to know anyway just what is expected of you in these tents where every day when you get off duty you find at least 1/8" of dust and sand on the floor and over everything.

I'm going to sign for a pass for to-morrow. They will be from 5 P.M. to-morrow night until 3 PM Sunday. May go in and see what Yuma is like. Probably not but I'll see how the spirit moves me to-morrow–probably go in Sunday noon if I go at all.

We just had our inspection. Most things O.K. but we have a Tent Leader, Corporal who for some reason I don't seem to be able to refrain from antagonizing so I can see me getting the dirt slung at me right and left from now on. I wriggled out of details twice since I started writing this–he'll get me soon–no doubt of that. He is in again–let's see what goes now? Seems to be in a better mood now.

Guess that will be all for today. Chow will be on soon and I am getting rather hungry. So, be good.

Love, Frank

September 16th, 6:40, Saturday

Dear Mother, Harry and Mike,

Ho! Ho! But today's tour and the prospect for to-morrow are gloomy indeed. At first we were awakened at 4 AM so that we would be on flight line early for our Orientation Flight this morning. Then we all had to wait, yours truly not going up until 10:30. The flight itself was uneventful but we did see a good bit of Yuma Valley from the air and I rode in the nose of the Flying Fortress most of the way. Can't say I was thrilled to pieces but they are splendid planes and truly merit the name they have made for themselves. The day has been a long one and I am tired–mostly from waiting.

Then the payoff comes when I come back from chow. Now they take 10 men each Sunday for K.P. and this is from 400 men. Yes my dears I get it to-morrow–all day from 4 AM till 9 at night. Direct assignment from a roster would not hurt so bad but the truth is I was given one (1) "gig" in today's inspection and that got me the job. Name tags must be on "shelf, footlocker, and bunk." The Lieutenant that was in yesterday and checked these and all were OK. Today he went through and apparently the one on my locker was missing today hence one gig–hence 16 hours K.P. Huba Huba. I don't think it is fair–I know I could raise hell but I also know that in the aftermath they would really fix me in the end. In other words, if

I did much now, the Squadron Administration would have to take some rebuke from higher authority, but then they would be rigidly on my tail for the next 5-6 weeks, so I can stand only to lose for standing up for what I know is right. Thank God I still have a sense of humor and can laugh it off–Bless it I have one solid week in now including the K.P. and only 5 more to go. I told youse before I felt I would get the business here but I hardly thought they would shoot it to me on such skimpy grounds.

Well, enough crying–maybe I'll be able to get a letter in for you to-morrow in spite of it all. Last night I got letters from both of you so cannot gripe about not getting any this evening. Hope to heavens that you received news that I got the box a week ago Friday. At Sioux Falls I could get used to the delay in letters but the lag in thought by the time I get an answer here, 8-10 days, just about keeps me befuddled all the time.

I am glad to hear about Jerry–hope he likes Farming–have his mother tell him that a reaper is a poor substitute for a cal. 50 machine gun on a B-29 but lady he is a lot safer in Texas than some places. Tell him to stick to farming a while if he can. All kidding aside these machine guns are splendid weapons–in Jap terms and designations they amount to cannon–the shells themselves are mean looking things–hope I can swipe one and send it to you. A man could not help but feel confident behind one of these babies and I'd hate to be standing in front of one. It is competent men behind these that have made B-17s so effective, for a fighter takes a real chance when he starts to fool with one.

After being in the plane I am quite satisfied with my spot. I believe it safest on the ship, coziest and most roomy–on top of that there is no substitute for a Radio man and also in order to save man power and increase bomb loads we are informed here that frequently on large formations the Radio Operator has to do most of Navigation since no Navigator is carried many times. It is a responsible job requiring skill imagination and initiative as well as a clear head at all times.

Still cannot say much for this group I am with in tent. Four of us out of 6 were slipped the shaft on this K.P. deal. I feel I never would have gotten it had the officer not been peeved when he checked up on the other fellows. All the rest have either bought their way out of it or been squawking in the orderly room but I think I'll just take my dose for a little work never hurt anyone–(I hope).

Of all things we had a good shower last night. First rain here since February–it was a relief–too bad there was not more of it. Well, I fear that sums up most of it for today. Be good, people and say a prayer for me cause I won't be able to make Mass to-morrow.

Love, Frank

September 17th, 7:35, Sunday

Dear Mother, Harry and Mike,

Just got off my tour of K.P.–long stretch from 4 this morning but it is over now and that is the main point. Start on my second week to-morrow and I just hope I can keep on the safe side from now on.

One of the boys got my mail for me. Harry's letter speaking of his mishap–Gosh, but it has me a bit worried to say the least. The extra work just will have to cease– and please take care–both of you and the money to me will just have to cease too. Lots of guys get along on less than I have and I feel as though I were directly responsible for the whole thing.

I know it is short but I'm slightly on the dead side right now–just to let you know all's well etc. It was probably easiest K.P. I've ever had but it is never any Sunday school picnic so I must go shower and shave and get some rest–also a few odds and ends to take care of so I avoid as much of these details as possible, although it still looks like personal discrimination to most of us. But it's only 6-7 weeks so what the hell + they can broil me in oil so long as I get out of here on time. Must be off now. Be good.

Love, Frank

September 18th, 7:50, Monday

Dear Mother, Harry and Mike,

Well, it is getting dark already. Seems I never get much done here and am still a little tired from two night's short sleep and the long day yesterday. Received no mail from youse today but did get 3 Gazettes and letter from Bealys (Norma). I haven't written them a second yet. Hate to do it on this paper and yet I just haven't been to PX for more.

School rolls along in an orderly and intense fashion although I cannot say that I can find the interest in it that I found at radio school. Many of the lads are trying and hoping to be washed out. For myself I think I'll take my medicine here!

I just had to look at the papers tonight. Did you note Marcella Peterson's picture with her new hubby in the paper? I can still remember a torrid night in a rumble seat with her. Jack long fixed it up and Jack Stolz took the "other one" and we went to Glen Park.

Please call Gazette and tell them of this address. Now it goes to the pool and I am late in getting it.

I apologize for brevity but I must fight my way to shower and shave and hit the sac but soon. Hope to do better to-morrow. Will need to be rested as we have Weapons examination to-morrow–also more Code checks.

Lots of love, Frank

September 19th, 8:10, Tuesday

Dear Mother, Harry and Mike,

Have finally taken refuge in the dayroom to write this one. I only hope lights will be left on later than 9:00. I received ticket for registered letter this evening but have not as yet been able to claim letter since P.O. closes at 5 o'clock and we don't have Mail Call till 6:35.

I did manage to get some of my stuff to the cleaners this evening. Of course that closes early each night except 2 when it is closed at 7:30 for sole benefit of gunnery students. Even at that the line is long and the prices here for cleaning have really thrown most of us. However, it is worth it to get your stuff in shape and insured against moths. I am referring to woolen clothing–of course we don't wear it but it bothers me if it isn't pressed and I am like Mother as far as worrying about moths is concerned.

I passed my Weapons examination today and last Sighting test. We had Code checks for next week today. If you don't pass you report for Code from 7:30-8:30 each night next week so I sure hope I got that. I don't know as I will get any writing done this week. Oh, I'll manage you fellows, but I just can't work the others in although I must write the Beals. It is really funny–this keeping on the go. No kidding–if you have a spare moment you actually feel guilty. Gosh I'm afraid I can't really tell you much new. A bunch of the boys didn't report for Reveille this morning so they scrubbed floors in orderly room this evening and will each night this week and apparently have the threat of K.P. over their heads.

We are still taking our parachute course from 5-6 PM each day. I sure hope that doesn't last too much longer. As the actual physical training end of it is set up, you go through 12-15 minutes of each of 4 phases each evening. 1. Tumbling and tumbling mats. 2. Jumps of 6-8 feet from stands using various tumbling techniques to break your fall. 3. Actual strapping on of harnesses and practicing landings and turns off of platforms. 4. You slide down an incline wire on a pulley which is attached to a parachute harness to which you are strapped and as you slide down you are released into sawdust pits. This last does a very real job of simulating actual landings. The course is darn good training and well set up. Many of us are apt to not appreciate it because it comes at the end of a rather long day whereas we should feel fortunate because we are the 1st class to get it. It is highly important (as I see it after having ridden in these planes) to be able to do these things in which we are being trained as rapidly and automatically as possible for there is little space and probably little time when the occasion comes to use that training. Incidentally have I told you that the Air Corps does not refer to a parachute as a last resort? No, it is spoken of merely as a "mode of transportation from plane to ground."

I turned another pair of G.I. shoes in for repair today–that makes three pairs of heavy rubber soles and heels I've gone through in almost 8 months. You know how I used to get a kick out of my shoes (figuratively!) well, I haven't changed and I do hope they don't issue me new ones cause the two pair I have are just right now. The lads tell me there is little danger of getting new ones but they do everything ass backwards here and I am ready for anything.

Guess that includes the day's activities so I'll rush off now and clean up for my sac. Dear old sleep will not be long in coming I hope.

Intend to get letter to-morrow at noon so will answer it that evening with anything else I may be fortunate enough to get.

Lotsa love, Frank

September 20th, 10:30, Wednesday

Dear Mother, Harry and Mike,

It seems that the "Interphone" course scheduled for this two hours is not completely set up so I am able to get this written during the day on the Army's time for a change.

I did find out that I passed my Code so that is fine. I just came back from Post Office where I got my registered letter. I had to get a pass from the orderly room first and finally managed to get ma letter. As to the letter I can't say much for I was looking forward to getting a nice juicy one but I suppose I should get that one tonight. But gosh fellows you sure went all out on the money end—it is grand to reserve it. Guess I can splurge now—sure hope you are not depriving yourselves. Don't know where the hell I'll spend money in this neck of the woods but you know me! I'll manage to get rid of it somehow. Gosh I hope I don't pull K.P. this Sunday—if not I can go to 8 AM Mass and Communion and then I'll get my breakfast in the Snack Bar over a Sunday paper. But I'm not planning on spending the Sunday in the mess hall—I did that last week and look what happened. Ah me we'll just have to wait and see I guess.

I feel quite smug. Have my clothes in cleaners so next thing will be going about getting Radio patches sewn on. I have 3 shirts in the laundry and as soon as they're back I can get this taken care of. Seems to be so many puttery jobs that you have forever on your mind and it is such an inconvenience to get them taken care of. Norm wrote me and asked how my shirt and sac supply was. Wouldn't you know—they never forget me—awful nice people you know Mom. Of course I have everything I want now but it was darn nice of her to ask—as if they didn't have enough of their own to worry about. Gosh I must write them but won't get to it tonight as I have haircut on the schedule. Was going to get it last night but cleaners kept me too long and I wanted to get a letter off to you fellows.

I'm glad to hear that Harry will be quitting Liggett's. I'm sure he will not want to, for public service work has lots to compensate for its drudgery and low pay in the people you meet, but since he is the mainstay of the 450 ½ 9th Street Thompson's, he owes it to himself and us not to take any unnecessary risks with his health. The main reason that a fellow can laugh and take hold and carry on to his best in a hole like this is that he feels secure that all the things he cherishes are being looked after and guarded by such capable hands. Let us keep it thus!

By the way I'm toying with the idea of a transfer to Merchant Marine. Doubt if it can be worked out from here but nevertheless I'm going to look into it—much better money and better experience than operating in a plane. I include this just to let you know that I haven't changed much basically. Still on the lookout for opportunities.

Have made inquiries about Engineering Cadet here but it is not open. Am sure I could get in Chemical Warfare O.C.S. but would rather fight my part of this war as a Radio Operator and Non-com than a Lieut. in a farce like Chemical Warfare.

Well, I'm afraid that says most of it for today. We will be off for noon chow soon and then 4 hours of school and an hour of parachute training—so, be good.
Love, Frank

September 21st, 11:55, Thursday

Dear Mother, Harry and Mike,

We went to noon chow exceptionally early today so fortunately are back earlier than usual. I rec'd two letters last night, one from Mother and Harry's. I also got the El'Chem. I see by the latter where all the young lads who came to work there shortly before I left and got married so rapidly are all leaving for the Army. Bob Wade, Chuck Shepherd, Dick Clark, Charlie Kamin and quite a few others are on their way by now. Wonder what happened—maybe the plant couldn't hold them any longer eh?

Thanks for the news folks and I'm afraid I can't reciprocate in much of a way. Just the old AAF routine you know. We had a required formation last night which turned out to be movies for our pleasure as was quite agreeable but it blanked the evening for me and I had planned on getting a haircut. Have to try to work that in tonight. Took my final in Sighting today 98% and we get final in Weapons to-morrow I believe. The first two weeks are the only ones where we get class room work. It will all be firing and flying beginning next week I believe. Of course our hour of Code and hour of Radio Mechanix continuation will go right on each day but very little more class room work in gunnery.

I hope I get a chance to write Gramp over the week-end. Don't like the sound of things. Sure would like to see him again at least once for this artery business cannot be cured at his age.

I wrote Ann a rather jolting little missive last time and am anticipating some type of repercussions soon after she gets it. Wouldn't be too surprised if she stopped writing me too. How are the elder Keoughs? I suppose the Davys are rooting along as usual. How is Mrs. Jopp, and Mr. and Mrs. Coleman and Lobianco's and their Pride and Joy. Latest rumour here is that all overseas training unit centers are very overcrowded— maybe by the time I get out of here I'll no longer be in the Air Corps. Ah well, the bright side of that is that they will have to start training me all over for something new again.

Say I see my time is about gone and I hear that dear old whistle in the distance so will have to toddle along now. Be good.
Love, Frank

September 22nd, 6:35, Friday

Dear Mother, Harry and Mike,

Things sure move around here. Good thing I managed to write before noon yesterday for at 6:45 last night we fell out for Pay Call and I personally didn't get paid till 11:15.

Last ones were paid at about 12:30. We still had to get up at 5:30 this morning and today was a ripper too. They take up all your spare time so you have little time to do anything.

I just got out of chow and before I go any farther I have to go to a Malaria lecture in a few minutes and then sign the payroll after that so I don't know as I will finish this soon.

The school itself has taken a slightly more interesting turn in the practical application of our Weapons and Sighting courses. This morning we were piled into buses and toted out to the "Range Estimation" Range. After standing in line over 5 hours for a $4 pay I was not too eager but it proved interesting. When we got out there, there were a couple of AT 6s buzzing around (Harvard Trainers). Under a canvas canopy on a long wooden rail there were mock (wooden models) machine guns—the only real thing on them being the sights. At each gun there were earphones. Behind all this there was a small shack which was in Radio Communication with the planes. After opening communications the planes swooped in and made mock passes at the machine gun emplacements. As the pilots came in they called off their range from us (marked on the ground) from a point 2 miles away. The radio picked up the pilot on his way in and this in turn was wired to headphones at each mock gun. The effective range of our gun is 600 yards so we got valuable practice in judging the range of a fast incoming plane. It really was kinda fun for those babies, most of the time, swooped in not more than 20-25 feet over us.

The afternoon we spend 4 hours in Preventive Maintenance Sheds where we were issued machine guns. We had to completely detail strip them and clean and oil all parts. 90% of these guns had bad parts in them and it was our job to dig out burred parts and replace them and get the weapons themselves in class A working condition. This is good stuff and for my money is the only way you really ever learn the gun. To-morrow we fire this same gun—only 30 rounds—just enough to dirty it up again so we can get more experience cleaning it again. We also will get our final written test in Weapons to-morrow. From then on it should be shooting and flying.

Later (at Malaria Lecture) I did manage to get my laundry—9 day service job—honestly my white towels are as white as when I first got them. This is indeed a satisfaction to me—shirts were done up nicely and I can now see about getting patches put on them. Even hankies - were ironed neatly—that is the difference between a G.I. Laundry and a civilian one which we have here—a civilian laundry still labors under the delusion that G.I.s are still human beings and like things neat and clean.

There is some medic beating his guns here now—this is really a riot—up till 11:30-12 midnight—then up at 5:30—solid school up to 5 o'clock—(2 hours radio, 2 hours on the range, 4 hours of weapons) from 5-6 we had a demonstration in the swimming pool of the Mae West life preserver and one man life raft. We ate and came here. I still have to sign payroll for month of September and we are supposed to G.I. tents tonight.

On a little brighter side—our section was selected as best of squadron this week so we get passes from 6 Sat Evening till 6 PM Sunday. This is really going all out on the part of the organization for us down here. Other squadrons cannot stay out overnight. Also all the other sections of our squadron are going to have to take drill and we are excused. Don't ask me how that happened. They'll get wise to us soon so we may as well enjoy what little freedom we can get while it presents itself. Of course I'm still not sure I won't get stuck with K.P. Sunday but I stand a good chance of missing it (I hope). I'll probably go into town to-morrow night—not that there's much to do there but I want to get my civilian shoes heeled and I hear that there is a shoemaker in town. Lights going out for movie.

8:30 Later

Movie was one I had seen before and after it I signed payroll—amazingly short line and quite painless and I'm glad that is out of the way. I saw Al Daher today and we plan on making Communion Sunday if we don't get stuck. We are separated by two classes but I see him in chow hall quite frequently.

No mail today so cannot comment so guess I'll get going—make ma bed, shower and shave and hit the sac in preparation for that last day of the week Saturday.

Be good, people.

Love, Frank

September 23rd, 10 AM, Saturday

Dear Mother, Harry and Mike,

A break in the schedule gives me a few minutes so guess I'll get started. We have final Weapons—

Sunday morning about 10:15 AM

Well, I just barely got a start yesterday. Another busy one and I did manage to get into town last night and no K.P. today—feel so free and fortunate today I hardly know myself. What I started to say was that on above mentioned quiz I barely passed but pass I did and that is the main point I guess. Yesterday afternoon we fired our cal. 50s on the Burst Control Range—each fired about 30 rounds which amounted to less than 5 minutes of actual operations on the firing line since the gun is capable of 750-850 rounds per minute. Then we had to clean weapons and return by bus and our guns to the armory. That left us a reasonably free ½ hour –> an hour before chow, which I well utilized in getting ready for town.

After chow I met Dan Hamernik and we took off for Yuma—6-7 miles away. We went by bus—the vehicles being of the 1934 vintage and they soak you 20 cents one way. Once in town we gave the place a gook looking over and had some good cold beer, which hit the spot as almost never before. We did quite a bit of window shopping and I bought myself a new O.D. Flight (overseas) cap as the one I have is quite spotted. Of course I won't use it here but there is a good chance of going North or Northwest after here and I wanted to have it on hand. They have a U.S.O. here which is quite superior to one in Sioux Falls. They ran a dance last night and little Francis

242 • LORETTO M. THOMPSON

George tripped a few in the good old manner. We then did some more looking—had a couple more beers and high-tailed it back to camp for the dear old sac. Don't ever know what we G.I.s will do if we ever again settle back to civilian ways. We all start to yawn about 9:30 or ten and from then on it is anybody's money who will have courage enough to suggest return to camp and bed. Staying up at all late gets us, that is all. But I didn't really hit the hay until 1-1:30.

Our passes are good for only 25 mile radius which permits only visit to Yuma or Winterhaven a small town, gas station and general store arrangement just over the state border in California. While bars close at 12 midnight in Yuma alcohol is sold in Winterhaven until 10:00 AM on Sunday so naturally a lot of the G.I.s go there. Also the gambling laws are apparently less stringent in Cal. and it is done on a wide open basis there.

I may go over just to see one of these places but could not see it last night—also it is very easy to get a ride to Winterhaven (about 15-20 miles) but it is hell thumbing a ride back again early in the morning. I rather doubt that I'll go in town this afternoon as I have lots of writing to catch up on and this is only day I can get much of it done.

Al Daher came around this morning and waked me for 8 o'clock Mass. We could not go to Communion for although we arrived early there was a very long line for Confessions and there being only one Priest we were not heard. However we plan to go early this afternoon and attend the 5 o'clock number as far as Communion. After Mass we went to Snack Bar where I had 2 beautiful cups of coffee and large sweet roll and butter. It was quite a relief.

Terribly sorry about not writing yesterday but I think you'll understand—I had not been out of Army regulations for over a month and could not resist temptation to get to town last night.

I guess a little of Yuma is in order. There are a great number of Mexicans, Negros and Chinese here which is to be expected in a border town. I do honestly feel sorry and ashamed of our Officers here. There is nothing for these "hot pilots" to do except drink and when they do they don't fool. They wind up with some of the weirdest women and drunker than hell. They pick up too many of the 14 to 16 year old variety to suit me. It is a deplorable situation—of course they are not allowed in U.S.O. and if there is such a thing as a better class of girl who will suffer a soldier, I believe you'd find them only at the U.S.O. here. In the Paradise Club here Officers get stinking drunk—(G.I.s can go there too) and then they become prey of the lowest form of woman—it is a crime socially for prostitute sticks out all over them and they generally hold some insignificant job clerking in the day time but they really clean up at night. These pilots are young—what I mean—some of them beardless as yet—they are inflated with importance of their job and their wings and they have seen too many movies about that "Go to Hell"–"C'est la Guere" attitude. Socially they are not matured but there is plenty of liquor and they really make the most (or worst) of it.

The club I spoke of is more like a stage for a puking contest than an entertainment stop. Women voice the come on loudly and brazenly and all that is lacking are tiers of bunks to spare the inconvenience of all that sand. Let's forget the social end of it—just imagine how we gunnery students feel when we see our Officers—boys alongside most of us—can't hold their liquor—throwing up everywhere. These are the men we have to follow—have to put our lives in their hands—have to trust them when we know what they went through the night before. Of course all of them are not and cannot fall prey to this free experimentation of youth but there is too much of it. Here, as in any place else, a man can conduct himself as a gentleman and keep clean and above reproach if he is man enough to do so. Indeed it is so much more to his own personal advantage, if nothing else, if he does so. Sympathy is all I have for these guys—from what I've seen here I hope few of them ever depend on a good word or demand undying loyalty from me.

Say I really do go on, don't I? Just getting some of the accumulated spleen out of me I guess so don't pay too much attention to it. I expect to spend most of the rest of the day writing and cleaning up. A high velocity wind has blown this sand into my bed while I was at church and I'll have to get it all beaten and aired before I'll want to get into it tonight. I must write Beals and Gramp today and there are several other odds and ends to take care of including church this afternoon.

Sooo, be good youse people. My special Sunday blessing to you.

Love, Frank

P.S. Got letters from both of you yesterday which was really the cat's meow.
F

P.P.S. Forgot to mention that this is end of second week—4 more to go—5th week we go to Datelan where we take operational phase checks in flying—radio operation and gunnery combined. Things do roll along eh?

More love, F

September 24th, 12:45 PM, Sunday

Dear Harry,

I write in answer to your last. God bless you old man, wish I could tell you more about what will happen and what assignment I'll be getting just 4 weeks from today, but I won't know until at best 24 hours before I'm on the train. Of course I'll let you know, by night letter if possible, as soon as I can. What follows should serve the dual purpose of giving you the general idea and also of reestablishing the whole idea in my mind.

Please do not feel disappointed if I wire and say I'm not going to be able to make it when the time comes. This is the overall situation. Westover with 15 days is about all I'll accept as a delay. Yes, I have the privilege of refusing any delay. You see this delay would go on my furlough time. There is no sense in kidding—after, shortly after, I get out of here may be the last time I'll be home until the day I'm discharged. I have decided on the following after talking to a Tech. Sgt. from the pool on the subject. It is from the pool after graduation that I will get my shipping orders. A lot of fellows the past few weeks have been getting 7 days to La Mort, California. Even for fellows in Chicago this leaves them only 1 ½ days at home at very best and if they take it they will have burnt out a good bit of their furlough time and will not be likely to get another one. On the other hand the best policy to me seems to be to refuse any such inadequate arrangement–go directly to new base and take chances on getting a 15 day furlough from there. I doubt very much that they would send me over without at least 1 trip home so if I give up the first chance I'm much more likely to do better by direct application to the C.O. of my new Post. Westover with 15 days would still be ideal but I fear flying weather is closing in there and in all honesty I dare not let my hopes run away with both of us.

Now let us get to something I have never mentioned before in a letter home. The damned old subject of money. It is not easy to save in the Army. I have written home about all I have done and I have done little although I have really wanted for nothing. A few beers and cigarettes and clothes in good shape keep me hopping. What you and Mother have sent me has been of inestimable help. You know yourself how far your 20 or 25 goes at home and in G.I. town's prices unfortunately are always boasted it seems to take you over the coals. The situation is just this. If things go as I plan I should have 50-60 bucks saved when the crucial moment arrives at the end of this course 4 weeks hence. I cannot be sure that this will bring me home although it certainly should–one way at furlough rates. The government pays your expense at 3¢/mile direct to your new base. Any deviations you make as going home is your own problem. I will be well reimbursed if I can get Westover. However that won't come till I report there after delay so if you could possibly hang on to a couple a bucks and should I need it I can let you know. I'd like to know on this score for if you're strapped I can borrow enough from the Student Commandant here but am not too keen about the idea. If I don't get or take delay from here money will be no problem as I will be drawing Corporal's pay and Flight pay when I reach R.T.U. and I shall have more than enough to make it.

Note I stopped here for some time. Guess I'll send this to the office and hope that you get it after your vacation. I do hope at any rate that they won't call you about it while Mother is around. I'll just have to take that chance–this shouldn't get there anyway until Friday or Saturday at earliest.

Guess that is all for now Bro so take it easel (sic) and don't worry about this cause should I get the chance I'll make it home if I have to crawl. Be good.
Love, Frank

P.S. When I get ready to leave I'll telegraph the office. If you're not going to be there have someone accept it for you and call you at home–you can tell Mom it is with reference to your work, the call that is.
F.

September 25th, Monday

Dear Mother, Harry and Mike,

   Huba Huba and Hello from Yuma. This morning we embarked upon our actual gunnery firing. We fired 50s all morning and it was a lot of fun to say the least. Three of us took turns on one machine gun and I can truthfully say that I did a better than average job scoring among the highest in the squadron. This does not make me too elated though for I started well on the Carbine too and sort of fizzled out on the tail end when I fired for record. Also we had steady gun replacements and were shooting at stationary targets. When it gets tough is when you find yourself in a bomber moving at 225 miles per shooting at a fighter which is flying at you at at least 100 miles per hour faster than you are going. When you figure the effect the forward movement of the bomber has combined with leading your fast moving your target–then the problem gets complex. This morning the main purpose was to train us in Burst Control–that is making the most of a short burst–that is not to waste ammunition in uninterrupted fire and risk burning out the barrel of the gun. To-morrow we fire shot guns from moving trucks at clay pigeons–the sport of kings eh? All this I realize can't interest you too much but I am forced to live it all my waking hours so I apologize for raving on.

   We also started "Jam Handy" today. This is shooting at planes in pursuit curves on a moving picture screen. Very much similar to some of novelty games now in most corner drug stores and hotels. This is fun too. We started a two weeks course in Aircraft Recognition here today. This is not fun. In fact I believe I will have to go nights of my own volition if I don't want to wash back if the work in the same subject I did in Sioux Falls is any criterion. More Code and Radio Mechanix and our first session in PT rounded out the tour of duty. PT is not long here, but an Eager Beaver shavetail gives it and it is rugged what there is of it. Of course being away from it for a full month didn't help much either. It is a good thing they don't drag it out for in this heat I'm sure most of us would drop before they finished. Big treat today when after evening chow I got all clean linen issued. First clean we have been issued since night we arrived which is just a month and a day. I also got repaired shoes from supply this noon at chow time.

   Tonight, with all my free time, I sweated out a hair cut which I really needed and also purchased me some new laces at the PX for my G.I. shoes. This rounds out the day. Mail call netted a letter from Tess–and one from Bill Hughes still at Sioux Falls. For the past 2 Thursdays I have been going up to the pool expecting he and John had arrived. Bill is having his hands full with John who has been incommunicado with his wife for the past month. Kostishack wrote his wife and gave her hell and for once she didn't reply with love and kisses. When I was there I used to volunteer to mail his spleen letters and hold em til he cooled off. Or I'd razz him till he felt cheap. After all, his wife is pregnant and has only about 3 months to go. She worships him but it is hard to expect anyone to take indefinitely the stuff he is prone to hand out once in a while.

Well, guess I'd better run along now—even now feel a little guilty about above—I hope to heaven it doesn't happen but that is the way it looks to me—if only one could do something, but you might as well try to stop the wind and the rain.

Have to shower and shave and make up a nice clean bed—bedding came at opportune time for even beating didn't get out all the sand. Don't feel bad about Perry's, Mom —there's nothing wrong with you—you loveable bundle of Mother. I have the same stuff here. 1st time in the Army where I have felt that blood will be drawn—fellow in bunk over me insists on lounging in my bunk—have caught him twice now and next time I swear I'll tuck in my head and start swinging. Oh he weighs at least 180 and is a heavy well-built lad and I'll probably get my clock cleaned but by heaven he'll know he has been in a fight before I get through. The 1st time I was nice about it—yesterday I raised the roof and almost came to blows and next time that is what it will have to be. He is one of the dirtiest living individuals I have ever come in contact with in the Army and I won't have his stinking hide on my blankets.

Ah well, these little things—that is why we have wars—some people will never understand or respect the rights of other people. The only way you can talk to them is by hurting them physically or otherwise.

Well, absolutely must go now—goodness 3 pages (nope 6) won't have anything to say to-morrow.
Love, Frank

September 27th, Wednesday
Dear Mother, Harry and Mike,

Well, we fired the 50s again today. To-morrow we shoot skeet on Stationary Range. Laundry had to go in tonight - another chore. It is ever something. I can see I'm going to have trouble—too much Huba Huba in this tent.
Later

Have moved to dayroom now—should keep a better train of thought here. Biggest event of the day a letter from the Otts—strange that I should get an answer to what I wrote last night—no it was the night before. Herein, in registered letter of today's receipt, I finally did get Mrs. Ott's answer to polite yet poignant questions I put to them some time ago regarding both of them working and the football. God I hope they are not sorry—of course she makes it look very logical, sane and the only thing under the existing circumstances. Also she told me a couple things quite personal that I often suspected but never did quite believe I'd ever hear them admitted. I guess I'm too suspicious or what have you but I do hope she is correct.

I was very fortunate on the mail end today. This noon I got aforementioned letter at P.O. and then at mail call tonight I got a letter from Mother (Sunday edition) one from Norma P. and one from Ann. Also a couple copies of N.Y. Times Magazine section from Gramp.

Gosh your Sunday's sure sound good—Glad you are spending more of them together. From what Ann says Mary is due very shortly now—there should be lots of

Huba Huba around there when the event occurs. Say I did get stamps about a week ago–apologize for failing to mention it. It is hard for me and I'll bet you two can see it too–this long lapse of time between writing and reading. Sorry Folks–next post I promise (hope & pray at any rate) to get a little nearer home–at least a little further from the unbeaten wastelands of U.S.A.

Had two beers tonight with Dan Hamernik under theory that all work and no play is nicht so güt. I go so long without some type of relaxation and I find myself getting up more tired than I went to bed. We are rising at 4:45 these mornings. The morning schedule is fun but that afternoon is a pisser. I fell asleep in Code today. Sgt. Instructor didn't yell at me right off. He waited till he had put helmet on me (still sawing wood) and then thundered a bawling out (ass chewing, here) about "Didn't I know enough not to wear a helmet in class"–big joke–fraid I was a little to dazed and sleepy and startled to appreciate incident to its fullest but the rest of the class roared at me and so that left everyone in a good mood–me bewildered and class continued.

I fired 240 rounds this morning–lotsa fun bang bang and all that–shot guns tomorrow–hope I improve–it really doesn't much matter except to me personally. Your scores don't count for graduation as long as you have certain, the required, number of rounds fired on each range. The basis of this policy as I see it is that if they disqualified a man on a low score we all would be trying to disqualify also they figure that even a very poor shot should be an expert by the time he gets in all the shooting you get here.

Gosh fellows–it latens (I coin my own languages as I go along). I must off to bed. Didn't write the Otts–please explain to Mrs.–maybe won't be able to write them until Sunday–anticipate night classes in Aircraft Recognition this week and pay call will be Saturday night sooo, Be good.
Love, Frank

September 28th, Thursday
Dear Mother, Harry and Mike,
Pen is out of ink thusly the borrowed pencil. Shot skeet this morning and got worse instead of improving. I got my Gazette today with correct address–please relay this as I can see now I won't get a chance to write much beyond my letter to you folks each day. I also got registered notice for a package which I will get to-morrow–am all in pins and needles and won't be able to get it till to-morrow.

Not much of anything to report. We have next week here at the base. We continue Aircraft Rec. and our radio work and shoot at moving targets with 50 cal. machine guns and also shoot shotguns at more clay pigeons from the lack of moving targets.

The week after next we move to Datelan for a full week. There we take final phase checks and do our actual shooting from planes and more radio checks in the ships themselves. Datelan is about 60 miles away and a week from Sunday and a week from that Sunday are consumed in moving out and moving back in again. After Datelan we have only one more week here. I'll say that is good in more ways than one. I shall be glad to leave here. It will only have been 2 months, but that is plenty of *this place. It has been a real experience being here and to say the least it is healthy weather. Do you remember how I used to cough in the mornings at home? Used to blame it on cigarettes! I don't think I have coughed once here. The weather though is far too hot for me to concentrate on anything. When I'm physically limp my mind just doesn't seem to function as alertly as it would in a cooler climate.*

Little premature to talk about the next Post but I sure hope I get Westover Mass., for it is the closest one to home. This training is known as R.T.U. or Replacement Training Unit. It is actually only an advanced school in Gunnery and Radio Operation—all done in a practical way. I am a long way from a flying Radio Operator or Gunner. I don't know how long the training will be—it varies as I hear it according to what they need at the time. Latest news is that these units are terribly overcrowded. So that can mean anything. Also 40% of R.O.M.G.s who graduate from here are washed out at R.T.U. The Air Corps makes K.P.s out of them or grave diggers or what have you. At any rate I figure I'll be around into next year maybe well into it and should the climax in Europe manifest itself soon maybe they'll put me on a farm too.

Sooo, in three weeks I should be getting ready to ship again. I do hope I get everything O.K. here. Aircraft Rec. is the present worry. I plan to spend to-morrow's free morning in that department. That is after I get my package of course.

Well, I must run along, shower, shave and all that—maybe I can get a little sac time to-morrow too—we shall see. Be good, people.
Love, Frank

September 29th, 8:15 PM, Friday
Dear Mother, Harry and Mike,
Am very busy little boy as usual. If I had not received package today I'm quite sure I wouldn't be writing. But such a noble donation certainly is an exception and more than worthy of my utmost gratitude. It was indeed a dandy. The sox precisely what I asked for and shaving cream and blades most opportune. I cannot get blue blades or any Gillettes here and I can see I shall have to guard them against borrowers. I just about had run out of cream so what you sent will help indeed. Please thank Mrs. Keough for the candy—I'll try to write her Sunday. It vanished in about 10 minutes. I urged the boys for if I had kept it the footlocker—all food stuffs draw large quantities of little red ants. I still have some of the peanuts—am saving them for some beer some night. Fruit cake is dandy—have it stored in barracks bag and am hoping to wash it down with some milkshake when I get a little free time. Only thing wrong with the box was tooth powder which came open and Lyons was everywhere in the box but it harmed nothing for everything was well wrapped.

The tie was welcome as you can always use them. I still have a few I've never worn but every little addition helps. The Yardley's relieves me of guarding and budgeting what remains of other box. Profuse powdering after shower each night is an invaluable preventative against any heat rash or jock itch as the boys call it here. All in all it is a real pleasure to get a box from home—more so when you get it from people who know how to put em together. You indeed anticipated my needs and gosh thanks so much. Candy even bought at the PX is too soft by the time you get it outside to eat it to enjoy it at all but for some reason what Mrs. Keough sent was well intact but not for long. If I have forgotten anything let me say that the box came very well intact and I certainly enjoyed receiving it. Such a thing is a real event to me here.

A little explanation of my hurried attitude which I can see has reflected itself in this letter. This morning up at 5 AM and then we figured we were to have free morning but orderly room planned a lot of detail work–I myself dug a 1 ½ foot ditch around barracks. This is to keep ants from getting easy access to buildings. I did manage to get off long enough to get to P.O. Of course there was school this afternoon. I passed my Code check so will not have any night school in Code next week. I just really got out of school for right after chow I went to an Aircraft Rec. review. I am quite certain I will fail examination to-morrow. That will mean I'll have to go nights for that next week. The thing is hard for me and I am not alone so you can see my day has been well filled in a weird sort of way. Even if I should by luck pass the thing I'll go nights voluntarily for altho (sic) I won't wash back because of flunking 1st week quiz, they will wash me back a week if I don't make 2nd week quiz. That, I would like to avoid, if possible.

I just got Harry's letter today before chow–vacation sounds swell and I find pleasure in living just a bit of it with him in my mind's eye. He says he'd like a little Yuma heat. I feel I'm quite used to it now and believe me brother you don't know what you're talking about.

To-morrow means more shooting and classes in the afternoon. Must run along now to grab shower and shave before lights out so I can get my required shut eye.

Please relay my "thank yous"–do it myself as soon as I can sit down for a couple hours and write it out. I may not get to write to-morrow. Few things in town I must do–if we get paid tomorrow I'll be late getting into town. I'll try to write anyhow.

Thanks so much again people–must be off again.

Love, Frank

P.S. Finally received my ballot–another aye for F.D.R. as I see it. Huba Huba F.

THE DECISION

Present Day

Another story my mother would tell us about our father was when she had asked him when he had made the decision to become a medical doctor. His answer was, "When I was in the Army, in a tent, in the desert." As I typed the Yuma letters, I waited, rather impatiently, for the letter home telling his family of his decision. Thus far, no such revelation or decision had been included in his letters, yet here he was, in the Army, in a tent and in the desert. Like his family, I was meant to wait until he chose to reveal his intensions.

Timing is everything and I was actually typing the Yuma letters, which I usually did while I was traveling for work, when my work schedule brought me to Phoenix, Arizona. So close, yet so far. My colleague Kevin and I had to work a trade show, and had very limited free time. Though we were quite busy, I could not ignore the tug I felt to drive the three hours to Yuma, to visit the still active base where my father had been stationed. We discussed it, and there was a pocket of time between when we closed the show early one night and opened later the following morning. We also discussed renting a car, or taking a bus, but throughout these discussions, Kevin in no way indicated that he would join me. He was certainly helpful in coming up with alternative plans to accomplish the trip, but was not too keen on a six-hour round trip drive in the desert, which he made perfectly, albeit gently, clear.

Kevin was not only my work colleague, but my friend, and the husband of one of my best friends. He knew all about the letters and what I was doing, and he supported me with enthusiasm each time I'd enter another dimension of discovery. Though supportive, he was also pragmatic, and a realist. Who in their right mind would purposely drive six hours to visit a base we may or may not be able to get into? At breakfast the morning after the brainstorming session, I had pretty much decided that I was not going to go because I did not want to go by myself, coupled with the fact that I'd had no luck with my calls or emails attempting to get authorization to visit. Since the base was currently an active U.S. Marine Corps base, I needed a sponsor to get in. Without a sponsor, and without a travel companion, I was resigned to not going and to trying to get back another time. That's when Kevin said that he would go with me. Oh joy, oh bliss, as my father would say.

I never asked if Lucy had anything to do with his change of heart, I was just grateful that he was going to join me, so we ordered our rental car and headed to the trade show booth. After the show closed, we got the car and got on the road. Three hours on any road is long and arduous at best, but on a straight road across the desert, those three hours were painful. It was 110 degrees and we hadn't even thought to bring any water with us. There was literally nothing out there but road and desert. We were tired and hungry, but we pressed on without incident until close to the end of hour number three.

Still a ways out from Yuma, Kevin calmly mentioned that we should start looking for a gas station. Not sensing any urgency in his nonchalant comment, we then traveled about 5 more miles before we saw a sign that there was a gas station coming up in ten miles. That's when I inquired as to how much gas we had, and Kevin sheepishly commented that he hoped we'd make it the 10 miles. Panic set in. Here we were in the middle of nowhere, with no water, spotty cell service, the sun was setting so it was getting darker, and we were about to run out of gas. I started taking several deep breaths to help me remain calm. We drove the next ten miles in complete silence and most likely on fumes.

Once we'd coasted into the gas station and filled the tank, and all anxiety was relieved, we continued on and arrived at the base around 5:30 p.m. The office where the individual to whom I would need to speak had closed at 5 p.m. I explained to the Marine at the gate that we were from New York, and had just driven three hours to get there, and showed him one of the Yuma letters, with its unique YAAF letterhead of a coyote with a cap and a machine gun, dated September 1944. The Marine looked at it with so much reverence, Kevin and I both felt it. He asked us to wait in the parking area outside the fenced-in base and went to speak with some other Marines. After about fifteen minutes, he returned with an expression of defeat on his face. He was unable to reach anyone and since we did not have a sponsor, he could not let us in. Could we come back tomorrow? Of course, we could not. We thanked him and took photos outside the base as proof of our unsuccessful mission, grabbed a bite, and headed back to Phoenix, this time with a full tank of gas.

YUMA, ARIZONA - PART 2

1944

October 1st, Sunday

Dear Mother, Harry and Mike,

I missed yesterday - please forgive. I completed another week reasonably success-fully. The extra time I spent in Aircraft Rec. paid dividends indeed, if I hadn't spent it I dislike to think of the consequences. I did manage to pass 6th hour examination with an 82, also made Code and another 100 in Tactical Procedure so I am not required to make any night school formations thank heavens. In spite of this I intend to go to Air-craft Rec. evenings next week for I know full well that I need the extra time. Yesterday morning we shot 50 rounds from shotguns mounted on trucks moving at 25-35 miles per hour. The targets were fixed - it was lots of fun and went far too rapidly. Next week we spend 3 mornings there shooting at clay pigeons, which I can see will be fun but not too easy for my marksmanship capabilities. So much for school.

Was glad when I didn't make K.P. team yesterday. We were paid during noon hour and right after chow last night I went into town, had nothing special to do but it is a real relief to get away from the Post for a few hours anyway. Had a few beers, danced at U.S.O. for a couple hours, had a bit to eat and then made the midnight movie which proved to be hardly worth sitting through. While drinking beer I met the fellow I wrote to you about who is in the Dental Clinic - Permanent Party. He is a darn nice chap name is Tommy Kilcoyne as I understand it. He is leaving for home next Tuesday on a 23 day furlough. Too bad only permanent party gets the furlough breaks - at any rate he took Mom's name and address and said he'd stop by and say Hello to you for me. I know you'll treat him nicely - he is a good egg - little cocky but he was dandy about digging up information for us last night - Harry - if he comes when you're around treat him to a drink if you have the booze to spare - you know - have one for me. He told me last night of quite a few casualties among fellows I know - mostly older than myself - one that struck me closest was Loyal Bogart's death - did you fellows know? There is really a crime when you sacrifice manhood of his caliber.

Of course after midnight show I didn't get back to Post till 3 AM or a little after. Al Daher woke me up this morning at 7:10. It is darn white of him to bother. He is one of those sleeping alarm clocks - he gets up in plenty of time and then tramps from his squadron to mine, wakes me, waits till I dress and wash and then we go to church together - made Communion this morning. Then we went to the Snack Bar for breakfast. Al Harrison joined us there and we had a good bull session on school etc. Just to linger over coffee and to go and come as you see fit gives me untold pleasure on these free Sundays. After that we went to PX where I got some cigarettes and met some more of the lads just arrived from Sioux Falls. More Gaff - we are much worse than your Bridge Club we G.I.s but is almost like going home again to see these lads you lived with some months.

This afternoon, Daher, Hamernik and I plan to go to the Chapel where they play recorded classics for an hour or hour and a half. It is air conditioned, quiet and comfortable not to say uncrowded so we shall take our writing and do it there this afternoon.

I have about 6 or 7 letters to write this afternoon and hope to get a little sewing in this evening. So you can see we keep on the go even on Sunday but on Sunday it is a pleasure. The limitations on your activities during the week serve mainly to make Sunday even better. Dan and Al, I believe, plan on going to show this afternoon but I have too much writing to do and I must get it out of the way. I know that beyond your letter each day I won't be able to write much more since I plan on making classes at night. Then too next week I go to Datelan (week after next that is) and I have no idea of what the mail situation will be. I expect it to be about same set up as Greensboro range and I don't know whether or not I'll be able to do much writing from there. So please don't get too disgusted if you don't hear too often from me in the next two weeks, not as regularly as usual that is. You know I'll write when I can and don't you dare let up on your end - pretty selfish proposition isn't it?

Well, I have Keoughs, Otts, Beals, and Gramp to write as well as Bill Hughes in Sioux Falls and little Ann so I'd better get a going or I'll never finish today. Heard from Gramp and Beals yesterday with the Gazette. No letter from youse but expect a couple today. Be good, people -
Lotsa Love and my special Sunday Blessing,
Francis George

October 2nd, Monday

Dear Mother, Harry and Mike,

Huba Huba again. I received three letters today - 2 of Mother's and one of Harry's. Harry's was much better and let me tell you that those airmails are sure welcome. I am writing in the dayroom. Supposed to be Fire Guard from 9 till 10 PM tonight - am goofing off - Let us pray no fire occurs. Needless to say I did not accomplish the writing I intended to yesterday - Got off only 3 - will have to try to work a couple extra in to-morrow if possible. I had no idea my letters met with Thompson's approval - needless to say they are not monuments of composition and I find it very hard to find much to be interesting about. Then too, by the time you write the same thing over a couple times, you become disgusted with the insignificant event you're embellishing and the search for new subject exhausts itself rapidly. I know that I often write you fellows merely a chronicle of events which cannot help but bore you but I feel you understand and the main point is to let you know that all is well and that I'm bitching in the same old way.

I sort of suspected that Gramp would have this one and that read the letters - you know that anything I write is more tangible news of the 450 1/2 Ninth Streeters than they have ever had of us even though they were only a block away - it is more than they merit! However my devotion for Gramp is something built of admiration and perhaps something left to me by my father - his personal concern when Harry was not working was something new I found in him. To Gramp alone do I write - If the others bask in reflected admiration it is from their own ego - certainly is not intended for them. I feel Gramp has always admired you to a great extent Mom - I always think of how he wiped up the kitchen floor for you - and I always get a kick out of the remarks of the fellows when I show them his letters bragging a little about his clear hand at his late stage in life. Any direct display of my admiration we know would be taken wrong and misconstrued so I would refrain from it as much as possible. Enuf of this!

Today we did more shooting - 400 rounds and Harroola it's a cal. 50 not .60! Made 5th in my flight. We arrived late enough to miss PT I had chow and showered and shaved and went over to see Tom Kilcoyne (spoken of yesterday). Didn't get to talk to him much but he says he'll call you fellows at least - he leaves to-morrow noon. Didn't get to spend much time with him as he was busier than expected. Sooo here I am right now. Can't think of much new - we will be shooting all afternoons this week - shot guns one day and machine guns the next. We will be issued flying suits this week in preparation for our trip to Datelan next Sunday. Next week will be crucial one but up to this point I have refused to worry much about it. If I don't make it one week I will in the next one or two I figure, so that is that. Am certain we won't get passes next Saturday night.

Say - I'm not too keen about the war news of late - what say you - looks like the stalemate that the Germans are playing for. If a decisive break is not made within the next two or three weeks I fear at least another 6 months before they can clear out the rats.

Glad that Jerry O'H. manages to stay on - he must be having some time of it. He has a good thing - not a lot of responsibility and gunners don't work hard for long as I see it from here. One thing I get a kick out of is the way other countries grade Air Crew members and train them. Take the Japs for instance - a Jap gunner gets about 10 months training and yet Yank Gunners are reputed best in the war. Also the British - pilots fly as Sergeants and about the only commissioned officer on a British Bomber is the Radio Operator. The standards for British R.O.s are a good deal below the ones we have been required to meet too.

Come to think of it I have 2 Gazettes I haven't read as yet so guess I'll beat it up to the tent area - make sure all is not in flames and then undress - read the Daily Blot & Blur in the latrine and by that time it should be about right to wake up my relief and hit the sac myself. So I shall say the usual Be Good.

Lovey Dovey,

Francis George

October 3rd, Tuesday

Dear Mother, Harry and Mike,

    I am well settled on my bunk tonight with a little extra time so I will try to answer to better satisfaction the 3 letters I got yesterday. Didn't have them with me when I wrote when I was supposed to be on Fire Guard last night.

    Oh, we have no radio, but there are a couple near us. Probably just as well in a way for the other radios bother us plenty when we are trying to get some sleep here at night. Funny you're speaking of Ethel Smith. Just to see and hear her again is the reason Al Daher and I saw "Bathing Beauty" again on my last night in Sioux Falls. One thing they do have is a station in Yuma which devotes most of its broadcasting time to the Gunners. At almost any moment of the day if you can take time to listen you can hear the best recordings from Deep Purple up to Bing's and Frankie's latest. Is Fred Waring off the air? Boy will I ever miss him.

    I was sure you'd agree with any transfer. Believe I will wait till next Post before I investigate too much. If I am sent where I hope to be sent, Westover Mass., I shall be near Boston and should be able to get any available information much more rapidly there.

    Don't get me wrong about the Town of Yuma. Some guys can't find anything to do but little Francis George has a hell of a good time. When they hear me say that here right away I get that disgusted look and then they ask me where I'm from as though I were a Hick. But for a good time in the Army I don't require much. If a fellow perseveres he can get hold of a fairly decent (looking) doll at the U.S.O. but you have to best the hordes of competition. I don't like the drinks too much but I do eat a bit–enjoy having it brought to me and like the best places. My passes here are spent in conversation and healthy argument over beer or coffee and something to eat. I enjoy people and personalities and without a lot of Helling I manage to enjoy to a great extent any free time I manage to get. Also Yuma is a different town than when Don was here. Formerly there were camps, infantry–tank & artillery which numbered over 200,000 men trained out here! Now there is only the Airfield here.

    One thing I want. Please send with least possible delay the bag I took to and shipped home from Ft. Dix. I will need it when I ship out of here as one I have is almost shot. If it is not there or Perry's have it please let me know at earliest possible opportunity. I will have extra shirts and things that I absolutely don't want to put in barracks bag this time.

    Going to try to get some sleep now so be good, guys.

Love, Frank

October 6th, Friday

Dear Mother, Harry and Mike,

    I am a very bad boy! Just a note day before yesterday and none yesterday. As per usual I have been on the go but I'll confess that last night I missed for I wanted to see "Kismet" with Ronald Coleman. It was the first time since I started school–for the very reason that it is about all you can do to get in and make bed check. First a line starts at 6 PM to get tickets–½ hour before show they start to sell tickets–then you line up and wait for doors to open. It has to be something I exceptionally want to see for this waiting in line is just not the thing for me. I do enough of it because I have to. The show was good entertainment but not the exceptional thing I expect when I go to see Coleman. It is unusual, spectacular and achieved its main point in a G.I.s camp of taking you completely away for a couple hours. Beyond that I can't say so much for it–Marlene is too old for her part say I.

Huba, Huba–I passed my Air Craft Recognition! That was also a cause for a lot of celebration last night. The rumor goes that 40-60 will be washed back a week because of it–Glad I have it out of the way here. In the next few weeks we all expect changes in the course here. Air Craft Rec. will be discontinued and 2 additional weeks will be added–2 weeks of what–I don't know. Don't know whether to be glad or sad about it but I don't think I'll be too sorry to miss it. This change will not affect us in any way as I hear it. Also I believe that that is the reason Hughes and Kostishack are not here from Sioux Falls. They both washed back just long enough to be taken by an extra 4 to 6 weeks added there. I honestly don't think they did it intentionally because they were mourning pretty badly when I left and Hughes in particular is very anxious to get to gunnery.

How are you guys doing in the World Series? Heard part of the first game and liked it but yesterday's game was not so good, although it was a good game as far as baseball is concerned.

Later

Started this letter after noon chow. We were called out to go to the range–did a few policing details there, no firing–listened to a great 2-6 game by the Browns on a radio the Lieut. brought and at present am back in the sack–must have 1 ½ hours till PT–Easy day today!

One of the main reasons I have been brief of late is that I have had a rather annoying head cold. Last Sunday night it turned cool–way cool and has kept that way–only at night of course. It has still been hotter during the day than the weather we get at home. Unwarned of course I slept with only my sheet on and awoke with sore throat and the sniffles. It developed into the usual cold which in the heat of the day proved a hell of a discomfort more than anything else. Didn't lose the old taster at any point and ate well but I did try to get to the sac as early as possible each night. Took the usual aspirin and Baking Soda–Vick's inhaler–Vick's up the nose and kept bowels regular. Do I sound like an old woman? Well, in the Army if you don't take care of yours truly no one else will. Also a cold next week would hinder if not disqualify me from flying and I didn't want that. Consequently it is about gone now. Thank goodness. Colds are difficult to shake in hot weather so I feel quite fortunate. Last night I got me some Sulfadiazine pills–same kind which I felt helped us so much in Greensboro. Al Daher had some he had gotten in the hospital. Incidentally yee old time of colds must be about present at the Falls and it might be a good idea if you fellows took a couple of the abovementioned pills now and then.

I just read the schedule for Sunday. We rise at 4 AM in preparation for going to Datelan. I feel quite sure I'll be able to write you fellows each day so please do the same. Don't think I'll get your letters till I get back a week from Sunday but you never can tell–they may get em to us. We go out in trucks or rather buses and take only minimum of G.I. issue and flying suits which we will be issued to-morrow. Leather jackets, pants and boots–sheepskin lined for it gets cold in those high altitudes so they tell me.

As far as gunnery is concerned we have only air to air firing–air to ground and camera missions remaining to complete. Our whole squadron–orderly room personnel and all move to Datelan with us next week. We will do a good deal of flying at Datelan and our last week as I understand it should be all flying.

Even for the day off I don't seem to have much news–pretty routine–as long as it stays that way I'll have no worry so be good, people.

Lotsa love, Frank

October 7th, 6:30 PM, Saturday

Dear Mother, Harry and Mike,

Just back from chow and will have to stop this letter soon for I have a formation to meet at 7 o'clock. I was foolish not to take paper to the range with me this afternoon for I had time to write as it was we set some traps for the boys shot very little and literally sweated out the whole afternoon.

Tonight's session will be in regard to to-morrow's trip to Datelan. It is 60 miles away and we go in buses. Have to get up at 4 in the morning to get ready and eat for an early start. They have Mass up there for us so I shall be able to make it there I believe. We drew flying clothes this noon. If anything looks out of place here it is their leather pants and jackets and boots sheepskin lined. We carry them about in all the heat and altho (sic) they seem cumbersome and a great bother here, it really gets cold when you get up there so I believe we shall be glad of them.

Last letters from home, one this afternoon–are full of Gramp's illness. I feel very badly about it but it is the same old story. When you're so far away much action seems futile. Harry says don't come home–little does he know that I couldn't get a release even an emergency furlough on anything happening to Gramp. It has to be immediate family or someone who lived with you in civilian life. I could probably manage it by talking fast but of course the thing is that I can't come and go even with the Army's O.K. for peanuts. If you want me home say so. I just this minute talked with a lad who has had 2 emergency furloughs–he says they don't go on your record as furlough time and that I could get one on account of Gramp. How true the dope is on this field remains to be seen so I'll leave it up to you. In my eyes the money is the big thing. They would have to drag me back here from Datelan but that could be easily done. Mother knows what has to be done at that end with the Red Cross and *that adequate and complete steps must be taken to avoid confusing the whole works. If, by the time this reaches you Gramp is still alive but does not look like he will recover and if by some strange shake up of emotion Gramp should want to see me, which would be in contradiction to any sense of values I have ever possessed, and if it seems feasible to you people—take action at home or rather have Marge do it and for my part I shall come scurrying home as fast as the rails will carry me. I suppose it is weak to leave it up to you fellows but I'm not there and in any case Haroola will have to act for me.*

I have to hurry off now. Expect to be able to do a better job of writing next week. Nothing new here except moving to-morrow—lots of confusion—so, be good.
Love, Frank

October 8th, Sunday, First from Datelan

Dear Mother, Harry and Mike,

Up at 4 AM this morning, a hurried breakfast and packing and rushing about and on a truck starting out at 5:45 this morning. We arrived at about 9:30 and got off our truck only to have squadron which had been out here last week immediately take our places for the return trip.

As I see it from purely the Post stand point this place would be more agreeable to me than Yuma itself. It has the advantage of being small. The permanent party consists of about 240 men and then a new squadron of gunners comes out every week—about 400 men. So we are definitely in the majority here. We have to wait for no one but ourselves in chow, at the movies and we have a swimming pool here the same size as the one at Yuma but here we are the only ones to use it. The permanent party live with their wives in a trailer camp here. The trailers are owned and equipped by the Army. There are quite a few women and children here. Of course the women are all married and there is no place for we Gunners to hide from indignant husbands in those trailers, besides most of the women are pregnant but to me it is good to see again the process of almost normal life still holding very much its own. Under strained circumstances to be sure but the meetings of married couples here with their children and baby carriages—men in fatigues and women in house dresses leaves you with a slightly nostalgic feeling but definitely leaves you more a human being.

The mess is very good here, served in the cleanest mess hall I have ever been in. The Officers and civilians eat there too so it has to be good and they don't dare murder good food and then throw it at you. As yet, of course, I have no idea as to what our program will be here. Radio and Gunnery final phase checks to be sure but how and when I don't know as yet. The K.P.s here are drawn from the pool at Yuma and unless we screw up quite badly I don't believe we should stand any of that.

Today, after we arrived, has been an essentially easy one for me. Since I lost sleep in the morning I took advantage of the opportunity here this morning to catch up on some of it. Have done a lot of lying around.

Most inopportune and typically Army was the formation at 7 PM last night. They took that particular time to give us six morality lectures and review the Articles of War—Lectures by Medics, Chaplain and Sqd. C.O. accompanied by movies we have all seen at least 4 times already. But it is an Army regulation so sweat it out we did.

For the first time last night I saw and listened to remarks made by our Sqd. C.O. He's a 1st Looy and carries my blessing and admiration with him if that means anything. He is young but darn capable and above all likeable. He said last night that regulations required that 3 men lecture to us about sex morality and venereal diseases—he said it always happens in the Army—the Company C.O. jokes about it—the Chaplain tells you not to and the Medics tell you how!

He outlined his policy of a Commanding Officer namely that if you leave good men alone they will come around all right, with better morale and essentially better men. He had the past 4 weeks of "laissez faire" to substantiate him and I know you have not heard me mention him before for I had not seen him. I don't even know his name now. He is a good egg, comes from the Infantry and the type you'd be proud to follow. He is the only example of this type of Officer that I have come in contact with on this field and his type is rare in my experience with the Air Corps. As a rule A.C. administrative officer smell to high heaven when it comes to commanding efficiently and still being a man. Of course my admiration was considerably augmented when I saw him receiving at the Alter Rail at Mass this afternoon Huba Huba—he must be Irish—He's from south Chicago at any rate.

The trip out here was essentially uneventful. At one point the whole convoy stopped while we all went out to water the desert lilies. A couple cars went by but we stood our ground and kept watering. In Dad's old story the little duck going Quack Quack would have had a May frolic about that time. Also the whole convoy more or less surprised 2 rather bewildered young women. At the side of the road near a culvert was parked a large Oldsmobile and the 2 gals from it were at one side of the road doing what we had just completed a few miles back on the side of the road, such Hubas you never heard and 2 very astonished gals had very red FACES. You see nothing ever happens on these wild barren stretches of desert—the little ladies normally would have been fully correct in assuming that no one would pass for passing a car out here is the exception rather than the rule. How were they to know Sqd. #2 was on the move much less that we would sweep down from the mountains at 50 miles per 400 strong and surprise them literally with their pants down.

Well, I guess I'll close here—this lazy life is getting me, so with my special Sunday Blessing I'll say, be good.
Lotsa Love, Frank

October 9th, 6:30 PM, Monday, 2nd from Datelan

Dear Mother, Harry and Mike,

Ahoy from Datelan Arizona. The duty day is at an end—just finished chow. Expect a mail call in a few minutes so hope to get something to answer before I close this.

Today was essentially uneventful.

Later

Went to sweat out mail call but it seems that mail truck broke down or some such B.S. so we will probably get it in the morning. As I was saying—today meant just ground school for us mainly review with the subjects upon which we will be tested here. It was rather boring and since I find it so hot here and the air conditioning so limited I must confess that I was prone to doze now and then.

To-morrow morning we fly at least 4 hours. We will get camera missions (shooting at actual pursuit ships with film instead of ammunition) or shooting live ammunition at targets towed by B-26s or just a high altitude mission. We don't know what it will be until 20 minutes before flight when we are briefed.

This place is quite barren for almost anything but I find after a couple bottles of beer that they take the trouble to really cool it. It was really good, believe me. Well folksies, since I am to be up at 4 AM on the morrow altho (sic) it is not yet 8 bells I think I shall take me a shower and shave and get me to bed. This four o'clock stuff is a lot of malarkey—wouldn't mind it if it were really necessary but we won't get in the air till after 8—just lay around class rooms or the flight apron and wait till the Fortresses arrive from Yuma. So I'll ring off. Be good, people.

Love, Frank

P.S. Mail just came in—Sat 5, 6, 7th letters. Jolly good to hear from home as usual. Have been quite down about Gramp but am exceedingly pleased that things look not too bad. I shall write him to-morrow—but when he was so bad I didn't know what to do—or do you realize how hard it is—not just to keep a letter going but when a man is very ill I wouldn't know what to say—I'll get one off to-morrow or else. Now I must clean up and sleep!

More love, Frank

October 11th, Wednesday, 3rd from Datelan

Dear Mother, Harry and Mike,

I took Mother's suggestion and let the rest go and wrote to Gramp last night. Six pages and I hope he gets some pleasure out of it and I do hope he improves rapidly. I received letter from Harry today in which he says nothing of Gramps so I assumed the no news is good news. Naturally if things had taken any radical turn he would have told me. I also got a letter from Fran tonight. God Bless those people on 440 they just don't forget a fellow. I owe them letters—don't know when I'll get to catch up—one is all I can get out from here in an evening. We fly again to-morrow—up at 4:00 AM and when you have to be on the ball, as you must in the air, sleep becomes even a more prime requisite than it would be normally.

In last night's letter to Gramp I went into detail about our 4 hour mission of Tuesday. I hoped he might get some pleasure from it but I know you fellows are a little better informed on those things so I'll not go into a lot of detail about them with you.

When we get up at 4 we are on the flight line at 5 or 5:15 and the sun is just coming up over this corner of nowhere and nothing. It is beautiful to see—even saw some natural mirages yesterday. As the sun rises you start to get uncomfortable for you are sitting on the apron sweating out a B-17 from Yuma in a leather sheepskin lined flying suit. You have a thousand things to do before you fly such as drawing parachute harnesses and chute and guns and ammunition. We were briefed by both Radio & Gunnery instructors and taken over what we were responsible for. Not much really and yet 9 students on the ship had to repeat the same things and it takes time particularly when at high altitudes you're on oxygen.

To me it was fun altho (sic) I dare say I can see why some of the fellows were bored already. We flew 2 hours high altitude and 2 hours low yesterday. I hope we fly a 4 hour high one to-morrow for I'd like to get those out of the way. It is uncomfortable flying on oxygen—more bother than physical discomfort. We shot film at attacking Bell King Cobras at high altitude yesterday and we fired live ammunition at a sleeve target towed by a B-26 at low altitude. Times when we weren't shooting we practiced on interphone, tuned up transmitters and contacted other 17s in the group with blinkers.

Today was quite boring. The other half of the squadron flew today so we drew details and some classes. We also saw the developed films we shot yesterday. This afternoon after classes I took off with Dan Hamernik for a swim in the pool. We then casually trotted over for chow and ate slowly chewing the fat vigorously. It constituted a good time for me. At first we had to go to chow in formation but they seem to have given that up now and we have been going as we will. Makes you feel almost human again.

To-morrow afternoon we start a series of phase checks—Sighting, Weapons and Air Craft Recognition. Hope to heaven I get them all but I'll be darned if I'm worrying about it. If I don't make em so go it—I'll get another chance but I don't really want to stay around this neck of the woods any longer than is absolutely necessary. Sooo here's hopin.

We will return to Yuma Sunday and then providing all checks have been passed we have only a week of flying and radio operating ahead of us—in other words two weeks from today by the Grace of God I should be on a rattler for somewhere away from Arizona—Huba Huba.

Well, must buzz off now—shave and sleep so, be good.

Love, Frank

October 12th, Thursday, 4th from Datelan

Dear Mother, Harry and Mike,

Got 2 letters one from each of you this evening which made the day complete. This will probably be a shortie for I am very tired and have had a full day and now have *little time to finish this. Flew 2 hours low altitude camera mission this morning. I was really beaten when I came down–must have been too much activity on oxygen at high alt. Don't ever believe that crap about the glamour of the Air Corps–its hard work and I for one am glad of it–makes me feel less like a boy scout and more like a man.*

This evening a lecture was scheduled and given. It was supposed to be orientation– the C.O. started to give a lecture on "The British–Our Allies." This sort of thing may have gone over good in the last war's Army but people, these guys, 80% of em, are so far better informed than their officers–it's a laugh. It ended up a joke–the C.O. is still best I've ever known but we knew, and he knew, that he was out of his class. He had no sooner opened his mouth than he was bombarded with facts and questions that absolutely floored him. But he's a sharp cookie and acquitted himself fairly well. Bouquets to him.

Well, 2 more days here. Took & passed phase checks in Sighting & Weapons today. Do hope I make Air Craft Rec. to-morrow. We took these checks after noon chow–after being up since 4 AM and flying. I was tired and had a splitting headache but got by fine. I laugh about being so completely bushed but it is to be expected. Somehow I am last man on my crew's roster so it fell to me & 2 other fellows to police plane of brass & links after we fired at high alt. today. That is too much work when you're on oxygen and so I am feeling it as we all are. It is still an experience and I find I enjoy it. I don't wish to pat myself or my job on the back and please don't talk this around but according to the way we figure here from what we've had and what we know is yet to come the old Radio Operator is the most highly trained man in the plane second only to Pilot & Co-pilot. A damn good operator is a rare thing but I'm learning and sure hope I make the grade and next two Posts. It would surprise you to see the way fellows fall apart emotionally when they're on O2. It is psychological of course, but it is certainly something to be reckoned with. A lot of the fellows by now dislike, even hate flying, as R.O. It is plenty rough in spots but I take pride in what I have been able to learn and believe me what I do will be the best in me.

Of course we will get more radio checks in Yuma before we leave but if I keep on the ball I shouldn't have much trouble. The meals today have been splendid–you feel you must be doing your best for a lot of men do minimal and monotonous jobs to keep you and your crew in the air. To my mind the most credit for these bomb- ing raids really belongs to the conscientious men competent Mechanics on the ground. They don't get much credit but in their hands is the balance–they make or break you.

Still no news of Gramp which indeed is good news.

I must write the Beals but as ever youse come first–that is enuf said. Have not heard from the Otts–probably letter was lost like others ???–if it's got green foldable in it–you can bet I'll be watching for it.

Well, I must hurry along now. Still have shower and shave to take care of and get to bed. Kinda dished but with your letters my morale couldn't be better.
Lotsa love, Frank

October 13th, Friday, 5th from Datelan

Dear Mother, Harry and Mike,

I am trying to get this done early today. Had Aircraft Rec.–think I passed–will know for sure to-morrow also had a blinker check in Code. If I have these behind me I have only Radio and Code at Yuma next week. I'd like to finish this line for "Until we Meet Again" is on at the theatre this evening and I'd like to take it in.

We fly again to-morrow morning. Today I saw camera shooting movies that I took while shooting at King Cobras yesterday. They were not too good but at least I got a grade on them. Some fellows or rather the majority of our crew could not get any grades at all off their film so I was fortunate there.

Don't know, as usual, just what we will have to do in the Air to-morrow but expect preventive maintenance at high altitude. This entails fieldstripping a .50 cal with oxygen mask & gloves on at about 20 thousand feet so it should not be too bad. I did this same stripping in check yesterday in less than 3 minutes so I should not have too much trouble altho (sic) the high altitude has funny effects on all of us.

Right now I am supposed to be at PT but I suspect they will never miss me. I want to get a shower and shave before chow so that I can get in line for the show early. To-morrow is our last day here and early Sunday morning we go back to Yuma. Our last week–Huba Huba! Of course we will be flying all next week too but I'm glad I am looking back on most of the course instead of forward to it as I did three weeks ago. Oh Yuma has not been so bad but you tire of it reasonably quickly for there is little to see, little change in anything and the old yearn to get on the move gets you sooner here than in most places. It is a good thing you are kept busy for much spare time would start you feeling discontent and looking longingly at the old rattler as it changes through each day. Well, I'm going to have to scurry if I expect to make chow and that show so, be good people.
Lotsa love, Frank

October 14th, 1:20 PM, Saturday, Last from Datelan

Dear Mother, Harry and Mike,

Am not long out of the air–just finished lamb and sweet potato dinner. Missions were not at all strenuous this morning. We had a Preventive Maintenance High Altitude (fieldstripping machine gun at 20,000 feet) flight and then we went right down to the ground–not higher than 300 feet and shot the guns at stationary targets in the desert. It really is a bumpy ride when you are that low and we had 2 or 3 fellows get sick but things worked out fine otherwise. Our plane was about the 8th one in here from Yuma this morning and we were first ship in the air and the first one down. We finished all our work in the air about an hour and a half early but had to stay up for not only are we required to have a certain number of hours in the air but also co-pilots train here and have to have so much stick time. So we got in a little sac time on the plane believe it or not.

Tonight the Sqd. has a beer party in the mess hall–I just hope they have plenty of beer. I know that is almost too much to want but right now I could guzzle a barrel by myself. Don't imagine I'll get to bed early tonight and then too I have to arise early in the morning–turn in bedding and get packed and ready to return to Yuma.

My pen keeps running out up here–haven't had a chance to fill it well. I was almost heart sick this morning–thought someone had swiped it but found it later in the Suntans I had worn to the show last night. Habit and precaution have dictated that I always carry it with me and when I changed last night to go to the show I put it in my shirt without realizing it. Gosh what little you carry with you gets to be part of you in the Army. My watch is very much on the blink–I attribute it to warm dry climate and changes of altitude–many of the fellows have found that theirs are on the fritz too. Sooo expect it home one of these fine days when I can get it packed and sent properly. I intend keeping it until I am issued a G.I. watch which I should get within the next three weeks–either here or at R.T.U. (next station). The watch is not completely useless for in a pinch it keeps good time for 5-6 hours at a stretch but beyond that it is no go.

We are fortunate in that we have 2 free periods this afternoon. We are just hoping that they don't find some detail for us to do. All we have this afternoon is Code and Radio Mechanix.

And so I am just about ready to leave Yuma–not so much the place itself for like most of the Army I have not actively or in any other wise disliked it but I am in favor of the changes as they come. My attitude is that unless I can be at home I would just as soon keep on the move–seeing new places and learning new things is the substance of the real kick I get out of Army life.

Please say a little prayer that I get Westover Field–since I've been in the Army I have not wanted to bother God with my little wants but I sure hope he sees fit to have me sent to Mass.

So much for hopes–there are plenty of wild rumors floating around here these days but from some of the fellows who I knew at S.F. and who graduated in the past 3-4 weeks I received careful instructions not to believe any of this malarkey so I'm trying to remain oblivious to it all.

Didn't receive anything from you guys yesterday altho (sic) I did get a letter from Ann. She seems quite het up about her job and getting quite a kick out of it. I guess Mary is due any time now and they are worried for fear Joseph will not finish this semester at Clarkson. I guess he is due to receive his "Greetings" soon now.

Well, I guess that is about all the dirt from Datelan, Arizona. Am quite sure I won't get to write you again till to-morrow afternoon some time. We will have to go through the old settling routine again. Honest I can move now at the drop of a hat– you get so it comes as natural as rolling over in bed. Hope yee old bag arrives soon

as I will be wanting to get all my clean things ready for the next long trip. Please be good, people and I'll be drinking of you tonight at the beer party.
Love, Frank

October 15th, Sunday

Dear Harry,

This will probably be the last letter I'll write to the office on this subject. Huba Huba—the time for action is near at hand. Leave us not get too jubilant for a good swift kick in the emotional pants may be the only issue but a hope such as I have now is one I have never even had the opportunity of nourishing previously.

To the business at hand—I will know—if I graduate—next Sunday afternoon what the verdict is. In any event I shall let you know by night letter, which you should have a week from to-morrow morning—at the office of course. Should I be shipping to home (gosh that sounds good) we more than likely won't start till Tuesday or Wednesday. On the way at at least 2 intervals I will try to let you know of my progress by succeeding night letters. This is in the way of a safety precaution in case something inadvertent should occur. You will be the only one at my destination to know that I'm on the way so I needn't remind you that should I not turn up in a reasonable time you will have to take steps to trace what the hell bar in what city I'm delayed in.

I will let you know if I need money—your speedy action is seeing that I get it as soon as is humanly possible will aid immeasurably. Telegraph it and unless I state otherwise send it to Flexible Gunnery Pool, YAAF, Yuma, Arizona—Name & Serial No. I hope I won't need it but I can't find out how the hell we will be paid upon leaving here. I do know that what we will get will be only a fraction of what is due us.

You should get this by Friday morning and if for any reason you want to let me know anything, an Airmail should get to me before I ship out.

From today's letter received I'm very grateful about bag being on the way. Just one more item I would leave to your own sound judgment. If I am coming home as you should be informed of a week from to-morrow I want you to do precisely as you see fit about telling Mother. I would in a way like to completely surprise her but if you feel that she would get more pleasure out of anticipating my coming or if you think she would be hurt about our being in cahoots or if perhaps you think that she might want to make any arrangements about her time (Bridge Club, etc.) I want you to use your old noodle. My reticence in my one and onlys regard has been that I don't want her disappointed. So if for any good reason you cannot or do not want to hold it—after you are sure I'm on my way—do just what you think is right about telling her. I have written Mother that I wouldn't tell her if I could get home—I'd just appear so I think she'll understand but I am not there—I'd very much like the surprise idea but this is not just my Delay en route—it's ours—all three of us. May God grant it to us—I have tried so hard not to let you know but I do so want to be home for a while again.

Hope I am not leaving you in a dilemma. You're my rock of Gibraltar and I know that whatever you decide will be perfectly O.K. Here's hopin any how
Love, Frank

October 15th, 5:20 PM, Sunday; Back at Yuma
Dear Mother, Harry and Mike,

Back at Yuma again! We arrived about 11:45. I'm writing in pencil for it is handy and I'm going to go to church in about 20 minutes so will have to leave this and return to it.

I suppose I should start with the beer party last night—it was a honey. Really best G.I. event I've ever been a party to. Lotsa beer and lotsa singing with an accordion and piano for accompaniment. Along about the 7th or eighth bottle I held up the little container and started singing "Have I been away too long." My capacity has certainly suffered from being not in continued contact with yee old amber brew but I judge that it is only my capacity which has suffered.

Of course the beer ran out too early but it was a good thing for we were all in the mood to kill whatever was there so if we had had much more you never can tell what would have happened. The C.O. was right on deck all the time. He has that rare ability of being able to be one of the boys and still retain all his prestige as a commander. He drank with us—led some of the singing and ripped off a couple solos. We were all rosey when the beer gave out—right away I thought I'd better get clear of the mess hall if I didn't want to get in on the cleaning up of the place. Sooo I grabbed Dan Hamernik and we streaked for the nearest exit. Alas—we were too late—the C.O. had stationed himself and Non-Coms at all the exits so that those who were there could not get out. Well, I just had to pull the old, but still expedient, "into the latrine" and from there out the window—ah good old Yankee ingenuity.

We were allowed to sleep in late this morning—indeed no whistles till 7 AM. We had a good breakfast and then cleaned up barracks—turned in bedding and packed. By that time buses and trucks had arrived to take us back. Whoops—have to go to kirk now—be back shortly.

After church

The larger part of the day has been devoted to a lazy and half-hearted resettling. Half-hearted for if all goes as we hope we will be moving to the pool next Sunday. There are still a few things they can get us on yet—new regulations require more than twice the number of hours in the air as formerly but we all hope to meet all requirements.

Enough of this I must get ready for bed. Expect a very busy week ahead. Be good, people.
Love, Frank

October 16th, 9:00 PM, Monday
Dear Mother, Harry and Mike,

Just finished taking my Gunners Final Comprehensive. To put it mildly, it was a Bastard of the first water—if I wash back on anything—that will be it.

Received no mail from you people today but I did get 3 Gazettes and a letter from Coach—Franklin E. no less. He slipped a couple greenbacks in, which to me at this time was quite acceptable—any loose change is just before you ship any place, for somehow you always manage to spend more than you plan. I was rather startled to hear from him for he has written but once before so I will have to settle down one of these evenings (when the hell I'll get time I don't know) and write a rugged reply.

There is nothing new here at the moment—fewer & fewer fellows going to Westover Mass each week which is not too good a sign.

Fraid this is destined to be a shortie—no flying today but we'll get it for sure tomorrow soo I must hit the sac—start lobbying for conclusion of poker game progressively on next bunk any minute now. Be good, people.
Love, Frank

October 17th, Tuesday, 5 more days to go

Dear Mother, Harry and Mike,

Just got back from flying—looks like we are not going to have to make that lecture this evening. Flew high altitude camera and low altitude air to ground missions. During Flight we also made radio contacts with the ground. Boy those babies on the ground sure are good. Maybe it makes some of the fellows feel inferior but to me it is as though you had a big brother on the ground there—patient, very aware of the strain you're under, courteous and efficient. They are there to help you and they sure do a great job of it.

I had hoped greatly to get some mail today but we didn't get back to the squadron till 7:30 PM & then it was all I could do to get me something to eat before mess hall closed.

Well folks, I must make up my sac and get ready for bed. I know I'm not writing much—but I'm well and trying very hard to keep on the ball. Hope someone picked up my mail and brings it in a little later when that lecture is over. Be good, people.
Lotsa love, Frank

October 18th, Wednesday, 4 more days to go

Dear Mother, Harry and Mike,

Perhaps I can do a mite better job today. All depends on whether we fly this afternoon. As I see it we should have a minimum of 2 more flights to make up our required 24 hours of flying here.

Flying itself will soon be relegated to routine—the most fascinating part of it will come at the next Post where, after a little instruction, I expect that we will be operators on cross country hops. That is what is really going to be fun. From the start, Gunnery did not appeal to me very much—the gun is still a nasty tool and a good one but until I see someone else shooting at me I don't believe the firing of it will hold any extraordinary thrill for me.
Later 5:30 P.M.

Well, we didn't fly this afternoon. Seems that the Colonel is going on inspection tour on the morrow so that we are restricted to tents for a G.I. party this evening.

That is really the best part of this tent business—all we ever have done is to throw water on the wooden floor so that it looks wet and that is about all that can be expected. Won't get mail until after chow so I'll hold this open till then.

We saw pictures of film we took yesterday. I did much better today. We also had to do a lot of cleanup work down at Operations. This too is in preparation for tomorrow's inspection. Taking orders from an Officer is one thing but cleaning up after them is something I cannot see—Oh well, ours is not to reason why—eh?

One of the boys just brought in my mail. Peculiar that I should get your Sat., Sunday & Mon. letters all today. It was good to get three at once. No bag as yet—maybe to-morrow.

Glad to hear that Harry's cold is on the mend. I got the whole story of that one in the three letters. Sat—its eminence—Sunday—the "effects of Sat.'s treatment & Sunday's re-treatment and finally Monday's back at work feeling better which is good to hear. It is probably too late now but I hope Harroola wasn't too hasty last Monday evening—don't blame him if he was but I wrote my sentiments on that before at Datelan.

I guess I'll have to scurry along to chow now so behave yourselves and be good. Love, Frank

                                            October 19th, Thursday, 3 more days to go
Dear Mother, Harry and Mike,

We flew today so to say the least I am rather tired. It is not so much the actual flying that is tiring altho (sic) much hard work at high altitude does get you—what bothers me is the waiting around—the drawing of parachutes and guns and a thousand sundry details which must accompany each mission.

Our missions were easy ones today—both camera, but one was on the blink so that instead of 2 men firing at one time we had to take one at a time which accounts for the length of the thing. We went up about 1:15 and didn't return to yee old terra firma till 7 bells. I believe we will have one more session in the air and that should do it. Our Liaison Transmitter was not in operation today so that simplified and in fact relegated to a null our radio activity but we will just have to make up the work next time.

It's not like it was at Datelan as far as eating is concerned. Here when you come down late you have to be content with makeshift meals and since I try not to eat too heavily when I know I'm flying I am a little hungry now. Have saved out a couple apples so will have them before hitting the sac.

You must have noticed that I haven't been bitching about the weather lately. Well, here it comes—last night I took flying clothes to bed with me and arose clad in sheepskin jacket—yup it really is getting that cold nights & 2 blankets too. The guys all give me the business but you know me and how I just love to be cozy.

After eating this evening I went over and got some personal articles Al Daher had locked up for me in his foot locker. Things I didn't want to leave around while I was at Datelan. He goes to Datelan next Sunday morning. We went to the pool to look up our Sioux Falls buddies but found out they're due to get here probably next Thursday so I shall probably just miss them.

I found out that all checks have been passed and I am pretty sure of graduating Sunday just so long as I get my required flying in. The last should be made up to-morrow or Saturday so I'm not worried there.

Received only 2 Gazettes today–and I have 3 I haven't been able to read as yet. No bag as yet. Hope I'm not worrying you fellows too much about that damn bag–I can always find something to replace it altho (sic) I can't see spending the extra Jack if it is on the way. If it's not here Saturday I'll just have to get me one.

Hope I hear from youse to-morrow. Please tell Beals and Otts etc. that I think of them each day but cannot manage during these two weeks.

Guess that will have to be all for today–lights have been out–am writing in day-room–still have to shower & shave so, be good.

Oodles of love, Francis George

October 20th, Thursday Friday

Dear Mother, Harry and Mike,

You can see how the time slips by me at the heading of this one. Well, it is very near the eve of our graduation–can't say that any of us are too popped up about it but we are glad of the job done and of course a little anxious to find out where the next place will be. We have done very little of any consequence today beyond taking some code and seeing film we took on yesterday's flight. Not much done but still they continually drag you out and you police this and that and waste away the day. I've been taking a good deal of liberty lately–not a good idea to be sure this late in the game but I hate this waiting around in the sun. They even wanted me to take PT today–can you imagine that? Well, I walked out of that one but I'm going to watch my step the next day or so for the boys are all goofing off and the orderly room is picking them up and they're doing a little night K.P.

I got Haroola's letter today. The badminton sounds good–often wanted to take a crack at it myself but never did have the time while I was going to school. There is too little new to report–have to see my boy Al Daher this evening about a little sewing deal–need a haircut badly so that will fill my evening I expect.

Later

Sewing spree developed into a full evening session so I'll have to try to work haircut in to-morrow. One of the boys just came in a while ago with a peach pie. It seems that he went to chow out of formation–was caught so the First Sergeant, deciding that, since he was so anxious to get to the mess hall, he liked it there, gave him a little K.P. there this evening. I have been elected to divide said, still hot from the oven morsel, into 5 equal portions. Upon vote we have decided to send the same man back on K.P. each night but he'll have to do better than one pie.

Fraid that's all for this one folksies so, be good.

Love, Frank

October 21st, Saturday, To-morrow we Graduate

Dear Mother, Harry and Mike,

Get all set for another shortie—seems as though that is about all I can get out these days. This morning for some reason we were left strictly alone. It was in a way a sad situation—we could not leave the Sqd. Area—we were afraid to go to orderly room for passes, to PX for haircuts etc. for fear we would be put on some detail.

Whoa!

This is a great deal later. You can see from above that I honestly did try but time just wouldn't permit finishing this yesterday. Right now it is about 6 PM Sunday. I'll run through the cycle of events as they have occurred just to give you a rough idea of what went.

At 12:45 yesterday we were called out & required to report to the flight line. We happened to be among the few crews who did not fly but we were supposed to stick around until 5 doing policing details and odd jobs. Personally this waiting around is one of the few things that really gets me. Honest work I don't mind but this crap they hand out just to keep you busy is a real pain to most of us. So little Francis George turned in his oxygen mask and took off for the PX for a haircut. By the time I sweated out the line and ate chow we were called out for pay call and mail call. I received your slip for a registered letter - I hope you are not worrying about it—just in case youse guys are worried about it I'll try to ship this air mail since I didn't reply immediately upon receipt. I have not as yet been able to get the letter—P.O. closed when I got the slip and of course the same story today, Sunday. Whatever is in it, you may be sure will find a more than welcome packet—my saying this after all that former stuff about not needing it—well, I shouldn't need it any more. When I ship out of here I shall be getting flying pay so if I have managed on what I have been getting I shouldn't have any trouble whatsoever henceforth. Lord knows I marvel at the way you fellows manage!

To get on with the story—at 7 PM we had a formation for turning in flying equipment and at 8 PM another to attend a lecture. After the lecture—almost 9:30 I met Al Daher and Dan Hamernik and we had a couple beers. I said goodbye to Al, since his squadron left for Datelan early this morning. I have been with him since we shipped together from Greensboro to S.F. so it was a little celebration—those 2 beers we had. I soon returned to the sac for with my aforementioned limited capacity, the effect of those 2 beers plus a long day left me ready for my sac.

Arose this morning at 6:50—forwent chow as I intended to make Communion. Always try to get there before shipping. Sad part was that could not get heard at Confession this morning so will have to make it to-morrow evening. Had breakfast after Mass in cafeteria—civilian style Huba Huba—the cantaloupes here are still something beyond what Niagara's Truck Farms have produced. Upon return to barracks (whoops I mean tent) I packed all my belongings. At 11 we had our Graduation Ceremony in the Post theatre—quite impressive for a G.I. article but short and sweet and then on to chow. After eating we met a formation where we were issued wings and then we marched back to the pool. So here we are again right where we started from 8 weeks ago. This time we are shipping out–same processing as when we came in. Where to? Fraid that will have to wait but this I know for sure–there is no shipment to Westover Mass this week–my usual run of luck and yet I feel that the Good Lord directs these things and whatever I get will be for the best. Still no bag in spite of the fact that I tore up most of the Post looking for it–Harry those gals must have wrapped so that it looked like gold bricks and has been delayed. At any rate I'll be here about 3 more days so it should turn up by that time. The overwhelming influx of students here has apparently subsided for there are few student holdovers here in the pool. Hence we graduates are going to pull K.P. For some dark reason I'm not on the list for to-mor-row–here's hopin I don't catch it.

Guess that's most of the dope for today Folks–my special Sunday blessing to you two lovers.

Lotsa love, Frank

P.S. Try to get some real stationary to-morrow. F.

October 22nd - Telegram

HARRY THOMPSON

ACCOUNTS PAYABLE DEPT CARBORUNDUM CO NFALLS

DEAR HARRY LEAVE HERE WEDNESDAY EVENING. SHOULD AR-RIVE BY SUNDAY AT LATEST TAKING SPECIAL TRAIN SO CANNOT BE PRECISE ABOUT ARRIVAL MORTGAGE THE HOMESTEAD

FRANK

October 23rd, 11 A.M., Monday

Dear Mother, Harry and Mike,

Thought I'd better get this off, perhaps a little sooner than usual today. I have fond hopes of writing Gramp and the Beals today. This morning I did not arise until 10 minutes till 9. Wow did I sleep! It rained again (?) last night. Quite a thunder bar-rage all night and for some reason I was quite restless. Didn't fall right off as usual into the Arms of Morpheus but tossed quite a while. I didn't hear the 1st call, or even 2 lads from my tent answering an earlier call (3:15) to K.P. They tell me that whistles blew everywhere but I didn't awake till the Master Sergeant of the pool came in and personally rooted my tail out. I honestly hadn't heard a thing so that my conscience isn't hurting and there weren't even any threats so all's well.

When I got up and dressed I went immediately to the orderly room and got a pass to leave pool area for the P.O. Not to underrate in any way the green foldable but I sure did appreciate the letter. 15 bucks again no less–Boy, it sure is great to get it and I think you'll understand when I tell you how I will most likely spend it. Seems to me I always spend money when I'm shipping for so many odds and ends and eats–this boy sure spends it on his stomach and I just love to invest a little tonsil lubricant every now and again. They just had noon chow call but it seems that they have two *in the pool—another at 12N so I'll stall here and make the last one. I'm not too hungry since I just got back from PX area where I took advantage of my pass to P.O. to get me coffee and what for. Rank extravagance I'll admit—2 mornings in a row now but aside from Sunday mornings—this morning was 1st G.I. breakfast I've missed—I keep on trying to justify myself.*

I told you my incident about my sac—that is the trouble with having a lower—fellow buddies come in and want to sit down and they always seem to land on my sac which is one thing I won't stand for. Last Friday the boys had a big poker game and the usual thing happened but this time there were about 6 extras in and I'm sure the guy who pulled it wanted to get me going—all the others knew about it and were just waiting to see the fireworks—sooo I told him to get his ass off—he did and asked me why—I know they all were waiting for a long harangue from me and I could see I was due for a razzing so I just told him I'd be damned if I could see where I owed him any explanation—his head dropped about 4 inches and we all laughed at him instead of me. You just have to stick up for what's yours or you'll be walked on all the while.

I'd appreciate it if Harry would wise me up on some of this election dope—outstanding issues etc. I have been able to get so little of it. Harry—if you can beg borrow or steal a copy of the Congressional Digest dealing with the subject please do and ship it to me.

Right now a lad named Zona is ripping off some sweet and solid jive on his sax— Gosh it sure sounds good—"I don't want to walk without you Baby." Well, I guess that cleans up most of the dirt of the day. I do hope yee old bag arrives today so I can get my clothes segregated and ready for a clothing check so Be Good, people.
Love, Frank

FRANK'S FELLOWS

Present Day

There was no denying it: For the first time in my life, I felt as though I actually knew my father. What an inconceivable gift he had left us. Though not literally, for the first time in memory, I could hear his voice. So many things I never knew about him, yet learning of these things made perfect sense. Several things he mentioned caught my attention. For example, we have always been a musical family. Many of us played instruments while others were gifted singers. I never knew my father was a singer. I asked my mother if he had done much singing when they were together and if she knew he loved singing so much. She said she never knew that about him. Then there was the dancing. I asked if they went dancing, and she said, "Of course," but she was unaware of the considerable amount of dancing he did while he was in the service.

Another thing that piqued my curiosity was the people who wrote to him. When I asked my mother, she recognized only a couple of names, but could not remember who they were. Venturing to the local history department at the Niagara Falls Public Library, I met Courtney and Helga. I didn't have much to go on; only that I knew where he'd lived in the 1940s. We started with the city directories. It's amazing what you can learn from city directories. Helga and Courtney would pull three or four at a time, going all the way back to 1918. I was able to determine much about the Otts, the Tenth Street Thompsons, the Perrys, and even the relatives on my mother's side of the family. I found my father's high school yearbook, and read the mantle speech he had written, which I found as applicable today as it was in 1939. I was able to trace him back from high school, to junior high school and from Ninth Street, to Chilton Avenue. I knew from the obituary he was born in Buffalo, and the genealogy site indicated his home was in the 25th Ward; however, that was in Erie County and I would have to continue my research at the Buffalo History Museum.

I learned that the O'Haras were neighbors across the street on Ninth Street, and that Jerry was five years younger than my father. It appears that his mother was Pearly, whom my father referenced in his letters, and that the Keoghs were also neighbors, as were the Otts who lived next door until 1933. The big mystery writers were the Beals. I gathered from the letters that they were in Canada, but had a Niagara Falls, New York post office box; however I had no luck in learning anything about them. Clearly they were close friends of his mother's, and therefore of the family, but I struck out trying to find the connection.

Some of what he mentioned in his letters also resonated with me, such as his comment about Gramp and his "artery thing." This made me wonder if my father's heart condition was hereditary, but to find out for sure, I'd need to take a trip to city hall's office of vital records to read Gramp's death certificate. I added it to my list of things to do. He also mentioned the demonstration of the Mae West and the life raft, and I found myself wanting to tell him to pay close attention, as both would save his life. Then he mentioned his plan to swipe a machine gun shell. I had to laugh again. I knew for a fact that he had done this because my youngest brother had the shell in his collection of military items my mother had given him.

Finally, I was curious about his friends Hughes and Kostishack. It seemed like they had some great times together, and he was genuinely unhappy that he had moved on ahead of them. I wondered what had become of them after they washed back and my father continued on. As for Hughes, all I knew was that he was from Syracuse. Back to the genealogy site I went. Here, sadly, I struck out. Other than the info my father had mentioned—that he'd been a foreman at the Syracuse Laundry, was married and had one daughter; had no college; and was age twenty-six in 1944—I was unable to find out anything more about him. I chalked this dead end up to the fire in St. Louis in 1973 that destroyed upward of 18-million military files.

After Bill Hughes, I sought out Johnny Kostishack. I had a little better luck learning what became of him. I was able to find his grave, just outside Pittsburgh, Pa. He died in 1989. He had married, but I was unable to determine if he'd had any children. I again suspected that the fire had played a role in minimizing yet another soldier's life. Next on my list was Al Daher. Once again, I came up short. Last was Dan Hamernik. I had much better luck there. It appears that Dan died in 2009; two months shy of his eighty-fifth birthday, and is buried in Maryland. Documents indicate he had become an aeronautical engineer and married in 1951 in Arlington, Virginia. His wife hailed from his hometown of Mt. Carmel, Pa. It was comforting to learn what I could about my father's friends, and that many had lived long, full lives. These men meant something to him, that was very clear, and therefore they meant something to me. I often toy with the idea of digging into the whereabouts and life stories of my father's pals. Who knows? Maybe someday I will.

From where these men were in their training, anticipating where it would take them, they had an ear to the radio and an eye on the paper as much as possible. Favorable progress in any Theatre of War would give them some indication of what lay ahead. Clearly, they had an ear to the radio and an eye on the paper as much as possible given that favorable progress in any Theatre of War would give them some indication of what lay ahead for them. A few times he wrote home mentioning that news of the war was good, and indeed he was right. Throughout the months of September and October in the European Theatre, British troops liberated Brussels and Antwerp. U.S. troops liberated Luxembourg. Romania signed an armistice with the Allies, as well as with Finland. Canadian troops captured Calais, France, and in early October Prime Minister Churchill was heading to Moscow for a conference with Stalin. Germany was not enjoying such good news. The U.S. Army patrols had entered Germany near Aachen, where German troops eventually surrendered to the Allies after twenty days of fierce fighting, which had resulted in the city being reduced to rubble, while in Le Havre, the German garrison surrendered and in Athens, German troops evacuated. In the Pacific, the U.S. celebrated a victory over Japan's Navy in the Leyte Gulf, and the first bomber missions were successfully flown from the Mariana Islands by B-29 Superfortresses striking the Japanese base at Truk.

The letters stop for about two weeks, which was due to my father's delay in shipping to his next base. The idea that he wanted to surprise his mother was no surprise to me. Neither were the comments he made in the upcoming letters; that he would never do that again. I say this because my youngest brother is in the Army, and has been for over thirty years. During the Iraq war, he was stationed in Bagdad for eighteen months; in keeping with the family tradition, my older sister wrote him everyday until he returned. As expected, this worried all of us terribly, especially my mother. Just prior to shipping out, and unaware that my father had done the same thing to his mother (we hadn't discovered the letters yet), he decided to surprise her. The story goes that the surprise nearly landed her in the hospital, and I'm guessing my father's "surprise" may have had the same impact, as both my brother and my father acknowledged they would never surprise their mothers again. Learning that my father, who my youngest brother had never met, would do exactly the same thing to his mother is another of those non-coincidences that kept cropping up as I continued coddiwompling, unsure of where I was going or what I would find when I arrived.

Letters from Frank's Fellows

Interspersed throughout my father's letters were a few letters from his pals, which he either sent home to Mother and Harry, or that were actually sent directly to Mother and Harry. I thought you'd enjoy reading them as much as I did. I hope I've guessed right.

Letters sent to Harry from Frank written by John | Johnny - Frank's bunk buddy referenced previously in June letters from Sioux Falls:

Dear Frank

At last! it has come; that proclamation in regard to my pass privilege.

My friend I have been struck down from behind, Quislings have laid their work well - dejection overwhelms me - I have been betrayed.

Tell me O'Frank, what have I done to deserve all this - have I not kept my antenna at 1/4 wave; have I not refrained from the beat frequency.

By the great horned toad! What am I to do in two hours - surely they would allow me more than just a round trip bus ride!

I retrieve my hat from the ring - I no longer fight - they have torn the oscillator right out of me, my transmitter is still. Look, dear comrade look for yourself, the following are two excerpts from that super structure - the new schedule.

1. 12:15-13:15 mess; and mess can they rightly call it - never have I seen such a conglomeration of garbage at one assemblage.

2. PT shall henceforth consist of 1 hour and 10 minutes - I can only say, "take care O mighty ones, least I develop into a monster and devour you with thine own fire - for this then have they stuck two hours for my private life, two hours when I was happy, when I sang and communed with nature and the paroled latrine. For this they have plucked my song, stilled my laugh and blocked that which nature intended to stay open, namely my secondary output.

I am struck dumb; words have not yet been invented to give vent to my feelings. There is but one passage I remember faintly from an old oriental play - I translate freely - "Fuck them all" -

I tell you, Frank, I have had enough. I have begun to pack prior to my leaving and I promise you mattress covers will not be optional.

I speed this to you post haste - take care lest these demons swoop down on you.
Johnny
P.S. Long isn't it?

———

Dear Frank

Aye, verily though I had walked into the valley of death, have I entered the gates of Sioux Falls Air Base - home of the mentally insane - As the gates clamped shut behind me I was stripped, stripped, O'Frank, of all reality; such was the nightmare I entered upon, I shudder as I write and my resistor drops.

Every hour on the hour new directives are issued, each destined to take its place in organized confusion.

To-day, dear comrade, I walk upon my toes, verily, lest I uncommittingly step into some forbidden zone - as I leave the barrack I offer up to my Lord a prayer for guidance through the maze of glittering rank.

I tell you, Frank, common sense has lost all semblance, neurotic utterances are the law.

Flee my friend, flee while there is still time for soon it - and I underline it - shall be piled so high every man will be issued a shovel as he leaves the barracks in order that he may make his way clear.

I must move now friend for to stand too long in one place would prove fatal - It rises at one foot per hour - Hi Ho I'm away.
Johnny

Dear Frank:

Tears pour from my eyes and my hand trembles as I write this - for to-day! To-day I have lost all faith in human nature. This day shall be recorded as the most dastardly in all animals, from this day our children will designate time - Infamy" At its blackest, for on this day, my dear Frank, this 15th of June 1944 they have taken away my last possession - namely our daily news broadcast.

I can say no more, for tears blind me; I only ask of you, my faithful Frank, to be kind to me to-night when I return to our bivouac and if late in the night the bunk springs sing there tell-tale song - I will not be tuning my antenna to its proper resonance, nay it will be but the results of the rocking sobs of a broken man.

Farewell my staunch friend, I return once more to the fray. They can do naught more than pour salt in my open wounds.

Dazedly yours, John

P.S. Spare the rod and spoil the child - they have broken my rod (half mast) and ruined a man.

—

June 20th—From Bill Hughes to Harry

Dear Mr. Thompson,

I am writing this to thank you for obtaining my stamp for me.

Frank insists there is no talk of money so I'd like to further thank you for the gift.

I assure you it will be as greatly used as it is appreciated.

As Frank has probably told you he and I are together every week end. Doing numerous things and I'd like to state here, to you, that you have one swell brother. We really have a good time to-gether.

He has told me so much about you that I can see where you two are a lot alike in many ways.

Well, enough rambling, I'll close now and once more thank you for the trouble & inconvenience you went through to obtain my stamp.

Frank's friend,

Bill H.

P.S. Please don't tell Frank what I said about him as he'd probably think I was, shall we say, "speaking the oil."

—

July 1st—To Frank's mother from Johnny Kostishack

Dear Mrs. Thompson,

I don't know if Frank has written you about me, but I thought I'd write anyway - I hope you don't mind too much.

I met Frank for the first time several months ago when we boarded a train at Greensboro to ship out to Sioux Falls - I guess we hit it off right away, for that night we shared a lower berth, and from that day, til now we've been buddies. Why even to-day I have the bunk above him.

It's funny how well we've come to know each other in the months we've been in the Army. Your son has been a fine influence on me, Mrs. Thompson, and I guess in a restless way I helped ease his monotonous Army life.

By the way, I want to thank you for the food you send Frank. I don't know if he mentions it or not but every night after school, he and I have a little snack and I don't tell Frank, but I offer a little prayer after we've gone to bed that a certain fellow's mother enjoys our Lord's blessing.

You'd be surprised how well Frank is doing at school; he is really absorbing a good fundamental radio knowledge.

Please don't take any offense of my writing this way without any introduction. I just wanted to thank the person responsible for giving me such a swell buddy -

A pal of Frank's

Johnny

TAMPA, FLORIDA

1944

Return Address:
Cpl. F.G. Thompson
A.S.N. 12,107,602
2nd. Det., 3rd AF Repl. Depot
Plant Park, Tampa, FL
Air Mail

November 9, Thursday

Dear Mother, Harry and Mike,

No doubt you have been worried but since there is no telegraph office, an airmail will have to serve the purpose. Using Bealy's stamps as per usual.

The trip down was uneventful and rather tedious. As the Beals, Harry & Coach no doubt told you, I met a lad from the Falls, Weicht I think it is, and we made the entire trip together—picked up a couple more fellows at Washington, so I had plenty of company. Out of Washington only one reservation was available on the Meteor so we all decided to take the Sun Queen. Accommodations were quite poor, but we managed to sit all the way—others were not so fortunate.

We arrived in Tampa this afternoon 2 hours behind schedule as is to be expected with these southern R.R.s. Were we sore when we found that a contingent of permanent party were there to greet us. We had planned on cleaning up—eating a good meal and seeing a movie or something and reporting at about 10 P.M. but we were herded into trucks and driven here—reported in, have beds made up and eaten chow. This place takes the fur-lined bath tub after some time at home; it is all I can do not to hop a rattler back tonight. Think I'd better sell that return ticket but fast before temptation proves too much for me. It is really not bad—it is warm here as is to be expected—pleasantly so. We are quartered—the whole depot is built around a stadium no less. Our quarters consist of all the room under the cement bleachers. And the Officers are in tents like we had at Yuma out on the playing field. Mess hall and all are under the bleachers—it sounds a lot more down to earth than it really is. Walls, floors, and all are concrete but there must be at least a thousand men here. Some of the guys having to use yee old Army cots since bunks were not available. They'll only have em for a night I think since a shipment goes out to-morrow making more room.

Say folksies, this is piss poor stationary but all I could get. I must get going as I have still to get cleaned up and a million things to get settled before I hit the sac. The main point is to let youse know that little Francis George is ragged, fat & sassy and quite consumed with groping his way about. I was right I think about being here not more than a couple weeks but as far as I can find out now assignments are made to four fields near here (one at Gulfport Miss.) and no one has said anything about Australia. Looks like we'll get 2-2 ½ months more before we move out.

Well guys, guess I'd better hustle along now and get things straightened. Be good–
Lotsa love,
Huba, Huba, Frank

November 9, Thursday; Just before Lights Out

Dear Mother, Harry & Mike,

Thought I might as well start this one now. I do hope you get that Airmail in time to reduce a lot of worry. I do expect to get a pass out of here to-morrow night but I can't be absolutely certain so thought since there'd be a chance that I couldn't wire to-morrow night I'd better settle for an Airmail to you–do hope you'll understand.

Try to give you a few impressions of the trip and the Depot. There are indeed too many traveling–of course who am I to judge–but it seems to me that far too many are moving about for efficient operations of the R.R.s I rode on. The Pennsylvania, of course, was O.K. to Washington but from then on–OH brother! I know that we got on the last coach of the train out of D.C. and we called it the coal car. Most of the coaches were old to start with and for myself I can easily stand the discomfort of the old style seats but the dirt really gets me down. We had a pretty good time on the way down–these gunners are really operators–they don't know when they're licked. I saw one guy (married with a set of twins + ?) spend at least 6-8 hours working on a very cute brunette. Now, if they're married I'll take a chance, or if mother is along, I'll take a chance, but when they're married and mother-in-law is with her–too much for me! But not too much for some of these jokers. Such caring of children too–Heaven knows babes in arms and tots should not be on the trains–well, in one case, this young kid I was with was working on two little mothers–holding one in reserve I guess. Well, he got both little ones to sleep finally only to have the most desirable one arrive at destination and leave the train at the crucial moment. And when he came back from putting them in a cab at Savannah, Ga. I guess–the Navy had taken over with the other one, so he had labored hard in vain. In Washington–too bad we were confined–we had hoped for seats on the Meteor and had to keep reporting back on the hour to check on any developments but unfortunately we were still in possession of but one seat at 1 PM (the zero hour for reservations) so we had to take the 2:50 out.

Next Day–Friday about 3:30

Have finished processing–managed to check vaguely on insurance–will be more than 55.10/month–wanted to get at least an idea of that. Also to my dismay–Engineering Cadets are now open, but my Sec. Number (Radio Gunner) has a priority second only to Air Crew and from the information I have received here I cannot be sent for the course–but that's the way it goes ya know "c'est la guerre." However, I'll get my assignment to O.T.U. and try there. Right now I expect to be here not more *than a week—Guess we have a good chance for assignment to 8th Air Force in England after O.T.U. but lots of time to worry about that.*

Am going to have to take a couple courses in some improvised school they have here. Camouflage, Chemical Warfare, and the inevitable Code Will try to see the 1st Sergeant this afternoon about this permanent detail while I'm here—I hear they have marches—5-10 miles afternoons first to keep you in trim so I may be able to get out of that. I should be able to get a pass tonight—good from 5 PM till 6:15 AM. This place is really O.K. from what I can find out and already have experienced and of course O.T.U. is the "Best Life in the Army" so I am rather looking forward to it.

The lads here are groaning—we all find that we'd have made out much better had we refused delays. That was my intention at first—from here we would have been given 15 days with traveling time automatically. Most of them have a good point I think—they feel the Army is screwing them "Why don't they come out and tell us" they say—Well, in a way, I feel it is still a good idea to take what you can get when you can get it. Received mail from home today, forwarded from Yuma—and slip for the bag. I'll ship the bag back home and believe I will put in extra shirt & pants for I hear that at the next base they'll take that stuff from us when we enter—I'll let you know when to ship it back to me.

Latest Rumor—Have to march in an Armistice Parade to-morrow. Gee that getting mail from home is rugged. This sure would have been heaven in the Army had we come here directly from Yuma but it's a piss poor excuse for home. Well, I'll read this over now and see if I've forgotten anything and address envelope. OH—have not received any money as yet but will endeavor to pay my honest debts as soon as I get some. Huba Huba—at least they don't waste any time around here—Little Francis George detailed for K.P. at 5 in the morning—List just posted—Guess I never will miss it—trouble is that my name is too easy to spell. Anyway it should get me over that furlough so, be good, people.

Lotsa Love, Frank

November 12, Sunday, 2:10 PM

Dear Mother, Harry and Mike,

Well, Happy Birthday Fellows. It is a lovely day in Florida today—Hope you are having the same. Incidentally we are wearing O.D.s for it cools off here but the weather is really great. My uniform is not in what I'd call Grade A shape but they told us at camp that we wouldn't have time to get them cleaned so I'm a wearin it as is. The best I can say is that it looks a great deal better than some I've seen about.

They woke me at 7 AM this morning and after shaving I ate my pancakes, bacon & cereal & coffee & rousted myself over to the Dental Clinic. All they did this morning was take X-rays—good thing they didn't try more for I was there until 11 AM. It seems I have one baby tooth that has to come out and also have a wisdom tooth coming up under another one so the former must come out—I also fear that they will find more trouble when they take that baby tooth out for I think there are cavities on either side of it in the permanent teeth. Well, that remains to be seen. I'll be given an appointment and I'm not looking forward to it.

After the clinic I went back & cleaned up and dressed for church. Then I ate a large Duck dinner–gee I really put it away. They really did a good job cooking it; the dressing was good as was the gravy–beets–tomatoes–cookies–ice cream & coffee. Zona ate with me and then we took right off for church. We walked into the main part of town and arrived in plenty of time for the 12:30 number. It was low Mass and kinda nice to look over (Forgot my missal again) all the lightly dressed dollies. Don't know just what the afternoon will bring after this–try to look over more of the town I guess–like to do a little dancing this evening–see if I can find some. Guess we'll get goin now–should write some letters but since I'm here & I don't know for how long, I don't want to say I was in Tampa & didn't see it so, be good people.
Lotsa Love, Frank

November 11th, About 9 Bells, K.P. all done.
Dear Mother, Harry and Mike,

Well, I'm disturbing a precedent by writing after K.P., but I'm not too tired, so here's a line for what it's worth. Here you don't keep same job all day–change after each feeding so altho (sic) 2nd and 3rd of day was really rough the rest was not as bad as might have been expected.

Went to town last night. Tampa is really O.K. if you ask me but of course you can drop a good deal of cash before you get through an evening. Went in with Zona of the saxophone last night. Hit a few of the better bars in the hotels–it is a great officer's town–not that they grab off everything but they have the jack, cars, etc. and do a rather better job of it than we G.I.'s. However there is no real substitute for a real Casanova and you can readily see that the Enlisted men are getting their share. We looked mostly last night and not bad looking either–spent a good deal of time and dropped a coupla bucks at a Charity Bazaar roulette wheel in back of Sacred Heart Church in town. Will undoubtedly go to Mass there to-morrow. Some of the boys are going into town tonight even after K.P. but I can't see all the primping & fussing to go in with nothing definite on the line. Sent out cards last night–I'm asleep at the switch I guess. Never thought of the 12th being Sunday but I didn't get & couldn't get into town before last night but I'm thinkin of youse two and a wishin you a lovely day and envying a little your Sunday at home and that toilet seat that I didn't have to put 2 protective layers of paper on.

I just got back from the mess hall and I find that I am required to report to Dental Clinic at 7:45 in the morning. Guess they want my Sunday morning too–Ah well, I know the Dentist wants my teeth X-rayed–is worried about those 4 premolars that never did grow in my mouth so guess it will be a good idea to be there. Could get out of it I suppose but I wish he'd find something to ground me–that is the only way I could get in Engr. Cadets. Why the Hell didn't we puncture one of my ear drums eh? If we'd done that at home I'd have been all set–Maybe! At any rate I find myself quite indoctrinated into Army routine–didn't even scream when they said absolutely no! Guess I'll have to hurry and get in my 30 missions so that maybe I can get back and make it then.

I had thought seriously of going in for church to-morrow after a long snooze but I see that with a dental appointment I'll have to be up, but Masses are various on Sunday to-morrow in town, so I can take my old sweet time & maybe get off a few letters in the morning.

Tried to buy cigars by the box in the PX this evening since I thought it might in some way alleviate your Christmas Gift problem for Coach and Grandpa–at any rate Coach asked me to try to get him some so don't tell if you want em for him for Christmas.

No Gunners wings available here! We even take em off our blouses at night cause some of the lads want in badly. They sell them only in the Jewelry stores so I will have to see what I can do. Of course they rob you blind but it's the same old story–when you want em–you want em!

Well Folksies, I must run now have to shower & leave note with C.Q. (Charge of Quarters) to wake me in morning for my dental appointment.

Tell Coach Tom Rotella is here, also Chap by name of Smith I knew at North Junior–have seen Joe Calaty also Ernie Cofrancess, a fellow who went to S.F. from Greensboro with me & was in 1241 till he washed out in Code. He is PFC now–Career Gunner–awaiting assignment to Crew as I am–No lack of familiar faces–

Be Good, people.

Lotsa Love, Frank

November 13, Monday, 12:15

Dear Mother, Harry and Mike,

Must get going here! This is part of yee old lunch hour. Have no idea how long it will last but we shall see what we shall see. Have received no mail from home as yet–could hardly expect to–did get a bunch a Gazettes from Yuma today, also another slip for the bag but I won't call for it just yet–it's safer in the Post Office!

Yesterday proved to be a good one and a long one, and Zona & I were tired when we arrived back at the Sac about 1:30. After I wrote you we started walking. We saw quite a bit of Tampa–Had planned on taking in a movie but in town there was nothing that looked good or we hadn't seen. On Friday night we had looked into most of the Hotels and so we snooped into those we had missed. Finally we returned to the Tampa Terrace to spend our beer money. We each bought one and then the bar keep who apparently was a little off the ball started throwing his mistakes (you know rye & ginger instead of 7UP) our way on the house. We decided that it would be a good idea to leave there shortly and after inquiring from several sources (surprising how hard it is to get information even at the U.S.O.s) finally found out where the better residential district was and then we hopped a trolley & took a long ride out around the Bay (Tampa Bay). Lovely homes and beautiful landscapes and an unimpeded view of all of the Bay–saltwater air and all that. We got off & walked quite a ways and returned to town at about 5-5:30. (Out of ink!) By then in spite of our big Duck dinner we were hungry so we splurged & returned to settle, quiet reserved & clean atmosphere of the Tampa Terrace and had ourselves Pot Roast which was dandy at 2 bucks a plate–all the trimmings but I've eaten better out. Food is high here but so many of the fellows have taken sick that I'll be darned if I'll eat in any of these Café etc. Tuesday Morn 7:45 AM

Well, I didn't get a chance to finish this thing–will explain as I go along. Sunday after dinner we went to church in the evening. Sounds like I'm getting too churchy in my old age I know but they are running a Mission there this week so we decided we would try to make it since there is a chance it may be the last one we'll get a chance to make in this country for a while. It is rather rugged–the seats are very hard and there is none of this 20 minute sermon stuff–it's a least an hour besides Rosary & Benediction–starts at 8 PM and we won't get out until 9:30-45 too late to see a show after unfortunately. So you can see why I have been in town past 2 evenings, of course we don't know that we'll be able to make all of it but we hope so. There was a shipping list yesterday & expect one Friday which may take us. After we left church Sunday we started back to camp & while going over one of the bridges we saw a boat–seemed to be loading G.I.s so we investigated. The M. P. told us that it went Mac Dill Field out on the end of the Bay & if we wanted to take the round trip to hop on. So we did–it was a 2 hour trip–it's run for military personnel at Mac Dill Field & is a free G.I. service–so per chance should I get my hook on something sweet it would be a good cheap boat ride.

While in the Service Club I noted in a book about Tampa that "If you haven't tried a Cuban Sandwich you've missed something." Soo, after the boat ride I decided that I needed one–walked about a mile beyond camp before we found a "Drive in" place where we could get one & we waited about 45 min. for that. The sandwich is a Florida version of a Dagwood special having ham, pork, salami, cheese, pickles, mustard etc. wrapped in leathery Cuban bread. Pretty darn good too!

Finally got back to camp after that. In the morning we were scheduled for Camouflage school. We were there from 7:30-11:30. These ground schools are much better than any G.I. lectures I have been to. Of course Officers are required to attend with us so they have to be pretty good. In the afternoon–just as I left the beginning of this we were required to wear our Gas masks for 4 hours. This proved to be a farce for after we put em on they took us to a movie & we all took them off. After that we came back and lined up to be paid what was still due us from our pay at Yuma. Drew 6 bucks on this one.

Right after that I hurried to shower & shave and eat. Sunday I had inquired & found a place where I could get some pressing done "while you wait." So we beat it into town at about 6 PM to get pressed for church. Got Blouse, cap & pants done and then we had to kill time till Kirk. Scouted around till I spent 3.50 for a pair of wings–type I wanted were not the "stamped out" variety of both pairs I had home but are originally made in 3 sections & welded together. Want them for bracelet I told Mother of–they are completely flat on the back. I can't get any miniature wings here but will keep trying–figure I'll want about 6 of those.

After that we had a milkshake–OH I got a Blitz Cloth too which are as scarce as hens teeth here. Then we went back to church where I dropped 2 bucks for a rosary– needed one–could have gotten cheaper one but wanted very small variety–can keep it in change purse of my newly acquired wallet which I sure have used here. After church we took in one of the 3 Carnivals in town–looked mostly–we had 1 beer & a Cuban sandwich and came back to the Stadium ready for bed at 10 or 10:30. So you can see I've been on the move.

I have written no one as yet but will do so as soon as I can. May get some done this PM if I feel like it. I must write Otts & Beals and do the thank you number–everyone was so grand and still the occasion is so rare that you get a similar unlimited chance to get out that you feel that as long as there are things you want to do you should take advantage of it. I dislike the unsettled living here in the Stadium but the food has been good and all in all–this place is the best I've known in the Army.

I was supposed to go on one of those little 5 mile hikes this morning but I was called out for a dental appointment at 9:45. I'm not looking forward to that cause they'll probably pull 2 this morning and G.I. pulling is not what it's cracked up to be.

Well, I guess that takes us up to date. I should get some mail from youse guys to-day–soo, be good, people.

Love, Frank

P.S. Hope you have called and changed that Gazette address

November 15, Wednesday, 11:30

Dear Mother, Harry & Mike,

How the Hell are youse today? Since yesterday I've had a number of things hap-pen–the main event being the pulling of a wisdom tooth. I was scheduled for 9:45 yesterday morning and was pulled out of formation at 7:20. I wrote you people and then tried to sleep with the result that I awoke just 1 hour late for my appointment at 10:45. My first impulse was to talk to the 1st Sergeant about it but remember-ing the harangue he gave us about meeting appointments on time I figured he'd be hardly sympathetic so I decided to just take off for the dental clinic and brazen it out. Fortunately they were rushed over & had not particularly noted my absence soo they put me on a list of fellows who were to have the work done at Mac Dill Field that afternoon. We went out there, 7 of us, in an ambulance, had noon chow there and soon after the fireworks began. I drew a hell of a good Neural (?) Surgeon. He was one swell guy & couldn't see why the Hell pull the thing if it wasn't bad–since it wasn't above the gum yet he didn't think there was a tooth there so another X-ray was taken. I understood then–the tooth had grown parallel to the gum instead of perpendicular to it. Sooo one whole side of my mouth was killed and the dentist started to work. What he did was to cut open the gum, then split the tooth with an automatic hammer–that piece came out easily but the other hunk held out at least 20-30 minutes of prying, chiseling & hand hammering. When it finally came the roots stayed behind & had to be dug out separately. Of course the Novocain killed most of the pain but I could feel the crowbar in there and the old jawbone was pretty well shaken up. The payoff coming when shortly before dinner time the dope started to wear off. I did manage to eat dinner under some difficulty. If they think they are going to screw me out of a meal by pulling a tooth they're crazy! At any rate I get 2 days off to recover from it but of course that knocked my plans for making the Mission into a cocked hat for I knew they would pull my pass.

You know–the old story–if you're too sick to work–you're too sick to use a pass. Something had to be done so I got dressed anyway and contacted one of the boys who was going to stay in last night and drew his pass. Have to try the same thing tonight. I just hope it works. I knew that last night would be the worst of it so after church I went to a bar and got a few shots of heavy rum & Zona & I hustled back while it was still affecting me. I slept face down on a towel–for the thing was still bleeding in spite of stitches in it. Boy did I sleep. Didn't wake till reveille & then I walked over & knocked off until about 11 when I went to PX for some milk. Don't' believe I'll attempt anything real solid till this evening. Yee old alcohol was a boon in this case–I know that the Army is a darn lonely place to be sick & I just couldn't see myself roaming about this darn stadium when I couldn't sleep.

Well, I guess that does about all of it. If I don't sleep this afternoon I may get some letters out or maybe some washing done, we shall see what we shall see–still feel a little tired for some reason. Be good, people–no mail as yet–maybe this afternoon.
Love, Frank

November 16, Thursday, 9:40
Dear Mother, Harry and Mike,

Don't have much to report today. Of course I'm supposed to be on detail at present but after finishing the job experience has generally taught me that it is foolhardy to return and look for more to do.

Went to church last night. It is nice to get in every night but it is too bad we get out too late to get into a movie–would be fun to see one. Any way we went to one of the Local Clip Joints. I've seen how they work these things in Western movies but here it's done on a modern scale. It was not a high class place of course but it was jammed. Pretty good little orchestra–they charge 25¢ to get in but like a great many of the places here–they serve no beer, mixed drinks only–of course we didn't know till we got inside. All the waitresses and gals from the floor shows are dressed in smart civilian clothes and at any time you can prevail upon them you are supposed to buy a drink (I guess) and they'll dance with you–drinks run 60-70 cents a throw. Zona & I had one which we nursed from 10:15–11:15 & then when there was no sign of a floor show we took off.

Kinda disgusted in a way—lots of officers there and some of those babes were really something—horror heads. Lots of those young kids are well taken before they leave is my bet. But they are young and with lots of jack and enjoy being taken. These Southern Belles are so darn demonstrative—the expressions—the gestures—the sighs—the moans and the body language is all over done to a gooey stage in my opinion.

There is a shipping list this afternoon—don't rightly think I'll be on it but can't say for sure. If I am I'll let you know by another letter sometime today—at any rate keep writing here until you get another address from me. Hope I get some mail at 11 AM this morning. It should be here by then.

One more thing—I got my travel pay yesterday—intend enclosing 60 dollar money order in this letter—please don't give me any argument—Harry gave me 30 and we spent all his and I know he's doing without right now—also 20 dollars extra it cost youse guys to get me down here besides all it cost to have me home. If you can't see it that way please keep it for me cause if I have it here I'll sure as hell have nothing for it—or keep it for Christmas as my Christmas present cause I don't know what the Hell I can get either of you here—am never out when stores are open. If I run short I'll wire home for some anyway.

Am going to see if I can get a money order now so, be good, people.
Lotsa Love, Francis George

November 17, Friday, about 10:45

Dear Mother, Harry & Mike,

I'll start this now—probably have to finish it at a later time. I want to get down to mail room & see if I have received any mail. I sure hope so. This morning I went up to Mac Dill Field and had stitches removed from my gum. Am scheduled for another extraction on Monday—jaw is fairly well healed and most of the swelling gone but it is still tender in spots.

Yesterday afternoon I did some washing and am thoroughly pissed off—you hang stuff out to dry and little fellows walk up & swipe them. I just pray I never catch anyone at it. Put out three pairs of Jockey shorts—2 new ones were stolen—the old pair they left—I guess I'm lucky that my shirts and 1 Sun Tan shirt was left. It's not so much the shorts but to figure you've been living with such bastards.

I survived a shipping list yesterday. Undoubtedly due to the fact that teeth are being fixed. Hate to see a lot of fellows I came down with ship to Avon Park but that's the way it goes. Zona still here—we went to church last night—5 nights in—3 to go—we feel pretty lucky that we have been able to make em all so far. This shipping business again—that's when they swipe the stuff—ah well, lucky to get off as lightly as I did.

There is not much new to report. I fully expect to be leaving here next Friday—probably not before for I don't believe there will be a shipping list next Tuesday.

Well, hurray for our side—4 letters no less—they sure do a lot for a fellow—probably wouldn't care now if they took the whole barracks bag—whew, what am I writing? All the same it makes me feel well that you two are well and Miker is still sniffin around.

Gee Mom, you speak of those 9 days, they sure were wonderful for me. That is you two sure made them the (best) 9 days in my life so far. I'm afraid you made too much of me–one thing I regret is that circumstances made too much of a fuss over me–not enough time to just be home and I keep thinkin of what I couldn't eat.

With Harry's and Mother's letters I received one from Norm 3¢ stamp mailed the same time. 3 PM mailed on the 14th so I guess Airmail doesn't help much. Reason for delay of my first letter now that I think of it was probably Armistice Day & then the ensuing Sunday. I'll keep a close check on your next letters but I don't think Airmail will help us much here in Florida. And then chances are Mississippi–Gulfport is next. Personally I would much prefer Gulfport to Drew or Mack Dill Fields near Tampa.

Al Daher tells me he got only 7 days to Lincoln Neb.–just imagine & he lives in N.J. So I was mighty lucky I guess. Al was 2 classes behind me–the class after us–boys from N.Y. State–got 16 days to Westover and so it goes–pretty hard thing to beat. And so the three of us can start to sweat out the next one. As things look to me now–it just ain't in sight no how but that's the beauty of the Army–maybe they'll be contrary to our advantage just once.

I have already written Beals–now that I see that it is possible to get mail in this Stadium I'd better write the Otts & Gramp and about 6 of the lads I'd hate to lose track of. Haven't written Ann–that hurts too but reason tells me it's better that way. Once I get this mission out of the way I should be able to get some writing done.

Don't know how I'll make out at O.T.U.–they tell me missions are 6-8 hours long and when you figure in briefing and orientation periods & preparations prior to each mission I don't expect I'll be too good on the writing. As R.O., I'll have to send in position reports every half hour–weather reports & probably a million & 1 other things–expect to be busy as a Cat on a Tin Roof. On top of that I haven't touched a radio for almost a month now–should be great at the start O ho!

I get a big kick out of the flying officer's "Peace Overtures!" Most of us have taken chicken sh— from Brass for a year or more and now when crews are made up here the boys are Huba Huba–back slapping and such camaraderie–they come over to our quarters to meet the Radio Man–hope they don't try it on me for I don't take kindly to such "about faces." However flying personnel, officers that is, are generally a pretty fair & liberal bunch–they have to be to get results.

Have another formation soon now so will have to git. Be good, Folksies.
Lotsa Love, Frank

November 18, Saturday

Dear Mother, Harry & Mike,

Don't know how far I'll get with this–I have to go on Guard Duty–you know "who goes there?" & all that tripe. It's not bad at all–should really be on 24 hours working 2 hours and off 4 but I have an easy post–the PX, and am on duty from 12-3 PM and from 3 PM–6 PM off then on from 6 till 9 and then through.

It's too bad to miss the Mission but it will just be the one night and I should be able to get to church in time to have my Confession heard.

Last night after church I went to a U.S.O. dance. The whole set-up is really nice here—all the U.S.O.s have patios in the rear where the dances are held out under the stars plenty of girls and some of them rather nice too. Had a sandwich and a beer before coming back. I had found out yesterday I was to be on Guard and since I had no idea of what kind of a deal it was to be I wanted to get back and get some sleep.

Last night I had trouble getting my pass. Seems the 1st. Sergeant got the impression I was late for my dental appointment yesterday and had my pass pulled—when I found out and tried to see him about it he was stinking drunk sleeping it off soo in order to get out I got one of the other boys' passes. They better not pull that crap on me tonight.

Well, I'm off for chow, my mail and stand Guard—finish this during my relief.
3:30 PM

Just got off Guard—tried again on the mail score with better luck. Received Mother's Tuesday letter. It was not canceled till 10 AM on Friday and I got it this afternoon at 3:30—not bad, what?

Duty in the PX is not bad at all, although the 3 hours on my feet was starting to get me—my relief was 15-20 minutes late at that.

It is nice to hear that you are so busy—believe me I think you have the right ticket doing your shopping now. I suppose if I were smart I'd pick up some things here now but I never can get in when stores are open except Saturdays and last week I had K.P. and this week Guard Duty so my hands have been sorta tied.

Well, kids I have to shave and wash up—maybe get a haircut grab a little sleep and be ready for the 6-9 PM number so I'll run along. Be good, people.
Lotsa Love, Frank

November 19, Sunday, 2:15

Dear Mother, Harry and Mike,

Well, here I am at my daily chore. The letterhead will tell you the place. Up to this point the day has been a rather lazy one. Last night I couldn't make Mission but managed to get in at 9:25 and have my Confession heard. Had a sandwich and glass of beer and then walked back to camp. Zona drew K.P. today but he raised Hell until they let him go to church this morning. He woke me and we went to Mass & Communion on the Post. It couldn't have lasted more than 25-30 minutes. After Mass I went to breakfast, which wasn't up to the Army's usual Sunday morning standard. Right after that I returned to yee old sac and slept solid until 11 AM when Brownell, another Mick, woke me and asked me if I were going to church—I rolled over explained that I'd been and dropped off till 12N. Then I hurriedly dressed and ate lunch. Since then I washed up—treated myself to a shine and walked here—in the heart of Tampa.

Town is pretty dull this afternoon because there is a big football game at one of the stadiums. Ordinarily I would have gone but Zona and I had planned on going to St. Petersburg for a swim this afternoon—of course his detail knocked that out and primarily I don't care much for going alone & secondarily I slept too late so I guess I won't see St. Petersburg this visit to Tampa. We both hope to go to Gulfport Miss. next Friday. Not such a hot town I guess but what is good is the Post Administration–so I hear–both fields near Tampa, Drew and Mac Dill are not so well spoken of.

Thank heavens tonight is last one of the Mission. We have really been kept going and contrary to most G.I.s we are looking forward to a few nights in the barracks writing letters. For myself I have made it 4 nights on illegal passes–last night, after being on guard all day, I was supposed to remain on the Post all night to be on call in case of a Riot. Thank goodness the Pass Clerk didn't know about that regulation!

Anyhow, Zona thinks he can make it tonight–we get the Papal Blessing you know–huba huba–so it will be done.

Don't really know exactly what to do with myself this afternoon–think perhaps I'll take in a show somewhere–have been wanting to for some time now.

I guess that is all for today Folks. I'll probably see a movie eat somewhere and wait at church for Zona–maybe find us a dance after church. Wednesday night all Catholic Soldiers are invited to the K of C for a Supper Dance so I hope I can make that. We were told not to bring girls as there would be lots of hostesses–well, we shall see.

To-morrow morning I expect to have another tooth pulled–it is the baby tooth that Kay (The Doctor) was going to bridge at the time he bridged the other one. It is not bad but is so close to the ones on either side of it that they both have cavities I'm sure. Will probably get a couple days off on that one too. Well, be good, people. My special Sunday Blessing -
Love, Frank

November 20th, Monday, 1 PM

Dear Mother, Harry and Mike,

As you can see, I finally bummed some ink for the good old "51." It seems good to [be] using it again. Received Harry's letter this morning at about 11:30. I had just come back from having aforementioned baby tooth pulled. Contrary to my suspicions there were no cavities on either side of it–doctor said that it was because gums were inflamed around the tooth that made it feel tender. So at present I am minus anything to fill the hole. I asked about getting a bridge put in–dentist said I might be able to get it done at the next Field. He said that my best bet was to try to get it done when things were a little slack. It seems that most of the "Cap and bridge" work is being done for fellows who have had front ones pulled. At any rate I'll squawk wherever I go for the last pulled tooth was directly under my bridge. The bridge has moved down a little as it is and there is not much sense in having a bridged tooth if there is nothing there for it to bite down on.

I should be in Class A now and ready for shipment next Friday and if it is Friday I believe I'll be going to Gulfport Miss. Ah well, time will tell on that score.

Last night after church we went to a U.S.O. dance–they are over at 11 PM so we were in before 12. Got the Papal Blessing at the last night of the Mission–it was

Bank night last night all right. Birth Control, Abortion and Death were well covered. One priest gave the whole business and to my way of thinking he completely defeated his purpose by his verboseness. He was a splendid speaker but Hell an hour or an hour and 10 minutes is too darn much. All in all I was glad I had had the opportunity to go–Zona rushed in last night after K.P. and got there before the Rosary was finished so he made it all–I made 7 out of 8–5 was all you needed.

At the dance later there sure were plenty of dollies and lots of nice ones too. There was one frill in Baby Blue Blonde and probably the loveliest thing I have ever seen off the screen. You could only dance with her 20-30 seconds before somebody with equally pointed ears cut in, but it made nice holdin while it lasted.

Don't know just what we shall do this evening. My pass is supposed to be held out because I'm quartered today because of tooth extraction. There is a dance here on the Post tonight. We may take that in or if I decide I really want to get out I may get someone else's pass.

"Goin my Way" is coming here so I'll want to see that if I can tomorrow night, also I've read a lot about Bob Hope's "Lady & the Pirate" [sic] so I may take that in one of these evenings. Also they have some pretty good Revivals here on the Post–like "How Green Was My Valley" & "Prisoner of Zenda." They do a great deal for the G.I.s here. There is dancing at least one place every night and sometimes 2 or 3 places. Plenty of free shows and at least 1 free stage show here on the Post each week. If I were sure I was not shipping Friday and could get out Thursday I'd take some of these Southerners up on a good Thanksgiving dinner, which are being offered here and there but if we move Friday we will be restricted Thursday evening so that lets that out.

One thing I will say is that I never hit a place where women strive to make so much of what they've got and wear so little. Such bosoms–such sweater stretching–such hip English and tight short skirts. Anywhere at any time of day I would say if a fellow were just looking he could see a nicely exposed thigh somewhere in the vicinity–you can generally tell what color underwear too if they happen to have any on. All of this of course augments that familiar gnawing inside which will be answered sooner or later–I hope I hope.

Hope that this has sufficiently made Mother shocked & indignant, & Harry drool, and tell Mike that if I see 2 more dogs brought on this Post by Officers I'll have him down here to clean the place up and to sit on my bunk all day–growl at intruders & guard my underwear on the line.

Must get going now–have a shirt to iron for that K of C Blowout Wednesday so, be good, Folksies.

Lotsa Love, Frank

November 21st, Tuesday 3:30

Dear Mother, Harry and Mike,

Have spent last part of the day listening to Survival Lectures and seeing movies. They were interesting to say the least, just another point the Army wants to get to you to help you in any type of emergency. The lecturer was Buck Ass. Private. He has over 3600 flying hours logged with the R.C.A.F.–just another guy who got screwed–from 252 dollars / month to 50–he tried to get into Air Transport Command and got the usual ride so here he is giving lectures with a General Duty Spec. number.

Received Mother's Saturday letter this afternoon. I believe it has been the teeth which have held me here this long but I'm afraid that I won't be held here much longer. Afraid–I use the term–Ah yes–getting definitely attached to the place. Ran into what looks to me like a very good deal and I'll be leaving probably Friday. Perhaps you remember the Bupa sisters–Ah yes Polish to be sure but they were two very attractive extremely well dressed little ladies. Well, one of them is a SPAR down here working for Marine Intelligence. Has been in SPARS 17 months & has been in Tampa only 2 weeks–spent all the rest of the time in Miami. She was waiting for a Bus - I passed–went back & asked her if she was from Niagara Falls. She doesn't like Tampa–no place to go–I rattled off dances & hotels which have dancing each night–yes said she, but you can't go those places alone! She told me she has her own quarters–actually besides uniform has only what amounts to a civilian connection with the Navy–from 8:30 to 5 PM. She is alone, lonely, and wanted me to come up & meet a few of the SPARS she works with. Of course I can't get out during the day but could call her I suppose. What a set-up–of course she tried to scare me off with deploring the morals of the South but I just stood there & drooled away. She is 3 to 5 years older than I am anyway. Thought I'd wait to see if I ship Friday before taking much positive action. Right now I've changed my mind again & would like to stay near Tampa–of course Gulfport, Miss. is only 70 miles from New Orleans I could still get to Miami from here. I'm not worrying about it–and while I could in some way direct my own destiny by going on Sick Call the morning I'm supposed to ship. I am not disposed to fool around–I'll go where I'm sent.

I intended to iron a shirt on my free afternoon yesterday but head ached from second tooth so I took a couple aspirin and slept. I'm sure getting plenty of sleep around here. Don't worry about teeth–they haven't kept me in a night yet. Tonight a U.S.O. dance & tomorrow K of C dance. Last night we saw Bob Hope in "Pirate & The Lady." [sic] Jerry is a lucky boy alright! Unless someone in my crew has not had a furlough in the past 6 months I'll go directly to POE after 10 weeks of O.T.U.

So Mrs. Ott has the wings–anything you do dear is O.K. & yet I kinda wanted Harry to have them. I can't buy small ones here for love nor money but can get size in between those and large ones you have for 2 bucks a throw. Let me know if you think I should get them for the girls for Christmas–let me know right away.

How about cigars–you haven't said anything about em–just want to know if you have got something already.

Guess that's all for now. Be good, Folks.

Lotsa Love, Frank

P.S. What will the Beals say if they see Mrs. Ott has the wings & I wouldn't let Al have em that night?

November 22nd, Wednesday

Dear Mother, Harry and Mike,

It looks as though I'll be off in a cloud of dust to-morrow around 4 PM. Yup I'm on shipping orders and have been assigned to a crew. Looks like a fairly good crew. I just went up to get the names of the fellows—all of them are white men except one—seems like a fair bunch—2 2nd Looys, Pilot and Co-Pilot—no Bombardier or Navigator assigned to the crew as yet. We will pick them up later in all probability or this may be an indication that we are to fly lighter ships than Fortresses, all hard to tell just now. A few of us who came down here together are on the same order—the "Old Guard" around here by now so that it shouldn't be too bad at all. Ah yes, the destination will be Gulfport Miss., I believe—will endeavor to send you a night letter from there as soon as I find out the address upon arrival. I'll more than likely be writing another letter to-morrow from here anyway. The one thing I hope is that they don't make New Orleans "off limits" for us. Too bad we will miss K of C Supper Dance this evening but that's the way it goes.

Here's the Crew
2nd Lieut. Sundin R.J. Pilot
2nd Lieut. Turner R.J. Co-Pilot
Cpl. Ferniza Flight Engineer
Cpl. Kimpel Gunner
Spencer (P.F.C.) Armorer Gunner
Sgt. Shaffer (Assistant Radio Operator) Gunner
And Little Francis George at the console of the Morse Key

Stopped abruptly a while ago in this letter—got the bright idea of seeing the Chaplain about getting out tonight. As far as I'm concerned the Chaplain is still a joke in the Army—he wouldn't help us. Sad part came when we found it was the Catholic Chaplain's day off so we had to see the Protestant—it was just T.S. as far as he was concerned. Soo I'll just have to let you know how I make out illegitimately—see what can be done later tonight.

Incidentally we will have our turkey dinner before we ship to-morrow. I know the holiday will be over when you get this but please don't feel bad about it. Holidays are just another day in the Army—they don't mean much if you are not with your own. I know you wonder at home but there are an awful lot of us in the same boat and when it's a collective proposition, and so large, well, as I say it's just another day.

This morning I got caught on a detail to clean up 2 baggage cars which we will use as mess cars on the trip—incidentally I understand it should be about 24 hours. The work was like K.P. and I didn't do much—you remember I said a good day's work would kill me—well, I don't want anything to happen like that.

A word or two about some things I find I will want and need. The Army provides you with good equipment and adequately however, you cannot always be sure that

Army issue in your plane has not been tampered with and upon the advice of men who have been over I deem it wise to begin trying to accumulate a few odds and ends which may prove to be of inestimable value to me. Of course I have in mind that Christmas is coming and I suspect that you two will send me a box - as you said when I was home it may as well be what I want. The following are things I would find most pleasure in receiving this Christmas.

1. A compass - they are put out on the watch case size with regular clasp & cover like old watches. It must be good, waterproof and above all small.

2. A knife - what I really want is one with a small light handle - good steel - double edged - blade not more that 4 to 5 inches long so that it can be strapped in an improvised sheath to my leg. A thick strong blade is desirable more than razor sharpness. Harry might throw in a small stone so I can keep it sharp.

3. A Tube (small toothpaste size) of Vaseline.

4. A small supply of quinine or aloprene or both. I realize this is almost impossible to get, but Mom might be able to help there.

5. About 3 German Chocolate bars

6. 2 cans (small) of bouillon cubes or anything you can find with a similar or greater amount of nourishment in a small space.

These things must be small and as described to be of much use - if you can't get them don't bother with anything like em but not it.

I suppose you are laughing, but in places I go from here these things will be sold out as they are here in Tampa. I learned respect for precaution and detail in the Lab - 99 times out of 100 you don't need safety or precautionary measures but that 100th time you'd give a lot to have prepared a little.

If you can get the knife and it's too long (6 inch blade Maximum) get a machinist to grind it down - it doesn't have to be pretty & shiny but it does have to be sturdy and strong.

I'd also like a small but sturdy screwdriver with a pocket clip on it like a fountain pen. This too wants to be short but strong as I intend using it mostly for making adjustments on the machine gun—not the radio.

That I guess takes in most of it—should I get any more bright ideas I'll let you know.

Will undoubtedly be able to write to-morrow—

Lotsa Love, Frank

THE CHRISTMAS GIFT

Present Day

After my many hours of typing and the many things I'd learned in the preceding several months, I was faced with how to share it all with my siblings. The break from his delay in shipping was the perfect place to break from my typing. His letters from January to October were typed, but sending a Word or PDF document to a group of individuals with varying levels of computer engagement, while the most economical means, did not seem to be the most meaningful. After all, these were the words of our father, the voice we had longed to hear for half a century. They deserved a more dignified manner of sharing.

The previous Christmas, as a family gift, I had created a family cookbook for my mother to give everyone. I had used a print-on-demand company, and the books had come out beautifully. They were spiral-bound and in full color, and the quality was top-notch. On my return visit to the website, I saw that I had many more format options and decided that I would have the letters perfectly bound into books and give them as Christmas gifts to my siblings.

For the next several months I reread the letters, correcting any typos, adding scanned documents, placing images of vintage movie posters, or items in the letters. These efforts were not professional-looking by any means, but they provided some visual interest and, in some cases, clarity. I collected images of as many buildings mentioned, vintage products, and planes he'd mentioned; book covers of books he'd read; and anything that would help deepen the reader's understanding.

The compilation was an unanticipated amount of work, but over the next few months I was able to get it together enough to send to the printer, complete with a basic cover design that provided the specific dates and locations of the letters, laid over a muted image of text from the very first letter. Once it was off to the printer, I set about having copies made of the various photos that had been enclosed in the letters. When the books arrived, I affixed an envelope that held the photos to the back cover and wrapped them up.

Christmas Eve is always a madhouse at my mother's, but filling the limited spaces between bodies is the essence of true love. In no other place and at no other time are we as poignantly aware of the closeness and irreplaceable relationship we have with one another.

At gift-giving time, I handed out my packages, and waited until each sibling opened theirs. Of course they knew I was working on the letters, but they had no idea I was compiling them into a book for each of them. I'm not sure what they thought at that moment, because I don't think they knew what to expect. Over the next several months, as they read their books, they too came to understand what I had experienced, and began to know our father as well, something we'd waited over fifty years to do.

It's difficult to explain, but as we read the letters, fully knowing our father's future, we all wanted to tell him he should pay particular attention to something or assure him that indeed, he would achieve a goal he had aspired to. My siblings and I would have these long discussions about him, his sense of humor, comments he'd make about redheads knowing he would eventually marry one, his fastidiousness, his love of family and faith. After fifty years of silence, we were actually talking about him and not as a stranger any longer, but as someone we actually were coming to know. They too were starting to feel a connection with him and, like me, anxiously awaited the next volume.

GULFPORT, MISSISSIPPI - PART 1

1944

November 24th Telegram
DEAR FOLKS ARRIVED GULFPORT 8 PM ADDRESS 328 ABU SO S
BKS 18-16 GULFPORT FIELD MISS GET THE MAIL ROLLING LOVE
= FRANK

Return address:
Cpl. F.G. Thompson 12, 107, 602
Combat Crew Mail Sect.
Gulfport Field, Miss.
328–A.B.U
Sq. S–Bks. 18-16

November 25, Saturday

Dear Mother, Harry and Mike,

Well folks, this is the first from Mississippi. I suppose I should go back a bit from the time we left Tampa. We were on shipping orders on Thursday and hence were left pretty much alone. We had a splendid Thanksgiving dinner–I shall try to enclose the menu. It was a rather festive occasion for the Army. We had white table clothes and napkins and there was fruit and pickles and celery & fruit cake on large plates in the center of the table. One thing that I hadn't been aware of before–soldiers can invite anyone to have dinner on a holiday with them. A good portion of the feminine population of Tampa seemed to be there–you can see from the menu that we fared a good deal better than most of the civilian population.

No doubt you fellows had a quiet and yet very adequate day. You might think I envied you your "nip" before dinner but I had that too. It was a stiff rum cake although how we managed it in the barracks is a military secret.

Perhaps you are wondering if we made the K of C dance? The answer is yes indeed! Of course Zona and I were both on shipping orders and hence were restricted however after trying all legitimate methods and still getting no results we were resolved to get out. The sad part was that all the fellows we knew were also shipping and since a new bunch had just come in–they were anxious to see Tampa. Finally we found one fellow who was on guard duty and wouldn't be able to use his pass so we had one–still there were two of us so we worked it by the simple expedient of one man going out and then handing the pass through the fence and then the second hopeful got out on it. It worked quite satisfactorily–wouldn't want to try that many places, but Plant Park was a cinch to get out of–lots of fellows were out all the time with no passes at all so we were amateurs. The dance was worth it although some of the usual wind was out of our sails for we knew that any acquaintance we cultivated would be in vain since we were leaving the next day. I hooked on to a blonde who was a swell sport and had a good time all evening. The Knights were good sports and I am a little sorry that we won't be able to go to a similar affair they are having on Dec. 9.

But to get back to shipping—we ate a good Thanksgiving dinner—made final preparations and then started out across the street outside the stadium to the awaiting train. To my surprise we were called off in the crews to which we had been assigned—Officers and all—we met them at the train and rode here in the same coaches with them. That of course, was good psychology on the part of the Army—still don't know how they did it. Our crew is of course very green—no men with combat experience on it whatsoever and still I think we have the framework for a smooth working team. The next 10-12 weeks will tell the story. The pilot is a tall (6'2" my guess) Swede from R.I. who has had over 100 hours transition in Fortresses. I am glad to say he seems like the type who at a moment had my confidence. He is young, boyish and yet seems to carry himself as though he would be very capable. The Co-Pilot is inexperienced, being a pursuit pilot who was transferred to Heavy Bombardment. He has never been in a 17. The remainder of the crew are about on the same status with Francis George as far as flying experience is concerned. To my mind, as I have always maintained, the quality of enthusiasm is priceless. This bunch seems to have it. Frankly, I would far rather have a young eager bunch to work with than that experienced know it all attitude to fly with. This way we will all learn together. The mistakes of one man, of course, will be frowned upon by all yet I look for indulgence in all of them and a fellowship which I have found to be the biggest lacking quality in the Air Corps. My Asst. Radioman knows nothing of Radio yet—he is a Sgt. and a former K.P. pusher I believe.

As I stated in my telegram we got here about 8 last night. About 27-28 hours on the train and I for one got little or no sleep. We were tired & hungry but in a couple hours we had been assigned barracks and had a meal under our belts. Here you can eat anytime you can or want to—the catch being that you have a mess pass which they punch each time you eat—3 punches only per day. And Mom, we got 2 sheets here. We are assigned to barracks by crews and all sleep next to one another. There are only 4 crews in our barracks—we have plenty of room, tables, easy chairs—indeed the best set-up yet! Say I have to take a shower now while there is still hot water (I hope) besides if I say it all now I'll have nothing left for to-morrow so, be good, people.

Love, Frank

P.S. Did you get money order?

Return Address:
Cpl. F.G. Thompson
A.S.N. 12,107,602
Combat Crew Mail Section Box 366
Gulfport AAF Miss.

November 26, Sunday, 2:10

Dear Mother, Harry and Mike,

Well, I have a lot on my mind today so here's hoping I can get most of it down. I'm in the quiet of our rather nice barracks, if it can be called that and I have thought of a lot to say so I hope I can remember it.

First the weather here. As you can realize, being right on the Gulf it is essentially damp. It was rather chilly when we arrived and the following morning it started to rain in torrents. I believe it let up last night for a while but there has been no let up today. The only times so far that we have ventured out was to eat and after noon chow we went up to see about the mail situation. I received 2 letters. Mother's of Monday and Harry's of Tuesday. As per usual it is good to receive mail. Ever so glad you could use the money and had the Christmas season in mind. Also it may help a little with plumbing session. I know a lousy 60 bucks won't go very far but every little bit helps. This morning they got us up for chow too late to go to Mass so we fully intended to go to 10:30 but the sac looked so good that we climbed back in after breakfast and I slept like a baby until 11:30–time enough to eat so we will have to go to the 6:00 PM Mass this evening. I'm not going near that bed until after church this evening. May take in a show later tonight but I doubt it. I still have some stripes to sew on and they insist upon your wearing them here.

I know you'll be interested in the set up here so although I know very little that is concrete about it as yet I'll try to give you the story. First and foremost–there are absolutely no leaves or furloughs from here except of the emergency–1st of kin variety. When we finish here we will be shipped directly to a Staging Area for 8-72 hours and then we are told that 98% of the bunch from here fly to the European Theatre. Not a too cheerful story to have to tell but there is no sense in gilding the lily. The European Theatre sounds rather good to me and of course our attitude has been that an awful lot can happen in 3 months and particularly in Europe. You see–with the present penetration in the South Pacific, B-24s have been used almost exclusively of course with exception of B-29s. B-24s go faster, farther and carry a heavier bomb load so it is obvious why very few B-17s have been used there as yet.

From what I can see now I will be a very busy boy. From what I can see from the schedule, we will be on duty 10-12 hours when we fly. We fly every other day– ground school on the intervening days and we get every 8th day off and that does not mean a free Sunday–maybe one or two free Sundays while I'm here. We will fly on 3 different schedules the first starting early in the AM–they wake you at 2:30 and the latest of course being night flying. Flights are at least 6 hours long and 50% of this will be at high altitude. Please correct the rather nasty inference I made to Mr. O'Hara about getting flying pay if you flew but 4 hours a month–being on the spot I find that is a lot of B.S. They tell us here that it's 4 hours/week. Please do not worry about my money–if I need it I'll let you know to be sure, I know you have the Bonds and if I'm in dire straits I'll sing out via collect telegram. Looks to me like the only thing I'll be needing it for anyway is for that 8th day off to go to New Orleans and for cigarettes and incidentals. Here we can go to a newly opened Non-Com's club where our Commanding Officers have told us the sky's the limit even to gambling. They give us this concession for the Miss. coastline is full of gambling joints and of course they don't want us in them. Also there is supposed to be lots of illicit bars–wide open soaking plenty and of course Miss. is supposed to be dry. They have been and I expect will be grand to us here and well they might be for at this point they must have our full cooperation. I'm still not sure of the pass situation but I think it is a 50 mile radius except on our days off. Also this particular county has the highest V.D. rate in Miss. and Miss. is supposed to have the highest in the country. I tell you this in passing–I don't believe you need worry about me in this respect for I still feel as I always did–when I do get it, it's got to be just right or not at all.

In Orientation lectures yesterday afternoon I got a kick out of the way the Flight Supervisor stressed communication and Radio men before anyone else on the crew. This was probably a slip of the tongue but it helped our ego a little anyway. All our training supervisory officers are young men and to me that makes it seem better for they seem a pretty regular and considerate bunch. In lectures in the morning, the sending position reports every half hour was stressed and before we fly we have a special session–all radio operators. Of course I'm shaking in ma boots–will undoubtedly ruin my pants first couple times up but I expect to get things ironed out. The thing being that the whole training schedule is run on a competitive basis. The radio boy of course is best method they will have of checking on what the plane and pilot is doing by way of the fixes etc. we ask for and receive from ground stations. Moreover if one member of the crew screws up the whole crew suffers so should you be the unlucky one you have 9 indignant men on your neck.

The problem of communication is an important one. I have felt this all along although as yet I know that the rest of the crew hardly considers it thus but they'll see it in short order I know.

Now to comment on latest communiqués from home. Don't worry about my money. We have a month's pay as Corporal coming and flying pay we will get from Yuma and ration money coming so that should more than cover my needs. Harry you should merely beat the Ginger on your shoes with the bristles of your shoe brush to get that soap out but you'll have to do it before soap gets hard! I still have to write Hamernik and Daher–would hate to get out of touch with them. I judge both of them will be flying B-24s for which I cannot say that I envy them. I feel that they are not too enthusiastic about it either. I would be careful if I were you people on the freeze situation–fuses don't burn out at leisure–there may be some exposed wiring somewhere and it would behoove you to have an electrician checkup regardless of expense. A fire is nothing to be fooled with.

My mouth still aches a little but I suppose that is to be expected. Curiously enough the gum around where the baby tooth came out is and has been a lot more tender than where that near operation was performed on the wisdom tooth.

To-morrow we process–same old crap–clothes and records. I will try to get new fatigues and new underwear to-morrow at any rate. Sign statement for the underwear for you can't have too much of it and it's a very cheap way to get it.

Don't believe we will start to fly until Wednesday at the earliest–maybe not even then. The food is O.K. here–we had steak for dinner with peas etc. best G.I. coffee I've ever had and what's more it is kept piping hot. As a rule there isn't much wrong with me that a good hot cup of coffee and a good furlough won't cure.

This one I'm not sure that you didn't tell me and yet I'm not sure–anyway I'll repeat it.

The four things the British don't like about the American soldier.

He's over dressed

He's over paid

He's over sexed

He's over here

Yesterday during the Orientation we had the usual explanation of the Articles of War. The representative was interesting and explained many instances where the G.I. is cornered by the technicality of the Law. It seems one G.I. went to a den of iniquity and after he got thru handed the little lady 2 dollars where upon she demanded ten. He asked what for and she said the "act itself." He refused to pay and she ran to the window and began to give the alarm to the police protection she was paying for. The soldier immediately, since he was smoking a big Tampa cigar–let her have it right in the seat. He was later apprehended & sentenced, the charge being–attempted arson on the rear end of a business establishment.

Well, be good, folks–that's all for now. My special Sunday Blessing -

Lotsa Love, Frank

P.S. Please note Box No. on address

F.

November 27, Tuesday

Dear Mother, Harry and Mike,

Well, I'll try to dash off a quickie this morning. Boy it's cold here right now and along with the dampness it is not too comfortable. When we came in from chow last night we made a fatal mistake. We opened up some windows because it was stuffy in the barracks and this morning we were all half frozen Burrr it were [sic] really chilly.

Today sometime we process–the old clothing and record checks. I believe we go down by crews and we don't know when this morning or this afternoon they will come for us so we will just have to stand by and wait.

Went to church last night at 6 PM. It is really convenient here—all we have to do is walk across the street. They have our Novena here on Wednesdays so I hope I'll be able to make it a few times.

Saw a movie last night—"30 Seconds Over Tokyo"—nothing extraordinary. I do want to see Cary Grant & Ethyl Barrymore in "None But the Lonely Heart," which starts this evening.

I believe Zona and I will become quite eager anytime now. There are things we want to go over together and also there are questions that we want to talk over with a good Radio Mechanic so any free time we get will no doubt find us down there in the near future.

I'm afraid there is little more to tell for the present at any rate. They have sent, from Plant Park, the change in my address to the Gazette so that should be taken care of this time. May find out more of what it is all about today and undoubtedly to-morrow so, be good, people.

Love, Frank

November 28, Tuesday 11:00 AM

Dear Mother, Harry and Mike,

I certainly have been the lucky boy since I've been here. Yesterday morning I got a letter from the Beals and last evening one from Harry & Mother—three all being forwarded from Tampa. This morning I got one direct from home postmarked 2:30 PM on the 26th—pretty good time I'd say!

It is too bad that Harry will lose time at work and I do hope this will straighten things up for him. It is a Godsend to have the bonds—If you'd rather spend mine first and not get in a hole some time when you need dough quick & I'm not there to sign them—just ship mine here and I'll get the money in a bundle and ship you a money order. Harry, of course, looked fine to me when I was home but a little haggard when I left—I supposed you both were bushed for I know I led you a merry chase. It will behoove him in so many ways to have his teeth looked over too. I am seriously thinking of getting another allotment—that is you would automatically get so much extra each month out of my pay. I don't want to have too much money of course—it is a bad influence and I'd only spend it foolishly. Didn't do it this time for I'd like to get one good pay from the Army—never have got one more than $36 at a crack. If I do get one it won't be right away.

12:00 Noon

Just got back from chow—Breaded veal—pretty good food here all in all. The box idea sounds good to me. Anytime now and anything to eat. When we fly it is for 6 hours and the mess hall packs us all a lunch so I'm sure me and ma crew would appreciate any little home baked item on these trips. Maybe some of those square cookies of the 3 different varieties—something that doesn't crumble too easily for we have to watch out for getting the ship dirty. I can see this place is going to keep me hungry a lot of the time. I froze in bed again last night—had on 2 blankets—overcoat over that and heavy underwear and Field Jacket around my shoulders. This crap will have to come to a screeching halt. Don't know just what measure to take tonight but believe you me I'll do something.

About the pins—I finally found some in Tampa but didn't buy. I paid 40¢ for them at Yuma—they wanted 1.80 a throw. I wanted them bad enough to pay for them but Hell I knew the PX was making at least a 10% profit on them at 40¢ and I just couldn't see it. I'll get—I think - 5 pairs of medium sized ones to send home—Al, Norm, Fran, Jean, and Mrs. Ott—maybe she'll trade what she's got for the larger ones if Harry still wants the small ones. Didn't get cigars in Tampa—imagine I can get them down here, but if you already have Christmas presents I won't rush about it. I will try to get Coach some after I get paid. They are expensive running 7-9 dollars a box.

Don't be too harsh with Jerry for coming home broke. After all that's about the way I did it and let me tell you—should I ever get a chance again if I don't have a red cent I'll be home. I'd probably enjoy being home more if I were broke anyway.

In a few minutes the Radio Operators have a special session—should get a better line on what's what. We had a formation this morning but not much of importance came up. Just general familiarization with Flying Administration. At any rate I believe we fly to-morrow—start about 4 PM—should get down at 11 PM anyway.

Yesterday we processed. I have more fillings I believe. I went chasing around to see if I could get a bridge put in. The Officers here were swell about it—almost got on their knees in apology, but they just can't do it—too much more important work to be done. A lot of boys have front ones out and that comes first. I was issued a very good leather—sheepskin lined flying suit—it's a dandy also parachute harness, flight helmets, and boots. I managed to get 2 brand new 1-piece coverall fatigues and I was given 3 new underwear pants which replaces what was stolen at Plant Park. Will try to get most of my stuff to cleaners this evening some time and I still have stripes to put on so I can see where I'll be busy if I do get some spare time. Have to go now so I'll leave this open till I get back so I can let you in on the latest.

4:50

Picked up quite a bit this afternoon—there is a gent dispensing with chicken shit details—here there are overseas instructors—they want you to get what you need. They're simple, direct, and they straightened me out (for one) on a lot of things.

Am going to try to see "None But the Lonely Heart" this evening so will have to eat and change clothes. Am still not sure if flying to-morrow—we'll see. Be good, people.

Lotsa Love, Frank

November 29, Wednesday 12:15 PM

Dear Mother, Harry and Mike,

Latest is that we fly this afternoon—start at 1:15 for briefing so this will have to be short of necessity. Received Harry's letter this morning—mailed on 27th at 1:00 and I got it this morning at about 10:30.

This sure is the life in the Army. I slept till almost 10:30—somehow managed to keep warm. No one bothers you here as long as you have no formation to meet. Missed breakfast of course but had coffee at the Service Club after I got my mail. Just got back from chow—Good Roast beef—fresh asparagus, mashed pot., fresh shrimps, lots of chocolate cake & best G.I. coffee yet.

Harry tells me of his coming operation—now he will be able to join those bridge sessions with his own little story. It was wise to recognize the thing and do something about it. I personally would advise a regular period of exercise each day—take it swimming or otherwise—it would tire you at first but it is really a habit you should try to cultivate soon now—not getting any younger Haroola.

Well, all is well here and am looking forward to flying this afternoon—have found out more about flying pay and will pass it along as soon as I have more time. Have to get going now so, be good.

Lotsa Love, Frank

November 30, Thursday

Dear Mother, Harry and Mike,

Well, today is our day off! Could have had a pass to go to New Orleans or Mobile but decided not to splurge till after I get paid. Besides I have some ironing etc. that I want to do and also most of my clothes are in the cleaners. We will be paid on the 10th on a supplementary payroll and plenty of time for that. Probably go on a big bender over Christmas—get a room, big meal and all that besides it is quite pleasant here.

We flew yesterday—I didn't do too well but then I didn't try very hard. We went up with Skeleton Crews—3 of them—pilots, copilots, aerial mechanics and R.O.s. All we did was shoot landings and I'm happy to say that ma pilot is a pretty hot cookie. The pilot of the other crew had me scared silly for a while but then he hadn't flown in 5 months. Glad I won't be flying with him! I didn't even contact the ground station once but boy the nets on this place are rat races. I got two letters today, one from Harry and Mother. Glad you gave Mrs. Keough a picture if she wanted one—she and I always did get along O.K. in spite of her frequent changes of temperament. Someone ought to tell Dorothy O'Hara what the score is, but then no one could tell me but still I'm a man (no cracks). Why doesn't her father tell her—that women at war business is dead against the precepts of the church. For girls the Army or Services is the easy way out—their destiny or future is dictated to them and they're taking no chances. My impression is that a good girl is an awfully lonely WAC or WAVE and I sure as hell wouldn't want to come back to a Service woman—I want something that is a good sport underneath but it's got to be feminine—they become too good sports and too understanding in the Army—you just tell her that she can't join my nudist colony if she joins up! By the way if Mrs. Keough gives you that compass have Harry make sure as Hell that it's O.K.—it might mean my neck someday. I would have taken care of those things when I was home had I been sure of just what I would need but you have to find out from someone who knows first.

I suppose by now that Harry's operation is all done. I do hope it doesn't bother him too much but you'll never know cause he never was much on saying anything about something like that. Went out to hospital a little while ago to see our Armorer who is having his tonsils out. We'll have to go back this evening from 6-8.

We are scheduled to fly again to-morrow. This flying pay deal is a mixed up mess. Boys from Yuma were put on permanent flying status as of Oct. 10th so as far as I can find out now we will get flying pay even though we haven't our hours in for this month. According to latest, that 4 hour deal a month is right!

I'll probably be writing a bit about flying so I'll try to give you a brief idea of what it's all about. On this shift we march over to flying line–Hanger where we line up crews and roll is taken. Then we go to Briefing room where we get a News Summary–latest weather reports. Missions are assigned. You are briefed by control officer and assigned missions & ships. Pilots then sign out with control and get S.O.I. for R.O. (special operating instructions). I had to sign out for headsets for entire crew and a Gibson girl (emergency radio) and go to communications and draw a Flimsy (latest radio operating data). We then are driven out to ships–after we put on flying clothes, harness & Mae West and draw chutes. Upon arrival each man according to his job makes his preflight inspection and after that we're all set to go.

Say I'll have to cut this short–my turn to use the iron and I have a lot to do so, be good, Folks.

Lotsa Love, Frank

December 1944

December 2, Saturday

Dear Mother, Harry and Mike,

I was glad to hear today the details of Haroola's operation and will anxiously be awaiting the report on the after-effects which generally are more unpleasant than the actual operation. I'll bet the big Boy appreciated the radio–we have none in the barracks at present but we are seriously thinking of buying one. Sometimes they are swell and others not so good especially when you want to write it is hard, at least for me, to concentrate freely on what you want to say if a radio is going.

I've been getting mail right along–got 2 day before yesterday so hardly expected one yesterday. I've felt so sorry for Zona for we'd go each day together. I'd get one or two and he would be out of luck. He sent a telegram just as I did and we couldn't understand it. It was almost the last straw but he got one today–some stupid ass put down on the telegram Northport instead of Gulfport so his wife had been returned all the letters she sent. Which brings us to a painful subject. I missed yesterday–rather early for that at a new field but it just can't be helped as I see it. When we fly 4 days out of every 8 we don't get up till 11 AM (that's on this schedule) we eat and have to report soon after chow for Briefing and flying. Before we go up, one of the crew picked up a packed lunch which is provided by General Mess. This we eat while flying. We are scheduled to come down at or around 9 PM and then we have to stick around "communications" till 10 for a "critique." This is a general going over of the work or troubles you put out for the day. These things handle the work while it is fresh in your mind and their length is arbitrary and adjusted to meet the circumstance. They are good things although the reaming takes place there too. This brings us back to the barracks with only one meal for the day at about 11 or 11:30 PM so we eat again and then we have to be at school at 9 the following AM. Sooo I think you'll see that on those flying days we have little or no time unless we do it early in the morning. I would do it then but no one wakes us till 11 AM so we all sleep right through. I'll do ma derndest you can be sure, but please understand if I can't make it as often as formerly.

Today we had classes from 9 until 5:30 this afternoon. We were then scheduled for 2 hours (no less) of PT but the instructor got soft and let us off. I hope they do a lot of that.

Up to this point it has been a good deal for the gunners for they have plenty of free time while we are flying since only the Mechanic, R.O. and Pilot fly during this first week or so. We didn't even take the Co-Pilot last time.

I did manage to keep nice & warm last night. Here is the formula: 1 sheet & blanket, single one blanket double–G.I. winter underwear top on–Field Jacket over my feet & overcoat from where Field Jacket stops up to my head. Also heavy socks on and wrapped in other G.I. heavy underwear top. It was the first really comfortable night so far. If you get to it before I do please tell the girls that these socks are Grade A for the air and I imagine I'll doubly bless them at high altitude. I'll have to launder them myself but it will be worth it.

School here is a great deal different than any G.I. school I've ever been to. If the boys want to goof off the instructors cover them up at the risk of their own hides. The instructors are almost all overseas men and they are a great bunch. Their theory is that they are there to help us–not teach us a lot of new stuff but to give us tips and help us on things they wish they had had help on. It is another remarkable job of psychology–we are all quite eager. The pilots have all been told by these combat men that the R.O. is the most important man on the plane. Already you can see the Buddy Buddy attitude on the part of the Ranks. Of course they have been scaring the living hell out of the poor pilots and copilots but the thing that surprises most of us is the ignorance of the pilots on precisely what radio facilities they have on their ship–the office of the equipment and its limitations. They'll learn here of course–that is what we're here for–at one time this course was only 2 weeks and its extension is indeed a good thing. We all want to learn at least the fundamentals of the other fellow's job and how to make the best team effort. I did a better job yesterday but am hardly satisfied as yet. I'll be glad when I can go up without another radio operator along so that I can organize my own schedule and get things done as I see fit.

More about flying pay. This I believe is the whole true story. In order to get it you must be put on flying status by a Flight Surgeon. This was done Oct. 10th at Yuma. You only have to fly 4 hours/month as I originally thought and it also carries a privilege that if you don't get the 4 hours in in any one month you can make it up the following month. Hereby you get paid the month you make the time up for the preceding month when you didn't fly. As this affects me–I won't get paid for November for flying but should get a double flying pay on the last of December. We didn't get paid us yet for November, signed payroll this evening expect it on the tenth. I should get "student" flying pay still due me from Yuma also rations due me from delay and my first full pay as Corporal. All this to let you know I'm making out all right and should hit the pay dirt at least by the last of this month sooo–if you're tempted to send me any money for Christmas just hang on to it. Let's leave it this way–if I find I'm running a little short what with what little shopping etc. I have to do I know that Harry will get paid early so I'll telegraph for a couple bucks if I need it. The only reason I'd need it is I sorta plan on hitting New Orleans one of these days, whichever one we get off nearest Christmas & New Year's so thought I'd get me a big deal–hotel room–dinner and all on the closest day I could get to Christmas. Sooo if I run a little short I'll let you know–otherwise you know I'll be getting more than enough for January–so don't be sendin me money unless I wire for it and if I do wire for it I'll have it back to you as soon as the Army gives it to me.

Well, guess maybe I'll take in a double feature this evening just by way of recreation–don't even know what it is–sooo, be good, Folks.
Lotsa Love, Frank

December 5, Tuesday

Dear Mother, Harry and Mike,

Well, I'm a bad boy–no letter yesterday or the day before–hope you are not worrying. The schedule here is pretty well jammed and we are due for a change any day now to getting up at 2:30 AM to fly–I should do better on the writing score on that shift. Here's hoping anyway.

To tell the honest truth not an awful lot happens. We fly one day and attend classes from 9 until 5 PM followed by a couple hours of PT the next day. They told us we would have plenty of free time here but up until today I have not seen much of it. I say up until today–it seems they took quite a few of our planes today to West Point no less for a review. That is the reason I'm not in "The Wild Blue Yonder" right now. Of course I would like to have made the trip this time but when some velvet comes up the rank steps in and I believe that the instructors want us Radio Operators so we students are "on call" in the barracks today. This morning they stuck in a lecture and I have just finished chow. The schedule is still new enough to be interesting and up to this point I have gotten quite a kick out of the flying. We have been assigned a Navigator–2nd Looy Shackelford, I think it is (name). This will or should make my job somewhat easier for up to this point I have been having to get position reports from the pilot and then figure out the latitude and longitude and then encode the position etc. in Bomber Code before sending it to the ground station. These reports have to go in every ½ hour–then at 14 & 44 minutes after the hour we have to listen in on a special frequency for weather and special messages or code checks. So you can see we don't do a lot of dancing in the radio room. I get a bang out of it for it still fascinates me that I can communicate by voice or code to the ground no matter where the Hell you are up in that sky. I suppose I'll get over it and you may be sure that I'm not looking forward to high altitude flights when the temperature gets to around 50 below. We have been flying so far only with Pilots, Engineers and Radio Operators of 2 crews so that the R.O.s split the work. Of course it is a relief to get off but also I'll be sorta glad when I can take care of things all by myself. It is a long session–day before yesterday we logged 6 hours & 50 minutes which is not child's play.

Sunday I received all the Novena cards–Mother & Harry and Mrs. Keough & Diane. To say the least a peculiar emotion overtakes me when I get something like that–feel awfully good all over and maybe a little weepy–swell to know that you have such fine souls rooting for you. I could hardly expect God to pay much attention to my puny and hypocritical attempts of faith but I feel certain he will answer yours. Three of us made Mass Sunday at 10:30–I can't quite get used to the full day Sunday business. I did know that I wasn't to fly today so I sneaked to the show last night to see Irene Dunne & Charles Boyer in "Together Again." It is a good show with a lot of laughs–I'm sure you'd both enjoy it.

I was glad to get Harry's medical report. Glad it wasn't too bad anyway. Boy– Mother writes of that homegrown attention and care given the ailing–Ka-runch I could sure do with some petting like that–list that first among the things the would-be soldier wants most. The weather here has been of the cold clammy variety–have a good system to keep warm now. At last we turned in laundry today–I personally turned in over 50 pieces–just hope and pray I get my own stuff back again but then it wasn't much good to me dirty!

If it is at all possible I wish you would try to get Dick Perry's address for me, also instructions as to how to write him–V-mail or otherwise. Since sometime in the future I expect to be going to that Theatre, some firsthand information on what to take or if he needs or wants some little thing you never know but what, I might be able to get it to him. We have been given some idea by the overseas personnel here so I'll have something to guide me at any rate. Of course this is all in the distant future but it never hurts to have some idea of where you stand. I have no idea of how you feel about it but most of us are exceedingly glad that we seem destined for Europe, could well be Italy too. In Italy your missions are a good deal longer so you get credit for 2 on every one you fly.

Just passing the following along as general information of interest. Of course we have all felt rather smug because we felt secure in the Air Corps–none of the slop & mud & hardship of the Infantry. Well, the prevailing concerns of opinion of the men here–overseas veterans–is that when they finish up in the European Theatre that many Air Crew men may be shipped right to the Infantry. Just imagine some men who have finished a tour of duty as Air Crew members have been shunted just there after all their hard work and subjection to the dangers and difficulties of air combat. Just doesn't seem on the level does it? This is the way they figure—to begin with there is a manpower shortage for the Infantry. Also at present—last figures I've heard & keep em under your hat—at least 13 thousand bombers in Europe of the B-17 variety. They cannot use them as yet in the China Burma India Theatre and in the South Pacific sooo if and when they finish off Germany—what the Hell will they do with all those physically perfect Air Crews? They can't leave them idle and the overseas boys here guess the Infantry. Of course it's all conjecture but it makes interesting, if not the most pleasant type of speculation.

Well, people, I must get on with my writing—have a lot to do yet today and there's no telling when I'll get the next chance. May go to the Non-Coms club tonight for a couple beers to round off the day also have some socks I should wash out—soo, be good.

Lotsa Love, Frank

December 5, Tuesday

Dear Harry,

It is high time I sat down and penned a special one to you. The most important thing I want to get across is something I have wanted to say since I was home. To another fellow, even your brother, it doesn't seem very manly to get emotional but it is important to me that I let you know to some extent just what it meant to have you at home when I got there and to have you there and with me while I was home. I honestly believe that the type of fellowship that exists between us and which God has permitted us to enjoy is not anything ordinary. Of course most of the lads went home to towns devoid of fellows they had known, where as I had a special dividend in you. Someone who still thought the way I did, had the same interests and who was ever ready to join me in my every whim and notion. You played no little part in making my time home the best furlough a fellow ever had. Thanks a million for holding together my family—for that lump in your throat at the station—for being what you are.

And now to my more temporal problems and ideas. I must let you at least understand that it is not laxness on my part that I do not write home more frequently while here. Of course this is the most important training I have had as yet and to tell the truth I fear that many of the details would hardly make cheerful reading at home—in a word I fear that much of it would worry Tess and there is no sense in that. For example the planes here are not the best in the world—in fact the first 2 days of flying netted me less than 5 hours and we flew in 6 different ships. They fly these crates so much that it is apparently impossible to keep them in the best of repair. We take em up and have to bring em down right away again. Best day I've had was Sunday when we got the whole day almost 7 hours in one ship. It was unusual! Don't let me give you the wrong impression—it is not so dangerous but just that it sounds so—that's why we fly with Engineers so that we come down before any chronic trouble exists—we get it before it happens. As far as I can discover there have been very few accidents here comparatively but you have to be ever on the alert—as the saying goes "Flying of itself is not inherently dangerous but even to a greater extent than the sea, it is unremittingly unforgiving of carelessness."

I want to get the Christmas situation straight if possible. Please let me know as soon as you possibly can how you stand on it. I would Air Mail this right now but to tell the truth I am flat broke. Will have been paid by the 10th on a supplementary payroll so should be able to get into action by then. Just what do you plan for Mother? I well realize what you have been up against being operated upon and all and you probably don't feel too well even now. I will be able to send you money by the 10th so let me know—if you don't write for it I'll just go to New Orleans and get something for both of you anyway so I leave it up to you. Let me know as soon as you can about above. Also as near as possible let me know how you will spend the holidays—essentially where you two will be for I may get a chance to call you. Lines of course will be crowded so I may not be able to make it on the holidays themselves but if I know you'll be home some night during Christmas week or sometime perhaps I can make it then.

I sincerely hope you two will not go overboard for me. As I have said before there are a lot of us together in the same boat. I think we fly Christmas day anyhow so my guess is that it will be harder for you people than for me here.

At any rate, be good and take care of yourselves. By the Grace of God we may spend the next Christmas together again—Here's hopin. Be sure to give me the dope soon.

Love, Frank

December 6, Wednesday

Dear Mother, Harry and Mike,

Well, we had ground school today again. Nothing of particular but we did see a couple good films on the importance of Briefing and after Flight Interrogation. It warmed up yesterday here in Miss. only to be followed by almost torrential rains. It has not let up for any substantial period today. We don't have anything quite like it at home in it just pours. We had to sit through lectures this morning drenched & chilled in a cold theatre. It is a wonder we don't all have colds. I didn't get any mail yesterday but did get two this afternoon.

Don't worry about the compass situation. I shall do just as you suggest and see my PX officer about it at my earliest opportunity. I'll manage one way or another to get those things if you can't, so don't get too het up about it. Mother if I were you I wouldn't worry too much about the house cleaning—somehow it is always there and it is one thing that will keep. Am glad you both are set to get tight New Year's Eve. Did you say you were going to Bealy's on Christmas? I got that impression somewhere. If you are, it should be a couple good occasions for you both. I too shall get a bit on the fluid side if I can manage it—be thinking of you both with each nip.

It is peculiar to me that you haven't heard from the Perrys. Don't they usually make Peace Overtures around the Christmas season? Just what goes at Bell? From

Recognition class here we know that the British & American air forces will not use the P-68, Bell's latest, and of course I got the idea they were through when I was home. Often wonder how and where Uncle Bob stands through all this.

Your letter reminds me again of the letters I must write, Brownie & Julius and Al Daher & Hamernik. I did manage about 5 yesterday but they went to Mrs. Keogh, Beals, Diane, and youse guys got your daily one so I just don't seem to get there. Also must write Gramp. Felt in the mood yesterday–too bad I don't capture the mood more often. Don't worry about my keeping on the ball in the air. I still have plenty to learn but I keep getting in everyone's hair because there are things I keep wanting to get straight. I feel that I get along swell with my pilot. I have been able up to this point to relieve him of a couple responsibilities. Although he is a master at handling that ship and a swell fellow he is still just a kid in lots of ways. I know you'd laugh at me chasing that big Swede about–he must take one step to my three - reminding him of things and keeping track of his flying clothes & mission folder for him. As long as we Radio Operators keep our mouths shut, you know we keep everyone in the ship pretty well baffled. They don't have any idea of how we do what we do–unless they've had some experience, most people can't read a Radio Operator's log intelligently. So we let on we're important and everyone seems content to leave us & our dignity quite alone. They don't tread on our toes & go out of their way to be decent. We're not so hot, but as long as no one else can do our job they consider us pretty important I guess.

Please don't work yourself to a frazzle Mom, trying to get boxes off to me. You have more than enough to do watching our invalid–"Snotty Nose." And I hope to heaven you don't go all out for Christmas–not just because I don't need anything but also because I know that some of my buddies are not so fortunate as me and we don't want em to feel too bad by comparison. Of course I share with em, but it hurts a little I imagine to see some joker get a lot from home.

Going to try to make U.S.O. stage show tonight–not much time to make it now–my 1st since I've been in the Army–Hope the bad weather keeps them away.

Be good, people.

Lotsa Love, Frank

December 7, Thursday

Dear Mother, Harry and Mike,

Just writing the date gives me an ominous sensation–feel like it should be recognized by some way or another–I had heard that they were going to have some sort of parade–some manifestation of the pendulant would be a little more appropriate to my way or thinking.

Is Haroola back at work yet? Under this sort of set up with Sunday a work day just as any other I feel I lose complete track of time and its passing. We all have trouble with what day it is to say nothing of the date. We are not flying again today due to the absence of our ships. They did stick in a special formation for Radio Operators this morning. We climbed out of the sac at 7 AM and the rest of our crews gave us the horse laugh. We had a lecture and demonstration on cameras. It seems that the taking of pictures during bomb runs will be another of our jobs. The Bombardier signals us and we take the pictures with large cameras, which are mounted in the belly of the ship right under the floor of our Radio compartment. It is obvious why it is important to get pictures of bomb runs but I hardly thought we as R.O.s would get stuck with the job.

Of course we have a lot of work to do here that we never would have to do in combat. While on a combat mission you just don't transmit at all. If you did the enemy would be able to take a bearing on you immediately, estimate your numbers and tell where and when you were coming. We just have to monitor certain frequencies at certain times to catch official messages. You keep your hands off the transmitter unless it is an emergency. Sooo since you have little actual radio work to do in combat the idea is to train you here so that you will be capable of meeting any exigency.

I have been getting quite a kick out of Zona the last few days. After declining definitely to the contrary he and his Ball Turret Gunner have decided to have their women down here. They are both busy as cats on a tin roof. Spring—the other fellow—isn't married as yet but intends to marry the gal when she gets here. They want to get a 2-bedroom apartment, which are supposed to be rather scarce in town and I certainly wish them luck. They're just like a couple kids and are having a lot of fun planning. They're going to try to get a place this afternoon. Far be it from me to judge the wisdom in it, but I'm glad to see them get so much pleasure from planning it. Here they will be allowed to go on separate rations and while they will have to maintain a bunk they will not be seriously restrained on their free time.

The U.S.O. show last night was not too bad. The entertainers were just a little on the amateurish side—the main trouble being that most people believe that G.I.s will go crazy over anything, and that's true that they will, but we still appreciate the genuine thing. They had 6 not too bad chorus girls but they couldn't dance worth a damn. Singers, specialists, comedian, ballroom, and burlesque exhibition dancers. It was a good couple hour stage show and I was glad that I went.

We were issued quilted comforters this morning so that there should be no reason for our being cold any more. If you note any lack of continuity in this just blame it on the Army (as usual). We just G.I.'d the barracks for the regular Friday inspection.

With planes gone some of the crews in our outfit drew 3 day passes—don't have to be in until 12 Midnight Saturday night. I guess our pilot must have been off the ball—have to tell him about it. Really doesn't matter much to me just now—if I had been paid it would have been another story. Our day off is to-morrow. I have been just keeping ahead financially but yesterday one of the lads paid me some I loaned him from Plant Park so that I'll be fine till Sunday when I understand we get paid. I have money coming from my regular pay & rations which I should get Sunday. We went up to the Air Inspectors and griped about flying pay still due us from Yuma. They assured us that we would get it in a few days. The trouble is that Plant Park checked us out as paid in full when we left there and we never did get our flying pay. We are told that a representative from here went down to Tampa to straighten it out 3 or 4 days ago. Also a couple of fellows got refunds on the unused portion of their tickets to Tampa so shortly after I got here I wrote for mine and hope to get that soon, although there is a good deal of doubt in my mind about actually getting it. Sooo there are three sources which should bolster my new wallet in the near future—better happen soon cause I haven't done a bit of Christmas shopping yet.

   Guess that takes in most of the dirt for today folks. So be sure and be good.
Lotsa Love, Frank

December 8, Friday

Dear Mother, Harry and Mike,

   Well, yee Old Friday is here again. Say where were all those reminders I was supposed to get on those Holy Days of Obligation—well, surprise, for once I managed to remember on my own. Today being our day off I slept in—seems we've been doing a bit of that lately—eating late at night too. We sleep in the morning till the last minute—through breakfast and all. Then we get up and rush like hell to wash, shave, make beds, and clean up the barracks. As a result of this we don't use the 1st punch on our mess pass sooo at night any time after 10 PM that we get in the mood we go over in the mess hall and eat the breakfast we missed that morning. That late they start serving breakfast at the mess hall. A pretty good evening here consists of going to the show at 6:30 and from there to the Officers (noncommissioned) Club and drinkin beer then back to the mess hall for late breakfast. That's what we did last night. Saw "Wilson"–thought they did a very good job with it. Then down to the Non-Coms club where we had 4 or 5 beers and listened to that good band down there. It is as good as almost any band I've ever seen. Swell selection of music—not much of that Jive business. Of course it makes you want to dance so I did manage to grab off a few dances—the other fellows weren't quite so lucky or maybe they weren't in the mood to try. We left at about 10:30 or 11 and went to mess hall for pancakes honey & butter, cornflakes and milk, fresh greatfruit (sic) and coffee. Thence to the sac, which reinforced with that comforter, was cozy and warm last night. Huba Huba.

   I hear we get paid to-morrow so I may go into Gulfport to-morrow evening. I want to get some washcloths and a couple more towels—get my clothes out of the cleaners and various odds and ends. Don't imagine I'll spend much time there because all I really want to find out is how to make connections to New Orleans next Saturday. There has been a faint suggestion that we may fly on the morrow but I don't think so. When we do start it will be on that 3 AM shift which is mighty early in the morning. Gosh folks, can't think of much more to say—am in there bitching as usual—no mail as yet—maybe later this afternoon. So, be good, people.
Love, Frank

December 9, Saturday

Dear Mother, Harry and Mike,

Today has been a quiet one as have the past few. I personally have been taking advantage of it in solid comfort, doing next to nothing, sleeping, all the eating I can manage—even doing some reading. I have Mother's of Tuesday before me and Harry's of Wednesday, the former received yesterday late and the latter just picked up. The mail situation is very good here.

So, Mom had a busy day—wasn't it ever thus around the Holidays but that's what makes em Holidays I guess. I did manage to write to Gramp a couple days ago—in it I told him I had a sneaking idea that I might go to England and suggested he send me addresses of the roots of the family tree there. Am rather anxious to see just what reaction to this will manifest itself. In days of yore the undeveloped system of transportation enabled a man whose roots spring from another part of the world to keep the family skeleton well buried. I have a hunch they won't want me doing much probing and they know sure as hell that is what I would do. Your mentioning Ruth Schaffer reminds me to ask you if you can get Mary Lou's address for me also verify spelling of last name—I never did get it right.

Harry I'd say it was rather nice of Steve to drop around. Also the 2 phones sounds good to me—just keep pinching them in the ass around there—make em kick you up-stairs if necessary—they are all so lulled asleep by their own security and self-satis-faction that there should be plenty of opportunity for the coming young man—cream always comes to the top but don't just let them homogenize you with the rest of the ilk.

Glad to hear you're going back if you are well enough—I know that it used to seem futile to me to hang around the house when ill with nothing to do—I got over it. You speak of my watch—I sure as hell need it—have done everything to get one down here but as G.Is ever do—those who went before spoiled it for us. We don't get watches till just before we go over now. It seems that the fellows all lost them when they were is-sued here so that they had to draw another. The Gov't. just couldn't keep up with the demand so we don't get them now until the last minute. The cigarette situation is fine here—I was thinking I might try to send you a couple cartons if they are as tight now as they were when I was home. Will try to do so when I get paid. Nope they didn't do it today and so it looks like we'll have to wait until next Monday. I honestly don't especially need the money until next Friday but it burns me up—you're ordered & have to comply at the snap of a finger but when the obligation is on their part you can piss and moan for what is honestly due you. The Army so stresses prompt-ness—the morale among the men would be a great deal better if Authority met their obligations as promptly and as cheerfully as we are required to meet ours.

Harry, Zona says that it was funny but he wasn't scared a bit. He is in the same barracks as us—I'm in Crew 440 and he is in 442—we only have 4 crews—20 men in the barracks and since he and I are R.O.s we go to classes together. He and I went about quite a bit but he has his wife coming down soon now I expect and I haven't been seeing much of him—he and Spring—his assistant R.O. did manage to get an apartment in town yesterday so I judge that soon he will be a busy boy rushing for town every spare moment he has. I have tried not to be so chummy with him lately for I know this is a big deal for him and glad to see him glean some happiness from his rather lonely state here. A single man is much happier in the Army!

Life being what it has been, I managed to get me a book at the Library yesterday—it is written by Nordhoff & Hall of "The Bounty Trilogy"—the title is "Botany Bay." It is as good as their other works. It is of particular interest to me for I have often wondered a bit about its colonization—I see I have neglected to mention it concerns the initial colonization of Australia. As close as I can figure, up until 1860-70 Australia was used as a destination for the transportation of petty criminals and incorrigibles—so stringent and unjust was the English prosecution of law at the time. It makes me wonder now, although it never hit me at the time—Gramp once spoke to me as being a cook there for sheep ranchers—also once last time I was home he spoke of having a tooth pulled on shipboard going to Australia—he explained how the Doctor was a Jack of all Trades and how successful the Doctor was at not losing a soul on the trip—he explained at the time that the Doctor on the ship got so much a head for the healthy people on the ship who arrived. Makes food for thought for we all have a hunch that Gramp never went to Australia in search of adventure. Harry if you get a chance—get the book and see what you think. Thas (sic) all for today Folks. Lotsa Love, Frank

December 10, Sunday

Dear Mother, Harry and Mike,

I fear this will have to be a shortie for I've just gotten out of church and I still want to try to make a movie tonight. It is a Bogart in Hemmingway's in "To Have & Have Not." Latest word is that we fly to-morrow so I won't get a chance to see it to-morrow night.

Received two letters today so I don't suppose I'll hit Pay Dirt to-morrow. I sure will be looking for that Box! No Mom, I don't think that it is strange Stenzlback's father not knowing what Irwin is doing—he was listed, I believe, as administrative personnel in the office, no telling what duties may have been forced on him by the exigencies of the situation over there. I'll bet the new teeth will be hard to get used to—the hole where they took out my last one is still a little tender so I can imagine how yours must feel.

Am awfully glad you feel better fell oh—things like that make a lot of difference some times.

Very little to report from here—start in the wild blue yonder to-morrow after just a week's lay off. Ground school today and the pressure chamber again. We were almost in wrong—reported 1 ½ hours late for pressure chamber and none of Officers showed up—we got reamed out good by school authorities and come to find out, just as we claimed, notice of our appointment there was never posted. So for once we were in the right. Just to make sure, our flying officers raised hell about it at the

Tactical Office–seems good to have someone hold up your end for you for once. Well, thas all. Be good, folks.
Lotsa Love, Frank

December 12, Tuesday

Dear Mother, Harry and Mike,

   As you have no doubt surmised by now I didn't make it yesterday. We flew and I didn't get up until the last minute, ate lunch, and reported to my formation. It was the first time we had flown with a complete crew & we had a new Navigator and Bombardier, also our Armorer who had had his tonsils out at the hospital since he arrived here. It was a pretty good trip and it is a lot better with me when we do have a Navigator. I can get the information I need much more quickly and efficiently. I had a little trouble with the radio not being as it should but aside from that all went well.

   The night before last I went to see "To Have and Have Not." By all means see it. It is obviously an attempt to do another Casa Blanca and I personally enjoyed it a great deal more. Lauren Bacall is new and showed it in spots but I enjoyed the thing more than any I've seen in ages. Just the type of movie I enjoy–I got a big kick out of it.

   Today brought a series of good things. First a package from home and what a box! Second, pay day and third, we got our laundry back. I'll try to deal with each individually. First the box. T'was indeed a dandy! To begin with I got out of class early today so when I got yee old donation I had it all to myself in the barracks. To be sure I don't like to be stingy with–indeed generous I am, but I like to do the dishing out as I see fit. So the full box of cookies is salted away. I have let the part box and bread to the wolves in the barracks and it is almost all gone now. I put away the cheese (God love it) and the sausage. I'm fortunate in having it cold (burr) here so it was fine upon arrival and will keep well. I'm saving cookies for flying tomorrow. I wanted em for our crew–if there are any left the boys can have em, but these are the guys I'll be with so we'll eat them together at 20 or 30 thousand feet. We get up at 2:30 AM in the morning so you can judge how nice they'll come in. I judge we'll be at high altitude to-morrow–I was frozen yesterday at 6 thousand I'll probably come down frozen stiff to-morrow. Don't know just how I'll manage the asparagrass but "will do" ya know. The boys are all yelling for more cookies but they don't know I have the others so it won't hurt them. Everything was in grand shape and thanks a million.

   We got paid–as I said–drew 42 bucks. I paid what I owed, bought cigarettes and some soap & shave cream, and have 37 left. Don't know how it will stand me with what I have to do this month–you know–much wants more, but I'll have to try to manage. Have to go to New Orleans and do a little shopping next Saturday–hope I can get out Friday around 2 or 3 PM and stay overnight in the city. On this 2:30 AM schedule we're through flying by 12 or 1 PM so we shall see. I tried to get wings at the PX but they don't have em now that I have the money to buy them–isn't it always the way? Maybe I can get them in the city or I may go to Keesler Field near Biloxi and see what I can do there.

The laundry was terrible—not exaggerating, the clothes were worse than when we sent them. They smell clean but goodness what a mess—nothing—nothing came back clean. I can see I'm going to have to do my own underwear and T-shirts if I want them anyways white—such a mess! Such moaning on all our parts—it was indeed a disappointment!

I guess that takes in most of it. As I said we arise early—all too early in the morning so with that in mind I guess I'd better get me washed & shaved and ready for to-morrow's session. I have no doubt that what it will be is a high altitude flight—oh well, it has to come sooner or later. Didn't get any letters yesterday or today from youse guys so there's not much to "write over." Received a letter from Coach and one from Beals when I got ma box. Don't know when I'll get to answer these. Going to try to get into town and pick up a few oddments to-morrow afternoon and evening. Guess thas all folks—be good.

Lotsa Love, Frank

December 13, Wednesday, 8:30 PM

Dear Mother, Harry and Mike,

Well, to say the least, today was a beauty. All of it. Up at 2:30 AM—breakfast and cleaning up, making bunks etc. rush to make buses, which leave the Tactical offices promptly at 3:30 AM. Roll call in the Hanger and thence to the briefing room. We flew our first Pseudo Combat mission today—formation of 42 planes no less. We simulated combat conditions, had definite target—the whole works—attacking P-40s and all. Of course in combat you would be on radio silence all the way unless you were in trouble, however here in order to keep track of the formations 4 ships, including the lead ship, had to send position reports—yup our ship was one of them. I had a rather rough time at first for all standard equipment was not on my plane, but after talking it over with the Pilot & Istr. Pilot, we decided on make shift methods, which proved successful and we made out O.K. I got in a goodly number of reports although not as many as I wished or as I should have, but none squawked and apparently the whole thing went off with as much success as could be expected for the first time. Some of the pilots not having any formation flying since they've been here. Our Navigator is right on the ball and really is a comfort and help to me. Incidentally those cookies sure did vanish—didn't have any left when we got back, they certainly were a treat—especially since we were up so long—up before 7 and not down till after 1—with Interrogations and Critiques and turning in equipment I didn't clear the line until about 3 or 3:30. I'll say we all were tired! But it was then that I finally got into action. Got a haircut, got ma clothes out of the cleaners, showered, and shaved—drew ma pass & off to Town. Not much of a town—not at all bad for a small town—as always just a pity there are so many G.I.s per town. I couldn't buy towels or washcloths for love nor money. Have to get them in New Orleans I guess. I did get Bus & Train schedules—now I'll have to see what kind of a pass deal my Boy Lt. Sundin can get for me. I do hope he fixes it so that I can get out early Friday afternoon. I am a bit tired—

I'll admit that. But I did get a pretty good meal in town and I will say that the women are friendly here abouts. Honest I could easily have had a couple but as usual I'm just not there. When it comes to walking right up and puttin the suggestion (any suggestion will do at the time) to them well, it grates against my delicate social nature. It is too damn cheap but I'll learn I guess - gotta get my lovin in some place along the line.

No word from youse guys again today, that makes 3 days running. Of course I got ma box yesterday - t'was grand but not a letter. We have decided that it must be the Christmas rush or something because fellows from New England & N.Y. are all in the same boat - probably get it to-morrow. Well, that leaves not much more to tell or talk about - ragged, fat, & sassy as usual and I think I'll go to bed soon now it's been a rough day - up at 7:30 AM for ground school so, be good, Folks.
Love, Frank

December 14th

Dear Mother, Harry and Mike,

At present I have washed & shaved and changed into O.D.s and am quite comfortable in the Post Library. Very little new to report. We fly to-morrow and arise at 2:30 AM again - Oh and with such glee. It is fun though and I would not be adhering to the truth if I said otherwise. The drawing of equipment and getting to the plane, loading it & giving it a rigorous preflight inspection is work and it's hard work while you're up there in a way, but it has its good points and I do get a kick out of it still. We'll see if I feel the same way in another couple months.

Glad to hear Mother's Christmas shopping was a success enough for her to get some pleasure out of it - as I remember last year she wasn't too het up about it. I note in today's letter I am to be on the lookout for another package. My Goodness - we just demolished the cheese, crackers, and sausage this evening and now another one - Huba Huba!

Today we had ground school only - not much new - mostly of a "refresher" nature. I personally get quite fed up on a lot of it, but by such repetition it seems that somewhere you can always pick up something new. And so it goes. I'm going to try to hit the sac a little earlier this evening - that 2:30 rolls around mighty quickly. Sooo, be good, Folks.
Lotsa Love, Frank

December 15th

Dear Mother, Harry and Mike,

This is indeed a rather hard letter to write! I received your first box yesterday. I had to unwrap the box itself for there is no place to keep a box that size. OH so many little packages done up in cute wrapping and Christmassy greetings - even Mike had a hand in it. I didn't unwrap a one for I do not want to rob myself of the pleasure of opening the many things Christmas morning or sometime thereabouts. I had just come down from flying a 1,000 mile cross country up at 2:30 AM and not released from flight line until about 3 or 3:30 PM. I picked up the box just after I got away and was feeling quite exuberant - then I went to get my pass to New Orleans only to find it voided by my pilot's applying for it 24 hours too late. Well, there I was - a whole box from home and a letter from our Big Boy telling me another was on the way and my only chance to try to get you fellows something for Christmas was gone My ordinary pass is good for only 50 miles so I hurriedly showered and shaved and did Gulfport all over again and then went to Biloxi and from there to the PXs at Keesler Field. There was just nothing to be had that I would bother sending home and my only other chance to find something would be next week in New Orleans but our day off will be Sunday so that is out. Of course I should have done it all at Tampa but at the time I could not get into the city while stores were open - one Saturday evening I drew K.P. and the other I was making Mission along with Guard duty. Once here I was too low on funds to do much in New Orleans and when I finally get some money my pass was voided. So there it is Folks - not ta (sic) thing for my darlins - somehow I can't see how I could have done otherwise but I should have found a way. I felt pretty low all day yesterday as I rather frantically toured as far as I could go but that's not much good.

Thus I hope you will try to forgive me a little - it is not that I didn't think about it I just lacked the required ingenuity somewhere along the line. You know what I think about money as a gift - it is piss poor but I hope you'll understand that it is about all I can do right now. Formerly I got a lot of pleasure out of shopping around and hiding presents and being in cahoots and stuff but I couldn't do it myself this year and then when I discover how the pair of you have been all out.

There is absolutely nothing here that I would put postage on and send you - there might have been something a month ago but there isn't now. Anyhow, I'm enclosing a money order. It is not much, but as I remember we always went a little over the line around the Holidays - maybe wanted a little something extra - I hope this may help a little in that direction - get an extra 5th and have one on me and get a brand new bone for Mike too. Take in a show and dinner in Buffalo - do something you wouldn't have otherwise and tell me about it. Please, please, do not deny me the pleasure of this at least. You know how I feel about money - I wouldn't do it if there had been any other way but since yesterday I have felt it would be my only recourse and it is.

Don't feel much like writing much more now - Start flying at a different schedule to-morrow - arise at 4:30 instead of 2:30 so, be good, folks.
Love, Frank

December 16th

Dear Mother, Harry and Mike,

Well, I'd best say something about that epic of despair I penned yesterday, feeling a little sorry for myself I guess - please accept the money anyhow - not much use feeling bad - it was all I could do so we'll say no more about it.

I'll try to answer a little more intelligently some I have received. About the knife - wanted it pointed - both edges capable of being sharpened to a reasonably keen edge thus (drawing of knife) small hand guard preferred. Now if it offers as much of a problem as it seems to have, I saw some in town yesterday which quite fit the bill so don't go too far out of your way to get it.

Glad Harry will get some good out of the suit; hate to think of its potentialities rotting in the closet - knock em dead kid! Too bad about the pictures but perhaps another day. And also glad that Harry is picking up the odd job complex. It is kinda fun and means a lot - just little things that have to be done one way or another. Have already started on cigarettes Harry. Please give me a little time as I can only get 4 packages a day but as I say I have started and will ship them on as soon as I can accumulate enough to make it worthwhile sending.

Yes I was wondering where the Hell those letters with the distinctive vertical writing were going. I understand how busy you are about now - don't like not to get them but circumstances alter cases and I know is being done by, in your best manner, as per usual. Say Barb why don't you tell me what you're getting the big boy! Don't worry about my finances you always knew I was never one to strap little Francis George. Also received $18.05 from R. R. today so look at the 60 dollars the way I do - 30 I got from Harry and 20 you gave me to get to Tampa which the R.R. has reimbursed me and the extra 10 hardly covers what you two bought for me and gave me for spending money on the trip so I'm still in your debt even with it. Thas why you gotta keep the twenty! I'd appreciate it if you would send on the woolen sox - they are made to order for this high altitude stuff. They keep the tootsies warm and you know me - when ma tootsies are cold, well, I'm just no good. Did you manage to get Dick's address for me?

We flew today - up at 4 AM - as I've told you I eat at night and then don't breakfast - figure I feel better that way and am not so apt to get sick if the going gets rough. We were briefed and were supposed to light into the Wild Blue Yonder at 7 AM but due to a heavy fog we couldn't take off till about 11 AM so we didn't have as much time flying as we would have had ordinarily. It was high altitude today - only had a couple hours of it - however type O2 masks made it easier for me although I'm quite tired now. Soon as I left the line I got my mail - read it on the way back. I ate right after that and then showered and shaved changed into O.D.s and here I am writing. We'll take off for church in another 15 minutes. Sure isn't much like (later after church) a Sunday when you are on the go but getting to Mass is the main thing. We'll try to make Confession to-morrow evening with the Novena - just think I'll be going to Novena about the same time you fellows will be there. I want to get to Communion - avoid Christmas rush you know - also have been doing too much flying without being in State of Grace. Have to stop that nonsense.

Had some trouble with my Navigator last Friday - he is a Southerner - what I'd call good at his job. (in spite of it). He keeps track of information, which I must send to Base every 1/2 hour. Well, in our 1,000 mile Cross Country I guess I was a little too persistent about keeping after him to give me the information I needed - he got a little raw about it and of course in a plane you don't have to take that crap from anyone.

However I feel that it is 75% of my job to get along with the men I will be fighting with and 25% to use every advantage of my skill and equipment to keep all feeling at ease and helping by getting information rapidly when it is needed. With this in mind I didn't say anything nasty although I sure felt like putting the Brass in its place.

Well, as it turned out I didn't have to get rough - the Pilot heard the aforementioned conversation and although I was busy at the time and didn't get to hear it - My boy Sundin reamed out the Navigator, told him that I was to have said information. You see if I don't come through at least once an hour, we have to turn back to Base and be assigned some other type of mission. As far as the radio was concerned on this particular trip, I was at a distinct disadvantage for the most effective antenna on the ship was not installed in it and in addition to that my receiver tubes were weak and though I could get through I believe at 400-500 miles away from Gulfport I could not receive answers to my messages, so without receipts for those messages they could be of no particular use to us. Also in order to get Army stations along the way I had to be right on the frequency, but the electric device, "a frequency meter," which I had on the plane, was inoperative due to worn out dry cells. So for 2 1/2 hours I was in a pretty pickle. The pilot was well aware of what I was up against and that the whole crew would only have to repeat the mission if we didn't somehow get straightened out. Then to have the lad in the nose get irate was almost too much for me and apparently too much for ma pilot.

That evening I went into town trying to shop but getting nowhere. The Navigator comes up to me on a corner, we shoot the Bull - he is trying to shop too - we both took off for Biloxi together and thence to Keesler Field and back to Biloxi. I left him there for I had to report before 12, but he was real chummy - is going to teach me some Navigation if I'll check him out on the Liaison set. Lots of Buddy Buddy stuff all at once - but that is the essence of this thing - if you don't have a 9-10 man team with precision you might as well stop trying right there.

Today everyone was in the Ball game again. We accomplished a good deal in spite of late take off due to bad weather. Will probably be flying gunnery missions again soon - like those at Yuma. We'll have overseas veterans as gunnery instructors this time and should get a lot out of it.

As I told you, I've just come out of church. They will have Midnight Mass in one of the theatres here. May make it or may try it in New Orleans haven't decided as yet. Have to wait and see if we can get Christmas day off - may have to fly - we shall see. I still have a pint in my footlocker that I brought from Tampa so I'll have some Christmas cheer at any rate.

I'll have to write Beals and Otts on the morrow, should do it tonight but believe that I may have me a beer or so and then go to bed. Those 4 AM till 10-12 at night days tire me - a good healthy tired and I sleep sound and undisturbed by Hell and High water.

I have ground school to-morrow - try to goof off PT to make church - we'll see. Guess this should arrive about before Christmas is a Merry Merry one to youse guys and be good -
Lotsa Love, Frank

December 18th

Dear Mother, Harry and Mike,

Well, another day, another dollar. Just finished the day's ground school and am now awaiting the call to a 2 hour PT session. Received Mother's Saturday letter this morning. You mention getting good out of things, makes me wonder just what's up but of course I don't dare peak so I'll just wonder. I may open things early for we have a rather good deal here over Christmas. We are through flying Saturday about 2 or 3 (or 4) with Sunday off - also have Christmas - Monday off so that means I may take off like a big ass bird Saturday afternoon and go to New Orleans for Saturday night Sunday all day - depending on the schedule we fly. When to be back; Monday or even Tuesday who knows? Don't know just what the hell I'd do there but trust me to find something.

Mother asked about Zona - his wife should be here Wednesday. About the paling business - I've been with fellows on my crew a good deal. Spencer (Tail) is married and off the Post a good deal during his spare time. Ferniza (Engineer) chums with another mechanic, one who went through AM & Gunnery with him. That leaves Kimpel (Armorer) & Shaffer (Ball Turret). The former is rather morose and sullen a good deal of the time and makes a poor companion. I believe, this is just a guess, that at one time he held a commission flying in Air Transport but was reduced to the ranks. As I say, this makes him not good in his nature to pal around with but lady if anything should ever happen to pilot or co-pilot it is reassuring to feel that there is someone else around who can really fly one of those big crates. Shaffer is a former cook, apparently volunteered for gunnery in a weak moment. He's quite a character - no breeding or background - left home & school at 15, but he is willing and a good man to have around in a plane. He outranks me by one stripe but is my assistant and helps me with the many things I have to be responsible for in the ship - he knows nothing of radio - I have hopes of teaching him but God only knows when I shall get the time or opportunity. Sooo that leaves no one I'm particularly keen about and leaves me alone if I wish to develop socially at all. Probably a good situation. Just as in civilian life if you would do just as you want you don't want to be too close to anyone or obligated in your activities. At any rate I've found one guy a Sgt. - Leonard - his people own a slice of Lorillard Tobacco Co. - seems to like the things I do so if I go to New Orleans I'll go with him or alone probably.

Whoops there is PT whistle - should get back to this later - don't go way!

Tuesday - December 19

Gee I hope you didn't stand around waiting for me to come back. Didn't manage to get back last night. They got us up at 4 AM this morning. Ate last night and again this morning so I'm keeping well fed anyhow. We had another Cross Country this morning and afternoon along with Camera Bombing in a couple of localities and used practice bombs on the bomb range. Lotsa fun - and 6 1/2 hours of solid work. Did a better job this time than I have I think - even to trouble shooting in the air and shooting fixes with the radio compass. Didn't get back here until about 4:45. Washed and then went to eat. Soon after I came back I picked up my laundry - much better job this time and then I had to get laundry ready to turn in - went to PX to get some more butts for Haroola - just about have the 2 cartons now - am trying to get hold of another box of book matches like those at Sioux Falls - soon as I do I'll ship them on.

Of course in the process of getting dirty clothes together I had to rearrange all the boxes from the first box in my footlocker - made what I'd call some pretty good guesses but will just have to wait to find out how good.

I received the 2nd box this afternoon - of course I spotted it right away in the Post Office and honestly I groaned inwardly for it looked so big - I wondered what the Hell now - I have a long way to walk and I was then and am now very tired. I picked it up and now am more curious than ever - the box is so light. Well, it is at the side of my bunk - have given up trying to keep Christmas boxes in inadequate places provided by the Army so we all have them lying around by our bunks - just no other place to put them.

Gee Folks, I'm dead tired - like to write more but it just isn't there. Be good, Folks. Lotsa Love, Frank

December 20th, Wednesday

Dear Mother, Harry and Mike,

Nothing much of importance today except that we found out the pass deal over Christmas. The Pilot, Lt. Sundin, applied for passes from Saturday at 4 PM until Tuesday at 9 AM so that gives us lots of time. Of course we'll have to see whether the Tactical Office will let them go through like that but it's more time than I've had in the Army. A couple more days and I'd try to make it home - alas such good fortune is not our lot but it's a pleasant thought. You like to think that there are only civilian limitations on your activities, but in reality there are greater things at stake. The Germans breaking through as they have is a bitter pill - too bad they just can't stand there and be shot like all good Germans. I guess there will still be plenty of our B-17s to do for a long time yet.

We had the usual ground school today. Had a 3 hour session of "Ditching." You remember Jack Stolz said we'd get that till we were blue in the face - well it has begun. You know - it's the procedure involved in landing your ship in water and safely abandoning it.

I received the third of the Thompson packages today. This one is heavy - Parcel Post job and has my curiosity at a peak. You know you should have given me instructions -

whether to open them or not - as it is, I haven't opened a thing and of course if there is food in any of them I wouldn't want it to go bad or unpunished for a minute longer than is absolutely necessary.

Sorry you haven't sent me Dick's address but I can well realize the difficulties on hand and particularly at this time contacting the "hard to get" Perrys. Don't know as I would have time to contact Dick now anyhow. We are scheduled to finish here, as near as I can find out, on or about the 15th of February. Soon after the first of the year I'll be asking you for some more stuff I guess. Up to this point I have an idea of what I'll want to take with me and I'll be asking to impose upon your good natures to get me some things. We have heard here that there exists a rather lucrative and advantageous barter system over in England and in France. The biggest shortages being in clothing - women's of the flimsy variety - stockings, underwear, brassieres, etc. Also cosmetics - lipstick being main item I guess. So please don't be surprised when I send money for some of these things. The veterans tell us that you can shack up with a gal one week for one stocking and then another week for the other. Of course I have none of this in mind but I'm told that it's the best way to get extra liquor or anything over in England. During the next couple weeks I'll nose around and endeavor to find out just how much I'll be able to get away with. They always tell you you can't take anything except what's issued to you but if we fly our own ship over I should be able to manage some way or another. Don't suppose I'll want a lot - going to have to cut down what I'll carry to a minimum. Think I'll get in cahoots with the Pilot one of these days and together we may be able to figure something out. I hear you get or could get 4-5 dollars for a lemon - think of what you'd get for a case of them?

Well folks, I think I'll hit the sac - seem to mind this 4:00 AM trick worse than the 2 AM one. Due to some mix-up in schedule we go back to the 2 AM one after Christmas too. By the way we get New Year's Day off too so I should be able to get a little tipsy New Year's Eve and still be able to sleep it off. Going to sleep now - am fighting a cold - hope I get the better of it now before it gets any start.
Lotsa Love, Frank

December 21, Thursday

Dear Mother, Harry and Mike,

Another long day today. Up at 4 AM and up into the "Wild Blue Yonder." It was a bad trip from my standpoint. The interphone system was bad - that is my responsibility, almost had to repair it in flight but managed with a few makeshift measures. Also my Receiver was bad - very temperamental - didn't want to play most of the time so I was really up a tree. It was high altitude - 5 of 6 1/2 hours in an O2 mask and me with my nose running most of the time, then it would drip out the mask & freeze on the table - OH lotsa fun. When we got down I got my mail - gulped some pork chops & French fries at the base cafeteria and hurried over to Ditching drill - just finished eating again at the mess hall and I'm a little poohed out.

I have Mother's of Monday & Harry's of Tuesday before me. From what Mother says there is something to eat in one of the boxes - I'll have to open one of em - one I think the food is in - maybe tonight. Boy oh Boy am I glad you two finally got a tree that looks O.K. - I sure would like to see that one. I received card from Gramp yesterday - one with 2 bucks in it (no comment). He had already written it before the attack.

The war news is terrible - strangely enough it has a very direct bearing on us. The last class of men to be trained in B-17s arrived here a few days ago - I believe they will work with larger ships - B-32 - Consolidated's new job, or B29s. You see, while things were going good, I can tell you now - the boys out of here we're getting 6 days delay but I'm sure I haven't a Chinaman's chance of that now. If this goes on much longer I doubt that we will finish training here in its entirety I hope they stop them soon!

Well, I'll have to toddle on now, would like to clean up - am very dirty - maybe take in a show & feel a little more like a human being. Be good, Folks.
Lotsa Love, Franks

December 22, Friday

Dear Mother, Harry and Mike,

Well, well, you grand people - I received your cards today - Huba Huba special ones too - thanks loads folks. I haven't opened packages as yet perhaps I have to confess I opened the Parcel Post job - I was right about the eats - golly is it ever swell. I didn't get a chance to examine it too closely - too many came in in a bunch as I put the knife to the box. I think the Fruit Cake will go a flying to-morrow morning early. We already killed one box of candy, and I didn't touch the nuts as yet. Believe I'll save them until one evening when I go to the NCO club for a few beers. I bet there are cashews in the little box - I'll see when I get to open it at my leisure. The fish should come in fine on of these evenings like tonight when I don't feel like moving for a snack. I haven't explored as yet those wrapped up things in the bottom - bottles is my guess, but of what? You can see it was a very hurried investigation - my main purpose was to see if there was a homemade cake in it - I sure wanted to make sure there wasn't for I didn't want it to get too hard before eating it.

Now to the plans for the Holiday as they are still in a rather fluid stage but we are New Orleans bound for sure. Sleeping & eating in Hotels for a couple of days should prove a welcome change. I decided to go with one of the lads in the barracks here - name is Calvin Taylor - boy from Tennessee. He is a pretty good chap and I flew with him when we were checking out the pilots - he is on crew 439 & I'm on 440. We are both radio operators & hence have that in common at least. Going to really take it easy I hope. We have passes from to-morrow at 1 PM until Tuesday at 8 AM. It's a pretty good deal and we hope to make the most of it.

I guess I'd better open things to-morrow before I leave for the city for I don't expect we'll be back till after Christmas - we want to get in & settled somewhere before to-morrow night. Don't suppose I'll be writing to-morrow but I'll try to let you know how I think old Santa treated me from New Orleans anyhow. From the quantity it looks to me that I'll do all right.

I want to get most of my stuff laid out sorta tonight - have all my brass to shine tonight shoes set and all. We will go very light - won't carry a thing except my brown leather case. First chance I will have had to use it.

I kinda wonder what our chances of flying are to-morrow. We are scheduled to get up at 4 AM and take off at 7:30 AM of course but in the first place Gulfport has been closed in today and we kinda think it won't clear up before to-morrow. They will keep us on the line until 12N anyway but we won't be so tired and will get off earlier too. In the second place my pilot "Sundin" has contracted a cold and may go on sick call to-morrow so if he does we won't be able to fly without the boss.

Sooo I judge I'll be taking off like a Big ass Bird on the morrow - it will be a decidedly different Christmas at any rate - damned different, eh what? They will have midnight mass and a big Turkey dinner on the Post, which, frankly, I rather hate to miss but we shouldn't do too badly as semi-civilians.

I also got a letter from Norm today - card from Beals and at noon a note from Norm telling me a box is on the way. People sure have gone all out for me and I truly appreciate it. Don't' really know what to do about Gramp - I won't write until I hear from you fellows more definitely about his condition - if he's well enough to hear it read to him O.K.

Well, I guess I'll get off to my polishing and getting set for to-morrow - Be good, folks - write you from New Orleans - Do hope you have a real swell Christmas. Lotsa Love, Frank

Still December 22nd, Friday
Well, Doggone Folks,

I just had a couple beers, it's about 11:30 and I still have to get up at 4 AM.

I had to jot this note - Yup, I gave way to temptation and am I ever glad I did - I did splendidly - I can't write much now - guys are yelling for the lights out so I'll have to hurry along. The lighter is swell - already tried it in the wind, but the thing that was perfect was that awful light box - Gosh that was a grand thought - funny that I shall get so much pleasure out of a 12 in. tree and some ornaments but it has made Christmas for me. We have nothing to suggest Christmas here - only a little fir boughs in the rafters - that tree has made it for me. I opened it last and my heart dropped when I saw the ornaments - thought you'd think we'd had a tree and knew we couldn't get ornaments - then I found the tree - it's the only thing we had - we trimmed it - I almost cried - stuff I'd seen since I was just a grasshopper, well gee, that sure did it. Just another few days has been made a holiday season for me with this touch of all I ever knew as Christmas as a kid. Well, you just don't know what this touch from home meant to me - or maybe you do. Lotsa the guys looked at me as if I were a fool - I'm so sorry for them - they can never have known the Christmases at home that I have. All the other stuff is swell I'll tell you more about the rest when I can write without 20 G.I.s on my neck about light - I started to open things up hoping there'd be something to wear to New Orleans - something clean - and sure enough it was all there - all I needed.

Write more later,

OH so much Love and Thank Youse,

Frank

December 24, Sunday

Dear Mother, Harry and Mike,

Today - Sunday & day before Christmas and I'm in the nearest big town to Gulfport. We didn't fly yesterday but we were kept at the line until 12:30 - if we loaded and unloaded that plane once we did it 6 times - each time our mission ready to take off or a change in mission and each time held because of weather. At any rate after we were released, I ate and got all cleaned up joined some of the boys and 3 others and we took off for Gulfport with intentions for New Orleans. Too bad there are so many G.I.s with the same idea. Keesler Field with its 20 thousand our 6-7 thousand and the Naval base near with 25 thousand. We couldn't get on a bus, were dubious about the train so we started to hitchhike and did it in pairs. The roads were all stacked with cars but there were G.I.s and a million sailors for every car. We broke up in pairs Taylor and I and Staeger & Morse together - decided we'd meet at the Roosevelt Hotel. And so did shortly after 7 PM evening. The difficulties on the road were numerous but I won't go into them here - you know that old Air Corps smile & personality must have been what did it. Of course New Orleans is overrun with Servicemen and it is a Navy town by virtue of its position ordinarily. However we are well set in rather nice rooms (civilians were refused) but we didn't have any trouble getting taken care of. Boy oh Boy could I ever get used to this! We got a 5th of Seagram's just in case we couldn't find anything to do and last night we took in the French Quarter, a dance (Girls in Formals) at the U.S.O. and although we tried we couldn't get into the Blue Room where Del Courtney is playing in the evenings. Maybe we'll go this evening if we don't find something better to do. To tell the truth a little Junior Birdman from Gulfport hit the sac last night at 12-12:30 - having been on the go since 4 AM the morning before we were rather tired.

Staeger being a Catholic, he and I slept together last night and left a call for 7 this morning. We rolled out at 7:45 looking like greased lightning and just made church in time. A Jesuit church is just across the street from the hotel so it didn' take long to get there. After Mass, we had breakfast in the coffee shop here - orange juice, oatmeal, waffles, bacon and coffee. Just a couple B.T.O.s and it sure is a pleasure to be served for a change. To the best of my knowledge the other two fellows Taylor and Morse are still in the sac. We won't wake them till later - I want to soak for an hour or two in this bath tub anyway.

I say Folks, you sure did grand by your serviceman for Christmas - as I put in my letter night before last - I haven't felt at all like Christmas until I started opening your boxes. Had received no other ones but youse up until the time I left yesterday. I surely owe my Christmas spirit and all the pleasure I derived from what you sent me to your foresight in sending things a little early and to your good sense in packing things - that special handling deal slows things up but I'm sure that that was one of the main reasons I got things so intact. Some of the fellows received boxes - candy and eats which were packed in 3 or 4 separate boxes and even at that had been opened, sampled, and tampered with. I wonder if I'll ever get Keough's or Beal's or Ott's boxes.

What prompted me to open things when I did was I had a hunch there might be some clean clothes therein - my underwear is so dirty from the G.I. laundry. I have on at present one of the shirts from Miker, a pair of those dandy sox and the tie. Yup I got all spruced up to come to New Orleans. I made a perfect nuisance of myself yesterday on the line - bet I lit everybody's cigarettes for miles around - finally my whole crew even to the officers would say to anyone within 50 ft. who they saw getting out a butt - wait Thompson will light it for you - he has a new lighter. Harry's gift of the missal was one I never thought of asking for - he must have noticed how battered mine was after using it 9 months in the Army. I'm sure its leather binding and cover will stand me in good stead - it will go across the Pond with me you can be sure of that. I'll try to send the other one home. The shirts are swell - indeed the cat's meow - maybe I could prevail upon you to get about 3 or 4 more of them. Pencil and screw driver are as requested - took them with me flying (on the ground) yesterday. That muffler is what I've been going to buy myself - it is a little ritzy to wear flying but looks none the less serviceable and you can be sure I'll be wearing it. We have large, what I mean large, jackets with big sheepskin collars but they don't fit close enough around my neck as I would wish and frequently my sanctuary - the Radio Room of a B-17 - gets quite drafty, especially if the hatch on top is missing or has holes in it. I get uncomfortable around the neck and the muffler you sent is of the heavy serviceable variety that I'm sure I'll get a lot of good out of. The sox are dandies!

Now to those other items which bring back days when I took them for granted - the pajamas and slippers - my dears they are perfectly elegant and just what a fellow would want down here however in my present position I find that are not practicable as I would wish, for example, I have no place where I can conveniently keep them - I'd have to stow P.J.s in barracks bag for I wouldn't be permitted to hang them up somewhere. Also the fine fanciness of them which is their finest feature would vanish beyond recognition after one trip to the G.I. laundry. In Yuma where I didn't need them I would have taken a chance on their laundry service but I've never seen the equal of the mayhem that is committed on clothes here. I can manage O.K. in my shorts to sleep in. I can change these each day since I still have 3 Jockey shorts and have accumulated 6 of G.I. issue - the P.J.s would become musty in a day or 2 in a barracks bag - they are too nice to wear and then ruin after one washing anyway. So I'm sure Haroola can get the good of them. I do hope you can get credit for the slippers - they would also be ruined in short order here or at camp and frankly, they are too much bother to tote around. The barracks floor is more like an alleyway at times than a floor - if I need slippers I use my shower sandals or my civilian shoes. If we dressed in combat as we do here I'd take them with me for warmth under my flying boots but we will be issued electronically heated suits - also you need G.I. shoes on in case you'd have to bail out so I'll send them back in hopes that they have not been paid for as yet. In a couple weeks I hope to be imposing on you anyway again, as soon as I find out what I'll be able to get away with at the staging area - have you got a spare shoe stamp?

As I said previously, the tree took the cake - ah tis a darlin. I was afraid to leave it up while I was away - you can't buy anything for a tree here and I feared some permanent party Joe would steal the whole business so I took her down before leaving yesterday and wrapped everything in the box and gave it to my Tail Gunner for he and his wife to have over Christmas. He was tickled pink - they live in a trailer (Govt. issued) outside camp and I know are having a hell of a time making the grade and I felt someone should get some pleasure from it if I couldn't. He'll return it Tuesday when I can look at it some more. It was a swell thought folks and the only touch of Christmas we had in the barracks. Have run out of paper here so if I've left out anything you can be sure it will get mention anon - all boxes arrived in best of order and you two made my first Christmastime away from home far better than I thought it could be.

Lotsa Love, Frank

December 26, Tuesday

Dear Mother, Harry and Mike,

Have just finished the day at Ground School and at last have an opportunity to write you fellows. I tried this afternoon but the lunch time is all too short to suit me. I suppose you will be eager to know just what happened to us in New Orleans.

I honestly had about the best time I ever have had in the Army - to say the least it was different. New Orleans is a great town - lots to see and discover and we did so but there is plenty left for another day - and how! After I wrote you from The Roosevelt Sunday - Taylor and Morse took off for a movie - supposed to be hot "Human Wreckage" and Staeger and I pursued the French Quarter at leisure in daylight in search of a good place to eat. The city, especially the French Quarter and Environs, there is an ordinance (City) that no building can be torn down - it can be remodeled but not destroyed. The streets are narrow as our alleys at home and the buildings start right up from the sidewalk. They are dingy, very old looking, and everywhere are shuttered doors & windows and wrought iron doors. Little windows in the doors with slides on them to peek out. This is all left over from the days when pirates were rampant along the Gulf. Saw a convent yesterday - built in the 1730s. The whole

atmosphere is positively musty - don't misunderstand me - I suppose some romanti-
cists would call it delightful but at first it really got me down - what the Hell was all
this rotten wood and stuff the famed French Quarter of New Orleans? Ah but there
is a secret behind it all. You actually have to know your way around to get anywhere
- Behind all these rotting facades are large modernly equipped cafes, restaurants, and
bars - night clubs etc. Bakeries & candy stores & everything that is really much in the
city as far as class is concerned in jewelry stores etc. is located there behind some
musty rotting front. Restaurants are obscured - you get the impression that they
are trying to hide them from the public instead of soliciting their patronage. And
are these places ever gems of cleanliness, atmosphere, and perfection in food and
service. These colored lads are fast - if after that last bite is gone you don't put the
fork down quickly on the plate it will fall on the bare table for someone has whisked
up and taken the plate and the next course is already there. We didn't take in "An-
toine's" for it was closed Sunday and Christmas there was too much of a crowd but
we plan to make eating there the main event of our next excursion. I'm sure you've
heard of the place - it is known all over the world. I'm going to go there next time -
have cold white wine and all Huba Huba!

Anyway, Staeger and I found a swell place to eat - we joined the fellows later.
While waiting at the hotel for Taylor and Morse, we went to the desk to pay for
Christmas night's lodging they told us to come back & pay in an hour. When the
lads arrived again we went down to pay and were informed that we could not have
either of them (rooms) - such a slap in the face but there was nothing we could do
and the bad part of it was we knew that there wasn't another hotel room to be had
in the city. We tried them all anyway - even to bribing Bell Hops and finally went to
U.S.O. where they told us that the Sisters of Charity had opened up some wards in
a new very large hospital they had there for we boys. The hospital is run in conjunction with Tulane University. As a civilian having no place to lay my tired head would
have worried me but not as a G.I. - just one of those things to deal with when the
occasion arises - when you're too tired to stand. After that we ate again at another
place La Louisiane in the Quarter - almost as good as the one at noon. Then, having
picked up tickets for a big dance being given at the Municipal Auditorium, we took
off like big ass birds for there. It was a nice party - gals in formals, good band and a
Christmas gift for each G.I. - men with a zero on the end of their ticket number got
ticket to the Sugar Bowl game next Monday - no I wasn't one of them.

I was really making time with one lovely Yvonne when Staeger and the boys came
up and said that they were taking off for Midnight Mass. I smelt a rat there - they
wanted me to come - Taylor & Morse are Methodists and Staeger and I had decided
in the afternoon that if we were to go to the dance we wouldn't try to make Midnight
Mass. Finally - I hated to do it - I let my dolly go and went into the lobby - it seems
our 2 left-handers had ran into a couple Mics and the girls had persuaded them to go
to Midnight mass and they wanted us to come along too. If I'd known what the story

was I could have taken the gal I was working on, but I had left her so went along. We had fun going through the Quarter to St. Louis' Cathedral but it was too packed even at 11:20 so we hurried to St. Mary's where at least we found a place to stand during Mass. It was long, sermon not too good - those Methodists really sweated it out We had to go back through the French Quarter to get a street car to take the girls home. My hair went up on end as we passed one dingy bar - a Sailor stood in front of it swaying from too much to drink with a nasty looking knife in his hand. There was murder in his eyes believe me. Some jiggaloo had rolled him for 57 dollars and he was looking for blood. Wanted us to help him find the guy but we were rather anxious to get out of there. Believe me it is no place to be late in the night alone - I hardly think anyone would try to tackle 4 stalwarts anyhow so we traveled there at any time in a bunch of 4 - lots a company and little to worry about because of our numbers. A lot of that stuff went on I guess - you have to be careful - only a fool would flash any money down there or travel alone after 12 at night.

   The street cars were packed - we couldn't get on so we hailed a cab. Took both girls home were invited up to Rosemary Boudousquie's (some handle, what?) home the next afternoon - Christmas day and then we took the cab all the way to the Charity Hospital where we hopped to sleep. I held on to the seat when we arrived & asked the driver the price - we had been in the cab for at least 1/2 hour - it was a revelation & relief to hear 1.50 - cabs are not bad at all in New Orleans. We then went into the Hospital waiting room where about 50 other G.I.s & sailors were waiting to get beds. They took us into the corridors to elevators - took about 40 up and came down telling us there were no more beds. Then one of those Sisters showed up and fixed up - not bunks or cots or beds - boy this should kill you - we went into a room which had about 40 operating tables in it - clean sheets and pillow cases on each and there we slept. They weren't too soft and you didn't dare roll over without getting off the thing completely but they were clean and fine and we slept like rocks especially since we had put what Seagram's 7 Crown we had left in a small bottle and carried it in my Zipper bag - we finished it before going to bed about 3 AM.

   Got up the next morning - big breakfast at The Roosevelt Coffee Shop and then we waited in a drug store while Taylor called home - he didn't connect - the rest of us were going to try to - Staeger from Mich - Detroit - Morse from Martha's Vineyard Mass. and Thompson of N.F.N.Y. but it would have taken 7-9 hours for all of us so we thought better of it. Around 12:30 we called up to Rosemary's house. Her mother received us very cordially - they hadn't had their Christmas dinner as yet she served us cakes & candy & wine - some of Rosemary's girlfriends showed up with some sailors. It was really a shame - we put the Navy to playing volleyball in the backyard with some of the neighborhood children and the girls out in the living room with us. Mrs. Boudousquie has a son in the Navy and was grand to us - the girls were grand too - almost begged us to come back next Monday our day off but it will be more crowded in the city then with the last of horseracing all over the country & Sugar

Bowl game. I'd almost go to see the Ballet Russe which will be there then but it is too much trouble to get there and get back. We sort of made a tentative date with them for 2 weeks from next Tuesday - the girls want to have a picnic and go canoeing in the lagoon - howdya like that - they were the most eager dolls I've hit in a long time - the Air Corps really took over & the Navy was left in the cold. We may rent a car next time - we'll see Huba Huba - I sorta fancied a gal I met, this Eileen Cochran - real Irish type - like Honey O'Haire with dark hair and blue eyes - Ka-runch.

We finally left - the girls saw us to the street car - I can hardly wait to get my teeth into that. The trip back was uneventful but terribly crowded - I can't describe truly how bad it was in those coaches so I won't try. So went my first trip to New Orleans - hope to go in a couple weeks again. Some town - no kidding.

Thanks for forwarding Don Hamernik's letter & thanks for keeping the money. I'm enclosing what he sent me - please have a couple prints made of the negatives so I can have a set - I only got actual prints I am enclosing. Don is flying B-24s and is not too pleased with them. I received box from Mrs. Keough today. It was all gone except the Christmas cookies about an hour after I opened it. Of course I took it direct to the Service Club and gorged myself on it at first as soon as I got it. I have saved out the Christmas cookies for our crew in flight to-morrow. I must go now I'll try to write the many letters I owe, some of them to-morrow. Have to get up at 2:30 in the morning so I want to get washed & showered soon and hit the sac. Please give me some word of Gramp. Be good, people.

Lotsa love, Frank

December 27, Wednesday

Dear Mother, Harry and Mike,

Not an awful lot to write about today after last night's opus. We were up at 2:30 AM and up at the flight line by 3:30 but weather had closed in and we were unable to fly. Of course they kept us up there till about 11:30 but I did manage to get some sleep along the line here and there. I came back, showered and dressed and am now in the Library. Am going to try to get a few letters out this afternoon but heaven only knows how successful I'll be.

I received no mail this morning but may get something when I try this evening before 7 PM. As yet I have not received boxes from the Otts and the Beals. All the fellows have been getting things the past couple days - kinda takes the good out of it for them it seems to me. Am I ever glad you sent mine early enough for me to get a lot of kick out of it.

I did put my clothes in the cleaners today. You just can't live in them 3-4 days running and expect them to stay put. Maybe it was a bum idea for I can't do much without them but then I didn't intend doing much over New Year's anyhow.

They will pay us on Monday next at 3:30 in the afternoon - already the fellows I went to New Orleans with are getting a little restless to be on the move again in spite of the fact that we all decided on the way home that it would be foolish to try to make it over New Year's. Maybe it is foolish not to make it for we have only about

6-7 weeks left in the Good old U.S.A. and then we won't be able to blow our tops here for a good while probably. Well, we'll see what the developments bring - I can always borrow some clothes, I hope, for over the week end - ah well, we shall see.

Guess thas all for now folks - it is really hard getting used to Army chow again after our splurge in New Orleans - Be good.

Love, Frank

December 28, Thursday

Dear Mother, Harry and Mike,

Yesterday after I wrote you I got 3 letters and one from Harry today so I was well off for mail. I also received the Ott's package. It was a little late but ever welcome. Heaven knows they sent it early enough - postmarked the 14th, but my guess is that the mails were more rushed than ever this year. The thing that struck me most was a small "pen" flashlight they sent me. I don't know why I never thought to ask for one for sometimes I almost impale myself in that plane when we are on the early morning schedules. It is difficult to preflight the plane when it is pitch dark and I bang myself all over trying. That little light will help a good deal!

Your Christmas and attendant preparations sound swell - just as it always was. Don't envy you your tree no matter how difficult it was to get the lights on; I have one of my own - getting real snooty eh? Such a liquor supply - should be a number of singed palates with it. I notice that the Thompson's are rather dubious about Gramp's condition but in later letters he seems to be coming along fine. I do hope he recovers and is not too much the worse for it. I will have to try to write him tomorrow. Couldn't see much sense in writing if he were very bad off. I guess the best idea is to forget the compass. I'll try to buy one, steal one from the Army. No, no box from DuPont - can't imagine why they wanted my address when I sent them my new one 3-4 weeks ago.

Harry seemed to have a swell time at his party - did you get any lovin? You didn't say. Also didn't Carbo kinda go all out for them - such reveling Huba Huba. Wait till the next depression - to suit the supply & demand of employees they will probably ball & chain them to the desk as per formerly Ho Ho - so you didn't make midnight Mass - I'll bet the Ottskis were easy to persuade in that direction. I really can't razz you two legitimately though for I almost didn't make it myself. Say did the Otts get you one of those special fruit cakes? I just finished mine and was it ever good - Karunch - the brandy & sherry which it was aged made it nice and wet and tasty. Dinner was skimpy this evening so I really ruined it.

Fran T. sounded real congenial - what happened? Harry the car deal sounds splendid - why don't you take him up on it? I would say off hand that both of youse did very well for Christmas - almost as well as I did. Harry describes the 25th to me and it sounded grand - real honey - if I'd been home you probably wouldn't have had so many invitations out and stuff - that at least is one good side of it - it is nice to be asked yourself for a change to Christmas, heaven knows that Mother deserved *at least one Christmas day off from all the hard work - we used to work you pretty hard Tess as I remember.*

Aside from the Cribbage, which I truly sweated out when I was home, Harry and Mother seem to have had a grand day. Complete with damsels 18 & 21 eh? Would I had been there to take a whirl at that myself. But in my hungry mood these days perhaps I wouldn't have been quite proper - I find that is what most of these women need anyhow. Sizzle Sizzle - I must needs behave myself, just went to Mass & Communion so I'd better be keeping my mind out of those channels.

Thanks for the advice on the lighter Harry. I had some trouble with mine so I got new flints and pulled the wick on it as you suggest. Works fine now except I have to keep filling it. Haven't been able to get the new packing completely wet down as yet. Keep filling it - we can get plenty of Ronson fluid here - do you have any trouble Harry?

Today has not been much of anything. Ground school and that's about all. However, we did get one slap in the face - no holiday off or even regular day off over next week end - the stinkers. This is no doubt to make up for 2 days we have been unable to fly so far. Good thing we had planned nothing such as going to New Orleans. Ah well, by the time a week from Tuesday rolls around we will all be all keyed up again and raring to go - that always makes the cheese more binding don't ya know. As I said, went to church at 6 PM and am off to bed shortly now since we fly early in the morning. Used my missal for the first time - it's a dandy but I have a terrible time fun muddling with the ribbon place keepers. Ah well, I'll learn I hope I hope.

I must be off to the sac now so, be good, folksies - OH, I almost forgot - I have found a new kindred spirit. I have fallen to the lure of the Cat. You know how I always hated them but this here is a cat with character. He even comes when he is called - pretty big fellah too. Well, with all the extra food in the barracks we have been bothered with quite a few mice. Our furried friend showed up yesterday and right off grabbed one before our eyes and gobbled him down - this mouse's legs were still wriggling as he went down in the last gulp. Of course this made us all hungry too - oh yeah. But he is a good cat and his luck has not been so good I judge today so Ron Zschau and I split a can of Canadian sardines with him. The other fellows from other barracks have been trying to lure him away because of his stellar mouser qualities and we in turn are trying to bribe him to stay. We have named him "malfunction" as in a machine gun. Be good, folks.
Lotsa Love, Frank

December 29, Friday

Dear Mother, Harry and Mike,

Today was another one we were supposed to fly but weather would not permit so they horsed us around all morning. It gets very tiresome and we would all really rather be flying in as much as we have a certain amount to accomplish and we will have to do it Hell or High water. In addition to no day off this week, we have to fly 5 in succession next week - it sure doesn't sound like child's play to me and I'm sure that it won't be. I won't mind it too much I don't think, just as long as they don't take a week from Tuesday next away from us - we want to do big things again then - Here's hopin anyway.

I received a package from Beals and Powers today. Another pair of sox - these great big babies and a lovely can of cookies - they've got nuts and cut up fruit in them and we all think they are the berries. Norm wrote and said something about a money order - I do hope they don't bother for they have been so grand to me and, which makes much more difference, so wonderful to youse guys. I must write to them tonight and also to Gramp since he seems to be coming along better.

Right now I am completely bushed! I planned on doing some washing this afternoon but, as generally happens, the lads prevailed upon me to take in a movie. It was Belita in some "Ice Serenade" or something. Not even average - not worth your time. Right after that I got sucked in on a touch football game, boy it was rugged. More hard work than I've done in ages but loads of fun - lots of laughs and it is a good healthy physical tired. I don't know much more to say. The weather - just as around Christmas in New Orleans is warm & muggy. It clouds up in the morning so we can't fly and the sun shines splendidly in the afternoon. Guess that is why we will be on the afternoon shift comes next week. As I see it we will get no ground school whatsoever next week. I think we have to have 150-200 hours of flying in before we leave here. We have only 50 and over half our time is gone. That is why - we'll really have to go some now.

Fraid that's all for now folks - be good - maybe I'll try once more for mail before 7 PM and eating - also have to take shower to get yee old sweat off me.
Love, Frank

December 30, Saturday

Dear Mother, Harry and Mike,

Again not much to report today. We had ground school again today and it offered very little of a new nature.

I did receive two letters today. Harry's & Mother's. Hope you have second letter about New Orleans by now - our good time really started to develop after that first morning. Harry sent me a fiver - it was very opportune old boy - I was down to 16 cents. By opportune I mean tonight would have been last chance for getting a bottle and 16 cents wouldn't have been much of a contribution towards one. To-morrow I will get largest pay ever in the Army but that is not tonight. Staeger, Taylor and I are going in on a bottle together - not a lot for anyone but enough to get a bit of an edge on. We have to fly Tuesday so we don't want to get too well oiled - anyway if we do, I have an extra pint in my foot locker I brought from Tampa so we should be well set in that direction. I'll send it back to you Haroola as soon as I can get a money order Monday or Tuesday - also get your cigarettes to you. I've had them for a week now and should have sent them before I went to New Orleans but I didn't and when I got back I was flat and couldn't send them. I managed to get most of a box of matches for you. I won't need them now - nor will you but I'll send them on anyway - you can't buy a full box of them now.

We get to sleep until late to-morrow morning. Ordinarily we would get until 11 AM but pay call is at 10 AM so as long as there has to be an interruption I can't think of a better reason for me.

Just one more thing. We will be flying continuously next week and if I don't manage to do much writing please try to understand. I will try to make a line or so each day to let you know that all goes well. I realize the past 2 or 3 have been short but there is just nothing to tell. At any rate I expect to be rather tuckered out next week but will endeavor to write so that you'll know all is well and I'm ragged, fat, and sassy. Sooo please be good, folks.

Lotsa Love, Frank

CONNECTING THE DOTS

Present Day

The skill with which my father masterfully crafted his letters to minimize worry at home was clearly evident. Often times while typing I'd have to remind myself that these were WWII letters, and there was a truly horrific war going on. Had I not known that, the lighthearted tone of his letters may have easily suggested they'd been written during peace time. The only indication of the enduring conflict was his occasional comment about the "war news." It seemed as though he and his crew kept an ear to the radio and an eye on the paper, though it's unclear how much they were actually told about the current status of the war. His letters may have been light in nature, but most likely he and his pals were all quite anxious to know what they were heading into.

In his December 20 letter, he made a reference to the "bitter pill" of the Germans breaking through, which sent me directly to my WWII encyclopedia to read about what he was referencing. He, of course, was referring to the counterattack in Belgium that had started the Battle of the Bulge. The battle would continue into early January and officially end on the 7th, being declared "an American victory." Years later, Hitler's minister of armaments and war production would admit that the German loss of that battle in Ardennes marked the beginning of the end of the war for Germany.

It was in this same letter that my father mentioned his crew had had "another ditching session." The few times he wrote about his ditching training, I found myself anxious; I wanted to caution him to pay attention, to somehow warn him that this particular training would be critical in six months time. I still didn't know the details of their ditching beyond the accident report I'd uncovered, and though I knew they'd all survived, I couldn't suppress the unexplainable way I felt when reading letters written in his present, while knowing his future, which for me was actually in the past. As I typed his letters I became accustomed to being in this strange emotional place, frequently wanting to forewarn him about his future, and each time feeling the distance between us was narrowing.

I'm not exactly sure when it was, but I knew I'd actually met his tail gunner Dan Spencer, twice. The first time was sometime after our father's death. Now reading about their friendship, I started to connect some dots. How kind it was of him to visit the family of his deceased friend. He only stayed a day or so, but I realize now it's quite possible he was checking up to see how his friend's widow and children were managing. His second visit came shortly after my mother remarried. He and my dad had sat for hours talking. Reading now about how close my father and Dan had been in the service, I wouldn't doubt that his second visit was a way to check out the man who would be responsible for his friend's family. No doubt he approved because the two of them got along as though they'd been friends for years. It seems that on this visit, my dad must have asked Dan the names and positions of the crew members in the crew photo, and then wrote them on the back, a seemingly insignificant thing to do at the time that would in fact become quite significant years later. It was among my father's letters and various artifacts I found a remembrance card announcing Dan's death on January, 23, 1996.

GULFPORT, MISSISSIPPI - PART 2

January 1945

Dear Mother, Harry and Mike,

Well, I hope you both had a very jovial New Year's Eve. I suppose you did since I expect you were up at Ott's.

Yesterday was a busy one to be sure for me. We had a pay formation and I drew as expected 124 semolians. Not bad, what? Will try to send a slice of it to you to keep for me so that I can wire for it in case I need it. More about that later. I can't get a money order right now, maybe in the morning. I also want to get those packages out to you folks - hope I can get it out of the way soon. Anyway, we barely made church yesterday and ate and were up at the flight line. There were so many flying we had to sweat out a plane. I put in a good day yesterday on ma radio - with things so crowded here it is a rare day that you do all you are supposed to, or want to, and when it does happen, to me, flying is really a pleasure.

We returned to the barracks last night and were at first going to drink our bottle at the NCO club but we were all too tired to get cleaned up so we decided on staying home. We had a big Poker & Black Jack game - I don't usually sit in on these things but thought the occasion - New Year's - merited something out of the ordinary so I did - lost about 3.50 but it put in a good evening. Before we had finished we had 2-5ths Schenley's and a pint of some Bastard Brew - never heard of it before - in the middle of the table. It turned out to be quite a party and I went to my sac about 12:30 very nicely oiled. What made it worse for all of us was that a change in the schedule fixed it so they got us up at 6 AM - pretty tough for some of the boys didn't hit the hay until 5:30 - stayed up all night playing cards - not for this boy. Not a very wild night for me but we had a lot of fun at any rate.

Well folks, I'm tired now - again - still have to wash up and odds and ends to take care of. I realize this is a poor & not very informative letter - we flew all day today too and will be at it to-morrow but it will be the late schedule I believe. Hope I wake up early enough to mail some of those things.

Be good, people.

Lotsa Love, Frank

Dear Mother, Harry and Mike,

Well, I'm behind again as per usual in this place - well, I warned you at any rate but I fear that is poor consolation. Finally today we went back to ground school. It consisted of 1 hour intelligence lecture and 6 hours of stripping, cleaning, oiling, firing, re-cleaning and re-oiling a machine gun - lotsa fun. This evening at 8 PM we are scheduled for a film assessment - that is the grading of film we shot at P-40s from our Bomber formation a few days ago. So you can see they keep us busy night as well as day. I do hope to get out early enough to write a few letters anyway. Yesterday morning I did manage to get up early enough to get money order and it is enclosed. Made out to Harry since he tells me it is easier that way. Five of it is his as of opportune loan over the New Year - if - I say if, you have a shoe stamp please call up Kleinhans and get me a pair of Matrix military shoes the same size as ones I have at home - they fit fine. If no stamp is available, please let me know as soon as possible and I'll endeavor to get proper authorization here. What I mean is if it is going to mean no privation on your part, or do you still have shoe stamps of mine in your second book? I can get one here I think but would avoid necessary red tape - it is a rule of experience in the Army - if they don't know you the better off you are. Probably mostly just laziness on my part. My shoes are still in good shape but I would have a new pair if possible to take overseas.

Later - after film assessment.

Well, we saw our film and after that went to Service Club and met Mrs. Spencer - our Tail Gunner's wife - we had a milkshake and shot the bull and I just got away. As I was saying - the remainder of the money, use to your own discretion or keep on hand for any little thing you may need or there is just a possible chance I'll wire for 10 or 15 before the month is out - I wouldn't have it if I carried it about. Please ship on any woolen sox also underwear and if you can get a couple more anywhere they would be greatly appreciated. I realize that I'm asking a lot but I always did - didn't I? I hope it is not imposing too much - seriously.

In your letter of Saturday Mom - sorry about the mail, but it just cannot be helped. We heard some of the repercussions about the rationing but it didn't make much of a dent. As far as sending me any canned goods you had better cut it out! You'll need all that stuff yourselves. Then too we eat at the mess hall almost any night we're hungry before going to bed so you can see the need for that before bed snack is fairly well taken care of by the Army here. We sure do appreciate any little baked thing though that we can take into "Wild Blue Yonder." How was the New Year's - see it is the 4th will be the 5th probably before I hear from you - I've had a few blank days on mail myself due to the holidays. Correction - the 6th can't get mail till 10 AM & have dentist appointment at 10 AM in the morning. Then we eat, brief and fly until 9 or 10 PM & mail closes at 7 PM so I won't get any to-morrow. War is hell isn't it?

Did Haroola get a Homburg - tell him to wear it with the gray suit - it always did merit a good chapeau. Thanks for Dick's address - I'll write him as soon as is possible - hope I can get to him in time to get a reply.

There is really not much new here - we brief and fly and radio operate - shoot 50 cal. guns & cameras - go to ground school and so it goes. Next big deal to look forward to is next Tuesday - day off. It can't be much for we won't be there flying until 10-11 Monday night. We have Tuesday off but change schedule for the following week and will have to be on deck at 2:30 AM Wednesday morning so you can see we won't have much time. Buuut I bet we make New Orleans - no one but fools would try but I bet we do.

I'll send this airmail to try to make up a little for my delays - splurged and bought 10 of them Hubu Huba - Well, be good, folksies - big day on the morrow - dentist at 10 - formation at 11:10 - eat - brief at 12:15 - take off at 2:30 - fly until 9 anyway - will be 10-11 PM before I get to barracks to my sac so I probably won't get one off to-morrow.

Lotsa Love, Frank

January 5, Friday

Dear Mother, Harry and Mike,

Received Harry's opus of the 1st this morning. I believe that they are undergoing some sort of personnel shake up at the mail room and things have hardly been satisfactory for me of late. Sorry you haven't heard much from me but I have written some and I suppose you will get them all at once. Your New Year's sounds like some of the things the Army deprives one of. Would I could have been with you but another day.

Things don't change much with me here. Yesterday saw Trombino one of the lads who went from Greensboro to S.F. with me. Also saw Jim Kucera who was in 1241 at S.F. with me - he started before me and was still there when I left. Both of them have arrived here and are starting training here.

We did have 3 Tech Sergeants just back from combat talk to us this morning. I suppose you think I'm getting on my ear but I want to get the things I need from home while I'm here and there is no sense kidding - I don't have such a long time left at Gulfport now. Harry - with some of that money please get me 1 doz. (12) lipsticks. Fairly good quality; ask Mother and Mrs. Ott about what to buy. Try to get them at Liggett's - maybe Norm will give you a knock down. The shoes and underwear and heavy knitted sox are important. They tell us soap and razor blades are plentiful - I'll load up with gum and cigarettes at my POE. If we fly over you can bet your neck I'll try to get a case of lemons over too. If I want any flimsies I'll let you know later. They told us the main thing was underwear, shoes, and heavy sox - any sox for that matter. Try to get the cosmetics in a small box - metal if possible and pack it as small and as well as is possible - I won't even open it until I get over. I'll write Dick tonight but hardly expect an answer from him in time. I must also try to write Gramp this evening - how is he anyway?

Well folks, this has been written during the lunch hour - have to be off to school again in a few minutes. I feel sure - if we get Tuesday off - we'll be on our way to New Orleans again. Didn't manage to write yesterday but did get Harry's cigarettes off to him so be on the lookout for them. Please, be good.

Lotsa Love, Frank

January 6, Saturday

Dear Mother, Harry and Mike,

I received Mother's of the 3rd and Harry's of the 3rd yesterday - will try to answer Harry's first for it is the shortest. I've had enough of this B.S. about a storm, buddy - so it snowed - how about more of the low down on any subject? You didn't say whether or not you were getting me some prints. Do you think you will be able to break Mrs. Gardner down so she will really help you out or are you going to let her remain merely a helper? How much was the bonus check or is that a military secret? Answer to question "like a big ass bird" refers to a B-17 airplane.

I am glad you got the New Orleans opus - really there is so little I do except when I'm having a good time that I can get on common ground with youse guys. It is hard for you don't know who I'm with and writing about them or my daily duty is hardly a subject we can mutually get our teeth into. You can bet your neck Mom - that is a threat - we'll do New Orleans one of these days together - maybe live here - I could take medicine at Tulane. I wrote Gramp last night - was a good boy - wrote you folks at noon, Gramp, Dick, Sally McPherson and Brownie last night.

Sorry if I seem villainous about not telling you whether or not I heard from Ann - you might have realized that in as much as I said nothing I have heard nothing from her. I did send her a card but put a 3 cent stamp on it and no return address. Maybe that was wrong too but as far as I'm concerned no word is the better way. Not that it doesn't and hasn't bothered me but what the hell - Melba Fix found out where I was - so did Sally and I got a letter from Lois Redans yesterday besides I'm still working on this set-up in New Orleans so I have plenty to keep me emotionally sharp in case I get a chance to exercise those emotions one of these fine days. Anything of a permanent nature in war time is just taboo with me - I hope I can stay that way!

I received a letter & letter and money - 4 bucks - from the Beals today. They really shouldn't bother with that stuff. It is more to me that they are grand to you people and so nice about writing and knitting for me. I can't convince them - wish you folks would try.

We tried to fly today - weather closed us in and we got back to barracks about 5 PM thusly I have a chance to write. My fear is that they may cancel our day off again - now someone tells me that maybe my boy Sundin may have forgotten to put in for passes for us today - oh trouble - if they're not in tonight then we won't be able to go to N.O. Monday night when we come down - may not get them at all.

Morale in the barracks among the crews is not too good today - seems some of the pilots have gotten Chicken Shit about addressing them as officers - the boys don't like it at all - some of these jokers better get wise - it takes 9-10 men to bring one of those babies home. We haven't had any trouble on our crew and I don't anticipate any but it makes us all sore when one crew gets their rear end racked. As a rule we are proud of our officers - boast about their ability and no crew naturally is better than your own. A good competitive spirit is very desirable but if the boys get sore at their officers things cannot run smoothly.

Well, I guess I have shot enough bull for today. May take in a show - I'll have to see. It has rained incessantly all day and is still hard at it. Be good, folks.
Love, Frank

January 7, Sunday

Dear Mother, Harry and Mike,

Sunday again and all too little like the ones I used to know. I did manage church at 6 PM for we had school all day. My church going partner Ronald Zschau (pronounzed without the z) got married today so I had to go alone since Staeger had the morning off from school and went this AM.

I think I have never seen such a struggle in a man, within the man himself that is, as I used to observe each morning in Zschau. He is 37 years old - far too old for this racket and yet like the rest of us, he would not change. He was my waker-upper in the morning - we have taken turns feeding coal to the stove which is at the foot of my sac - he has done most of the work - I just help carry in the coal. Every morning before he'd get up - like most of us he'd have a cigarette and look off into space. It was easy to see he had made a decision but still rather seemed to be in the throes of making it over and over again. I never said much for I knew what he was up against. Don't know as I agree with him but I cannot deny that he in a way has a right to what happiness he can glean from the mess that is the world today. He is a Catholic - the gal he married is likewise and the fly in the ointment is that he has been married previously. If ever a man sweated out anything - he has his marriage. In the church he is absolutely wrong - is now excommunicated - cannot receive the sacraments - whether he deserves a better break in life I cannot say. All I know is that each morning I'd lie with one eye open and watch him - it has been rough on him and though he has chosen the way of the flesh I hope the Lord forgives him for he is a fine fellow. He is more or less independent. He has an insurance business - is a broker in a small town in New England. I wish him happiness at any rate and hope I never face a like decision.

The weather here is in sharp contrast to what you have had - today was just like a beautiful spring day - wore fatigues with shorts on underneath period. Sounds worse than I ever saw it at home - just be careful folksies - and don't go stubbin tootsies on the ice. No am not getting the Gazoote (sic) again.

I do hope the cigarettes I sent arrive in time to be of some value to Harry. I can keep sending them as long as I'm here if he wants me to. Bordner writes me he is getting a supply of London Dock and going back to the old "Gargle Pots." I'm glad to hear that Haroola is getting prints made I'd like to label them for you so you'll know who the fellows are.

Of course I don't like Haroola's report of the State of Gramp - so none of us like the way he is maligned physically and verbally - too bad he never gave us the right to protest it.

Yes radio operators double on the tail guns in ships like A-26s and B-25s & B-26s. That is a good racket in a way for the ships are speedy - due to relatively short range, missions are short in duration and they are lucky in having no high altitude missions. No O2 equipment is being installed in them at all now. The catch comes in when they have 75 missions to a tour in Medium Bombardment whereas we have only 35 in Heavy Bombardment. Don't know but what I wouldn't trade should the opportunity ever present itself.

I went to make sure about passes for the 4 crews in our barracks - they hadn't been signed for, so I called up the pilot at his home and wound up by dragging down Co-pilots from 4 crews to get our passes in. These guys are damned liberal with their crew's time off - just another case of when you don't look out for yours truly, no one does.

At any rate we hope to be off for N.O. tomorrow night - let's hope nothing interferes. Sooo I am afraid I won't get to write Monday but will try for sure on Tuesday from N.O. again. I just hope we have half as good a time as we did the last time there. There is another formal dance on that we know of, so we may hit that and then there are those dolls too - we've even considered renting a car for a day or so - not too steep here for 4 fellows. We shall see - let you know the dirt from the scene of the digging.
Lotsa Love, Frank

January 10, Wednesday

Dear Mother, Harry and Mike,

Received Harry's of the 8th this afternoon and in it he says something about missing over the week-end - I thought as much but then, I haven't acquitted myself very well the past couple of days so I cannot say much. We did have our day off if it could be called such - off Monday night after flying at about 10 or 11 PM - we were to go on schedule #4 which would have brought us back for duty Wednesday at 1:30 and so we had passes made out for 10 Monday PM till 12 Wed noon but they changed our schedule - we had to fly this morning at 2:30 AM so we couldn't see going to N.O. arriving 1:30-2 AM Tuesday morning and having to start back Tuesday PM at 8:30 or 9. Wouldn't even have given us an evening there. We were as riled as G.I.s can get, but you do get used to these things. Went to bed Monday night after flying and arose early Tuesday - accomplished lots of odds and ends - laundry, cleaners, etc. I still do not have packages out to you folks - the boys have half persuaded me to keep the P.J.s - I will try to take them over with me, so cross that one off your list - still don't know what to do about slippers - they'd be swell to have in the right place but I haven't seen such a place since the induction center - let you know definitely as soon as I can. I realize this is holding up payment of your charge accounts - please bear with me - I may not be able to get over half of what I want to.

Gee Harry, I didn't know you wanted a black Homburg - isn't it just a little too oldish. I would have said a classy light Gray to match coat. My best Harry, with your date for Saturday, as always my best to you in all you do. Be a little subtle - if you need a physical workout, get a pig, but with Marg I would take her out consistently and play up to her banter and have lots of fun with her - after all that is the main point. Don't ever say it, but leave the understanding that it is platonic and you are playing the big brother. Most important is to be absolutely the gentleman and forcfcc und provide for her every whim but in an indifferent matter of fact way. This can lose you nothing and create in her a habit of being thought of [in a way] that women love and which, if done right, most men of today lack - that's your big point - by comparison. Then one day after lots of said treatment you'll be able to tell one opportune moment when she is weakening - that is when you nip it in the bud. Take the aforegoing (sic) for what it is worth - that is what I would do at any rate.

I too find the need of the she-male. Went to a dance last night at Community House in Gulfport. Had a good time, got hold of the most wholesome sweet smellin WAVE. She's really something. Hope to go in tonight and consolidate it - if I can find her. Her brother is an R.O. on a B-29 so we can talk about Radio anyway.

Think I gave you the enlightenment about Ann you wanted - My, I am surprised and surprised by your manifestation of what killed the cat. Haven't given the matter too much thought. I now have another problem - the Christmas card deal - what few I sent brought me sweet little letters from Lois Redans, Barbara Webb, and Agnes Holdman. Now the question is should I try to pursue any or all three of these via the pen - and should I be lucky enough to interest any one of them - what then - all blind alley stuff you know. Still I don't suppose any of them would have bothered to write if they hadn't had a little interest - ah well, they say men are scarce and I don't suppose it would hurt too much to dabble in it a little - what do you say?

Well, I guess that takes in most of it. In late after the dance last night - up at 2:30 AM to fly - since flying got my mail, ate, washed and have written this. Must write Beals and thank for the money order. Going to town tonight again - have bought Fitch shampoo - hoping for a killing - we shall see.

Lotsa Love, Frank

P.S. Have bought my Camels for the month so if you want any let's hear about it.

January 11, Thursday

Dear Mother, Harry and Mike,

Received Mother's of the 8th today and no I'm not blessing you for not writing - I miss it very much but I do understand how busy you get at times - I get a bit that way myself once in a while. I do think you should cut out the "unnecessary servile work" on Sunday though - not much good in going to Mass in the morning and working like crazy all day - 6 days a week is plenty.

I sent the money for the express purpose of getting the shoes and stuff I needed and asked you to get for me. If there is any left please use it. If I should need money I can always get it from someone - that's what you have a crew for. If you can't get lipstick - get some type of rouge.

Don't feel bad about not getting baked goods out. Heaven Knows that you have sent me plenty and sweets are not any easier to get at home than they are in the Army. We buy boxes of cookies at the PX and they serve the purpose. Also we are now getting a much better deal than formerly on the lunches we take with us from the mess hall.

Lots of the fellows had lots of stuff around Christmas - that is food from home, but when you are away as long as most of us have been most families build their lives around someone or something else and that is quite as it should be so as a result it is not often that I see anyone get a box from home.

I went into town last night - the first dance Taylor and I found we didn't like but the second one was not too bad. We got hold of a couple of school teachers one of whom had her car. They live in Pass Christian and teach in the High School there. The town is about 10-15 miles from Gulfport. They, with other single teachers, live in a house together - some fun, what? Well, at any rate we had a fair time of it and have not quite decided whether to treat em to the works or let them drool a little longer. You know these school teachers - duck soup. I was unfortunate in that I didn't find the little WAVE I'd had the night before - that really washed me ashore - well, I'll try looking for [her] again to-morrow night. Decided I should stay in this evening and do a little writing. Most of the lads have gone to see Winged Victory - the comments are quite adverse - quite as can be expected, the lads don't think enough was devoted to the Gunner. Don't know whether I'll go to see it or not - have to fly in the morning 2:30 AM.

Of course New Orleans is knocked in the head again this week - they have scheduled dental work - at least they let us know early this week - perhaps we complain accordingly.

I believe the Horrible Four will venture in to-morrow night to another dance - might as well give the local talent the once over in as much as we can't get to New Orleans. And with that there is not much new - we fly and go to school and get out in the evening once in a while. Even that is somewhat limited for, or have I told you, there is a 12 o'clock curfew in town and that is not so good either. Guess I'll run along now - have lots of letters to write but I'm in no mood tonight. I'll air mail this so that you'll know - use any or all of the money I sent - if necessary forget things I asked you to get - they're not that important - use it if it will help anyway - the reason I ask for things when I send money is that seems to be the only way you'll keep it. Be good, folks.
Lotsa Love, Frank

January 12, Friday

Dear Mother, Harry and Mike,

The paper will tell you where I am at just now. Indeed, offhand I would say it is the best and most extensive U.S.O. I've seen yet, bar none.

Came in this evening, to town that is with Staeger, Taylor, Morse and Ferniza, the latter is the engineer on my crew. They have all gone to a local eat shop someplace just out of town but I preferred not to go this evening. The main reason being, that in as much as it would have cost me 2-3 dollars and I had already eaten at the mess hall, I just couldn't see it. I've tried some of the half-baked meals here in town and if I want to spend that much to eat I'll do it in New Orleans where it will be worthwhile, that is if I ever get the chance to go again. A bunch of us are seriously considering ducking out on our dental appointment before our day off - I have considered the idea seriously but actually don't think much of it - after all that is as much being in the Army as anything else and moreover I wouldn't want my pilot to get reamed out because I wasn't on deck. He is too fine a guy.

He and I get along fine. He is just a kid but when he drives that "truck" he takes on a maturity that merits admiration and respect in my eyes. One evening when we were scheduled for film assessment he had had just a little too much beer - I didn't know it at the time but he told me later - well, anyway, the non-com - a Staff Sgt. in charge of photo scoring, started to raise hell with Sundin because we weren't there ahead of time. He was a wise boy, Lt. Sundin, he didn't say much - he claimed he wasn't feeling too good, but you know little Francis George when he sees one of his getting abused for no good reason at all - well, I opened my trap and I can get pretty sarcastic when I'm kinda sore. Apparently I did the boy up in lavender - Sundin still jokes about it - it was a natural reaction to me - the Sergeant's effrontery to an officer was colossal and in addition to that he was talking to my boy. Well, I blew up - must have held the floor for a solid 5 minutes. At any rate, since that time Sundin and I have seen eye to eye on a lot of things. On top of that I have been able to come through with repairs in flight and makeshift arrangements which have served the purpose of inoperative equipment so that I feel he feels he can depend on me, which is a great deal of the battle won. Say, guess I've done enough back patting for this one eh.

We were up at 2:30 AM (sounds barbaric doesn't it) this morn - flew high altitude again and for some reason I am and was really bushed at the end. We fired live ammunition out over the Gulf at 21,000 ft on O2. I returned - ate, showered and slept until 6:30 PM. I got tired of waiting for the rest of the contingent so went to the mess hall and ate there and thusly I manage to get time to write - otherwise I wouldn't have.

This is a little delayed in coming but I'd better say it while it is on my mind. My first reaction to my lighter was that the Thompson contingent had been robbed blind - couldn't get it in good working order for love nor money but right now it is a fine satisfaction to me. I tried various adjustments to no avail. Finally, I stretched the flint spring, got new flints, and changed fuel from Ronsonol to Energine. Now all is well and she operates like the blow torch I have always wanted - Goody Goody! A couple days after I got it, the cover broke off of its hinge - at first I was going to have it repaired but have changed my mind - it is a bit less bother not to have to worry about the weak hinge and the cover fits tight anyway. It really gets rough treatment - have to carry it and everything else I take flying in pockets - zipper closure in the knees of my sheepskin lined, leather flying pants, so that when I'm roaming the ship on my preflight inspection and when in flight crawling from nose to tail I am kneeling on it a lot of the time. It is a more than welcome addition to crew 440 and we all are getting the good out of fire when we need it. The large flame of course gets very small when we get about *10,000 ft.* up for there is not enough O2 to support a large flame - thank heavens it is a blowtorch to begin with - it is even hard to get a light from a match at that altitude.

Guess that is about all the news - expect to go to a dance shortly now. The lads will stop by and pick me up as soon as they are finished eating which won't be long now. Be good, folks.

Love, Frank

January 13, Saturday

Dear Mother, Harry and Mike,

Received Mother's of the 11th this morning along with the letter from Julius, Marg Crean and one from the Beals. I have more mail to answer than I can rightfully shake a stick at and not much prospect of getting it answered.

Last evening we went to a dance but it was not at the place I thought it would be. Had some fun but still haven't found the WAVE. I think we will have another try this evening being as it is Saturday night. On Saturday night we can stay out until 2 AM and then of course we fly or get ready to fly at 2:30 - ah tis a rugged life.

Things don't sound too good at home what with the confining weather and all. Also Mother's letters sound tired and as though she were doing too much. Harry - How about it? How do you like that - Nettleton's were the best you could do. I'm sure they will be fine and I'll be looking for them. The coming T shirts and shorts will provide just the needed reinforcement for my underwear supply so I'll tuck them away as sort of a buffer. Thanks a million for getting them for me. Glad the cigarettes arrived and were welcome.

There is little new here whatsoever - hope we fly low altitude on the morrow for then I do a good deal more radio work. I just don't bother much when we're up high, although they tell you to. For my money fooling around up there is taking too big a chance, so once I make complete contact with the ground I do little that might lose it.

Julius sent me pictures of an individual with a pipe which he hastened to remind me was "His Mike" not mine. Sure is a robust laddie isn't he - or should I have said pipe and then the person. I'll enclose a couple of the prints just in case you haven't seen them. Also another little poster swiped from the latrine for Harry's collection. Guess that's all for now folks.

Lotsa Love, Frank

January 14, Sunday

Dear Mother, Harry and Mike,

I realize that yesterday's was a short one and still, as I say, there is generally not a whole lot to tell. I received Harry's of the 11th this afternoon, which is froth with the intrigue and scull diggery of the Carbo Office. Personally as long as I wrote letters during my lunch hour I would just like to see anyone try to tell me what to do with it or what not to do with it. However I'm hardly on the spot and I bow to *others whose experience is greater than my own - I probably just get myself into more trouble as per usual.*

I'm getting a kick out of Dorshel's reaction to Mike Salupa - never come back to the Falls to live. Frankly, I think there are an awful lot of fellows who will wander from their established homes after this is all over. You can't travel about as a G.I. does and not soon establish some preference for a site for living and it generally is quite different from where the guy is originally from.

Yesterday was a school day and I took advantage of a break they gave us - last 2 hours off to write you folks and did manage to get a letter off to Julius. I try to get at least one a day off my chest in addition to writing you fellows, but I don't adhere to a good principle as a should.

Last night Cal Taylor and I ripped into town - at last I found my WAVE again - boy is she ever nice! It was murder trying to dance with her for more than 10 seconds running - the boys in blue seemed to resent the Air Force trying to take over a WAVE. They had me about 5 to one so I shall have to wait for another day - but it'll come Huba Huba. Did a good deal of dancing last night and really met some pretty fair dolls - no kidding. Well, Cal and I took a couple home - 2 of 3 that live in one of those new Government apartments - don't know just where the 3rd one was - we didn't miss her! I had a red-head - she was no child either, although Taylor's doll was about 19 years old - about right for him. We had coffee and did different things and talked until almost the last minute when we left and got a bus back to camp - it was really not such a good idea because we had to fly at 2:30 AM this morning.

I just got in bed - didn't even pull the covers apart - rolled over and got up again and that little fellow came around blowing the whistle - what a life! Well, I didn't mind it too much altho (sic) I don't think it would be a good idea to make a habit of such canoodling.

On top of my wonderful condition, we pulled a 6 hour high altitude mission - whew was it ever a honey (of a bitch) with the flight commander flying with us to make things just perfect. I was fighting sleep all the way altho (sic) the O2 helped somewhat to reduce my fatigue. People, I was really dished when I returned to my sac - didn't even eat Sunday dinner but made arrangements for one of the boys to wake me at 5 PM so I could make Mass at 6. That getting up at 5 was the hardest thing I've done in some time. Well, I did manage to get to Mass & on time too - Ron Zschau and his very attractive new wife sat ahead of me and of all things Lt. Herb Robinson - my Bombardier was right next to me - I had him figured for a Jew but I guess not eh what! Was surprised and glad at any rate to find that there is another Mick on crew 440.

So here I am in the barracks tonight - a Lola McKlelland, whom I met last night and who Taylor is dating tonight, wanted me to come along and get a date this evening. I'm sure glad I didn't say that I would. We made a fire in the stove - I think I'll have a couple beers now and go to bed. Be good, folksies.

Lotsa Love, Frank

January 15, Monday

Dear Mother, Harry and Mike,

Ground school today and not an awful lot doing. This afternoon we have our final communications examination - it doesn't mean a hell of a lot - you just don't "wash-out" or back at this stage of the game.

Well, we are all hopped up about our day off again. Ordinarily we would be off when we finish flying at about 1 or 2 PM and could take off from then until Thursday at 12M for we go on schedule #4, but Tuesday I am scheduled for a dental appointment at 6 PM so won't be able to leave until that is over with. The other boys are in the same fix so we won't leave until late Thursday night or Wednesday morning - have to see what goes after our session with the "Bone Breaker." My clothes need pressing, but guess I'll let it go until we get to N.O. - go to a While U Wait joint.

Nothing much doing, folksies - awful hard to dig up anything to say these days - we fly at 2:30 AM to-morrow so probably will get to bed early this evening. Last night after I wrote I got me a couple beers and the Staeger and I smuggled 1 apiece out - he had bought Ritz crackers so we opened the lobster paste and really enjoyed it before hitting the sac. I petted most of my stuff along - nuts and all and we all really enjoyed it more that way - we had it for the time when we wanted it and we all certainly have enjoyed the candy nuts and canned goods you sent me prior to and at Christmas. I still have some peanut butter and jam yet and have not as yet used up the asparagrass, but all the rest has gone & my locker has got to be known as Thompson's Grocery.

Guess that's all for today folks - I'm rugged fat & sassy & badly in need of a shave now so, be good.

Love, Frank

January 18, Thursday

Dear Mother, Harry and Mike,

Well, we finally got in a little time in N.O. thus I haven't written the past two days. I know I should have but these things happen around here in a very abrupt manner so I hope you'll forgive and understand. As you must have guessed from past letters and then this one, I have been having one Helluva time the past couple weeks - been on the go but good and having a wonderful time - too bad this session wasn't for 10 months instead of weeks. Well, to get on to the meat of the situation.

Tuesday night we could have and should have been on our way but dental appointments interfered so Taylor and I got dressed up after myself having 4 fillings (Taylor had 10) we took off like Big Ass Birds for the Community House. A dance there and we connected with 2 sisters, one a civilian visiting a WAVE. The Civilian gal was staying at the Markam Hotel in town - best one there - the WAVE I was with was a college grad. They were both blondes and quite attractive - we ended up by my putting the WAVE in a cab back to the Navy base, too bad she couldn't stay in all night, and Taylor squired the other one to the hotel. They were really grand girls - we call

Taylor "subtle like a bulldozer" and I fear he tried to force the issue a mite too far with little "Margie" and she got a bit irate at the boy - he should know his women better - they were sweet little chickens and you can't rush a thing like that - not when they're nice. They are from Texas. "Manning" is their name - Margie and Dorothy.

Well, we came in late that night, as might be expected - dodging the M.P. for we far over stayed curfew. We left a call with the C.L. to wake us up at 6 AM - finally got up at 7:30 and the 4 of us Cal Taylor, John Staeger, Dagget Morse (we call him the "Horrible Head" - he was hit by a prop - 7 stitches in his turban) and yours truly. We had bacon and eggs in town and hopped a 10:05 bus for N.O. Lt. Sundin, his wife, and mother went down on same bus. He sat with us and was apparently dreading a big shopping trip his women were anticipating. We arrived at N.O. about 12:30 and got in a cab and went directly to "Antoines" to eat. We had shrimp remoulade to start with - turkey - broccoli - diced French fries - chef salad - and some special dessert. Demitasse (black) - hot bread served and continually replaced when it cools - all very nice but I've had meals I enjoyed more - those at 450 1/2 . They keep the atmosphere very French and menu, I'll try to enclose it, is all in French. It is a farce though for they don't really have anything these days that's on the menu. We also had a domestique California Sauterne with the meal, which always makes the cheese more binding.

The dessert was plain vanilla ice cream but the sauce was the ovation. They bring a small copper bucket on 3 legs to your table and in it is cherries soaked profusely in brandy. The waiter sets the dishes of cream in front of you then he lights the brandy with a match. At this precise moment his assistant (very well trained) turns out all electric lights. That leaves only old gas lit lamps in one center chandelier lit - this of course directs all attention to your table watching the large blue flame issuing from the burning brandy & cherries. The pot is well stirred, the lights go on, and the ice cream is dressed up - topped with the hot sauce and served. I need not mention that it was extremely good.

From there we roamed the town a bit - not quite settled as to what we wanted to do. Taylor and I went to the U.S.O. while Staeger and Morse went to buy John a sweater. Taylor showered but I settled for a shave - not having done so since the previous night before going to Gulfport. Well, anyway, we called up our gals on Douphine St. and they proved to be eager as ever so we agreed to meet them at 7:30. At 6 we tried to get a room at Roosevelt but no dice. I have no idea why they would be so crowded this time of year and on a week day too - but after calling all the larger hotels, there were no rooms to be had. Finally through one of the bell hops we talked to a guy at the Roosevelt who runs a sort of hotel in a large old home - oddly enough it is called the Parkhouse. So we got a room for 4 of us for $6.50 - one swell bed and a day bed. As usual I lost the toss and so did Taylor - sooo we had to take the day bed. We barely had time to grab a sandwich and get out to our dollies.

Cal's girl is Rosemary Boudousquie and her mother is grand to us when we go there. The true crux of the situation was that the week before we were supposed to go down there - well, as per usual, we were screwed - couldn't go, but apparently we *didn't make it clear to them - they had arranged some sort of party - Eileen - my little baby evidently had her mother make a cake and all and there they were with it - all alone when like the "big greed" we didn't show. God love them - they were really hurt I guess - so altho (sic) they were all on deck when we arrived - the Horrible Four had a bit of ice breaking to do all over again.*

Eileen is sure an Irish honey and I had a grand time with her. We stayed at the house for an hour or so while Mrs. Boudousquie played piano, a lot of the old semi-classical ballads, and we all sang. Then we went down to the dock and got on a Mississippi River Boat - the "President" which you can guess is devoted entirely to dancing - fairly good band - lots of stray women - in short a good time was had by all.

Of course I'm not making the time I should with this dolly, but I've at least got the framework layed and with a couple letters, hope to have the situation well in my arms if I get a chance to go again. She is little - just about a perfect build - legs as good if not better than Kitty Keaty's - wore sheer black lace number - low neck - complexion I'd love to get a hold of. Drool dammit Harry - that's what I did last night. Anyway, we hit the sac at Parkhouse at about 2:30 AM - tired but happy if not completely satisfied. Returned to camp on an 8 AM bus - got in here at 10:30 and had a big breakfast - we had to rush so to get that bus that we didn't even have coffee before we left. We met our formation at 1:15 - place was closed in so we couldn't fly. Sooo here I am back at the barracks trying to catch up on the news to youse guys.

I did splendidly in the mail today - letters from Mom, Harry - Coach Ott, the Beals and a book from Gramp and a nice letter from Sally McPherson - she wants a picture - I don't suppose we have any of those small ones in uniform - now that I think of it I don't believe you had any small ones made - ah well we shall worry about that anon and anon. I received that grand box today. The shoes are swell, and are a good fit, and I have them locked in my foot locker - saving them for when I really need them. The underwear is a Godsend as are the sox. I have taken to washing out my own sox and civilian underwear - they do a hell of a job in the laundry here. I get them nice and white and feel swell underneath when I get cleaned up. The Beal's sox wash up fine - they run a lot but don't shrink too much at all.

Harry - from his letter - sounds like the usual busy boy. Next time you see Queen, Harry - give her a lusty pinch in the buttocks and say it's from me - you might even get a bang out of it too. Bridge sounds like a good diversion, wish I could get some of the boys here to play that instead of the usual Stud, Draw or Black Jack game. It would be a good idea to get a line on Hazel's Technique - even if it just knows what not to do. Advise you to keep Tess in her place about the magazine business - threaten her with opening your mail as a federal offense - that may help but I doubt it.

Mother—I'll try just as soon as I can to get a letter to Mrs. Keogh but with all my traipsing about of late you can see I'm way behind—but good—must owe about 15 letters at least. I do hope I can get some of them caught up this evening. It is an awful temptation to head for town tonight or go to the NCO club where they are having a swell Navy band and bringing WAVEs in too, but like all good things this must come to an end and the dough is getting a bit short. I have loaned 20 out and have but one more day off till payday—you might wire me $5, no more than that, because I'm sure of having enough if we should get a chance to go to N.O. next week. Received the 3 dollars and have already started accumulating Harry's cigarettes. Don't worry about the ties—I just have had a dozen or so pressed and cleaned. I sure will be looking for the box of eatables. You got me wrong about being away etc.—you asked me if other fellows didn't get boxes—and I was merely trying to explain why they weren't getting them. I know we're different—we three are pretty darn special people I'd say.

Glad I have the cosmetic situation well in hand now. I'll take care of them—hope you send the metal box. I must write Gramp again since I got that magazine. Another English one dealing with the Battle of Malta addressed in his hand.

If I were Jerry O'Hara I wouldn't worry too much just as long as I wasn't stopping any slugs. All our PFC. Gunners have made Corporal here. Yesterday in N.O., Staeger and Morse left us to buy a sweater and came back with their stripes on—very quietly—didn't say a word you know—and did Taylor and I razz hell out of them.

Well, I'll never get dinner or do any more writing if I keep this up. Have to go now. Lots Love, Frank

January 21, Sunday

Dear Mother, Harry and Mike,

Well, I am certainly a bad boy. Didn't write yesterday or the day before—this stuff will have to cease. Not that I was any busier than usual but I'm too easily persuaded of late. Friday after school I played football with the boys and after chow went to a dance at the Service Club. This place is a goldmine for women. Of all the girls that were there, there were very few who were from Gulfport itself. Most of them came in from outlying small towns. A few pretty good ones too but I fluffed that one. Should have taken at least one home but neglected to draw my pass early and when I wanted to get it, it was too late.

Yesterday we flew Schedule #4. Didn't have a formation until 1:15 PM. Taylor and I got up reasonably early. We got difficulties! Due to lack of help the Post dry cleaners don't get stuff back for 10-15 days. Of course this is no good to us for we hope to get to N.O. again come next Thursday. Finally we got dressed in O.D.s and drew our passes and carried clothes for half the barracks out beyond the camp gate where we can get 3 day service on it. We came right back and I went to mail call. It was sure a good one. Huba Huba—the box of eats arrived. I didn't get a chance to open it then but did the first thing when I got down from flying. We opened one box of cookies then and there, and with a couple left for breakfast it is gone now. I'm saving the other for when we go flying.

I no longer have room in my locker for some of the things, so my Mechanic has put the crackers and some of the canned goods in his locker. We all get a lot of pleasure snacking as you can imagine. The past couple times Staeger goes over to the PX and smuggles beer back for one or two of us writing or reading in the barracks. That makes it cozy. I have all my ties pressed now, just had em cleaned and the two new ones make me about 16 or 17 total. I have taken good care of most of them and not one is in a condition that I couldn't wear it. Sooo we are all set for a while. On top of that I got a box of cookies from Norm Bealy so we'll be well cookied for a while. The boxes of Hydrox are similar to ones we buy at the PX to take flying–they're the thing at high altitude for you can slip the O2 mask off and slip in a cookie and that helps for a little while. The large boxes of crackers are fine–we can only get the small ones here–when we can get them.

I guess it would be in order to answer the past 3 letters I have received. Harry you must feel Zoot in that new outfit–I've told my buddies about it and we all drooled together. Tell me–did Steve say he saw you in the Drug Store or did he miss you completely? I think the bridge idea is fine and the both of you going together should make for getting a good deal more out of it. I'll bet Mother often thanks heaven for such a son as you Harry!

Don't really need too many tips on school teachers–they weren't too bad. We really should have gone back this week and finished the job but that all important "finishing" it has been something we have managed to avoid so far and I expect we'll keep it up. It would be something if Milt and Jim Kehoe could get together–maybe the three of you could get plastered together some small evening! I received prints today–thanks muchly–I'll label them so that you'll know who is who and ship them back to you as soon as possible. John Staeger has a camera and we will do the same thing here as soon as we get a good day. By the way, can you get me any 828 category film? Here I am asking again. Here is the set up plain and simple. Would like very much to get 828 for John's camera but can use 127, 616, 116, 120, or 620 or Univex 00. Next to cosmetics, as near as I can find out, film and Gunner's wings have a high priority as a medium of exchange. I will be asking for odds and ends from here on in I guess altho (sic) right now I can't think of anything more you can get me. I know that it takes nerve to ask Dorshel for anything like that but tell him why I want it–to take overseas. If you'd rather I'd write him a letter please say so and I'll write him as soon as you let me know. I know this stuff will take money and also if I make New Orleans once next month I won't be too flush but please manage if you can without too much trouble.

When I get overseas I expect to be raised in rank although right now I have no idea of how far it will go. At the advice of overseas men, I'll allow myself about 50 or 60 per month and put all else in allotment to be sent to you people–won't be a lot at first but should get larger if I'm there any time at all. What I'm trying say is that if I do overdo it now I'll be paying it back as soon as I ship out. Another thing–I hope you'll send me boxes of candy as soon as you get my overseas address. Cal Taylor's brother has been over almost 2 months now as a Mechanic, Engineer Gunner and he has been writing Cal the dope.

I received El' Chem yesterday–will enclose a picture so you can get a glimpse of Sally–not bad at all. Maybe I'll get to write her tonight–we'll see.

We (ROGs) had this morning off so slept a little–went to 10:30 Mass and then I made my big mistake by playing football again. It sure tires me and they almost break me in half out there sometimes but we have lotsa fun at it and the PT here is so sketchy you really need something in the way of exercise to keep you trim.

Harry–if you need flints or more cigarettes let me know. Those are some things I can get for you. I sent 20 packages with Xmas tree and trimmings–sent it special handling so it should get there O.K.–sent it out yesterday morning.

About Air Force–We are temporarily attached to 3rd A.F. unassigned as students–we can, but do not, have to wear 3rd AF Patch. Stationary was all I could get at PX at the time.

Hope Haroola makes out to his advantage at Carbo in anticipated Shake up. He should, I know, and they better dread it or they'll have crew 440 to reckon with but good. We could bomb Hell out of that 2 bit establishment during an afternoon off. Guess that's all for now folks–be good.

Lotsa love, Frank

January 21, Sunday

Dear Mrs. Keough,

It was so nice to hear from my grand neighbor. Fraid I am a bit late with an answer but you will forgive me I hope. To tell the truth we have been out on a continual prowl of late–going to lots of dances and really getting a sample of this Southern women situation–not bad at all–honest.

One of the main reasons I delayed writing was because I had hoped we would hit the Mary Gold during trek to New Orleans but unfortunately the only good place we managed was "Antoines." Perhaps you've heard of it. It is supposed to be known the world over and of course we had been looking forward to eating there. The place has been in existence under the same family management for about 105 years now and they have distinctly preserved the old French atmosphere. The food of course was distinctly French–the menu–I sent one home this evening–is all in French. From what I've had of the language, I believe I could have managed all right but the selection was very limited due to the present shortages and we had to take what was on hand. We settled for turkey and didn't do at all badly. It was exceptional as far as the atmosphere was concerned and very good, but to tell the truth I enjoyed eating at the Mary Gold at home more. Of course that was when it was in its prime but I enjoy American styles of cooking much better.

We have hopes of bursting in on Mrs. Ressler's establishment the next time we go to N.O. Thanks a million for sending me her name. If we get there I'll be sure and ask for her and let you know how we make out.

I don't envy you your N.F.'s weather from what I've heard of it. I've been south the past two winters and the inconvenience of it all–all that snow–doesn't appeal to me too much these days.

How does Mr. Keough keep? I do hope he has been behaving himself. I still think you have displayed a good deal of wisdom in not choosing to travel this year. I well understand what you are missing in Fla. about this time of year for we fly over St. Pete's every now and again but conditions are really rough traveling and I don't envy any one more than 8 hours on a train at a stretch. We just went to N.O. and back to Gulfport about 3-4 weeks ago and it was murder–no kidding.

How are my two little gals at 454–I suppose they are having a big time with all the snow.

We had a big time in N.O. last Wednesday. Three other fellows and myself are lined up with some of the very nice local talent down there and we had a grand time. We spent most of the evening on the "President." Perhaps you know it–it is that large Mississippi River boat which is devoted entirely to dancing. The band was good and the company, all that could be desired. For my money that N.O. is some playground. We hit it as often as we can but they fool us around here. We are supposed to get every 8th day off but when the weather is bad and we miss some flying time, they take our day off away from us and we fly. As a result we have only been able to make it twice so far but hope to get there a couple more times before our time runs out here, which won't be long now.

Well, I guess that is all for now Mrs. K. Please sit down and treat me to a little of that noble script of yours again in the near future. Be good–till I hear from you soon. Love, Frank

January 22, Monday

Dear Mother, Harry and Mike,

Really not much to say today after that opus last night. We are waiting for the call (whistle) into the wild blue yonder. It has been closed in yesterday and today so I doubt very much that we will fly. But of course you can never tell here–if you but likes the weather, wait a minute–it'll change.

Best news today is that we fly schedule #3 after our day off Thursday next. Of course this is subject to change at no notice at all but we hope it won't be changed. This schedule will give us time to get to N.O. again this week and people–That's good!

Received Mother's of Friday this morning. I should write Gramp this evening. Did manage to write Mrs. Keough, Beals and Sally last night besides you fellows. If I stay in tonight I may get some more written–we shall see. I have a hunch Taylor and I will be on the prowl if we don't fly.

I did start getting Gazette again–day after I wrote the Otts so please tell them. Also start breaking it to them gently that it would be foolish to send it while I'm overseas–I think it would, do you?

I get a kick out of Hazel Sample and her man. Mother–N.F. isn't the only place where those things go on–I've sure seen some beauties around here. The crux of the situation is that, like European women–most Southern women believe in being married–that of course is a must, but they also believe in having some "lover" as they refer to it. I guess it makes the cheese more binding–nobody ever really knows who the little bastards belong to. Oh I am not familiar enough with the situation to really make such a blanket statement and it is far from general, but there is some of it I believe.

The war news is good–let's pray it stays that way. Vincent Shanahan in V-12? Just make sure that that is not the deal where they sign up for 6 years–ugh. The Navy does a better job on educating a man for his job–but these sailors lack something– ask any Gulfport girl. Tell Harry and Jim K. to have 7 or 8 for me–have to run now. Lotsa love, Frank

January 23, Tuesday

Dear Mother, Harry and Mike,

Well, I thought we wouldn't fly yesterday and I also thought we would fly schedule #3 next week and hence have lots of time for N.O. again. Well, I was wrong on both counts. We have been put on schedule #2, which calls for getting up at 4:30 AM and when we came out of briefing the whole field had cleared. You can just imagine how I felt about flying yesterday. All the fortunes of war–Ah well.

I think I'll go to N.O. anyway–it will be taking a chance of course but we're get- ting too near the end of the rope to bandy words or worry about a couple hours sleep. Don't know as yet whether the 4 of us will go–John and Daggett are not too keen about it–of course they have faithful heart interests at home but old Taylor and my- self as usual are rarin' to go so I shouldn't be a bit surprised if we manage it.

We have to go and get our clothes this afternoon and get all set. I know it sounds silly and insignificant–all this planning ahead but that is the only way you really manage to get anything done. Anyway it's more fun that way. Also we have a line on a couple college girls there–go to some Hoi Polloi school–forget the name right now, so if we find the company not too congenial, there is pa-lenty of room for expansion.

Nothing new here–final phase check in machine guns this afternoon–have to fieldstrip and detail strip a cal. 50–in 20 minutes to a half hour–blindfolded–some fun. None of this stuff worries any of us now as it did at Gunnery School–most of us are pretty sure of the stuff anyway.

Have to run along now–medical lecture first and then my machine gun. Be good, folks–
Lotsa Love, Frank

January 25, Thursday

Dear Mother, Harry and Mike,

Received a couple letters this morning. Harry's of Tuesday and Mother's of Mon- day. I detect a strained note–Sorry–did miss a couple days but had no idea that things were held up as you say. Please forgive and understand that we are rather confined and when we do get a chance to do something we get a kick out of, we just don't bother with much else. Kinda thoughtless that's true but we get a lot of disap- pointments here although the overall deal is good, still we actually never know when we will honestly be free and it makes an awfully fluid schedule.

I have received books from Gramp and the N.Y. Times Magazine today—must write him again. Peggy in the movies? What about her legs? She is a honey aside from that. Hope you have box with cigarettes and Christmas tree by now.

Yes indeed there is evidence of this course coming to an end. It is known as Class 0216 or 2nd month 16th day. No hope of extending it I'm afraid. We are top group now—next ones to leave. Somehow—if the Russians keep on we won't see much of anything in Europe I judge. As the intelligence officer put it the other day, "American forces were considerably het up and jubilant when they captured 3 miles of front and St. Milo—they were glad they got there before the Russians." No—No mustache as yet—wait till I get overseas for that again. They will probably quarantine us for 2-3 weeks and that will be a good chance to start anew. I imagine, from what I've heard, we go through a similar training program over there as we have had here. Probably be at least 2 months after we get there before we see any action. A hell of a lot can happen in that time!

Have received ma box from the Otts. Told you when I got Coach's letter and I answered it immediately. No word from them since—I am getting the Gazette now.

I got quite a kick out of Harry and his one man fashion parade—reminds me of how I used to feel when I got something new. It's a great feeling isn't it?

By the way Tess—I don't hear of you having anything new to wear of late. I do hope you're not cutting down. Too bad about the Oxen Yoke going "out." Ah well, a lot of things will "live again" one of these fine days. Let's hope it is not too far off.

Harry—don't get caught not "pissing on the green" in that penny ante game. The boys here have been coaching me along. Still haven't learned to shuffle nonchalantly yet. Good thing—they say you don't start to lose much until you can shuffle like an expert.

Guess that takes in most of the last two from home. Today is our day off and we decided against going to N.O. Cal Taylor has a bad chest cold and we have been doctoring him up. We wouldn't have had too much time there anyway I suppose. Would have been some Rat Race getting back to fly and this trying to do a good job when you're dead tired is not what it is cracked up to be. It has rained all day here and we're glad in a way that we didn't go. We sent a telegram to the girls last night and expected they'd be very sore but received a telegram from them this afternoon that they would like to come here Sunday if it is all right with us and if we can get passes for a while. As it is—we get up at 4:30 AM Sunday—fly until 2 PM so we'll have the evening with them I guess. Don't know whether I've told you or not but between here and Biloxi along the Gulf are places which constitute one of the larger Winter Playgrounds of America, although I'd never heard of it before. Plenty of high class hotels—dancing and luxurious gambling houses. So I expect we'll take them dancing somewhere. To be truthful the four of us can't quite figure it out. We all got letters from the girls during the week—didn't particularly mention having a good time last time they were with us in N.O. We were quite disgusted with it all. Then this—we wondered what their folks were saying about it—having met some of them and been in their homes we know that they are nice kids from nice families. We're not egotistical enough to think we have enough charm to bring them on a 150 mile jaunt and the man situation is not that bad at N.O. Oh well, we have ceased to try to understand them. We as G.I.s have nothing to lose. As Staeger says, if they were the kind you could rent a room and get some liquor we wouldn't worry about it but we don't know what the hell to think - every one of them is too nice to kick around. Sunday should tell!

I guess that says most of it for today. Saw a movie right after lunch "Music for the Million." Good entertainment - better than usual and the girl (not the little one) who plays the lead is definitely for me. Guess it's her voice that gets me.

Well, be good, folksies - have to arise at 4:30 AM on the morrow so am not quite sure whether I'll go to Gulfport or not. Looks like too much effort right now - the weather being what it is and my co-operator being down with a cold. Be good, folks. Lotsa Love, Frank

January 26, Friday

Dear Mother, Harry and Mike,

Well, there is not much new today. I didn't go to town last night - weather still not too good and besides I got worried about Cal Taylor. His chest cold was tight and they wouldn't do a damn thing for him on sick call - kept him flying too Sooo little Francis George slapped him in his sac last night - rubbed him good with Vicks, couple aspirins, and chiseled a couple good shots of Shenley's for him and then covered him up like a mummy. Poor devil sweat like a sucker but his cough loosened up this morning and he feels a lot better. I feel sorry for some of these fellows - they are such babies and don't know the fundamentals about keeping well. No one will take care of you if you don't look after yourself. Well, we got the kid fixed up fairly well now - a little good sleep should do the rest.

Got up at 4:30 AM this morning and after they had warmed up a Big Bird up we went into the Wild Blue Yonder. I really just went along for the ride for I no sooner got in the air and tried to get under way - I blew fuses, sparked, and almost expected it (the Liaison set) to blow up. It was of no use - neither transmitter nor receiver was any good. I tried for 4 hours - everything in the book and then a lot of make shift measures but to no avail. I was pretty sore! On the flight report, when we came down, I wrote a long tale of woe - really condemned the communications equipment on that ship. Ground crew didn't like it much - I stayed - helped gas the plane and when finished I met the Radio Maintenance men at the ship. Even there, on the ground, I tried to contact the local station but to no avail. In 4 hours I had analyzed the trouble I figured, but they just laughed at me - tried to tell me my business - I really burned but managed to keep my head. You may do the flying but you're not worth a damn if your ground maintenance crews aren't pulling for you. Strangely enough I knew more about the mechanical set up - circuits and all than they did and I tried to explain the *difficulty - either they didn't understand or weren't willing to admit that I knew what I was talking about.*

After that I had to go to communications and report. I reported equipment inoperative. The Master Sergeant there smirked - said he would go to the plane and check equipment with me. I was almost ready to give up. He thought I had been goofing off all morning - too lazy to work. I started to burn again - was afraid of result for I knew ground maintenance was not going to collaborate my story of faulty equipment. Then I thought to myself - I know I know my business and if I couldn't make her work I'd like to see someone else try.

So the Master Sergeant and I tore in a jeep and drove out to the ship. My heart sank when we got in but I stuck to the courage of my own convictions. When we got in, low and behold - maintenance apparently had checked closer - when we got there they had just finished ripping out the old set and had put in a new one - the ground boys told the Master Sergeant I was right and everything was fine. I made that Sergeant feel like a fool before I got through - that is what he was trying to do to me. People, was that ever a moral victory for we operators over ground maintenance and communications. I gave that old boy one hell of a reaming out. It's not nice to gloat but if you've never seen a Banty Rooster - I was it.

Guess that says most of it for today - I reckon they'll think twice before they subtlety call me a liar again.

When I finally got in I went to sleep - slept too late to get supper - haven't had a square meal since 5 AM this morning but that was where the Spam came in. We made a meal of it. Think I'll stay up long enough to eat and then sleep some more. Ground school in the morning and all day - may hit town to-morrow night - we'll see. Be good, folks.

Love, Frank

January 29, Monday

Dear Mother, Harry and Mike,

Well, I'm a bad boy again. Missed the past couple days - out playing around as you might expect but at this point I promise to try to not let it happen again regardless - even if I just say I'm kicking and such.

Received Mother's of the 24th yesterday with the 10 dollar bill safe and sound. Will airmail this so that you won't be worrying any longer than is absolutely necessary. I say again the cookies were grand and I noticed absolutely no difference in the shortening. We don't get any decent pastry and it really filled the bill. I saved the 2nd box and took it flying - did we ever finish them up - officers and E.M. really made short of them.

I don't think that requesting items by letter from overseas deal really holds good or is necessary. To make sure I'll inquire soon as possible. Lots of these things I've asked for, you don't use yourself but I understand that if you really have something to barter - between that and the black market - you can get pretty well anything you want. It is not previous to talk about these things. I had hoped that maybe B-29s may be coming here and we might be held here and trained all over in them, although I wouldn't relish going to the So. Pacific. Well, that just ain't going to happen I guess. I heard yesterday that we are due at the Staging Area on the 16th of February - for the love of heaven don't breathe this stuff around much - I shouldn't be writing it. Don't know how long we will be at a Staging Area but it sure won't be long. Not pleasant to talk about but the sooner I get over, the sooner I'll be back again.

The night before last I went to a dance - Taylor and I - found me a red-head, Frances Elam she was here with her mother visiting her brother who is a R.O. here also. I was really making town with that but unfortunately she leaves tonight or today or sometime. She lives in Jackson, Tenn. and Taylor had plenty in common with her - he always seems to have - what a line! Yesterday we flew. None of us thought we would - for my money it was closed in around here but up we went anyway. Not a hole through it anywhere so we did a 4-5 thousand foot penetration Huba Huba - up above the sun was shinin away and beneath nothing but fluffy clouds - couldn't see the ground no how. We flew high altitude formation and then dropped incendiary bombs. We got down late and even later finally got to town to meet our four New Orleans dollies. Mrs. Dowling had come with the girls and that made it proper - I felt better about that - somehow I couldn't see them coming here alone to see 4 pointed eared Gunners. We were disappointed for they wouldn't stay later than 8 PM but we were with them about 4 hours - danced at the U.S.O. My Eileen had the flu and couldn't make it but they brought another girl with whom I had quite a time. She is not nearly as easy on the eyes as Eileen but she is a lot more fun - now I'm between points - which one will I get if we go to N.O. again? Ah I do have my troubles don't I?

After the girls left we went to the best place in town to eat - "Angelo's" about a 10 minute taxi ride out of town. Steaks, French fries, bowl chef salad and beer - couldn't eat any dessert. We were disappointed naturally that the girls couldn't stay as we had planned on going all out - dinner & dancing at the Edgewater near Biloxi on the Gulf but we had our dinner alone - Staeger, Morse, Taylor and Thompson - came back to town after eating in time to catch the last showing of "Frenchman's Creek." Thought Joan Fontaine overacted it a good bit and also that there were more opportunities to make a good picture in the book than were taken advantage of. We got home reasonably early - before 12 - it was all right - didn't cost us much anyway. With what you sent me I still have over $20 and payday is Wednesday. Guess that keeps us up to date for now. Am writing during lunch hour so this will be sure and get out. Have to run to make my class now - Be good, folksies.

Lotsa Love, Frank

January 30, Tuesday

Dear Mother, Harry and Mike,

Well, we were off into the Blue Yonder early this morning. We were supposed to fly a DF (direction finding) mission which is the type of most concern to the R.O. It is a mission that calls for efficient coordination between Navigator and R.O. I was all set for lots of work but our Navigator - Shackelford didn't bring along equipment he was required to so the thing was called off. Have another crack at it I suppose. Didn't do much last night - went to see "Practically Yours" - MacMurray and Colbert - not bad but nothing out of the ordinary. Had decided earlier in the day to go into town but felt a little too tired so made it the show instead. Have just really gotten back from flying - got my clean laundry back and since I didn't make it to sign Laundry Roster for next month I had to hustle around and get one of my boys to send my stuff with theirs.

I have Mom's letter of Friday here - Yup it is just a year since I hit old Ft. Dix. Not a too pleasant one in lots of respects but there is no sense in complaining about it. I've been fortunate in that of the lots of company I've had - it has not been too bad. I've learned a lot about a lot of things - mostly about men. I needed that - I've learned it - and now I'm ready to go home but that's the hell of it. Ah well, if the Russians keep rushin maybe I'll be there sooner than we think. It will be grand to start living my own life again.

I spoke of receiving the "sawbuck" yesterday. Thanks muchly - I'm pretty well set - first month in the Army I haven't been absolutely broke or nearly so - sweating out payday. We will be paid to-morrow at 7:45 AM - it's early to get up but for payday I don't mind it. I do hope you get the box I sent - seems so long now that you should have it, although as you say things at home are jammed. Fran tells me (got a letter from her and Norm yesterday) that the situation is terrible. So many people have to walk - boy that's too damn bad. Someday someone will wake up in this country and Canada - War's Hell - Huba Huba. Evidently in my last letter to the Beals I must have alluded to Bobby's personal appearance. I don't know for the life of me just what I said but in Fran's letter she tells me very subtly not to mention Bob's looks again - you know subtle like a bulldozer. I was terribly sorry to hear about Shug Carrol's dad dying - he was an awfully nice fellow - always grand to us.

I am scheduled to go out this evening and meet my Ball Turret man's wife. He has been at me and at me so I figured to keep peace I'd better go. He just married about 4 months ago and I think he still isn't sure whether it was a good idea or not. Kimpel - my waist gunner had a date with a WAC. Frankly, I'd much rather go to the Community House and dance as I have been doing. Kimpel and Shaffer enjoy a different type of good time than I do, but to keep everyone happy I guess I'll go out with them for a while this evening. When I get fed up I can take off like a big bird whereas if I had a date it would be different. Shaffer wants me to dance with his wife anyway. As I say I'm not very keen about it but we'll try it once anyway.

Another pleasant thought - the Sergeant in charge of our flight and the Tactical office tells us this morning that we fly on our day off so that makes it nice.

Well folksies, - guess I'd better get along now - have only had one meal since 4:30 AM and I'm gettin that gnawing feelin in the stomach - Be good, people.
Love, Frank

January 31, Wednesday

Dear Mother, Harry and Mike,

Payday was today - drew some 68 dollars and along with that, what I had, gives about 90 in all. A tidy sum! I took out a money order to keep it, well, 40 bucks of it, safe in case of any exigency and also as a precaution against theft. If we get to go to N.O. to-morrow I'll be particularly thrifty - I want to be able to stock up on things when I get to a staging area. I understand that anything you might want is plentiful there. You have never said anymore about my watch beyond that it went in for adjustment. I don't think I'll need it now so I hope you are not sending it on. I should be issued one soon.

I received Harry's of Tuesday and Mother's of Monday today. As Haroola probably knows by now no N.O. last week. We're kinda hoping to go on the morrow - we shall see. Hope you three lads can get together - you, Jim & Lapoint. I'll try if I can to get some more cigarettes for Harry before I leave. We can get them by the carton at the staging area. I guess I'm writing too much about the last stop before leaving the States but it won't be long now. We cannot turn in any clothing for repair, salvage or exchange nor shoe repair now here. They're getting us in the mood all right. I don't like the idea of your having to wait until the first of April Mom to get anything new. One thing I may telegraph about to-morrow, whups - slip of the pen I guess - I'll just do it anyway. Thanks for getting extra lipsticks. Anything you have like that - please ship on as soon as is possible.

Went to town last night - first Kimpel and I tried to get a couple girls at the service club for we didn't relish going to a Honky Tonk Club with Shaffer & wife and our being womenless. Well - we almost connected but not quite. By the time we got in, Shaffer had decided he was not too keen about going so we just stayed in his room a while and talked until about 10 or 10:30. Then Kimpel and I went to a dance at the Community House and later went to the Town House, a restaurant where I had the best t-bone steak I've had in ages. It was really all "right." Tonight Taylor and I are going in again. We can't stay late but we'll have a crack at it anyway - we have a good time dancing - with no one in particular - just a lot of them. I still haven't learned to jitterbug - guess I'm getting old.

We are scheduled for photo scoring of camera film at 7 PM. I still have to eat - then clean up to go to town. By the way, the Rooshans are only 58 miles from Berlin by the newspaper not bad, what? I'd like to get to England just in time to see it finish. Then what the hell would they do with us. Nice way to kill time anyway. Since I got paid I got some more airmails - Huba Huba - quick communication these days.

No cold Barb - I sure cured Taylor - he's in fine shape now. Just is too lazy or doesn't know how to take care of himself I guess.

Have to run now - my Engineer is waiting so we can go and eat.

Lotsa Love, Frank

February 1945

February 3, Saturday

Dear Mother, Harry and Mike,

Here is little Francis George back on the line after a two day absence. Not a very good boy I guess. Received Harry's of Tuesday and Mother's of Thursday this morning so will endeavor to answer them before I tell you my adventures of the past couple days.

From every source we are hearing of the bad weather up north. It has been very changeable here but we all change clothes to meet the changes. Haven't yet been driven to wear my long woolen drawers as have most of the fellows. The dampness is penetrating and you just have to be careful to avoid colds. Don't like the sound of the Coal emergency - can't Harry manage to get bags or something through the plant? I do hope the thing clears up to some extent soon. My guess is that it is not so much a shortage of actual fuel as much as it has been the slowing up of transportation due to the weather.

The tax deal does not sound at all good - of course I have been wholly ignorant of this new change. As per usual we live from day to day and selfishly. The conduct of the war interests us only in so far as it hurries the conclusion of the whole mess. Frankly, I feel guilty at having as good a time as I have been having of late. By next month I should be overseas and will have an additional allotment settled on you fellows by that time. I'll get to work on the cigarettes immediately ... maybe I can get a few cartons to Harry from the staging area but I'm afraid they won't let us ship them from there.

Peculiar that you should write, Mom, about Communion, when I'm staying in this afternoon keeping away from eats so that I can go. Kind of hard to make it unless you make a special effort when we are flying at such varied times. We are supposed to fly every day this week. Got up at 2:30 AM this morning but were closed in so they finally released us at 10 AM. I hope you do get a box out to me. As I understand it, they want to finish up our flying by the 10th. Have to be in staging area by 16th - intervening time will be spent in final processing is my guess.

Now to get to the N.O. deal of this week. Thursday we were up at 4:30 AM. We really didn't know till briefing that we could get off over Friday. It came as a pleasant surprise also the fact that Lt. Sundin had put in for our passes. Immediately upon getting down from flying Morse, Taylor, and myself showered and shaved and got ready to go. Staeger was ill, something wrong with his stomach so he decided he'd better not join the Rat Race with us. We had to stand all the way on the bus - arrived in N.O. at about 8:15 PM. We went to La Louisianne to eat - it was dandy - then we called our little girls. We had not let them know definitely that we were coming for on last Tuesday the tactical office told us we would have to fly on our day off. As it happened two other flights had to fly - not us. When we called the girls - they were at a show so we went to Cal's girl's house as usual and waited for them. It was too late to do anything when they arrived - the situation was not good. All three had to work the next day and our passes were only good until 9 PM last night. Sooo the girls decided they would have to stay off work - Huba Huba and arranged to meet us at Rosemary's house at 12 noon next day. We had not gotten a room so it was a little late to start looking. Finally got one in a sort of boarding house. Not too good but served the purpose. They called us at 10:30 AM next morning. We had breakfast at St. Charles Hotel and were going to treat ourselves to a shave ala barber but the time was passing rapidly and we waited 15 minutes & decided we couldn't stay any longer so we took off for the U.S.O. borrowed razors and did the job ourselves. We were at the house by noon and soon took off with the girls. Started at a movie - went to the park - bleak day but lotsa fun - then we stopped at Dawling's house - that's Daggett Morse's girl's home where we rolled up the rug and danced and shot the bull with the gal's pappy. Finally ended up taking the girls' to dinner and caught a 10:45 bus back to camp - arrived at 12:30 - no trouble at the gate. We were lucky to get on the bus back at all and stood all the way on that one too. We were tired laddies when we got up at 2:30 to fly - glad we didn't go up. We went up in the locker loft in the hanger - jumped into heavy flying clothes and laid right down on the floor and slept until they released us at about 10 AM.

I sure found myself a bundle of Irish adversity in little Eileen. I owed her a letter and had to thaw her out on that score. She won't give me a picture - first girl I ever asked for one. She'll take a day off from work to be with me - tease the living hell out of me with those great big eyes but kiss her - not even a little peck. Haven't hit anything so tantalizing and yet so untenable in some time - that's what makes the cheese so much more binding I guess. Then she up and tells me she might have come but the first thing she ever learned was NOT to chase a man. Evidently she went to a wedding Sunday - claimed she had the cake to prove it - then she says she went to Confession and Communion Sunday and she asked God - "Please don't let Frank be angry." And God said he wouldn't be - So she maintained that I shouldn't be sore - I couldn't deny God's word. She's quite a little character - think you folks would like her - Hell Harry - just looking at her is a pleasure.

Well folks - that catches up on most scores I guess. I'm still rather tuckered out - think I may hit the sac for a while now. Hate to miss Saturday night in town but I think I need some good solid sleep so I guess I'll trundle into bed until church time. Lotsa Love, Frank

February 4, Sunday

Dear Mother, Harry and Mike,

Another day closed in today. We got up at 2:30 AM as per scheduled and reported - were briefed but due to weather we were unable to fly and so we slept up in the locker loft. I wish I had a picture of that scene for you. It is cold up there and we all put on flying sheepskins to keep warm. Once dressed in flying clothes we are all well upholstered and just drop on the floor. The entire loft was filled, that is the floor - so many men all sleeping. We were released just too late for me to make 10:20 Mass so if I go into town I'll have to come back on the Post again to go to the 6 o'clock number. And you can bet we are going in! Yup N.O. is coming to Gulfport again. I don't know what we've got that will make them come that distance and last time they stood both ways on the bus but they wanted to come when we called last night so who are we to say no?

John is going to take his camera with him and since the sun is really shining in sharp contrast to a dull bleak foggy morning perhaps we can get some decent pictures. There is a Tea Dance at the Community house this PM so I expect we will take them there - probably dinner someplace and I suppose they will have to leave early as last week. It is really a lot of bother for I have to come back, go to Mass and Communion and then back to town again. Maybe I'll bring Eileen in to church with me, that is, if she comes - the villain! At any rate it is undoubtedly the last time we'll see them so some effort of some nature is surely required.

I have been picking up cigarettes since yesterday. I have that shoe box my slippers came in and altho (sic) I can't promise anything I'll try to fill it and ship it on as soon as is possible - before I leave here at any rate. We are scheduled for processing the 12th - 14th so you can see that it won't be long now. Our crew is just slightly behind on minimums but I expect that we will fly our heads off the next few days in order to complete all our work.

Aside from what I have mentioned there is little new. Have to get ready now to get in and see my "Irish" - if she comes. Be good, folks.
Lotsa Love, Frank

February 4th - Letter from Dick Perry
(Lt. R.M. Perry, 5th T.C.S. New York, NY)

Dear Frank,

Just received your letter of January 5th and as you can see it took just about a month to reach me. Hope this doesn't take as long. You landed a good plane Frank and I think you are lucky to get the B-17. Here's wishing you lots of luck. I am flying a converted B-24 called a C-109 which is nothing more or less than a big gas tanker. Treacherous as hell. Before I forget, I took a census amongst my brother pilots about what they wish they had remembered to bring with them or would bring across now. So here's a few things to really consider if you have the room. If you fly across you can manage swell. About 10 of us all agree on the following -

A good supply of underwear and at least 2 sets of "longies"

A good supply of "hankies"

A small pillow (honestly)

Overshoes or rubbers

Extra insignia (the stuff over here is cheesy looking)

A good pocket knife

Some heavy socks and a good all around supply of light ones too

Get yourself at least 2 new pair of low cut dress oxfords. Enlisted men can't buy them here.

If you like to drink, buy some rye, bourbon, and rum. Lots of scotch and gin here.

By the way, I would appreciate it if you could get me a couple bottles of rye as I haven't tasted it in a year now.

Bring a cigarette lighter or two.

Shaving lotion, powder, cream, and as many razor blades as you can get.

Sounds like quite a list but all are very necessary items and are either virtually unobtainable over here or just absolutely unobtainable. Take my word for it.

If you come by plane bring everything with you that you will need for six months as extra luggage they might send by boat has a way of getting lost. Even if you have to sneak or smuggle it aboard. No one checked my plane all the way over - so don't let that worry you. If you fly over the Southern route get a case of rum or whiskey at Puerto Rico as it is very cheap there. Your officers can get it for you at the club. You can also get perfume by various means in S. America but don't buy those silk stockings as they are just a cheap service weight. If you come the Southern route you'll really enjoy it and I recommend picking up souvenirs at each stop if possible, if just post cards.

Over here you need ration points to even buy a 10¢ handkerchief, and as a matter of fact just about every purchasable item over here is under the ration system. PXs here mainly sell our candy ration to us (once a week) and have very little else to offer. You get a PX ration card.

If you are assigned here in England telephone me at my sqd. orderly room. Ask the Red Cross for the name of the town my group is near. I can then fly over to see you.

Well, I have sure made a poor job of this, but I hope you have at least an idea of what to bring over aside from what they will tell you at the POE.

Oh yes! Bring a camera and film as you will see a million things you will want a pictorial record of. Bring a supply of your favorite pipe tobacco also, enough to last until you can get more sent from home.

Well, I've covered everything of importance Frank, and I hope this has helped a little.

If you can get me a bottle or two of whiskey I would be grateful - but I realize you may not be able to.

I've "done" N. Orleans, too, and know what you mean. Well, here's wishing you luck and happy landings. Be seein' you I hope...
Dick

February 5, Monday

Dear Mother, Harry and Mike,

Monday and another day without flying. Yup, she were (sic) very closed in yesterday and again today so we slept most of the morning again in the Locker Loft in the hanger. We are getting so we depend on the fog rolling in so that we just get up at 2:30 AM, eat and then go to the hanger and get the rest of our sleep. At first I couldn't sleep comfortably but now I really knock off and get quite annoyed when someone gets me up. This has two aspects - this not flying. We get off easy for we are scheduled to fly every day this week but most of us would rather fly. You see we are watching the weather do us out of any chance we might have for a couple days home at the conclusion of this course which is coming rapidly now. I doubted all along we would get it - only a week ago there were rumors of it but no one speaks of it now for we haven't flown in almost a week now. A week ago we were well ahead but right now we may not finish completely.

I must tell you about yesterday. New Orleans came to Gulfport again and was it ever lovely. Eileen came - we must have them worried that we are leaving soon. Actually all it was a teaser for they weren't here long - not half long enough. We did get in early - met them on the bus and took a few pictures with John's camera. We took them to a Tea Dance at the Community House and later for a bite to eat. The stinkers won't let you spend money on them - won't eat much. Of course this is the nicest thing that has happened to me since I've been in the Army and I'm all for going all out but they won't play that way so that is that. They're as independent as Hogs on Ice and the only reason we can glean from their conduct that it makes any difference to them whether we leave or not is the fact that they do come down here. I doubt very much that I'll get to N.O. again while here all of which reminds me. Please rush me one of those small photographs (civilian picture) - the smiling version if you have one left. The lady requested a picture and I'd certainly like to comply. If there aren't any of those I guess one in uniform will be OK. Use your own judgment on which one you'd rather send. The lady wants a civilian photograph and I'd like her to have it but you're still the first lady on my list so I'll leave it up to you.

After we put the girls on the bus I rushed back to camp with John and made the last Mass here at the Chapel. I kinda wanted to bring Eileen here to Mass with me but they were determined not to stay that late so I didn't get in on the gloating I'd planned on. Went to Communion and then had a very slight bite in the mess hall.

Shortly after that John and I went back into town and met Cal and Daggett at the U.S.O. and then we started all over again. There is a new U.S.O. senior hostess there that really is a Grade A. She is from N.C. but mighty nice in spite of it. We all got talking with her and as usual we got to asking her to eat at Angelo's with us. Daggett dropped out at that point so that left three of us. She got a U.S.O. car and instead of Angelo's we went to the "Broadwater," a ritzy dine and dance place along the Gulf. We had a swell time - she, of course has made a business of appealing to G.I.s and she was playing above her game. She lives miles from Cal Taylor and he sure got in the punches. The four of us had a grand time They lady enjoyed herself I'm sure - why shouldn't she with three of us taking turns dancing with her - she is O.K. and that's no lie. We may go up to her place one of these evenings for a bit of a beer party - she is going to get two more gals - of course I say for John and Cal, Cal says for John and Frank and John says for Cal and Frank. We had a good evening.

Honest folks, I'm having more fun here than I've ever had in the Army. I think it is the company for we don't fool with cheap girls or drinking for drinking's sake. We *all like the same things and unless the place is nice we don't go there. Of course it takes money and I've never spent so much before on just pleasure - in or out of the Army but it is sorta our last fling in the States for a while and as long as I have held out enough to get home should the occasion arise I figure I may as well enjoy myself. Where we spend most of it is on eating and we don't stint there. We have heard so much from the fellows here who have been overseas and Cal's brother is constantly writing him V-mail to eat and drink milk while he can that we are beyond the point where we need persuasion - we just romp into the best place in town and order. The meals are awfully standard - shrimp cocktail, steaks, French fries, chef bowl salad - milk to drink with it, coffee to finish up with and apple pie a la mode for dessert. On top of that the hot French bread they serve at most places is really something.*

I guess that sums most of it up for today. Please send along either picture at your discretion - may even lose a pair of wings out of this deal too. She's very nice folks - wish I had more time cause with her I'd need it. Be good.
Lotsa Love, Frank

February 6, Tuesday

Dear Mother, Harry and Mike,

The stationary will tell you the place. A WAC just asked me why I'd come into town to write a letter and I told her that if I wrote it in the barracks I'd go to bed and never get to town. So here I am - had to be firm - refused deal to go to the movie in town with her - I was determined to write.

I received a dandy big box today and two letters - Harry's & Mother's. The box was perfect - the cake was oh so greatly appreciated for I picked up the box just after we came down from flying. Yes we finally flew today. There is only enough left for my Tail Gunner, Armourer, and Ball Turret man who weren't around to get a piece when we opened it. The cookies will go up into the Blue Yonder with us to-morrow. I am so glad to get them. Of course the mess hall packs us a lunch to take with us when we fly - 2 sandwiches, cookies and apples or oranges per man. Lately I don't know what they've been doing to them but the whole works seems to lodge in my chest and I have a burning sensation there hours after I eat the sandwiches sooo I have been letting them go by the board and feel better for it - but hungry when I get down.

No particular news of the day - we flew - fly to-morrow - up at 2:30 AM. There are two dances in town tonight so I thought I'd wiggle it a bit this eve. Cal came in ahead of me this evening for I had photo scoring of camera gunnery of a mission of a few days ago at 6 PM this evening. We may take a flyer and go to N.O. to-morrow. It is a long shot to be sure but is certainly the only way we'll get there again. Our passes are good for only 50 miles but if we go by bus no M.P.s bother you and we almost went this afternoon. Someday Harry I'll really give you a mild description of what keeps dragging me there whether school keeps or not.

I am very well set on the lip rouge score now. Have them tucked away in that tin box Mother sent - a few to spare too - couldn't get them all in. Also have a large supply of gum I've been hoarding two packs at a time. The sox are dandy - I'll bet they set you back plenty - all wool. I shall save them for special occasions and wash them out myself. The razor blades came in just in time - I'm plumb out and can't buy any here anywhere. Funny but we finished last of strawberry jam just sent just last night. All the boys were glad to see another added to our supply. They all call my foot locker Thompson's commissary. I am trying to get a box off to you people. Am trying to get stockings for Mom - or mesh - have not had any success so far. Will try places I missed in town here to-morrow and may make N.O. in time to try there again before the larger places close. Have been getting butts for Harroola - will get as many as I can before shipping box out.

The only thing in the box that was damaged was the peach jam and it was smashed to Hell. The wax paper saved it getting too much over everything. It is a darn shame - had my mouth all set for that but such is luck I fear. Hope the Ott's box makes the time yours did but no one else's ever seems to make it so well, does it? Latest dope is about 9 more days here - should get here in that time. That flashlight comes in so handy - I'd hate to miss having the makings to make it work.

I'm glad you are managing about the coal - it has always been a big thing to think about. How I remember how we'd gloat when we got the bin filled in the summer. Remember when it cut loose and with combined efforts we repaired it and I shoveled coal with Haroola that night until zero hour 6:30 PM then I bathed and danced till 3 AM with Mimi at the Ted Roy - Ah, them were the days!

I can well imagine how you feel about Sam going out of business - it will make things so much harder - dammit, as if there wasn't enough. You had nothing on me getting your throats blessed - John and I did likewise Sunday after Mass - so there. I forgot to mention it in yesterday's opus - Hope Dorothy O'H isn't sorry - sure like to meet her in England under those conditions. All of which reminds me of a brutal incident at the NCO club one night which, altho (sic) not typical of women in the Army, is rather poignant. A WAC, rather oiled - got up from table alone - said in a loud voice I came in the Army to replace a man and work hard to end the war - all I done so far has been being laid - she walked out disgusted in a huff and 4 or 5 G.I.s followed her.

No, I didn't think that the war will proceed rapidly enough to keep me from seeing some of it. I cannot say don't let it play the devil with you - it leaves me empty in the stomach when I think of it - our relation has been so complete - our Triumvirate. I feel that you two have been so good that God will keep me safe and we three together. I have been so fortunate - had my year in the States - I cannot ask for more. The sooner I go over - the sooner I'll be back. Thank the Lord I'm not in the ground forces where they stay till it is over. We will get some relief! There is absolutely no chance of getting home from here now I'm afraid. We are all on edge - witness restlessness of past 3 weeks - I'm sure my letters must have let that slip. We're all like that - it is emotional - not rational but we can't help it. The sooner we get going the better!

I think more of my crew every day - we are such a compact working unit and we are together - a bond between men exists that is so important to all of us. We like and respect each man - depend on him. Each feels responsible in that he knows the other 8 rely on him to keep us all in his particular job. We criticize and razz and joke and have worked hard. We are well trained and have decided to all return together - and so we will!

Well folksies, I must rush off tonight if I'm going to get in a wiggle or two - go to the Community House where it is formal tonight.

Be good - Thanks a million for the box -

Lotsa Love, Frank

P.S. Hope to have some pictures of the Horrible 4 and the girls for you before we leave - Huba Huba

F.

February 7, Wednesday

Dear Mother, Harry and Mike,

Well, the old fog rolled in this morning again - kept the Big Birds on the ground until 9 or 9:30 AM. We finally got a ship and were scheduled for an instrument check ride with an instructor pilot. As things worked out we let our gunners go and were to fly 2 skeleton crews but at the last minute audio instructor stepped aboard and had two students with him. He was to give the boys their final check in radio. I've had mine weeks ago and have accomplished all my minimums so I would have really gained nothing but a ride by going. I didn't want to let my boys go without me but Sundin said go ahead so I finally left just before they taxied out to take off. Sooo here I am back at my sack alone in the barracks. I've been making heavy inroads on that chocolate cake. I'll say here's one cake I've hogged to my satisfaction. It arrived in excellent shape and nice and moist. It is cold in the barracks so it keeps fine and is it ever good.

Cal Taylor and I think we'll go to N.O. this P.M. It is a good time for it for weather predicts bad weather again to-morrow and we'll be able to catch up on sleep if we don't fly. I hope Taylor gets off soon so we'll get an early start.

I got a grand letter from Agnes Holdman today. I'm a villain - I told her we might get an RON to N.Y.C. and would be banging on her door if we did - wanted to find out the reaction don't y' know. Aha, it was good and now I sure wish to Hell we could go. It is not impossible - we have been recommended for it, but it seems all our officers were late for briefing a couple days ago. That just about ruins us and costs the lads about $75 a piece. That is rather expensive anyway you look at it. If we did go - the farthest we could go would be Newark and I'd only have about 8-10 hours there but it is a nice idea to toy with. From the letter I judge all are fine and I really would like to see (?) Agnes again - just for the record. Ah women - I love them all.

It has been a rather lazy day - slept in the loft this morning - got in early from town last night. I expected to meet Taylor but didn't wait too long as I figured he would be making time with the WAC. If she'd been extra nice I would have found him just to pester hell out of him but she really wasn't worth too much effort I didn't think.

I can see I'm going to be busy the next few days. They won't do anymore laundry for us here and my gallivanting dirties the clothes so I'll just have to do a big washing soon. Gosh I guess I must sound like the busy housewife!

We are quite crazy to go to N.O. this afternoon - I mean we're nuts to undertake it! We won't have much time there - but after all if we can't do these things now - we'll never be any younger and we might just as well live 3 to the minute while we have the energy and inclination to do so.

I should write a lot of letters but I can't right now. Thought - as usual - I'd get this one off and then get off myself. Time is a wastin' and there is wood to be chopped - Huba Huba!

The soiled paper will attest to the proximity of the cake which - I should finish any minute now.

Be good, folks -

Lotsa Love, Frank

February 8, Wednesday

Dear Mother, Harry and Mike,

This will probably be a broken up letter. My Engineer finally got his radio from home and we are burning out the tubes in it in short order. We are so appreciative of good old American Swing these days Of course in the plane, between position reports and all the work I have, I tune in short wave broadcasts for my gunners to listen to - Crosby and all - but this isn't as often as we'd like it. Listening to - "I Didn't Know About You" - Dinah I think.

Now to get to yesterday's Rat Race. Of course our passes are (it is Dinah) good for only 50 miles - N.O. is 78 - also they're only good until 12 midnight. Taylor and I got in town at 4:30 - bus wasn't due until 5:30 so we started to thumb. We make it in two rides - arrived in N.O. before 8 PM. We called the girls and spent the evening - a while at Rosemary's home and then went to Eileen's. Mrs. Corcoran is nice people - she fixed a bunch of us and we had fun just horsing around if you know what I mean. We finally left on a 12 midnight bus - this time we got there in time to get a seat. We slept all the way back - arrived at Gulfport at 2:15 AM - grabbed a cab for camp and arrived in the barracks just before the fellows got up. Just a couple of Hot Rocks! We changed rapidly - cleaned up our barracks area - ate and were with our crews in plenty of time for briefing at 3:30 AM. We took big chances all the way for once we left Gulfport we were technically AWOL. Of course if we had been unable to get the bus we could have taken a cab - only 42 bucks worth! We felt good about working it but to take from our satisfaction - the M.P. at the gate picked up our passes for overstaying our passes - being out after 12 o'clock Gulfport curfew. I don't expect much to come of it - can't tell as yet - haven't been called for an interview with the Major as yet - if they only knew where I was Huba Huba Huba. Here I'll say it was *well worth the effort and risk - we had fun and weren't at all tired for we had slept 12-14 hours the day before. The boys on the crew all kid hell out of me but we have a good time out of it.*

I got Harry's letter today and also a great big box from Otts. Boy - the Bingo just started - almost give up the Big Birds to be in the Red Chair listening - "almost" - what am I saying?

The Otts' box was really grand - more food than you can shake a barracks bag at. I had my Ball Turret man "Shaffer" help me carry it from the mail room. All kinds of cookies - 2 loaves of homemade nut bread - enough batteries to run a Big Bird for a month - peanuts pretzels - it sure is a dandy box. I'll have to write them this evening. I just hope I can get over with the stuff I have. That is the chance I have to take - I'd never forgive myself if I didn't try at any rate.

Well, we're all spending tonight quietly in the barracks enjoying Joe's radio. During the next few days I plan to do a final shopping trip - main object stockings in Gulfport or Biloxi and extra wings at Kessler field. Also want to get hold of (steal) necessary tube replacements for Joe's radio and also transformers and resistors so we can play the thing overseas on a foreign power output or even on the planes own central power supply. Have lots of odds and ends to take care of. Really look forward to a couple days of nothing to do before shipping but, with usual restriction, to finish up everything.

We flew today - had a big radio day - my boy's missed me yesterday - that makes it worthwhile - they are my boys and they won't fly without me again - just think - if they had been forced down at N.O. and I hadn't been with them. That's too big a chance to take again.

Well, guess I'll run for today - hope to shop a bit to-morrow that is if I'm not restricted for this morning's job - we'll see. Be good, folks.
Lotsa Love, Frank

February 10th, Saturday

Dear Mother, Harry and Mike,

So sorry about your getting letters late but then I don't blame you for getting a bit peeved - just don't get so much so you don't write. Forget youse guys? - now fellah, shuffle or no shuffle, you know better than that. Am writing now at the U.S.O. dance - got a splendid deal worked up and have thrown it to the dogs just to write.

Had a terrible time getting out today. Had to clear flight line - flying clothing supply & dental clinic. Then I had to interview the Major about an M.P. report that came from Taylor's and my outing a few nights ago. We got by OK. - went in together and really laid it on - it was our first offense so he let us off with a reprimand.

Eileen is nice, Mom - she reminds me a lot of the way I bet you acted - can't figure her out at all but that's what keeps me coming. Plan on seeing her to-morrow - have a pass good until 12 M Monday so we should make it. Taylor isn't finished flying s yet so I'll go to Mass in the morning and take off in the afternoon - get some sleep while he flies. You should know by now about both your box and the Otts'. They were the berries and we are all getting a lot of enjoyment from them.

The picture arrived today - thanks again - I'm always pestering you two for something but I'm glad to get it - take it to my little Irish on the morrow. Haven't written Beals lately - God knows I should - will finish up with letters to most people just a couple days before I leave - we'll be restricted but good.

To-morrow will be the last time we'll have off here I believe - then we'll process and go to a staging area - Processing should take about 3 days I believe. My Tail Gunner Dan Spencer has his wife here and lives on the Trailer Camp outside the Post gates. My whole crew was worried that I was in wrong and wouldn't make it to see that "stuff in N.O." as they call it. Sooo he doesn't go to N.O. with the wife but he did get a pass and left it for me. When I write to-morrow I'll enclose the note - my Gunners - my Boys.

Guess that is about it for this evening people - see if I can't put finishing touches on Ione this evening - that should really be interesting. See if she can get a car this evening - Huba Huba. She has a blazing red formal on - not bad at all - really all "right." Taylor bets I can't make any time with her - don't think I can myself but will have a try anyhow - let you know how I make out on the morrow.
Lotsa Love, Frank

February 11, Sunday

Dear Mother, Harry and Mike,

Sunday morning and I just got back from Mass. John did get me up to go to 7:30 AM but they didn't have it this morning - instead they had 6:30 Mass at the Hospital so I had some breakfast and then went back to bed and the old "Bloodhound" got me up again at 10:30 and so we've been. I wasn't too worried about missing here for in N.O. they have a 6 PM Mass for Servicemen and if I'd slept thru 10:30 I could have made that one.

Yes we are still quite determined to take a last fling at N.O. but conditions certainly don't favor it. Taylor didn't have to fly this morning but is still at the flight line trying to get cleared so he can go. Right now it is raining cats and dogs around here. I do hope it lets up a while so we can get on our way soon and not get drenched. We thought we might do a little dancing on that River Boat, "The President" again tonight. Wonder how the weather is in N.O.

That was a rather hurried opus last night - it is hard to do a job of writing when so much is going on about you.

I didn't tell you enough about Eileen last night. She is 18 or 19 - maybe too young you think? She works for the Navy and is a stenographer for some Commander there. She gets rather annoyed when I run down the Navy - says it is her bread and butter. Yes I think their folks think we're O.K. We have met both Rosemary's parents - took her dad some cigarettes last time, which of course was the proper thing to do. The very nice blonde that Daggett Morse takes out - Rhodora Dowling - we've met her folks - I have a hunch I get along very well with her mother. Rhodora's mother is Eileen's Aunt so that makes things fine. Also met Eileen's mother - she is grand. Eileen is the oldest of 4 children I think. After her comes a girl - Pat - then the boys oldest one Michael - I think - the names are Irish, what?

Last night after I wrote you I did make connections with that vision in Red - her name is Ione - How do you like these Southern names - they just murder me. However the lassies is right there - we had a bite to eat and danced a bit after the U.S.O. dance and drove a bit in her Dodge coupe and then we finally took her home. I didn't leave her until about 3:30 AM - one of those nights when Mother would have said - "Well, let's have no more of this." But then women in long dresses fascinate me - maybe it's just women. She is a Senior Hostess staying at the Y.W.C.A. here now. She is permitted a key to side door because of her U.S.O. activities all of which, including the car, was damned convenient. She has only been at Gulfport about 3 weeks. She plans on moving to Marcum Hotel I think - good thing she's not there now and by the time she does go there I'll be gone. Brother, that dolly is dynamite in more ways than one.

Well, I got back last night, curfew was extended until 2 PM for Saturday night, but I was a bit late for that so I didn't take any chances last night and did the little fence number - through the trailer camp and the WAC Area - ah folksies, war's hell - this babe wants me around today - love to make it but have my heart set on N.O. weather or no weather, Ione or no Ione. Besides she's married - husband in Belgium which makes me feel like a hell - end quote.

Well folks, I guess that keeps us abreast of things for the present. Right now - since all the lads are off on pass - the fires are out - maybe I'll break down and build a fire - ah they can't put that fire out in me Huba Huba Huba - Be good, folks.
Lotsa Love, Frank

February 13 - Telegram
DEAR FOLKS PLEASE TELEGRAPH 20 OR 25 DOLLARS AS SOON AS POSSIBLE LOVE = FRANK

February 14, Wednesday
Dear Mother, Harry and Mike,

Well, Ash Wednesday and Valentine's Day in one. I managed to get the boxes I spoke of out this morning and also sending you my prized possession - my picture of Eileen. Harry spoke of wanting to see a snap of her - the snaps we took have not been developed as yet - also the picture was too big to carry about so after much deliberation I finally decided to part with it. Staeger and I have made a ritual of saying goodnight to her - so I commend her to your care - please put her someplace safe and ask Harry if I can still pick em?

I also sent a few odds and ends in an envelope. Stuff I won't be needing until I get back from overseas - never know, I may try Cadets again. Found out yesterday, when I had my Army record, that I was disqualified physically. This we all know is an Army dodge. There is no other mark of disqualification on my record.

I got the 25 dollars at about 9:30 AM this morning - thanks a million folks - you'll never know - I should have known you'd come through in a pinch but I certainly never would have blamed you if you hadn't.

I have spent all afternoon washing and ironing. Really been on the ball. They skipped me on last month's Laundry Roster so my boys have been sending my things with their laundry. I had accumulated a lot of things that I wanted to do myself - T-shirts sox and my Sun Tan shirts. On the latter, we have been getting very poor service so I decided rather than take a chance and wait I'd do them myself. Found out today that to-morrow we have lectures - final packing and ship early Friday for Savannah. That is just as they planned I guess. We'll be on our way Friday for sure as things stand now.

The boys have been at me all afternoon while I washed to go to town and have a sort of final dinner out with them. Haven't told them as yet that I would go, but I'm shipping and probably will go. This being Ash Wednesday I'll have to get fish but with the variety and preparations they have around here, that is no hardship.

We almost went to N.O. this afternoon, that is, Taylor and myself. I wanted to go again but couldn't see taking such a long chance at this time. Ordinarily if we had been held up by some extraordinary circumstance it would have been only a charge of AWOL, but since we're alerted for shipping it amounts to desertion if you are picked up and as per usual we wouldn't have passes to N.O. so I figured it was too long a chance to take.

It has been a beautiful day here today. Certainly a reminder the summer is on the way - I hope it's coming soon now, will somewhat relieve the privation around home. Despite the warmness, my clothes have been very slow drying - humidity is so here that even your wash - clothes - don't dry out from day to day.

Well folksies, I guess that is all for today - Be good.
Lotsa Love, Frank

February 15, Thursday
Dear Mother, Harry and Mike,

Well, as you can well guess, I gave in last night and went out with the lads to din-ner. Went to Paradise Point - had me a flounder stuffed with flaked crabmeat. It is a good place to eat indeed and we were sorry we had to wait until our last night in town to find it. We had to wait about an hour before we could get a place for 5 of us to eat but it was worth waiting for.

When I came in town, I stopped in and meant only to say goodbye to my little Southern Belle but it proved to be a long drawn out process. Add up her lonesome-ness, my natural affection, her big Pontiac coupe a warm night, the Gulf and the stars. Ka-runch - good thing I'm getting out of here. That is the kind of set-up every soldier dreams about - I finally hit it but it is too bad I'm too principled - or maybe she was, at any rate I landed in camp at 3:30 AM a tired boy - over the fence again.

Ah Gulfport would I had more time to spend with thee Huba Huba. Before she took up Recreational Organization she was a model in Miami - went to Georgia Tech college - name is Hogsed (I think) her husband played ball with the St. Louis "A's" and Detroit Tigers before he was drafted. She is getting too eager for me - wanted me to come in tonight - I could go over the fence but I think I'll stay restricted. Harry you'd really get a bang out of this gal - she is very snappy looking - lots of personality and the body beautiful. She wanted me to write but I couldn't see it - just think that knife in your ribs while you sleep some night. I wouldn't blame the guy either.

This morning we had formation. My clothes were not completely dry so I put them out again - just got them in after night fall and they're still a little damp. I have so much stuff the lads are going to help me out carrying it - I'll sorta farm it out. This morning was spent in final packing preparations barracks bags had to be turned in before noon. This afternoon we had final lectures from Commanding Officers. Apparently we were a rather exceptional class. You see lots of classes leave without bombardiers - we all have them - maybe we're destined to fly lead ships in formations overseas.

And so we are about ready to leave old Gulfport, Miss. - I guess I'm not so hard to please - the only place I was extremely glad to leave was Yuma and that was because I was coming home. Seven crews of our class (about 50 crews) are being held here - kinda hoped we'd be but no such luck - we have been on the ball too much. We were told today that 5 days would be the maximum in Savannah, Ga. but we have had letters from fellows who have spent 2-4 weeks there - some with furloughs too but don't count on it people - I almost expected to be held here - rumor was out that our crew had been recommended for Submarine Patrol along the Caribbean - a groundless one I find now - otherwise I expect I'd be on my way to you now. Ah well, perhaps we'll be lucky in Ga. They shouldn't be needing too many crews over there now. Contrary to the last time, I'll keep you posted if anything should happen - please - but then I know you won't count on it much.

We will start out to-morrow. I'll send you a night letter of address if I see we'll be there any length of time - I'll write as soon as I get there at any rate. I expect it to take from 12-20 hours to make the trip so I won't get to write on the morrow.

I have lots of letters to write - don't feel like writing them now - guess I'll take in a show - none of us feel much like writing tonight I guess - I'll do better from Savannah I hope - it has been an effort to write for the past two weeks. Better get in a stock of V-mail stationary people - that seems to be the best deal. Thas all for tonight
Lotsa Love, Frank

P.S. Make and take special care in writing serial No 12107602 from now on. Started wearing Nettleton's to break em in a little - they sure are the berries. Hope sox from Beals and bulbs from the Otts get here so I can get them in the morning - get last mail here tomorrow morning.
Francis G.

Frank's parents, Harry Theophilous and Barbara Agnes, 1914. They were married in 1916. "The Honorables" is written on the back of this photo

Frank & Mary on their wedding day, February 16, 1957

Frank's 40th birthday celebration March 8, 1961; holding Loretto age 8 months

Loretto's fifth birthday, not long after Frank died

Frank and Mary's seven children with their babysitter Missy Buhr

Pvt. Frank G. Thompson; photo taken at Sioux Falls and sent home to Mother and Harry

Box of letters discovered and sorted, 2014

Goldfish booklet cover and letter

AMERICAN DIVISION

GOLDFISH CLUB

SPONSORED BY
FLYING 185 NORTH WABASH AVENUE • CHICAGO 1, ILLINOIS

Dear Member:

We are pleased to welcome you as a member of the GOLDFISH
CLUB.

As you probably know, this exclusive organization is composed
of airmen all over the world who, like yourself, have survived a water landing.

Your insignia and membership card are enclosed. We also
enclose a booklet on the Club which will be of special interest to you as a member.

We look forward to meeting you personally if, at any time, you
find it convenient to visit Chicago.

We don't have to tell you that you really <u>earned</u> this membership; you can well be proud of it.

       Best wishes,

       THE GOLDFISH CLUB

MaxKarant:mhs   American Secretary

Please keep us informed of any changes in your home address.

Image of Heavy Date nose art

Frank's Blouse with Goldfish sewn to breast pocket

Bill Hughes and his wife; Bill's sister-in-law and Frank, Sioux Falls

Frank and pals in Yuma

WU2 NL PD YMA ARIZ OCT 22

HARRY THOMPSON

    ACCOUNTS PAYABLE DEPT CARBORUNDUM CO NFALLS

DEAR HARRY LEAVE HERE WEDNESDAY EVENING, SHOULD ARRIVE BY SUNDAY

AT LATEST TAKING SPECIAL TRAIN SO CANNOT BE PRECISE ABOUT

ARRIVAL MORTGAGE THE HOMESTEAD

      FRAN K

755A OCT 23RD-1944

Enlisted men in Frank's crew - Frank is in the middle, Gulfport

Staff Sergeant Ceremony; Frank in middle row, second from left
(radio patch on right sleeve), Horham, England

Enlisted men from Frank's crew - Standing: Ferniza, Thompson, Spencer;
Front row: Kimpel, Turner (Co-Pilot), Shaffer;
First photo of Frank with his mustache or "cookie duster," Horham, England

Frank receiving Air Medal, Horham, England

General Eisenhower inspecting Air Crews, Horham, England

Frank with Mike while home on leave, July, 1945

Mothers Day card Frank sent to Mother. Inside reads: A Spiritual Bouquet for you dear Mother from your ever grateful son. There were also two lines from scripture; "He saith to his mother: woman behold thy son." St. John XIX, 26 and "He saith to the disciple: Behold thy Mother." St. John XIX 27. On the back of the card is the emblem of the 95th Bomb Group.

Mother, taken while Frank was home on leave, July, 1945

Harry with Mike, taken while Frank was home on leave, July, 1945

Gloria and Roger "Big Sundin" with Loretto, September, 2016

Postcard Frank sent home en route to Sioux Falls in August, 1945

Linda Woodward and Beverley Abbott at the Red Feather Club, 95th Bomb Group Heritage Museum, Horham, England, 2017

Loretto in front of Heavy Date, Red Feather Club, 95th Bomb Group Heritage Museum, Horham, England, 2017

The Not Forgotten Association
requests the pleasure of the company of
Mr P J Thompson & Mrs L M Thompson
to a Garden Party
in the Grounds of Buckingham Palace
by kind permission of Her Majesty The Queen
in the presence of HRH The Princess Royal
Patron, The Not Forgotten Association
on Thursday 7th June 2018

2.00pm – 5.15pm
Lounge Suit or Blazers
(Medals may be worn)

Pour Mémoire

Invitation to Buckingham Palace Garden Party, 2018

*Peter being pinned by Art Stacey and welcomed as an Associate Member
of The Goldfish Club, June, 2018*

*Photos taken with
The Goldfish Club
contingency at
the Not Forgotten
Association Garden
Party, June, 2018*

*Left to right: Leslie and Kitty Stephens, Loretto and Peter Thompson,
Kate Burrows, and Art Stacey*

Frank G. Thompson, M.D.

Loretto with her step-father,
Paul McDonough,
at Father-Daughter
Weekend, 1980

Loretto with her step-father, Paul McDonough,
Father-Daughter Weekend, 1981

THE CURIOUS THING ABOUT GRAMP

Present Day

This last group of letters was very enlightening for me. To begin with, it's the first time my father referenced his plans to go to medical school and speculated about going to Tulane. That authenticated my mother's telling of his making that decision in the desert, in the Army, in a tent. I figured he most likely made the decision in Yuma, but never mentioned it in any letters. He must have waited until his delay, and subsequent two weeks at home, to tell his family in person. I also sensed some foreshadowing of this decision when he told his family how he was "doctoring" some of the men. On a more intimate level, I found his reference to growing a moustache enlightening. I had only ever known him to have a moustache, and learning that he'd grown it in Europe during the war, and kept it until his death was the sort of information you'd only learn from having a personal conversation with someone. That's how learning this about him made me feel.

As with most of what I was finding out through my father's letters, I continued to connect the dots. However, the one curious thing that kept coming up was my father's speculation about Gramp. What brought him to Australia as a cook and why didn't he explain himself? But it wasn't until I'd started the 1945 letters that I reached the point where I found myself asking, "What is the deal about Australia?" especially after learning that Australia was where at one time the Brits had sent their troublemakers. Having learned that my father was heading to England, Gramp's birthplace, that nagging voice started again, asking me, "What's up with Gramp? Why so secretive?" In a way, I wanted to find out more about him, so I could tell my dad—to answer his questions, though I knew that was impossible. I'll never know whether or not he found his answers before he died or if the questions remained throughout his life. Knowing Gramp died in June 1945, I wanted to warn my father to not delay writing him for too long because there wasn't much time left.

When I mentioned all this to my mother, she surprised me once again. For years we have had in our family home a perfectly preserved scrapbook, which was delivered to my mother by one of my father's cousins, though she is not exactly sure when. It seems that Gramp had traveled to England in 1920 to visit some family. I have yet to figure out the purpose of that trip, but he returned with this scrapbook, which was given to him by two of his cousins living in England. Inside the scrapbook was a letter explaining that the scrapbook was a gift to the Tenth Street Thompsons and was to remain at the house for all the grandchildren to enjoy. Somehow it ended up in the possession of this cousin, who was moving to Florida; she felt that it should be passed on to my mom and her seven Thompson children.

The significance of the book was the role it played in finding out about Gramp. If Gramp had traveled to England in 1920, his records would have been at Ellis Island; not knowing anything else, I started there. In the records I found the trip to England and his date of birth as well as his place of origin, Pimlico, Middlesex, just outside London, England. Based on his date of birth, I tried to determine when he'd emigrated to the U.S., and assumed that he had departed from England. Here was where I ran into a bit of trouble, as Ellis Island opened in 1892 and I could find no matching records for Alan William Thompson. That's when I considered he may have arrived earlier than 1892, which meant I needed to look at records from Castle Garden instead.

If you've ever investigated your genealogy, you know it can be a daunting task. While many records are incomplete, we are truly fortunate to live at a time when we are able to access these records with a simple search on the World Wide Web. In the Castle Garden records I located a male passenger, a laborer with no name, who had arrived in New Jersey in 1890 at age twenty-nine. I determined this had to be Gramp. At this point, I had hit a dead end and had to continue my search on the genealogy site. When I'd entered Gramp's name, I found information from New Jersey, Massachusetts, New York, and Niagara Falls. Jackpot!

As I built a family tree for Gramp, I found his siblings, spouse, and children, but in order to access any of the records from England, I needed an international membership. With my upgraded membership, my questions began to be answered, at least somewhat. I found the marriage license to Ada in, of all places, Australia. Not being sure what brought him to Australia in the first place, I did learn where he'd married Ada, that they were both from England, and that they'd had three children while living in Australia, with the first dying shortly after birth. I also learned that they'd emigrated with the other two children to the U.S., though I never found Ada and the children in any of the Castle Garden records.

The entire Alan William Thompson family tree started to unfold, and remarkably the pieces began to come together. I found other aunts and uncles of my father's, as well as cousins. In particular, one of my grandfather's cousins would become a stop on my and my father's journey, the Reverend John A Kempthorne, of Trumpington, just outside Cambridge, England. I'd also located Gramp's grave. Ironically, it was in the same cemetery as my father and I'd never known it. As my father appeared to have a certain closeness with Gramp, it was comforting to know that they'd both been laid to rest not far from each other and in a strange way were still in each other's company.

As my father's life slowly started to unfold, I found the genealogy site invaluable in solving mystery after mystery. To start from the end and work backward, for even the most experienced researcher is challenging, but the emotions associated with the findings are difficult to prepare for when the research is so personal, especially when researching your father. Feeling satisfied that I'd solved at least part of the mystery of Gramp and Australia, though unable to share my accomplishment with my father, I was forced to accept not knowing what had brought him to Australia in the first place, yet was relieved to know he was truly a mere cook all along—and not a criminal.

SAVANNAH, GEORGIA

1945

Return Address:
Cpl. F.G. Thompson 12107602
Combat Crew Center
Hunter Field Ga.

February 17, Saturday

Dear Mother, Harry and Mike,

As you can see I'm making it on borrowed stationary so I'll write small so as not to use too much. We left good old Gulfport yesterday at about 10 or 10:30 AM and got here at about 3:20 or 4. The trip down was uneventful for the most part. I did manage to get hold of a copy of "Forever Amber" - have you heard of it? It is really an excursion into the sensual - not a lot of pleasure to me to read it but have heard so much about it I want to finish it. I'm halfway thru now and there isn't much more she can do - have to finish just to find out what the hell the rest of the book is about.

Hunter Field is really a big one. The ramp is not far from our barracks and they have all types of combat crews and ships here - mediums and heavies and damn heavies. Am going to try to get in one of those 29s one of these days just to see what they're like. The place is really large, mostly in a spread out way - have never seen any place like it unless it was the Syracuse Bomber Base. From what I can see some good changes in clothing and equipment will come about here. We get our chutes, harnesses, Mae Wests of course, but we get heavy gabardine flying fatigues. Our G.I. fatigues were taken away at Gulfport. Also we get gabardine flying jackets with big fur collars - really smart looking.

I have seen quite a few R.O.s that shipped a week before me at Tampa. They went to Avon Park, Florida They have been here a week now. I don't know what that means, whether they will keep our class here until they are gone or send us all out together. From what I hear of the last bunch that left, only 8 crews did not fly over. Of course we should get a ship here but you can never tell. They seem to really go out for Combat Crews here - even have green felt poker tables in the dayroom. And what a game that was I watched in there - I've anteed pennies or maybe nickels but anything less than a buck or a 5 didn't stand a show there - Whew, I don't see how they do it - 25-30 dollar pot and a guy comes up with 4 aces. It's a wonder someone didn't come up with a razor.

They didn't give us too good living quarters here. The barracks are better than I've been in since the induction center but they are terribly overcrowded. I'm still with my crew of course and also the rest of the lads in our barracks at Gulfport. I do hope they don't' break us up for we've had so much fun together. Chances of course are far against it but you can never tell. I have no idea of how long we may be here - we were told not longer than 5 days but that is a lot of crap if you ask me.

Right across the street is one of those Post theatres - Mass there in the morning at 8 AM so I'll have to get someone to wake me so I'll be able to make it.

We have been told absolutely no furloughs Hmm - may be able to work something - How about Dr. Muldoon, Mrs. Durkin of Red Cross, and Mary Hogan over there. I'll have to talk with my crew about it first. Two men on the crew have to be off for a whole crew to get it. If I think anything can be done I'll call you, maybe before this letter even gets there. If nothing is at all possible I won't fool with it. Let me know if Dr. Muldoon - if you think he might think you, Mother dear, are near a nervous collapse or something - maybe we can do something. I'd want your opinion before doing anything so let me know soon if you can.

Well, I guess I can't give you much more dope now maybe to-morrow. Things will probably move fast now - Huba Huba. Be good, folks.
Love, Frank

February 19, Monday

Dear Mother, Harry and Mike,

Things go on here in a hustle and scurry - while we have been busy here, the past couple days until we go I expect things will move at a lazy rate. We are actually responsible for nothing now, nor will we be until we get a plane. I expect I will let a few things go here so for heaven's sake keep mum or I'll be behind bars for 10 or 15 years - no kidding. I've been waiting so I might be able to tell you something concrete - well, here's the dope. I expect to fly over - destination England and soon. This is not my last stop on this side but the next stop will be a POE from which I will be able to make no communication to you. (Probably get a letter out with 1st APO No. on it from this point). We are being wised up on a lot of things here - it is so hard to write and say nothing and yet it cannot do you folks any actual good or satisfaction and might do some harm so I'll let a lot of it lay. No furloughs possible of course and as soon as we get a ship we will be on our way.

We by now have new crew members, and unless we are absolutely devoid of luck we hope that a lot of us from Gulfport will finally wind up in the same Bomber groups together. I expect we'll wind up at the same place. We have not had final inspections here as yet but we expect them to-morrow or the next day. We may hang on here weeks after these final issues of clothing and flying equipment but then again it may be only days or even hours. It all depends upon when we get a plane. We'll have an opportunity to check our plane by flying it on a test run. These long flights are going to be a big and interesting job from the radio standpoint and it should be a real experience - I'm looking forward to it (what the hell am I saying). At my POE, I'll be getting an APO number - I'll endeavor to write you from every possible stop so that you will be hearing from me. Write please to these addresses so that I won't have to wait a month or so for mail. I'll write V-mail as soon as I get over there so get a stock of the paper on hand and Harry you'd better write more clearly - if not type your letters.

Haven't gotten Beals' or Otts' packages as yet - I do hope they forward the things here from Gulfport. I did get a letter forwarded from there today - not bad, what? We didn't get here until Saturday afternoon.

The food here is exceptionally good - and the mess hall is the best I have ever been in. A grade A restaurant could not compete with it these days - even to a choice of 4-5 vegetables - choice of coffee, tea, milk or cocoa - big slabs of butter in the middle of the tables. Of course here we have to eat on a schedule and we're not used to it - they spoiled us in Gulfport where we could eat at any time. I haven't been able to get up for breakfast as yet. To get back to fine conditions here - and what makes them possible - Prisoners of War. It fairly makes the fur on my nape stand on end - feel like growling. All the clean up boys at the Service Club are P.W.s too. They are all over the place. Their fighting is done and they're getting fat in a land of plenty - have you been reading what they are doing to our boys - quite a difference isn't there. They look smug and safe - I don't like it - almost see red every time I go in there and can't really understand why - maybe I instinctively hate them. Mom - they look so healthy and robust - why the hell don't they send them to college where they can play football? Oh Jesus, it riles me! Our boys who sign 104th or are AWOL a few hours don't have it as good. Who the hell are we saving this country for? If we beat the Germans we're going to have to come back here and run the P.W.'s out of our own country.

Ah well - I went to the mess hall and ate so much I had to sit down after dinner so I guess I'm not too bad off yet.

Well, I figure that I've given you just about all the dirt I dare - we are hoping to get a couple pictures of our crews in flying togs if we can do so before the authorities seal John's camera - the ones we have taken of the "Horrible Four" and the gals from N.O. haven't been developed as yet - hope we can manage it soon.

We are very much tied down here. The pass deal is good but our clothes are all a mess from that last week at Gulfport and traveling. We cannot get any cleaning done until we have had a show down clothing check so until then most of us will look like bags tied in the middle - just as well we get some rest I guess after that strenuous aforementioned week or two. So after today I guess we'll eat and sleep until they get us a ship. Be good, people.

Lotsa Love, Frank

February 20, Tuesday

Dear Harry,

Well, I've been meaning to write this little missive for some time now - thought a lot about it and besides I've owed the breadwinner of the family an exclusive one for some time now. Yes. I've given it a lot of thought and I had hoped for a place to write this where I might not be oppressed by so much noise, activity and distraction. But I have no other place - we're jammed like sardines in a barracks where we stay all the time due to a number of reasons. First, we are on call all day - have nothing to do now except stand by for our particular Big Bird. Secondly, as I have mentioned, my clothes are in a not too good state so that my pride wouldn't let me take advantage of a rather generous pass privilege in the evenings and last, we know the personnel is very transient so that we keep at best one man around to keep an eye on our belongings. So we stick around.

Harry ma boy your little laddie buck is about to go over and get his ars shot off! And the truth of the matter is I [am] scared shitless. We all are, so I'm not so unusual. Oh I'm not trying to dramatize it - a hell of a lot of darn good men have gone, but I expect we are all a little leery of the unknown. Truthfully we have a much better chance of survival than any who have gone before us in training, in their experience, in material and in our allies' hard won present advantage. I fully expect, if it is God's will, to return to you one of these fine days and begin anew something from which we all derived so much pleasure, happiness and security. But just on the outside if I don't quite make it let us call this a final confession or whatever the hell you will. Should I have to stay away, I don't honestly expect that what follows will influence you too much - I have been away too long and mainly I have failed for a year now to contribute the prerequisite of our triumvirate - my presence - my bitching, my morale, and least important, my economic support. However I would set a few things down here. A little advice I suppose you'd call it - even if you were in my obligation I would not try to insist you consider them too seriously for you are now the pilot. You're there and your judgment has proven itself so let's just call em ideas.

God knows I don't leave you much but you'll have 2 thousand cash from the Metropolitan and Mother will get 60 dollars a month or better from my government insurance. With her property this should, in a very modest way, make her almost independent. You will have to help some of course but it should not be too much and should in a way give you even more of an opportunity to shape your own life. I know we both in our hearts always considered it a privilege few enjoyed to live at home in our Piano Box with Mom and Mike, but as you continue to succeed in your work, you owe it to yourself and Mother and me to have a family of your own. Please name one of the boys after me huh?

If anything should happen to Mom, I advise you to avail yourself of the best legal advice and sign nothing without guidance. Beware of fair weather relatives and friends. Your breeding, so adequate and by one hand alone, must dictate to you to compromise with nothing and accept only the best and most perfect. This means friends, the selection of a wife, and in living a life in itself. You are blessed with honesty and truth. Guard them zealously as you go along. Another blessing is your nature, which so few understand. It is a distinct advantage to you for you are far less apt to be intimidated in life when only those close to you understand the depth of your comprehension, understanding, loyalty and abundant affectionate nature.

I know you will not sell out marriage for merely complete physical satisfaction but neither must you be duped by apparent complete companionship - no worthwhile woman was ever won without adversity. I wish I had your spiritual faith - it has and will be ever your best criterion in all things. And Mother - her common sense, intuition and foresight have ever seemed uncanny to me. If I ever put my church second, or it has been to her - I've worshipped her in every possible way - I think she knows that too.

I was most ashamed Harry when I hit the roof one night because you couldn't get a job and one day in Sioux Falls when you wrote me of a big chance you had and couldn't take because I was in the Army.

I was most proud of you when you came in with two jobs one night and also one afternoon when you bounced upon the High School Stage and walked off with what represented 3 years of sweating out night school. I couldn't stomach that deal and admitted it by doing so poorly.

I never did get to do much that amounted to anything but I can always take refuge in the "prevailing conditions." Anyway I always have excused myself that way. Honestly, seems like a man of 24 should have left a greater mark on life. Well, it still remains to be seen what I can do when I get back.

Only one thing I would admonish you for! You mustn't get stagnant mentally - you should get your C.P.A. before this thing is over if possible. If it keeps MacFarlane in a job - think where you could go with it. Personal application is about all that is called for now to get it and you should you know!

I suppose I may as well answer your 64 dollar question here. No on second thought I'll write a letter home tonight and explain.

I want you to keep on being a good boy Harry - awfully proud of having been of you two. You're still the best buddy a guy ever had and I have some pretty good ones now. Don't show this to Mother, not now anyway. I expect she's kinda peeved at me right now and rightly so - sooo I guess I'd better write - I noticed she hasn't written in answer to my night letter but you had to do it. I guess I had that coming. I'll write home now I guess.

My special Tuesday Blessing Fellah.

Love, Frank

P.S. Please keep close track of my birth certificate. It is important!

F.

February 20, Tuesday

Dear Mother, Harry and Mike,

Another day of just sitting around. We are on call during the day and in evenings are not too eager about doing much because of our clothes and also we don't like to leave what we have alone in the barracks. Many transient crews here and things disappear a little too readily. It is very crowded - not more than a foot between bunks, double tiered and it is cold. Have been getting real good use out of my slippers - the wooly ones with the zippers today - it is cold here - has rained all day and is uncomfortably damp and cold all the time.

I received Harry's direct to Ga. today - good to know we're in direct contact again. Glad you like Eileen - she was a great gal!

Guess I'd better get to Harry's 64 dollar question. I guess it is the main issue of the day. I repudiated a lot when I sent for that money I guess. Mom, I don't blame you for getting peeved in lots of ways and I can understand how you feel, but I wrote you before that if I had a chance to get home I'd let you know. I had my fill of that surprise stuff the last time. You're right when you ask "what has come over you." I know you think it peculiar that all of a sudden a good time should take precedence over my concern for your financial situation, over my financial independence, and the reputation I had, for I don't believe I ever asked for money before. All I can say is that it was my last chance to have a good time in the good old U.S.A. for a long time to come and I hated to miss it. I honestly never thought you'd think I was coming home - thought I'd made it clear that I'd let you know if I could come home. I'd never have risked hurting and disappointing you both that way. But as usual I see I'm all wet - I'm sorry but that doesn't help too much does it?

Furloughs are out here, too, unless of an emergency nature and then you have to have 2 men on a crew getting them before you stand a chance. I guess that takes in most of it for now. It's cold people - guess I'll hop into bed soon now - maybe I can keep warm there. Be good.
Lotsa Love, Frank

February 22, Thursday

Dear Mother, Harry and Mike,

Still nothing of too much importance going on today although we did get under way. It is indeed a lazy man's life eating and sleeping and doing little else. I do think I will try to take in a movie tonight. Haven't been to one here as yet for so far they have been showing what we saw at Gulfport a week or so ago. It is a funny existence - quarters are very cramped and since between my bunk and my Armorer and Ball Turret Gunner's bed there is more room than any place in the barracks (at least 18 square feet) the boys from old Crews 440 & 439 now 81 and 80 all congregate here. It is hard to get down to writing a letter. I haven't done too well by youse guys, but you hate to write with eight other fellows on your neck. I must write Otts and Beals soon but I don't seem to get to it. Otts' light bulbs arrived today and are very welcome. We have been using my "flash" a lot here for they turn lights out very early and it saves us a lot of groping around at night.

Now to get to today's happenings. We finally started the first of our processing today. This was the final record check we will have I hope. To-morrow we will be issued flying equipment and have final clothing check up. It will be a relief to get that finished and a worry too. That stuff, jackets and chutes and stuff costs like hell and you have to wear it all the time or have someone watching it for the permanent party here have taking ways. This is particularly directed towards the 45 automatic pistols we get and fur collared jackets and summer flying suits. We will get a hell of a lot of stuff and it weighs plenty and we are only allowed 116 lbs. but I figure on beating that some way or another. Of course the more difficult problem will be beating regulations again at POE, but I'll worry about that when I get there.

As I told you I've been reading "Forever Amber" - darn near finished now - it runs about a thousand pages. I'm getting a little fed up on it just as I did "Gone with the Wind" - sort of having to force myself to finish it and not having too much success.

I finally did manage to get some clothes to the cleaners - had to sneak them in because we're not supposed to send them until after we have had a final clothing "Show down." Frankly, we are all getting a little on edge. We feel if they are going to get us out of here - let's go - the sooner we go the sooner we'll be back. Then too, if they can't get us planes - let us go home for a week or so. Absolutely nothing is accomplished by sitting on our dead ass. We are all dying to get home but it is nigh impossible from where I am sitting. The Pilot doesn't want us to try to get an emergency for he doesn't want to lose the group we are with at present so that is that. Unless the whole group gets it the thing is out. We keep telling each other that if they can't get ships for us they should let us go but you know the Army.

Well folksies, guess I'll finish up "Amber" till it is show time. Try to get to the Service Club to-morrow and catch up on my writing - Be good.
Love, Frank

February 24, Saturday 9 AM

Dear Mother, Harry and Mike,

Got up very early this morning and tried to start this opus at the barracks but a new shipment of crews came in from Drew Field, Tampa, Florida and bedlam reigned so I finally gave it up as a bad job.

Yesterday was a big one and busy and tiring. Got up reasonably early to get my clothes completely straightened out for final show down. I have so much extra that I hardly know where the hell I'll get it all in. We went over in the morning and started and finally had to go back after lunch before we could get the entire crew cleared.

It was in a way a good deal, like being issued first equipment at the Induction Center but on a much grander scale. We were issued plenty and it is all exceptionally fine equipment. If I ever had any doubts about American Airmen getting the best they were dispelled to my complete bewilderment yesterday. As I've told you we are allowed only 116 lbs. and by some remote chance my equipment scaled exactly that when I finally cleared. Sad part is that I still had a laundry bag of towels, sox, underwear, etc. and my furlough bag full of personal things still in the barracks so a large part of the later part of yesterday afternoon was spent in farming out excess weight. Some things will be shipped in my Bombardier's foot locker by boat and the rest will be carried by my crew. They absolutely forbid any Sun Tan shirts and when I finished I still had four of them. The 2 stiff old Army ones I had gotten at Sioux Falls, the one

Norm altered for me and the broadcloth one you sent me at Sioux Falls. They threaten to break us if we are caught with any, but things are too far along now for me to let a little thing like that stop me. Besides all the enlisted men on the crew except Kimpel the Armorer can wear my shirts so we all agreed we should keep mine and expect we'll manage. I also managed to screw the government out of an extra pair of O.D. pants. I figured I'd need them in England for you can get no dry cleaning done over there. We are allowed only 3 bags. We got a B-4 bag for our personal clothing. I think you know what they are - Dick had one when he was home. Only mine is not heavy canvas it is completely of heavy shiny rayon like the pants football players wear these days. Zippers everywhere - it is a brand new type and a dandy. We also got an A-3 bag to carry flying equipment in. This is heavy canvas and at present I have everything important in it. It is made so that you can put a lock through two zippers on it and am I ever glad I have my lock. That at last allays some of my fears about having things stolen. We also got a Musette bag - that knapsack I brought home that we got so much in. In these three bags must go all we carry overseas and if you could see what we got yesterday you'd have been bewildered too. I didn't know me arse from sour apples. Where and how the hell to put it - that was the problem. Quarters are so crowded and yet I'm signed out with about 700 bucks worth of stuff so I spent my time until the lights went out last night getting things straightened out. Finally, just about made it but am having to use my Engineer's - Joe Ferniza's Musette bag to get the last of it in. Jumping Jimmy what a job! We have everything now from soup to nuts - not much use going into it all but I can well understand now why you can't get nylon or elastic or zippers. People I think I've got it all right now.

Today marks the beginning of our second week here and a lot of the boys from Avon Park who were here a week ahead of us haven't left yet. Yesterday was the only day they really needed us here and we could have had a whole week off but I guess it just isn't in the books for us. Any time within the next week we should be assigned a plane and from then on things will move more with the rapidity and preciseness we originally anticipated.

I received two letters from Beals yesterday and one from Chuck Bordner. From what he tells me things in Research have really taken a turn from the old R&H lackadaisical attitude and being as we put it "DuPontized." Evidently they are having group discussions now as a routine thing. A big point is being made of exacting the maximum amount of ingenuity and thinking power from the lesser lights. This was never done before - a junior chemist there was only a glorified poop boy when I was there but apparently Dr. Tucker, the new director, wants to accentuate the positive and utilize much of the brain power that exists up there, which heretofore has been left in a less than dormant state. Bordner was nice when he said "Things are changing so that I hope you will want to come back."

Of course I will want to - for a while anyway.

Well folksies, I guess I'd best shove off now - try to write Gramp, Beals, Otts and some of the others today while I'm here - I hope. Be good.
Love, Frank

February 25, Sunday

Dear Mother, Harry and Mike,

You see I'm here again for enough peace and quiet to try to write a decent letter. Yesterday I got two letters from Mother - first I had received from her since I've been here - it had been almost four days since I had gotten any mail from home after Harry's first one. Got another one from Haroola today. I left here yesterday only to find out that we are to have a factory briefing at 4 PM - we had it. It amounted to only code sending and receiving checks for R.O.s and blinkers. We expect to get a ship to-morrow and fly our calibration mission tomorrow PM. That means leaving for our POE the following morning before 7 AM.

I had all my shots at Gulfport, Mom, and I can assure you that we will not be here much longer as you can see from the above. I fear I'm going to lose my best buddies if we do go as we expect to. Taylor's Bombardier is in the hospital and is not expected to be able to get out in time to go with us. I don't like it but we all hope that we'll meet again in a pool at our final destination. If we do get a ship on the morrow I'll have plenty to do to get my radio sets just as I want them. This time is mighty important.

Our flying suits are Gabardine instead of leather, sheepskin lined Harry because the latter is really not warm as we found out at Gulfport. These things are heavy and are lined with Mohair - Grade A what I mean. I will do my best to get you some more cigarettes Harry. I'll have to mail package COD as that is the only way we can get the stuff out of here. It has to go through a government window in the processing section. I don't think I'll be taking too big a chance.

Was quite relieved to hear boxes had arrived. Yes Mom, those stockings represent quite a rigmarole - what burnt me up was that they were only 42 instead of 51, but I had committed myself and had to take what was available. Glad you like cologne too. I was beginning to get worried about whether you'd get them or not.

Last night I finally went into town. Five of us went finally wound up at a formal dance where no Jitterbugging was allowed. It was really nice - we had a bunch of nice chicks but this curfew deal really cramps a man's style. I was in favor of going over the fence last night but was outvoted so we got in on time.

At present I am waiting for John Staeger - we're going to Mass and Communion I believe - should have gone this morning but I sacked it until 11 AM.

This evening I'm going in to meet Sgt. Shaffer's mother - should have gone in before but had nothing clean. Situation is not much better now but I suppose we'll manage.

Our pilot Roger Sundin was worried about us - came in barracks a couple hours ago and wanted to loan us all money since I don't expect we'll be here to get paid - what a man - all the fellows envy us our pilot - he is grade A believe me.

Well my dears, it is 5 PM and I want to get over to Confession before Mass at 6 PM - have to eat here after Mass I guess so I'll have to run - so, be good.
Lotsa Love, Frank

February 26, Monday

Dear Mother, Harry and Mike,

Well, here I am again. I find it is much easier to write here. That barracks is really bedlam what I mean. I'd better say this while I think of it. I have 1 carton of Camels for the big boy - will try to get more to-morrow - as many as is possible before I leave. Here is the deal. I'll try to ship them home in a leather furlough bag. Inside will be cigarettes and I hope and pray that they get there O.K. The bag does not belong to me and also inside will be the address to which I wish you would forward it. It is my Engineer's bag so if they come (the butts) in the bag please forward it to California. I may have to send them C.O.D. as that is only way to get them out of here unless I'm lucky enough to get out to city P.O. with them, which I doubt.

We did not get anticipated plane today. We now hope it doesn't come until - well, for a couple days more. We'd like to be paid here. There is something about being shorted on flying pay at POE so we'd rather get it here than fool around getting it on the way out or on the other side.

I went to a movie this afternoon. Errol Flynn in "Objective Burma" - not too bad for a strictly action picture. Took first PT today since the one time at Gulfport. I felt I really needed some exercise for we are all getting lazy with not much to do around here. I haven't made up my bed in 2 days now - there is always someone lying on top of it because Joe puts his radio there in the morning. What a life - not enough order in it to suit me. Guess with the airplane still an uncertainty I'll have to do laundry to-morrow by myself - am accumulating yee old pile of dirty clothes. I received Harry's letter today and also sox from Beals - finally forwarded from Gulfport. It sure took them a long time, what? Please thank girls for me - they are grand - I may not get to write them again from here. All depends on to-morrow's developments.

Went into town last night and met Sgt. Shaffer's mother. They are typical country people from Pa. We took his mom out for a couple hours. Thought she might like to see some of the places in town but everything was closed down so we settled for a bite to eat and Shaffer & I left for camp. He has more than his share of in-law trouble and I don't envy him but he's a big enough boy to handle his own problems. He likes to take them to everyone, which I don't admire but as I say that is his problem.

Well folksies, that is about all for right now I guess. There is a dance here at the Service Club in an hour or so and another one I think at the same place in town as I went Saturday night. Haven't quite decided where I'll go so guess I'll have to let you know on the morrow. Be good.
Lotsa Love, Frank

February 28, Wednesday

Dear Mother, Harry and Mike,

Well, we're still here contrary to a lot of things said and the apparent general practice. Got paid today - should be in town tying one on I guess but I thought I'd better stay and get ma letter written. We are rather on edge - supposed to be getting a plane any time during the past three days but no soap as yet. Maybe we'll go by boat yet. I hope not. We are the next crew to go - next 17 crew that is - have been for a couple days.

I'd better start with the night before last. Went to town looking for a dance some-where but it was no soap so I wound up in Tavern, which is the bar grill and night club arrangement at the DeSoto Hotel, which is the largest and oldest hotel here. It is really very nice. I met Shackelford, our Navigator and after a couple beers we found Co-pilot - "Lips" Turner and his date in a dark corner. We promptly set out to spoil his evening and I'm afraid we very nearly did. I finally found me a sweet little thing and the Navigator was with me and I'm quite sure he was trying to beat my time - he thought he had her but I hope I know better. Anyway we made a date with her for last night, both of us, I told her to bring a playmate for the rank. Anyway I was supposed to call her yesterday. She is an accountant with some shipbuilding firm here and altho (sic) I tried to get her about 20 times yesterday I couldn't get her. She was out of the department every time I called. We were at the appointed place on time but she and the girlfriend didn't show. Don't blame them in a way but it was the first time I'd ever been stood up and it didn't set too well. Sooo last night I had my first fill of beer since I'd left home on my delay. OH I didn't get tight but it sure reminded me of the night when Harry and I used to operate at home. I was really rosy but got back to camp with Shackelford before pass was out. I don't enjoy a drinking evening and no women but made the best of it.

Well, after several tries today I finally made contact. Seems she didn't care to be waiting around the DeSoto alone without the telephone call to substantiate the date we made. She was sorry so we made it for to-morrow night. I'll let you know Harry how I make out. I don't think she's married.

We still have not been doing much around here - not much I can write about. Think we'll play football to-morrow morning for we are all getting logy from the inertia here. Most of us have lost our appetites and don't feel as peppy as we should and exercise is the answer to that. Will try like blazes to get cigarettes out to-morrow. Guess I'll have to get them into town and send them from there - they are getting chicken about it around here. I'll try to sneak em out to-morrow and get them out. Have lots to do to-morrow too - all contingent on whether or not we get a plane. I have had leather name tags made for my flying clothes and I'll have to have them sewn on. Then too there is the inevitable laundry which keeps accumulating no mat-ter whether school keeps or not. But then am I telling you Mom? We had some crew pictures made yesterday too. I look pretty rotten in them but the main point is that you both get a look at the rest of the crew - you know how I look! I'll send a couple home - or rather I'll pay for them and they'll send em from the PX.

A note on shaving, Harry - try Gem single edge or Schick injector if you can. Shortage of double edged blades has driven me to change about. I believe I'm getting better shaves and am just passing it on remembering how tough it has always been for you to shave.

Well folks, I owe lots of letters but won't get to it tonight - going to try to clean up the pig sty which is our section of the barracks. Glad I stayed in tonight - everyone is in town blowing their wad and only a few of us are here so I can make any changes I want to and there'll be no squawking so guess I'll get to it. Be good, people.
Love, Frank

March 1945

March 1, Thursday

Dear Mother, Harry and Mike,

As you can see I'm using borrowed stationary. Have lost track of mine! Such a mess around here! Received Mother's letter today and I'll get to her P.S. right now. I wrote Gramp a last letter and told him that I was sorry that he did not see fit to send me addresses of my distant relatives but I told him regardless I intended to find out what was what and who was who over there. I inferred I smelt a ripe rat, and that I meant to "ferret" it out. I don't suppose they'll like that at all but they have 2 choices. One to leave me in the dark and let me find out as I will or can and admit that a sultry stink exists or to rush a few addresses to me. Ah well, it matters not too much to me - betcha I find them if I ever get over there though.

Enough of that. No plane again today so I finally connected with that gal in town and got her to bring a playmate for Lt. Shackelford so it looks like I'll get in a little dancing tonight. Shakelford would like us all to think he is a social lion but he impresses me as to be one of those who "never had it better." He seems to have trouble with some of the boys. I certainly would rather go out with Taylor or some of my boys but he happened to be along when I was promoting this deal so in as much as I feel a little sorry for him, I fixed things to include him tonight. Perhaps I'm speaking too soon for maybe his rank will swipe my girl tonight but I don't think so. Shackelford will have to learn a lot of things the hard way it seems to me - you just have to be a gentleman - bred one (thanks for giving me a reasonable right to that Mom) before you can impress any girl - slut or otherwise. An act of Congress hardly does the trick. Robinson the Bombardier is the big operator on our crew for my money - he's really smooth and darn good looking too. He is second tallest on our crew so you'll be able to pick him out when you get the pictures I will enclose the receipt for pictures so if you don't get them in two or three weeks you'd better write and ask about them. Also will enclose information pertaining to option on insurance payments and pension.

Things roll along here much as usual. We get in a lather twice a day and expect a Big Bird of our own but it hasn't come as yet. I honestly expect one in the next three days. We all are getting a little tired of loafing and mainly we're afraid they might decide to send us to C.B.I. Theatre and none of us are too keen about that. With Spring on the way, if those Yanks and Russians keep going as they have, they won't need a lot of crews. We hope to get over and get our preliminary training in and fly a few missions before they finish up over there and then get home before a new assignment comes through. So much for speculation.

Well my dears, I have to get ready for my big deal tonight. Lots to do - mostly get some clean clothes out of the debris around here. Have a couple day beard to cut up too. Be good, folksies.
Lotsa Love, Frank

March 2, Friday

Dear Mother, Harry and Mike,

Well, I had my big eagle last night and had a rather good time. The set up at the DeSoto Hotel is rather like the Roy, OH except that it is much roomier and classier. We danced a good deal to a fairly good band. She was a good dancer, a good conversationalist - took her home in a cab, got my little lovin, and had an evening of good clean fun. Shackelford got the date I arranged for him rather tight and I don't know really what he did - mostly blow I judge, but he got a date again tonight. His technique is a little raw for me and I doubt that I'll bother with him again. I had a really good time - ma gal has a car or rather her father has and maybe we'll go for a long drive in the country one of these fine days - that is if we stay here. I got in in plenty of time not to have my pass pulled (just lucky there) so I didn't have to resort to the fence. It is not quite so easy to come in over the fence here as it was at Gulfport - as evidence. Joe Ferniza (Lobs) Engineer and Bob Turner (Lips) - Well, Lips and Lobs got tight together the other night and, one taking care of the other, they got a cab and came into the fence - over it, walked two miles through swamps and then my boy Jose, who was doing the navigating led both of them right into an M.P.s shack. Both of them were leaning upon one another for support but for some unknown reason they were not disciplined or penalized but you should have seen their clothes - apparently they started jumping from log to log which was O.K. but then they started to miss the logs and that was rather sad.

Enough of the social side for now I guess. Got Harry's of the 27th and Mom's of the 28th today. Harry your diagram of the C House gives me a good idea of it but if you were a G.I. you would have sweated out the coming of the fellows - two girls at a bar are always waiting for a couple fellows who never show tsk tsk! Then before they can say Tom Collins you date them or her for the next night and leave but fast before you are committed to buy drinks for both of them.

Please don't try hard, if you have been, to bother with anything for my birthday. I do not need anything but an armful of loveliness and then to be able to come home after I throw her in the door. It just isn't sensible - hope you didn't get compass as I have been issued equipment which, although I myself do not know the extent (not *allowed to open), I'm sure there is a compass in it. Glad you told me of the coming balls from the Otts. We fool around a lot and my boys and I sure would like to get hold of a football. I told them all I dropped a not too gentle hint for a football and they've been asking me when it is coming. At other bases we could draw balls but we can't here. We're constantly on the alert and they're afraid we'd take it with us. So we are out of luck. I only hope they get here in a hurry for I have a hunch we'll move on the morrow - no not to-morrow but Sunday - should get a plane to calibrate to-morrow. If we don't get one to-morrow I'll almost quit looking for one!*

Awfully glad the income tax will not be quite as staggering as you originally antici-pated - it sounds pretty rugged to me - to tell the truth. By the way 4 cartons of ciga-rettes are on the way so look for them. If we're here over the week-end I'll try to do it again - we'll see about it. Have not been having so full and so good a time here as at Gulfport. I can see putting money into lots of things but not a lot of liquor and that is mostly what goes on around here. Also Taylor and I are not operating together. We think pretty much alike as far as spending is concerned but he hit something in town and has been going in every night to take care of it. He was alone at the time he met her - if I'd been with him I'd have razzed him out of it for she is a little below our standard. He has been in bad shape lately - he called his 1st love in St. Louis the other day and she cried and told him that she had just given the Postman a "Dear John" letter - seems she found another guy she likes and after all Taylor isn't there. I never knew him to drink much but he was tight the other night - said he wanted to put his hand in his pocket but was so numb he couldn't manage it. Tonight he seems to have a hotel room deal with this doll - bad business but I've seen lots of that in the Army. Glad I've never gone in for that stuff. Are you relieved Tess to know that I'm still sweet and clean and pure and nice? Maybe my little Kay Geer will change me with her pappy's car but I doubt it. Guess I'd rather be hot & bothered than hurried and worried and tired!

Well, I have to get going - staying in tonight - must do that laundry to-morrow - still have some organizing of my flight plan to do and some packing. Be good, folksies. Love, Frank

March 3, 1945, Saturday 7:00 - Letter from Harry

Hiya bro

Well, today was only a half day at work & I was very glad for that. I hardly had enough will power to get myself out of bed this morning & I don't think I really woke up till 10 o'clock.

The big change in our department hasn't occurred as yet & now Lord knows when it will happen. I think we'll have a pretty good hint though when they change over our billing machine. I think that's what is holding them up. Also the new cost system is a mystery to even the boys of the cost department & they are having a hell of a time get-ting it rolling. There are some changes though. There was posted on our bulletin board Thursday A.M. a four star notice. (1) All employees were to be permitted to smoke at their desks anytime during the day (2) a coke machine had been installed downstairs for the convenience of the employees (3) the girl's rest room was to be locked & only used for girls who were ill. (4) Those who were in the habit of recreating (that's the word they used) in the rest room would be allowed to gather in the lunch room as soon as it could be cleaned up from its noon day meal & before they started their evening meal. Quite a change for Carbo, eh what?

Of course everyone practically took full advantage of all the points. I noticed Steve reading it & he seemed rather disgusted. He said, here he had been jacked up twice in the last 2 weeks for the laxness of our department & then the company goes & makes it easier. He was really sore. As a consequence I still take my smoke in the washroom. Charlie Anderson, second in command, stated that he didn't think it was right at all. So that's a pretty good criterion of Steve's thoughts for Charlie loves his pipe. Even though none of us in the department appreciated the mixture he smokes. It's "Brindleys" & smells like it.

Gib lit up his pipe yesterday for about 10 minutes in the afternoon but I think Steve got him in the vault & sort of explained matters to him for I saw them both coming out of the vault & Gib had that Cheshire look about him. On the Coke side, they ran the one machine so much the first afternoon that they had them bring in another. I guess there was even a line to Coke. Both machines are like that one they had down at the YMCA that night we went square dancing. One holds 59 bottles & the other 39.

I was over to see Gramps last night. He looks about the same but his foot troubles him. Says he can't sleep half the night because of it. He said he had received a nice letter from you but didn't bring it out for me to read or say anything more about it since Uncle Bob & Aunt Cecelia were there.

He did mention however about you asking before for addresses in England. He stated last night that only one he knew & where they lived was his sister, 82 years old who lives on the outside of London, who he said you certainly wouldn't be interested in. Another was our dear Bishop Kempthorne who lives in Cambridge & is at the present very ill and then Vera Marshall who lives near Liverpool, I think they said it was Portsmouth. This last one is the only one they seemed to approve of so we'll see what you do get. Of course I didn't push it for fear I might seem too interested but I think they'd feel more at ease if you didn't see anybody over there who knows them. You know those "skeletons in the closet" can make an awful racket when they're disturbed.

Well, today was the day our "old faithful" went out of business, Good old Mary Lobianco. Mom said she was almost in tears, that is Mary, when she phoned in her order today.

I went over to pay the bill & talked a little with Mary & wished Sam good luck. Mary said it was going to feel funny at first but they'd just have to overcome it.

I'm thinking of going out tonight I have had the urge to see what the Prospect Oval Room is like, now that it is decorated, so will probably take it in tonight. The places *close now at 12, which is good in my language although you hear squads around tonight, they even had an article where a speakeasy has been raided already.*

Well, if I want to get out tonight I guess I better get going. Think I'll take a bath & feel sweet & clean & pure & nice.

So, be good and good luck & stick with single girls.

Love, Harry

P.S. Yes, we ran out of Air Mail Stamps. So what? Mmmm?

March 4, Sunday

Dear Mother, Harry and Mike,

Well, another Sunday has rolled around and we are still here. I'm tempted to say probably not for long but I've been saying that. At 6 AM this morning Taylor's crew got a plane and they are either briefing or flying right now and since we are directly behind them it is reasonable to suppose that we will be next. Of course we've been on deck for some time now and truthfully I'm anxious to go. We are all getting on edge and on one another's nerves and it is not at all good.

I heard Strauss's Crew (Taylor's pilot) being called and assigned this morning at about 6 AM and listened for us but we were not listed as yet. May come at noon, 4 PM or may be a few days yet. I got up at 7:30 when the boys left here and went to breakfast and then to 8:00 AM Mass at the theatre, which is just across the street from the Combat Crew Area. Think I may go to the Service Club for a second cup of coffee soon but it is quite a jaunt and I thought I'd better write first.

Yesterday was a full one. In the morning a large group from Mac Dill Field came in. That still leaves a group from Avon Park - boys who were here before us, our bunch - only 8-10 crews left now, a bunch of Drew Field and yesterday the lads from Mac Dill. Anyway I had decided to wash yesterday and so had John Staeger so we got together and fired up the water to get prepared. They have permanent party barracks orderlies who are supposed to do these things keep place clean and keep water hot but they never seem to do it.

Staeger had been trying to date a blonde WAC at Processing for the past 4 days with no success so finally yesterday she relented but it seems she had a friend so I more or less got roped in for her buddy. These kids were what I've known existed in the WACs but had not seen much of. They were nice girls - no kidding. We danced and had a few drinks at the DeSoto and while it was not so much for John and I I'm sure they had a rather good time. The one I was with was Norma Kelly - she was cute and nice and not a bad dancer. When a girl orders a Tom Collins you know she hasn't been down town too many times and that's what Staeger's date - Thelma Kranshaw was drinking not so with Kelly - she was having Bourbon and ginger ale and it was on either 4 or 5 of them that she got quite high. God Bless her it was a good thing she wasn't with some of these old Army wolves - no kidding. But I took fairly good care of her if you know what I mean. Never had a girl get kinda high on me before - she was just full of fun that's all. Well, we brought them back to camp and they took us up to the so called "Date Room" they have. Such a display of bare-faced slobbering up there. Nothing out of line of course cause the lights are going full blast and people are sitting in easy chairs and 2 of us necking to beat hell - on top of this an M.P. walks through from time to time just to make sure that someone's emotions doesn't get the better of someone else. Well, I'm telling you it was a riot no matter how you look at it. All the way to the WAC Area were couples in Olive Drab just loving the hell out of one another. Huba Huba Huba! Never having dated a WAC before I'll say it was some experience. Haven't decided whether it needs duplicating again or not, but I rather doubt it.

Well, I guess that is about all for now. Just that I did get my washing done - both shirts done up yesterday afternoon and starched if you please. How do you like that?

Think I'll post this - I'll try to write again this afternoon if I get a plane - may be my last chance here. In any case when I leave here the Army will let you know my Temporary APO number. Cards and V-mail have already been made out - the latter for permanent APO - so as long as I keep on the ball I believe things will run along rather smoothly. Please don't worry if you don't hear from me days or a couple weeks on end. These changes of station take time to accomplish and must be done as quietly as possible. Weather may or may not hold us for a long time anywhere along the line. Be good, folksies.

Love, Frank

March 5, Monday

Dear Mother, Harry and Mike,

Well, still here and no visible signs of leaving yet. When it does happen it will move so fast I won't get much opportunity to write about it. Went to see "A Song to Remember" last night. By all means see it! Be sure to get in at the beginning otherwise you won't enjoy it to the fullest. Paul Muni is very good and it is the most exceptional movie I've seen in a long while.

Our boys on crew 439 just ahead of us left this morning for POE. We are the next to go on our shipment but latest information I can glean indicates we have a few more days here at least altho (sic) I can't vouch for reliability of information. Joe Ferniza, my Engineer, got up at 5:30 AM to eat breakfast with the boys - help them recheck their plane and wave handkerchiefs as they took off. I'm sure they hated to leave us behind as we hated to see them go. The 5 E.M. on their crew and on ours have been as solid as 10 men could be. We were so close that it hurt to watch them take off in their big bird, particularly when we have none as yet. We were commissioned with many things to do for them and at 7:45 they left us for parts unbeknownst. Ah but we'll catch them somewhere, but till then we wait impatiently for the means. We have missed them a great deal today and I know that they didn't want to leave us. After getting a plane they seemed to change a great deal - lost a lot of their life and pep - said they knew it was coming but the actuality was still another thing. They were issued 45 automatic pistols last night along with a short bayonet which is a very good knife - all I could have wanted. We'll get the same when we prepare to leave. They left our barracks last night, loaded their plane and stayed last night in a barracks which is playfully called the "Alert Hotel" here. They slept there last night and awoke Joe and I early this morning to go and eat with them. They are at destination by now - airplane travel is a great thing. I tell you these things now for when it comes to us I doubt that I'll have time to write about it.

A good bit of my time yesterday and today has been spent perusing the "Line" maintenance shops, begging extra equipment so that I can do my job better and make my crew more comfortable and secure. It has been a revelation for always before I have had to almost sell my soul and then sign a million forms. Here it reminded me of the way I used to expedite things at the plant by knowing the right guy to go to. It is or was surprising to find that merely a smile - the time of day - and asking with humility can get you almost anything. My pilot and crew are proud of me I'm sure, for just the few extras I have gotten for them and a couple new innovations I have made. I have tried to remember all the little angles about which I asked and heard of. About now being on the ball begins to pay dividends.

I got a letter from Dick yesterday. Haven't heard from you fellows in 2 days now. It took my letter just a month to get to him and just shy a day or two of a month for me to get the answer. I have shown it to most of my crew and it has been helpful. I'll try to get him what he wants - got two of my gunners in town tonight working on it. I'll try to enclose the letter so you can see what I mean. I got the box from the Otts today. That package didn't lose any time getting here. It was mailed the third and here today. My lads, as well as myself, are overjoyed to get the football and baseball. I must write them tonight. They sure came through - I'll admit I hinted but I hardly expected it to get here in time. I picked up a pair of sneaks here today so I'm all set.

I have also picked up a nasty head cold here during the past couple days. Nothing serious of course but I have felt very uncomfortable the past couple days - nose running, etc. I've been hitting 100 Empirin compounds I bought at Gulfport - am I ever glad I have them! Just have to sweat it out I guess.

Well, you nice people that is about it for today - guess I'll have a few beers and hit my dear old sac. On Dick's advice guess maybe I'll get my old shoes fixed in the morning and take them - they have rubber soles and heels. Be good, folks.
Love, Frank

March 6, Tuesday

Dear Mother, Harry and Mike,

Tuesday afternoon and we're still here. I suppose we'll be moving soon for 3 of us, contrary to orders, put in dry cleaning this morning and can't get it until Thursday. We figured that was the quickest way to get a plane so we dood (sic) it. I also have both pairs of civilian shoes in to have heels put on. Went all out this morning for I got fed up on waiting. I can't see getting clothes pressed and repressed and just pressing dirt in. The things were dirty - no two ways about it so they're getting cleaned now.

I still very much have my cold but it is just a question of sweating it out I guess. Head has felt so heavy. Just got a Benzedrine inhaler and it has helped a good deal. The boys brought me some whiskey this afternoon - Seagram's 7 Crown of all things. If I manage to get it over I should get a pretty penny for it - here's hoping. Our crew total must be a case or more but we're not going to worry about the weight problem now. I received Mother's "shorter" of the 2nd. Let me know how Gramp liked that last letter - bet it didn't go over too well.

Plan on going to movie this evening since my O.D. clothes are in the cleaners. Very little to do or write about at present. Should have dated Kay for this evening I guess but I know that there is no such thing as dry cleaning in England and I very much wanted to have a final good job done. You do your own cleaning over there, so I hear, in 100 octane gas but there are plenty of places to get pressing done.

Well folksies, aside from a bit of a cold I'm ragged, fat, and sassy and rarin' to go. Be good, people.

Lotsa Love, Frank

March 7, Wednesday

Dear Mother, Harry and Mike,

I am very late getting to today's missive but just as I said in yesterday's, as soon as we turned our clothes in to be cleaned we got a ship. Was awakened by PA system this morning blaring and we all cursed as they passed out 17s to other crews, but we did get one and today has been spent in checking our plane and getting ready for an early morning departure.

They will awaken us at 5:30 AM and we'll be on our way by 7:30 or 8 AM to POE. Nice way to get there by plane eh? We checked our equipment thoroughly today. It was a satisfaction for I can tell it now. Planes we flew at Gulfport were wrecks from being on the go 18 hours a day. It was risking a lot to fly them and our class lost too many good men in merely the training period.

We have a brand new ship and it's a beauty. Everything is up to snuff what I mean! I did not get maximum satisfaction out of my Liaison Radio but it was in perfect shape and I guess I just wasn't used to it. Got in all that was required but little extras I wanted to do I didn't quite make. Will manage those tomorrow during flight I guess.

Spent the entire day running about for the Army but it was a relief. Ate with an appetite for a change and the cold is just about gone so it was a good day for me.

I have been in a muddle all day - started for the Service Club once but came back. I really wanted to telephone but finally decided to write and spare you the uncalled-for excitement. By the time you get this I should be through POE and already arrived at final destination. A card has already been made out to you so that you will get a temporary APO number a couple days after this and then I'll be writing V-mail as soon as it is possible. Probably be asking for things right away - haven't changed you see. I received a grand letter from Beals today. Norm said she was not getting out and sent letter in lieu of a Birthday Card. Also got Mrs. K's Birthday Card. I should write but it is late now and I still have to get cleaned up for to-morrow's session so please thank them for me and I'll write them soon.

I just hope you fellows are not doing extra for the eighth. It will sure be an exceptional ride on my birthday anyhow! At any rate I hope you'll just skip it this time as I suggested as there is nothing you could get me that I need and I don't know where the hell I'd carry it.

We drew knives and guns this evening and then I picked a few more radio accessories I figured I might need. Most of the boys have gone to the show but I am puttering around as per usual. I still have to get some more APO cards out to folks at home.

There is a tendency to think that this is a big step or something but honestly, it does not seem as important to me as some of the other shipments I have made. We still have training to undergo when we arrive and this is after we, as a crew, sit around in a pool until we are needed. Sooo you can see things have still a ways to go. Just a little more travel involved than usual. Travel in distance that is, for in time it will be shorter I judge than some train trips I have made while a G.I.

Received Harry's letter today about changes in his sweat shop. Hope things look up - Haroola when the hell are you going to up and tell Steve you're moving in? I'll make an effort to write from POE and would appreciate it if you'd drop a line to me from time to time until you get my first V-mail even though it takes a month to get to me. Will be a bit of a bonus when I do get it don't ya know.

I shall have some planning of my own to do before we leave - that is in the radio line. They didn't brief me - apparently don't think that the radio contacts as too important from here but I figure it is a good opportunity to get in some good experience so I'm making a bit of a plan of my own. You know - just an eager beaver. As I said I still have cards to address and clean up so guess I'd better get a going.

Be good, people and you'll be hearing from me as soon as is possible on my part. Lotsa Love, Frank

March 9, 1945–Postcard

Notice of Change of address
Cpl. Frank G. Thompson
APO No. 19042-CJ-81

March 10, Saturday

Dear Mother, Harry and Mike,

Finally I'm down to writing. Rather hard to know exactly what to say at this stage of the game although I've been given a rather precise idea of what not to say.

The main point is to let you know that I'm ragged, fat, and sassy and having what would be considered quite an adventure under any other circumstances. For that matter I believe the whole crew has been getting quite a kick out of our travels.

What I'm learning and appreciating most I guess is my crew. I've said before that they are a swell bunch but working with them in situations which up to a few days *ago were completely alien to us all and watching everyone perform makes you feel proud to be one of them. Our Pilot and Navigator have been hardest put I believe, but you'd certainly never know it. They are really on the ball and we all have every confidence in them.*

Another thing I've come to appreciate is the extent and overall services offered us by the Air Transport Command. Every exigency has been provided for in the air, and every possible comfort afforded us on the ground. A lot of men have done a lot to see that there is absolutely no operational hitch or delay in our project and a good many more work solely for our comfort and safety. Not just eating and sleeping but even at the remotest points the good old Catholic Chaplain is on deck at all times even more so than when at home.

How I wish I could say more but it would do no particular good that I can see. We are all well—thanks only to the (this word was torn out of his letter) that I can sit down long enough to write this. I wanted you to have my temporary APO number so you can write to it instead of Hunter Field.

Be good, people.

Love, Frank

ONE RETURNS, ONE DEPARTS

Present Day

To say my mother is sentimental would be a gross understatement. While she is not a hoarder by any means, she has kept many of her "worldly treasures," as she refers to them, particularly if they have a story attached, which most of them do. Among her most coveted treasures are a beautiful set of rosary beads and a silver watch that she received from her "soldier." As I typed more letters and began to learn more about soldiering, the war, and my father, I wanted to know more about her soldier. Apparently when my mother was in middle school at St. Mary's in Niagara Falls, her class had been asked to choose the name of a soldier to write to during the war. That was in 1943. She was thirteen years old and in the seventh grade. It intrigued me that she was writing her soldier while, at the same time, her future husband was preparing to go to war.

My mother's soldier was William "Buck" Roffle and after another visit to the genealogy website, I was able to piece together a bit more about him. He was three years older than my father, and had attended LaSalle High School, so it was unlikely the two would have known each other. Among my mother's treasures was also a photograph of Buck in his uniform. As I reviewed the records returned from my search, another "non-coincidence" presented itself. The military records show that he'd enlisted in 1941, on July 9th, my birthday, again. What are the chances? Of all the dates he could have enlisted, and he did so on my birthday. I began to consider these "something bigger" instances as my father nudging my journey onward, offering me nuggets to inspire me to continue.

Buck's family owned a restaurant in Niagara Falls and his brother owned a service station that sold auto parts and cars. City directories indicate that when he returned from the war he'd worked in his family's restaurant and then as a painter. Prior to enlisting, he'd worked for his brother at Roffle Service Station. During the war he was stationed in the European Theatre of Operations in the UK. As hard as I tried, I was able to learn very little about his tour of duty. I was able to ascertain that he was part of the Tank Destroyer Group—possibly the 2nd Tank Destroyer Battalion. I did find a ship manifest indicating he was a passenger departing from Liverpool, England to New York City, New York, near the end of the war.

I actually knew a little about the Roffle Service Station because my mother would tell us the story about how her mother had wanted her to learn to drive.

Being the obedient daughter, my mother had agreed, and my grandmother set about arranging for anyone and everyone they knew to take my mother out driving. The family car was a station wagon my grandfather used for his painting business and was always laden with paints, tarps, ladders, and brushes. If the family ever wanted to go on an outing, all the painting paraphernalia would have to be taken out of the car before they left and returned to the car when they arrived home. From the stories I've been told, my grandmother was quite the schemer and I'm certain having my mother get her drivers license was part of one of her grand plans. In the end, all the "driving lessons" paid off and my mother got her license in 1953. When it came time to buy a car, it was Buck Roffle who took my mother car shopping at his brother's business where he helped her purchase her first car. It wasn't too long after that purchase that my grandmother (had already) planned a road trip to Washington, DC with, of course, my mother driving.

On one of my many research trips to the cemetery, I decided to take a different exit route than usual. As I eased my way down the narrow gravel road, a large headstone with the name ROFFLE caught my eye. It was close to the road so I stopped; I put my car in park, thinking, *What are the chances?* As I approached the stone and the lettering became clearer I realized I had happened upon Buck. I had seen several Roffle headstones on my past visits, but had never stopped. By finding him in a section of the cemetery that I had never been to before I felt I was meant to include him in my story. I told my mother about my discovery and that Buck was in the same cemetery as Frank. She never knew what had happened to him. My mother still says the rosary every night using the beads she received from Buck. On special occasions, you will find a silver watch adorning her wrist, the watch he gave her when he returned home from the war.

As I returned to typing letters, I realized that while Buck was on his way home from England after serving four years, my father was just preparing to depart for his own tour of duty. His destination? England. He and his crew departed from Savannah, Georgia on his twenty-fourth birthday. My mother was sixteen years old.

HORHAM, ENGLAND - PART 1

March 19, Saturday
V-mail postmarked March 26, 1945

Dear Mother, Harry and Mike,

Well, here we are in England—The Midlands to be more precise, but I'm afraid that is about as specific as I can make it. We, that is the crew, are all quite well with the possible exception of slight head colds, which was to be expected with the movement.

At present our personal problems are many and varied and can generally be summed up as those any individual entering a different country during war time might encounter. I, myself, have been unable to get on speaking terms with the English money but I will figure that after a couple "thro pence ante" games it will iron itself out. As long as I don't iron out my own resources too great, an extent in the learning, it should provide a good method of acquiring ease with the system.

Coming here, we had some opportunity to get a glimpse of the English countryside. It upholds quite ably all the commendation spoken of it and then some! The neatness and thrift which are typical characteristics of the people are quite apparent in their farms. The people themselves, to my first impression, are quite friendly and eager to bid you the time of day. This in itself helps - as you can well understand—they call us and refer to us generally as "Yank." The food thus far has been all right and the main point is that there is plenty of it.

Quartered here, along with Air Force personnel, are a good many Infantry men who are just really recuperating from previous action. After talking with a Staff Sergeant last night, our part of the war seems like a May frolic compared to some of the things they have gone through. Just coming from the States we are quite apt to complain about the natural strangeness of things but after talking with this lad I find my attitude undergoing a rapid readjustment.

As I expected—most things are rationed—although generally your share is quite adequate. I would appreciate any standard brand of candy bar you can get or some Fanny Farmers—preferably the former. About here V-mail limits me. Be good, folks.
Love Frank

March 21, Wednesday
V-mail postmarked March 24, 1945

Dear Mother, Harry and Mike,

I have finally been assigned in the Air Forces after fooling around for over a year. We arrived at a new base Monday and I believe that it is from here that we will eventually see what this show is all about. Of course we have the usual training period to go through which we started this morning.

Living conditions here are really fine—there is no doubt that as long as you have to fight a war—this is the way to do it. Although I have had little contact with anything actually English as yet—it is obvious that privation and conservation are of utmost importance here—quite in contrast to our own people—they are quite aware of the war here. In spite of that, our quarters, food, and general living conditions are as comparable to our own as is possible. First time I've eaten off plates since I've been in the Army. I can see where my next big purchase will have to be a bike. Everyone rides them here on the Post and around the countryside—indeed there is very little distinction. Had my first English beer last night—it is called "bitter" or "mild" and I sampled the former last night. It is rather stale—not too much flavor but it goes down very easy and really packs a wallop.

We won't get any passes until we are actually on operations but then we get 6 hours each night and 48 hours every two weeks, which is not hard to take. Intend getting in touch with Dick—may get to check with Red Cross tonight—also the Bishop who should not be far off. Well, people, have to get this to a censor so you'll be getting it.
Love, Frank

Friday, March 23

Dear Mother, Harry and Mike,

Not an awful lot to report these days—going to school again as per usual. Tried to find out where Dick was last night but it was no soap. I'll have to wait until I go to London I guess before I can find exactly where he is. It will be quicker to write him which I no doubt will do soon.

How is everyone in the little old Piano Box these days? It has been some time now since I've had any news but that certainly is to be expected. By the way, be sure to let me know what happens to D. O'Hara—did she volunteer for overseas service—maybe I'll run into her.

Have not as yet bought me a bike. Am waiting around for a bargain. A pound here is supposed to be worth about $4.03, but the Yanks have made it rough for themselves here, and the boys who have been here any length of time claim they spend a pound here just as they used to spend a dollar at home. From what I hear they all see the Yanks coming in London.

We had ourselves a pint or so this evening on top of ice cream, which did not set too well with little Joe Ferniza, the engineer, but the rest of us weathered the storm O.K. Guess that's all today folks.
Love, Frank

Sunday, March 25

Dear Mother, Harry and Mike,

Well, all is well here in England as far as yours truly is concerned and I'm sorta wondering how you are. Some of the boys got letters yesterday so I expect I'll be getting some of the local news soon now. Today was Sunday but unfortunately I didn't have an opportunity to go to church. The training program is pretty full so I guess I'll just have to go to-morrow evening.

We have been having some dandy weather here lately. It certainly reminds me of home but the general dampness everywhere is quite different from home. My general bad luck with bicycles is still with me but good. I borrowed my Ball Turret Gunner's bike to go to the Red Cross last night so I could get me some hot coffee before turning in. As per usual I left it outside and someone made off with it. There I was snooping around for a bargain and before I know it I owe ma boy 9 pounds and still don't have a bike myself. Ah well, so it goes! I still haven't written Dick–thought I'd get to it tonight but I've been persuaded to go to the show. Guess I'll be off now so, be good, people.
Love, Frank

Wednesday, March 28

Dear Mother, Harry and Mike,

Well, I did get me some mail today. Didn't actually realize how much I'd missed hearing until I got three letters today and just about ate them up. I know you won't think much of these V-mail "notes" and yet it is the fastest method. I have not been too eager about picking up the habit of writing everyday for fear that when I do miss a day you'll worry more than usual so I guess I'll just write a little less often - when I can and I'm sure you'll understand.

I got my rations today! As I've said before they are quite adequate but I did get me some Camels today which are the first I've been able to get since I left the States. I would try to send some to you but I doubt very much that any package suspected of being cigarettes would get very far under any mail system these days. In this regard let me say that some cookies would certainly be getting appreciated.

Don't know as I told you before but we lost Taylor and Staeger and Morse and crew at Iceland and have not as yet been able to find out what happened to them. I have been very well schooled of late and expect a great deal more to come. The news today seems quite good and everyone has listened to it rather closely.

Some of the boys went to town last night and while I gather they had a good time they don't seem too eager to return soon. As per usual I am a slow starter on this going to town business and with the blackout and all, you cannot see a great deal in the evenings so I believe I'll wait until I can go somewhere during the daytime. As far as the gal situation is concerned things are quite as Jack Stolz described them only more so. With that in view I deem it to my advantage to go somewhere when I get the time where there are not quite so many soldiers. Of course I'll try to make London one day for they tell me that that is really the hub of English life. Heard some pretty weird stories about it and I sure do want to take a look into them.

Thanks a lot for the Index. I sure got a kick out of the Wes Peters' incident. I must write Gramp but have not been doing any writing lately except to you people. Take it easy with Mary Harry - discretion was ever the better part of valor.

Makes me feel good to hear of your latest purchase Mom - how about more of the same? It is also good to hear about Mike. I know you'll take good care of him - just watch his associations that's all.

Take good care of Lois, Harry, and I'll be thinking of you at the Brock next Saturday. Myself - I expect to be at the Red Cross at a dance. One week they have a dance for G.I.s and the next week for the officers. The same girls come each week. Our officers went last Saturday night and the girls told them they'd rather be with the enlisted men. Why? I don't know but I intend finding out Saturday I hope I hope.

We have movies here every night which are free and I've been going evenings but they're having "Buffalo Bill" tonight and to-morrow, which I thought was lousy so guess I won't bother with that one. Guess thas all for now people - Be Good.
Love, Frank

April 1945

Easter Sunday - V-mail

Dear Mother, Harry and Mike,

Am writing you this just to give you the latest "poop" and to more or less assure that not too many breaks occur in my not too steady stream of letters to you. I'll write you a regular one to try to answer the "Deluge" of mail I got yesterday and today. It sure makes a difference in the way you feel at the end of a day to find a line from home. I got 12 yesterday and 5 today all of which gets us up to date from you to the 22nd. Not bad by airmail, what? By the way 6 cents takes a letter airmail overseas! I enjoyed the birthday cards, and how, and the Easter ones arrived on the snoot on Easter Sunday which was good timing I'd say. All of which brings me to the point that I'll be shy on the Easter end again so please understand and forgive. A million reasons as usual—no place to buy and since they didn't pay us yesterday I didn't even have enough to cable as I planned but you know I'm thinking of you constantly and have pretty well in mind what I want to get you both when I get the jack and get to London or somewhere where I can do the job right. Of necessity must make this short. Church this morning and Stations Good Friday. Be good.
Love, Francis George

April 1, Easter Sunday

Dear Mother, Harry and Mike,

Just finished V-mail one—now to get down to a little more of the specific. Had to borrow this paper. It is the one thing I didn't bring—it is rationed in little pads but don't worry on that score I'll send them on "bum wad" if necessary. Of the 12 letters yesterday I got one from Sally McPherson with a snap—Huba Huba—not bad! Better than I remembered and the lads all approve too. Also one from D.A. Brown, V-mail which was mailed on the 23rd so from that, your airmails of 22nd got here just a day later, so decide what you want and let me know. Also letter from the Beals—namely Fran. Also Diane's and Gail's cute card. There were 2 birthday cards. Of the 5 I got

today–2 were cards and three letters from the ones who mean the most–just a second till I get them lined up in chronological order and I'll start a-answerin'.
2 minute wait.

The Birthday cards were grand–bet you picked them special. Kinda makes me wonder what the hell I'm doing all the way over here–ah well, so it goes.

March 5

Glad weather is clearing or has cleared at home for I guess your winter has been a ripper. It should be spring in England too I guess–things are starting to bloom here. Alter this morning was decked with daffodils–looked lovely and it makes you feel good to know that they go to such trouble for us. I for one appreciate it. How goes it without Mary? One thing I'm glad of–it will get Mother out more frequently and that is good for anyone. You speaking of dinner–we had chicken & dressing today. We don't have an awful lot of fresh meat here but it is adequate and the cooks here use plenty of ingenuity to make the canned variety different and tasty so that we do quite well. Don't worry about "offending" the Thompsons–it is a little late for that. I told him what I thought. I inferred that to me the deal had a strange smell and I told him I would "ferret out who's who and what's what in England regardless." Does that sound too strong–if it does that's rough I felt strong that day.

So Shero is out of olive drab–good for him. I've often wondered where he'll wind up at. I always felt he sorta dirty-dealed me but then I had it coming for I only used him! I do hope you get crew pictures soon now–be sure and let me know. As far as I know up to this point none of the fellow's folks have gotten them. First letter I wrote from England I asked for things (as usual) so there should be no question there.

March 6

Harry you seem to be getting to be quite the Gad about–good for you. Just make sure these guys you are carousing with will bring you home O.K. That's one thing I (in uniform) never had to worry about. Before I was in it, we brought each other home–after, I was always sure the M.P.s would get me if I misbehaved too obviously.

March 7

Your paper is O.K.–It carries the written words that mean so much to me and that really is all that counts! I'm surprised you didn't enjoy "To Have and Have Not" more than you did. They say that movies take the individual away in that he is in his imagination (the observer assumes the lead roles). In that direction I can account for all of us G.I.s enjoying it so much. What a dish–"I'm hard to get–all you have to do is whistle–you know–close your lips and blow." Huba–Huba.

I believe you show wisdom in holding on to the property. Something tangible is always marketable and staunch reinforcement to the peace of mind.

March 8th

Bowling scores of the 8th are very good I'd say–Just keep it up. You "cream" the pins as the boys here are "creaming" their targets and you'll be an excellent bowler. Glad you got cigarettes finally. Wish I could have sent more but there latterly at Savannah they were hard to get. I had about 6 packages shy of a carton myself when I started out. Seems to me they should have had them there but they didn't. We get 7 packages per week here but my Navigator doesn't smoke so I can pick up any extras I need.

March 9th

Bud McCurton could have made it but the only way I see is as a fighter pilot. My guess is that he'll stay in the Army after the war with permanent rank of Captain. Is he in the Air Corps.? Glad you gave Otts the cigarettes - I would have suggested it had I sent you more than I did but I wasn't sure how you felt on the subject.

March 13

(don't know what happened to 3 in between!)

I didn't send Ann my APO number. I thought you understood. It hasn't been easy in lots of ways but it has been the best way I figured.

OH - here's the 12th

Doesn't Pearly approve of what goes on in the trains these days? Too bad she didn't observe more before she let her little girl walk into it. It is lots of fun if you are taking part in it believe me! My engineer brought a brassiere with him he took off one gal in a train. Those "sit up all night" couches are much more fun & satisfying than a sleeping Pullman as peculiar as it may seem. Something doing every minute. I'm so glad you are to see Oklahoma. I envy you in that to be sure. Sorry about the "every-day letter" situation but I hardly deem it wise to let you expect a daily letter. There is just no percentage in it. I'll write as much as I can and reasonably often. It is only because I'm Combat Crew that I can do that.

Guess that will have to be all for tonight. I love you both so very, very much that you better be good and take care of yourselves.

Lotsa Love, Frank

Tuesday, April 3

Dear Mother, Harry and Mike,

Have had no word from you since Sunday and I'm wondering whether or not you have received my permanent APO I had best be patient I guess for we only had it for a little over two weeks.

There is little news to report beyond that training goes on and we are all just a little put out because they won't pay us until the tenth. I guess we can sweat it out till then and it may be a good idea for my pilot tells me we are quite likely to get a pass around that time. Here's hoping we get paid before we get the pass. If we do get a pass I don't suppose I'll have any idea of where I'll want to go. Of course I'll want to see London but I'm far more interested in seeing a bit more of the country and investigating some of the smaller places. I suppose I could run up to see the Bishop but I am advised that the best way is to start in London "So you get to know it sooner."

Hope you did get compass and send it on for they have taken my kit, which had one, away from me. I sure hope I'll be hearing from you soon now as it sure helps a lot - Be good, people.
Love, Frank

April 3 - Tuesday

Dear Mother, Harry and Mike,

April 3rd makes me a little reminiscent. That was the day I started radio school last year. As you can see I've come by some of that thin variety of paper myself and so I'll try to answer a few of the letters I got a couple days ago up to the last one.
March 20

So glad you finally heard from me (interruption) - I was about to bargain some candy bars for some eggs. A little English country boy comes in and gets my laundry. G.I. Laundry takes about 2 weeks and you can only send 9 pieces so although it is not too reasonable I have availed myself of the luxury of frequent changes of sox and underwear. Especially the former for unless you do, your feet are cold all the time. Showers here are about a mile away and I generally borrow a bike to go there. Needless to say I don't go as often as I did under these conditions as I did in the States for there is no guarantee of hot water and I choose only optimum conditions, being careful to avoid too much risk of catching cold. Thus I change frequently and make that do.

As I was saying it is good to know that you got the first letter. Be sure to keep me up on all the latest poop about our little Red Crosser D. O'Hara - would like to run into her over here. Jerry certainly seems to be taking his time - Is he in B-24s or 29s?

I feel very pious as I went to Communion this afternoon. Got up too late to make it Sunday and yesterday we flew a short practice mission so I finally got there today. Oh ho! So Harry is going to have to wear colored shirts - now he'll know how I feel deprived of the "family" white ones.

Thanks again for Easter cards - one from Mike too - so nice of him to remember me. Be sure and get him a big "T" bone steak for that job. I'd sure like to have him with me now. Really not much sense in getting a dog here even though I've been sorely tempted to do so. When you leave here they'd quarantine the pup for 6 months before they'd ship him and when he arrived in the States they hold him another 6 months so that takes the good out of it.
March 21

Those bowling scores 148, 177, 154 certainly look good to me boy! If you can keep that up I'd say you were really getting to be quite the Kegler. Maybe I shouldn't Kegel with you when I get back - you're getting too good for me.

Sandhurst sounds good - I don't blame you - I'd sure get some of that come summer if I were you. The picture of Mary Munday was cute so please thank her for me and give her a little pinch on the buttox, which I'm sure will do both you and her a lot of good. By the way if Dorshel is still wondering about me - give him my permanent and tell him to get busy.

Well, I guess that takes care of most of the questions so I'd ask nothing better than to get some more soon. I still have the Davy girls to write and the Beals and the Otts (haven't heard from them) and Gramp and Sally and Dan Brown. Don't know when I'll get around to that but we'll see.

Guess I'll have to be buzzing off now so be good, people -
Lotsa Love, Frank

April 4, Wednesday—No letter
Flew Mission 309: Kiel, Germany; Aircraft 42-97194

The primary target of this mission was to attack submarine installations at Kiel, Germany. 37 B-17s took off for this mission from the 95th Bomb Group, with 37 returning. One had been diverted to Sweden with two engines out due to heavy flak damage at the target. A total of 1,407 B-17 and B-24 bombers, from three air divisions flew this mission, making up 49 bomb squadrons. This was my father's crew's first combat mission. Their ship was named Good Pickin, and the report indicated that she sustained major battle damage. Big Sundin's crew was at the back of Group B. Their target was secondary to the Torpedo Boat Harbor, their target was the Fried Krupp Germaniawerft A.G. and at 10:34 a.m. they dropped six 1,000 lb. bombs from an altitude of 25,600 feet at a ground speed of 285 mph. Flying behind the lead in their Group B formation, was Heavy Date, with tail gunner Ray Perry.

April 5, Thursday—No letter
Flew Mission 310: Nurnberg, Germany; Aircraft 44-8272

The primary target of this mission was the rail flyovers east of Nurnberg (sic), Germany. My father's combat group was unable to attack the primary target due to clouds obscuring their vision and therefore attacked the secondary target, which was the main passenger station at the rail yard. A total of 1,354 bombers from three air divisions attacked Nurnberg (sic) that day, with the help of twelve groups of fighter escorts amid moderate to intense and fairly accurate flak. The ship they flew was Lisbeth II, and in formation, directly in front of Big Sundin's crew was none other than Heavy Date.

Friday, April 6
(First V-mail letter with new rank: Sgt. F.G. Thompson)
Dear Mother, Harry and Mike,

About time I got to this one I guess. I see I have an airmail here that wants a stamp. Stamps (airmail) here are rationed so I have to wait until I get my ration before I can get one. I should be able to get it this afternoon! How is every little thing in the "Little Old Piano Box?" As you can see I'm ragged, fat and sassy and they are keeping us quite busy in our capacity of "not quite Senior Birdmen." A chap came into the squadron a day or so ago who was in same barracks with me at Sioux Falls. It was good to see him for he is the first of that bunch I have run into. Have not as yet heard from Dick but suppose I could hardly hope to so soon. Received V-mail from Fran B. and Chuck Bordner along with yours of the 22nd. I'd say it was a good deal having the Red Cross as customers entirely now - for their convenience and yours. What is this I hear about a riot at the Falls at the market over chickens? The kind with feathers on? Hurray for Melba - plain to see she won't wander much longer. Fraid I've run out again - very unsatisfying aren't they?

Love, Frank

April 6, Good Friday

Dear Mother, Harry and Mike,

I am finally breaking down and writing a real letter for a change. Check the time it takes to get there and let me know how you'd prefer I write - via V-mail or like this?

I am out of school a bit early today so I thought I'd best sit down and dash off a few lines. I wrote Dick and Cal Taylor. I told Dick I'd leave it up to him as to the method and time to see him as I don't expect any appreciable pass time for quite a while now.

Was very pleased to get three letters and Index day before yesterday and am anxiously hoping for some more today. I can see right now that I'm hardly going to fully appreciate receiving V-mail but we'll see when I get some. As yet I've written no one in the States with the exception of you folks and I suppose I should get on my horse but I honestly don't have a hell of a lot of inclination.

We have been learning a good deal lately. It is all quite important and if your plane is in an important position the R.O. really earns his salt. The opinion here seems to coincide with the general view at home - that fighter attacks are of not too great importance these days for which we are all truly thankful.

My going to school lately has made it bad for getting to church these days although I hope to make "Way of the Cross" this evening at 7:30. Don't know just what the set-up will be Sunday but I hope they arrange school so I can make Mass. At home you had room to complain about these things for there was certainly no excuse there but here it is another story. Tried to get to Mass yesterday morning but left school just a little too late and the chapel was jammed to the doors and we couldn't get in no how.

As I said before, I'm looking forward to going to the Red Cross Dance tomorrow night and I'll let you in on all the details. What is the news on Don O'Hara and how about John Dick?

Weather here has been a bit cold and rainy although we do occasionally see the sun and it is cold, damp, and overcast most of the time. As usual I traveled with everything but the kitchen sink and so am quite well set on all types of clothing. I have plenty of cigarettes even though they're not Camels and we are all getting on quite famously. Most of the boys have been very fortunate in getting rid of their colds and I was glad to say good bye to mine in Savannah. Sgt. Shaffer, Ball Gunner, had trouble with his ears and has been grounded the past couple days, but we all hope he'll get over that soon. It doesn't make much difference now as we have yet to do any serious flying.

Things on the front are taking what we view as very good turns. The prize joke here is that "Monty is regrouping" or "Monty is massing." All the Yanks over here complain about the overall emphasis being laid on Monty's advances while Patton's comparative greater gains are little publicized. Of course here in Britain 50% of what a man makes is taken as income tax at the paying source. When people are taxed like that you have to give them something for their money but even so it does not seem right to most of us to hear only about old Monty.

A galaxy of rumors are everywhere here these days and along with General Arnold's statement that all aircraft and personnel will be transferred to the C.B.I. after this is over here has not gone too well with the veterans here. He also said that before 6 months the Air Force in the C.B.I. will be trebled so take it for what it is worth.

Some of the lads are eager to get going - others quite dread it and little Francis George just sits around patiently awaiting his lot and honestly believing that no matter what we do or where we go it will be for the best of all concerned. The main thing here is that I have objection to (this is beyond the rather primitive "honey pots") is that Gunners seem destined to pull some K.P. here. It seems that they have been taking so many permanent men into the infantry that they are short of mess personnel. I hope I don't catch too much of that.

I really don't need anything and we're all ragged, fat, and sassy - about the only thing I would like is some of that Kickapoo Joy Juice if you have lots of ingenuity in sending it. Don't take any chances about it though for if it was caught coming they would prosecute the return addressee. Sooo I guess that is about all for now so, be good, people.

Love, Frank

April 7, Saturday—No letter
Flew Mission 312; Kaltenkirchen, Germany; Aircraft 42-106993

Attack on Kaltenkirchen Airfield. 143 aircraft from the 8th Air Force with full fighter escort were part of the 1,311 aircraft from three air divisions that flew this mission. Bombs blanketed more than half of the only runway and airfield, the landing area, station buildings and stores, as well as the south dispersal, barracks and stores. The clouds that partially covered the field made photographs difficult. Of the three bomb groups from the 8th Air Force, the 95th was the only one that did not lose any bombers to enemy aircraft. The 100th BG lost two and the 390th BG lost one. This mission, Lisbeth II flew behind Big Sundin in formation where they were surrounded by six enemy aircraft - Me 262s and FW 190s. Big Sundin had his own troubles contending with two Me 262s. One flew through the formation from 3 o'clock, toward the lead ship under the formation with a P-51 on its tail. The second came from 11 o'clock, level, and into about 500 yards of Big Sundin, and then pulled off. For reasons unknown, my father's group was the only one not attacked in their formation. That day they drew Pretty Baby from the pool to fly the mission, and flying ahead of them in their group was Heavy Date and her crew, including tail gunner Ray Perry.

April 8, Sunday—No letter
Flew Mission 313: Eger, Czechoslovakia; Aircraft 42-106993
Back up in Pretty Baby, the target was a marshalling yard in Eger. The attack hit sorting sidings, the locomotive depot, reception and carriage sidings and the goods depot including goods wagons and one factory-type building near the marshalling yard. Two of Big Sundin's bombs got hung up over the target and had to be jettisoned in the North Sea en route back to the base. The mission statistics listed a total of 1,223 bomber sorties by B-17s and B-24s of which 1,184 were effective, dropping over 3,000 tons of bombs on the target. Total losses were recorded at 10, nine in the heavy bomber attacks and one fighter escort. Despite the losses, the mission was considered "very good." Heavy Date had the day off, and Ray Perry's pilot, Glovick, flew in Little Joe for this, their 35th and final mission.

April 9, Monday—No letter
Flew Mission 314: München-Riem, Germany; Aircraft 43-38106
The first priority target was the München-Riem Airfield, which was about 5.5 miles east of Munich, Germany. Among the targets hit were three hangars, 25 aircraft of the 47 visible ranging from small to large, station buildings, dispersals, landing grounds and runways as well as workshops, the ammunition dump, the perimeter, and taxi-tracks. Low clouds forced Big Sundin's group to bomb lower than the briefed altitude. Sundin was in the third force of six group formations. 228 B-17s dropped almost 600 tons of bombs on the air field. Flak was fairly accurate and considered meager to moderate. All told, 31 ships had minor battle damage, 5 had major damage and four B-17s were lost that day. Big Sundin flew Starduster for the first and only time, and up ahead in their formation was the ever-present Heavy Date.

April 10, Tuesday
Flew Mission 315: Burg, Germany, Aircraft 44-6475
Big Sundin flew Round Tripper in Squadron D for this mission; neither Heavy Date nor Ray Perry were along on this one. The first priority targets were the hangars and runways of the Burg Airfield, just outside Burg, Germany. Unlike the previous missions, this one was wrought with malfunctions and failures ranging from electrical systems and scopes to transmitters

and rack malfunctions. In addition, cameras and engines were malfunctioning, but the worst were the losses of one bomber to enemy aircraft and a second that crash landed due to damage from enemy aircraft, of the latter fortunately all the crew reported O.K.

Sundin's group arrived over the target eight minutes early. Sundin reported seeing one Me 210 and five Me 262s. The attacks came from two Me 262s and one Me 210 starting 6 minutes before bombs away. Flying at 18,500 feet, the first Me 262 attacked from four o'clock low, then the second, and finally the third. Two Me 262s were shot down by P-51s, but four minutes later, two FW 190's attacked, from the same direction. The first exploded before it reached the bomber formation; it is unknown what happened to the second. Sundin's crew claimed one enemy aircraft, which would later be confirmed to have been shot down by waist gunner Kimpel. Unsure of the time of the other two attacks, one just before the first and the other about 10 minutes after they had hit their target. These attacks also came in from four o'clock, straight on, but broke off at about 9 o'clock under the tail. No fighter support was in sight.

The flak at the target was meager to moderate, but the distress of my father's fellow airmen was severe and, in some cases, deadly. Shortly before bombs away, two B-17s were hit by enemy aircraft and blew up. No chutes were observed. Then, about 15 minutes after bombs away, one B-17 from the group behind my father's ship was hit by enemy aircraft and went down in a spiral. No chutes were observed then either, but the crew did see the escape hatches coming off. All attacks that day were only on Squadron D. The Burg mission was reported as having a "fair" result, though in all it claimed 20 B-17s and one B-24 between the three air divisions whose 1,315 bombers flew the sorties that day.

Of all the missions I read about, this is the one that disturbed me the most, and it must have disturbed my father the most as well because there was never a letter from him on the day of a mission, in all those letters, or through all those missions, only this one. I've tried to keep my mission descriptions somewhat brief and concise, although they are some 60 pages on average; however this particular mission to Burg was a total of 139 pages and was not declassified until 2010. Each page created a visual that has never left me, which helped me understand why, on this occasion my father wrote home, caused me to read much more meaning into the first and last sentences to his loved ones after returning safely from Burg.

April 10, Tuesday

Dear Mother, Harry and Mike,

Just one of the unsatisfactory type - purpose to let you know that all is well and me and my crew are all fine. Weather has been a bit on the chilly damp side as is to be expected here but I find myself longing for one of those days when the sun seems to be soaking into your bones. I got lots of mail tonight - it is wonderful to come in to some mail. Glad you received and like the pictures of the crew - glad too that you have, and are writing to my present address - latest I've had is Harry's of the 28th. The Beals have been grand about writing - I must owe them 5 or 6 by now but can't make the answers just yet. Their sox are a Godsend! Must get some rest now and have my laundry to put away. Please keep well and watch my boy Mike and please don't forget the "Big Sundin's" crew in your prayers.
Lotsa Love, Francis George

Wednesday, April 11

Dear Mother, Harry and Mike,

Today has been a beauty - lots of sun for a change and it is rather unusual here. Generally we have an overcast which makes the day rather dull.

Things are going fine here as you have probably read in the papers. Big doings every day and it does us all good to see what a splendid job the boys on the ground are doing and I judge we are doing O.K. too. I was so glad to get mail last night and also glad to hear that you might be getting me some candy bars. Never ate much of that stuff at home but there we had those good old cakes and pies. We are all looking forward to a pass one of these days but I fear we will have to wait a while longer for that now. I guess I didn't tell you the only good news - we recovered Shaffer's bicycle and on pay-day I didn't owe him the 9 pounds I expected I would. So I have about 10 pounds now equal to about 40 dollars to have me a rip-snorter when we do get a chance to go on pass. I guess that is about all the dope I can legibly get on this one so, be good, people.
Lotsa love, Frank

Saturday, April 14

Dear Mother, Harry and Mike,

I have plenty of letters of yours to answer although I haven't had any during the past couple days. However, before I start on them I want to tell you a bit about what I've been doing extra curricula the past couple evenings.

The night before last four of us, Shaffer, Ferniza, Spencer, and F.G.T. borrowed bikes and set out for a town some 3 miles distant. We had ourselves some Bitter and Mild, chased around after what few women there were - gave our gum to Kiries and started back. Joe and I ran into a couple Land Army girls so we detoured - put them on the bikes and rode them home. They must have iron bound bottoms to take that stuff but you know us - we were irritable. Anyway they put us on a work detail the next day as long as we weren't working and we didn't care too much for that, sooo we saw the Big Sundin and we got passes and we took off again in the afternoon. This

town was further and we didn't have bikes but we bummed a ride on a Jeep and trailer. Friday was a good day to go for it was Market Day and the Pubs were open all day. We made the most of it you can be sure. We almost bought a horse and buggy too but we decided to wait until next payday. Of course you can get almost nothing to eat except Chips (French fries) and sausage or fish. We had to settle for that. We did a lot of looking around and finally wound up at a dance that evening. We had a fairly good time and I got my first real impression of English women. Lord knows they have been hit hard as far as clothes and shoes are concerned but I conclude that most of them don't make the most of what they have got. They lack that old Yankee ingenuity if you know what I mean. We hope for a pass to London soon now but we'll have to wait for more new crews to become operational before we can go. Weather was beautiful the past 2 days but today has ended up in rain which has chilled things off as per usual.
March 26

I did miss going to Communion Easter but went the following Tuesday - I guess I was lucky to get to Mass Easter. While I think of it I did manage to write Gramp and the Beals a couple days ago. Also I bought some English Bloater Paste for Gramp and will send it on as soon as I can get it wrapped. You can be sure that I'll write either Leon or Mrs. Devitt if they write and I can manage it. Again I'm glad you liked the picture. The little fellow you speak of is Joe Ferniza - of Mexican parentage. He keeps us all laughing most of the time. You ask me what I want. Any canned foods or fruits you could send would be greatly appreciated. Some tomatoes maybe. They told us today that a slight shortage exists on food and it manifested itself in this evening's meal. We eat just about anything in sight these days. We can get eggs and they get them for us for breakfast - you walk into the mess hall - up to the stove and tell the cook how you want them. Not bad what?
March 28

Biggest News of all I forgot to mention - the death of the President! We felt very surprised and rotten about it all at the same time. I said I thought he'd go if he got this last term but I thought he'd linger in sickness. The English people realize they've lost the best friend in America they've ever had. It is a shame for as the representative of the U.S.A., he was known admired and had done international political business all over the world. Now the first groundwork - the trusting of a representative will have to be done all over again. It is a pity for the country, for the soldiers and the forgotten American working men. They didn't treat him kindly and their time for repentance is yet to come. Hope you had a good time at that dance Harry and conducted yourself as I would have wanted you to. No the Thompson's never sent me any addresses or such so I guess we'll have to manage without them. But ask I will.
March 30

Bowling scores sound good - just keep it up that's all. Don't blame you Harry for wanting movement of some description in your job but from my present place I

would hesitate to advise you. Do as you think best as I know you will. Seems to me you are established there long enough to be worth more responsibility and more pay.
March 31

The Yanks certainly are forging ahead these days aren't they? It sure looks good to us although there is no apparent end in sight as yet. Won't be, I guess, until the Nazi Regime gives way to some other group. They won't do business with Hitler - we know that.
April 4th

I guess in this one we'd better get a few things straight. First on the mail situation. I've been trying to do better and hope you don't get too disgusted with me. As with this one - when I get a chance and the time I try to write a longer one. I can see you don't quite understand what we're up against here. How often does Mrs. O'Hara get a letter from Don or even from Jerry and he's still in the States? How often does Mrs. Jepp get one and her Bob is working in a hospital where he can write with ease. My dears, you just can't write about what is filling your whole being. Same way on the church situation. I am in a combat zone - I am subject to orders and I can't be at Kirk and executing those orders too. I don't think I'll be able to go to-morrow again so please pray for me. I do my best to get there during the week. They have Mass once each week day and twice Sunday but sometimes you just can't make it. Sweetheart you're telling me that church is a must? Mustn't worry about Jerry getting home Mom. At best I can say it this time - somebody has to fight this war. I could have had an extra blouse and had it cut down merely for just calling for it at Gulfport. Mike Salupo offered to get me one but it was too much bother at the time. Air Corps personnel are the only ones who can wear a Battle Jacket you know. Anyway they are starting to issue a snazzy one, which is not cut down but was designed and fabricated as a Battle Jacket. Some of the groups have them over here already. Only Master Sgts. have them here as yet but we hope to get them soon now. We haven't named a plane as yet for we left our new one at a pool when we came over. We fly the 336th ship but there are too many crews for each one to have a plane of their own. Hence no St. Christopher's medal but I have one around my neck - Robinson - Bombardier has one too.

We just got an inkling where Taylor and Staeger are - hope to look them up when we get a chance.

I might add this little note in passing. This Bitter we drink has the same effect on one as beans only worse. We have a terrible time among us. In the Big Bird or in the barracks we are all little Bowls of Roses and at times can hardly stand one another. It creates an almost impossible situation at times and we've had a lot of laughs out of it.

Well people - big day on the morrow so I have to shave and get to bed. Please don't mind me and keep writing.
Lotsa Love, Frank

Sunday, April 15—No letter

Flew Mission 317: Royan, France, Aircraft 42-102455

There were a total of 17 bomb targets designated in the area around Royan where there were two German forts, just south at Pointe de Grave area near the mouth of the Gironde estuary. Little remained intact after the final attack. Flying Lucky Lady, Big Sundin's squadron was assigned the first priority target. This mission marked the introduction of the use of napalm by the US Air Forces, a highly flammable incendiary bomb made using gasoline thickened with special soaps. The mission was rated "fair," most likely due to numerous malfunctions, most of which included bomb rack malfunctions. 1,345 aircraft, of which almost 1,000 were B-17s, targeted 17 German strongholds, coastal, and flak batteries. 1,277 aircraft dropped over 2,800 tons of bombs, of which 1,200 were napalm, destroying the entire town of Royan. No flak was reported, and all aircraft returned with no battle damage. The report I read was labeled S E C R E T on every page, and was only declassified in 2010, a testimony to its severity. Though the significance of this mission may not be recognized in the history books, to the crew of Lucky Lady, although never spoken of, Royan would remain their most disturbing mission.

Thursday, April 19

Dear Mother, Harry and Mike,

Here I am at last to give you the latest "poop from the group." I do deserve harsh words this time for being so lax but the reason is that our pass came through Sunday night after we had put in a long day - from 12:30 Sunday morning until about 2:30 in the afternoon.

Of course combat crew passes come through on very short notice so late Sunday evening we heard and there were great groans amid the shining of buttons and polishing of shoes.

The next morning we took off for the English capital! Incidentally we are extended a fine courtesy here in respect to R.R. travel. I suspect the U.S. pays for it in the end but, unlike home, here on any pass 48 hours or more we sign up for a travel warrant and we travel absolutely free of any charges.

Once in London we went to the Red Cross and registered for two nights - it comes to about 40 cents a night there. Of course there were many things we wanted to see and do. Unfortunately my crew does not enjoy the good time that Taylor and the rest of us got so much kick out of in New Orleans and since you must travel with your crew - only ones that get off with you and only ones you know in London - we had a rather riotous time - for me that is. I did manage to work in a few things I wanted to see and am enclosing bottom half of a tour we took. Spent best part of an afternoon in Madame Tussauds Wax works. Managed to get through a couple book shops and a couple antique shops. Boy they certainly want money for anything you want to buy in these places. Couldn't see investing in anything until I get hold of someone who knows their way around a bit - they see the Yanks coming - even restaurant waitresses have explicit instructions to jack the price up when Yanks appear.

We spent one evening in Covent Garden, which is a large dance arena. One of two bands play all evening in shifts and it is really a well set up place. It is very large - music is good and the place is tiered with balconies where there are tables and chairs and you can snack while you intermission. Girls - they are there by the hundreds and there are some mighty attractive ones too. However I'd say you have to be mighty careful what you get hold of. Here everything is on a strictly mercenary basis. They have the typical American trick of picking up a girl and seducing her completely licked here. Some of the fellows took them home - got all worked up and then she sprung some hard luck story and asked 3-5 pounds for the night with bacon and eggs for breakfast. It is really a riot - little revolting at first but after while you can't do anything but laugh. Then, at night of course, prostitution is rampant everywhere - they call the gals Piccadilly Commandos or Rangers and you almost have to beat them off with a club. That particular business is a lucrative one here for as you know British income tax of 50% is taken out at the source so that most incomes fall very short of what they once were. No one can check up on what those dollies make and then too they can't draft them for work unless they can catch them and they are constantly on the move. There we have the supply and you can just imagine where the demand comes in when all these boys - particularly the infantry etc come in. Those fellows aren't paid month on end when they come to London so that they probably have accumulated 5-8 months pay and do the English ever know it. Also the Air Forces get good money! This same thing started in N.Y.C. not so long ago but police disguised as sailors cleaned them all out - but not so here. The Yanks are really having a Hey Day and don't quite realize how much they are paying for it. Lest I give completely the wrong impression - just as anywhere else in the world, anything worth having must be sought and just before leaving I believe we found about what we were really looking for.

The second evening we spent in a large Pub in Angel, which is a good bit outside of London. They had an orchestra and we did some dancing with plenty of women there - in abundance. I found myself way outside the city proper after the underground had stopped and I didn't know where the hell Piccadilly was. I finally got a cab - they're cheaper here than at home if you're not drunk and can haggle with them - and low and behold there was a Commando already in it. She and the driver insisted I take the ride to where she was going before coming back to where I wanted to go. Whew - what a rat race that was! Anyway I was glad and took a little pride in the fact that throughout I came out unscathed - thank the dear Lord for that.

The following noon we took some girls to lunch from a Government Shippers office and they are really quite nice and would seem to be well bred English girls of middle class families. We could get their names but their people don't approve of

Yanks (which is in itself a good sign) so to get in touch with them again will have to be done through the office.

I wanted to take in a play but one running with A. Lunt & L. Fontaine was sold out. Next time I'll go to DuPont's Sales offices and see what can be done - they should be able to get me tickets. On eating - it is hard to get anything to fill you and coming back on the train yesterday I was glad I had had the foresight to hang on to some K-rations. We found two places where we could buy steak but although it was the best eating I've done since I came here it was mighty sketchy steak. Liquor was our biggest expenditure. We paid about 13.50 per for two 5ths, which the officers got us here on the base and 18 dollars / 5th in London. Seems to me I paid for a lot of liquor I didn't drink but then I'll know better next time. That says most of it I guess - now we are patiently sweating out another two weeks and pay day before we can go again. Also on the 21st of this month the Group has a big party in honor of our 300th mission which was put in shortly after we arrived here and which, incidentally, permits us to wear the Presidential citation. That promises to be a big affair.

Of myself I am very well and none the worse for wear. The war news is splendid and I suppose you noted Eisenhower's statement that strategic warfare is over. That means our effort is of a strictly tactical and support nature now. Haven't worked since Sunday - we all wonder how much more work there will be for us here. Our crew is nowhere near finished and it looks very probable that we'll see the C.B.I. one of these fine days. Had hoped to see a bit of Paris while here but may have to be content with flying over it.

Have had no mail since Sunday since they hold over mail when we're on pass and I won't be able to get it until this evening. Try to write again then - may have a few more impressions.

Be good, people.
Lotsa Love, Frank

April 19

Dear Mother, Harry and Mike,

Well, here goes number two for today. I thought I'd have some mail from you folks-ies after being away for 3 days but no such luck. I did get a letter from Sally McPher-son - she is a grand person and writes a darn cute letter. Keeps me up on all the latest dope from the office angle of DuPont which helps. She also sends me that overseas copy of the Gazette. Don't really know how or why I rate all this, but it's nice work when you can get it.

This day has been one of complete rest for me. I got up early with some of the lads who had to fly a practice mission and had breakfast early. Came back to the sac and straightened things up - got my O.D.s together and was at the new dry cleaning estab-lishment bright and early with them. I didn't wait for my boys for I wanted to take them in and get them done. That proved to be a fatal mistake for the other 4 hot rocks went down later - told the people there that they were going on furlough and had to have stuff tonight. Well, they got away with it and are going to get their clothes tonight. They had the squadron party in mind and I had forgotten about it so I guess I'm just stuck. Ah well, I'm not too enthused about this brawl anyway (sour grapes).

I did have a call by phone from Cal Taylor last night when I got back. He had called the night before. I couldn't get near the Red Cross phone last night so I'll have to try again tonight. I sure would like to meet up with those boys again - we had such good times together. In London we met up with the Pilot on Zona's crew. He (the pilot) and Sundin are big buddies but we didn't manage to meet any of the rest of the crew.

Anyway getting back to "My Day" - after I took my clothes over I went to the combat library where I wrote you a letter. Also wrote Chuck Bordner - he seems quite interested and always gives me the latest poop. After that I ate (it takes me so long to write) and then bought my PX ration for the week, returned to the squadron - slept about an hour and then took in the afternoon movie. Got in in time for mail and then ate again - ah it's a great life. Sooo here I am. Can't think of much more to say so I'll say Cheerio (I'm a-learning) and be good.
Love, Frank

Friday, April 20
Flew Mission 321: Oranienburg, Germany; Aircraft 43-38333
   Having flown their last mission in early April, Ray Perry and his crew became official members of the "Lucky Bastards" and returned Stateside. Not so for Heavy Date, who remained in the pool awaiting her next crew. Today was Big Sundin's first of three missions in this Big Bird. The Oranienburg mission targeted seven towns forming an arch west of Berlin from north to south. These targets consisted of marshalling and railroad yards, passenger station, station and carriage sidings, and business and residential areas. There were 11 group formations of over 300 B-17s. Of the 35 aircraft that took off from the 95th, 33 returned. Two aborted, one due to engine failure, and one had a supercharger fail. None of the 35 aircraft sustained any battle damage.

Saturday, April 21

Dear Mother, Harry and Mike,
Just a line or so to let you know all is well with this segment of the family circle. I am at present all dressed and ready to start taking in some of the main events of our 300th mission party. I'm waiting for the boy to come who picks up my laundry and he better get here soon now. Have not been doing much lately to speak of. Today has been some day - a very busy one for ground personnel for this party business is really theirs. They all have been here some time now and hence have steady girls in neighboring districts. They all have their girls on the base and believe me the sky is the limit. Also have about 54 barrels of beer in the mess hall - 50 gallons/barrel.

Tomorrow they are even going to have horse races with pari-mutual betting. The racing will take place around the air strip perimeter - special U.S.O. shows at the theatre tomorrow and a midnight show tonight.

Taylor called me again this evening. English phones are Hell. I could hardly hear him - however we are making arrangements to get together soon.

Well dears, must be goin off now - I stand a good chance of getting to church tomorrow for a change so I don't believe I'll make much of a night of it.

Be good, my dears.

Love, Frank

Sunday, April 22

Dear Mother, Harry and Mike,

This has been a lazy Sunday - one for which I have been thankful. As I said before they went to a great deal of trouble to give all personnel on the base a good time on this 300th mission celebration. Last night there were three different dances on the Post. One at the Officers club, one in the Combat Crew mess and one in the NCO club. The first and last the enlisted men on my crew could not attend. Naturally we couldn't go to the Officer's dance but merely as "Buck" Sergeants we could not go to the NCO dance - you have to be Staff Sgt. or better. Sooo we took in the one open to us. It started out quite sanely but that didn't last long. They had a colored band which was really O.K. In another section of the mess hall they had (I've been told) 54 barrels of "Limey" beer. Now what a mess that turned out to be. The stuff was ankle deep on the floor before it ran completely out. There were a few fights and much angling over a shortage of available women. Spencer and I managed to get hold of a couple. I've run into some cold propositions in my day but that [one] was really a problem. I finally warmed mine up a bit but it took some doing. I left before 12 at night and was fast asleep before the rest of the boys returned.

I got up about 10 this morning, went to Mass and Communion and came back to the barracks and roused the rest of my boys. We all went to chow then - they had real steaks for us - fried individually and not baked. They were darn good eating let me tell you. It took us a long time to sweat out the line for there were lots of boys who had guests and then too the boys had broken so much pottery and lost so much silver the night before that we had to slowly take our turn. After we had eaten we came back to the Sqd. and armed with reading material we returned to the Post theatre and sweated out a U.S.O. show. It was quite good. At about the same [time] they had Sulky horse races around the runway perimeter and a musical in one of the hangers. So you can see there was plenty doing all over the Post yesterday and today.

One thing that impressed us a bit around here is the English girls regard for Rank. In London it was quite the same thing. In London I hadn't bother to change my stripes and last night I went down with a field jacket on. It is a woolen one, which was issued shortly after I got here. I have sewn nothing on it and didn't even wear wings yesterday and I found myself quite distained. At home the girls seem to notice to be sure, but they realize that in the citizen Army of the U.S.A. the Rank doesn't necessarily bespeak the man. Here the officers have told me that the girls would rather go out with E.M. than officers so you figure it out.

Well people, I guess that is about all for today. Today was a holiday so no mail call so no mail. It has been over a week now since I've had word from you two. I expect it is a hold up on those Airmails somewhere along the line and I expect mine to you are held up too. Ah well - war is Hell - just be good, people.
Love, Frank

Monday, April 23

Dear Mother, Harry and Mike,

I'll get started with this now and expect I'll have to finish later this afternoon. We have not been actually real busy of late for we have been doing some practice flying and have been having some false alarms on the real thing.

The way things look to me they are due for a radical change soon. Probably start PT soon and lot of detail. They have been trying to get us in the latter score lately but we try to get up early enough and clear the area - you know they can't put you to work if they can't find you. Weather has taken a turn for the colder and damper of late. We had 2 1/2 beautiful days for our pass in London but the weather is hardly as pleasant here.

Well, I was interrupted as I expected. We lost our Bombardier. That is, he was put in a pool I believe for lead crews. Sooo now we have what is called a togglier. Our waist gunner and armorer will be advanced to that position in the nose and I believe we get a new waist gunner. I hate to lose Robinson - he was the only other right hander on the crew and a mighty good boy, but that is the way it goes. He was by far the smoothest operator of the officers and it was a pleasure to watch him work. He was the oldest officer on the crew a year younger than I am. All this leads up to the point that being eager for knowledge and having been assigned nothing else to do for the afternoon I went with Kimpel to be checked out as togglier. Not that I ever expect to do the job but I figure that anything you ever learn [won't] go to waste.

I got back to find Mother's letter of the 11th and Harry's of the 12th. First I've had in over a week. I had a hunch something was wrong - I never thought of that. What a mess it must have been at Perry's. It is terrible! I don't believe it has soaked in completely yet - I hope it doesn't. Yes, their big topic of conversation is gone - it is such a shame and, although it was hard to swallow at times, I feel so terribly sorry for them - all of them - for as an officer in the Air Corps he was their beacon in life. They live so much by comparison with the other fellow and yet they haven't had the easiest of lots - would that God might have spared him for them. I was going to write you that I wondered why he hadn't got in touch with me - I brought some Seagram's 7 Crown with me that he wanted and have had a hell of a time hanging on to it. Doesn't make a great deal of difference now I guess.

My boys, that is, the enlisted men, are not a too happy bunch today. It seems that last night they went to a local pub - Ferniza, Kimpel and Spencer and came back rather well oiled. Not drunken I understand, but feeling good and very talkative. I don't understand why I wasn't with them; mostly I guess because I feel Ferniza & Spencer don't drink beer often enough and when they do they drink too much. Anyway they went direct to the officer's barracks - roused the boys and raised particular hell as I understand it. I was in bed when they came in here last night and they woke me up. Anyway the Rank didn't care much for the intrusion and although things were very rosy and buddy buddy this morning when we thought we were going to fly - it develops that someone of the Officers tried to prevent our next promotion and also had withdrawn the next passes for London for the aforementioned 3 E.M. This is a sad state of affairs - glad I missed it but I have to live with the boys and it makes a rather delicate situation. It is too bad the boys had to do it - no matter how chummy you are with officers you just can't barge in on them. Myself I am dubious about any social contact with officers. The Army won't have it and actually I believe there would be some question in my mind if I would seek it even if we were all civilians. You know that old story - you can choose your friends. At times they act a little too young - inexperienced with life itself I think - they are still experimenting with things that they should take better care of. I guess they don't realize that much of their future depends on how they conduct themselves these days. However aside from the social end I have the utmost confidence in them in their respective jobs - they're all damn good and I'm proud to follow them.

Well folks, I guess I'd better buzz off - it would be rough if the Rank decided to read this one wouldn't it - they censor our mail and they haven't read any of them as yet. They have been rather good to us I'd say.

Be good, people.
Lotsa love, Frank

April 24, Tuesday

Dear Harry,

It is high time I owed the bread-winner of the family a letter so I'd best be at it. Mother's very terse letter of yesterday bringing news of Dick's death has had a bad effect on me. It was not so much what she said but rather the brevity of the letter itself which affected me. It is quite plain that she is worried heartsick and it will be even worse now I suppose. I can't say don't worry myself for I do a bit of it myself and knowing Mother's nature I can hardly see any solution - the big pity of it being that it does none of us any good.

Perhaps you'll understand why now I have been purposely far from regular on my letters to you fellows. It is mainly that I don't want you to get to looking for that letter every day and then worrying extra when it doesn't arrive for some reason. Try to remember that no news is the very best news you can have. If anything has happened the government will let you know sooner than my airmails could ever get there. Then too if you ever get an M.I.A. (missing in action) don't hope too much but just remember that right now chances are better for getting out of Germany than they have ever been. You must know from the papers that right now things are better for the type of war we fight than it has ever been. We have the best equipment obtainable and we have plenty of fighter support! To me - these P-51 pilots and our ground crews are the real heroes of the war. Let me tell you this - if you ever meet a 51 pilot - buy him a drink or take him home to dinner - I personally would kiss their rump in the middle of Falls Street and give them an hour to draw a crowd - they are wonderful.

Of course the Luftwaffe is supposed to be dead but we have seen them - John K (waist gunner) got official credit for shooting one down - we found out yesterday. It was one of those new "jet jobs." As a rule, the 51s don't let them get in that close but they were busy elsewhere the day we were shooting at that one. They sneak into a formation and are almost gone and the damage is done before you know it. Most of the 51s get them before they get too close - one will hand them off, then when the Kraut turns to run he gets just so far and runs into a couple more. They herd him off into a corner and shoot the living piss out of him. We have seen some combat, but we have painfully few missions in and it is a long haul. Personally, I have visions of seeing the C.B.I. one of these fine days. With bases so close as Iwo Jima our Big Birds should almost be able to make it. Can't say as I'd like it as well - too much water and too many bugs - and no London but they tell me you don't have much choice. I've seen Paris from the air and the outskirts of Berlin and a lot of other places so far out believe me, old 450 1/2 - 9th Street will look pretty good one of these days.

Our base is quite well laid out. It is widely dispersed as is to be expected but places we are required to go they have trucks to take us - places we get to of our own volition we manage by foot or bike. Movies show from 2 PM - last one at 8:30 and we have a Red Cross Aero Club where I go and get my hot tea every night before going to bed. The food is fine and shows that a lot of ingenuity has been made to give us Spam in a different way. We do get chicken and steak sometimes and ice cream about 2 times a week. Boy - it is heaven compared to what a lot of our boys are having to go through. Every morning we fly a mission we get eggs fried just the way you want them - fruit juice every morning and when we get back we get a big double shot of Cognac or Bourbon. A couple of those really send you on an empty stomach after being in the air 9-10 hours.

During the days we don't fly we may be doing practice missions or going to school or just dodging the duty Sgt. I have done a good bit of reading over here but hardly the writing I should have. Just is hard to know what to say to people and still you want to hear from them so much. I have written Gramp once - will have to soon again I expect. I got him some Bloater paste but have been unable to get a box to put it in.

Haven't as yet heard any word from the Otts - I suppose I should write them but I never have the required ambition.

Women here are sure some proposition. What we met in London were certainly a mercenary bunch. These country girls out around here have very red complexions including their legs - they look sorta purple. Some of the gals we saw at Covent Garden were really lovely but you never know what you're going to get there. The best bet I'd say were these office girls we met our last few hours in London. I told you we stayed at the Red Cross last time, well, for each room they have one or two girls to make beds and keep them clean. Man that was a riot - they were only chamber maids and really nothing to fool with but did you ever wake up in the morning to find a young and attractive gal sitting on your bed - one arm over you looking down - Huba Huba. We really gave them a hard time, but anyway, they told us which room to request when and if we go back. The place we stayed was formerly a gentleman's club and this room is one of the smaller ones. Only 6 bunks with a private bath. What a wicked deal that would be!

If I can possibly arrange it next time I think I'll try to get my travel warrant made out for from here to Cambridge - to London and back to here again - just sorta look over the place don't ya know.

Well Bub, I guess that is the bulk of the poop from the group today. Be good and keep prayin so that one of these days God willing we'll all be back together again. Love, Frank

THE REVELATION

Present Day

It was as surprising to me as it was to my father to learn of Dick Perry's death. I didn't expect it, though I'm not sure what I was thinking, after all they were fighting a war in which tens of millions died. After reading my father's letter to his brother, my heart went out to him. At this point, I wasn't quite sure if Dick was a friend, classmate, or relative, but after reading that he'd died I found I could not go on typing until I found out just who Dick was and how he fit into my father's life.

The first thing I did was reread the letters I'd already typed to find every possible mention of Dick Perry. This was much easier than having to reopen the hundreds of letters I'd typed up to this point. Gotta love technology. In doing so, it struck me that there was a tone of familiarity with the Perrys that went beyond friendship and was more personal in nature, which led me to consider that my father and Dick may have actually been related. Back to the genealogy site I went.

Accustomed now to the references made to the Perrys vs. the Thompsons, my first approach was to look at relatives on his mother's side of the family. On several occasions my father had referenced Aunt Maime, and knowing nothing about my grandmother's side of the family at this point, I started my search there. I found that she had a brother Frank George, no coincidence there, and a sister Mary Ellen. I asked my mother if Maime may have been a nickname for Mary Ellen in her era and when she said yes, it all started coming together. I found that Mary Ellen, Maime, had married John Robert Perry, and Dick was their eldest son. My heart sank. Dick had been my father's cousin. No wonder his death had hit him so hard.

With this new knowledge that the Perrys were related, I went back with this new perspective and reread all the mentions of Dick, Maime, and any other Perry. It was clear that there had been some sort of ongoing sibling discord that seemed to resolve itself and then reappear, not unlike most families; although my father's letter to his brother alluded to some of this, it was also clear that his grief for his relatives was deeply felt. Once this had all settled in, I couldn't suppress wanting to know how Dick had died and if my father had ever found out. In a strange way I felt that I should try to find out what had happened to Dick for my father's sake. I wish I'd have left that mystery unsolved.

Armed with only Dick's name, the unit he flew in, that he'd been a pilot, and the type of plane he'd been flying, I went back to all my research links and came up empty. I then tried a Google search for his name; only one link came back with an identical match. It was a website for the East Tennessee Veterans Memorial Association. The page was honoring Kenneth R. Rader, 2nd Lt. and crewmember along with Richard M. Perry, 1st Lt., two other crew members and two passengers who had died in a non-battle accident on March 27, 1945. Also listed was the type of aircraft and the ship serial number. This was a pivotal discovery. I knew that having the ship number, I could go to the website where I'd found the accident report for Heavy Date and learned about my father's ditching. I had this sense of foreboding. Did I really want to find out what had happened or was it better left alone? I debated this for days and finally made the decision to find out what'd actually happened to Dick Perry and his crew.

HORHAM, ENGLAND - PART 2

1945

Thursday, April 26

Dear Mother, Harry and Mike,

I hit the jackpot today with 4 letters from 450 1/2 and I guess I'd better get going in the way of an answer. I have been and will, for a few days, be flying my missions in ground school. Operations regularly put so many crews on a ground school schedule to prevent them from getting rusty so that is it for the present. They needed a few radio operators for something - took one I guess from a couple squadrons. In our squadron they put 3 names in a hat and drew one - mine wasn't drawn but another fellow in the barracks who came here with us. Well, it turns out today - they wanted men with some combat experience - he is going to A.T.C (Air Transport Command) which is not too bad. As far as combat danger is concerned he will be relatively free from it. I am glad for him for he is married. He is quite immature about a lot of things but he seems quite happy about it. For some time now I have ceased to speculate and hope about these things. Wherever God sees fit to put me I will make the best of it. At any rate I should not have been too keen about leaving my crew. That is just about all the poop from here - nothing doing and we all wonder how long it will last.

April 8

Purchases of April 7 sound dandy Harry - I'm still hoping for a look at you in Homburg and new coat - must be quite the man about town - Huba Huba. In as much as you speak of it - my lighter has never been worth a darn - may try to send it home soon and you see what you can do about it. I just have to get a box now - tried all over the base to find one this afternoon but no luck. I want to send Gramp's fish and then we all got the Air Medal yesterday so I want you to keep that for me. We earned it a couple weeks ago and we finally were presented with it by Major yesterday.

April 9

I'm glad you both had such a swell time on your Saturday. A word about the mail. You say Mom - no use wasting money on airmail stamps. You haven't as yet told me how you'd prefer I write - V-mail or air mail. Please let me know and I shall comply- until I hear definitely since I'm fairly well stocked at present I'll continue with this method. I get your letters all mixed up - some written a week before I don't get until ones written two weeks later. This may account for the incongruous way I answer most times. In spite of this I prefer something I can get my teeth into so please continue the airmails. It distresses me naturally to hear that Gramp is getting steadily worse - I do hope I get to see him before he bows out.

April 13

So the Thompsons have finally acted on my disturbing presence in England? Well, that is rough! I plan on going to Cambridge next pass if only for a few hours. I may as well get the poop and I have nothing to lose but a little time. Hope I get there before Marg's letter - puss should come around again within the next week or so sooo we shall see.

Well, I finally got one addressed Sgt. at first we sorta had a competition - no body wrote that they got it we just changed return address. However the answers were so long in coming we sorta lost interest. I didn't want to say much for frankly, I expected another stripe before you wrote back but things have slowed down so much now we may not get it here now.

I agree, Perrys shouldn't be too optimistic about Dick. I'm feeling badly but what more can one say or do? Yes, I have been getting air mail stamps. No need to continue sending them now - I have fortunately found a good source for them. No word from Leon or Nell as yet. Glad you are getting money - I was going to ask. If we ever make Staff Sgt. I should be able to cable more to you. I'd give a dollar a lb. for a fresh chicken - one that I could chew right about now. I dream of them fried or roasted with dressing. I read in Stars & Stripes where Niagara Falls had another little session - Man beats woman and apologizes saying he thought she was his wife. My crew razz hell out of me for of Niffles gets in the news and they don't seem to care how!

April 14

Good thing you got Marg out anyway Harry in spite of no dance. When you asked her what she wanted to do she really came through didn't she? How was that session? Ah, loves young dream - smooch smooch. It is much simpler here. You walk up to the gal in question and say "Shall we have a go at it?" and there you are - park bench - doorway or what have you. You more than did justice in a description of "Oklahoma." I certainly would love to see that - maybe we'll have a week-end in N.Y.C. one day and see it again. The music is what I love - Did you see "A Song To Remember?" Well, anyway, a good evening here is Tuesday. I go to Red+ Aero Club early for my tea and a girl comes in from neighboring town to play piano. She has a lovely touch and plays anything you want. Even "Chopin's Palonaise." I go over and listen - you know how you associate events - particularly the first time you heard a melody. I stay until I feel blue enough for one night and then I leave but I love to listen.

April 18

Am looking for that box and you can be sure you'll hear about it when I get it. Brownies - mmmm. The ones you sent Dick one Christmas traveled for a couple months before he got them and he said they were O.K.

I've given you what I think - that we'll fly the Big Birds and not the Great Big ones in the C.B.I. We have a start here - enough to be considered experienced enough to go to a new theatre without any transition. We all hope to go to the States first but are hardly planning on it. This of course is all plain thinking ahead on my part - absolutely no official word whatsoever. Another thing - let's get this war over and let's get to London a couple more times before we worry too much about that.

Thought I told you about watch. I use Lt. Bob Turner's personal one. Would like to have mine but don't send it unless I specifically ask for it. No - I haven't written my "Little Irish." Got a letter in Savannah and one here. God love her she is so innocent and wholesome and immature. Not much use in teasing myself thinking of that these days. Good thing I got out of there when I did - I probably would only have tried to defile her sweetness eventually. Well, why not - somebody will if I don't. But then I had one in Gulfport. Boy it was a good thing I left there but just don't give me a chance to go back Wheeee!

You're speaking of Mike - I'd give my right arm (almost) to get hold of one of the Police jeeps they have around here - Gee but they are beautiful little fellows. Tell Mike and make him jealous.

Think I'll go and see "OH Frankie" now in "Step Lively" again if I can get in - Be good, people.

Lotsa Love, Frank

Saturday, April 29

Dear Mother, Harry and Mike,

Well, it is extremely difficult to sit down and write with little or nothing to write about. Haven't received any word since Thursday but that is plausible for I got four then.

Weather surprised us this morning with a bit of snow and I was really surprised when I traipsed off to school this morning. Some of the Master Sergeants around the place here - Crew Chiefs and Line Chiefs and such got a trip to Frankfurt and others went to Koblenz. They say these places are really leveled. You probably read General Arnold's statement in commendation to the Eighth Air Force for now the works they did can be fully appreciated. That is no kidding - some of them are a complete mess - you have to get the whole picture from the air to really appreciate it.

Conditions in the crew as regards officers and E.M. have made little progress. It is hardly my place to say or do anything so I sit idly by, but it is not too easy. Seems like a well integrated team damn near disintegrated and now it is slowly picking itself up. I hope somebody does something soon to straighten things out - they aren't worth much the way they are to my way of thinking.

They are having a dance for the G.I.s this evening over at the Aero Club - haven't quite made up my mind whether or not to go but you can bet if I can find me something decent to read I'll be a stayin here and reading it. Feel quite sure I'll make Mass with no trouble whatsoever to-morrow. I suppose I should write a lot of letters but there is little to write about as you can see. Main point is I'm well and quite well fed and as happy as can be expected under the circumstances and as far as I can see the aspect shouldn't change too much in the immediate or very near future so, be good, people - sorry no more info but it just ain't.

Lotsa Love, Frank

April 30, Monday

Dear Mother, Harry and Mike,

Still not very much of note has been happening around here. As the day's date will indicate today is Pay Day and we are all patiently awaiting the Eagle who is scheduled to hit the Bomb Run at 1 PM.

Saturday, much to our dismay, we were moved out of our barracks and assigned to another one. We are reasonably well settled by now although at the time the order was given I was at school and I returned to find the old barracks empty. Joe and Shaffis moved my stuff thank goodness! It seems they have decided to make a day-room here in the squadron for us and as per usual they picked the barracks we were in to be the new recreation center - thusly we were moved.

Conditions in our new quarters are rather different since we are no longer quartered with some Ground Crew men. All the fellows here are Combat Crew and are quite experienced. Two crews here are lead crews. They have been here some time and don't have many more to fly before they finish. These veterans really have things fixed up in here for their comfort. They have their own food supply and coffee. The place is papered with pin ups and maps and pictures of planes. They have spared themselves nothing which they could contrive to provide little comforts and conveniences for themselves. It is really quite some set-up.

Yesterday after Saturday's snow it rained and sleeted all the day with occasional sunlight just to prove it couldn't make up its mind. The boys and I were becoming quite restless so I call up Taylor and suggested he and his lads meet us in a place that was common to both of our bases. He poked around and finally found out that after they arrived there, there would be no means of transportation back for them so he suggested another place. We didn't know much about it but we said sure, sure! Lt. Sundin was going and Turner too. Well, we nosed around and found absolutely no means of getting there or returning - the weather grew worse - the Rank reneged but since I'd put on clean underwear and was ready to go, likewise Spencer and Ferniza, we refused to be discouraged. We had told them we'd be there and we were going. We asked everywhere on the base of how to get transportation - a matter of 30-35 miles confronted us. Each one told us it was impossible on a 6 hour pass - that it couldn't be done! That livened us up a bit and after each one of these admonitions we grew more determined. Thirty five miles is a real trip over here! Well, we started out via the thumb. Almost any car or truck will pick you up - even civilians will do it in their tiny cars - as long as you are in uniform almost any G.I. vehicle will take you - the big trouble being that you can walk for miles and nothing passes you. Petrol (gas) is very tight over here and about all that does pass you is Army cars but they are few and far between as compared with the States. Well, to make a long story short, we made it there and back by the very skin of our teeth. We got our first hitch in an ambulance - Spencer yelled when it stopped. Where the Hell ya going boys? Turned out to be a Lt. Colonel and Major in the thing - Ka-runch!

Second hitch in another "meat wagon." These boys were out to drink and we stopped at every pub on the way and even made a few detours. We finally arrived in an RAF truck and got to the Red Cross - designated meeting place only to find our boys had let us down and they didn't show. They had a swell dance there - some of the nicest gals I've seen - it was the best set-up Red Cross I've been in. Just like one of the better U.S.O.s at home. We couldn't stay long and the poor director of the Red Cross looked like the end of the world had come when she told us "There is no transportation to where you want to go - absolutely none!" I don't know what she expected us to say - she was crestfallen. We weren't really worried at the time but actually we almost wrote a little treatise on how to make Privates out of Sergeants on a 6 hour pass. We did get back and within the limits and it was quite an experience. Next time the boys will have to come and see us! OH yes - by the way we have about a two inch blanket of snow here today. Nice weather for the last day in April, what? Got Harry's of the 17th yesterday while I was away over the countryside.

Don't know just what I'd do about Marg, Harry. I'd have queered things for better or for worse by now I'll bet. Biding your time is undoubtedly the best policy there.

Also got Mother's of the 21st.

I'm sure looking for those boxes and hope they'll be here soon. Have to have something to add to the local kitchen here don't you know. Hope there is some Nescafe in one of them, then I won't have to travel to the Aero Club evenings for my hot drink before bedtime.

Left this letter a while to get paid. I got 9 pounds 17 shillings (around $4.03 - shilling 20¢ sooo I'm back with a little monya (sic) again and it feels good. Did manage to get something done today that I've wanted to do for some time. Am having a subscription of "Yank" sent home - thought you both, particularly Harry, would enjoy it. We don't get paid flying pay until the 10th, which should run another 10 lbs. I've been wanting to get you both something from here and don't know just what it will be. Could send some home (money) but I feel as long as I'm here I should get you something that is really English. I imagine you both realize how hard it is to get anything decent - much worse here than at home and then the things you can get are out of this world as far as price is concerned but I figured I just didn't know where to go in London. If there is anything you want over here and think I could get it be sure and let me know.

Sterzlback's parents are grand. They were always so grand to me. They and the Macks are always abject lessons to me and why I generally get myself in a mess in any barracks when some G.I. starts to spout off about the Jews. I never knew there was so much discrimination against them in the States until I got in the Army. Too bad Mimi couldn't wait - she'd have been one swell person to live with in my opinion - big disadvantage was that I'd probably have to have taken a 10% cut before I could have made any real progress.

Well, I guess that is about all the dirt at present. OH, those pictures I sent of the EM, I couldn't get one of John Kimpel the boy who shot down the fighter. He is a rather reticent lad about most things and besides he sent them all home I guess. One of me stinks as per usual. The officer is Major Sweeney - good looking dog, what? Have to run now - um hungry as hell - hope my candy bars last until your boxes get here. I had a full box of Mounds and Welch's Fudge bars but they are on the way out now. Be good, folks.
Love, Frank
  P.S. How about a fruit cake please.
F.

May 1945

Tuesday, May 1—No letter
Flew Mission 322: Chowhound 1; Hague; Holland Aircraft 44-6475

On the day following the news of Hitler's suicide, Big Sundin's crew took off in Round Tripper on a very different type of mission. Their target, The Hague, only this time they were dropping food, not bombs. Sundin was one of almost 400 B-17s tasked with dropping over 700 tons of ten-in-one rations in The Hague and Rotterdam areas. On this mission, Sundin's crew was in the A group, and flying in formation next to Round Tripper was none other than Heavy Date. At 10:02 that morning, flying at an altitude of only 300 feet, Round Tripper dropped 90 boxes. The reports indicated the results of this mission were "very good." As I read about this particular mission, it occurred to me that my father would not have known how ten years later his humanitarian contribution to feeding the starving Dutch people would take on a more profound meaning when he learned his future wife's father was a Dutch immigrant with family still living in Holland during the war.

Wednesday, May 2
First letter with S/Sgt. F.G. Thompson on return address

Dear Mother, Harry and Mike,
  We are all rather enthused with a circular which has just come out with General Arnold's signature attached. Of course we are not postmasters at the art of interpreting these things but the way it reads to us is that in the future they have one of the following in mind for us - either stationed as part of an occupational Air Force here or returned to U.S.A. for further training before shipment to the C.B.I. with furloughs. Nothing was mentioned about direct shipment to C.B.I. This is not a bad deal from either viewpoint since if once returned to the States we would probably be there at least 6 months which is good. Then too sitting over here for the duration and running no risk wouldn't be bad either. We were all elated for we got promoted to Staff Sergeants today which puts us in the higher price bracket and entitles us to privileges of the 1st 3 grades of enlisted men. We'll have to be on the ball to keep it. Pay, base is 96 and then flying pay

boosts it to a total of 144 and then 20% of that for being overseas amounts up to 160 something which is not to be sneezed at. Engineer and R.O. on B-17s are supposed to make another rocker but under the circumstances I would say we are mighty lucky to get what we did.

As far as work is concerned we've changed our theme song to "Angels of Mercy" and it's all right with me.

I changed my bunk today. Uppers are desirable in "Limey" bunks for the bottom one is too close to floor and you get your blankets dirty in the lower. The place I got was all fixed up by the boy who left it and I'm surrounded with pinups and shelves. Even have a bed lamp for late reading.

Just got the dirt about Germans surrendering in Italy which is good and of course the "Stars & Stripes" carried story of Hitler's death today. I wonder if there is any truth in it. Over here I suppose the peace should be coming soon but it seems that the policy of the government will be to minimize any celebration until victory in the Pacific can be celebrated as well. I don't know just how the British people feel about it although I talked with an RAF pilot the other night and he is not too keen about it from what I gathered.

They are putting a new dayroom in the squadron and they had us working on that today. We oiled the floor and did some painting and cleaned up around the place.

I've been eating like a horse lately. Cast pride aside I have and have been resorting to all sorts of evasions to get me seconds. Been pretty lucky too.

Well folks, I'll have to run now need a haircut and I should sew my stripes on. Never did sew Buck Sergeant Stripes on and the Big Sundin doesn't like the idea. Guess I've given you most of the news so be good, folks.

Lotsa Love, Frank

Thursday, May 3

Flew Mission 324: Chowhound 3; Utrecht, Holland; Aircraft 43-38333

The mission target for today was Utrecht, and once again the purpose was humanitarian in nature. Referred to as a "Mercy Mission" on the report, the notes the pilots included in their interrogation reports told the tale. One pilot noted that near a small town the Dutch people "wrote SOS Hunger painted on ledge along side pond." Another wrote "SOS written on sea wall. Also sign 'Hunger'." Tasked with dropping food supplies for the civilian population in Holland, four squadrons, totaling 395 released more than 700 tons of rations at altitudes of 300-700 feet. Sundin was Squadron C in formation, once again flying Heavy Date. Though the mission was rated "excellent," the interrogation reports from Squadron C were not declassified until 2010. As far as I could tell, the only indication of why was that two crews had spotted a "yellow-tailed B-17 on the ground - didn't look like a crash landing - no activity about the ship." Another crew reported "tail gunner thought he saw a white life raft - no personnel seen - information given to lead ship." While these ships were no longer in combat, that did not mean they were no longer in danger.

Thursday, May 3

Dear Mother, Harry and Mike,

Am sitting here on my newly acquired "upper" listening to one of the boys play a small accordion and not bad either. Music of any kind always helps me - Huba Huba. Have been doing a bit of flying. Flew with the Big Sundin today - flew in nose mostly - radar navigation - lotsa fun.

Nothing much more to report. I guess they will be starting us to some sort of school here soon to keep us busy. That is just until they decide what is to become of us I guess.

Received Harry's of the 26th today. Seems he's had a cold! We have all been getting them here what with the change from such nice weather a couple weeks ago to the snow and sleet of the past week or so. You know the usual head colds - just sweat them out. No boxes as yet - hope they arrive soon.

Got letters from Sally and Den Brown today so I suppose I should get on the job and answer but I'm not much in the mood tonight as you can see I'm trying a pencil tonight. Pen is not so good for I can't get any good American ink for it. Limey stuff is not so hot - it clogs up the pen. I guess I should be able to get some in London. Pass should come middle or last of next week I guess. Big headline in Stars & Stripes today - 8th A.F. goes back to school. They are already getting chicken-shit about things here and it is due to get a lot worse. That is always a sign of domesticity so I thought you'd be glad to hear it. I must write the Beals & Otts too I guess. God knows I don't hear from the latter unless I write first. I also have me a good sized washing on hand so you can see I have plenty to do if and when I get me some spare time. I don't know - some of these times I don't seem to get anything done. We have to attend Pond discussions these days and then we don't usually get up till late, although I like to make breakfast when I can. You can see it is a rough life - the kind you get fat and lazy on.

I was pretty sore last night when I finally got my laundry back. Boy was I sore - they took three of my good pairs of woolen sox - ones you sent me at Gulfport. I've been guarding them and wearing them only for good and then the bastards swipe them. If I don't get them back I'm going to see the Provost Marshal. They also got my Tee shirts. Oh the life of a Gunner is Hell. We haven't joined the NCO club as yet but are seriously contemplating joining - even tonight maybe. I could really go for some brandy right now. When V.E. day comes we're going to drink my Seagram's 7 with a vengeance.

I'm thinking seriously of getting checked out in Navigation. I know something of it and have already used most of the radar & radio aids. I figure it doesn't hurt to know as much as you can about any phase of the work for you never know when that little bit extra will pay mighty big dividends. Harry's news about his move to Gib's job is good. I hope he gets more money - he should demand it. What are the aspects for getting ahead from it though. Anything with the word "clerk" added on to the end doesn't sound good enough to me for my boy but then I don't think anything is good enough for him. It is a satisfaction Harry to see you move ahead - go to it boy - the world is your oyster if you're not afraid to work and have initiative and above all enthusiasm.

One of the lads has been pestering hell out of me. He has wife trouble but good. He got two letters asking for a divorce (not been hitched more than 6 months). He wrote explaining away a few details - his wife & mother don't get along - then he got second letter requesting break so he saw Captain - lawyer, got things arranged and now today he gets a letter - all is forgiven or forgotten and letters are already on their way asking her to sign waivers for a divorce. He is Lutheran & doesn't believe in divorce but felt if she wanted to leave him he wouldn't hinder her. So now he is pissed off and doesn't know what to do. I'd be inclined to laugh but it is really pathetic. He really doesn't understand women - you have to be gentle with them I'd say. Also it is mostly a case that both of them are uneducated. They cannot express how they feel or what they mean on paper - you should see some of the letters - they're sad.

Well folks, I'll have to buzz off. News just came that Holland & Denmark have capitulated - not much left over here now. Be good, people.

Lotsa Love, Frank

May 5, Saturday—No letter

Flew Mission 325: Chowhound 4; Utrecht, Holland; Aircraft 43-38617

Once again, dropping food to the Hollanders, with one difference. This was the only mission my father flew with a pilot other than Big Sundin. Much as with other "Chowhound" missions, there were four squadrons dropping over 700 tons of food rations. Nothing was out of the ordinary, other than when one crew spotted a "life raft from a naval vessel - empty." Another reported they saw "many red, white, and blue flags, and green, white, and blue flags displayed today." A final crew observation read "Dinghy - heard on radio and called in; Sub - heard on radio and called in." Other than seeing a burst of flak and on further investigation, seeing the Germans fire a red flare, the day's mission was without incident. However, this was not always the case. On a similar mission over Utrecht, in two days time, Squadron A reported "A/C in water - looked British - 20 dinghies - surface vessels nearby." But it was not a British plane, it was American, and another crew reported "dingy empty." The pilot's interrogation report was blank and only notes "Down in Channel - MIA." Still another pilot reported "B-17 ditched - two chutes in water - plane was on fire - and explosion." The final pilot report read, "Circled area of ditched Fort - found wreckage at 1530 - left at 1735 - rescue planes still circling - PBY picked up 2; cutter 2; trawler 1; searched area mainly north of area first places where men seen in water." Reading this, I was even more worried about Big Sundin's impending ditching.

The final report of this ship's ditching read:

```
One aircraft flying ahead of aircraft 8640 re-
ported the aircraft flying at about 1500 feet
when a fire broke out in 2 engine, and the air-
craft dove to put out the fire. Failing to do so,
the engine exploded and the aircraft ditched,
breaking up as it hit the water, remaining
afloat. This was 1527 hours. Two aircraft were
circling, Air Sea rescue were circling. As many
as 20 dinghies were on the water. The CP and
the Togglier are the only persons on board now
alive. The report the 2 engine on fire, the CP
coming from the radio room to use the extin-
guisher and to feather the prop. They bailed
out approximately 1530 hours about 12 miles off
the English Coast, the aircraft flying steady
and level about 300 feet off the water. Togglier
saw Navigator and Photographer leave the nose
before him, both chutes opened.
```

These men met with an indescribable fate within 24 hours of V-E Day, yet Big Sundin's crew all survived their ditching. How that happened was yet to be discovered.

May 6, Sunday

Dear Mother, Harry and Mike,

I'm all set here today ready to write a big letter and I hardly know what to say. I have been nursing a bit of a cold along - nothing serious. Has not been too much of a discomfort to me for I've been keeping busy and that way it doesn't bother too much.

I flew yesterday with a Captain Thomas. He is finished but wanted to fly one of these mercy missions so Turner went as Co-Pilot and I went along as R.O. This was the first time I'd been over Holland since Krouts there capitulated. I don't know where they kept all the Dutch flags during the German occupation but they were everywhere yesterday. They waved to us from bridges - horse stops, road junctions, everywhere. It was a wonderful sight - Krouts down there shaking their fists - tulip beds cut up to spell thank you - yes delivering groceries to them was certainly worthwhile. Makes you feel a little better to be dropping something constructive instead of those Hell raisers.

I was glad I flew yesterday for when I got back I found they had put my boys on K.P. - a sort of modified [version] of it but detail none the less. I got to Mass this morning at 11 AM. I know you'll be glad to hear.

This morning crews with over 25 missions were alerted for shipment home I think. I was hardly prepared for such quick action. They turned in flying equipment today and will leave within the next week I guess. I have no idea where we stand but as long as they let us stay here and fly once in a while I'll be content. We should be due for a pass middle or last of next week. I plan to get to Cambridge for a while anyway but will no doubt spend most of my time in London - all depends upon my reception in Cambridge - need I say more.

If we are going to be here a while I guess I'm going to have to get me a gal of some description to fool away my time with. Only one I've met so far that suits me was this Dorene Burgess in London but I guess I'll just have to look around some more.

The weather today has warmed up, thank goodness, all of which reminds me I've been waiting for such a day to wash (clothes) and take a shower. It has been so long since I've done the latter that I'm ashamed to count up but when the weather is cold there is no heat over there - it is a good 1/2 mile away - the water is generally cold and I just won't take a chance on catching cold. Then I got one (cold) anyway and guess I can risk it now.

Spent almost a pound getting stuff for my uniforms. Cloth wings - Presidential Citation ribbon & Cluster - C.T.O. ribbon and Bronze Star - Good Conduct ribbon & Air Medal. These "Limeys" soak hell out of you and so your money goes, however if we are here much longer I should manage to save a bit. We are all getting decked out for it seems to make such a difference here. Also took my woolen field jacket over to be cut down this afternoon. I don't know just what to do about a dress battle jacket. They should issue us one but only ground men are getting them. I can buy one in London for 3 pound 10 shillings (about 14 dollars). The officers would buy it for me I think but I think I'll await developments. Well, I guess that's about all for now folks - be good.

Lotsa Love, Francis George

May 8

Letter from Gramp, written by Aunt Ruth

Dear Frank,

On "V" Day we are thinking of you. I came up from Brockport on Sunday night to spend a few days with Dad & today he asked me if I would help him to write a few lines to you—so this will be a joint production.

We have all so much enjoyed your letter from England, which has been passed around. It was good indeed of you—to find time to write us—your mother and Harry have probably advised you that my sight has failed recently, which makes it rather hard for me to write & that, in addition to my foot, makes it difficult for me to accomplish much.

It was interesting to us to hear of your first impression of England. The country being so very small in comparison to the one you have become used to of late but we know–that if you have the opportunity to travel around a little you will find very much of interest. We do not know just what part of England you are located but if near Cambridge try to see my cousin Rev. Dr. Kempthorne who lives in a village close by the city of Cambridge–(Trumpington) where anyone will direct you to Maris House and he and his wife will be so pleased to see you. Should you be in the vicinity of Liverpool–you might look up Elisa (?) Vera Marshall–(Grandma Thompson's niece) who lives at 36 Leylan Road Southport (suburb about 20miles from Liverpool) she would give you a real welcome.

The news which we have today would indicate that the most of the fighting is over in England–but there will be plenty of cleaning up to be done.

Harry tells us when he was here visiting the other evening you have visited London. Quite some place! Or at least was–when I was last there (1921). Everything is quite different from U.S. cities, perhaps to you not so interesting or convenient, but from an historical point of view–well worthwhile.

All members of the family with the exception of myself continue in good physical condition today–but being unable to walk.

I have not seen your mother lately but Harry tells me she keeps well.

Should you have the time or opportunity to write me from England or any country you are likely to visit you know how glad I shall be to receive any news you can write me.

We send you our affection with love and best wishes to you.

Grandpa and Ruth

May 8, Tuesday

Dear Mother, Harry and Mike,

Well, today is VE-Day–heard Churchill speak and everything. NO doubt you people are very elated–I hear of big doings in N.Y.C. and also London. And well it might be–we all have cause to rejoice and thank the good Lord for being so kind to us. And then too the debt civilian Americans will never, never be able to repay–the debt owed to the men that did the job for them. Oh I don't mean guys like me but the fellows who really had it rough–the ones who really know what it is all about.

To a lot of us here it is a little anticlimax. We have known it was about over for a couple weeks now but we've just been tickled over a longer period of time, that's all.

I flew with co-pilot while he took instrument check yesterday. We had advance information then so when we came back we broke open the Seagram's 7–assembled the crew and started a little celebration of our own. We all had a nice bun on–then went and ate dinner then back to the squadron got dressed in Class As and were ready to really go again. We all got bikes–don't ask me from where but we had them. Sooo we cycled into a small pub about 2-3 miles distant and we started to put away the Bitters. We had a big time and closed the place up at 10 PM. Incidentally it was still light–twilight ends here at about 10:45 or 11 PM. Sooo we started back–a round about way but we had the right directions. When we came to a crossroads we stopped to reconnoiter. I knew where we were all right. Well, the Big Sundin tried several times to go swimming in a small pond there. He had his blouse off three times but we finally convinced him he shouldn't. We decided that Turner and Sundin were too far gone to continue operations so we gave them a flashlight and sent them home. Ferniza, Spencer and I went on to the Dorms of the Women's Land Army. We sure raised Hell there. Women leaning out of windows in flannel nighties all over the place–Say we even got in the place for a while. I was afraid to go too far for although communication is poor and I don't think police or M.P.s could have got there in time to get us–those Land Army gals are really ruggedly built and they could have beat hell out of us if they'd wanted to sooo we took it as easy as possible under the circumstances. Say–already they're telling us "Your job is over." Want us to go home I guess.

Anyway, we left to come home. I did pretty good–only fell off the bike once. When we got back the base was going crazy–looked like a Fourth of July–boys all had flare pistols and flares and were really using them up. You could hear 45 slugs whistling by all over the place. Thought the barracks would burn down there for a while if ever those flares got started on the roof.

Ah but this morning was rough–you know big head and butterflies. Have spent most of the day reviving myself. The officers are at it again I judge for an announcement came over the P.A. system that free Martinis and Singapore Slings would be served from 5 PM until 12 midnight or until supply was exhausted at the Officers Club. Sooo I imagine they are all at it hot and heavy again. I suppose we could go to NCO club (nothing free there) or we still have two 5ths of Seagram's left but one night like last night holds me for a long time.

We got paid again today–now have 18 pounds on me which amounts to about 72 dollars. I want to spend some of it on youse guys in London if I ever get there again. Don't like to carry that much money on me–sure feels good in a wallet but it is not too safe there.

This morning we had to go to the line and do a special job of cleaning guns for some Group Inspection I think. I see by the bulletin board that after to-morrow we go on a 6-day work week program so that is that. All the fellows are speculating about what will become of us. I suppose there is an outside chance of our going directly to the Pacific but I don't take much stock in it - I hope not anyway. A big group leaves here within the next few days. A special teletype order was posted that their processing would be splendid. Some of them are recommended for instructors, some for B-29s or B-32s. Gunners and Engineers who go on very heavies will have to have some more technical school before going to B-29 R.T.U. but sadly - not so for the R.O. All they have to do is check us out on this new high frequency set - we have our code and procedure. On the other hand I thank Goodness that I am an R.O. for if we should be kept here to fly transport or patrol they will most likely dispense with career gunners and armorers and fly 5 men crew - pilot, copilot, navigator, engineer and R.O. I personally would just as soon stay right here another 6-8 months flying transport or what have you As I see it ferrying wounded men or anything from here to the States would really be a sweet deal.

I should be able to do better on the writing deal now - we'll have to see, but I've been flying almost every day for the past week and that makes it kinda hard. Lately I've become a movie addict - huba huba - I really hit them all now whether I've seen them or not. "Laura" is coming in the next month or so - want to see that - missed it in Gulfport.

Well people - that will have to be all for now. I know I haven't told you what you want to know most but I don't know myself. We're due for a lot of chicken here soon now and that's about all we know now.

Be good, people.

Lotsa Love, Frank

May 10, Thursday

Dear Mother, Harry and Mike,

Well, I suppose I should start with what I've been doing. Got two letters today - feel very good about it - mail man has been on pass so haven't had any mail for 3 days, which is indeed a hardship for me. Yesterday I did very little of anything all the day but lie in the sac and sweat out the line at the PX. They restock there Tuesdays and if you want choice articles you get there early when they open on Wednesday. I had two rations of cigarettes so got a carton of Camels - Huba Huba - and two cans of tomato juice along with other items so I felt as though it was worthwhile.

Later in the afternoon Spencer persuaded me (he twisted my arm) to go to Ipswich with him so we took off on a "Liberty run." It was VE day + 1 and they were still celebrating. We had to walk far from the main avenue before we could get any brew. Somehow many of the hometown lads managed to get home of all things, on VE Day + 1. Most places were sold out. We hit two places, both very crowded, and Mom, they ignored us till we walked out in the first place, and in the second they tried the same stunt but we stayed till we both got a bottle of light ale. You see the Tommies are coming home now - in fact a lot of them were home and the "Limeys" were going to see that their own got what there was. It was quite natural I guess and yet it hurt. It seems to me that in Los Angeles, Chicago, N.Y.C. or even Niffles that anybody's money would have been good on a day like that. We really don't quite understand - you see an English Pub caters to a neighborhood or family trade. The whole family goes there to relax and each family or individual goes to a public house as they are called and refers to it as "his own pub." If you meet a girl and suggest a drink she'll suggest going to "her pub." Even so - we're not veterans but we do wear the uniform of the U.S.A. and although maybe not quite as often or as long, but we have just as definitely risked our little red asses as they have. We did it for the same cause and

I honestly believe we materially did help - and then they seemed to begrudge us a drink even when we were paying for it - Hell they should have given it to us.

Right now I feel we are in the same position as a nurse who is lured; the friends and relatives are overjoyed to see her come in to stay but when danger of the patient is passed they are very glad to see her go. I can't honestly blame the English for they have taken quite a beating - All the girls were forewarned and appeared quite confident in their tin panties but what they didn't know was that these Yanks all carry Boy Scout knives with a long wicked can opener on it. Yes, they have had enough. Anyway we ended up at a dance last night - had a fairly good time - Oh my ego - I cut a girl - then two different ones cut me - then the first one bundled me up when she came up and asked for the next dance - whew - war is Hell.

I got in last night to find I was up for a mission or sightseeing tour today. 8th Air Force is flying skeleton crews (pilot, co-pilot, navigator, engineer & R.O.) who carry 10 ground crew men in a Big Bird over to see the havoc we wrought in Der Deutschland. It is a nice idea - those ground crews have been here some of them for 2 1/2 years and they deserve to see some of it. It proved to be about a 9 hour flight - Belgium - Holland - Germany - Luxemburg & France. We flew at 1,000 feet or less and you can see plenty from there. Europe is beautiful really. Germany is lovely to look at from the air. Brunswick, Frankfurt and Hanover, and London was bombed but that was child's play compared to these places - I judge most of them useless for anything.

I saw famous Rheims Cathedral in France - parts of Rhone Valley - well there is nothing like it at home. The small towns are so quaint and neat. We went over the Ruhr Valley which is referred to as Happy Valley by airmen. Flak was so thick there that you could walk on it. I saw enough Flak installations today to make me sick to my stomach. Those bastards wanted to shoot us down I guess. And then there was Paris - one day I'll go there. No sense trying to describe it. It has been called most beautiful city in the world - nuff said. Saw Eiffel Tower - Arc de Triomphe - Notre Dame - Palais de Justice - Saint Chapel - the Seine and its little islands and bridges. One squadron landed at Brussels today to bring over POWs and brought champagne back with them. I hope we get a crack at that one of these days. France and Germany - Holland and Belgium are well worthy of any praise they've ever received. I'd love to visit them - like to get a "working" knowledge of Paris.

Well people - I'll make this all for today. We start 7-hour day schedule of school to-morrow - still have to shave and get my cup of tea - be good.
Lotsa Love, Frank

May 11, Friday
Dear Mother, Harry and Mike,

So we started back to school today and although we haven't been presented with much as yet we will be thoroughly reviewed, it is my belief, on all phases of Mechanix and Operation so that we'll be completely ready for our next jaunt by plane, if we should go by plane, if we go anywhere. Not too definite is it - that's what we think too.

The point system for discharges came out in the Stars and Stripes today and although it has created quite a hubub the fellows don't really pay much attention to it. You see we are all (supposed to be) highly trained specialists. Even the gunners come under that category, I think, so we have no chance of getting out until the whole business is finished.

As I've said before I'm glad I have radio school behind me for if there is any chance that they keep skeleton crews here to help with transport that is what will do the job for me. Now that I have a decent rating I'd' just as soon sweat it out over here doing transport work but we'll have to wait and see. Also in this line - a radio operator would receive little additional training in the States if he were returned. The other side of it is that he also would need little introduction to Air Transport Command work and could step in in a moment for we used their system and procedures while coming from Savannah to the E.T.O. In summing up the sad, but most important factor is that we are a battle experienced crew and have had enough combat experience to be shoved in at the drop of a hat. Not enough of it to be ready to be released but enough so that we are far from green. I guess that takes in most of it for now.

While I think of it - I meant to include this in yesterday's letter. When I was in town a couple days ago I did get some English light ale. It was very good! If you remember Gramp always liked Grandma Thomas's brew, well, I never tasted anything which tasted so much like the old Home brew - it is really good.

Now let's see if there aren't some questions here in your past few letters I can answer. Please send me some Tuna Fish if there is any available. We have Spam! We have been doing better on the eating lately and then too we are not anywhere near so hungry as we were a few weeks ago. So Jerry O'H. still keeps them guessing about even what he flies in. Well, I hope he is not in a B-24. If I write one day and am a Pvt. again just know without opening it that they ordered me into a B-24. Give me a "Big Bird" any day. Fortresses were designed to bring the crew back. Ford's engineers built a Bomb Bay and then made it fly when they designed the 24. That is my opinion - they're just too fragile and temperamental for me. Not drinking too much Mom - seems to me a point in your past 2 or 3 letters. It is a good idea to keep me on the ball. I like it often but am content with it once in a while. It is rather hard to get here although you can get it any evening on the Post. Only place E.M. can get hard stuff is at NCO club. You have to be Staff or better to join (which I am now - ahem) but I haven't been over as yet. Have to be off to school now - will finish later.
Sometime Later

Well, went to school this afternoon - really didn't amount to much - had had most of it in school but they try to keep us from sleeping all the time which is not a bad idea for idle men are discontent men. Anyway, I got back early and went to the movie and then ate. The movie was a "Limey" one and they like the melodramatic and it was just that. Not too bad for putting in an afternoon though. The chow today has been good - don't know why - they didn't feed us that well when we were flying combat.

Now to get back to some of those letters.

It is funny you're speaking so much of French fries lately. Here, with the war, ice cream and sweets are out of the question so the little treat for the kids and adults and G.I.s is to get three pence or sixpence (5 & 10 cents to you) worth of chips (French fries). Fish & Chips get a big play over here when you can get the fish. Harry, you take good care of de la Spusier for me - when I get there he and I will both go out and "check out" a Niagara Falls Commando - we might even take you Harry - if you're a good boy.

I did write the Beals when I wrote Gramp - put on an airmail stamp - probably someone screwed up some place - going from here to Canada with a U.S.A. stamp. Well, no telling when they'll get it so I'll try to get one off to them this evening to their Niagara Falls, New York address.

Been hearing lotsa rumors as usual today - no sense in getting all of us down in the dumps or up in the air so I won't bother to pass them along - too many of them anyway! Well people, I'm going to write a couple others off tonight - (of all things) sooo, be good.

Lotsa Love, Frank

P.S. Sent Babs a cable this morn. Hope it doesn't scare you.

F.

Monday, May 14

Dear Mother, Harry and Mike,

Well, I am delinquent for two days now but I hope you won't be too sore at your laddie Buck. Nothing much of real import has developed here with the exception of a more definite school schedule and the initiation of a flying schedule. It seems that to-morrow night we start flying a schedule similar to what we flew at Gulfport - the sad part of it is there is no New Orleans to jaunt off to on a day off. Which reminds me, yesterday marked 4 weeks since we had a pass and it doesn't look like we are going to get another very soon. In a rather disgusted mood yesterday we all started out, Ferniza, Kimpel, Spencer and I. We hit a couple of the larger towns in the vicinity stretching a 6 hour pass into a 10 hour number.

They put on a bit of an air show over London yesterday. Our crew didn't get in on it and I'm not too sorry - we saw parts of it while we were philandering and it really looked O.K.

Rumors persist here that we will go direct to the C.B.I. - I certainly hope not, although I guess there is not much doubt that we would be finished sooner if we do go direct. Myself I'd like to get home for a while again - you know - steaks and stuff.

Going to town last night we find many of the bloody English first starting to express their contempt of we Yanks - now that the job is done. As I say, I don't blame them - the boys are forever pulling things here that they would never try at home, but nevertheless it does not set too well. I'll be extremely careful where I spend my money from now on. If all the rest of us would take that attitude, these "Limeys" would soon yell uncle for they are still very grasping for the "Yankee dollah."

I think the girls still love us anyway - I think you understand that nowhere in the world is a woman as well and equally treated by a man than she is in the good old U.S.A. Britain will never forget this war - she wasn't invaded by Germans but it will take generations to get the Yanks out their systems and blood strains too.

We have been doing little lately! Don't know just yet how this flying will come. Maybe every other day as at Gulfport - we'll have to wait and see. Only 18 crews left in our squadron now - some of the lads left last night - flying home - lucky devils - but then they had almost finished their tours. I think at least six more crews are to be cut and sent somewhere - we all have to wait for that too. At any rate I doubt that we'll be among that last six since I believe we are due to stay here a while longer.

Well, people I'm afraid that's about all for today - it's short, I realize, but there is just no dope and I seem to be reporting rumors as news so I'd better stop here.

Be good, people.

Lotsa Love, Frank

May 15, Tuesday

Dear Mother, Harry and Mike,

Well, today I got a box mailed on April 6 so you can see it took a bit better than a month to get here. The Hershey bars are as welcome as anything could be. Our ration here has become a bit better but what I intend doing is trading what bars I have on hand for some eggs and then I'll have these to eat. The brownies are whole and in good shape physically and as far as edibility is concerned they are an indeed welcome relief from the crap we can get here in the line of pastry. Their freshness varies in proportion to the wrapping. Those which were very well wrapped are dandy - the others where the paper peels off easily are not quite so well preserved. We're flying tonight so I reckon I'll take de "Swag" along and we'll all enjoy it.

Say the mail for the past couple days has really been getting here. I got Harry's of the 6th yesterday and Mother's mailed May 9th today. I suppose that with victory, mail gets 1st priority (I hope) at any rate I'd say that was pretty darn good.

Today we had to go to a movie which showed the method which will be used by the Army for releasing some of the troops used in the ETO. There is very little encouragement for the Air Corps man and that is as it should be I suppose. As for myself and my crew we have little bitch coming for as yet we have hardly done anything. It is really enough for me but the Army doesn't see it that way.

Let me know when you can where Dorothy O'Hara is located in the E.T.O. I don't suppose I'll get a chance to see her but then when you get in those big Birds you never can tell where they may send you. Glad you received and liked pictures - Spencer we call the "Grasshopper." This was aptly taken from the Aesop's fable of the Grasshopper and the ant - you know the Grasshopper had a good time and the ant worked all summer & saved for the hard winter. Ferniza is the ant - he also is an admitted expert on Aesop and quotes him at the damndest times - used to do it in ranks at Gulfport and turn the formation into a riot.

I have been very busy of late trying to doctor myself up with this Limey cold. Have had it almost 2 weeks now. At the infirmary they just give you pills and medicine and unless you're running a temperature you never get to see a medical officer. You can see it is not serious because I've had no temperature but it is still a darn nuisance and uncomfortable as the dickens. Finally got me some Vick's and put a start on it last night - hope to deal the final punch to it tonight - we'll see.

There is still not much news. Say I want to say something and don't exactly know how. Was Rita Jane Niger's husband ever heard of or is he still MIA? Please don't say anything to anyone of what follows for you know the human equation in all things and I'm very apt to [be] mistaken but in the movies shown to us shortly before V-E Day I caught a glimpse of a chap that certainly looked like Rita's Ian. The thing that got me was that the fellow was in an American uniform - not Canadian. Pictures were of rescued POWs - Likeness was quite noticeable. I thought it might have been him so just sorta ask around to find out if he has been reported living and let me know please.

You wanted to know what a Togglier is. Well, when we fly any position other than lead ship in a formation, we drop bombs using a smoke bomb dropped by lead ship as a guide. Actually no bombardier is needed so they "check out" an enlisted man who pulls the toggle switch at the right time. It is without a doubt the easiest job on the ship. No, I wouldn't want it - just like to keep up with the other fellow's job so I stand a better chance of understanding his problem. I like to know as much about every job on the ship as I can. Has anything more been heard from Earl Richardson?

Well, I suppose I'd better be gettin on - we are still on a day to day schedule here as far as school is concerned so that can change any minute. We were supposed to fly 4 hours cross country tonight and two hours of co-pilot transition starting at take-off 10 PM and land at 4 AM but the x-country has been canceled so we just fly transition I guess.

I understand that the RAF has been flying men from the continent to England. Too bad they won't let us do that. We could really haul them. If they took the turrets out we could carry 60-70 men believe it or not.

Ah well, I await my destiny with a great deal more patience than I would have a year ago. God has been so good to us and I am content here as long as they'll let me stay.

Be good, people.
Lotsa Love, Frank

May 16, Wednesday

Dear Mother, Harry and Mike,

Well, I'm at it a bit earlier than usual today. We flew in the dark a couple hours last night and apparently because of it we have done nothing all day. It is a bit like a summer resort camp here today. Everybody doing just as they darn please. The nicest thing about this new school program they are initiating is that they have neither the space nor equipment as yet to really do a lot with it so as a result it has not become too stringent as yet.

I have yet to take some dry cleaning over today and send some laundry off which constitute my biggest problems at present. Rough isn't it? Cold seems better today than it has in past two weeks - seems to loosening up for which I am thankful indeed - it has been annoying.

Best rumor of today is that a pass seems to be in the offing which is good news in any man's language. I suppose I'll spend all my good money but I hope to get around a bit more this time if it has to be on my own and also I want to get a couple things for you guys, if possible, in London. I expect to be robbed blind, but then I may never get over here again, what?

Right now the weather is lovely here and I suppose you're having nice May weather at home too. When it is nice in England it is very nice. From what I hear on this pass deal we may get a day or two extra out of it so despite all my resolutions to go to Cambridge I may abandon said scheme and try to make Scotland for a few days. All the boys who have been here some time say that Scotland is the place to go and if I can make it I shall go there. It won't cost any more for transportation for I believe that is still free to us - it just would take a bit more time. The Scots are supposed to be more like the Americans than anyone in England - not much of the military up there - 12 hours by train unless I can get me a Big Bird going in that direction. All is rather in the embryo stage so I'll have to wait and see.

We took up the brownies into the blue with us last night. Frankly, they tasted a bit moldy to me but rest of the boys - Turner, Sundin, Ferniza, Spencer, Shaffer & Kimpel sure ate them up and enjoyed them but good - but they weren't what they should have been to me. Guess I'm a little too particular - been that way about too many things I guess but it is too late to change now.

Made a deal last night for a dozen eggs - have to get all peppered up for my next excursion into civilization. They'll fry them for me at the Red X so I'm all set there.

Well people, I believe I'll dash over and get my PX ration for the week. Not much to report - all's well - so, be good, people.
Lotsa Love, Frank

1945 May 17 AM 6:49 - Telegram
MY LOVE AND GREETINGS ON MOTHERS DAY WISH I COULD BE
WITH YOU LOVE FRANK THOMPSON

Friday, May 18

Dear Mother, Harry and Mike,

Spent a rather busy day for me yesterday. Went to radio school for a while, attended a compulsory movie and did a bit of dry cleaning. I don't care much for the job they do at the local dry cleaning establishment - they just don't do the job, sooo Joe and I journeyed out to the line, drained ourselves some 100 octane from one of the Big Birds and we did ourselves a real job. Have to run over and get the stuff pressed this afternoon. My flying fatigues (best loved garment) were covered with grease and oil from carrying machine guns to the plane before a mission. I got them nice and clean now - have to get a couple rips fixed up and the old zoot zoot will be almost as good as new again.

Went to see a Limey movie last night - it was really pretty good. Last night we initiated our policy of sticking around the base. We all went to the NCO club. It is really all right over there. Their bar is not too bad at all! You can get scotch, cherry brandy or gin and good old bitters. They have a darn nice lounge - all upholstered furniture - really OK. No drinking allowed in the lounge incidentally - radio and recording there too. Then at about 7 PM they put on a buffet feed - that's for me. Boy, they had the best ham there last night. I had me a great big ham & cheese sandwich and with a glass of brew I was all set. We had a good evening all right. It costs a pound to get a membership and they return it to you when you leave.

Well, I guess we are really due for a pass in the next day or so. I had hoped that we might get a couple extra days but I guess that won't work for the EM. In other words, the officers, if we start on pass Monday, don't need a pass and can take off to-morrow afternoon whereas the enlisted men have to wait until they get their pass before they can leave. So it is not so good for us. But if we do get a few days it will be O.K. - it is getting a bit tiresome around here.

This morning we flew some camera gunnery. You know just like at R.T.U., you shoot film at a fighter plane from the Big Bird. We had a P-51 out there - those babies can really make those pursuit planes do tricks. It was a lot of fun to watch him - the whole business was a lot of fun - it is some difference - the last time we sighted our guns on a ship coming in it was German jet planes and they were playing for keeps - so were we!

We really shouldn't have flown today. At Gulfport they never would have let us in the air, but up we went anyway - ceiling was only about 200 ft. or less. Going up was not bad but getting down again was a ticklish business. I should get a chance to write again before we go on pass and I'll let you know then what my "Flight Plan" is. Until then I guess I've given you most of the latest poop - so, be good, people. Lotsa Love, Frank

May 19, Saturday

Dear Mother, Harry and Mike,

Well, another day and not much to report. Please bear that in mind when people ask why the hell I'm not doing a better job on the writing just tell them that there haint (sic) much to write about now.

The pass, which yesterday seemed a delightful reality, seems to have retreated into the recesses of Army ambiguity so there we are - you know as much about it as I do. Another thing - Radio Operators according to the Stars & Stripes will be held regardless of points. Not that I had any real hopes nor has any Air Force personnel - I only ran up 44 points anyway.

Went to a local pub last night and had a couple bitters and sweated it out until the fish & chips man came last night. It was really O.K.

So we spend our days not doing much - Spencer - after he has been losing steady at Black Jack & Poker now is content to play checkers with Joe for a shilling a game. I am busy in the middle of Lloyd C. Douglas's latest opus "The Robe." It is quite good - quite well done and should make a very good movie.

We are now all worried about the Grasshopper (Spencer). He has not received any mail from his wife - today makes 11 days. He got a letter from his mother about 5 days ago saying his wife had been over and was going out with a friend - but didn't say girlfriend. It was real funny at first - he wrote the missing word "girl" in the letter and we have been razzing hell out of him. We start - "We will now devote 10 minutes to cheering up Dan." Then we sing "Somebody Else" and "No Letter Today." Then we tell him that some buddy of his at home has probably been working in conjunction with his wife to get him an extra 8 points for another youngster. As I say, it was funny at first, but now 11 days, well, that is not good. We all inwardly hope there'll be something for him today.

Spencer is quite as likeable as his picture portrays him but he is an inveterate gambler. He is really quite a lady's man but although it would be hard for a woman to understand - I don't see how anything he has ever had to do with the gals here would affect his affection for his wife. In weaker moments he blurts out that he is no good and if he is anything it is due to his wife - he thinks the world of her - he is 25 and they have a little girl 4 or 5 years old - cute as a bug's ear.

We took a farce physical exam today which really only amounted to filling some forms to state that we were ready for further overseas service. Another thing - or did I tell you - we are getting more crews here! Evidently they are experienced combat men transferred from some outfit which is on its way home. They're not here yet - let you know more about it when I see them.

Well people, I fear that is it for today - if we go on pass it should be this afternoon sometime but the outlook is not too bright. Be good.

Lotsa Love, Frank

Wednesday, May 23 - Letter from John Staeger

Hi Frank,

And the rest of the next best crew in the E.T.O.

Thanks for the compliment (S/Sgt.) but we happen to still be a lower class known as "black ass" sergeants or buck. Some of us have "it" and some of us don't. (We don't - none of us.)

I'm really ashamed of myself for not having at least written to you. No excuse, Sir. That Sunday night that you boys came down to the Red Cross must have been a misunderstanding on someone's part. Cal said you were to be there around six or six thirty. At seventy-thirty all hopes were lost and he tried to call you at your base Red Cross, but didn't get you of course.

I know what it's like trying to make connections from here, so can appreciate your futile attempts. That hop we had the second time you were here surprised us. They popped it on us late in the afternoon. However Morse and Johnson weren't on it. I was down at a hospital four miles from here to see an infantry boy from home. Got back at eight and found we had an eight-thirty take off.

As for us getting to Ipswich, it can be done. We can get a train from there at 0025. Don't know for sure what time we can leave here but will find out and call you at your Aero Club next Thursday (31st) evening at 7:00-7:30, or Friday at the same time if I can't get through, or one or the other of us can't make it.

Not much late news as to what is going to happen to us. Plenty of rumors. They scheduled us for ground school and flying and they do have facilities. We've been flying quite a few night missions and have had quite a lot of ground school. Mostly things we had in basic gunnery school.

Just came back from a 48 yesterday (This morning at 0400). My brother is over here and I have spent three of my passes with him. He is way down near Torquay. It takes quite a while to get down there but I can usually squeeze forty hours out of a 48 down there. Man, has he got a deal. Wish I were a Navy pilot. I'd settle for a "super big bird." If I ever get back to the states I'm going to try to get back into "gadgets." My grand total of 33 points sure won't get me out of this damn Army very fast.

No, I never did hear from "Wabbit Twacks" or Kranshaw. Maybe if I'd written first it would have helped. I did get the "pics" from Gulfport and Savannah though. I've ordered prints of the best ones. They sent too many of some. I gave Cal some to send Rose Mary. Those weren't so hot. Especially the one of you and Eileen and that "thing" I had. Boy, was she a honey. The one of you boys was perfect. Cal still hears from Rose Mary and also that Savannah "babe." He doesn't write her, but she has been keeping some sweet ones coming. Maybe she'll pull another Rock Hill deal on him.

We have a hop in an hour and I must get a letter off to home.

Give all the boys my regards. Here's hoping we can do some good soon. Hope to see all of you. Till then, best of luck.

As always, John

Thursday, May 24

Dear Mother, Harry and Mike,

Here, here, I'm way behind but as you can probably guess we got our pass. It was a 72 hour number this time and we didn't find out until rather late Saturday evening it was to start Sunday at 6:30 PM and end yesterday at 6:30 so I had to rush to get ready in a hustle. We showered by flashlight on Saturday evening and felt ourselves very lucky to have hot water to do the job in.

Fortunately the truck left Sunday at 9:30 AM for the station. Mass is at 9 AM and recently the priest has no sermon at the 9 o'clock number until after mass is finished just so those going on pass can make it and skip out after Mass itself is over. I made it O.K. and we all took off together Sunday morning. I was determined to go to Cambridge and my boy Shaffer wanted to go along. I wasn't too keen about it but he pulled that "well, if you don't want me" routine, so I just couldn't say no. Shaffer and I took the necessary change at Stowmarket and had to wait a couple hours for a train to Cambridge. Upon arrival in Cambridge I went direct to a Red Cross Canteen. I had only the Bishop's name to go on but did rather well with that. He was listed in the telephone directory and after we'd had some coffee I called. Mrs. answered - I explained who I was - little difficult if you know what I mean. The English are not quite as informed on the phone as we are but she soon placed me and I said I'd like to call if it were convenient and bring one of my buddies and she said of course to come immediately. We got a bus - they live in a small village just outside Cambridge. It is on the edge of the borough of Cambridge but quite a distinct separate quaint little community. There are no numbers for houses there - each place has (each house that is) its own particular name. The Bishop's house is Maris house. We did not stay long for I had promised to meet the rest of the crew in London. They received us rather warmly I would say and seemed quite hospitable. We weren't there longer than 10 minutes when "Tea" was ready and we sat down over a hot dish and carried on our discussion from there. My few times at Thompson's at tea time stood me in good stead - it was one of those quite homey situations which is accomplished quite casually - mainly conversation and mostly use of the fingers to accomplish the majority of the eating. Oh Shaffer - I had coached him a bit before going in - he got on quite well letting me talk my head off for both of us but the thing that baffled him was when they served him a piece of tart. Quite like a pie but in a much smaller scale. He had no tools at his place save the usual knife and he had not watched Mrs. Kempthorne managed hers with her fingers so after a quiet sigh, he proceeded to do the job with a knife. If there was a real breach of etiquette it was on their part for he had no fork - should have asked for one but aside from that everything went quite well.

It was at tea that Mrs. told me that two days before they had received a letter from Marge which stated my coming was imminent. Well - I had hoped to beat that letter there - thought I had but I said "Oh she did write? Well, what did Marge have to say?" Well, the old gal insisted I read the letter. It was rather well done for the gal on Tenth Street - her usual typed communiqué but very few errors in typing - some in spelling and she still types on both sides of a sheet of paper. Frankly, I have always been rather startled at anything she ever writes for, with all due respect, the gal does herself credit by the spoken word - not so good on paper.

My coming was confined to a post script. Quite typical for them - the section was too long for a literary post script, but I guess Marge will ever try to relegate her brother's sons to that "after thought" category. It quite amused me - also she referred to me as "very attractive young man" which you can imagine skyrocketed my ego into limitless oblivion. The Thompsons know, but they hate to admit it, that they have no finer representative for their family - thanks only to your guidance Mother.

Perhaps you remember how well informed the Bishop's wife was concerning most things. I was glad I'd had a reasonably decent course in Modern European History - I was satisfied that I'd held my own. My impression is that this branch of the family, however connected it is, rather looks down on the Thompson clan. I got the impression that the bishop was quite pleased with me - maybe they expected I'd be a wild Indian or something. They were as a whole very, very kind to me and insisted I stop by again should I be in the vicinity. The Bishop has a heart condition but both of them, I'd say, are in darn good shape. He has to slow down of course but, for a pair as well on as they are, they are well preserved.

Their home is a simple cottage - quite typical of the English philosophy of living - retire to the quite countryside in the waning years. The community itself is typical. I was glad I went. I had not, before I left on pass, received Mother's letter regarding the silver but Harry had written me something about it. Mrs. offered to help me get something, however I didn't stay over for a couple reasons. First not knowing how I'd be received, I promised the boys I'd be in London that night. Second it was the Whitsuntide Sunday here - it is called a Bank Holiday - probably analogous to the Holiday we have for Labor Day only I believe it is of some Anglican religious significance. At any rate shops closed on Friday and did not reopen until Tuesday so I'd have been stuck in Cambridge a couple days. We had made plans to take a room in London so I figured I should be there, moreover I more or less was afraid that the old lady's selection would hardly agree with my own. I had in mind something quite modern and I could see from the furnishings etc. that her ideas would hardly coincide with my own. Also Shaffer was with me so I did not give the whole thing too much serious thought. However, I hope I can get back there once more. My impression was that, although it is a large place, Cambridge is essentially built around the University. I saw some rather good etchings and a painting or two I wouldn't mind having. They were not too steep either - done by students I think.

I think I'll finish this letter on this sheet for I want it to get there without delay. The matter I want to get straight and would like as fast an answer as possible is this silver proposition. In all, I spent a day or day and a half scouring London for something. I wanted plate because it is more serviceable and more likely to be within the limits of my pocketbook. Unfortunately, for the past five years no plate has been produced in England - cutlery - yes, but I was shopping for a silver service - sugar bowl - creamer - perhaps coffee pot and tray. Any plate you can get is second hand - saw quite a good looking one for about 40-50 berries but it had a bit too much gingerbread to suit me, but I would have bought it if it hadn't been second hand - couldn't see sending you anything which someone else had used.

The one outfit I did like was really beautiful - modern - classy looking - solid silver - about 64 pounds - between 240 and 250 dollars. I don't know where you would put it Mom - it was a little out of my line at the time but if we're here a couple more months I could manage it. Or if you are interested in cutlery let me know. I spent a lot of time looking about - Red Cross woman went with me to Hammersmith (section of London) she met me in the morning and spent some time with me taking me *from place to place but it was no dice. Tried a number of places off Piccadilly and on Oxford Street but it was not much use. I could pick up sugar bowl and creamer alone for from 40-60 bucks - or would you rather have the money? Don't worry about my strapping myself. You know your little boy - It seems a shame to me not to send back something quite typical of England now that I'm here and yet I'm not certain what to get - There is a place that does coats of arms on lovely white scarves - tried to get fixed there but you need British ration points so I'm out of luck there. I have plenty of money - more than is good for me perhaps, so name your poison mom. Let me know as soon as possible please. We may not get another pass here even at that but we'll see - maybe I'll do better if I could get to Scotland - I'd better close this for now. Lotsa Love, Frank*

Thursday, May 24

Dear Mother Harry and Mike,

Well, this is my second today. The first was a bit hurried. We had some visiting General on the field so we had a review down at the "Line" so I thought I'd better get the first one off since I wanted some information in that one; this one I can take a little more leisurely and if I don't get it done today I can finish up to-morrow.

Incidentally censorship has been lifted. I am close to a village called Horham in Suffolk County. We are 2 or 3 miles from a small town of Eye and 10-12 miles from "Diss" where we catch the train for London. More or less centrally located between large towns of Ipswich and Norwich. They have "Liberty Runs"(6 hour pass) to these two places 5 nights a week but I'm not too well disposed toward either town and then we can only get in in the evening. A truck or bus takes you in at 6 PM and picks you up at 11 PM - distance about 25 miles. Also trucks from the base meet all incoming London trains at Diss so we can get there any evening. Eye we get to on bicycles and Pules at Horham or Hoxne we manage the same way. Most of the time we are more inclined to stay on the base for unless you want women, you can have a better time right here. So much for location - I think you can find it now on a large map of England.

Well, let's see now, I guess I left off on my pass to London at Cambridge. We got a train out that evening dodging the rain drops but the rain had stopped when we hit London at about eleven that night. We went to Central Red Cross where we picked up a note telling us where the rest of the gang was - same place as before. On the way we met Joe and we all went back together. We had arranged to get a room at this Red Cross Club, which was formerly the manager's lodging. Just 3 double bunks in it - enough for the E.M. on the crew and one over. It is as good as a hotel really, for that particular room has a bathroom adjoining so we had our own private bathtub, wash bowl, and toilet.

Next morning we all slept a bit late - I was glad, for traveling all the day before had kind of petered me out. To tell the truth weather conditions and everything else were against our having much of a time. It rained a lot of the time and then this Holiday business had driven a lot of people away from London, but it seemed to have driven a lot more people in. The rain, in turn, drove them into the shows and try as I would, neither the Red X or myself could get me tickets to the Lunts in Love and Idleness or Gay Rosalinda (Der Fledermous) the two stage productions I wanted to see. I spent part of the afternoon trying to get tickets and the remainder in the art gallery taking a glimmer at the Exhibition of the Royal Academy of Arts.

That evening I started out with the boys - we had a steak (horse, I think) dinner and then went to a pub. We really started for a dance but didn't quite make it. About an hour after we got in the pub the beer ran out and we started drinking scotch. This sort of deal burns me up for I knew they had more beer for they would sell it to us on the sly for a chaser. In other words, they'd turn off the beer to sell the inferior scotch at 50 cents a shot. Well, the longer I stayed the sorer I got. In addition, my boys were busily engaged working on a couple rough characters. I don't mind going down Piccadilly teasing and pricing the Commandos but hell, you don't have to associate with them - look for them and buy them drinks. My boys seem to enjoy fooling with this God damned spawn of the gutter. I honestly try to be a good sport but it just isn't there. If I got drunk enough I suppose I'd check one out like the rest but if you must have it I say, get something and at least have the pleasure of seducing her - why pay for it? Well, I left - it was pouring rain but I couldn't stand it. Those Limeys' taking your money and calling you "sucker." If they said it under their breath I wouldn't mind.

Well, I finally made the dance quite drenched but the old O.D.s soon dried out and I had some fun dancing. Wound up with a British Service Gal - not too bad at all. I told you the last time we went to London we'd met some - what seemed to us - nice girls. Well, the one I liked I couldn't get hold of. You see when I'd last seen her she wouldn't give me her home address or telephone number - she said her folks wouldn't think it proper if I called, for we met them under rather peculiar conditions. I'll tell [you] about it sometime, or have I already? Well, I had the office phone number but due to the holiday they weren't working so as they say in the E.T.O., I had "had it." The next morning I resolved to call her at the office early but although I left a call at the desk no one awoke me and I burned out another morning in the sac. I called at noon to get her for lunch but line was always busy.

Spent the afternoon looking for silver - I've already told you my difficulties there. Also had a hell of a time trying to find a place where I could get my clothes pressed. Went to one prosperous looking place and the proprietor was kind enough to send me to a place - his comment was very British "You Americans are too clothes conscious - an Englishman would wear a suit 8-12 months without getting it pressed." Before it got too late I got to a public telephone and called up Dorene. It is rough in the U.K. - it seems she had a date - well, I was annoyed and decided I'd better sell myself over the telephone but quick. Finally she said she would break the other date and I met her that evening at six. We had dinner at a Chinese place and went to Covent Garden and danced all evening. I really had the best evening I'd had in the U.K.

The next morning I went to Hammersmith and all over again in search of silver. Had lunch with Dorene at noon and then we had a couple drinks in the Pubs until 2 PM, met the officers and all came back together on the 4:05 train. We had had a rather good time in spite of the weather and the Holiday. As soon as we got back I went over to see "Laura" playing on the Post.

It certainly did us all good to get away for a while. Things get stagnant when you stay in one place too long and don't accomplish very much there. It did me a lot of good to have a night out with Mrs. Burgess' little girl too. She has quite a cute figure and quite a pretty face - good company and not too bad a dancer. Incidentally I got a big kick out of when they'd have a "ladies excuse me." The girls cut in then - there actually is a preponderance of women - it's really nice work.

Well, guess I'd best be getting along - so went our second invasion of London - didn't actually accomplish a thing but I tried hard anyway. Be good, people.
Lotsa Love, Frank

Saturday, May 26—No letter
Flew Mission 335; Cooks Tour 3; Ship #43-38333

This mission was not listed on the website for the 95th Bomb Group. I would soon learn the purpose of this mission and what actually happened. Once again, Sundin was flying Heavy Date, however this time she did not return to the base. To this day, she remains on the bottom of the North Sea.

May 30, Wednesday

Dear Mother, Harry and Mike,

Well, let's see people I'm a bit off the beam here. This is my first since last Thursday or Friday and I don't blame you if you are peeved at me. I honestly couldn't help it we have been doing quite a bit of flying - routine training missions you know - that was up until Saturday and when we got back someone had decided we were to get a 48 hour pass so on Monday morning we were off again to London.

We just got back a few minutes ago and I thought I'd dash off a few lines. I had a pretty good time this time - not so much rain and I got to see a bit more.

When I first got there I went along with the boys and we all got pressed up. We had been caught with our pants down in that respect, for we hardly expected to go on pass again so soon. After that I ran all over London to get me some tickets for the "Lunts." I finally got two - they were not good seats but all I could get so I called up my little Dorene and we took in "Love and Idleness." It was an experience going to an English theatre. We had a drink at the bar first - got our seats - ordered coffee for the "Interval" (Intermission). It was very well done - light comedy but quite good. The next morning I slept in as I was tired from a strenuous week before. Actually I shouldn't have gone on pass - would have done me more good to stay at camp and sleep but you know a G.I. - he just can't let a pass to London slip away. I managed to see Gramp's London Tower while there this time. It is closed to all civilians. I had not tried to get in before for all information I could get was that it was completely closed. However they do take people in uniform through twice a day on a conducted tour. You cannot wander about and it is hardly as worthwhile as it would be if you could go and look as you please. More about that later. Also went through a German Submarine on display on the Thames. Went dancing last night and had quite a good time - did very little drinking and it can be assumed from that that I chubbed very little with my boys. It is nice to know a nice girl to be with - you enjoy things a lot more that way.

Well, people this missive is merely meant to be a hurried explanation I will do better tomorrow - still a bit tired and am going to have myself some sleep. I have lots of your letters to answer - will get at them soon - honest - I'm not neglecting you honest! I have lots of things to tell you. Rumors are good and persist that we'll have orders to fly home in the next 30 days so save the puttying job for me. (I know you know better than to take this too seriously but it sounds awfully good). Box arrived Sunday with Snips and Tea and Stone - it was Grand and couldn't have come at a better time. Going to try to fix me some soup now and get some sleep.

Lots and Lotsa Love, your own, Francis George

FINDING "BIG SUNDIN"

Present Day

I had been typing letters for about eighteen months and had bound one volume, which I'd printed and gifted to my siblings for Christmas 2015. It was now August 2016 and I was feverishly typing the final few months of letters before the next break at the end of June. There were no letters the entire month of July; my guess is that he'd returned home. I was in the middle of the April 1945 letters, and like any reader anxious to find out what would happen I had to discipline myself not to steal to the end of May's letters to find out if my father had written home about the ditching. I never would have imagined the next treasure I'd unearth.

It was August 10 and I was home in the evening typing letters, when I noticed yet another letter with the signature of the pilot on the outside. I had seen this before, and realized that there were other letters also signed by different officers. I determined they must have been censoring them. That was when I started to wonder what had happened to the pilot, so I did a Google search for "Roger W. Sundin"; it returned five listings. Two of the listings were from the Army archives. One was the accident report of ditching, which I already had, and two were from an article about a marketing firm in Boston, Massachusetts with the name Sundin Associates. What were the chances, I thought, given that the pilot was from Rhode Island. When I went to the article, I found the website for the firm mentioned. I then went to the website and there, on the About Us page was the CEO, Roger W. Sundin, Jr. This was not a coincidence. I wrote a message in the Contact Us, inquiring as to whether or not I had found the family of my father's pilot from WWII and if not, would they please let me know. I indicated that I had some letters in which the pilot was spoken of very highly by my father and if this was the right family, I'd be happy to share them. What follows are the remarkable emails we exchanged.

August 11, 2016
Hello Loretto,

You have indeed reached the right family. I am actually Roger, Jr. My dad was a B17 pilot during the war. And we will celebrate his 93rd birthday with him this Sunday. He and his wife live independently in Maine (he did decide to stop driving this year).

Just last year, we put together an album including any of the photos, letters, and telegrams that had survived from his service. Anything you could share would be appreciated.

And by the way, how did you come across our web site?

Thanks.

Roger, Jr.

Roger Sundin

Sundin Associates, Inc.

34 Main Street • 3rd Floor

Natick MA 01760

—

Good morning Roger Jr.,

Oh my Lord, I cannot believe I've found you AND your father...and that he's living, you are so blessed. I am overcome with emotions...

I went on to explain the whole story, about my father's early death, his letters, and how I came to search for his father.

Many of the letters mention your father, and my father had nothing but praise for him, and believed he was truly blessed to have him as his pilot. I also have a copy of the accident report from May 1945 in the North Sea when your father ditched the Heavy Date. I can send you a copy if you don't already have it.

I'm attaching a crew photo, which you've probably seen. My father is first on the bottom at the right. I'm guessing your father is first on the top at the left. Let me know if I am correct. Also the Heavy Date nose art and photos of the actual letters I am typing.

Besides my mother, there are very few people still living who knew my father. He would have been 95 this past March had he lived. I am trying to learn as much as I can about him so that I may share this knowledge with his 7 children, 14 grandchildren and 8 great-grandchildren. Please wish your father a blessed and happy birthday this Sunday from Frank Thompson's family. I will tell my mother I have found your family. She will be thrilled.

I told Roger Jr. that I would collect the letters in which his father was mentioned, answered his question as to how I found his website, and closed with the following request.

Please forgive my lengthy reply; I am beside myself to know that your father is still living and that I have found him. You cannot imagine how I feel right now. Please share my story with your father whenever you feel it is appropriate, and if he has any willingness of spirit to provide me with the honor of meeting with him and talking about the time he spent with my father, I would be on a plane to Maine in a heartbeat. If not, I completely understand. Just knowing he is alive and well brings joy to my heart.

Kind regards,

Loretto

—

Hello again Loretto,

First things first. You are correct in that my father is at the back left in the photo. He was 6′ 4″ at the time and many couldn't figure out how he could get in and out of the cockpit - especially in an emergency!

The crew photo looks very familiar. I will review our photos tonight. I don't believe we have ever seen a picture of Heavy Date.

We will be seeing my dad on Tuesday, Aug 16. I will bring him up to speed on our connection. I am certain he will be as overcome with emotion as you.

We will pull together anything from my dad's album that would be of interest to you. Most of what we have learned is an oral history. He has a very clear recollection of his time in the service, and has visited the airfield in England where they were stationed.

Looking forward to receiving any information regarding my dad's service in the war, and his connection to your father.

Roger

We exchanged a few additional emails. I shared that I, too, had connected with the 95th in Horham, England, as well as with The Goldfish Club.

. . . I have connected with the 95th in England, and they have invited me to visit the base, which I am hoping to do next year sometime. I've also connected with the Goldfish Club in the UK. They were able to help me with this info after some dedicated research. I'm sure your father remembers this, how could he not, but maybe he doesn't want to remember...

My father remained in contact with Dan Spencer prior to his death, and then Dan did come to visit us again when my mother remarried - I think to check out my step-father on my father's behalf - but he has since passed as well.

. . . I am grateful for your kindness and kindred soul, and will look forward to hearing about your conversation with your father. I will also work to collect anything I have that will contribute to your father's album. My father sent many things home, so I have quite a collection to sort through. I will be back in touch as well.

Kind regards,
Loretto

—

August 19, 2016
Hello Loretto,

As you know, we met with my father to celebrate his 93rd birthday this week. I can tell you he was astonished that you had made contact. He well remembered your father - especially their time in the North Sea!

I know you said you would like to visit him, and he said that would be "wonderful." The other option is on the phone, but I don't know how well that will go as his hearing is much better in person.

Please let me know what you would like to do and I will facilitate.

Roger

We agreed to touch base in a week to set a date for my visit.

. . . Wow, how exciting that his memories are still so clear after all these years, and that he has a willingness to share them. This is not always the case with many Veterans, as I'm sure you are aware.

Yes, I absolutely would love to come for a visit. I concur, the phone would suffice, but frankly, I'd be honored to meet him in person...someone who actually knew my father . . . I am beside myself. Plus, it's just so much nicer to have a conversation face to face, don't you agree?

Let's plan to touch base again next week, and Roger, I can't thank you enough for facilitating this once in a lifetime opportunity for me. Your kindness abounds and I am extremely grateful to you.

Have a great weekend!

Loretto

HORHAM, ENGLAND - PART 3

1945

May 31st, Thursday

Dear Mother, Harry and Mike,

Slept in late this morning - late for around here these days - they want to get you up at 6:30 now that we're not flying combat anymore. I scraped around and got me some coffee and now am back in yee old sac waiting for chow. We have a class from 1 PM until 3 so I expect I'll have to break this somewhere and finish later. We don't have much to do these days when we're not flying but you know the old story - the less you have to do the less you want to do.

I suppose I'd best get to some of the changes here on the base. I think I've told you most of them - best one here in the barracks is that some of the new crews came into the squadron from another outfit which I judge has gone home. They brought a radio with them and now we listen to the AEF programs all day. They rebroadcast Hope's, Benny's, and a lot of other programs, and we thoroughly enjoy it. Incidentally, these crews were told when they came on the base that they would be on orders to ship out to the States by June 15. I don't expect we'll go with them but it is a good sign. Also while "tooling" about the area in the Big Birds we noticed that a great number of fields formerly occupied by Yank Bomber or Fighter Groups are now absolutely empty and devoid of activity - they seem to be moving them out all right. The best part of all the rumor business is that I haven't heard one in about three weeks which would indicate we are going direct to the C.B.I. I'd love to spend some time at home first - How about that?

I got your Mother's Day card Mom - it was awful nice to get. I'm sorry my cable didn't do better than it did as far as time is concerned. I had purposely waited until the Friday before and clocked times it would arrive with Special Services and fig-ured according to what they told me that it would get there on the Sunday.

I am quite well set as far as clothes are concerned for Herb Robinson's locker finally got there and I had stored extra sox, T-shirts, the two sweaters Aunt Maime knitted me and my Sun Tan shirts in it. It took it about 2-1/2 months to get here. I also had my pajamas packed in there so now I go to bed in the U.K. in solid comfort. This week I got to bed as the "Blue Hornet" - next week I suppose they'll dub me the "Tan Hornet."

Coach's condition doesn't sound at all good. I hope I get to write them before the week is out - we'll see. I still have a letter started here for Gramp I must finish today but I wanted to write you fellows first. I had started it - was interrupted by the flying spree and haven't gotten to finish it as yet.

I don't think there is any doubt about our going to the C.B.I. - the big question is will we get home first and if so will we continue on in our lovely Big Birds or will we be delayed and trained in B-29s or B-32s. If the latter case I believe we'd kill almost another 6 months in the States, which would be a bit of the all right.

Harry, when we went to chow one evening I told the boys what you said about Joe being the only one who enjoyed getting the Air Medal - well, they all got a big kick out of that. I guess I should have been more explicit about the Air Medal. We got it - everyone does who flies 6 missions - then you get a cluster for each 6 missions after that. Let's get this straight - we have not so many ribbons. We have the Dentyne wrapper (good conduct) which is the laugh of the Army. We can wear the E.T.O. ribbon with two bronze stars - 1 for battle over France - One for battle over Germany and the Air Medal. Also the Presidential Citation. We can wear it with 2 clusters over here with our group but should we be separated from the group we can only wear the ribbon itself for we were attached to the group only when the last Citation was awarded. That should take care of that.

I can well sympathize with you over your radio trouble. I know that when we have trouble up in the Blue well, there is just not much that can be done and sometimes you really want those radios. How is she coming along now? Haven't heard much about it lately - is she O.K. now?

There is a lot of nasty business going on in London now. The Tommies are returning, there are some shootings! I hope I never get into London in uniform when they all return - there sure will be hell to pay.

Don't say Jerry is "at last" on his way to the Pacific. I was just lucky to get over here for the beginning of the end. I guess that was the bonus I got for getting through my Tech schools as promptly as possible. Sometimes I could have kicked myself for not purposely screwing up along the way - especially at radio school but I guess trying to do your best pays dividends in the end. He may have fooled around a long time but it wasn't his fault and all to his good I'd say more power to those that can stay out of it say I.

Guess that will have to be about all for today people - save something for to-morrow don't-y'know - Bing has just come on too, sooo be good, people.
Lotsa Love, Frank

May 31, Thursday

Dear Harry,

Well, old boy following my lifetime policy of letting you in on all the poop, I'll get this one off, which should serve the dual purposes of informing you and also keeping something for the record. Under no circumstances do I want you to let Mother get her glimmers on this or anyone else for that matter. Mother for it will only worry her - anyone else for they will probably voice a tribute to my conceit. I'll tell Mom when I get home.

I just thought when you spoke of Rita Jane Niger in her last - I hope you don't let up in that respect. You see I have faith that your prayers will be answered but I am dubious about my own. God was certainly with us Saturday last - it was your prayers I honestly believe that saved six of us - we were in dire straits for a few hours and were rendered safe through a course of events that could not have been coincidental - there was a greater force at work for us - that is all there is to it. This too should explain why I didn't write for almost a week also our additional pass to London.

I left a letter to Gramp to attend a discussion which is held in the Post theatre every day and attendance at least once a week is compulsory. It was on the G.I. Bill of Rights. Joe and I went to eat and then to PX to sweat out a line to get our weekly ration. We met Shackelford there had a Coke and left. On the way back we met Sundin, Pilot, and Turner Co-pilot in a truck. They had been looking for us. It seems we had to "slow time" an engine on a plane. So we took her up - tooled around the area and came down. We ate late and found out that we had a D.R. mission the next day, (Dead Reckoning). It is a navigational training mission and so we went to bed early for we were up early in the morning. We got up - went to a more or less token briefing where we found out we were to fly out over the North Sea. Also in addition to Pilot, Co-pilot, Navigator, Engineer, and R.O. who must fly with every ship, we took our Bombardier, Herb Robinson who hadn't wanted to fly that day, didn't feel like it, but the squadron Navigator wanted him to go along and get checked out on D.R. navigation so that made six of us. When we got out to the Big Bird we found out that a C-1 maintenance man was supposed to go too. C-1 is the automatic pilot we call it "George." He didn't show up at take-off time so we went up without him. The weather was bad - we couldn't fly over the stuff, so we flew under it. I was supposed to send in - position report every hour - so that about ten minutes after 9, I called up the Navigator for a fix. The Bombardier told me that he was taking a double drift wind reading and would call me as soon as he was through. I was tuned up on my radio on an emergency D.F. frequency as soon as I had left the coast and had called in and obtained a fix which was 7 miles off according to the Navigator - the trouble with accuracy was that we were too low for good transmission. When I found I couldn't get a fix for position report from the Navigator I tuned up to the base ground station so I'd be ready when he got ready to give it to me for it was late already. When I had asked for it the pilot had heard me and said we were too low to send it then. We were too low for comfort!

I was unhappy because it is not much fun getting there - all alone doing nothing so I called up the base station and got a frequency check O.K. and maximum signal strength. I was about to call again when I heard the co-pilot over the interphone giving the order "Prepare to ditch." I'd better explain here that ditching refers to landing your aircraft on the water when you are run out of gas or in dire distress. We were losing altitude fast so I immediately changed my radio set up to the emergency and by that time the Navigator and Bombardier had come from the nose thru the Bomb Bay to the radio room. All members of the crew take places seated on the radio room floor with hands locked behind their necks when you ditch for there is a terrific impact when you hit. Figure it out for yourself - we hit the water at 105 miles/hour. When Joe got back to the radio room I sent him for the emergency radio - he got it - closed the door and took his place. I was hopelessly trying to get in an S.O.S. to the D.F. station but I knew that by that time we were far too low I was sending in the blind for I had to listen on the interphone for the "Prepare for impact" order and tell the three boys who were seated so they'd be ready. The Co-pilot had kept asking me "are they ready?" Finally I said they were and in a few seconds he gave the order - I relayed it to the boys - they got set - I pulled my chute and stuffed it between me and my radio to absorb the shock and then we hit.

Water came in from all places immediately although the actual shock had not been as bad as I expected. That was a tribute to a darn good pilot. As soon as we had absorbed the first shock we started to climb out in turn from the radio room hatch - the cover having been taken off and thrown out when they came back. Joe got out first and pulled the handles to release our 2 - 6 man rubber dinghies from the cowling of the ship. I got out second to last and it was then that I finally discovered why we ditched. The number 4 engine was burning - still going in the water - flames about 6-8 feet high. When I got out Herb, the bombardier, tried to lift the radio out but couldn't so since the water was up to his waist so he got out and into the dinghy. I was reluctant to leave the radio so I finally got hold of Herb's knife and tried to cut it out. With the impact the radio had become jammed in a rack we use to house radar jamming equipment on combat missions. It was impossible to cut her loose and I left the top of the ship just a few seconds before she went down. We had to push our rubber boat away to avoid being hit by the tail which was the last section to disappear under the water. Then we were alone - nothing on the horizon but water - it was cold, too, and no radio. This was unfortunate for we knew there were ships - at least two within 50 miles of us and we'd have been sure of rather rapid assistance had we had our radio to let them know our plight. As far as we knew no one knew that we were down - it was a chance in a million that my S.O.S. had been picked up when we were so low. We were a bunch of sad looking sacs. The four of us who had been in the radio room were drenched to the skin.

We sat there about 5 minutes checking to make sure no one was hurt and then, there was where Providence entered in. A beautiful Big Bird came over us - we frantically grabbed flare pistols and flares and shot them off like crazy - yelled like mad men altho (sic) we knew they couldn't hear us - at first it looked as though they wouldn't see us but they did - circled us to send in a fix to Air Sea Rescue and stayed with us to keep us company. After about an hour in the water it started to rain - we covered ourselves with oilskin sheets provided in the dinghies - it kept the water off us but it fell in the bottom of the rubber boats and our feet were in water all the time. We were shivering so that the dinghy shook.

Shortly after the end of the second hour in the water a British plane arrived with a small boat tied on the bottom of it. The B-17 that had been keeping us company *buzzed us and left. That ship had been on a D.R. from our base just as we had but it was a wonder that their course so closely followed our own. We waved her a grateful goodbye and turned our attention on the RAF ship. It made 7 or 8 passes at us and finally dropped the boat. None of the chutes on one end opened and when we had finally paddled to it in the dinghies we found it splintered to pieces. The plane blink-ered us that a Launch was on the way and so with the rain we covered up and settled down to wait. I think I even dozed for a while - but I was too wet, we were all cold.*

After another hour or so another B-17 from our group showed up. The Warwick (RAF) had not left and that made two planes keeping a vigil over us. We were never without company in the air - it was extremely comforting to say the least. Another hour or so elapsed and another RAF Warwick came with another boat. This relieved the first one and after a couple passes dropped us the wooden boat tied under him. It was a perfect drop - only about a city block away from us and all chutes opened this time. She settled neatly on the surface - we paddled over and climbed on an almost dry boat. After cutting loose the chutes (wished we'd saved them) Joe and the Big Sundin got the two motors going - they were outboards mounted - a third away back from the bow - the plane signaled us by blinker a magnetic heading to steer and off we sailed under our own power. That little boat had everything on it. Most important at the time was cigarettes.

The plane had not left us - they were still guiding the Launch to us. At 5:10 we sighted the Launch but with our little boat we were independent as hogs on ice. We were glad to see it really. Once aboard it was a story of love and kisses, they had warm woolen clothing for us hot soup and tea - even some South African Bourbon. We ditched at 9:30 AM and were picked up at about 5:30 PM very little the worse for wear. We didn't get back until 1:30 that night for it seems we went down dead center in the North Sea - just as far from Norway as from Scotland - about 155-160 miles out. Once we made land the Navy took over for we wound up at a Navy Submarine base. They fed us 2 quarts of good Scotch and hot ham and eggs. We went to bed in nice warm English blankets. Joe got sick from drinking too much but got some sleep later. The WRENs woke us at 7 in the morning with a cup of hot tea - Oh it was rough - we had breakfast with the Naval officers and I got to Mass and we got a chance to go through an English submarine before we left for an RAF base where a Big Bird picked us up and flew us back to the base.

Well, fellow that is it - we returned about three PM Sunday and at 8 they told us we could have a 48 hour pass if we wanted it. So we took off for London. Herb bombardier didn't go - had to have his back x-rayed and Shackelford had to be left at RAF base for treatment of head injury and shock and exposure but aside from that all we sustained were minor lacerations. Sooo I hope you at least will understand why I didn't write for a few days - have to run off to lunch now - expect to take a X country over Ireland this PM so, be good, old boy and please keep remembering us - we sure need it!
Love, Frank

LOST AND FOUND

Present Day

Finally, I knew what had happened when they ditched in the North Sea. The letter my father had written to his brother was so descriptive; I could envision the entire ordeal. It was one thing to know they'd ditched, but something completely different to hear my father's voice explain it in such detail. I now had two pieces of the Heavy Date puzzle—the accident report, and my father's letter. Knowing they'd all survived to live their lives after this event had never caused me a heavy heart. It was more like solving a mystery. This lighthearted perception of their accident poorly prepared me for the next mystery I had decided to try and solve, however, which was the mystery of Dick Perry's accident.

Committed to finding out about Dick Perry's accident, I set about my search as I'd done when searching for the accident report of my father's ditching. To this day I don't know what I was thinking when I embarked on this particular search because what I uncovered disturbed me so much that I could not type letters again for a few months. I was haunted by what I'd uncovered and rebuked myself for ever having decided to go somewhere I should have just left unknown.

When I searched for my father's ditching, I knew going in that the entire crew survived and went on to live their lives; although my father's was short, he did not perish in the accident. This was my mindset when I approached the search for Dick's accident, with a sort of levity and curiosity to solve the mystery. Regrettably, I realized I was not in the right frame of mind to uncover the tragedy that was the end of Dick's life. To this day it breaks my heart.

Upon locating the accident report on the Aviation Archeology website, I purchased the report and awaited its arrival in my inbox. In the meantime, I poked around the Internet and learned that Dick had flown with the 9th Air Force, was a member of the 61st Troop Carrier Group (TCG), and was stationed only 105 miles away from my father in England. I couldn't find much about his tour of duty, but once the report arrived, I read with a heavy heart the outcome of that fateful day, March 27, 1945.

The report was covered with stamps: SECRET; RESTRICTED, S E C R E T. I knew from the initial website that the mission was non-battle, and I also learned that the TCG was responsible for transporting cargo, troops, or fuel during the war. Dick indicated in his letter to my father that he was flying C-109s, which he explained was a converted B-24 "tanker" used to haul fuel. However, on this particular mission, Dick piloted a C-47A Skytrain, known for carrying troops, cargo, and towing gliders during the war. The accident report indicated only that the pilot's mission was "ferrying personnel."

On board were the pilot, co-pilot, navigator, engineer, two passengers—a glider pilot and a ground officer - and a radio operator. All seven souls perished that day. They took off from their base in Barkston Heath, Lincolnshire, England en route to Saint-André-de-l'Eure, France, approximately 380 miles one way. The weather was overcast, with visibility only one to two miles in light drizzle. The report indicated that Dick was flying into instrument weather, where the pilot cannot see because he is flying in the clouds and must rely on navigating by referencing only his instruments in the cockpit.

Eye witness reports indicate the sound of engines approaching, flying very low in foggy weather. The valley would not have been visible in the heavy fog. As the plane flew straight on, its left wing hit some trees as the ground level changed, tearing most of it off and causing the right wing to rise. It continued that way through the trees, uprooting many and bursting into flames when it came to rest, where it burned for two to three hours. The crash occurred less than 100 miles from their destination. I had to stop reading; my heart was too heavy to continue. I can't imagine those final moments of that flight. What a horrendous way to die, after surviving almost 1,000 hours of flying time and being so close to the end of the war. I think it will never stop haunting me.

When I was finally able to continue reading, I probably shouldn't have. Included in the report was a map of where the accident had occurred and also the degrees of injury to the personnel. To make things worse, there were copies of photographs of the wreckage. I had to put it away and did not revisit Dick's accident report again for two years.

I resumed typing my father's letters a couple of months later, which brought me great joy after such heartbreak. During my hiatus, I poked around the genealogy site a bit more to determine Dick's final resting place. Of all things, he was in the same cemetery as my father. One day after an appointment I had nearby at Mount St. Mary's Hospital in Lewiston, I went to the cemetery office and asked for assistance with locating Dick's grave. Heather at Gate of Heaven located his grave for me and copied the map so that I could easily find it. It was surreal to learn that Dick was laid to rest not far from my father, and not buried abroad; he'd been there the whole time. I found him resting next to his mother, my Great Aunt Maime. I took some time to reflect on his short life and contributions he had made to our nation, said some prayers for him, and walked back to my car with an all-too-familiar heavy heart.

—

When I began this journey to my still-unknown destination, I had no sense of the places I would go or the people I would meet, but more unexpected were the opposing emotions I would feel along the way. In one moment I found myself excitcd, the next heartbroken, still the next elated. While at times it was full of ups and downs, I must admit it was also a bit addictive. I could not seem to get enough information, history, or facts to satisfy my hunger for understanding. Each time I would catch onto a thread of my father's life, I couldn't stop myself from unraveling it until I felt content I had reached a satisfying conclusion. Of course, in some instances I knew that was impossible, but in some instances that desire to know brought me face to face with experiences I otherwise would have missed completely, experiences that have deepened my life and stole my heart, experiences like meeting "Big Sundin."

After a little back and forth with emails, Roger Jr. and I arranged for me to visit his dad. I was actually going to meet THE Big Sundin.

Hello Loretto,

We are good to go for your visit to Maine on September 24-25!

When you have firmed up your schedule, please let me know and I will keep my Dad informed.

My wife - Geralyn - and I will also be in Maine at that time. We look forward to meeting you and listening to the conversations.

In the days preceeding my visit, I continued typing with the hope I may learn something of the ditching from my father before I met Big Sundin. My flight was Saturday when finally . . .

—

Hi Roger,

Just typed this one Wednesday evening.

It is a letter from my Dad to his brother in which he describes the ditching.

Thought you may like to read it.

See you tomorrow!

Loretto

SEPTEMBER 24, 2016 —MEETING "BIG SUNDIN"

To say I was anxious, excited, or nervous would be understatement. It's difficult to describe how I felt as I packed up my letters, a printed version of the most recent letters, and the previous book of letters, photos, and memorabilia to share with Roger and his family. I also had questions. Lots of questions and I was hoping Big Sundin would be able to answer them—or at least some of them.

Ninety-three years old. Was he a lively ninety-three or sedentary? Was his memory still sharp or fading? Would he only have certain memories, or would the letters serve as the catalyst to perhaps bring suppressed memories to the surface? All these questions kept rolling around in my head while my heart was hoping for a warm and informative reunion of memory and man.

The flights were on time and uneventful, just the way I like them. The airport was small and not busy, with a two-person queue at the car-rental desk. I texted Roger Jr. that I had landed and was in line, and that I would be on my way shortly. His response was comforting "... having a grand time listening to real war stories." This small communication set the tone for me and helped to calm my nerves.

I didn't even take a moment to compose myself when I arrived. I just couldn't wait any longer. The suspense had been building for weeks and finally, I was going to be face to face with Big Sundin. I collected my things, and made my way to the front door. The bell was answered by Roger Jr.'s wife Geralyn. She embraced me with a warm hug and I knew at that moment that everything was going to be fine. We both admitted it felt as though we had known each other for years, reuniting after a long absence; we were not complete strangers.

My next hug was from Roger Jr., then Gloria–Roger Sr.'s wife and finally, there he was, walking toward me, all six feet plus of him, smiling and vibrant, Big Sundin. As we hugged, I told him I felt like I was meeting a celebrity. He laughed and we got right down to business. I was shown to "my room" where we unpacked all the things I had brought with me, then we made our way to a beautiful sunroom overlooking their wooded backyard.

Roger Jr. had already printed out a copy of the second volume of letters that included the mentions of his dad, and was happy that I had also brought along printed copies to leave with them since their son was very interested in reading them as well. Now we had two sets. Of course mine had arrow stickies on numerous pages where I either wanted to show an actual document that had been included in a letter or where I had a question about what was being referenced in a letter itself.

I had the best intentions of trying to keep my questions in some sort of order, but once we all sat down it was obvious there was no way our visit was going to be orderly. Everyone had questions, some had answers, and none of the questions followed any sort of order. It was basically a free-for-all and we had a grand time. One question or photo begot another question or document and then another and another. This went on for a solid four hours. At some point, we had managed to decide on our dinner choices, and Roger Jr. left and returned with dinner. I never noticed when Geralyn and Gloria snuck away and made all the meal preparations prior to Roger Jr.'s return, which is when we all moved to the table and continued the conversations, reminiscences, and anecdotes. The afternoon flew by, no pun intended. We were all so energized and engaged that there was never a lull in the banter. I remember feeling the comfort of visiting family with much catching up to do. It seemed that when one of us came up for air, another jumped in and took the rest of us in another direction.

Finally, around 9 o'clock in the evening, Roger Jr. and Geralyn reluctantly decided they should be on their way. They had a two-hour drive ahead of them to return home. After sharing warm goodbyes and more hugs, they left only to return a few moments later having realized we had not taken any photos. With photos and selfies on our phones, they departed once again with assurances that we would stay in touch and continue to share our findings with one another. Those few hours together created a bond I knew would never be broken.

How to explain the dialogue? That is a challenge. I was prepared, and had brought my smartpen with me to record our visit, but as Big Sundin was telling us different stories filled with animation and remarkable detail, though I wished I was recording him, I didn't want to stop him and ask permission to, I just wanted him to keep going. I felt the request would have broken the flow and spirit of the exchange, so I decided to forget it and took notes to help me remember.

What left the most indelible impact on me were Big Sundin's very explicit recollections of events from over seventy years before. He recalled them as though they had just happened, sharing precise details, some of which I had an inkling of and many that were new to me. I will try to share them with you now.

THE DITCHING

Roger Sr. seemed to recall very specific details of the ditching from 1945. His memory was remarkable.

"The day happened much as Frank had described it in his letter," he told us, but he added a few details that my father didn't know, and a few more that both he and my father knew, but my father chose not to share with Harry—at least not in his letter home. The first of which was the antenna situation.

We all knew from my father's letter that they'd had to fly below the clouds, and were very low over the North Sea.

"In order for the radio to communicate with the base, Frank had to drop the antenna, which was a long cable with a heavy weight on the end of it," Big Sundin explained.

"When flying at a higher altitude the antenna would be dropped and trail taut below the plane, but because we were flying so low, when your father dropped the antenna to contact the base, the weight on the end of the cable hit the water and yanked the entire antenna from the plane."

The next situation revealed to me was when my father got the order to "prepare to ditch," and he got busy getting the other four crew members into position. We knew from his letter that he tells Ferniza to get the emergency radio, which Roger Sr. referred to as the Gibson Girl, the nickname for the emergency radio transmitter.

"Ferniza got the radio, and got into position. The position of each crew member was based on their height, and since Ferniza was the smallest, he was the first man." They were sitting in a toboggan-like position, with all four men on the floor of the radio room.

"Shackelford, the navigator, would have been against the bomb bay door since he was the tallest, between his legs would have been Spencer, Robinson, and Thompson in some order, and lastly would have been Ferniza." According to Roger Sr. "It was Ferniza's job to hold the Gibson Girl tightly between his legs during the ditching, but apparently he didn't hold it tightly enough because when we hit, the radio transmitter went flying toward the bomb bay, harpooning the bomb bay door." At that point, the crew would have started getting out of the ship, freeing the dinghies, and escaping before it sank.

As the radio room was quickly filling with water, Robinson, the last crew member to leave the plane, had tried to free the radio from the bomb bay door with his knife. When he couldn't get it to budge, he climbed out of the plane. Roger Sr. recalls that my father was determined to get the radio free, "He took Robinson's knife and went back into the sinking ship to try to get the radio from the bomb bay door." When the water got too high in the compartment, my father gave up and left the sinking ship.

"What Frank didn't say in his letter was that the radio was already submerged and he had to dive underwater to try to free it," Roger Sr. explained. As the water rose he was forced to abandon his efforts and escape the plane shortly before it sank. My father may have intentionally neglected to include this detail in his letter to Harry, but Roger Sr. said "While we were in the dinghies the remainder of the day, Frank told me about his final desperate attempt to free the radio, describing how he dove under the rising water with Robinson's knife, trying to cut it out of the bomb bay door," where it most likely remains to this day.

"Another thing," Roger Sr. recalled, "I'm not sure your father ever knew this, but an RAF base actually had received Frank's SOS. The only problem was that they didn't know where it was coming from." This in itself is remarkable since the plane's antenna, which my father had let down previously to call up the base station, had broken off as they quickly lost altitude from the burning engine. "Your father knew no signal went out to the base station or the D.F. station before the ditching," which Big Sundin said my father had shared with him when they were adrift; it was more understandable why my father was so determined to free the Gibson Girl. He knew it was their last hope to communicate their plight.

Roger Sr. also reminisced about the ship that saw their flares in the North Sea and called for help. From basic training to their deployment to Horham, England, Roger Sr. "had never been separated" from his fellow pilot Snyder. Their military careers had mirrored each other's, and although they had different crews, they had remained together up until their return to the U.S. in July of 1945. On May 26, 1945, several missions were scheduled from the base. The crews rarely knew which crews were flying what missions until they returned to their quarters afterward. It wasn't until Big Sundin's crew returned to Horham after they had ditched that Roger Sr. learned the plane that had spotted them floating in the North Sea and radioed for the launch was flown by none other than Sundin's good friend, Snyder.

FRANK

Roger Sr. also shared some of his thoughts about my father, "I never knew your father's name was Frank!" He was always referred to as 'Thompson.' Roger Sr. continued, "Your father was a true leader." In my father's letters, he referred to other crews having trouble between the enlisted men and the officers—it appears primarily with regard to respect. Roger Sr. said "That was not the case with my crew, mostly because of Frank."

"Frank would not tolerate it," he said, and with the exception of one disciplinary action with the engineer, Big Sundin had no problems with his crew, which again he attributed wholly to my father. He also said, "Frank knew how to get things"—extra things they may need for their missions. One such thing was ammunition. "I was not supposed to know about it," Roger Sr. said, "but I knew that Frank had managed to finagle more ammunition out of supply, and he would strategically place it throughout the ship in order to balance the weight." Roger Sr. told me, "Your father was a born leader," and if he had stayed in the service, someone would have "grabbed him and made him an officer." Roger Sr. was actually "surprised that my father wasn't already an officer, because he certainly seemed like one to me."

SAYING GOODBYE

My room at the Sundin's house was actually Roger Sr.'s room. Once we all retired for the evening, this became more apparent—it was like a small museum. All around the room were photos and images of B-17s, museums they'd visited, memorabilia, and right there on the bookshelf, in this bedroom in Sanford, Maine, I found the identical photo of the crew that we have in Niagara Falls, New York, showing both Roger Sundin and Frank Thompson.

The next morning, Glo knocked on my door to be sure I was up and told me breakfast would be ready shortly. I readied myself, packed up my things and headed out to the kitchen. In the dining room, Glo had set out a lovely breakfast for the three of us that we enjoyed while our conversations resumed. We had already determined the best time for me to leave to get to the airport in time for my return flight, but our talking once again took us in many directions and suddenly we all realized it was time for me to leave.

Leaving them was sad, since meeting had brought us all such happiness. As Glo hugged me goodbye, she said, "I hope this isn't the end." I replied, "No, it's just the beginning." Roger Sr. and I exchanged hugs as well, and I quickly departed with many thanks. Since our visit, Glo and I have become "pen pals," writing letters, sharing thoughts, and of course, getting more questions answered by Roger Sr. I have continued to visit Roger and Glo as often as possible, each time settling into a routine of spending time together. Through our letters and occasional phone calls we have become quite close, quite like family. Whenever I think of Big Sundin, I do so with amazement. Had it not been for his skill as a pilot, at twenty-one years of age, my family would not have existed. I not only have him to thank for my father's life, but for my life as well.

HORHAM, ENGLAND - PART 4

1945

Dear Mother, Harry and Mike,

Well, I suppose this will have to be a shortie for I have little to say for myself. Am going up to Red + and hope to receive a call from John Staeger. Yes we are still trying to get together and we might make it this time - I hope so.

There is little doubt in my mind that some sort of movement will be underway here within the next two weeks. What it will be is hard to tell - we hope it will be towards home but it is hard to tell.

Gosh I'm not getting very far with this one, am I? Well, I went up to get my phone call from John last night shortly after I started this and it didn't come through so I guess I'll have to write the boys again. Went to see a show after that and thusly didn't get to finish this.

Nothing of import has been doing here - some classes today - regular squadron routine and little else.

We really began appreciating that last box I got last night. The food ration here has been cut two or three times lately. Of course in as much as we're not on combat anymore we don't need as much - I myself find myself wondering how what I eat keeps me alive but it dood (sic) it. Last night we got out the stove and made tea and soup around. We used a lot of fuel but that was to be expected for the only thing we have to cook in is our canteen cups - they hold a pint and are of aluminum which dissipates the heat very rapidly. Have to try her again tonight. The soups are dandy and sure hit the spot before hitting the sac.

Did I mention I was very glad to get the tooth brush? We can only get one every eight weeks and they are not much good so the Dr. West will come in mighty handy. The powder also comes in very handy - it is next to impossible to buy decent stuff over here. Can't say as I'm too daft about the maple sugar candy -never have been but by golly it is candy and that is the main point isn't it?

To tell the truth I am getting a bit restless again. Just back from pass last Wednesday and raring to go again. I honestly very much doubt that I'll ever see London again - just when I was making time with that gal too - but that's the way it goes in the Army.

Well people, I guess I'll have to close this one - nothing to tell - I am in there pitching vigorously. Be good.
Lotsa Love, Frank

Tuesday, June 5

Dear Mother, Harry and Mike,

I am very bad on the writing these days - no excuses really - just not enough to say to make anything worthwhile. We have been spending a lot of time in movies of late - today in particular we saw a movie this afternoon and a G.I. show this evening. Neither were too bad and it is a good way to put in time. Oh we're not discontent, but most of us are a bit restless. We'd be happy to stay here a good while longer. The big trouble is that we have plenty of spare time of late and they won't let us do too much with that spare time. We are eating quite well and getting plenty of sleep, really resting up what I mean.

We have been doing a bit of flying lately - got us up this morning at 5:15 AM to drop some 20 practice bombs. You feel better when you're doing something else like that. Justified, a bit, that you are actually earning your money. I got two juicy letters from the Tessa today so I guessed then I'd better hop to it. Glad you finally got some letters from me - things must be congested - these large troop transportations are a tremendous job. Just remember if a letter doesn't come on time that some G.I. Joe is getting home to his loved ones and that - just the thought of it - is worth a million.

Managed to get me a 12 hour pass yesterday and went cavorting about the country a bit. Main purpose to see Shackelford who is in hospital some 12-15 miles distant. Nothing serious, just not been too well of late - hope they don't ground him. He's temperamental at times no doubt but he is a darn good Navigator.

By the way, I'm expecting, by the time you get this or shortly thereafter, to receive a bit of Literature from "Flying" magazine. Please do not send it over here to me just keep it - unopened please.

Well, I suppose you will be interested in the latest rumors - I notice from your letters that some of the boys are getting home and if I read between the lines correctly - you are wondering just where your wandering boy will wind up. I'm afraid I can't help much - just chalk this down as what I'll call a good guess. It might possibly be more than a guess, but don't spread it around at all for you know how the Army has a way of screwing you up when you think you have the angles figured. We will go to the Pacific Theatre somewhere in B-17s, which I judge will be used for medium bombardment over there with the advent of the B-29. We will be home for a short time and should get some time at home, I think. We may not get to States for 2 or 3 months, but I doubt seriously that it will be that long before we get back. Return to States just the way we came here. There is my hope and guess - hope it makes a pretty reading as it does writing. Say one to St. Christopher for me cause it is a long way. Lotsa Love, Frank

June 13, Wednesday

Dear Mother, Harry and Mike,

Well, I am really ashamed to start this one - almost forgotten how to write - I bet you think I have, but tis not so you see. I have a good reason you see I'm waiting from day to day hoping that I might have some official confirmation of that last letter of mine to write to you. Things looked very good there for a while and to be quite frank, they still have a pretty good appearance if you ask me but still nothing very definite.

I suppose you have been terribly worried about me but I am as well and as ornery as ever - more so if that were possible. I got a letter from Mom yesterday - I'm so glad Rita's Ian is O.K. - I was sure I was right - that it was he and yet the American uniform puzzled me - I figured him for the Canadian Air Force. So wee Ann caught the bouquet - whew that's bad - should I get home I'll just have to steer clear of that. She is a determined gal when she gets her mind set on something - I found that out last time. I've been getting at least a letter a week from Sally - I guess I'd better get to answering soon or she'll give me up for lost. Again Tess you're keeping after me for drinking - believe me I don't undertake to write when I'm in my cups. Been doing very little hoisting since V-E Day - been doing very little of anything as a matter of fact. Censorship has been on and off so many times lately I don't know just what the status is now. Same with training program here - now you see it and now you don't. We have had a good deal of spare time lately - can't get off the Post of course except at night and I haven't been trying - only Limey town that appeals to me much these days is London - I'd sure like to hit it again - just once more.

We have been playing quite a bit of cards lately. The poker they play around here is too steep for me - it runs about a shilling (20¢) a chip and I can't afford to lose that kind of dough. What we have been playing a lot of lately is dear old Sarah Tidley's "500." The lads don't play any Bridge so we settle for that. And then the movies - we see every change and an occasional U.S.O. show. Get my cup of tea at night and some cookies and save my candy bars for before going to sleep. Actually we have been getting very little training lately and personally I welcome most any chance to keep from getting too rusty.

Today I paid about 80¢ for a little better than a quart of fresh strumberries (sic) - are you getting any at home? They sure prove a welcome change to us. What do I do most - I sleep - I've really been logging sac time of late - sleep at the drop of a hat. Indeed it is a very lazy existence and yet I am not too prone to complain for I can remember days when I would have given a lot to have a full day's sleep and then too, each day I spend here I don't have to put in in the C.B.I. so I actually can't lose if we stay here another month or so.

I guess I'd best get this off pronto before this good intention goes on the rocks. Be good, people.

Lotsa Love, Frank

1945 June 30 AM 8:10 - Telegram

DEAR MOTHER HARRY AND MIKE BACK IN THE STATES AGAIN EXPECT TO BE WITH YOU WITHIN A WEEK MORTGAGE THE HOMESTEAD LOVE= FRANCIS GEORGE

BIG BIRDS

Present Day

From the time my father arrived in Gulfport and found out he was destined to crew a B-17, he had nothing but admiration for the ship. Even his cousin Dick told him, "You landed a good plane Frank and I think you are lucky to get the B-17." As often as he spoke about his plane, I couldn't help but wonder what it was like to fly in one. Even listening to Big Sundin tell his stories of flying a "Big Bird," I'd imagine the image of this huge plane and these young men, flying into such dangerous situations and living to tell about it. Understandably, there were a few truths about those flights that remained dormant and untold until I started asking questions.

I was reluctant to ask about the specific missions, though occasionally something would trigger a memory that Roger would openly share, but I did want to know about their flights to and from the States, and was surprised to hear that their crew may never have made it to England at all. Roger explained they had left Savannah after they got their plane and headed to Bangor, Maine, where they stayed overnight. En route to Bangor, Roger buzzed not only his own house in Rhode Island, but also Shackelford's in the Tidewater area of lower Virginia, and Turner's in Albany, New York. The next morning, the navigator didn't show up. The crew went ahead and got the plane loaded, when Shackelford finally arrived in a Jeep after having gone to the infirmary. What Roger learned much later was that every time they flew a mission, Shackelford would vomit into his hat, and each mission he would show up with a new hat. Some of the crew knew this, but no one said a word to Big Sundin.

From Bangor, they flew to Thule Air Base, Greenland, and had lunch. This may have been the reference that was blacked out of my father's letter. The crew spent the night and then took off for Iceland in the morning. En route, the crew took turns sleeping, and though the plane was on automatic pilot, one of the three in the cockpit was charged with staying awake with the navigator. At some point, the navigator saw the plane was going off course, and realized that all three, Sundin, his co-pilot Turner, and engineer Ferniza had fallen asleep—the result of staying up half the night playing poker. Now, seventy-four years later, Roger admits that he had told Ferniza and Turner, "You two guys go to sleep. I'll stand watch—but I nodded off—my fault."

Shackelford called to Roger on the interphone, which woke him up and put him into action. In order to figure out where they were, Roger had to fly a search problem. "Shackelford was mad because of the extra work, and he let us know about it," Sundin recalls. There was some scrambling to get back on course, which would have kept my father very busy making all his corrections, all the while listening to Shackelford's complaining. Roger said, "He was not a happy camper from the beginning—probably because he was sick, but it may have also been fright." Once Roger found the position head for Iceland, he was able to get them back on course and they landed safely in Keflavik, Iceland, for another overnight.

The next morning they were off to England, but had orders to land at the RAF Valley military base in Anglesey, Wales. It was there that they had to leave their brand new B-17 and board a train to Horham, England. A little-known fact is that close to 1,000 Army planes disappeared en route from the US to foreign locations. Praise God Sundin's was not one of them.

—

As I mentioned, I was reluctant to inquire about the missions beyond what Roger openly shared. I had found all the declassified mission reports online and had been printing them out and sending them to Roger. When he read them, he would comment about how he didn't know there were so many planes on a particular mission or about how he'd had to abort one mission. However, one particular mission really seemed to bother him more than the others; the mission over Royan, France. As I summarized in an earlier chapter, this was the mission where they dropped napalm bombs. The napalm bombs were particularly dangerous and Roger had told my father, "Don't, for God's sake, use your key!" This was the first mission that the crew knew they were hitting buildings and underground places, where people and soldiers were; they never spoke of it. If you've ever spoken to a military veteran, you're most likely familiar with how they will share a piece of memory, and then become silent and go somewhere far away—where they see something we will never see, and know something we will never know—and out of respect, we do not pursue the subject further.

—

All these Big Birds and I'd only been next to one—the Memphis Belle—when I went with my high school friend Leslie to the National Warplane Museum and air show at the Geneseo Airport in Geneseo, New York. That was the first time we'd seen a B-17. We couldn't go into it and, much as I tried, I could not imagine what it was like to fly in one. It was at this event that I learned there were several B-17s that traveled the country and offered rides to the public. The following summer, a co-worker told me a B-17, the Madras Maiden, was coming to Buffalo, and that this was one of the planes offering rides. I found the information in the paper and called the company, Liberty Foundation, spoke with Kyle, and got all the particulars. Sadly, I learned that the only available seats for passengers were on dates I was going to be out of town. I promised myself I would take that ride the following year.

As it turned out the Madras Maiden did return to Buffalo the following year, and I was the first passenger to sign up for a seat. The morning of my long-awaited flight in the Big Bird, the sky was overcast and gloomy. I prayed it would clear up. My sister-in-law offered to join me and take photographs so I grabbed some coffees and picked her up. While we drove, the clouds dissipated, and the sun shone bright in the bluest sky I'd seen in months. I had no doubt I was being watched over. When we arrived, there were already people milling around the plane. The Liberty Foundation had a lovely display of items related to their organization, as well as to the B-17 itself, but I headed straight to the plane.

Ours was the first group of ten to fly that morning. We were able to go in the plane while it was parked, so my sister-in-law, who actually loathes flying, went inside and took some photos. In short order, they cleared all the visitors out of the plane and gathered our group for a "briefing." Well instructed, we all boarded the Madras Maiden and buckled up. The engines were loud and there was a lot of smoke coming from them as they were started and warmed up. After a time, we started to move.

I was surprised at how tight the plane seemed. I had imagined it would rattle about, but no, it was as smooth as could be. I hardly noticed the lift off and just like that, we were heading into the wild blue yonder. As promised, we reached the point where we received the sign that we could unbuckle and walk around the plane. I couldn't get to the radio room right away, but figured I'd get there eventually, so I started where we'd been seated: in the waist. Directly across and next to where I'd sat during takeoff were the two waist gunner .50-cal. machine guns. I remembered how my father had spoken about them during gunnery and was amazed at how heavy they were, and that these guns were the only flexible-mount guns on the ship, requiring some strength to maneuver.

The tail was off limits so I made my way past the ball turret and was amazed at how small it was. How anyone fit inside it and then fired guns from such a cramped space was beyond my comprehension. Next I was in the radio room and there it was - the radio operator's desk, complete with seat, telegraph key, and receiver. I sat down and looked out the window at the two engines with the blurred shape of their spinning propellers. I was energized beyond what I'd anticipated I would be. I knew it was loud in the plane, but at that moment, everything went silent. In that solitary moment I felt closer to my father than I ever had before, knowing that was his seat, this was his plane. It was very emotional. I finally knew what it was like to fly in a Big Bird.

SIOUX FALLS, SOUTH DAKOTA - PART 5

1945

August 8, 1945–Telegram

MRS BA THOMPSON
DEAR FOLKS ARRIVED SIOUX FALLS THIS MORNING ADDRESS
95TH BG 336TH SQD SFAAF SIOUX FALLS SD LOVE= FRANK

Wednesday, August 8, 10:50 AM

Dear Mother, Harry and Mike,

Well, about a year ago when I was getting ready to leave here I hardly expected to be back in the same Service Club at S.F. I left here for Yuma on August 21 last year I believe.

We got in the camp at about 3:30 AM this morning after having left Dix on Sunday at about 5 PM. Time we made up to Chicago was very good - less than 24 hours, but from there on, progress was very slow. When we got in last night they gave us this poop, which I suppose to be authoritative. 11% of the men here will be discharged - 3% will be sent on to combat (that's right 3%) and the remainder will be given permanent party jobs with the Second Air Force. Please don't get your hopes up too high for, as I see it, I may very well be under that 3% and hence back to combat. If so, I believe it will be 29s for that is the only bomber they are working with in the 2nd Air Force. Will enclose letter on back of which is list of bases I may be at - none near home as usual.

Beginning of our processing starts at 4 PM this afternoon so that I don't suppose I'll have any complete idea for 3 or 4 days, but you can be sure I'll let you know the verdict at the first possible moment. You can be sure also that if I get a chance at a permanent party I'd not volunteer for combat, although I feel the latter would be a much better deal. It is hard after being treated like a man to return to the old C.S. and this 2nd Air Force is reputed to be the worst of any outfit. I'm sure I'd rot mentally at a quiet job somewhere but I guess I could stand it - figure it would be better for all of us.

The trip to N.Y. was eventful enough. Two little ladies got on at Rochester and no seats - being gentlemen another lad and I volunteered our laps which were not accepted at first but later our twosome became a foursome - all the way to N.Y. Ugh such a business. I left the rest of the foursome at Grand Central went to Pennsylvania Station and checked luggage, got some breakfast and then slept until 11:30 having had little shut eye all night. I ate again went up to Times Square for a look around, got uniform pressed and then called Fellemen's. No answer so I assumed that no one was home so I took myself to see Phil Spitalny and his gals. Really was very good - picture was "Incendiary Blonde" - well worth seeing just for "What did you want a make those eyes at me for" number.

After show I caught 5:20 local to Trenton and finally got to Dix at about 9 PM. We were alerted and restricted to the area upon arrival and almost suffered dire consequences by sending you telegram next afternoon.

I saw Herb Robinson as I was leaving Dix - he was on same train - he had a wonderful 30 days too I guess. Getting on the train I was outmaneuvered - I drew a "cattle car" - Troop Pullman. Boy was it ever dirty - Ah well, just another experience. I always did wonder what they were like - Now, Oh now I know. Bunks are in 3 tiers - I had a top one and our car was the last one so you figure it out. The center of gravity in one of those things is low - but I was high and then that last car really gets snapped at the tail end. We all figured we had enough R.P.M.s to take off there for a while as that first night was spent hanging on for dear life.

At Chicago, they joined our train with another coming from Dix just behind us. That made about 30 cars - I estimate 800-900 men so you can figure the big time we had upon arrival and only two meals on the train yesterday - some fun.

I enjoy an advantage over some of the lads here as I'm familiar with the Post. It is too small for all the men they have here actually and you can guess what probably has been happening to that nice little town. It will probably never get over this session.

I guess we get passes into town after we process, which takes about 3 days so maybe I'll have a look at it soon - undoubtedly too overrun to have much fun there now.

What do you fellows think of this Atomic Bomb business? Oh Lord, what have our chemists done for the world in this or should I say what have they done to the world? I'm not particularly the squeamish type but would that this had never come. It is almost as though a world stinking with sin and destruction were preparing to destroy itself. God must be tiring of man's independence and ego and while his mercy is limitless so is his justice. Maybe it doesn't scare the Nips but it sure scares me.

Well folksies, I guess I'd best run along and sample the chow around these parts. Expect to be doing a bit of K.P. any minute now. Used to be that only Pvts, PFCs and Cpls. drew it - now you can't get near the place I guess unless you're Staff or Tech. That's all right if they want to pay me 96/mo. for K. P. - I'll take it!

Not too much sense in saying a lot about my 30 days home. These brief reprieves from the Army are never adequate no matter how long they are. You people made it grand for me but I just don't fit in yet. Won't be able to I guess until I can again, God willing, take my place with you. Thanks so very much - take care of yourselves my loved ones cause I'll try to be lookin out for me for you.

Lotsa Love, Frank

August 9, Thursday 9:40 AM

Dear Mother, Harry and Mike,

Well, I'm writing actually before breakfast this morning. This every day business will get me and you in bad habits I know but I guess that's O.K. here in the States. I say before breakfast for I just got up a few minutes ago and cleaned up and it is too late for breakfast. Ordinarily I'd run over to the Snack Bar for coffee but it is raining here quite heavily so I guess I'll just wait for lunch. Food here is somewhat better than it was before when I was here but that still doesn't make it too good.

Found out yesterday that purpose of this field is to get men moved out to their next assignment as quickly as possible. I can see what they mean for the place is flooded with men. Here you are classified into four classes - classification which fixes your shipping status from this field only. In other words, that class you are put in may very well be changed by the classification officer at the next base - anyway these are the four classes as I understand them.

1. Men who sign waiver to go overseas for another tour

2. Men who will be sent as permanent party (afterwards abbreviated as P.P.) to 2nd A.C. bases who will eventually be sent overseas as soon as some 60,000 men in 2nd A.F. who have not been overseas are sent.

3. Is known as a Bastard Class - men who have not quite finished a tour or have not quite enough points for discharge. As I understand it these go as P.P. to 2nd A.F. bases with little chance of seeing action again.

4. Men eligible for discharge who go as P.P. to 2nd A.F. bases to take temporary jobs and unit discharge on the quota in that field.

This leaves me, I believe in class two, which could quite likely be changed without waiver at next station and I could be shunted into B-29 training. At any rate I figure I'll be in States for a while yet. Don't get too het up about this for I have not been processed as yet nor will I be today. We'll just have to wait for that I guess.

Gee, they have men and more men here! I've seen few that I know. It is funny how you walk about looking into people's faces figuring you should see someone. I understand from grapevine that Shaffer came in yesterday but haven't seen any of the E.M. on our crew as yet - only officer has been Robinson. It is kinda lonely but they will be here soon I guess although it is a major operation to find them in this place even if you know they're here.

Crews will definitely be broken up here. It will be pure luck if you ever are returned to your original group - ground men standing a better chance than flying personnel. They consider a tour here 18 missions or 110 combat hours. We fall short on the missions by about 10 and are behind about 30 hours so my guess is that the whole crew should see action again if the war lasts another 6-8 months - not as a unit of course.

Well people, I guess that is about it for today. The weather here is a good bit cooler than at home. Wish right now I had a field jacket but will have to wait until I can get one issued at processing. It is nice in the day time but quite chilly at night and then it's raining today. Well, be good, people.

Lotsa Love, Frank

August 10 (I think), Friday 3:20 PM

Dear Mother, Harry and Mike,

Well, today has indeed been one for the books! Got up about 6:30 for breakfast and into mess hall in time to hear latest from Japan. It sure sounds good doesn't it? I can't see letting Hirohito returning his so called "Prerogative" anymore than we would have allowed Hitler or Il Duce to remain, even as nominal head of their countries, but then I suppose it is just as well I'm not administering the job. If peace does come, in reality, our real troubles will just have begun, but then we all want to be free at our earliest opportunity to cope with our own specific personal problems as soon as is possible. Not a lot of excitement here we all just hope it will end soon.

I started my first day's processing here today and have one more to go. I am as I expected in Class 2 which means redeployable or eligible for duty in the South Pacific. As I said previously this may mean permanent party job for a while but I think it will mean duty under Training Command immediately. More radio school I believe more gunnery and R.T.U. If there should be no cessation of hostilities that would mean that I'd get, I figure, at least 5-7 months here in the States which would be all right. However, if the war stops before I can get shipped out to training command it is anybody's money how long I'd be pushed around before I finally got out. What I'm getting at is this - just a guess again but if I were in a training group at time of official cessation then since such a training group would be purely superfluous, I might stand a good chance of getting a more rapid separation - but then who cares just as long as they won't be shouting at me again, what?

When I came here I had a goodly number of points and would have had almost 50 with 2nd Battle Star, which remained uncounted. Well, they revised it - personnel at 95th had made a mistake I know of but hoped it would get through. You see they had given me points from date of enlistment whereas you should only get them for months of active duty. They caught it here and I now have only 33 points so if they discharge according to points I'll be a long time getting out.

I met John Kimpel last night and we went to the show together - on him! My total capital at the moment being just 46 cents. I get a partial pay to-morrow so I should be fairly well set then I hope. They are taking orders for a book of 95th Bomb Group activities - 8 dollars - be nice to have so, I'll have to see if I can't manage it but it is a lot of Jack. John wanted me to go to town with him this afternoon but I couldn't see it. I have some letters to write and clothes to hide from tomorrow's clothing check. I stand a good chance to get another B-4 bag to send home but I almost can't see it. It is taking something that doesn't belong to you. Better I should buy one of my own - maybe I'll have a change of heart - we'll see. They have no records of what you have or haven't here so those two jackets are safe at home I guess.

There is very little to do here and so many to do it. You actually have to stand in line at latrines. Tomorrow I finish processing and am sent to permanent "T" Squadron. From there I am eligible to be put on orders, but some R.O.s have been around here 5 weeks now. In such a squadron you get a Class "A" pass good for 100 miles at any time. You can even get a job somewhere while awaiting orders as long as you are around for morning roll calls and pull your share of K.P. and details. Rough life eh? And three meals a day too. I'd kinda like to work on a farm - 8 bucks a day but I fear a good day's work would kill me.

I would not send on the check if it arrives until we are sure I am getting your mail here. Also in that regard - if you can afford it - get me a couple pair of serviceable slacks - if the war ends - for by the time I do get home clothes will probably be scarce and with a couple pairs of pants and what I still have I should get by O.K. till things loosen up.

I do hope you are both keeping well! Formerly I hardly realized with just 9 days at home just how things were going but with 30 days at home I got a better eye on things. Not that the pair of you don't get on dandy without me but maybe that's just it - you get along too well. What I mean is I'd just as soon be around to do my bitching by word of mouth rather than by the pen - understand? I guess it can't be too soon for any of us.

Well people, I guess that takes care of most of the poop for today - be good, people. Lotsa Love, Frank

August 11, Saturday 3:50

Dear Mother, Harry and Mike,

Well, I finished processing today and am assigned to a more or less permanent squadron. We are alerted here on 12 hour notice to ship but I understand that most flying personnel stay here for some time.

I don't know a soul in the barracks here, but I saw Shaffer last night and I guess we're going to the show tonight, that is if I can make it in time. Also Spencer got in today so that makes four of the five E.M. here - Joe hasn't shown up as yet but then he had a long way to come. Turner is here but I haven't seen him as yet.

I got a partial pay of 10 berries - not as much as I would have wished for but we'll have to make it do. I can get a few of the things I want. I'll be able to get a job here somewhere I think so I won't have anything to worry about in that direction.

News has been coming over all day and it sure looks as though the war may soon be over although no one seems too excited here. Hardly expect the G.I.s to get too excited - it will mean lots of red tape before most of us get out. Rumor has it that an 8 hour day PT and drill schedule will go into affect here next week - we'll have to see about that.

Gosh folks - there is very little more to tell. I believe I'll be here for some time now but of course cannot be sure of that. They have put permanent personnel on a 7 day a week schedule and are trying to get men out more rapidly. The place is terribly choked up and I guess shipments are not moving rapidly.

Well people, I'd better hurry off - I have to get me some Air Mail stamps before Post Office closes at 5 PM then shower & shave and eat. Will probably go to show with the boys this evening on the Post. Be good, people.

Lotsa Love, Frank

Sunday, August 12, 11:30 AM

Dear Mother, Harry and Mike,

Well, here we are again. This every day business is rather a useless effort for from day to day there is little new to report. As yet no assignment, no K.P. or detail but the latter I expect Monday or Tuesday.

Last night they seemed rather sure that the Japs would accept surrender terms but I have heard nothing today. We have a new C.O. here on the base a Col. Kane I think. He's called "Killer Kane" and the Gravy Train here promises to come to a screeching halt. That is always the way when I get somewhere it seems. The easy way goes out and the C.S. is on the ascendancy but then I'm quite used to it now. I have a Class A pass now but little inclination to use it particularly over the week-end when things will be worse than ever.

I have plenty to do this afternoon and I seriously doubt whether I'll get much of it done. I want to write some of yee old bread and butter letters one of these days - but it seems useless to initiate correspondence when I'm not sure whether I'll be getting anything in the mail line at this address. Think I'll wait until I am sure of it. Also I have a suit of Sun Tans - a couple that badly need laundering - I should do that for the sun is shining today.

Made Mass at 10 AM this morning. They had it in a theatre as they used to - it was really packed. I must be sure to make the Feast of the Assumption on Wednesday - hope I remember.

Went to movies last night - not much satisfaction in going really. You have to get in line an hour or more ahead of time to even get in to get a seat so that it is hardly worth the effort. However there is nothing else to do so we stand in line. They have not been permitting you to take books from the Library, there are so many out, so I just had to borrow one without their knowledge. I've been able to pass a lot of time with it but when I finish I'll be a bit lost. It is a collection of 4 books - "Spy Stories" by Eric Ambler and really not too bad.

Guess that's about it for today folks. Be good.

Lotsa Love, Frank

August 14, Tuesday 12:15

Dear Mother, Harry and Mike

I missed yesterday and you can probably guess the reason why - yup - a bit-o-K.P. Actually it was the easiest K.P. I ever drew. I was tipped off by the night C.Q. (charge of quarters) how and what job to get so all I really did yesterday was count the number of men who ate and sweep the mess hall porch a couple times. This fellow who gave me the tip was a lad I came to know in Yuma - last 3 days there. He is trying to fix it so that I can work in the orderly room nights. That is every other night I'd work and have every other day off. This I figure would be O.K. since I wouldn't pull K.P. or detail and I'd have every other day off - the work would be of an office nature. As I say he is working on it - I hope it comes through - probably find out tonight for sure.

I took in a show last night - "You Came Along." It is strictly Air Force and of course all of us enjoyed it a good deal - you really have to be a G.I. to appreciate it completely I think, but I'm sure you fellows would enjoy it. I went with Spencer whom I saw at the mess hall yesterday. He had a good time I guess but to him and Shaffer, family complications were brought on by their 30 days, in fact we are all quite eager to get home now. Joe hasn't arrived as yet as near as I can find out - at least none of us have seen or heard of him being about.

I'll have to get over and see if I draw any mail today. Also since I haven't the cash I'm going to try and have that book of the 95th Bomb Group sent home C.O.D. I'm sure I'll be able to send you the money before it arrives, but if I don't order it now we won't have it and it would be a crime not to have it! Sooo with those items I guess I'll be spending the best part of the afternoon in line at different places.

Things are tightening up now. 1st call at 5:15 AM and Roll Call out in Company Street at 5:30 - really rough - and then they got me up at 4:00 AM yesterday morning. Ah well, guess we'll live through it O.K. Guess that is it for today folks.
Lotsa Love, Frank

August 16, Wednesday, V.J.-Day + 1

Dear Mother, Harry and Mike,

I'm late at this today but after all V.J.-Day doesn't come every decade and I have been sort of recovering from last night. Monday I had made arrangements that I should meet Spencer and Shaffer in my barracks about 5:30 last night and so we did. Dan and I decided to go to a show—it is not worth the wait in line really but there is nothing else to do. Shaffer didn't want to go so we thought we'd go anyway. Then Shaffer told us he'd seen Joe so we thought we'd go see him first. On the way there, the news came over officially—we stood around a taxi cab and listened to it come over the radio. Then we went and found Jose and all three of us started for the movie—then someone got the bright idea that we should go to town. We all changed clothes—I had a pass but not so Spencer and Joe so we had to borrow some for them. And off we went in a cloud of dust.

All you could see in town was a wave of khaki—it was murder! There was plenty of liquor everywhere—all the girls were out kissing the fellows and things gradually gained momentum and all hell broke loose. The fellows stopped cars—pulled up the hoods and ripped out electrical connections while the driver pleaded with them. The G.I.s were all trading hats and ties with the people for civilian models and they started a quaint custom of cutting off everyone's tie just below the knot. One Model "T" Ford was torn apart and set fire and they had to call out the fire department. We got some liquor and soon we entered into the spirit of the thing. Everyone walked down the street with his bottle and glass and had a wonderful time. Believe me "anything went."

They called off the curfew and put on a multitude of extra M.P.s but they bothered no one aside from picking up those who couldn't walk and seeing that they got back. They had large trailer buses in town to pick up the boys. Yours truly drug in at about 5:10 A.M. and there wasn't a soul at the M.P. post at the main gate. I just got in bed in time to hear the whistles waking the lads up but I slept through all that until about 9 AM when barracks chief woke me up to tell me I'd better get out of the sac before the Captain made his inspection. I had me a bit of breakfast at the Snack Bar and made 11 o'clock Mass. Boy I've had a head as big as Prospect Park all day but then you see we couldn't buy coke or ginger ale for a chaser so we had to buy bottles of beer. Then it got to the point where we didn't want to carry part empty beer bottles around sooo we'd have to have another little meeting of the board of directors so we could use up the beer chaser.

Well, it was really something. Sure wouldn't want to suffer like this frequently but it is O.K. once in an Army career I guess.

I saw Harrison yesterday and he in turn told Dan Hamernik where I was. Dan was around for a while today–he nor Harrison got in any missions–they were both in B-24s. Dan has been here over 5 weeks. Evidently they are just not shipping re-deployable ROGs out.

Well people, thas about all for today–hope you had a bit of a time last night–we did the best we could here. Be good.

Lotsa Love, Frank

August 16, Thursday 3:45 PM

Dear Mother, Harry and Mike,

Well, I finally got a letter today. I thought it was the very terrible mail service here that was holding things up. Didn't you get either of my telegrams–one from Ft. Dix and one a few hours after arrival from here? That kinda burns me up. The thought, the effort, and the money completely wasted. Also you wrote on a Saturday and here it is the 16th before I got it. I did better than that in England. It is very good to look at the familiar "vertical" also got pictures from Harry today–where are the ones with Tessy in them?

I'm supposed to find out definitely about this night job this evening after chow. Hope I'm not sticking my neck out too much–well, we'll see about it. Better I should be busy at something or other than just sitting around reading and walking about.

I think Joe and Spencer took off for Minneapolis yesterday. That is O.K. for them for there is not too much of a way they can check on them but I have to answer a roll call every morning so it would not be so good for me. They haven't processed yet nor been assigned to a "T" Squadron so I'd say they stand a good chance of getting away with it. Here's luck to them anyway.

From Stimson's Statement and clarification for it, I read in paper today, it doesn't look to me as though I'd get out for a year or more anyway–well, at least no one will be shooting at me I hope! I don't know what they'll do with us but that remains to be seen–as far as I can see all re-deployable R.O.s are staying right here–none of them are leaving, so in that connection please ship on the sandals and thanks muchly for thinking of them in the first place.

I got me a copy of "North West Passage" today and went to the movie this afternoon–"Johnny Angel" not bad entertainment but nothing too unusual except the story itself. Right now I'm waiting to go to chow and then I'll go up to see about that job. It is a crime to see all this manpower just lying around. Col. Kane–C.O. of the Post ordered all men to stay on [the] Post until 5 o'clock so that meant no farm work but the order was rescinded and some of the boys are at it. Hamernik said he tried it one day–meals were very good but I leave it to you to judge–he hasn't gone again. Must be hard work eh? I don't think Airmen tried it at all. I think I'll try to find me a job every other night tending bar someplace where the knock down is fairly good Huba Huba.

Well people, I guess I'd best go up and see if I'm on shipping orders yet. This is just a waste of time I honestly think but I'm supposed to look so I do. Be good.
Lotsa Love, Frank

August 17, Friday

Dear Mother, Harry and Mike,

Well, another day another dollar. That about says it all. Today has been a busy one for the Post, but it has not concerned me as far as I can find out, so that is that. Shipments out of here I have judged as slow but today things really speeded up a great deal–to such an extent that they restricted all transient personnel to the base until Saturday evening. There are many rumors going about–none of which I give much credence and I believe, as ever, the best policy is to wait and see just what develops. It has been very hot here–quite different from when I first arrived and vainly wished I had a field jacket. I have been doing a good bit of sleeping and reading and smoking. I let that job go by in the orderly room last night–could have had it but my idea has always been the less they know of you in the orderly room the better you get along.

I had had great plans for today–was going to work tonight at a steel mill at 55¢/hour and go out on a farm with Dan Hamernik in the morning but this restriction knocked that into a cocked hat. Frankly, I needed some money and I was just getting underway. I couldn't see working in orderly room when I could be getting paid outside. Reason I've waited around is that I suspected quick shipment and also plenty of K.P. and details but neither dangers seem to imminent at present so I started getting underway. Also planned on seeing a "Red" Olsen in town I knew from being here previously–met him about 16 months ago at K of C. He's an ex-marine 1st Looey and an engineer here in town.

Harry you must have a sixth sense or a bit of mental telepathy when you sent that 10 spot. Yes I got it today and was it ever a Godsend. I wasn't completely broke but what with cleaning and stuff here, and last Tuesday night's session, I was getting to the point where I was watching the number of cakes and coffee I was indulging in. Then, too, how the hell do you manage it just as your vacation begins? Thanks an awful lot folks–I'll see that you get it back as soon as I get what the Army owes me. I know that you don't intend for me to return it but then maybe you'll be able to use it as advantageously as I was when I have it. Incidentally I think I've seen the end of flying pay. Thank goodness I was able to make a rating–and let's hope I'll be able to keep it for a while.

I fear there is nothing new to report here. It is all very hazy to me. Almost looks as though the Japs haven't quit yet doesn't it? Joe and Spencer are still gone, to the best of my knowledge–I hope they don't get caught. The best rumor here is that soon this is to become a Separation Center, although how it could affect me I can't quite see. I don't believe it till it happens anyway folks. Things seem to be slowing up a bit here on the "coming in" angle and speeding up on the "going out" although I actually don't believe they know what they want to do with the fellows. Just where in hell will they put the guys from the Pacific if we're still lying around when they get back? Ah well, time should tell.

Ats (sic) all for tonight. Thanks for funds again.
Lotsa Love, Frank
P.S. Couldn't see about "Power" today due to restriction–try tomorrow
F.

August 18, Friday

Dear Mother, Harry and Mike,
Have had a busy day today doing nothing much as per usual. I did go swimming this afternoon with Jose and to the movie this evening. At the pool I saw Sundin–he had been what would be called AWOL in an enlisted man for 18 days and they got off Scot free. His wife is expected to produce on Wednesday next so he'll be going home again next week–rough life. From what the Big Sundin tells me all the officers are trying to get out with a vengeance. Herb going to the doctor–something about neurotics and Turner wakes the boys up at night yelling about the flak–"if I get it, you guys will go with me" seems to be his favorite cry in the night. Sundin says he'll try to get a dependency discharge and with Shackelford grounded and just shortly arrived from England I guess that sums up that. Somehow I guess I'm a good deal too sentimental. I'm so glad to see them all and just a bit disappointed when I do.

Joe and Spencer got back from being AWOL last night. As usual Joe got off O.K. but Spencer got caught. The C.O. was easy on him–he was lucky he didn't get broken but the Major just chewed him out and he's had to sign in every hour on the hour in the orderly room today. It is a wonder he wasn't broken.

I think they've shipped out almost 5,000 in the past couple days. Another big bunch goes to-morrow. Still no shipments concerning yours truly. We all had an opportunity to become permanent party here today but I can't see it. There is a long cold winter coming here soon and also they are libel to hand you a clerk's specification number and you'd be called essential so I didn't bite at the bait. All these things you do or don't do you hope will work out O.K.–I'll probably wind up in the desert someplace but that's the chance you all have to take.

I've drawn detail for to-morrow so people I guess I'd best get some sleep so I can be on the ball to-morrow–Be good, people–
Lotsa Love, Frank

August 20, Monday

Dear Mother, Harry and Mike,

I have been putting off writing today–mostly been horsing around getting a Power of Attorney and finally succeeded. The legal red tape was negligible but finding the right Army personnel proved a different story–shoved from pillar to post–you know the old Army game. Will enclose it with this opus.

I got three letters today–Mother's, Harry's and one from the Beals all on the subject of V.J.–the day or evening itself or day prior to it–all of them full of the repercussions that it should bring in our lives. I don't want to be a wet blanket but people I look for at least another year in the Army–it will be a hard one but well worth it waiting if we can all be together permanently again. In that direction, of squadron here, called in all Radio Operators and Armorer gunners and told them point blank that no one seemed to have any idea of what was to become of them. They got them together for the purpose of doing a little screening. They gave a little speech and then told everyone to go except those who had some clerical training or experience–no one stayed! Of course what we hope is that we will be of sufficiently great liability so that they will release us, which is of course too good to be true. Then too, if they want us for something else they will have to train us for that–meanwhile our knowledge of our job declines as we sit around and get rusty.

Yesterday I was on a mail sorting detail. Not hard at all–I took off in the morning at about 10 till 10 to get to Mass and then worked a bit and again in the afternoon. When I got back Spencer was waiting for me. He is thinking of bringing the wife down also the youngster–he wanted me to go into town with him and help him since I know my way about town a bit. So I cleaned up and we went in–we got the poop at Travelers Aid. There are plenty of rooms available at present but of course a 3 ½ year old presents another problem. We took in a free movie and dance at this Coliseum afterwards–pie and coffee and back again. It was an enjoyable cheap evening and proved to me that a man is a fool to stick to the Post. Most of G.I.s here aren't around long enough to discover the good deals and many of the rest just want to get tight and they don't sell beer on Sundays here. Sooo I expect I'll be going in more often now.

There was plenty of room to dance and more than enough girls and they are particularly luscious and wholesome out here. They've added a couple more dandy U.S.O.s and if a guy can't have a good time here he's nuts. Sure the town is mobbed, but 80% are aimless and don't know or care what they do beyond walking the streets.

About the "Power"–as you can see it is a "Carte Blanche" to what Harry refers to as my inheritance. That's what I meant it to be and do with it what you will, my only reservations are personal property I wish you would not dispose of–my grey pinstripe–my B-15 and coveralls and my 1/3 share in Mr. De La Spusier.

Here–I haven't answered any of your letters as yet directly but that should make good subject matter for the morrow. Chow is about to come off so I guess I best be getting on. Be good, people.

Lotsa Love, Frank

August 21, Tuesday 7:45

Dear Mother, Harry and Mike,

As you can see I'm in town and thought I'd better get this one out from here. Say, I forgot to enclose the "Power" in the last letter so I sent it on in separate envelope–you should get both of them together. Incidentally you'll probably get this one before the other two since this will be mailed in town.

Dan Spencer and I came in this afternoon–yes in spite of being restricted to the base. You see he worked in the G.I. laundry last night so he got a pass to come in all day today–he also hit one of the boys in his barracks for a pass for me so I came too. We haven't done much all afternoon. Spent best part of it in a hotel room with a couple of gals and drank their liquor. BUT we figured they didn't have any dough and we sure as hell didn't have any we wanted to spend on them so we cleared out about the time they were going to change for dinner. One of them had a new routine–she was going to scratch my back but she had to have me lying on a towel on the floor to do it. As much as I was dying to see what came next I couldn't see me stretched on the floor getting my uniform all dirty for that. Ah well, maybe I'll run into that kind again someday.

There is little new at the base although there is a good deal of unrest. Last night I read a bit after chow and fell asleep–then awoke at 9:45 got undressed and went to bed and slept all the way through. The big reason is that the C.O. has ordered that there be an all night guard in the barracks. This guy sleeps across from me and has to have the light on all night so I have a helluva time getting to sleep most of the time. Reason for the guard is that $900 has been stolen in the squadron in the last two weeks. No, I was not totally immune–they got my bathing suit. All of which makes me feel damn sore but what can I do except be glad that is all they got away with. Jose is on K.P. today so that takes care of him but good and it rained best part of the day so that ruled out the farm work but it looks like it will be a good one to-morrow so maybe we'll be able to make it then. I may as well be doing something. I hesitate about taking this steel co. job for you never know what you'd have to lift on a job like that, so since I'm not destitute I let that go.

Dan is now trying to reach his wife via the telephone to tell her to come down here. I almost think he has decided to go permanent party—he's only about 240 miles from home here but the bad part is—so I hear—these P.P. boys here will be moved to March Field, Cal. in October when the A.F. shuts down here. Also he'd be getting a clerical specification number and my guess is that the clerks will be the last out. That's why it doesn't appeal to me.

My guess is that R.O.s will be moving out in 1-2 weeks so we'll have to wait until then to find out whether I'll be in New Mexico or Arizona or some such Hell Hole. Guess that's all for now people. Be good.

Lotsa Love, Frank

August 22nd, Wednesday

Dear Mother, Harry and Mike,

I started this and then had to bum some ink. I was lucky to chisel some for they don't sell it in the PXs anymore—don't have it around here at any rate. I got a letter from both of you today which was good going for me. I managed to write Jean Logan today and I'm glad I did that. I suppose I should undertake to answer some of your previous letters and those of today—wait till I get them out—

Harry, you seem to be meeting a host of new women lately—how the hell are you making out? Just be sure to keep them all on tap until we can examine them at our leisure—Huba Huba! What's the idea of letting Lois beat you at tennis—you really don't have to be that much of a gentleman you know. Say by the way how is the Gibber boy doing these days? Is he still embroiled in a mess of women—ah to be such a desirable Casanova! You seem to be getting in plenty of driving practice—that's good—we have the auto robe—almost a driver—all we need is the car—what? I'm glad "Yank" started to arrive—I had considered that 2 bucks a complete loss. I'm sure you should get some pleasure from it. I had ordered it in time to get the V.E. issue, which was what I wanted to keep but I guess we're out of luck there.

Sounds like V.J. at home was fine—I liked Mother's phrase "under control." Harry got around quite a bit! I was glad everyone got a day or two off—that really makes it seem like a holiday doesn't it. Mother—I was in pretty good shape when I got in a week ago Tuesday night too. I'd say we were pretty well crocked about 45 minutes after we got there—to town that is, but it wore off and I only had about 3 beers the rest of the evening. When I lost track of the boys I had a pint of PM in my pocket and I never did have any of that. We wound up, or I should say I did, in one of the local homes where the bottle fell out of pocket and top broke so I left it there. You see target for that night was a singer in one of the road houses out of town. Finished up at her house, with her mother eating egg sandwiches and drinking coffee. Some Buck Sgt. was trying to take mother to the Kasbah (7th floor) while I found that at about 4:30 AM the younger generation with whom I was busily engaged in conversation (?) grew tired and I had to put her to bed. I said put, not take. When I left—aforementioned G.I. was still trying. Ah these G.I.s—never say die!

Today I find we have another C.O. on the Post–a Brigadier General Travis. We all had to go to a lecture given by him and it was pretty good. He claims he's going to do a lot of things–here's hoping he can, although, I frankly don't believe he knows what he's up against. First he is going to improve the chow–that's fine! Also, by middle of next month he plans to have a system whereby no one will be here more than 7 days. Also, I find out that orders are made out here and that he will try to see that we get shipped to bases near our homes if possible. This is admirable but I hardly expect much luck there although there is a remote possibility. Another thing I discovered is that shipments are not restricted to list of 2nd A.F. bases I sent you but you can be sent almost anywhere in the country. We can hope anyway but it is a long shot as I see it. Also, minimum no. of points for not going out of the country is 54 so there is a possibility of my going overseas again–we may as well face it. I can't see how myself–they'd have to train us in another airplane. A group of R.O.s asked where they stood and he said if they would delegate a man to come and see him in his office he'd try to straighten the thing out for them. All of this was very democratic and very nice–too smooth to work in the Army I fear. He said when he trained in the training of Bomber Crews he had been so tough he was known as a S.O.B. but he said at that time rigid discipline had saved lives–now he can't see any reason for being tough. He sounded out with "remember that you are just as big a pain in the ass to me as I am to you and I'll do everything I can to get you men out of here as soon as is possible."

As I say all of this is great–I hope he can do it, we'll see.

Well, I guess that is most of the poop right now. We are restricted from 7 AM tomorrow until 11 AM. So I guess another large shipping order is coming out. Got in last night from town at about 9:30. We had a couple beers and got in early for we intended going out on the farm. The trouble came this morning when very few farmers came in (ground still wet). There were about 300 of us and only about 75 were taken so that was that.

Dan called his wife last night and she is coming in Thursday at 5:15. No one on the crew has shipped out yet but I hear that Lt. Turner is getting a discharge next week (only 42 pts. for a 2nd Looy). Sundin's promotion to 1st screwed him out of it for 1st Lt. needs either 54 or 62 I forget which. That's it people–Be good.
Lotsa Love, Frank

August 23, Thursday 3:15 PM
Dear Mother, Harry and Mike,

As per usual I fear I have not a great deal of poop from this end. I received Mother's of Monday today. It makes a great deal of difference once things start to run a bit more smoothly as far as the mail is concerned and I can count on getting something every day or so. Of course I still don't trust the system much since I've worked there and seen it in operation.

I'm glad that Harry has enjoyed his vacation–he has more than had it coming–judging from the letters I've received from him he has had himself a time indeed.

Yes, I'll have to write the Beals again now–I am two or three behind and that's not so good. They all sat down and dashed off a few lines V.J. night which was quite like them and showed their usual thought, which was appreciated.

I can see I should have thanked both of you for the 10 spot and as much as I hate to write about money I fear I will have to. If you can possibly manage it, I wish you would try to send me another tener after you get your Gov't. checks around the first of next month. I think I will be needing it then for as yet we have signed no payroll and from the grapevine I suspect that we will not be paid here on the last of the month. Don't ask me what they expect us to get along on, I guess we are supposed to sleep and eat and that's all. Here, with nothing to do all day, you find your money slipping away for coffee and ice cream and an occasional beer. Haircuts and pressing and cigarettes and movies. You know how it goes. As I figure it now the Army owes me, at the end of this month, about a hundred bucks. That is exclusive of flying pay for 2 months, which amounts to almost another hundred. Another interesting development–this General is trying to see that we get our flying time in so we can collect flying pay. As I have explained it to you before, as long as you're on flying status (and I am), as long as you get in 4 hours per month before the end of three months you can collect. Here they are attempting to fly only those who are in their third month but I'm going to try to lie my way into it if I can, for what I'm afraid of is being shipped to another base and being taken off flying status and losing the cash.

I had planned on picking up some extra change working and still hope to by working, but the farm was kicked in the head again today when they restricted us. Also, since they put this restriction on that you can't leave the base until 5 PM, you can't look for a job in town very easily in the evening. So that is the state of affairs.

Went into town last night with Dan and we looked for a place for he and his family to stay after we had clinched a reservation for them at a hotel for the first few days. Went to the K of C and had a beer later–I was surprised that Mr. Murphy there remembered me–they were (he and his wife) quite nice to us. It was the first time I'd been there since I got here this time.

Well folks, I guess that is most of it for today–shipping orders have been read and I'm not on them as yet–probably won't be for some time. Be good, people.
Lotsa Love, Frank

August 24, Friday

Dear Mother, Harry and Mike,

Well, I guess this will have to be a shortie for there is little new to report and this one is close on the heels of yesterday's. I have signed up to fly to-morrow–I guess that is the biggest development to date. I really shouldn't have but I'm afraid they will take me off flying status at the next base and I want to be sure of getting those 96 fish. As I understand it, we start early in the morning from Sioux City, Iowa and go somewhere in Colorado on an RON (return over night). I hope I can get the time in at any rate. I suppose that the best idea would be to wait a week and get three *months in but I don't know when I'll ship and I want to nail this thing down while the nailing is good.*

Spencer's family came in last night. They're set at a hotel for a couple days but they'll have to get something else soon. If they do get satisfactory living quarters, I imagine he'll sign up for permanent party here for he figures he'll never get any closer to home.

Believe it or not people, they have started processing men here for separation. My guess is that they go from here to a base near home to be turned loose. These fellows are of course well over 85 point men and it doesn't concern me in the slightest, beyond that it is good to see that things are actually getting underway and also the sooner they get these high point men out the sooner the rest of us will stand a chance. Anyway here's hoping that we all get a chance at that separation soon.

You've never told me whether or not you got my two telegrams—the one from Dix and the one from here. Please tell me about it because if you didn't I'll report it to the air inspectors. If mine didn't get through chances are some other fellow's didn't either and somebody is really knocking down someplace along the line. Thas all people, Be good.

Lotsa Love, Frank

August 27, Sunday 4:05, Walla Walla Time

Dear Mother, Harry and Mike,

Just a line to let you know I finally hit the State of Washington. OH I'm not assigned here—just dropped in from S.D. via a bomber to get my flying time in. I had signed up to fly as I wrote you the other day and then I found I was scheduled to fly and also to be on K.P. so I took what I considered to be the lesser of the two evils thusly I wound up in Walla Walla Washington—furthest west I've been I guess. They got us up at 2:00 AM yesterday and we had to take trucks to Sioux City—a three hour trip by G.I. truck is no May frolic. Anyway, we didn't get off the ground until 6:30 PM yesterday and in all it took us 10 hours to get here and we had one stop in Boise, Idaho for refueling.

It was a long time all right and the trip was a very cold one. I sure wish I had had my flying clothes for all of us almost froze, but then it is quite a trip. We were weathered in here this morning so I believe they have postponed take off until to-morrow morning. We brief at 4:30 AM to-morrow I believe, of course we cannot get off the base. It looks rather nice around here to me and I'll bet Walla Walla, the town, is O.K. I see where they have a Mass here at 5:30 this evening and I am grateful that I should be able to make it.

It is pleasant to be here for they have rather nice snack bar and PX facilities and believe me it is nice to be able to walk in and be waited on immediately instead of standing in line for an hour or so. I find the bag Al gave me ideal for I packed towel and all in it and that is all I brought. Crews here - it is an R.T.U still going strong - have been flying to Sioux City and flying 8th A.F. personnel so they can get in their flying time - is a part of their training. I don't envy them for that kind of flying is hard work - I'd say it is almost too much.

Guess that's all from this end of the country so, be good, people.

Lotsa Love, Frank

August 28, Tuesday

Dear Mother, Harry and Mike,

Well, I'm back at Sioux Falls again after earning my 96 bucks flying time for the past couple of months. Bases at Sioux City and Walla Walla were both quite a relief as compared to this place and while we were away a galaxy of new reforms have been added. There is no use getting wound up by writing about them for they only make life here less livable than it is already.

I was quite tired when we finally arrived last night so I took me a shower and climbed right into my sac and had little trouble getting to sleep.

I find that they are beginning to ship radio operators. Hamernik is going to Clovis, New Mexico - some others to March Field, California. I'm not sure as to whether I'm on orders or not. They post them in the orderly room but right now there are so many fellows looking at them that you can't even get to them. I'll be sure to let you know as soon as I find out anyway.

I was going to work on a farm again today with fellow named Goodliffe but they restricted us again so that's that.

I really should have some mail today since I haven't been able to pick it up for three days, in fact I think I'll let this go until I can get it - then maybe I'll have something to write about.

10:10 PM

Well, I didn't get my mail but I have something to write about - I went to work this afternoon at Sioux Steel Company - only got in 4 hours this afternoon but I'll try to go in in the morning. It only pays 55¢ an hour but that's not the point too much - it is a relief to be doing something instead of rotting here on the base. Also I'm shipping Friday to March Field, California. I don't know when Friday but there's where I'm headed. Not too close to home, what? It will take from 4 to six days I understand. I can't find out much about the place except that all of us re-deployable Radio Operator Gunners are bound for there and I think we're going to school. Also I think we will be grounded.

I spent the evening listening to T Dorsey aggregation. It was terrible trying to see him here on the base for there were a million G.I.s there but we managed. Well, I' better close and get this off - try to write a couple more times before I leave here - let you know more about new station if I hear it - be good, people.

Lotsa Love, Frank

August 29, Wednesday 7 PM

Dear Mother, Harry and Mike,

Well, here I am after a hard day at Sioux Steel. It is probably the hardest work I have ever done but it is far from the hardest there is. I got in 8 hours today and the old bones are beginning to ache. I thought I'd better write before taking a shower and getting to bed. I had one of the fellows get my mail while I was working today and I drew 4 from you fellows and 3 from the Beals. I've just finished chow and reading letters - it is indeed good to get them!

Not an awful lot to report - still shipping to March Field and cannot get transferred east. Don't know what it will be all about till I get there. I may as well tell you now not to expect anything too good to come of this - it is very possible for me to go overseas again. If I did, I hardly believe it would be flying but more in the radio maintenance line.

Got up at 6 AM this morning and punched in at work at 7:45. They are allowed to pay only on a weekly basis so we don't, unfortunately, get paid each night. I should get in the neighborhood of 8-10 bucks to-morrow at quitting time, which will eliminate any need for your sending me any money.

I spent my last for lunch today but have three oranges saved up for lunch to-morrow and may get me a steak for to-morrow night's dinner. I'll be able to pick up the few odds and ends I need and have enough to send you fellows a night letter when I arrive at new station. There is a slight possibility that we may get paid before we leave here. That is partial pay - they pay no flying pay here nor have I as yet been paid rations for my 30 days at home.

I'm very glad to hear all the latest poop from home and I fear I'm not going to be able to do justice in answering the 4 letters I got today but I'm very well - a bit tired and am absolutely not doing anything which is too much for me, but it is so long since I put in a good day's work. Sorry this won't be airmail - ran out of stamps and didn't quit work until 5 so could get none at P.O. Be good, people.

Lotsa Love, Frank

MEMORIAL DAY

Present Day

It was when I was typing letters from August and September of 1945 that I realized my father had returned to Sioux Falls, South Dakota after the furlough he and his crew had received upon repatriating in June. The entire month of July, there were no letters. Again, without reading ahead, I continued typing in the order they had been written to learn where he was headed next and what his next assignment would be. While in the throes of my typing, my cousin contacted me to see if I was interested in going to see Mount Rushmore in South Dakota over the Memorial Day weekend. This intrigued me somewhat; however it wasn't until she said that we would fly into Sioux Falls, South Dakota and drive to Rushmore that I decided to go.

Over the coming weeks, we planned our strategy. We would spend the first part of Saturday in Sioux Falls, searching for the locations my father wrote about in his letters, and then we'd drive through the Badlands and arrive in Mt. Rushmore that evening. In addition to Mt. Rushmore, we wanted to visit the Crazy Horse Memorial before driving back to Sioux Falls early to catch our flight back. It was an aggressive trip for sure, but I was excited to actually see some of the places my father had written about.

Prior to leaving, I had reviewed all the Sioux Falls letters and created a list of places to see while we were there. I also did some research online about where we might find historical information about the technical school on the base, and other places he mentioned such as the Cathedral, the Knights of Columbus, the Carpenter Hotel, the movie theater, the university one of his conquests had attended, and more. I found the historical society had in its archives several documents that had been donated by veterans and their families from Sioux Falls, and hoped that I may be able to see the documents on our visit. Armed with as much as I was able to glean in advance, we embarked on our journey of discovery.

On the Saturday we were to tool around Sioux Falls the weather was sunny and warm, which made our "sightseeing" much easier to navigate. I had tried to map out an efficient route, but as the day progressed, that became a moot effort. We started the day heading for downtown on a route that took us past Augustana University. We soon learned that Memorial Day weekend may not have been the best time for this escapade because many businesses as well as the university itself were closed for the holiday. This was our first disappointment of the day as I knew that one of the barracks from the original base was currently being used on campus as an art classroom, and I had hoped to see it. When we couldn't get into the library where the historical materials were located, we took a photo in front of the university and carried on. The next stop was the YMCA. The building had been altered during an expansion, however much of the original building was still as it would have been in 1944-45 when my father frequented it. After inquiring within, we learned that there was an individual on staff who had historical knowledge of the YMCA; however he was not working that day. The staff was very helpful and provided us with his contact information. Once again, we took a photo and carried on to our next stop, the Carpenter Hotel.

Located on the main strip of what must have been the city's business center of Sioux Falls back in the day, the Carpenter Hotel stood tall and proud. In fact, much of S. Phillips Avenue was unchanged, with many of the buildings restored to their original state. We found parking on the street and headed to the hotel only to find out that it had been converted to apartments and required a key to enter. Through the window we could see what appeared to have been the hotel lobby, complete with an elegant winding staircase and front desk area. Disappointed that we were unable to venture in, we revisited our list to see where we should head next when a couple arrived at the front doors on their way out; we quickly scooted in before the doors closed.

The lobby was somewhat bare, but having visited many historical hotels, it was easy to imagine it during its heyday. The floors, walls, and stairs were marble with accents of wrought iron and brass drawing your attention to the architectural details. Directly above the lobby, the stairway ascended six floors and each landing was clearly visible thanks to the natural light coming from windows on each floor, providing much-needed illumination to what would otherwise have been a dark, somber lobby. It appeared that part of the hotel had been divided at some point as an Irish gift shop was located within the original hotel structure and accessible from the street and through the lobby. There was also a small cafe off the lobby, which was closed, but hanging on the wall adjacent to the cafe doors we found a nicely framed photo of the lobby, complete with the front desk, as it would have looked decades before.

Not wanting to trespass any more than we already had, we decided to take a look around the Irish gift shop, Mrs. Murphy's Irish Gifts. That's when it occurred to me that my father had referred to a Mr. and Mrs. Murphy in his letters, and I wondered if this Mrs. Murphy may be in some way connected to his Mrs. Murphy. Once the proprietor was finished with his customer, we approached the counter and began our inquiry. We explained why we were in Sioux Falls, asked about their Mrs. Murphy and found there was no connection between the two. We then shared the list of landmarks we'd already been to visit and those we had yet to see, and once again we were provided with new insights and directions. We learned which museum would house the documents I had hoped to view, also the location of the Knights of Columbus and the Cathedral of St. Joseph, complete with a hand-drawn map. With our newfound information, and much appreciation, we said goodbye. Before leaving for our next destination, we took a short walk up and down S. Phillips Avenue where we located the movie house and several shops, one of which, we later learned, was the former Chocolate Shop frequented by my father and mentioned in his letters.

Our next stop was the Old Courthouse Museum, which housed one of the two Siouxland Heritage Museums. Anticipating the holiday weekend may once again derail our research, we proceeded to the information desk to inquire about the documents I wanted to see. As luck would have it, Adam Nyhaug, the registrar for both Siouxland museums had "drawn the short straw" and was actually working the holiday weekend. We were sent up to speak with him.

Once again we explained why we were in Sioux Falls and the particular documents from their archives that I was interested in viewing. That is when Adam explained to us that those particular items were not housed at the Old Courthouse Museum, but in the other Siouxland Heritage Museum location, the Pettigrew Home & Museum, which we learned was closed for the weekend. Feeling defeated once again, we were deciding where our next stop would be when Adam had a revelation. Apparently a student from the university had been doing research on the technical school, and had requested the identical documents I was seeking. They had been brought over to the Courthouse Museum for her to work from, and Adam said there may be a chance that they had not been returned yet. With that, he left us for a few moments as we looked at each other, wondering, "What are the chances?" Before long Adam reappeared with an archive box containing precisely what we had come to see.

There they were: the Technical School: Army Air Forces Training Command booklet, a yearbook-type booklet titled Army Air Forces Technical School, another booklet titled An Illustrated Letter, and several photos and albums. We scoured all of them as quickly as we could mindful we had a few more stops and then a long drive to Keystone. Thanking Adam for all his help, we made a donation to the Siouxland Heritage Museums, exchanged contact information, stopped by the gift shop and then were on our way again.

Our next stop was The Coliseum, which now served as a multi-cultural center, but when my father was there, it was actually where many of the dances were held. It too was closed, but we took a photo of this massive structure, which very much resembled the vintage postcard photo I had found online, and then carried on up the hill toward the former Knights of Columbus, stopping first to visit the Cathedral of St. Joseph en route. When we were at the Irish shop, the proprietor had told us that we should not miss the Cathedral. He explained that in recent years all the Stations of the Cross had been restored to their original colored versions after years of the color being removed. He said that they would have been colored in the 1940s when all the servicemen, including my father, were in Sioux Falls. He was right. The Stations were gorgeous. It was truly moving to walk around the Cathedral knowing that some seventy years prior my father had done the same thing. Suzanne and I both agreed that if we came back to Sioux Falls we would definitely add attending mass at the Cathedral to our itinerary.

As my father indicated in his letters, it was not easy to find the Knights of Columbus from the Cathedral, but like him, we were persistent, and eventually found ourselves in front of an event center bearing a plaque with the Knights of Columbus crest dated 1947. As was the theme of the day, the event center, was closed so we were not able to see inside. We took it in stride and walked around a bit before heading back to the car. On our way to the car we encountered a couple of men walking around the yard with metal detectors. As we passed them, it was clear they had just discovered something, so we walked over to see what they'd found. There, in the one man's hand, was a coin from 1944. Suzanne and I were in agreement: another non-coincidence.

RIVERSIDE, CALIFORNIA - PART 1

1945

September 4, 1945 - Postcard

Dear Folks,

Doing fine on this first leg of trip. As you can see the people on the way are taking good care of us as usual. Will telegraph upon arrival.

Love, Frank

September 6, 5:03 AM–Telegram

DEAR FOLKS,
ALIVE AND WELL AT SQUADRON E 239 AAF BU MARCH FIELD
CALIFORNIA PLEASE WIRE TEN DOLLARS LOVE=FRANK

September 5, Wednesday

Dear Mother, Harry and Mike,

Well, I suppose you people have been in a sharp flurry awaiting this one. Although I got in yesterday morning at about 5 AM I had to wait until I could get some sort of a permanent address before I considered it feasible to write. No doubt you've answered my telegram by now and I hope you have started writing–Thanks!

The trip was uneventful except that it was very long and drawn out and I had a bad time with the food situation. After about the first day and a half out, the food on the train started to bother many of us and there was no recourse but to try to supplement, or should I say replace meals on the train, with what we could get at various cities where we stopped. I am still bothered by a mild form of dysentery and stomach cramps which if not better by to-morrow will force me to go on sick call. The pains are not serious–like gas pains mostly but hurt like hell and are spasmodic in occurrence. Bowels are open but stools are runny and the intense heat here doesn't help much. I haven't done much about it for things are really SNAFU here. They didn't even expect us here as near as we can figure and they don't even know where most of us are quartered so that has been what we have been trying to get cleared up. No one can tell us actually what we're here for but we have been finding out things all day by the simple expedient of digging out the right people and probing into forbidden places.

I was rather worried when I shipped for our orders read "men earmarked for OJT" and the word got about that it stood for Occupation of Japanese Territory. Well, we found out today that it means "Other Job Training." Also we went to the trouble to be processed (no one cares or asks you to process here) and we bid for instructors jobs. I believe we are in a squadron now where we will be used as instructors or used as maintenance men on the line. It seems that we will be settled here for some time. All men on the field who have not been overseas are being pulled out and are going, and we are here to replace them. With some luck I won't leave again I don't believe. I say "we" all the time—there are three of us—met on the trip down on the train—Bob Forgit—Mass. and Mike Grailey from Philly—2 very nice Catholic boys with ideas similar to my own. They are very clean upright lads—quite a contrast to my old crew. By the way Shaffer and Spencer are here too. Spencer is trying to get a job on the skeet range and I haven't seen much of Shaffer. What they really want to assign you to here is cooks, bakers, clerks, M.P.s or truck drivers, also supply men. We thought we'd like to be instructors so we are going to buck in that direction. Maybe get sent to an instructor's school someplace on detached service and then back again. There is also the question of flying—I'm not too keen about it but as long as I'm going to be in uniform at least another year I may as well be making what money I can, however unless flying is thrown at me I doubt that I'll take it.

The Field itself is the best I've ever been on. They have stucco buildings—green grass everywhere. It is a permanent field. Right now I'm in the temporary section of it—they call it "Dusty Acres" but even that is O.K. Two storied barracks with latrines right in them—really all right—2 sheets to a man—we get a Class A Pass in a couple days, which can be used any time you're not on duty—good for 150 miles. Buildings are far from what I ever expected to see at an Army camp. They have permanent homes for Officers and Non-Commissioned Officers and their families. Grand PXs, movies, bowling alleys, and swimming pool. It is a splendid field and the chow is exceptionally good.

Don't know when we will get paid as yet—that is something we'll endeavor to learn for sure to-morrow. Money spent mostly on food on the trip is reason for collect telegram for I am quite broke. At present I am due June, July, and August pay less allotment deductions and partial pays of $115 received at Dix when I left for home and $10 received at Sioux Falls. I am due in addition—3 months flying pay, overseas pay for June and ration money while on recuperation furlough. I don't think I can get a furlough from here in the very near future but I'm working on it. Will try to get in flying time to-morrow so I can get flight pay for August before I'm taken off flying status, which will be very soon here if I'm not off already.

Don't worry about me people—this place looks O.K. and I should be rid of the cramps in a day or so and if my luck holds and I get me a decent job and things will be O.K. Be good, people.

Lotsa Love, Frank

Return Address
SSgt F.G. Thompson 12107602
239 A.A.F B.U. Sqd. "E"
March Field, Cal.

September 6, Thursday 8:30 PM

Dear Mother Harry and Mike,

Well, biggest and best news for me today came about an hour and a half ago when I found out my money order had arrived. Boy, that was sure short work and thanks a million I don't know when I was ever so broke, had been saving one cigarette all day for before I went to bed–now I have a carton. Worst of it was there is no one whom you could borrow from for none of us have been paid in 2-3 months. And do you people ever lift a guy's morale–well, I guess–ask for 10 and get 15–gosh did the guys ever ogle but I just explained that my Mom was one in a million. Spencer's came too, but Grailey's has yet to arrive–maybe I can let him have 5 till he gets his. They would not let us send a C.O.D. wire from the Post here so we had to nose around and finally got Red Cross to go good and that was the only way we made it. They had to guarantee C.O.D. wire. Thanks a million–I figure I have about 160 dollars coming so I'll see what I can do when I'm finally in the bucks. No word about being paid as yet.

I got myself a job today–Bob, Mike, and I, and a host of others–we will be ground station operators until they can fit us into ground school as instructors where we may or may not fly. I thought you'd be glad to hear that. I start to-morrow and we work 6 hour shifts. I figure it as a very good deal but too good to last long for right now it is so terribly over-manned they don't quite know what to do with us. It is a rather responsible job - I'd say you really have to be on the ball, at least I will for I don't ever want any Joe in the air to want something from me on the ground and not be able to get it.

Also I found out I had credit for flying time for June, July, & August so that's set. Will try to get set for September maybe but I doubt it. Will take out request for furlough to-morrow–have hardly too good outlook on results but here at least you can try–what a place!

We had to go outside the gate to pick up the money order and then we had no passes. An M.P., we could have worked on, but they have civilians in police uniform here–well, we talked our way out but of course no place to cash checks on the base here. Well, across the road is Camp Haan and we swung a deal there. Such a business but we made it and one feels 100% better with some of that green foldable in your pocket–really good!

I'm in the Service Club now–big dance going on but hardly feel ambition to try for a killing tonight–will try next week. We had to stand the worst retreat I ever stood tonight–about 2 hours and the old dogs hurt so I guess I'll try to get a beer–haven't had one in ages - and hit the sac.

Please have heels fixed on my low cuts at home (Army plan caps) and send them on. Do you need any cigarettes? Army ration has been boosted to a carton a week now so I can get you some with no trouble at all.

At last I have a foot locker and am getting settled a bit—it is a relief, believe me. The gals at this dance look grand—have to give em a go after pay day. Thanks a million again folks—cramps almost completely gone today and feeling pretty chipper. Be good, people.

Lotsa Love, Frank

September 7, Friday

Dear Mother, Harry and Mike,

Well, it is getting late and I suppose this will be a shortie. We had a rather busy day still nosing around trying to secure our positions as far as a job is concerned. We discovered a new deal in radio and are starting tomorrow. It involves work with Cathode Roy apparatus in a D/F station here. There is no flying to it and it offers enough time off so that I figure maybe through a part-time job in the PX I can make 50% of my base pay or as much as flying would net me. This is all in the future of course but I am trying to work it out. The job offers quite a bit of time off and that will make it nice even if I can't turn that time into money.

The food here is the best I've ever had in the Army bar none. They actually even try to make it look appetizing too. Soup 2 meals a day and always a selection of 3-5 vegetables. It is really all right. Saw latest Shirley Temple picture tonight. It is quite funny and quite well done if you appreciate Shirley, which I never have completely, however you'll enjoy it I'm sure and get a lot of good laughs out of it.

Haven't seen Dan as yet today and don't know just what he is doing but Shaffer is due to return to the mess hall—maybe I won't eat then eh?

The furlough situation looks fairly good if I take it soon but I sort of shy away because my ticket would cost about 70 dollars, which is out of the question right now. Don't get het up about it, it may just be a mirage and I'll do the most expeditious thing about it anyway when the time comes. Technically we are not assigned to a squadron as yet and nothing can be done about passes or furloughs until orders are cut and we are assigned.

Have to arise early in the morning to get a start on new job so I'd better sign off! Be good, people and keep well as I am.

Lotsa love, Frank

Sunday, September 9, 9:40 AM

Dear Mother, Harry and Mike,

Well, I didn't write yesterday for it was a busy Saturday so I'll have to make this do for today and yesterday. Mike and Bob and I got up and went to 8 o'clock Mass and Communion this morning and I just returned from having bacon & eggs at the PX—getting real flush—that will have to cease!

Yesterday during the morning and afternoon Bob and I work out and around the DF station and we go out again this afternoon—we'll have Monday off. Mike decided he didn't want the job so he's going to continue to work at the ground station. We're going to put up a small prefabricated house out there this afternoon I guess to house gasoline supplies for the power units. I guess I'd best tell you about the job.

D/F means Direction Finding. Aircraft call the ground station to ask for bearings when lost or as navigational aids. The ground station has a direct telephone line to D/F station. At the station they call us when such a request comes in—we shoot the bearing on a Cathode Ray outfit out there and transmit information to ground station. They in turn relay it to the airborne aircraft.

The D/F station itself is located 6-7 miles from the Field and consists of a couple shacks housing equipment, power unit, and gasoline supplies. When you work there you are all alone, but you have so many men now that it looks as though none of us will have to work very long at a single stretch. In the main shack they have a bunk for sleeping, which is quite permissible on the job—they have typewriter for knocking off letters and such—lots of reading material—cooler for butter and milk—hot plate for cooking and percolator for coffee. As things are now, days off are frequent and you may work 2-6 hour shifts a week and one overnight shift of 18 hours. The thing is in operation 24 hours a day. It is not hard nor particularly time consuming since training here has been cut down and now they are on a Peace Time—Saturday afternoon & Sunday off—schedule. You don't do much work but they have to have someone there all the time just in case transient aircraft need assistance.

I was particularly glad to get it for with the time off I can probably fix up some deal in the PX to work for half my base pay and also the leisure on the job will enable me to get my writing done and probably I will devote a good bit of the time to brushing up on some of my college work in preparation to getting back to school one day. At the present it seems to have plenty of possibilities—they also have 2-3 radios out there so I'll be able to listen to commercial broadcasts and also be able to keep my code speed up should I be so inclined.

Last night Spencer and I went into Riverside for the evening—we didn't even have a beer but went to a dance at a Recreation Center in town. There were plenty of girls and not bad at all. We danced all evening and then took a couple girls home from North Dakota—that's where they're from originally. One is a nurse and one a school teacher. They have a 6 room apartment. Yesterday in the country, out near the D/F station, I saw lots of turkeys—the land here abouts is almost only good for poultry farms for there is not much water. Well, we asked the gals if we brought up a turkey would they cook it and did they ever fall in line sooo if and when we get paid we are going to try to get a bird and then we'll go up there for a good home-cooked meal. They're going to make us a big thick apple pie too Huba Huba. The girls are sisters—Fay is their name—look like Swedes and should be good cooks. Got in early 12:30 last night but the days were a bit tired. Well folks, I guess I'll have to hustle—have to eat early chow for they'll be picking us up soon to go out to the station.

Bob and I plan on hitching to L.A. tomorrow. I believe tickets are available for broadcasts and we may strike luck there, also we want to get to Hollywood Canteen before it closes for good. We're going to make it a cheap trip—thumb both ways and sorta live off the town when we get there if we can. Sooo with some luck I should be writing from L.A. to-morrow. Be good, people.

Lotsa Love, Frank

Tuesday, September 11

Dear Mother, Harry and Mike,

Well, I missed yesterday but you see I was very busy in Hollywood! Guess I'd better start from the beginning though. Bob Forgit and I worked Sunday with Master Sgt. Csotty (Scotty) and erected a small prefabricated house out at the D/F station. I worked in my jockey shorts and came off with a nice burn. Anyway when we got back we got passes and took off for Los Angeles (henceforth L.A.). We decided we'd go "on the town" and see what it had to offer.

We got 2 hitches into L.A. (62 miles) and went directly to the U.S.O. to inquire for free lodging. The K of C has a dorm under St. Joseph's Church so we walked over and signed up for bunks and then returned to the U.S.O. for sandwiches and coffee. We sat down to read paper for we had inquired as to dancing and there was none so we didn't have much place to go not knowing anything that was free. Soon one of the hostesses came over to talk with us and a few minutes later got a girl for Bob and I danced with her. We stayed till the gals had to go home and then Bob and I took aforementioned hostess home. She is Ruth Wagoner in her last year of training as an Army nurse. She is not too bad but hardly anything special. She wants us to come again and will get a date for Bob. This I'm leery of for Bob is only 19 and doesn't drink and I'm afraid he'd get stuck but we'll see another time. The gal has a diamond that would bowl you over but I guess it's not my place to complain. Anyway we got back to our sacs and got some sleep. I'll swear there were bugs in the bed but I fought em off till I fell asleep.

In the morning we ate some oranges we had brought and splurged for coffee and sweet rolls. We got a bus for Hollywood and went to N.B.C. We were lucky—they only had 15 tickets for the Lux Theatre and those for overseas men but as I say we were lucky. We went to Hawaiian Theatre to see "Queen for a Day" broadcast—not too good and then we toured U.S.O.s getting free sandwiches, doughnuts, and coffee, milk, and punch. After getting our fill we went to desk at U.S.O. and asked about "Meet the Mrs." broadcast. It emanates from Earl Carols Night Club in Hollywood and we wanted to get in and see it without paying $1.65 cover. We were told that uniform is ticket of admission and upon inquiring as to location of the place two WACs standing there said they were going and we could go along with them. We had half hour to kill so sat down and played 500 rummy till time to go. Broadcast was

O.K. Club is a honey and prices to match–thank goodness they were selling nothing while we were there.

After that we ditched the WACs for although they were very nice and quite attractive we knew they'd cost us money and that was not the object–the target of the day as it were. Soon after that we got tickets for a John Kirkwood broadcast–Ivory Soap–he is really a good comedian and has a good show. From there we went to DuPont's Cavalcade with John Hodiak and the fellow who has a lead in Ziegfeld Follies picture, can't remember his name. From there to Lux Theatre–Experiment Perilous with Virginia Bruce, George Brent, & Paul Henreid.–Not bad, what? After that we went to a U.S.O. where it was Hot Dog Night–stuffed ourselves with dogs and tomato juice, coffee, and cake & milk. From there to another U.S.O. where we shaved and cleaned up and then to Hollywood Canteen where we saw & heard Ann Miller–she is really something in the flesh–Karunch, and Rosalinda–used to be pianist with P. Whitman and also Cas Daley. There were some others too but can't remember them. We had more to eat there and then got bus back to L.A. I really had to hunt for a beer joint–you have to really probe for one. They are all cafes and clubs mostly the latter down here. Well, I found one & had me three beers & Bob had a couple cokes–this was the major expenditure of the trip. We slept same place as night before and got up and made it back in 8 hitches by a bastard route, but made it in 2 hours and had breakfast in Riverside–ten miles outside of camp. Total expenditure for both of us was less than 2 dollars.

Really didn't have to go so cheap for I had plenty of money but I figured it wouldn't be plenty to tide me over the month if I spent it promiscuously so that was that. Anyway if you go on the town once or twice you take the time to see the worthwhile free things from which you would get sidetracked if you decided to spend some dough. At least it was fun for once and we proved to ourselves that it can be done.

We worked from 11:30 until about 5:30 and ate this evening. Figure on taking in a show perhaps here with Dan Spencer and Mike in a half hour or so.

No word about pay as yet also no mail as yet either. Prospects for an extra job look pretty good so far–will try to find out definitely to-morrow. I will leave question of large expenditure of money on a furlough up to you people–if you think it is worthwhile I'll take it when I can get it and come home. Prospects look good in this direction but you can never tell so don't get too excited.

Most of the boys have had mail but not me as yet–none forwarded from Sioux Falls either. Ah well, it should be in soon I guess.

I plan on washing in the morning and getting a few odds and ends straightened out. Be good, people.

Lotsa Love, Frank

Wednesday, September 12, 7:00 PM

Dear Mother, Harry and Mike,

I finally collected some mail today for which I was very truly thankful–it is so good to hear from home again. After getting nothing for over a week I began to wonder what was up. I have received nothing as yet forwarded from Sioux Falls. I received letters from you people mailed on 6th, 7th, 9th, & 10th. That's darn good time I'd say–mailed the 10th and received the 12th. The others had been accumulating I believe for I had been going to the wrong place for my mail. You should be getting my letters by now fairly steadily.

No we weren't near the wreck, but I heard about it. Guess it was pretty bad but we were very fortunate–only mishap was cramps which soon disappeared. Again I was extremely glad to get the 15 dollars–I still have larger part of it and should be able to manage–I'll have to for I'm quite sure we won't be paid now until the end of the month. The picnics sound grand–you people certainly manage to do your "ruffing it" in comfort but then that is the only way if you can manage it.

"Alive and well" in telegram was to dismiss worry on your part, not incite it. I wanted you to know just that in least possible words and since I'd heard of train wreck I thought you might be worried. I have not as yet received card for my signature–sample for bank–why does the bank want it? Is it a joint account?

In your next letter please find out for me the address of Bill Edwards Senior. In L.A. I ran into Mr. Kelley. Met him in a line waiting to get into a broadcast in Hollywood. He is a brother of the Kelley of Kelley Business Institute at the Falls. He asked if I knew the address and I said if he'd give me his address in L.A. I'd try to get it for him and forward it to him. You never know who you'll meet do you?

I worked (?) today 12-6 PM. We played 3 hundred pinochle out there all the time. Saw about job at N. C.O. Club today–was told to come back first of next week. I start working a regular shift at D/F next week Monday I think. I also made out a furlough application today–asked for from Nov. 1–Nov. 25–25 days which includes 10 days traveling time. I don't know what effect it will have so I certainly am not planning on it nor should you! Did a bit of washing this morning and have some more soaking. I do hope you are sending on old low cut shoes as soon as possible as shoe situation is very bad. My G.I.s are shot & it takes a month for a pair here, also Nettleton's are very nearly shot from continued wear. Guess that does it for today–Be good, people. Lotsa Love, Frank

September 13, Thursday

Dear Mother, Mary and Mike,

Received letter written Monday and mailed Tuesday this noon - really very good service to say the least. I'll be darned if I have it with me now, although I thought I had it, but I got a bone to pick anyhow. What's this stuff about you people not being all I expected when I was home? Those are not the exact words but they are the general idea. I wrote and told you that I was the one who didn't fit in and you know

528 • LORETTO M. THOMPSON

it is well as I do. Two people certainly couldn't have done more than you two did and Mike too. But then the dog didn't recognize me at first but he got used to me. I didn't fit in immediately because, well, I'd been living a bit of a different life - do you honestly think there was more you could have done - I hardly think so. You let me go and pampered me as if I had done something when actually it was very, very little. It is my fault and problem and I'll have to iron it out myself and once I can get home and make some definite progress in assuming mine permanently then I don't think I'll have any trouble. It was like having what you wanted and needed and still not being able to touch it for I knew I had to return to the Army and perhaps go to the C.B.I. Please don't feel that you let me down if anything it was quite vice versa - you two are a helluva lot more than adequate for me you know!

About a box - please don't bother just yet. Sure would like one but it is almost too hot here for that just now I think - just like Yuma at times here. Hope you are getting shoes on the way and that will suffice for present.

We stayed in the barracks all day today for we were told we'd be called to be paid, but as usual nothing came of it. I did a good bit of washing and finished most of it up. Have been able to get occasional box of soap chips here lately - how are you doing?

Went to show this evening, had a couple beers and wrote Beals and youse guys and I guess that takes in most of it. I found I could get goggles exchanged, which was a relief. Not much new poop here people - have to get a settled shift first and my start of extra work 1st of next week.

Be good, people.

Lotsa Love, Frank

September 15, Saturday 6:30 PM

Dear Mother, Harry and Mike,

Very little to report from here of a new nature except the day's happenings. As I told you they are going on a "Peace Time Army" basis with Sat. PM and Sunday off and as a result we had a stand by inspection and Review Parade today. The former was not bad, the latter was a real pain since it was very warm and the lads as well as the WACs were dropping like flies on the parade grounds. Here of course is the beginning of the Chicken and the C.O. told us to forget that we were in the Air Corps because we were now in the Peace Time Army. Just the beginning of the rough stuff, which seems to start at fields shortly after I arrive. I seem to be late for everything but just as long as I was a bit late for the serious combat I don't think you'll hear me complaining too loudly. C.O. also spoke of breaking men, which is inevitable I suppose—smallest group in the squadron is composed of Pvts. So don't be too surprised if you see Pvt. on the headings of letters again. I certainly hope to keep my nose clean and if I keep on the ball in the squadron, and am out in God's country on my job, I should be able to steer clear of most of the Chicken. However you know the old story—if they're after you, they'll get you sooner or later. I believe that a lot of that stuff is coming—it is bound to where there are so many stripes.

I'm in the Service Club now–Dan and I are going to a dance this evening–sorta keep contact with those two gals who said they'd cook that turkey–maybe after Monday we'll be able to buy one.

This is a poor letter I know but lateness of parade and lecture wouldn't permit getting mail so I can't write about stuff you guys have written about–won't be able to get mail until Monday now. It gets your goat but it doesn't help much. I understand that a lot of stuff held at Sioux Falls has finally been forwarded and it will be a relief to get that.

Say there are two items I need very much and absolutely cannot get here. They are towels and wash cloths. I certainly would appreciate 3 (no more) large towels (any color at all) and half a dozen wash cloths any color. Anything will be greatly appreciated even if they have to be orchid or orange. Washing out the underwear and sox doesn't bother me too much but getting at my two (2) towels every 3 or 4 days is getting me down. I guess that takes in most of it people. I read "A Night in Bombay"–Bromfield all afternoon and will soon finish it. My lovely tan acquired too rapidly is peeling off in an awful fashion–I look speckled and dirty for it has peeled all over and it dirties up my sheets as it peels when I sleep. I'll have to start again on it I can see that.

All for today people. I'm as content as I possibly could be so far from home so, don't worry and be good.

Lotsa Love, Frank

September 16, Sunday 6:45 PM

Dear Mother, Harry and Mike,

Well, I am finally at work on my own. I'm out here all alone in the D/F shack. There is no flying today so I don't expect much business but perhaps there will be a bit in the morning. I hope, so far I'm anxious to see how I make out doing the actual thing. It is quite comfortable here although there is no company as yet. I say as yet for I expect the coyotes to start about 11 PM or having been forewarned. I have the radio on and am listening to the Bayer Aspirin program - I suppose maybe you are doing the same at home. As I've told you before, I started this afternoon at 5 and will be here until 12 noon tomorrow. We have a bunk out here - hot plate and coffee pot and all the "makens." Also fresh eggs, butter, and bread so it is not bad at all. I brought out paper to write on and a fiction book from the library and an advanced algebra book to work on. I may take some code too just to keep up so you see I have plenty to do.

Went to 8 AM Mass this morning with Mike and Bob and we had coffee and doughnuts in the PX afterwards. I spent afternoon in library and got me some fresh milk and came out here in a Staff car - really a rough day.

Got in last night at about 1 AM with Dan. We went to a dance (30¢ a throw) and had 2 bottles of brew afterwards. We took home the Fay sisters again and all turkey dinner is awaiting is our being paid to-morrow. They are very grand girls - remind me a good deal of the Beals - just grand people - even offered to get the bird too but I couldn't see that since if they cook the dinner and let us come up to eat it- 6 room apt. - that is more than enough.

We are getting so we recognize a lot of the gals who go to those dances and we have a pretty good time - good clean fun you know. I had something very nice on the line last night but decided to let it go in favor of the turkey deal - a bird in the apt. is worth 2 in the bush or even in the tall grass I figure. I never saw a place where it was so hard to find a beer joint. They stop selling beer at about 7 PM for they make more on cocktails and you just can't get any brew.

But leave it to Francis George - must have inherited that from my Grandfather Thomas - I smelled one out and we had a couple last night. Tomorrow I see about extra job, I hope and that it is all on the roster as far as I can see. I really should do a lot of writing out here but I'll probably just finish this and then read and listen to radio until time to sleep. I really should have a couple brews out here, what? Guess I'll be getting on to my books people - maybe have some coffee and toast before going to bed. Be good, people.

Lotsa Love, Frank

September 18, Tuesday

Dear Mother, Harry and Mike,

Well, we did get paid yesterday but all I drew was 20 bucks so it was hardly as gala a day as I had hoped for. That straightens up my base pay up to and including August. I had had $115 at Ft. Dix and 10 at Sioux Falls and then the 20 here. That plus what is deducted for allotments consumes my 96/month for 3 months. I still have 3 months flying pay + rations for 30 days coming. I suppose we'll have to fight now to get that.

Yesterday Mike and I went to NCO club for work and worked last night at 50¢/hour for 8 hours. I don't know when I'll be able to do it again for they don't seem to have many open nights the rest of the month when they'll need help. Also my working schedule is so erratic that it is a bit difficult to make both things jibe. The work as "Floor Boys" and it consisted mostly of picking up beer bottles and dishes from tables and carting bottles to storage bin. Also setting up of tables for bingo. It was not hard at all and we had the occasional beer on the house.

I'll have to see what I can do - if they'll let me come in at 6 PM instead of 4, I could manage very nicely 3 or 4 evenings a week and of course the money would be nice too. If I can't manage latter there I'll try PX or gas station. I'd like to work the fountain with Grailey since he too is an old "Jerk" but they have 2 WACs working it now.

I work at D/F to-morrow afternoon from 12-5 and then don't go again until Friday afternoon at 5 when I work the all night trick including Sat. morning. This is good for I'll get out of Saturday Parade & inspection. That will mean working out there just 3 times a week which gives me plenty of free time as you can see, which I'd like to turn into cash somewhere if possible. It won't be that good for long for we are due to lose three of the fellows soon on discharge points I think. I was sorry to miss Les Brown last night because of working but that's the way it goes.

Received no mail today so this will be a bit short. Please by all means send me ma Goldfish so I can gloat. Mail has been coming through splendidly so I cannot complain there. Hope mine has been getting to you as well and from your letters it seems to be doing just that. Thas all for now people - Be good.

Lotsa Love, Frank

September 19, Wednesday

Dear Mother, Harry and Mike,

I'm down to my daily dozen in the Service Club, which is located conveniently just across from our barracks. I have very little to report in the "New" line. Not working today - don't until Friday afternoon when I take that long trick again which as I said is a relief in that I avoid Saturday inspection and subsequent parade.

Bob Forgit got word yesterday regarding his furlough and he goes, I believe, a week from next Saturday or Sunday. I just received Mother's letter concerning my own hopeful chance of getting home. On the contrary, I found you explained it well Mom, and I hardly did expect you fellows to put up any cash for my getting home. That was all right from Yuma - I needed a bit of help then getting only $19 a month. You see I expect a bit better than 100 bucks in a lump one of these days from the Army - the reason I asked your opinion was that I felt that that money could be better employed by you fellows at home to clear up a bit of this Peter and Paul situation and with your letter of course I am more certain of it now. It would be selfish to spend it for my own pleasure coming home when it would ease things a great deal at home. I should have qualified the question more I guess when I asked it. At any rate I suppose I'll have to take it if and when it comes.

There is a place in Hollywood where you can board and bunk for free, so I could probably spend time off there. And then you know little Francis George - he might see the board of directors or something equally expedient but then it is too far away to plan much on so let us just let the matter lay completely. You can bet at the time things come to a head I'll do just what I deem fit. The main question I wanted answered was your practical advice on how to dispose of my own funds - not yours, which I realize are adequate but far from abundant. I absolutely do not blame you for thinking that I'd need help - that kind of asking of late seems to be the best thing I do however I hope it won't happen again as I have been in arrears for some time now with respect to what is due me. I've pretty well made up my mind what to do so let us await developments.

The extra job situation here does not look too good as yet for my own working hours (few as they are) do not jibe well at NCO club or any other place I can see as yet however the PX takes you on a sort of day to day basis so maybe I can get in there.

I'll see in the morning about that. I can't take on NCO club again the rest of this week or next. At the PX I could go in if needed and if I didn't want to go or wanted a couple days off I could just take them.

The sun finally came out today and feels good - think I caught just a bit of a cold from the dampness during the past couple days. Guess that is all for now people so, be good.

Lotsa Love, Frank

September 20, Thursday

Dear Mother, Harry and Mike,

Well, Dan and I have been much in a flurry since yesterday when we found that Sgt. Csotty had gotten a turkey for us. We called up the girls and told them about it last night and then went in to - ah make the final arrangements. Unfortunately the oven is not large enough to take the bird but the gals borrowed the landlady's electronic roaster so that is all set. We are going to have it on Sunday since that was the day most convenient for everyone.

Three girls stay in the apartment - the other one is getting married to a lad just discharged and they will be there Sunday too. We stopped by at the house at 8 PM last night and the girls and aforementioned G.I. were just finishing their dinner and asked us to join them in pie a la mode (apple) and coffee. Of course they had to twist our arms but boy was it ever good. Most pie I've ever had bar none can't touch yours Mom, but this was very nearly in the same category. It was excellent - they use the same type pie plate as you do and it was big and thick and juicy. Anyway we're going to have more for Sunday dessert. I thought when Csotty bought the bird the farmer would kill and clean it but no. Csotty was keeping it in his refrigerator but I figured that was too much figuring they'd need space for over the weekend so I got a Mess Sergeant to put it in mess ice box till Sunday. Sooo you can see we have had more than combined assistance of all - wish we could all enjoy eating it. Everyone's been so grand I feel a little guilty about it.

It should be a good dinner though cause those N. Dakota gals seem to know their way around the kitchen. They're grand girls and very much country although the one is teaching and the other is a nurse - obvious effort by concerned parents to see that they were educated. Of all things we spent the evening up there looking through their photograph albums. Sounds pretty tame all right but it was fun for a change.

I go to PX fountain in about 10 min. to see if they can use me today - I work to-morrow and Saturday at D/F. Al Donohue and his band will be here this evening and I'd certainly like to take that in. I talked myself into an extra pair of pants - Sun Tan today which once cleaned will be handy since you have to wear them working at NCO Club or PX. If you have not bought towels as yet - don't bother I bet that gets your dander up and I don't blame you but PX had some today for first time in 4 months - only one to a customer but Bob Forgit got me one so I should be set. They are white. Request for wash cloths still goes and I hope you're not too annoyed with me. Well people, I'd best take off if I'm going to work today - Be good.

Lotsa Love, Frank

P.S. Please send Perry's address on 58th - I don't have it and would like to write.

F.

September 21, Friday

Dear Mother, Harry and Mike,

I'm using Service Club stationery again today since mine has about run out - such delightful pastels they provide for us. I work tonight and in the morning so will be busy for that time. Received mail only from John Staeger today so can't answer anything. John and Cal Taylor and the lads we trained with at R.T.U. are in Tampa at Drew Field where a large portion of the 8th and 15th Air Forces were sent. He says same conditions prevail there as at Sioux Falls and things are not much fun because there are so many men.

Did I hear correctly yesterday when they said they'd start to discharge 800 thousand/month? Also this two year number whereby all with 2 years in can get out. I hope so for if they take it from time of enlistment I have 3 years in and if they don't I'd just have to go until February of 1946.

I didn't work yesterday at PX - maybe next week I hope. Saw and heard Al Donahue last night. It is a good aggregation and yet I can't say I would call it particularly outstanding. By all means see "State Fair" movie. I enjoyed it more than any movie I've seen in ages. It is in color and I'm sure you'll get a great deal of pleasure from it.

One of the lads who works at D/F was called on an emergency furlough last night and left this morning - his mother is ill. This of course complicates things and I suppose I'll be working same shift as this week now.

We have a swell bunch working out there and to my way of thinking it is too bad we can't get to know one another better but you work alone out there and so you can't get better acquainted on the job. I've been playing a pit of pinochle with them in the barracks (no stakes involved) and so am beginning to understand the game better.

I think I'll write Doc Bordner one of these days, perhaps to find out how the ground lays - I figure I can't begin to start getting an inkling on things in general as they may affect us if and when they may decide they don't need Mrs. Thompson's little boy, who wasn't cut out to be a soldier in the first place. It may be a year or more before I can get those plaid ties again but this unemployment business which seems so prevalent warns of what a Hell of a mess things may be although I don't actually expect there will be much trouble getting my old job back again - I hope I hope! In effect I believe in looking into the future but can hardly see planning anything of a very definite nature.

How are the Otts - I haven't written them from here but did from Sioux Falls and as usual have heard nothing from them.

Have almost definitely decided to learn to Jitterbug here. They have classes teaching it on Monday nights here at the Service Club so out here I deem it an important social asset to learn.

I picked up a copy of "The Doctors Mayo" in the library today. It is a rather ambitious looking work but looks rather interesting so I shall have to peruse it at the D/F station today and tomorrow.

Things are very clouded here again today regarding the weather so I don't look for a busy afternoon and evening and there is no flying on Saturday so that cancels to-morrow morning. I should be able to get in a good bit of reading and/or writing.

I guess that takes in most of the poop for today fellows so, be good.
Lotsa Love, Frank

Monday, September 24

Dear Mother, Harry and Mike,

Well, I'm a bad boy. I've missed for a couple days so will try to make up in this one. Saturday I worked in the morning and since I didn't get a particularly good sleep I slept in the barracks all afternoon. I got in too late for parade and also late for inspection but I missed Saturday chow and the evening meal was terrible so in the evening Dan and I went into Riverside and got a couple steaks which were really good. We saw the girls at the dance later and made final arrangements for the Turkey Dinner on Sunday.

I went to Mass with Mike at 8 AM Sunday - came back and woke up Dan and we picked up our bird at the mess hall, some butter and peaches and off we went. We got to the apartment at about 11 and had the bird in by 12. We ate it about 5 PM and did I ever stuff myself. We had, in addition to the turk, smashed potatoes, dressing, peas, a salad, rolls, olives, apple pie, and coffee. It was closest thing I've been to having Sunday dinner at home - we had a bit of Tokaj wine to start with too. Frances Fay and I cooked it so we got out of the dishes - Betty and Dan got stuck. After dinner the girls got dressed and we went to see "Rhapsody in Blue" and back to the apartment again for coffee and cold turkey. It was a 14 1/2 lb. bird live, but it sure looked sick when we left. I think all 6 of us really enjoyed it and it certainly was grade A with your little boy. Those girls are certainly grand - I guess I told you Betty is a nurse and Frances starts teaching at a nursery school just outside of Riverside today. It certainly is and would be a wonderful "set up" but I think I'll sorta stay away now because these particular girls are far too nice and fine to fool with and for the next few years I can't see much of any future in anything but fooling so I'm afraid that will be that.

Mother asks why Dan instead of Mike and Bob - well, Dan met the girls in the first place and also Mike does little or no going out because he intends to be married soon after he gets out of the Army. Bob is quite young and although he is good company he doesn't drink and runs around very little so since I met the girls with Dan we got the turkey together. I'll be seeing very little of Dan soon now anyway. His wife comes here in a week or so. She has a lot of courage I'd say. We asked the girls about places and the gal that stays there with them a Sybil "something" is getting married soon and they're holding it up because they can't find a place. They are impossible or almost so to get here.

If you recall that address of Bill Edwards I wrote for and Harry sent - well, I wrote Mr. B.H. Kelley as I said I intended to and received a letter from him Saturday. He wants to know if I am a son of Robert or Harry Thompson and nephew of Emily Bartlett. It seems his wife was quite friendly with Emily. He wants me to visit them - to bring my Buddy (Bob Forgit was with me in L.A. when I met them) and to plan on staying overnight. He expressly asked us for next Saturday - the 29th and said they would take us to a big show at the Hollywood Bowl. Talk about coincidence Huba Huba. Of course I'd like very much to go but after scouting around I find I can't get away as I have to work next Saturday and also Bob goes on Furlough next Sunday. I can't get anyone to work for me for they all have to be on deck for parade on Saturday morning so I guess I'll have to write with thanks and ask for a rain check. His name is Ben Kelley - write me and let me know what you think. I guess it's a small world after all isn't it?

I guess that includes most of the dope for this time people. I am at work now - have been interrupted at this a couple times to take bearings but as usual it is quite comfortable here. Guess I'll get back to my book now so, be good, people.
Lotsa Love, Frank

September 25, Tuesday

Dear Mother, Harry and Mike,

Didn't make it yesterday for time was pretty well consumed working at NCO club. They found work for Mike and me with a vengeance - mostly because we are dependable I think. I'm signed up for plenty until 15th of next month and it won't be too bad I don't think. Thursday I have to work as what Mom didn't bring me up to be, but that's the only night and it only consists of opening beer (that's all they sell there) and collecting for it. The other days I'm signed up for fountain work or on the floor. I can't say I'm too keen about it or some of the guys that work there but it is work and added money and that's what they have over there that I'm after.

I have interspersed the hours around my schedule at D/F and I'll be pleased to at least have a bit to show for some of my spare time. Nothing much has happened during the past couple days. Dan Spencer was finally assigned to truck driving at the motor pool and that killed his golden goose working at the gas station. He had to move from this Sqd. and barracks so I don't expect I'll see very much of him now. He is trying to get a furlough right away anyway.

Please don't plan on my furlough - I have already put it off for later than November and the best bet will be to see how things develop. Mike and I will try to get ours together so we'll have company coming and going for it is a long haul anyway you look at it.

I finally got another pair of G.I. shoes today - it is a relief for the others need repair badly - now I can have that work done.

We have also been putting in a few hours at the Club during the day. That is yes-terday and today. We have been cleaning a stove. Oh, what some people won't do for 50¢/hour it is terrible. I have to go back to work now. I go to D/F for overnight trick this afternoon at 4:30 - I'll get plenty of rest.

This is a hurried letter but I had to let you know I'm ragged, fat, and sassy and glad to be quite busy in quest of the almighty dollar. Be good, people.
Lotsa Love, Frank

September 26, Wednesday
Dear Mother, Harry and Mike,

This is the second time I've set myself down to write youse guys. I sent the other "shortie" but since I figure I'll have little time to write to-morrow I'll mail this one then. Also I'm writing at the D/F station about 6 miles from nowhere and couldn't mail this thing if I wanted to.

To-morrow I assume the odious task of tending bar at the NCO club. This pays 62¢ per hour instead of 50¢ on the floor. It is the only night I'm scheduled for it, so don't worry Mom. I'm getting in, I think, on the soda fountain soon - that pays 62 also. As I said the help over there isn't too congenial, however, the only thing they have over there that I'm really interested in is the cents per hour, so I'll go a ways to gather up as much of that as I can.

Another opportunity has presented itself here to me today. There is a good chance to go back on flying status here and it is extended only to those men who have less than 50 points of which I am one of the unfortunate number. They are going to need flight instructors here soon and it is quite a temptation to collect the extra shekels. I'm going down to see about it in the morning or afternoon. It can't hurt to hear what they have to say at any rate. I honestly am not too keen about flying again - especially in a B-29 for having been in them on the ground a few times I see no easy way for the radio operator or instructor to get out easily. If the work were in 17s I'd take it in a minute if I could get it. I'm not asking your opinion for I think I know it. Also, I'm not keen on these mountains they fly over here - I don't think I'll fly again unless I get a chance as operator with A.T.C., which I figure would be too good a deal to let go.

Say, that suggestion about that chocolate cake sounds wonderful - please send one if you can spare the sugar - thinking about it here in my solitude I could sure use one - ka-runch.

Some bad news - for me at any rate. I left my low cut shoes at the club last night and they were stolen. I don't have much hope of getting them back so I'll have to get me a coupon here and get me some. This is just by way of telling you people my little trials - please don't bother with any shoes for me for I'll manage myself on this one. I think I should make out O.K. here in town or the PX.

This next, I don't know whether to tell you or not. It will get out sooner or later so I guess I may as well spill the beans, but please don't make any plans that can't be easily altered. Things come up daily in the Army which are unforeseen and continually upset personal apple carts, so promise not to plan and I'll tell you - Did you promise? OK! Furloughs have been extended from 15-30 days with a maximum of traveling time of 10 days - I'd get 8, I think, sooo I have delayed mine and changed request so that if it goes through as planned, and I have good reason to believe it will, I'll be getting it sometime around the 5th-15th of December. I thought you might like it if we could all be together this year at Christmas and New Year's and I know it would certainly be all I'd want for Christmas, so I've tried to arrange it that way. It delays it more than a month, but I thought we all would rather have it that way cause gee, I hate to be away from home at Christmas. I talked to Master Sergeant in charge - he had planned on letting me go in November but he said he'd let someone else go and then I could make it in December. Also (ink ran out) I could probably work at Post Office when I get home. It will be an expensive proposition but I think I can manage if I can get the time I've spoken for. I wouldn't talk this thing up too much for it is too far away just yet and just a hope with all of us. I plan to write the Beals tonight and I don't intend to say anything about it to them as yet. Youse guys use your own judgment about it. I don't think any of us will mind the delay too much if it comes through on schedule.

I've got myself booked pretty well at the NCO club to work the rest of this month and first half of next. I work there 9 days of the first 15 so if you people don't hear from me so often or so, well, will you please consider I'm a busy "bartender" and forgive me. I figured I could get work in in the first half of the month and then could spend the money at my leisure the second half. I want to go to L.A. a couple more times. Needless to say - if you really want to do anything, the prices on everything are "terrible" there, but I should get there a couple times more. Also, I've written the Kelleys and asked for a rain check, also my old drawing teacher Jenevere Tomkins is living in L.A. - she gave me her address when I saw her in the bank at home a couple days before I left for the induction center - she was leaving for out here at that time.

Soo people, I guess that more or less takes care of that for the present. I work till noon here to-morrow and start at the Club at 4 and work till 12. Saturday I work here at D/F from 12 until 6 PM and Sunday I get some more time in at the Club. I have all day Friday to myself, but in the morning I pull barracks orderly and have to swap and mop. I'll be busy but I like it better that way - sorta feels like working for yourself again instead of for the Army. I have a couple more to write (in pencil) so I'd best be going.

Mike is working at the ground station tonight. He calls me every hour to annoy me and to keep me awake. We have a direct line from here to the station, which is only means of communication out here. The stinker better stop that stuff for I plan to hit the sac at about 10 PM and he better not keep me awake. I'll write or try to write a couple more now before I make my pot of coffee and have some toast and jam. Be good, people.

Lotsa Love, Frank

Friday, September 28

Dear Mother, Harry and Mike,

Well, I've had good intentions but slipped up a bit. I wrote you at D/F station day before yesterday but left it at the shack so it will probably arrive with this one.

I received Harry's letter today and I'm so glad to hear he's been able to get to a couple shows and is having his vacation. Mom, after last night I find I've missed my calling. Ah, the life of a bartender - such a business! I told you I was going to have a whirl at it - I also told the boys what you said about "bringing up your boy." Mike is going to get a couple pictures of me "at the bar" as soon as his camera gets here. Don't worry Mom, I didn't enjoy it that much.

Today Mike and I spent mostly checking up on our status in the Army and our pay and furlough rations still due us. They will have to write to Ft. Dix to get my ration money OK'd and it will take 2 or 3 weeks I guess. Funny that Harry should ask about points just when we checked on them today. I have the grand total of 39 so don't look for me too soon to be home for good. I didn't get extra Battle Star I'd hoped for but that is not too bad. I don't actually think I've been in much chance of going overseas again now - haven't worried too much about it since I've been here. I don't think there is much chance of it now.

Say, I got my shoes back today - more luck than good management. Picked them up at the Club after work and was I ever glad to get them. I put them in for repair today and will get them middle of next week.

I was very pleased as punch to get my Goldfish - I'm going to sew him on soon - I'm a bit proud of it don't y'know - sorta my only claim to fame.

Bob Forgit leaves on furlough for home Sunday and also we stand to lose a couple fellows who work with us at D/F. They have over 80 points and will be moved to a separate squadron soon. We have some more new recruits and are checking them out. Also, Mike found he had 77 points (he got in 26 missions) and he also is due to be moved after the 80 pointers are shipped out. What is really holding things up is that the Air Force has not as yet got its own Separation Centers in operation as yet. As soon as they do, I'm sure things will move along much more rapidly. We were very lucky today for we found one of my old R.T.U. buddies at Unit Personnel and he got all the information for us. He got Mike an extra Battle Star and sorta padded my points for me. We are very fortunate in that respect for in almost all departments here on the field we have buddies and hence an inside track. It is good for a change instead of having to buck permanent party as transients.

Guess that's it for today people. I work to-morrow and hence get out of parade. Mike helped me with barracks orderly today so it wasn't at all bad. I work Sunday at NCO club and really go at it from there.

Guess that's all for today so, be good, people.

Lotsa Love, Frank

September 29, Saturday

Dear Mother, Harry and Mike,

And so Saturday night rolls around and I don't expect to do much beyond going to Confession this evening. I was very glad to get ma box today - Boy didn't that make time? I have shoes on but as yet have not sampled cake. Plan on doing that tonight with a quart or so of milk. The towels and cloths are sure welcome and I'm ever so glad to get them, also the shower slippers. I'll use the latter shortly as I plan to clean up a bit before hitting the sac or going to church. Got to shampoo ma locks tonight.

Shoes really held me in tonight but now that I have them I don't figure on doing much. Suppose I could go into the dance tonight but Dan is giving these Fay girls quite a rush. It isn't right and I'll have no further part in it, although they're certainly old enough to take care of themselves. He goes on furlough Thursday I think and then he brings the wife back with him. His method is expedient enough for he tells them he is married in such a way that they think he is kidding. Anyway he takes out the one I like and I wouldn't hurt the other one by making a fuss over him. So much for that.

Received letter from Ben Kelley of L.A. today. He tells me to make his home "my western home." He seems enthused over my relationship with Thompsons. Wonder what he'll think when I tell him I hardly know them. It seems his son married a girl who formerly roomed with a Mrs. Jackson who rented [from] Granddad. Quite involved but there it is. She has red hair and name was Marion Zegler. Mrs. Kelley's maiden name was Hazel Pettit of Lockport, N.Y. - does it register at all? Anyway, I'll go to see them next time schedule permits. Mike will go with me I think for we want to investigate possibilities of getting 2nd & 3rd class radio operator's commercial license.

They had parade today - it was a long drawn out affair in the hot sun and plenty were carried off. Glad I didn't have to stand it. I just managed to get my mail and box and eat before going to work. Didn't even get a chance to open the box. Work was easy and I worked with a couple of new boys checking them out. We listened to Illinois Norte Dame football game. That sure was a sloppy game but since the Irish won it was OK.

I guess that is it for the daily report fellows. Thanks a million for the box. They're grand to get - will murder the cookie tonight but good. Be good.

Lotsa Love, Frank

October 1945

October 1, Monday

Dear Mother, Harry and Mike,

Well, today is finally pay day. I have already been paid at the N.C.O Club and hope to get money soon from Army. I am anticipating my pay a bit but I've seen it and am finally getting last of my flying pay. I'll get in line as soon as possible but I want to mail this right after I get paid for I have to go to work right after that.

Sooo please find enclosed money order for 100 bucks. It is not very nice to send it and tell you what I want done with it but I'm going to anyhow. If it is needed for other things please use it as you think best however, I would appreciate it if you would consider my suggestions. As usual these suggestions arise from selfish motives but that is what I want. Primarily, I want dentist paid in full–some 40 bucks I believe. Then I can and will bitch like hell if Mother doesn't wear that bridge. That is a must! Hardly needed for appearance, but wear it Mom, more sake of health and also to prevent deterioration of other dentures to which it should be hooked. A word of warning; if you don't start wearing it soon Mother, gums will contract to a point where it won't fit and the needless expense of another fitting will be entailed. I couldn't say much when I was home cause it wasn't paid for. It has bothered me to some extent and I want it taken care of. So there–I can get real high-handed when I'm so far away you can't get your hands on me.

Of the remainder, I owe the house 25 dollars, which 10 I got in Sioux Falls and 15 here. Also, owe house account another $20 rations, which I get from Army for food consumed while on furlough. I realize that I ate a helluva lot more than that but the Army allows me only 65¢ a day for food so I'm passing it on as I got it. Five more dollars should cover towels I asked for and repair of shoes and no price could make up for that chocolate cake. That leaves about 10 bucks, which I suggest be put toward final payment on plumbing bill which was outstanding when I was home.

Well, that is that! I send a century and then proceed to spend it for you but I'll feel better that some of these odds and ends are straightened out. Especially Dentist and Harry can go over at earliest opportunity and get a dental check. In that regard I expect to get tooth pulled in Tampa bridged in here as soon as I get enough spare time to go over and agitate for it.

This continued after Pay call and getting money order and cigarettes. I have plenty of money to get along on so don't worry–you know little Francis George doesn't stint himself. Also I've taken into consideration future couple months so let's have no malarkey about this.

I have to go and eat now–am taking sad remains of cake with me to D/F. Work there from this evening till to-morrow noon. Put in hard night at NCO club last night–must hurry now–be good, people.

Love, Frank

October 1, Monday

Dear Mother, Harry and Mike,

I just rightly arrived at D/F station and so I thought I'd settle down and write a more leisurely line to you. I'll get this one in the mail to-morrow so this should cover and take place of to-morrow's effort. I get back to [the] Post about 12:30 PM so I won't have time to really write for I work at NCO club to-morrow evening, Tuesday, and Wednesday night also. I was quite satisfied with my pay and I hope you get money order O.K. and that it is some help.

By the way, in passing, I might recommend "Love Letters" to you in the cinema line. It is quite good–Jennifer Jones and Jose Cotton more or less a psychological love story similar in type to *Rebecca*. The gist of it will remain with you some time I imagine. I missed Joan Crawford's opus "Mildred Pierce" but would recommend that also not only because I hear the best of it but also because I believe little Joan has taken a beating and if helping the box office will help her I'm all for it. I think she has received raw deal from numerous studios.

Harry, I'm finally going to send signature on card. Am at a loss as to what to put it in without folding it but rather than delay any longer, I'll fold it and send it on. Apologies for delay. I know I'd piss and moan if I asked for something and you guys didn't act promptly and I have no excuse–will do considerably better next time.

One question I want to ask. I believe that you mentioned bank account in my name. I honestly cannot see the wisdom in that. I would rather you had it in your name Harry, being head of the family, you would have ready access to it for the common good. I may not be right in my impression so will withhold any further comment pending clarification from you.

Work at Club last night was hard for they had a dance. It is a lot of work but I'm glad to have it especially since I'm not kept too busy or fatigued here at D/F. Help situation there has not improved but we hope it will. Here I am telling you my working troubles but I always have and it's no time to stop now.

Well people, I guess I haven't much more to talk about. I have rather ambitious evening planned. I have a number of letters to write and a copy of "King's Row"–bet the book wins out a little later. Be good, people.

Lotsa Love, Frank

October 3, Wednesday

Dear Mother, Harry and Mike,

I was glad to get a letter today from the Tessa Girl–I was beginning to wonder if something were wrong and someone were sick.

I have very little to report. I had planned on getting to town today to get me a pair of swim trunks but the Sergeant in charge of D/F came around and asked me as a favor to work this afternoon. I was glad to help and waited around only to find that deal he wanted help on fell through so I had stayed in camp in vain.

I have been reading King's Row–I find it quite intriguing although it is quite on the sensual side. I don't know why I left this letter go until the last minute today– I have a rather amusing incident to tell you but there is hardly time to write it today. It has been a long time since I bit on the sucker as I did yesterday–I'll try to be sure and tell you in to-morrow's missive.

I'm fine–been doing also a bit of sleeping today since I worked at NCO club last night. I work there on the Soda Fountain tonight and at D/F to-morrow afternoon. Goodness but aren't I the busy boy. Feels good for a change. Well folksies, I have to shave and get ready to "Jerk" tonight. Be good, people.

Lotsa Love, Frank

Thursday, October 4

Dear Mother, Harry and Mike,

I'm at D/F with Master Sergeant Csotty and should be able to write a decent letter for a change. I worked at NCO club last night on the Soda Fountain and got a kick out of being a Soda Jerk again. I was quite busy and the evening passed rapidly, which after all is the main point. I'd rather work there than any place at the club for you are free generally from any interference and intimidation as far as the stock is concerned. I don't work again until Monday I don't believe so I'll have a bit of free time.

The incident I spoke of in yesterday's letter happened when I was out here last time on an overnight shift. I had trouble getting to sleep and hence when I woke at 7 AM the next morning, I was tired. I got up and got my power unit going–checked the equipment and hopped back to the sac. At 9:45 I was awakened by a voice–"He is either asleep or dead!" I jumped out–jockey shorts and T-shirt only and opened the screen door to let in a Captain and Master Sergeant who said they were from Air Inspectors. They had come in a Staff car–gal driving was getting quite a kick out of my dazed, unclothed situation I think. I climbed into my clothes and showed them around, demonstrated equipment and after answering a number of questions they left. Being afraid that they might inspect other units of communication I called General Station and told them to be ready and incidentally told them I had been caught asleep. I made coffee and then proceeded to check power units for gas, oil and water.

On the way back I heard phone ringing and ran to get it–I was "awake" this time–I sired him and explained I had been checking units. Twenty minutes later another call–I had to check on one of men's working schedule out here for them. Finally, before leaving I got a call from Air Inspector's office–Master Sergeant in charge telling me to file delinquency report in form letter and present it at their office in 24 hours. This now was serious–I figured I was due for a good going over. I asked about form of letter and was referred to Technical Library. Here at last I smelt a rat– finally I discerned Mike Grailey's voice and did I ever burn. All calls had been from Ground Station and did they ever roar–I could hear it over telephone. Such a business and I don't believe I've ever been razzed so much. They call me "sleepy" now! Was I ever chagrined and I never even suspected–such a business. It has been ages since I bit on one like that and I still hear about it every day–in the barracks and at the Club–boy if I never learned to take it I sure am now and with a vengeance–it was very funny–even if the laugh was on me.

I received two letters today, which was good. Glad to hear you have taken into your head to do a little more formal studying in your subject Harry. Have you given up ever trying C.P.A. exams? Is this study directed in that direction or do you feel yourself getting out of touch with basic workings in your specialized job? I've said before and state here again that your C.P.A. would be surest way I know of insuring yourself a future in what may become a chaotic commercial and industrial world when the haze of this damn war clears and they start to get ready for another one.

No Mom, don't worry about me doing too much—I have not much taste for killing myself in the Army. They had their chance, I hope they never have another. Work here at D/F could hardly be called such since it is mostly of the "being here and knowing exactly what to do variety" and the maximum number of hours I can put in at the Club is 96 in a month so I hardly think I'm over doing.

Well people, I guess that does it for today. I don't work tonight and am in the mood to really "tie one on." Let you know how I make out folks—be good.

Lotsa Love, Frank

October 6, Saturday

Dear Mother, Harry and Mike,

Well, Saturday again and we just listened to the Tigers even it up and I love to see those boys win. The lads have the Norte Dame game on now. I figured I'd better get some writing to you people done since I didn't write yesterday. Went to San Bernardino Thursday night. Had the usual beers, got hold of a couple gals and when I missed transportation back to the field I didn't wind up here until 9 AM yesterday morning. I got razzed about that—well, the fellows think I'm a Heller anyway. I worked last night at the NCO club—I certainly didn't feel like it at the time but glad I did now. We had inspection and parade today. I had no excuse to get out of parade today so Mike and I "goofed off" and were lucky not to get caught. We did stand the inspection though. I work the long trick at D/F from this afternoon until to-morrow—at 12 noon. It is really not work now for all training flights have been stopped here—no more crews training here whatsoever. The B-29s are expected to be moved out shortly. The only ships that will want our D/F help now are Transient Aircraft. This makes it easy on the Ground Station too where Mike works. Big news here is that the place will soon be a Separation Center. Already men in Squadron "A" have been moved from permanent part of camp to make room for this development. Squadron A's old quarters will house the Separation Center I guess. Also all men with 80 points and over will leave here—will be gone that is by the 15th of this month.

Mike and I have been seriously investigating opportunities in civil life for R.O.s and we plan on going to L.A. to get information and perhaps take exams for licenses very shortly now. The main trouble being we are pretty well booked at the NCO club until the 15th.

I'm afraid I haven't much poop for you today people. I'm well on the way through "King's Row" but have been saving last of it to finish out at the station.

Work last night was hard to say the least for I worked with a Joker that certainly didn't pull his weight. Of course it is not hard work, but I churn inside when I feel I'm being taken for a sucker. Won't hurt me though I guess.

Well folks, I have to get in touch with D/F now and find out what I have to take out there with me in the way of food. I also want to shave and stuff so just remember to be good.

Lotsa Love, Frank

October 8, Monday

Dear Mother, Harry and Mike,

I was glad to hear that you got the money order and doubly so to know that it came in handy. It helps me to help a bit when I can—makes you feel like a civilian almost, ya know. Let's start wearing the teeth, eh? Don't worry about my getting home if I get the chance. If it comes, as we hope it will, I'll get about 40 days and Honey I'll be home if I have to walk!

I didn't write yesterday—didn't get in from work until about 12:30. After eating, we listened to the Tigers win Sunday and then went out and played some tennis with 3 of the lads—it was fun and I sure can use the exercise. Claude Pilcher and I went to church at 5:30 and managed to work in Benediction and the Rosary. I played some Pinochle with the lads until time to go to the show and then took that in. It was the "House on 92nd Street" pretty good on the work done by the F.B.I. protecting Atomic Bomb.

This morning I haven't done much and this afternoon I go to work at NCO club at 4 PM. Went to Air Corp supply today and got me a leather jacket no less. They don't issue field jackets or overcoats here so I says (sic) since it gets chilly in the evenings I'd better have something to keep me warm, so Mike and I went over and talked ourselves into a jacket a piece. Now if we can get hold of those records and destroy them we'll be all set. Ain't we terrible?

Just finished a bit of washing and was glad to get that out of the way. We find we are not going to be able to get in all our time at the NCO club. That is unfortunate indeed but still we get a bit of dough we hadn't planned on also a little more spare time which will come in handy too.

Well folks, I can't write with much continuity now. My Tigers have tied it up at 7 all and the game starts on the 10th inning sooo I guess I'd best buzz off—be good, people. Lotsa Love, Frank

October 9, Tuesday

Dear Mother, Harry and Mike,

After that masterpiece of incoherence yesterday, I guess I'd really do better today. Received no mail today so that lets that out. How did you like that game yesterday? Wasn't that ever a heartbreaker? I was sorry to see the Tigers lose after tying things up so brilliantly. If only that Joe hadn't been caught off second trying to steal just before Greenberg hit his homer things would have been finished up really. Oh well, I hope they come through O.K. to-morrow.

I received letter from John Staeger yesterday and of course I'm always glad to hear from him. He sent photos we took at Savannah and Gulfport. They are not too good but I was glad to get them. I sure miss those guys—haven't met any like them before or since Gulfport. John is working in an orderly room at Drew Field just outside of Tampa—Jim Fahl, Engineer on that crew is at Mac Dill Field nearby where I had work done on my teeth while I was at Plant Park. Cal Taylor is at Alexandria La., where their crew crash landed during our training at Gulfport and Daggett Morse is at dear old Gulfport the lucky stiff. Just as on our crew their Pilot and Co-Pilot have been discharged. It certainly rubs against the grain to see the "Wheels" get out first—after all, we risked just as much as they did. They had all the training and got the good money and all the privileges and it hurts to see them beat us out on the discharge deal too. Ah well, such are the fortunes of war I guess.

Worked last night at NCO club and will be there again tonight and to-morrow. Contrary to what I said yesterday I found out last night that we are well scheduled and Mike and I should be able to get in most of our time this month. If things go as planned I should be set by the 20th of the month so I'll have some time to spurge a bit in L.A. if I can manage to trade some hours here at the D/F station.

According to a roster system in the squadron, I find myself on K.P. Thursday. I've been here over a month now and of course Staff Sergeants and below take their turn. It is not bad here—they let you go when work is done and call you back so that won't be bad. It comes on a good day, which doesn't interfere with work at Club and very little with being out here at D/F. I'm out at the station now. Out in the sun, which I get all too little of and am trying to remedy a bit. We have Power Units shut down and Csotty is in the shack sleeping—really rough, what?

Well people, I guess that is about it for today. Can't think of anymore dirt so I'll let her go at that. Be good.

Lotsa Love, Frank

Thursday, October 11

Dear Mother, Harry and Mike,

Well, things have been happening here with a vengeance but before I begin I'd best tell you that I've been a very busy boy of late. To begin with, I worked at the NCO Club last night from 4-12 midnight and then had to get up early to do K.P. I had left a call for the C.Q. to waken me at 4:30 AM but he didn't so I was lucky to report by about 6:45 and just beat the Mess Sergeant to the job so it was O.K. I drew "the China Clipper" today but they have no clipper here at our mess hall and you do them by hand but it is a small mess hall and we had 4 men on the job so it wasn't bad at all and I got off shortly before 6 PM this evening. At present it is 6:55 and I'm at the D/F station on the "overnight" trick so you can see I have been up and at em. It is hardly as bad as I realize it must sound but at present I have a bad case of ants in my pants.

While I was on K.P. today orders came out for my transfer. Not off the field but for a change in duty from the D/F station to the Separation Unit, which starts here Monday I believe. It will mean a change in Sqd. and of course furlough plans knocked in the head. Work there would be of a clerical nature 7 days a week, 6-8 hours a day. Well, you can imagine how I felt, for although I put in hours here, many of them I can sleep and this is really a good deal since I get plenty of opportunity to work extra at the club. Furloughs will probably be non-existent under this new deal and when possible only 15 days, also work would be of a clerical nature, which I don't give a damn for. Pardon me while I go and get drunk or something - I'm really in a mood to piss and moan for after being so well set I can't see myself in one of the worst set ups around. It is too damn confining and will probably mean that I'd be branded in some "Essential" category and in the long run would be one of the last to get out of the Army.

Well, you know lil Francis George - I couldn't see taking a thing like that lying down I did the best I could. Of course my job is of a skilled nature - it is actually simple enough but you must have a knowledge of Code and some experience. At present, with the exception of Csotty, who is in charge, I am oldest most experienced man here. Anyway, I went to Communications Office and talked with officers there. They want to keep me quite badly but of course this transfer came over their heads and they are losing men from all sections. They were making a list of the men they were claiming they really needed and I'm on it but the big crimp in the thing is that these orders for transfer are already made out and come from Commandant of the Field and since the Separation Center is to be the main and only function of March Field, this new thing has the 1st priority on men. All this is the main reason for my being here tonight. A notice is already posted for me to get my transfer orders from the 1st Sgt. at the squadron but I'm stalling for time and playing dumb for I'm afraid if they once get me moved I'll never get back again. Sooo it isn't actually necessary for me to be here tonight after pulling K.P. but I figure if I can play dumb until perhaps Monday maybe by that time they will be able to get orders to hold me - if not, I'm sunk I fear. I have to prove where I've been so this is the best way to do it I figure. Also Csotty is the man who would have to work here if I didn't, and I want him in there in the morning to plead my case out, he couldn't do that if he were out here in the country. Ah such a business - take some plain and fancy bitching with a grain of salt people if they don't manage to hold me. I'll keep you posted of course and watch for a change in address - I hope not, I hope not, I hope not!

I'm glad you had the watch fixed - don't just know when I'll be a man of sufficient stature to wear it, but I felt so terrible when I lost Dad's razor in England. It wasn't much as far as value goes but when I think of "My Old Man" up there watching over me every day, I like to have something near me to remind me that I have to go some to parallel the success he had, and my Mom made, of life.

Say, this has really become drawn out hasn't it? Guess I'd better stop now. I have my battle jacket here and plan to do a bit of sewing before I sleep tonight. I may have to go before a couple Colonels before this thing is settled and I'll want to be dressed for it. Anyway, this is [the] last sheet of paper so be good, people.
Lotsa Love, Frank

October 14, Sunday

Dear Mother, Harry and Mike,

Well, I haven't been much on the writing of late. As my last letter indicated, the little world and rather lucrative set-up I had for myself around here tumbled down around my ears and I see myself starting anew. Ah well, I put me on a clean pair of pants yesterday and Mike and Bill Siebolt and myself went to San Bernardino just to sort of loosen up a bit. I finally reported today since my spies told me things were beginning to get rough and I felt I'd better get over there. I am now a Counselor for men separating. Have to prepare myself to answer any questions they may have and help with any problems. It is not bad really - quite easy and interesting although it hardly gives me the free time I had. They are on a 7 day week over there and they are trying to get every 4th day off for us. Also, today our work at the NCO club folded up for now they have men whose only duty assignment is to work at the Club so that lets any hired help out. Just another change to get used to and a lot of brand new angles to work on. As you can probably guess this finishes any furlough plans and I seriously doubt if we will get any at all at the Separation Center. Of course there still is a chance I may get reassigned to D/F and Communications but I hardly give it too much credence now. My two years of college never did me an ounce of good in the Army and here at last it almost turns up to be a detriment. Yes, that is what happened - it seems they went through our records and anyone who had any college training got stuck with this counseling job. Please don't misunderstand - I'm not being or feeling bitter, it is just another one of those changes you must school yourself to expect and be ready for, although I hated to see my nicely arranged Army life be slipped out from under me so abruptly and so completely.

Anyway, we set out to have a good time last night, Bill and Mike and I, and we had a few beers and went to a dance and had an all round good time. Good clean fun don't ya know. Of course Mike isn't interested in women, but we got him to break out last night and he claims he had a lot of fun dancing while Bill and I were working on a couple sisters who go to U.C.L.A. One I was with - blonde, finishes in a week or so and starts to teach - the other one continues school. They live in Fontana, not too far from here, so I'm told and of all things Dad runs a winery and one of the landmarks near their home is a Wine Cellar - Oh Baby that's for me. Their name is Moranrick, I think - wouldn't be a bit surprised if they were Polish, they are quite refined and their people called for them after the dance so you can see there was none of our taking them home - darn it. Anyway, we think we'll look into it since one of the Lieuts. at the Separation Center lives at the same place and we sorta figure we might get a ride there and back. Town is only about 13,000 and is where Henry Kaiser built the first Open Hearth Steel Furnaces west of the Rockies. Oh yes, we're interested in steel now - anything that accounts for that sturdy Polish foundation.

Hours at work now are 7:45 in the morning until 5 PM so you can see I'll have to be on the job. Just like a civilian clerical job really but I'd still rather have an Army job and be making a little dough at a civilian job at the same time. Hope the furlough business doesn't strike you too hard, but with 39 points I just miss going overseas again so leave us not complain and rather stop and count our blessings for we have much to be thankful for. I fear I'll get to be too much of a socialite and spend too much on this new deal when I have reconciled myself to settling down to working hard to try to accumulate a little extra dough that I hope I'll be needing one of these days when I get home. I guess that just isn't one of our talents - that saving money is it people?

Well people, I'm getting a bit hungry - may try to get me a beer and hit the sac soon for I have to be around to "counsel" in the morgen (sic). Be good, people.
Lotsa Love, Frank

October 15, Monday

Dear Mother, Harry and Mike,

Well, after my first full day on the job of listening to someone else's troubles, I can claim no ill effects. It is quite interesting and refreshing in a way, that you feel you are able to help in a way, some of these lads who are returning to struggle with civilian life.

Things are under manned over there at present so we get no day off this week and will start getting some time off next week I guess. It is confining to say the least, but we have hopes for a better set up in the future. I have a great deal to learn as you can imagine. You'll never know the problems some of these jokers can dream up or some of the situations you can find them in. Of course, we have little actually to do with a man's personal problems but in a man's enthusiasm or depression, personal details bleed into the discussion of his economic problems and we generally get the whole story.

Hardly know what to do with myself tonight. I suppose I should stay home or at the barracks but I think Bill Siebolt and I will go into Riverside and see if we can't find us a dance somewhere. We'll have to be back early of course for I found myself arising at 6:30 this AM in order to be ready to report promptly at 7:45. It is really rough when I haven't been getting up until I damn well pleased.

Well, I guess that is about it for today. There is really no poop to speak of. Many of the fellows in the barracks here are leaving for Separation Centers and I'd say that the barracks, which was completely full when I got here, is now barely half full. A lot of the lads were transferred to the Separation Center - I should move myself but I'm waiting around to see if the boys at Communications have any luck in holding me - or I should say getting me back now.

I guess that is just about it for today people. I know it is short, but I'm fine - not doing much of anything to talk about so, be good, people.
Lotsa Love, Frank

October 16, Tuesday

Dear Mother, Harry and Mike,

Well, as was the case yesterday, there is very little new to report. I put in my day and little of extra interest happened. The furlough situation is quite dead and I also made a quiet bid to get out of there today. Also my former section head, a captain, *spoke to them about it but it is just no go absolutely at present and I look for very little change in the future. We passed 60 men through today and yesterday and we expect to put 90 through to-morrow. I think we are really helping some of the fellows - some of them are so bewildered and seem to hardly know what to expect of civilian life. It is peculiar for it seems to me since most of us have spent an appreciable amount of time wishing we were home and planning for it, we should have some idea of what to do with ourselves. So many are prepared for so little - it is too bad.*

I plan on moving my living quarters to Squadron "L" soon now, probably to-morrow so please note change in address when you write.

Mike will leave here soon now. He has 77 points and there is a notice on the board for all men with 70 points or more to clear the various agencies on the field as they will be discharged by Friday. That sure is good news for Mike for he wants to get into civvies and get situated and started so he can get married as soon as is possible. I hate to see him go for he has sure been a good buddy but I'm glad for his sake of course.

I find I can work another 3 nights at the NCO club this week and also have a lead on a job at the G.I. laundry, which I intend looking into. So the extra job outlook is not completely dead yet. It is a Post regulation that no one can hold a job off the Post so that lets that angle out.

Last night I didn't do much. Went into Riverside and there was no dance. I want to go to-morrow night for there is a dance in there then. Bill Siebolt went with me and got hold of a blonde with a car. She had a couple buddies but I absolutely couldn't see either one of them so I cleared out but quick. I seem to be losing a lot of my zest for what that "pick-up" stuff represents and boy oh boy, there is plenty of that stuff around California. I had me a couple beers and came home. I guess that does it for tonight folks so, be good.

Lotsa Love, Frank

Return Address
S/Sgt F.G. Thompson 12107602
420 A.A.F B.U. Sqd. "L"
March Field, Cal.

October 18, Thursday

Dear Mother, Harry and Mike,

Well, things have been rolling along at a fairly good rate here. Got 60 men out today and worked only in the morning. We are set up to handle 4 times as many but the bottle neck comes in the finance and unit personnel end of it. They do not have enough people left there to be able to handle the volume so that slows things down. The way things are going now, I believe that all men permanently stationed here will be discharged here from now on. They are trying to get the 70-80 pointers out now and the 60-70 category are all ready to go. Mike leaves in a couple days now and I sure hate to see him go for he has been a swell buddy. He and I have accomplished a lot of things together but he is on his way out now and I'm glad for him. He got notice very suddenly today and has had to "clear" the field and has been transferred to the Separation Squadron. I expect to see him in the processing line to-morrow or the next day and he'll be on his way home soon.

Had myself a really good time in Riverside last night. Bill Siebolt and I started for the Municipal Dance - 30¢ a throw but wound up at the U.S.O. number for free and we really had a good time. Yours truly got lined up with 3 or 4 gals and I'm feeling good today but tired. Took one home - Frances Carlson - goes to Occidental College in Pasadena - not bad at all ma dears. Really wanted to take a blonde home but I missed the boat - I thought she was well spoken for because when I'd cut, it was always the same 2 or 3 guys who cut back. Well, just as Francis stops by to say nite nite - the blonde stops by and I think she was alone - ah such a shame - well maybe I can get to that another time. Batted a thousand last night for the third Gal was a red head and she was all right too - cute as can be. Yesterday I didn't know a girl around here to take out, now I know 4 pretty decent looking ones. This includes WAC in the Office at work - she seems to be looking for trouble so I guess maybe we'll have to shoot a few bearings with her some dark night on the tennis courts.

Well, here we go again - chopping wood! I have a copy of "The Valley of Decision" now and am reading that in my spare moments so you can see I should be well taken care of.

Guess that is it for today people. Be good.

Lotsa Love, Frank

October 19, Friday

Dear Mother, Harry and Mike,

Well, there is not much change in events at present. We got 90 men out today. I wore my leather flying jacket to the roll call formation today and 30 minutes later an order is posted that "sweaters and leather jackets will not be worn as an outer garment" so that cooks that. I was chilly and since no field jacket has been issued or will be, I wore it. Well, we'll just have to be careful wearing it from now on - doesn't do me much good having it that way.

I get a day off of all things to-morrow. Bill Siebolt wanted me to go into L.A. - he goes to see his sister who lives there but I can't see going in to-morrow. Mike goes through the Separation Base to-morrow and I want to be around to help him fill out a form 100, which will really carry all his qualifications and be of a good deal of use in helping him get a job as a radio operator when he gets home. He helped me move today and I'm now in Sqd. L living there. Mike has been told he'll be through and discharged sometime Sunday afternoon, so I reckon he'll be shoving off then.

I believe I'll get things straightened out in my new barracks to-morrow - also have a bit of sewing to get done. They insist on your wearing your rank over there at work. I only have it on a couple shirts now and my battle jacket also I have to put 4th Air Force patches on the left shoulder and 8th Air Force on the right shoulder. It is a lot of malarkey if you ask me but that is the way it has to be. I have accumulated a good deal of extra clothing lately. Lots of the guys have left clothes in the barracks. Of course, I can't wear all this stuff but I can exchange it for new stuff that will fit me.

I'm planning on going to a dance here on the Post tonight just to see if any of my dollies have showed up, don't ya know? Went to see Spanish Main last night and enjoyed it very much. One of those old ships and sword fighting pictures I enjoy so much.

I guess that takes in most of it. No mail today for me but I believe that is due to change in squadrons and it will be coming through O.K. soon.

Guess I'll get going now people and have a go at some of those dollies so, be good, folks.

Lotsa Love, Frank

October 21, Sunday

Dear Mother, Harry and Mike,

I'm afraid I lead a more or less dreary life these days - that is as far as writing much to you of interest. It is just like an office job of course and gets more confining as we put more men through. Managed to get 120 out today and this will of course be increasing as time goes on. My only annoyance is that as long as I must be tied to routine, I'd just as soon do it at home in the bosom of my family. Sorry that I've been missing the boat on the Air Mails but the Post Office was closed yesterday and today so I'd sorta had it in that respect. Haven't been able to get any mail either so that doesn't help much. I should be in line for a real "take" tomorrow.

I am getting through "The Valley of Decision" and really enjoying it - get it if you still can from the Beals - I am considering it quite worthwhile.

Last night Mike decided he'd ship his barracks bag and carry a small bag with merely the necessities so we decided a trip to town was in order. We went in and got him a small bag and then we decided that a beer and a steak was in order so we really treated ourselves. A bit later we took in a dance at the Municipal Recreation Hall - met the Fay Girls - took them home and finished off with coffee in their apartment. We had a good time kidding them. Dan Spencer had told them before he left that he was married. Guess he was afraid of possible consequences when he brings the wife and youngster here with him. At any rate, they have not quite gotten over being "taken in." According to what they said, they had, at one time or another, discussed the possibility of either of us being married and they decided if either of us were, it was me and not Dan. They said I was the "conservative type." Boy did old Mike ever razz me about that - not a Big Time Operator but "The Conservative Type." Ah well, it's safer that way.

We got in late last night and I just made work in time. Both Mike and I had been to Confession last night but schedules today - his getting his final discharge, and my working - fixed things so we couldn't make Communion. Don't think I'll make it tomorrow night for I am working at the NCO club. One of the last trips over there to work but I should be able to get to 5:30 PM Mass and Communion Tuesday evening.

Went to a movie this evening - Franchot Tone's latest effort. It was O.K. but I'd hardly put it in the "good" category. For me it was a few laughs and that's about all.

Well folks, I guess that's it for today - not much new poop. I'll just be here awaiting discharge, which I consider it lucky if I make it by next summer - maybe not even then. I'm not complaining - I should say not - some of these guys are pulling permanent K.P. and Police details and I certainly hope that's not for me. Sooo people, be good.

Lotsa Love, Frank

October 23, Tuesday

Dear Mother, Harry and Mike,

We have been at it, here at counseling, rather hard the past couple of days. With the present personnel working here, the goal for enlisted men is about 240 and we got out about 180 yesterday so we should be going full blast soon. The bottle neck at finance should soon disappear for they got 150 trained men in yesterday.

The job is settling down to routine now and getting a bit boring with it all however it hasn't become too bad as yet. Received letter from Harry of the 17th and that is all I've had from you people since about last Tuesday. I know you're writing and as soon as things solidify a bit again here at the base things should move smoothly in that respect again.

Got a letter from Sally with one rather good looking photo - she's been holding out on me that's all I gotta say. Looks like she was poured into that swim suit.

I worked at the club last night checking membership cards at the door. It was quite uneventful and I took the "Valley" with me and read on the job most of the evening. I'm getting pretty well through it now and have enjoyed it.

I get another day off to-morrow of all things. Bill Siebolt and I plan to go to Fontana and look up the girls we met at San Bernardino almost 2 weeks ago. In as much as I can't get home, I may as well see as much, or should I say as many, as I can. This extra day is part of a 2 day off a week deal they're trying to get for us and eventually they are going to try to get us the 2 day successively instead of every 4th day off.

Haven't as yet tried for work at Officers Club but I will as soon as I get straightened out, probably early part of next week. I hope I can get hold of something - we'll see.

I plan on going to L.A. next Monday - I have Sunday off, but am going to trade it to one of the boys who wants to be with his wife on Sunday. Maybe I'll get a chance to see the Kelley's then - we'll have to see.

Gosh folks, I can't think of much more to say. I'm right in there pitching these days - eating too much and I bet I'm taking on weight. Shaffer, the old Ball Turret man has taken on 20 pounds since he has come here - wonder if I have. The G.I. issue still fits O.K. so I guess not. Be good, folks.

Lotsa Love, Frank

P.S. Finally was able to get some airmails today so here it comes.

F.

October 25, Thursday

Dear Mother, Harry and Mike,

Well, I got me a letter from each of you today and one from Norma. Also received El' Chem and a copy of Post Yarns from the plant, which I'm always glad to get.

I suppose I'd best give you an idea of what I've been doing for the past day or so. We started out Tuesday night at 6 PM in quest of the girls and Wine Cellar at Fontana - we found the place but no girls so we went on to Ontario and since that was quite dead, we finally wound up in Pomona, which was about as quiet. We had a few beers and finally decided to stay there all night. The next morning, we horsed around Pomona and then went back to Ontario at about 11 AM. We went direct to the Junior College there where we knew one of the girls was enrolled. Found her and spent the afternoon with her and one of her chums. It was fine except that both girls live so far out in the country that if we had taken them out that evening we would not have been able to get them home that night. One of the girls lives a full 2 hours ride from the school so we gave that up as a bad job. They get back and forth on chartered school buses and nothing in the way of a commercial line comes near their places making the situation quite impossible without a car.

We then put them on their buses and struck back to Riverside and finally wound up at the regular Wednesday night U.S.O. dance. The girl I had taken home last week was not there and I was just really beginning to enjoy myself with a different number when she showed up. She wasn't dressed for the dance - had been working overtime - it was her last day of work before she starts back to school. Anyway, we climbed in her car and she drove us to her home and did a quick change while I did a tumbling act in the parlor to muse mother. Then back to the dance we went - only had about an hour left but she seemed to think it worthwhile so who am I to complain.

I find I'm going to have next Monday and Tuesday off so I plan on going to L.A. and maybe stop in and see the Kelleys. I don't know whether Bill will be going down or not - he generally goes to see his sister who lives there. I imagine I'll be able to see this gal down there Tuesday for she will be at school - it is a temptation but I'll have to see how the expenses run. Actually it is a cinch to blow 50-75 berries an evening in L.A. - the prices are rough. Besides, it is getting too chilly here evenings for many outdoor maneuvers - I'll have to decide when I get there.

Well folks - I guess that sums it up for today. I have quite a few odds and ends to take care of this afternoon so I think I'll get on the ball. Be good, people.
Lotsa Love, Frank

October 25, Thursday

Dear Harry,

Mother's Birthday present is on the way. I got it in Riverside today and do hope she likes it. I am having it mailed to the office to you and you might write and let me know what you think. Please have it wrapped decently and have the card made out from you and Mike and me. Take it eisel (sic).
Love, Frank

October 28, Sunday

Dear Mother, Harry and Mike,

Well, I'm a bad boy - not having been much on the writing lately. Yesterday we were very busy getting 210 men out and I was so bushed after evening chow that I hit the sac and slept until 10 PM. I got up and went over to the Club and had me a couple beers and then went back to the old sac again. Oh, it was not so much the work that tired me - it was really the evening before.

Among those going through here yesterday was Bob Walsh. I think you should remember him - he lived on 7th street and was in Mrs. Draz's class with us. He was a year ahead of me in school. He was in the high school fraternity too. I hadn't seen him since high school for he had been going to Ohio State and working out there during the summer months.

It was sure good to see him and we really hashed over little old Niffles. He has changed a good deal - the Army I'd say has done a lot for him. He always had plenty on the ball but socially he never had a chance to develop. He was a Technical Sgt. flying as R.O. with A.T.C. for almost 4 years. That was really a good set up. It seems that he now has a number of good connections out here and also a girl whose father happens to be on the inside of a few business deals and has been giving Bob tips on the market. Boy, doesn't that ever sound reminiscent of the last war? Bob plans to go to Yale on his G. I. Bill of Rights - guess he wants to finish up with the Hoi Polloi. He says he has a job all set in Chicago and that although he's going home for a while - 2 weeks or so - he never wants to be there long again. He's afraid the town will drag him into a rut again! I was glad to see him - he actually didn't recognize me with my cookie duster but he came around later - I'm awfully glad he seems to have life's problems solved for it never seemed to me that he had had much of a chance at home.

Friday night Bill Siebolt and I had decided to go to the U.S.O. to a shindig there. I called up Frances Carlson and stopped by for her at her home and more or less spent the evening with her. She doesn't drink or smoke or even eat as far as I can see. She is pretty good company and her folks whom I've met seem quite nice even if they are Masons. She manages to be quite baffling being quite adept at a "Come On" the likes of which I have only seen here in Calif. and then when she gets you all worked up she tries to turn you off like a faucet. I'm not particularly interested as usual, but it's fun fooling around. Ah women - I haven't found two who react alike yet.

Well folks, that does it for today. We'll soon have the lads coming through again today. We expect as many today if not more than yesterday - have to run now people - be good.

Love, Frank

October 31, 1945, Thursday

Dear Mother, Harry and Mike,

Well, I've been a busy boy of late. Have had past couple days off and spent most of em in L.A. It was raining practically all the time so I say to myself that is a good time to call the Kelleys, which I did. I was alone and went up there for dinner and stayed all night and had breakfast and then left. Mr. and Mrs. Kelley work at the Post Office from 8:30 PM until 5:30 AM and are at it 6 days a week getting Friday, Saturday or Sunday night off. I didn't see much of them except in the afternoon and at supper and spent the evening over a bottle of Calvert's Reserve with their son Dan and his wife–formerly the Ziegler girl. Yup, Mrs. Kelley is the gal dad used to go with in Lockport–she claims he was ready to settle down but she was only 17–a likely story. She of course was anxious to know what the Thompsons had to say when I had written them. At which I made no bones about telling them that I was quite the Black Sheep in the family and since my grandfather had died I had had little or no contact with them.

I had a great deal in common with Dan's wife Marion for she trained with Eileen Daley (who is expecting) Flo Murphy, the Tyree girl and a lot of others I knew. She also knew many of the priests. It is the same old story there–Marion is Catholic. She told me at breakfast that the Kelley's are not–she had heard from the Jacksons, tenants of Gramps, how the Thompsons were very dogmatic–she said "you can sway the Kelleys." They have a little girl 3 months and she blurted out that she thinks the second is on the way. She is a swell person–they all are, although I didn't feel that I made much of an impression on Mrs. Kelley. They were grand to me in every way and I feel I put them out although they made me at home effortlessly. Dan is at "Muroc" north of here. He got in 3 years ago when he and his buddies enlisted together and have been kept there these three years as a unit. The group was a dance orchestra and of course he has been fortunate to be so near to home and not go overseas.

There were lots of things to do in L.A. last night but I just didn't feel like doing much. There are a couple girls I know down there now but the spirit just didn't move me. It was still raining so I took an early bus home, got me a steak in Riverside and got to bed very early. In a way I feel sorry for Dan and Marion Kelley. He is prepared for nothing having a couple years in U.C.L.A. in music and now feels that music makes a poor life work. He has a family now–his wife is capable of making a decent living–they are staying with his folks and he doesn't know where to turn. I met a good many G.I.s in L.A. who have been discharged–some are working and none seem too happy–they have nothing to believe in. Many are drawing unemployment insurance and just loafing. They seem to think discharge means that they are entitled to live on the country. I expect some pretty nasty results from this in a year or so. They don't understand that all they've really earned is the right to make a living in the finest country in the world in the same unhampered manner their fathers did.

I don't know what prices are at home but I can say they are terrible here. No wonder men strike–costs will have to go down considerably before anyone can make a decent living wage at the present scale.

Best news I've heard in a long time is that Mike is getting his hamburger on Sundays. Things are readjusting themselves to normalcy in some respects anyway.

I finished Valley 3 or 4 days ago–feel like I've lost a good friend–have to get me another book soon now. I plan on trying to get a job at the Officers Club sometime this week so maybe I'll keep busy there–I hope so! They have followed the spoken statement with a written formed directive that furloughs for us are frozen and that is positively that.

We don't get paid today but are supposed to get it to-morrow. I'm not sadly in need this time as I usually am since I still have cash on hand and also a bit coming from the NCO club.

I met a chap I went to N.U. with at an L.A.U.S.O. Club Monday–Denny O'Sullivan– he is flying R.O. with A.T.C at Mather Field right now.
Friday–Nov. 2

Boy, I started this and didn't mail it. I certainly have been off the beam and will take quite quietly the berating I know must be on its way to me now in the mail.

Wednesday we started out for the dance here at the U.S.O. and sort of got way-laid–it was more than sort of. We got a ride into Riverside with a 1st Looy and we mentioned that Artie Shaw was playing that evening in San Bernardino–he wanted to go so we went along with him–he twisted our arms of course. Only we never did get there. He was one of those "Let's stop for a drink" guys and so we did. Finally got to San Bernardino and wound up with three nondescript girls. The fact he had a Torpedo Pontiac and a couple bottles of 100 proof bourbon in the car only made the cheese more binding. Don't enjoy that type of evening but Bill Seibolt did and I guess the Lieut. did–me going along to be a good sport. No, I'm not getting to giv-ing you the Bob Mitchel Routine, you see I got the other one of three, which believe me should have been the other one of a couple thousand. And Harry knows that I generally don't get taken that way. Well, I guess you have to be taken in once or twice anyway. Finally wound up at the barracks in the morning at 5 or 5:30 and I was really a beat boy all yesterday having had only a couple hours sleep. Got to bed but early last night and slept like a top. I came in town this evening to see if I could find out where I could get tickets for San Francisco Opera Co. presentations. I think I can get them, from what I hear, at a drug store here in town only they're closed now. I'd like to take in a couple operas during the next week or so but what I really want to hear is the Don Cassock Choir which will be on the 11th I think. I got all the poop when I was in L.A. last but hated to buy until I found out what days off I was scheduled for in the near future.

I got a letter from Doc Bordner today. I had written him a nondescript sort of letter not mentioning anything about coming back hoping he'd give me the dope. In this letter he more or less advises me to come back to work until I get 5 years with the Co. and then he says I can get any kind of leave for going to school I want thus assuring myself of part time or summer work when I start back to school as a steady diet. He of course assumes that I have 5 years service. I started there Nov. 14, 1939 and worked until 26 of Jan. 1944 so I'm a bit shy on the 5 year deal. Anyway he says there is a great exodus of men at the lab. Don Woodbridge is going to Princeton to work for PhD. as well as Fred Leighton who starts at Wesleyan sometime soon. Bill Bacon who started there shortly before I left is going somewhere to work for his PhD. so the boys are going to be really shorthanded.

Bordner, as you know, is now the Head in the lab and I'm sure he'd go to bat for me in any situation. Sure I've got a lot of plans for the future but I first have to get Mother's and Harry's opinions on them and that will tell most of the story. In any case, my plans call for returning to work for a while until I stabilize myself and my outlook.

Well people, I guess that's most of it for now—I must get this in the mail—I'll probably think of more to-morrow as I try to get back to the standard daily schedule. So, be good, people.

Lotsa Love, Frank

MARCH FIELD

Present Day

The year I discovered the letters, I was employed by a small manufacturing company and responsible for sales and marketing. My job required quite a bit of traveling around the country, visiting customers and working trade shows. I was with that company until 2016, when I was recruited and moved to a larger manufacturer. After about a year with them my job was eliminated; my second experience with downsizing. Needless to say looking for work is never fun for anyone and a full-time job in its own right, but as always the Lord provides and within a few months, I was back to work for a company that had four branches, one of which was located in Riverside, California.

My first trip to Riverside was packed full with meetings, and some customer visits. As I drove with my colleagues, I mentioned that my father had been based in Riverside during the war and that on my next trip, I intended to add an extra day to my stay and try to locate his base. While we drove, I explained my project and the discovery of the letters, and that the base was named March Field. Moments after I shared this with them we saw, across the highway, some huge vintage airplanes. It was very exciting to see all of them, but what stopped all three of us from talking at the same time was seeing the sign for the facility: MARCH FIELD AIR MUSEUM. What were the chances?

We drove to the next exit, turned around, and headed back to the museum. With our tight schedule, there was no time to actually visit the museum, or even make contact with their people, but we drove up to the sign, took some photos, and headed back on our way. All three of us were amazed that, of all the places we'd been that day, and all the highways we'd been traveling on, we would come upon the exact air base I was talking about, and that it still existed as yet another air museum. I knew I would be back.

———

My next trip to Riverside was again full, but this time I'd done my homework. Prior to traveling, I'd extended my hotel and car rental another day, and I'd contacted the March Field Air Museum in advance of my visit. Karla, from the events department, was most helpful with coordinating my visit, including a meeting with the museum's curator, Jeff Hulihan. I'd shared with them that I had a number of letters my father had written while he was based at March Field and that I'd like to donate them to the museum. We arranged the date and time for our meeting and I finalized my travel plans.

Upon arriving at the museum, I was struck by the amount and quality of work they had done to commemorate those who had counted March Field as their permanent or temporary "home" while serving our country in WWII. The museum was located in a huge hangar, with an adjacent building, and there were numerous plane exhibits outside. Clearly a great deal of work had gone into preserving the history and detailing the legacy of the base. Once inside, I indicated that I was meeting Jeff, and browsed the gift shop while awaiting his arrival.

I had brought along some actual letters from March Field in addition to the bound copy of the letters I had typed. Once in Jeff's office, I shared these with him. In true museum curator form, Jeff was in awe of how well-preserved the letters were. We discussed the proper handling of them, the best way to store them to ensure they remained as pristine as they were currently, and that's when Jeff told me about the Vincent J. Rogers, Jr. letters.

We ventured from the office out into the museum; Jeff spent a great deal of time with me, showing me various exhibits, explaining how each one was developed, and his plans for future exhibits, but we spent most of our time with the Staff Sergeant Vincent J. Rogers Jr. Exhibit. Jeff explained that this was the first exhibit he'd built upon accepting his role as director of collections and exhibits. While I am always intrigued by the many stories and personal histories I've encountered throughout my various visits to military museums, this particular story captured my attention.

Vince originated from the Buffalo, New York area. He served in the Pacific Theatre in WWII, elevating his rank to S/Sgt. Enlisting in 1942, he attended radio school and gunnery, similar to my father, albeit at different bases, and he was an ROG. in B-24s. Vince never made it home. His plane received bad fuel prior to taking off from Tarawa atoll, in the Gilbert Islands located in the central Pacific Ocean. Their mission was to hit the Marshall Islands. Circumstances were such that all men who were lost when both planes exploded were buried side by side next to the runway. Only three of the ten men onboard survived. All these years later and officials could not locate Vince's remains in order to bring him home. The museum worked vigilantly with officials, to the point of building a separate display named "Finding Vince," where museum visitors could contribute to the effort.

This story was so moving my mind was reeling, but what happened at the end of Jeff's telling of it brought the two of us to tears. It seems a family member had walked in one day with a box of military items, including a stack of letters Vince had written. Piece by piece, Jeff was able to tell Vince's story. The hours dedicated, and the research involved, created a bond between Jeff and Vince that is difficult to communicate. Much as I'd developed a close relationship with my father through researching his life, Jeff had developed a close relationship with Vince. It was at the end of Jeff's story that he turned to me, and requesting confidentiality, shared with me that he'd just been notified that, through DNA testing, they'd finally located Vince's remains and he was coming home.

A week or so after my visit, I saw on the local television news, and online, the story about Vince Rogers Jr. finally coming home, being repatriated after seventy-five years. No doubt Jeff would like to have Vince's final resting place close to him in California. I can understand why. Vince's story has not left me, nor has Jeff's. I am captured by yet another story that could not have been told without the discovery of a box of letters.

RIVERSIDE, CALIFORNIA - PART 2

1945

Dear Harry,

Very pleased to hear that bag arrived and was O.K. Glad indeed you liked it. I saw it in a window and it just happened to catch my eye–thought it looked like class but needed Tessy's personality to give it that final umph.

Now our big problem is Christmas. I don't have many ideas beyond that I could pick up some odds and ends. I snooped a bit in L.A. Monday and Tuesday but it is hard to snoop if you don't have an idea of what you're snooping for. I had an idea maybe we could pool our funds and get a watch but the gal has a watch she never uses and it is nicer than we could afford. I can't think of anything–haven't been able to for a month or so now–how about you? Lord, I'd sure like to be home Christmas!

Please keep me in the know if you get any brainstorms. I'd thought of a lapel watch or maybe one of these new wrist gold jobs. I felt awfully bad that you had bought a bag on Sat. and I shipped ours from here on Friday afternoon. I'm beginning to believe in mental telepathy–what say I do hope you could change it and be sure to use your best taste on the gloves. I have tried to get nylons thru DuPont–Doc Bordner will keep me posted but no luck in that direction as yet nor is much to be hoped for I guess.

Been busier than hell at work here lately. Talking 1 hour-1 1/2 hours to 8 men a day is no frolic but I'll keep putting on through if you do. Be good, Haroola.
Love, Frank

Saturday, November 3

Dear Mother, Harry and Mike,

Well, yee old Counselor is on the job. Not many going through this morning but I guess we'll have a full afternoon - it was ever thus when I sure would like to hear that Notre Dame Navy game. Last night after I wrote you people, I went downstairs in the U.S.O. and looked in on the dance. I certainly didn't intend to stay but of all things I ran into a girl from the Falls and had a few dances with her. I hadn't shaved and I had on the "strong" shirt so I didn't force the issue to any extent. She was Ruth Schule and she is working out here. She graduated from LaSalle about the same year I did from high school and she knew a lot of people I had known. It is kind a nice meeting someone from home once in a while.

I guess I'd best get to some of the questions you people have asked. About Christmas - please don't bother with anything for me. I know I need not appeal to your reason about this for the facts are quite self evident. There is little I need and I can't see stocking up on G.I. clothes, which I hope to have no use for in 6 or 7 months. I would like a couple of those fruit cakes like Mrs. Ott sent last year. Small ones are nice cause you don't have to eat all of a big one when you open it. I need shorts badly if there are any available at home but I expect they are as short at home as they are out here. Little sentimental odds and ends are grand to get but I just don't have much use for anything in the line of little extras and they cost. Soooo I hope you will tell anyone who asks. There will be many items I'll want when I get to be hanging out at the Little Old Piano Box again, so please don't worry or bother yourselves about my Christmas. I'll get by very nicely, although it will be quite lonely I suspect. I'll just plan on seeing a football game or something.

Harry - succumb to temptation about those jackets as far as I'm concerned - it would be a good idea to get the B-10 cleaned. Please try not to let anything happen to the B-15 for it was close to me all the time overseas and went on all missions with me as well as that little swim. Those jackets are no good to anyone if you don't use them so I'm in favor of it. I don't care what happens to the fatigues - much! By all means wear them - I wouldn't wear them to do dirty or hard work in and I hope you won't either. I want them dry cleaned, not washed.

A cake would sure go good Mom, only if the pair of you can spare the sugar. We have plenty of sweets here - pie and cake at the PX and on the job I find myself going often for coffee and but it is hardly "the kind Mother makes."

We are going to get Sundays off here now. I'm glad of course to have Sunday to myself but don't like it as far as going any place is concerned for everyone is on the go over the weekend. I think we may get another day off besides. At present they are screening 50-59 point men and we should be getting to them soon now. The ranks of dissention have widened here of late for we have been discharging all Aviation Cadets. Later in the afternoon

(That was a rough decision on that Notre Dame Navy tie.) Anyway, these Cadets, some of them have as low as 5 points and are getting out. It goes against the grain to be sure but I guess there is a chance they may be drafted again, although I think it unlikely.

If there are any items I can get you for your Christmas shopping, let me know. I looked at some plastic cigarette cases for women over there and thought of Mrs. Ott about $7.50 and classy looking - what do you think? Also have all types of dolls and stuffed fuzzy dogs etc. if you want any of that stuff for the children, let me know.

I just found out that I have Sunday off this week and Monday too, so I'll be free from this afternoon until Tuesday morning. Think maybe I'll be off to L.A. again with one of the boys taking in some free shows and stuff and do it as cheaply as is possible. I feel that I may never get here again and it seems a shame not to take advantage of the opportunity to see what I can while I can. But as ever, I don't want to spend much.

Well, I guess that takes in most of it for today. I'm all cleaned up and ready to go as soon as we're through here. I may as well be on the go for as Chuck Bordner wrote "have a grand time and get it out of your system while you're young (says the old man)." He sure is a good boy and I must write him but I hate to appear too eager all of a sudden like. From what Sally writes, things are not going too good at the plant - men with 4 kids drawing 29 dollars/week but these things are not too often affected seriously in research so we shall see.

Getting some more of the lads through here now folks, so I'll have to be a goin.
Lotsa Love, Frank

November 6, Tuesday

Dear Mother, Harry and Mike,

Well, since I had me a couple days, namely Sunday and Monday, I thought it would be a good idea to get away from it all and go to L.A. and vicinity, which I did. Bill Sielbolt, Jerry Braheny and I started off together, but we soon lost Bill for he was quite anxious to get down to see his sister while Jerry and I were in no particular hurry.

We hitched down in the evening with a rather attractive gal in a 42 Chevy Coupe. We gabbed all the way down and then twisted her arm into having a drink with us when we arrived. She recommended we go to the Meadowbrook, where Artie Shaw was playing so we took off for the place when we left the gal. Her name is Dara Schuler - she works in Palm Springs and was coming to L.A. over the week-end to be with her people and see a friend of hers. Anyway, it was about 10 PM when we got to the place and being misers at heart, we couldn't see the $1.20 admission that late in the evening so we thumbed a ride into Hollywood and got ourselves a bed at the Methodist Church. We bought a pint of 3 Feathers to keep our spirits up and had a short snort before going to bed. We had a sandwich and coffee at a very Chinese place where tea is served in little earthenware cups without handles along with your glass of water and napkin. Also, you get a little baked wafer in the form of sort of a bow in which are baked little paper fortunes.

We got a good night's sleep and were up at 8 AM. We washed and shaved at facilities provided by the Methodist Church and then walked over to the Church of the Blessed Sacrament I think it is. Same parish as Irene Dunne and Pat O'Brien. They have a canteen there and we had breakfast on the Right Handers both before and after Mass. (Say did I mention that I got to Mass last Thursday? It's a wonder, I generally forget completely about Holy days in the Army). Anyway, Mrs. O'Loughlin recommended a restaurant to us - a Jewish place where we got a very good chicken dinner complete for a dollar. She writes for radio - those people connected with the entertainment always seem to know where the good cheap places to eat are. In the afternoon we called up our little Dara - complained that we two Hayseeds weren't getting around much and wanted to know what she was going to do about it. Dara impressed us as being one of those Smart Gals who lives alone and likes it - anyway, we knew she had a car and that is quite essential out here. After we called and had arranged a date with her and her gal friend, we were inclined to kick ourselves in the butt for we figured they'd want to go to some ritzy place, but after all we still had the initiative and we figured if it looked like too much, we'd just fade out - we had nothing to lose.

As it was, they were very considerate and after driving us down the "strip", which is where Cira's and all those other high class joints are (where you pay 50 bucks to stand in the knee deep carpets) we went to a place called the Casa Blanca. Very nice indeed - no cover or minimum - a very nice orchestra - quiet and a good sized dance floor, not crowded. We had a good time dancing and the girls insisted on stopping at 3 drinks - Jerry and I had 4 costing us close to 3 dollars a round for 4 of us - me with my beer - the girls' martinis and Jerry's bourbon. When we left, we went to one of these "Drive Ins" where you honk the horn and they come a running with a tray that hooks on the car door. We had sandwiches and coffee and shortly after had to take Jerry's girl home - had to go back to her apartment - she had to work Monday - Dara had it off. So we took the gal home and then went to the Hollywood Guild Canteen where Jerry and I had registered earlier in the afternoon. Here we let Jerry out - Huba Huba - it seems the little gal wanted to play so we went out to the ocean no less. And me, trying to be the sophisticate and man of the world, with all that beer damned up in my kidneys - oh my achin back! Beer is a great drink in more ways than one. Anyway, I finally got to bed at about (ALONE) 5 AM. I'd learned she is about 26 or 27 from what I could figure when she got out of school - has been married and divorced. She seems to be O.K. - you know most of these California women are phonies. I was glad when this didn't end up as things usually do out here - she says "This thing is bigger than both of us" and away you go. The evening was expensive to us, although it was certainly a cheap one by standards out here. Gosh the girls even left their coats in the car so we wouldn't have to bother checking them. Goodness - what consideration - but you ain't heard it all yet.

Dara called the Guild next day - Monday, about noon - I'd just awakened. She was going to the opera Monday evening and said she'd be driving back if we wanted to go, so of course we were glad because that meant we could stay Monday evening and still be sure of getting back to camp in plenty of time. Sunday afternoon, I forgot to mention, we had free tickets to a stage show "Opening Night." Now I know what a going flop looks like, all I have to see is a big success now. It was a musical and not too bad but it certainly wasn't catching on in Hollywood. They had only a handful of people in the audience. One act really made me nervous! A Dr. Giovanni called fellows up from the audience and then proceeded to frisk them of their wallets, wrist watches, even suspenders. I almost died when he pulled a box of Trojans (Harry will know) from one sailor's pocket and the guy didn't even know it. All the rest of the time - even now since I saw that, my hand keeps going back to my wallet in my hip pocket. Lord knows I'm not laden with cash, but I'd sure hate to lose what I have got. I guess that takes in all of Sunday. Monday we slept in until 12 noon and then got some breakfast. We were at the Hollywood Guild - another free deal only this one is *a soldier's dream. It is laid out in a residential district and they have a big pool there too. The thing got so large; they've been using neighboring houses to bed the fellows in. They have free meals there as well as beds and everything else. We had fried eggs, sweet rolls, coffee, stewed prunes. We had eaten supper there the evening before - good thick Swiss steak, boiled potatoes, spinach, chef salad, coffee, chocolate milk, and choice of 4-5 kinds of pie for dessert. I don't know how they do it all for free but it sure is OK. The Jews are the ones who seem to be doing it out here, every place you go they are the ones.*

Sunday afternoon we saw Cavalcade of America again, with Claire Trevoir looking very lush in black - really stacked is the gal. Also saw Hoagie Carmichael. He is really good - you can't help but get a kick out of him. He knows his singing is corny but as he says "after all, they pay me for it." He sat down and played and sang 4 or 5 numbers after the broadcast - really put on a show for those who had come. We got tickets to see Weekend at the Waldorf (free again) and saw that in the evening. We got our little bottle out of storage - we sure petted that pint - finished her while we waited to meet Dara and when the gal came, we started back for camp. She's quite a woman - I'd heard things like that happened out here, but never thought I'd see the day. Guess I'll have to be journeying to Palm Springs one of these fine days.

Work has been going O.K. lately. We have a new Major in charge now, so I suppose there'll be a lot of changes coming soon. I think they plan to slow things down on enlisted men in order to get some 350 officers out in the next couple days.

Well people, I guess that's it for today. I sure owe a lot of letters, so I'd best be getting to them. Be good.

Lotsa Love, Frank

November 7, Wednesday

Dear Mother, Harry and Mike,

There is not a great deal to report from March Field today. We have not been really busy today since they are trying to get a lot of officers out and few enlisted men have been going through. This has fortunately given us a bit of free time during the day. Spent most of said spare time today snooping about for a job. Tried all places on the Post - could have started immediately at the Officers Club as a bartender. Yes, I kept in mind your admonition, but even stronger than that - it has been my experience that the man at the bar is too easily intimidated - drinks are expensive of course and I don't want to handle the money or the officers. They may need men on the soda fountain soon, so I may get that.

Jerry Braheny and I went into Riverside this PM to see about work, part time at the Govt. employment agency. There is very little available at present, in fact nothing for us except dishwashing or something like that. Waiting table is out for it is a Post order that we cannot work off the Post. Anything where you come in contact with people would be out if it were off the Post. The thing that sounds the best to me so far is damn hard work - setting pins at the bowling alley. It pays 10¢ a line and one fellow I talked to has averaged around 7 dollars a night for working 8 hours. Best I could put in on my job is about 6 hours. Features about it that I like is that there is no limit to what you can make per month and also it is run on a day to day basis - you get paid each night when you finish and sign up each day to work - in other words you can work when you want to and can be off if something comes up that you want to take in. Bad part about it is that it is darn hard work - although I'm sure it wouldn't kill me, I'd be sore most of the time. The exercise would be the best thing in the world for me and the "something to do" evenings would keep me out of mischief. Maybe I'll take a whirl at it on the morrow - maybe not!

I turned in my Air Corps equipment including my B-4 Bag. Hated to see it go, but I hadn't intended to try to steal it anyway and wasn't using it so that is that. Sorta winds up the passing of an era for me - Junior Birdman no longer.

Weather is cold here, people. I finally got a Field Jacket - one of the new long ones and it is fine. How is it at home? It gets quite chilly here and I'm glad of my O.D.s - I have an extra pair now that I found. Guess that's it for today - little chums - Be good. Lotsa Love, Frank

November 8, Thursday

Dear Mother, Harry and Mike,

Things are a bit slow here in the department so I'd best be getting my daily dozen out. I stayed in last night - went to the Service Club and wrote a few letters, which I have owed for a time. I generally go to the dance at the Riverside U.S.O. on Wednesday night, but last night I didn't - decided I'd catch up a bit on the letter situation. I didn't figure my little (that adjective really doesn't apply here) Frances Carlson would be there since she is now at school. Bill Siebolt went, as usual, and now I'm sorry I didn't go too. It seems Frances was there after all - had taken off from school just to come up for Wednesday night dance - he says she was looking for me - Huba Huba - it must be that cookie duster that gets em.

I am tempted to go over and set up pins tonight at the bowling alley - I'll have to see how early I get out of here and how the spirit moves me.

The meals are getting a great deal better here at the Separation Base Squadron. Imagine, they actually had large steaks for us today - really good eats and we've started getting baked goods for dessert too - cakes and things.

There are a lot of colds going around here lately - hope I'm going to be able to miss them. The cool weather evenings and mornings and the rather warm noons make it difficult to dress properly. Some of the boys are still wearing Sun Tans but that will be all through on the 15th.

I guess I'd best take this opportunity to wish both you nice people a very, very Happy Birthday. Maybe it is a little premature, but I can't be sure when this will arrive so I thought I'd best slip it in now. God willing, we'll all celebrate the next one together - I do hope so. I love you both so very much - please take care of one another until we can make that twosome a triumvirate once more.

Lotsan (sic) Lotsa Love on your birthdays,
Love, Frank

November 10, Saturday

Dear Mother, Harry and Mike,

Well people, I missed yesterday but I did get a newsy letter from Tess. I see where you people are well at yee old cleaning as per usual. We are getting this afternoon, Sunday and Monday off because of Armistice Day - not bad, what? A lot - well, most of the lads on the Post will have to parade over the week-end, but in the Separation Base we do not have to, which gives us all this time to ourselves. I don't know for sure what I shall do with it - work some I guess. Yup, I picked up after the Keglers last night. Harry I laugh when I think of you and your boys going out to Kegle and calling it exercise - fellows you should set pins for a while if you really want exercise - man it is kinda rugged. I admit being a mite stiff today but plan on going back this afternoon and evening to loosen up. I felt myself getting susceptible to colds and feeling a bit lazy as I used to at home and I judge it to be merely lack of exercise soooo I figure I can keep in shape and still kick up a few two bitses (sic) at the same time.

It is hard work - no question about it but I figured hard work never hurt anyone and if kids can do it so can I. A chap named Willis went with me but I think he has had enough - got his nose full. They pay us 10¢ a line and I made four berries even last night - not working all the time of course. I started about 3:30 and took 30-40 minutes off for chow and was through at 10:15 so that's not too bad. I only worked 1 alley - boy these guys who work, two of them certainly do go at it, but then they're use to it and I haven't been sufficiently broken in as yet. I plan to have a go at it again this afternoon and evening and then, if I feel like it, take off for myself on Sunday and or Monday.

There is not a lot new here as usual. 50 point men come up for Separation on orders very soon now, but they froze all lads working in the Separation Base. This has been expedited but it means those of us who are left will have to work harder and no extra day off. That will keep me close around anyway, but I don't know how I'll get my Christmas shopping in on a Sunday. Well, we hope these things will solve themselves and we're hoping for some additions to the staff, which may or may not come.

I feel bad about Christmas, too, Tess, but we have no right to complain. If points are lowered to my category before the 1st of the year or shortly after, I still can't get out because I need at least 2 years service, which I won't have until January 27. Leave us just sweat it out - I am so grateful myself that I didn't wind up a memory! It has been some experience for me, even though we feel it is being run into the ground now, when there is no excuse for it.

There are so many things I want to plan and do and while I hold them tentatively in my mind, things will have to wait until we can get together on them.

How about a few hints on the Christmas situation. I am glad you see things my way as affects me - if you do send things please don't go all out for I have no foot locker to keep things in here and if I can manage it I will not be on the Post over Christmas. Don't go all out on a money order or extras this time. I said don't once before in a telegram from Chicago and youse guys didn't heed - I mean it now as I did then.

But we can get you fellows an odd or end or two. Whatcha want most Tess other than a mink coat? Say, that's an idea - how much for a new fur coat? I'll guarantee help with a 50 buck down payment and an extra 20 a month to get one, only it's got to be a good one. How about it? Can you buy one on time? We have to be gettin a new one soon anyway and it makes it nicer if you can get it for Christmas. Talk it over you two, but if we get one on time, it has to be in Harry's name that the thing is bought - I'm going to raise Hell about charge accounts when I get home anyway.

I guess that's it for today folks. Please let me know soon what you decide - we may as well have something to show for our money. Be good.
Lotsa Love, Frank

November 13, Tuesday

Dear Mother, Harry and Mike,

Well, there is not a great deal to report as per usual. Saturday I set me a few pins and felt the results quite rigorously on Sunday. Went to 11 AM Mass on Sunday and set me a few more pins in the afternoon. It is quite rugged work but after the 3rd day, my muscles had become quite acclimated to the added exertion and I was in good shape Monday morn. They had Open House here yesterday and permitted civilians on the Post and let them climb all over everything to their heart's desire. They had a big review at 10 AM and I was truly grateful that since we worked in the Separation Base, we didn't have to be a part of it.

Jerry Braheny and I left the base at 11 AM to set out for Palm Springs and Dara. We got there in a couple hours and the place itself, I'd say, is vastly overrated. It is supposed to be a resort town for the movie colony - why, I still don't know. It is very much spread out and really nothing extra at all. Prices are sky high for almost anything but we weren't doing much buying.

We picked up Dara in the afternoon and she proceeded to show us about a couple of palm canyons around there - all just dandy, but you know I'm not much of a scenery fancier unless it's that two-legged kind. Boy, do they ever dress extremely down there. We saw all kinds - some characterized by style and most of em characterized by sheer lack of basic material.

We had dinner down there - I had me some prime ribs of beef, which were the best I've had since we got that last 11-3/4 lb. rib roast for the three of us before rationing went into effect. In the evening Dara had a date for Jerry, and we went dancing and had a few drinks. Dara had arranged with her boss, a Mr. Reed, to take us back this morning for he was going to L.A. at 5 AM in order to be there for some series of *meetings. There is no U.S.O. in the place and since it was about 1:30 when we had a last bite to eat, Jerry and I didn't feel much like paying for a hotel room only to have to get up by 4:30 to be on deck to be picked up by 5. Sooo we took Dara home - about that time she was insisting we don't wait for Reed but instead, take her car and drive it back here to March Field and then take it back to Palm Springs sometime during the week for she wouldn't want it until the following Sunday. This was all very nice - sort of a G.I.'s dream - bring a coupe here and all that stuff, however at this point we are smelling a grandiose rat. It would have been O.K. getting here, but we'd have to take it back and another evening at Palm Springs, which by this time we are having none of. Also, I can't see accepting the responsibility of the damn thing and I cannot understand the gal letting a couple G.I.s make off with her machine. Ah such a bunch of situations you can run into here in California. I'd heard of such things about this place but could never quite believe them.*

Anyway, Jerry and I take the car down to where she works and sweat out the coming of Brother Reed. We had to talk aloud to ourselves to keep awake and it really got cold down there in the early morning. Reed brought us home to Riverside - he's a darn good egg - and I feel sure we will not journey to Palm Springs again - I saw John Carrol Naish anyway.

I saw Bob Forgit Sunday - he just got back from his 30 day furlough and Dan Spencer was in to see me this morning. He has brought the wife and baby down with him and of course no place to live. That is really going to be a rough proposition. He was working while home and bought himself a car - they remind me of the Perry's always doing things on a shoe string.

We start working hard again at the base here this afternoon and I guess the "Lucky Bastards" should be coming through soon now.

Jerry and I expect to start working at the Officers' mess in the coffee shop tonight.

Boy, I'm really bad on this one - started it day before yesterday and haven't finished it yet. We have been very busy here separating lots of men - 320/day. It keeps you busy all the time hence I don't get time to keep up on the writing here. Also, Jerry and I have been working at the Officers' mess for 62¢/hour and we get in 5-1/2 hours a night, starting at 6 PM. It is a pretty good deal - in fact darn good - 3 of us work a fountain with only 8 stools and we have 2 men making hamburgers. It does get busy sometimes I guess, but has been easy the past 2 nights. Bill Siebolt gets out Friday or Saturday and even I had a scare yesterday. It looked like they might count my 16 months in the E.R.C. as points, but alas - no go.

Most of the men I went to R.T.U. with are leaving now and men I've known rather well from Yuma, Gulfport, and in England are getting out. I'll be stuck quite a while yet since I lack the two years service requirement. We get new faces here in the department daily and the old guard has almost completely left. Oh, I didn't mention that we get our evening meal at the Officers' mess. It is better of course than ours and we enjoy it. Also it is still new enough that we are enjoying ourselves eating egg malts,

hamburgers, etc. to our heart's content. It is so decent over there that like all things in the Army, I fear a change for the worse for that's the way it goes. I don't look for us to be so busy in the Separation Base for long - it comes in spurts, but this one has really been a lulu. Guess I'd best get this off now - here come some more lads with problems.
Lotsa Love, Frank

November 16, Thursday

Dear Mother, Harry and Mike,

Just a line or two to let you know I'm still doing business at the same old stand. We have been very busy here for the past 3 days getting out over 300 men a day. Bill Siebolt got out today as did a few others I knew rather well. Jerry and I worked last night at the Officers' mess. They feed us well, don't care what we eat, and we are quite happy at our work evenings for the present. The Army job is altogether too demanding of late to be any good. I'm beginning to think they want blood. Am very glad you like the purse Mom, and also that the pen works OK. I had hoped Harry would use it at work. The only thing I didn't like about purse was the plastic clasp but it looked O.K. and was a rather snappy looking job I thought. Saw it in a window two weeks before I bought it and kept going back to look at it and finally bought it—that still doesn't help me on the Christmas proposition. How about that?

The lad "Willis" I told you about who went to set pins with me the first night has gone to hospital. Had a recurrence of rheumatic fever and will be in 2-6 months. No I don't think it was work alone that did it. He leads a fast life and he has a rough price to pay for it now.

We work again tonight—I want to get my 72 hours in as soon as is possible so I can splurge with the pecuniary returns—it was ever thus. Doesn't look like I'll be going anywhere for some time now—being occupied with the job evenings and since we're getting so little time off now—only Sundays.

I haven't written anyone but you folks at all lately.—please explain for me and I'll try to do better when we stop discharging so many—over 900 in past 3 days is pretty good. I had a bad scare on Monday—thought they were going to count my E.R.C. time as points—16 months of it—but alas no go. Or did I tell you? There is little news. I am fine—eating very well of late and often—lotsa egg shakes again and will be getting too fat no doubt. I guess there is no more poop for now people—am leading very sterile existence for the present—Be good.
Lotsa Love, Frank

November 17, Saturday

Dear Mother, Harry and Mike

Well, hyar (sic) we are on Saturday again. As I had more or less expected, things let up a bit today and I believe we may get the latter part of this afternoon off. I will be working tonight also to-morrow. Expect to try to get in about 10 hours to-morrow—may as well get the time in when I can. I have planned on getting Wednesday *off, for my little Frances will be at the dance Wednesday in town and I'd like to see her again.*

Hope Harry does all right on this deal coming up at the Beals. Gee your descriptions of weather at home leave me in a nostalgic frame of mind. I've known so little of rough weather since I've been a G.I. I'm very glad you like the pen etc. Harry - hope you will get some satisfactory use out of it Harry. No arguments with me about pens though. I have always thought that Sheaffer pens write nicer than any other but my objection to them has been that they are forever going on the bink (sic). Hope yours doesn't. It is hardly as expensive an outfit as could be bought but they are hard to get out here as yet, also it will give you a chance to lose one outfit before we get you a better one. Only Parker outfit I could find within 50 mile radius of here was a 50 dollar deal, which was a bit out of my class at the time.

I hope I may get a few letters written this afternoon, but will have to see. I still have a bit of washing to do this afternoon.

Gosh folks, there is little to tell at the moment. We have a pretty good time working evenings and have been eating quite a bit on the officers. The fellow who hired us over there will leave soon on a dependency discharge, so we're waiting to see just what that will bring. Right now the set-up over there is almost too good to be true.

Can't think of much more for the present people - be good.

Lotsa Love, Frank

November 19, Monday

Dear Mother, Harry and Mike,

Well, I should be catching a bit of Hell in the near future. I just opened my stationery box and found letter I wrote on Saturday and then didn't mail it. Woe is me—I'll mail it along with this one—intentions were good anyway.

As per usual, there is not much new or happening when you are busy working. We (Jerry and I) worked Saturday night and then went in Sunday at 1 PM and worked until 11:30. Not so hot an idea working Sunday when you really don't have to but we did anyway. We went to Confession and then Communion Sunday morning at 8 o'clock Mass. We had C.Q. wake us up at 7 bells and so made it in plenty of time. Even got in on the Rosary Saturday evening—my goodness are we ever being good lately—to be honest we were caught—had to go to work Saturday evening so didn't stay for Mass then.

We have been eating but good—steaks yesterday noon—turkey last night and then steaks again sandwiches to fill up the empty holes in the evening all very Kosher.

Somehow we have this morning off—nobody wants to get discharged I guess—what am I saying—nobody scheduled at any rate. How are youse guys doing at home—boy I sure get to thinking about being there these days—thank heaven the end is in sight even if it is a long way off for yours truly. Latest rumor—Separation Base here closes on the 15th of December so I guess I don't get out here—there will be a jet fighter group here after the Separation Base closes. Am not sure about this of course, but believe it is pretty straight dope.

Almost died last night–we had a Brigadier General come in looking for a sundae. I drew him, of course–I would, but we got along fine–he was a pretty good egg I guess. He came in with a Wing or two or three of the 50th Air Force, which we will be discharging very soon now I expect.

We work tonight and to-morrow and then take off Wednesday. Me to go to a dance in town and see Frances, and Jerry, who is getting low on funds, to come here to NCO club and try to win a few bucks at Bingo game they have here for members. I guess I told you Bill Siebolt left–if I get a chance on the way east again I'm supposed to stop in Lincoln, Neb–Bill says he'll get me a date with a corn fed blonde and we'll "pitch a bitch." (That pitching deal refers to a–"Gee its drunk out tonight" good time in case you have gotten any wrong ideas.) Drinking was never a thing Bill and I never got along on–he likes bourbon and I always drank beer–ah well, we managed at times.

Well people, I guess that constitutes most of the poop for this one. Sorry the late ones are not more newsy but I'm fine and getting along dandy from day to day. Can't activate much news when I'm busy most of the while–maybe that's just as well! Be good, people.

Lotsa Love, Frank

November 22, Thursday

Thanksgiving

Dear Mother, Harry and Mike,

I was certainly glad to get your letter yesterday. I had been a bit worried about the pair of you to tell the truth. I don't recall any whole week's stretch that I didn't write - maybe letters will gang up.

Your nifty big box came yesterday and it was sure a load and grand to receive. It came right after chow, but even so we sat right down and ate up most of the cookies. The gloves are dandy - I almost bought myself some at the P.X. the other day, but they were of inferior quality to these and I'm glad now that I didn't. It does get chilly out here - some fellows had heavy over coats on in town last night, I have all the can goods stashed away in my locker - that will keep fine and the crackers and cheese will go swell with beer some evening at the NCO club. That cake is due to be murdered any moment now and I have the fruit cakes set aside - I think we'll get some wine to finish those up with. I say fruit cakes - Mrs. Ott's box came yesterday too, so you can imagine how well stocked I am now. It is grand to get and I like to put it away, except for the baked goods, and eat it when the mood hits me. I took what was left of the cookies and some of the nut bread over to Willis, who is the lad with rheumatic fever in the hospital and he was very glad to get it.

Yesterday at work was easy - it comes in spurts - we had the afternoon off and Jerry and I took the opportunity to go to San Bernardino and do some Christmas shopping - he did some shopping but I didn't - haven't seen anything I particularly like as yet. I work at the Club today 10 hours - don't like the long shift but it will be easy over there today and they are grand to me - want me to get in all my hours so I can collect full pay so I can't very well complain. The dance at the U.S.O. didn't come off last night so I took Frances to the show and we had a bite to eat last night. She is a nice gal and good company and we have a fairly good time. She doesn't drink or smoke and won't eat much or anything out so it certainly isn't expensive.

I'm going over to eat myself full of turkey now at the officers club - I won't have many more nights there this month and will be better able to space them next month. I hope to get to-morrow night off and bring Frances to a dance here on the Post - they better have a dance that's all.

Thanks a million for the box people. - Just how much you put into it is reflected by how much it cost just to mail it and it is greatly appreciated. Don't send anymore can goods because it weighs too much in a box and I can get that stuff here at the Commissary I think - I'm quite well stocked now to say the least. I slept in until 11 this AM and now I've got to be goin off to work - I'll do a better job on this on the morrow. Be good, people.

Lotsa Love, Frank

November 23, Friday

Dear Mother, Harry and Mike,

Well, perhaps I can do a less hurried job this morning. I worked last night and afternoon - got in 10 1/2 hours and after tonight will have only two nights to go to get in my 76 hours. Jerry has all his time in but he's going to work for me tonight cause I've got a date with Frances to go to a dance here on the Post. Don't know what kind of a time we'll have but she says she has always wanted to come out here so she's going to get her chance this evening.

I'm still crowded in my wall locker for space now that I have it loaded down with food - I'm going to have to make some serious dents in that stuff very soon although beyond the baked goods and candy and hiding the gloves, I have done little about it yet. Can't find ma can opener but that one's easy for I can get things opened at our own mess hall easily.

Mom, you say keep what you want in the box. Well, it was all grand and beyond yesterday's comment on the can goods, I can't think of any of it I don't want. Baked goods go best of course for we are well fed here, especially since we are working at the Officers' mess. We bring (home) to barracks hot hamburgers when we're through at night. We (Jerry and I) plan on getting a bottle or so of wine to kill the fruit cake at the NCO club one of these nights when we're not working.

I was glad that I worked last night - it was very slow and we sat on our tails most of the evening. Time went fast and we had turkey over there too. They had plenty - even smoked ham and all the trimmings, but in my opinion, the cooks over there sure ruined the dinner. They couldn't hurt the turkey, which was good, but the gravy (which to me is all important) was terrible and dressing, tasteless. The turkey itself was fine and I filled up on it "straight" but as I've said before, Holidays just don't exist as such when you're away from home. We're not unhappy or particularly blue - they just don't mean anything that's all.

I must write the Otts - it was nice of them indeed - all that trouble and money in a box when a letter would have been even more welcome. They sure don't bother with me when I'm away do they? I think of them often - I wrote from Sioux Falls - am I supposed to write and write - I got tired of that the first time I was at Sioux Falls.

On the Christmas deal people, I feel the same as I previously stated. Oh Yes, I'd like a box, but put a cake in it and maybe a half dozen of any kind of shorts and let it go. Please don't bother with a lot of Christmasy stuff because, well, my crew enjoyed it last year and the "Horrible Four," but honestly I feel embarrassed when I get a lot of stuff for most guys don't get much and you feel silly when you get all the stuff I did last year. I still have sox that have never been worn. I only have three good ties left but Bill Siebolt left me five which, when I have them cleaned, will be more than plenty. Anyway, I have at least 6, which were issued at one time or another, and wear these on the Post and at work. I can use two or three new Tee shirts for the old ones are ripping out at the shoulders and I figure I'll always be wearing them anyway so they are a good buy. I have 11 on the go here, which keeps me going fine. I strongly advise against the money deal - it is needed far more at home. If I continue to work at the Officers' mess, I'll be getting some sort of pay there on the 15th of next month, which should suffice if I'm short.

I still don't know what Barb wants and I'm through asking. I'll use my own judgment, sink 25-35 bucks into something and you'll have to rave about it whether you like it or not. I know I haven't said much but we all know it is foolish in my case.

Well people, I guess that's it for today - I'll have to run along now - we have a full afternoon ahead whereas this morning we only had one group. Be good, people. Lotsa Love, Frank

Saturday, November 24

Dear Mother, Harry and Mike,

Well, things roll along as per usual and at present we're having a boost in the number of men going through. We don't like to be worked hard but we take pleasure in the fact that the more we get out the sooner we'll be separated ourselves.

As I told you yesterday, I didn't work last night but had a date with Frances Carlson. I brought her out here on the Post and we danced till 11 or 11:15. I had a good time and so did she, I think. She wants me to write her so she can have me down to L.A. to one of their school dances. Don't know how I'd like that, but may as well have a go at it I suppose. She reminds me a lot of Liz Donahue only she is personally more fastidious and hardly as worldly wise - or if she has been around she doesn't let me know it, which is in her favor. She is a big gal, but well proportioned in most directions - has a younger sister who is almost 6 ft. Her people are grand to me when I'm there so everything is Kosher as can be. As I said, I can't spend any money on her since she won't eat and doesn't drink. She's a good kid and I enjoy being with her.

I intend working at Officers' mess tonight and sometime to-morrow for a while. May as well accumulate time and dough there while I can.

Aside from that, there is little new. Couldn't get mail today and won't be able to get it tomorrow since all personnel except our squadron had to parade today and to-morrow is Sunday. I can see I'll have to register a bitch with the Air Inspector on that deal.

Guess that's it for today people - I have to write Otts a thank you for the box - also Sally - she even sent me a Thanksgiving card - Huba Huba. Be good, people.
Lotsa Love, Frank

November 26, Monday

Dear Mother, Harry and Mike,

Just a hurried note to let you know all is well and I'm still at March Field. I worked all day yesterday so got no opportunity to write. Made 5:30 PM Mass by taking off to get there. I started a letter to the Otts on Saturday and it isn't finished as yet. My goodness I'm a busy boy. Don't care for so much work but everyone has been so good to Jerry and me at the Officers' mess that we hate to leave them in a hole. Many of the fellows who formerly worked there are getting discharged or have their time in so we are really getting the brunt. I hope it won't last much longer for I'd rather have more time to myself even if it does mean less money.

Things have been steady at the Army job so I don't get much chance to write there anymore. I expect it to slow down some but that remains to be seen. I feel very bad about Mrs. Sheppard. I sent a card - she probably got it when relapse occurred - I never do the right thing at the right time plain to see. I owe quite a few letters and just don't get time to get to them. I hope to be off sometime this week though.

Harry shouldn't get annoyed at the way these women carry on at the parties - what has he? - Principles? So Sally finally got spliced. I envy the lad the physical pleasure he'll get out of that deal but I hope he is strong that's all. Whatever gave you the idea Sally was the blushing type Mom? Tain't so!

Guess I'll have to run now folks - meals past 2 days are bad - they are holding cooks who are eligible for discharge until they are replaced and the boys just won't cook. S'all for now. Be good, people.
Lotsa Love, Frank

November 27, Tuesday

Dear Mother, Harry and Mike,

Well, I dood (sic) it again! Letter I wrote yesterday during lunch hour I didn't mail and so just got it off today. As I remember, it wasn't much of a letter just yee old facts in general. Don't know really what to make of this one to tell the truth. I finally managed to get tonight off and to-morrow too so I'm again to get me more sleep for a couple nights. Not that we don't do well when we work for we are generally in the barracks by 11:30 PM and sleep in until 7:30 in the morning. We hurriedly shave and get dressed, make the sac and sweep the area and then rush to work, which is just across the road. We sign in and sneak out to the P.X. for coffee and doughnuts.

I, myself, am fed up with working so steadily for it gives me no time to do the things I should do and those things I want to do.

The fellow over there, who keeps track of the help, has taken a shine to Jerry and me and likes to have us there as often as is possible I guess, but anyway we have a couple evenings to rest and relax now.

Work at counseling has certainly stepped up. Too much so, for at the present rate we are unable to put before the fellows many pertinent facts and they are all so hopped up that they cannot think to ask questions. It is too bad but that is the Army I guess. No news about my getting out as yet - even the latest favorable rumors do not affect me. Bob Forgit got out today and a couple others too. That makes about all the lads I came here with - I'm holding her down alone now but cheer up people - it can't last forever - I keep telling myself!

I do hope Mrs. Sheppard is better - I don't know what Jim will do - poor devil she has given him all of herself but little else that he can salvage. Just another abject lesson on no children.

I am at the NCO club now and expect to eat chow. Jerry and I expect to eat ourselves a fruit cake and have a drink or two this evening while we catch up on some letters we both owe.

I'll have to think about getting me some Christmas cards soon too I guess - looked at some in San Bernardino the last time I was there but they were pretty steep I thought. I think I'll snoop around Riverside tomorrow night since the stores will be open there. Frankly, I didn't care much about who I sent to last year because I was on my way to war and had no right to expect I'd be blessed enough to survive. This year it is different of course and I feel it is one thing that must be taken care of.

I received a letter from Shaffer with 5 bucks in it yesterday or did I tell you? I had loaned it to him just before he left for he was flat. I was certain he'd send it but was wondering since he took his time about it. He says Turner (co-pilot) is going to school now.

Well folks, I guess that's it for this one. I expect to shop and perhaps dance a bit and get in early. Be good, people - sorry there is not much news but I'm behaving myself pretty well and that just don't make for news. Be good.
Lotsa Love, Frank

November 29, Thursday

Dear Mother, Harry and Mike,

Well, we have ourselves another night off and are pleased as punch. We work to-morrow and Saturday I guess. We wanted to go to San Bernardino Saturday but may just as well work I guess for there will be so many out then with pay day coming on Friday and Saturday. If we have to work Sunday, we'll try to get Monday off so we can do our shopping. Stores are open in San B. Monday evenings.

Last night I watched the dancing a while and then returned to camp after having a bite to eat. I joined Jerry at the NCO club - he had won himself 5 bucks at bingo and was feeling pleased as punch.

We worked hard again as counselors again today but it is due to slack off to-morrow I understand. I received a grand letter from Tess today but still no info on Mrs. Sheppard - How about that? I guess she must be doing better or you'd have written.

Better answer some of those 5 pages of Mother's I guess. Yes, I found out what the price of those cakes were - now I know what I'm asking for - it was still marked on bottom of both boxes. It is a good thing I wasn't around when little Bobby consumed the cake - Heaven knows I don't care too much about it but I bet I'd have opened my trap. Leave us hear no more of that "our Duty" stuff - it puts a crimp in doing anything nice. Let us not get that Thompson dollar and cents and all because it's the thing to do attitude!

So glad you enjoyed the Ice Show. I'd like to see one myself one day. Ballet Russes is in L.A. now as is the Student Prince. Please forward me, at all possible speed, the name of company who put on Student Prince that Harry saw. I'd like to take Frances Carlson but wouldn't want to if it is same company Harry said did a putrid job of it. I'm glad you are well on the way with your Christmas shopping. Poking around is such a drain on one's energies. I wish I was as well along. It would be nice if you did get something for Mary Ellen - I have wanted to write for past month or so but was afraid it would look like an overture for Christmas.

The fruit question is out Mom. I had investigated it some time ago. You cannot ship it out of state by law due to plant diseases and anyway, they are not in season here now.

I have no hopes of getting out before I have two full years of service in, which will be 27 Jan 46 and it will be at least 3 weeks after that. Don't plan or look for me even then because there is talk of freezing Army personnel one of these days. We might as well face it - there will be trouble in Asia, and Heaven only knows how that will work out.

I guess that is most of the poop for tonight my dears. I wrote Sally last night and completely forgot the card she sent me. Sooo I must pen her a little white lie of some description now. Be good, people.

Lotsa Love, Frank

December 1945

Sunday, December 2

Dear Mother, Harry and Mike,

Well, I haven't written in two days now. Have been working the past couple of evenings and have been so busy on the Army job that I just couldn't work it in. We were paid yesterday but we even had to sandwich that in - goodness - looked for a while like we wouldn't get it. Also got paid at Officers' mess yesterday and collected a few outlying bucks so I have a very cozy financial feeling today.

Have done very little but work past couple of days so I have very little to report. Last night, since NCO club is opened late Saturday night, we went there after work and had a few beers. Also got in a little nickel-dime poker. We had brought extra hamburgers from Officers' mess with us so we had a gamblin, drinkin good time for about 2 hours. We then hit the sac and got up in time to make 11 o'clock Mass.

Had chicken for dinner and I'm working at the club this evening.

Jerry's brother, sailor from Frisco, arrived today and will be here for a couple of days. We're going to try to bunk him in the barracks with us - have to see how we manage. Jerry and I both have heads this morning - we had about five beers a piece but that is the price you pay for not being in practice and then trying to drink any quantity of 3.2 beer.

Well folks, I guess that is about it for this one - no poop but you're lil boy is O.K. and getting along fine. I hope to get off to-morrow night and go to San Bernardino - have to see about that tonight. I still have to get me some Christmas cards. Be good, people. Lotsa Love, Frank

December 3, Monday

Dear Mother, Harry and Mike,

Enclosed please find money order for Harry's Christmas present - 1 bowling ball and case to go with it. If price comes to any more, please let me know at once. I should have sent cash sooner for I have had it but wanted to make sure where I stood. Harry be sure to get a good one - don't know where you order it but I suppose you do. Make certain you get pre-war ebonite and not this synthetic deal. It has been estimated here that that is what it will cost, if it is more at least order it and let me know. I insist that this one be on me. It is too bad to have to get a present like this but you want it bored to fit your hand, and besides, I wouldn't know the size and weight you prefer. I hope you'll have it by Christmas but I realize it is late so do the best you can with my best wishes for better scores and a too early Merry Christmas.

I worked last night and have this evening off so will journey to San Bernardino this evening to more or lessly (sic) finish up my paltry Christmas shopping. I'll have to get cards this time or else. Jerry got today off by virtue of his brother's visit and I will meet them at S.B. this evening. They have an uncle there and plan on looking him up I understand.

Work here for the Army is heavy as usual but we hope for a let up. I fear I have little to report in any line. Work at the soda fountain has been a snap for the past couple nights for all the Wheels are out spending their pay - it makes it easy for us. Tuesday

I started this yesterday and then didn't get it off very promptly. Went to S.B. last night - got me a few Christmas cards and that's about all. Met Jerry and his brother there. We toured a few of the night spots and drank a good bit of beer (have to get back in trim so I don't get those hangovers).

We are very busy here at counseling again today. Guess I'd best close this now or I still won't get it off. Be good, people. Lotsa Love, Frank

December 6, Thursday

Dear Mother, Harry and Mike,

As per usual, there is not a great deal to report to the old homestead - just a general report again this time I guess.

Things here come to a pretty pass here on the base - chick is really getting a good deal worse. They had men permanently assigned to NCO club and the new C.O. of the field went in and closed the club and sent all the personnel to typing school. Also they have been picking up men in the P.X. during duty hours and putting them on K.P. All this hasn't affected us too drastically but you never know when they'll unearth some regulation that will affect us.

This is news all right, but I for one do not know how to interpret it. They will close Separation Base here on the 15th of December. This has been rumored for some time but it is straight dope now. What that means to me I don't know. They may ship us as counselors to another base to do the same job - I may get another assignment here. None of us have any idea of what will happen to us or what base we'll be at for Christmas. As trained, experienced, Separation Base personnel we stand no chance that I can see of getting away but the best deal I can see is being shipped somewhere - almost anywhere - I can't get any further from home can I? If I get a choice, it will be Mitchel Field, N.Y.C. or Rome, New York, if the latter is opened. It is too bad I didn't have 2 years service for I would have been able to get out here I think.

Jerry and I worked last night and hit the old sac early the night before so that takes in most of my activities. Just one word about the foregoing paragraph. I wouldn't send anything out here if you are planning on it before the 15th or 17th of this month for perhaps by that time I can let you know where I'll be.

Guess that's about the works for today people. I received Harry's letter - feel quite badly about Mrs. Sheppard. I wonder whatever will he do now? Hope I'll have time to write more in detail on the morrow - am quite rushed since I'm sandwiching this in on the job and am jerking sodas later this evening. Be good, people.
Lotsa Love, Frank

December 12, Wednesday

Dear Mother, Harry and Mike,

I'm at work writing this as per usual. I'm starting early this morning and I'll try to sandwich in enough material between each man I have to interview this morning to write a decent letter.

Jerry and I worked last night. I hadn't planned on doing so but one of the boys who works there wanted to see the gal friend badly so who am I to stand in the way of true (?) love. Work was steady as ever here yesterday and looks as though it will follow the same pattern until we close the Separation Base on Saturday. I still have absolutely no idea of what they will do with us when we finish here. There is the usual galaxy of rumors of course, but even the Wheels don't know the answer as yet.

I have this evening off and will have to see about any future schedule at work since I'm not too eager this month. We wanted some Scotch for Christmas and the Mess Officer is getting it for us. I stayed and closed up the place the other night and they are very appreciative hence the Scotch - Whitehorse or Hague and Hague I believe. Also, at a tavern where I stop in for my beer or so in San Bernardino, they got hold of some for us so now we'll have more than we know what to do with.

I received a letter from Doc Bordner yesterday and he tells me of all the lads who are returning. He apparently took it upon himself to inquire about my job status both with Al Jennings and Cass and he says my job is waiting for me when I return, which is some satisfaction or should be to all of us. I heard from Sally yesterday too, but no mail from youse guys - I'm sweating it out this morning since we go to Riverside this evening to finish up the Christmas shopping I hope. I have a good many cards to write too. Of course they are very plain and simple ones but you can't expect too much of a G.I.

I heard from you fellows today. I am so very glad the money for the ball filled the bill - I wish I could say as much for Mother's present - I still have no dope on that as yet. I'd better get a line on it soon for the stores won't hold the items for me much longer than Friday, so if I have no word by then I shall proceed as I see fit. I do hope the next letter helps some. No fair opening anything that comes to the house now until Christmas so please leave us have no cheating.

I should write Frances Carlson about the dance deal - maybe I'll get to that this afternoon - I'll have to see. I cannot think of much more news at present. Actually there is very little doing by me, although I do not expect to be doing much anyway. I got a card from the Dan Kelley's in L.A. - no doubt I could have fixed myself up for Christmas there but it is not particularly to my liking. I have been tempted to get the baby some sort of stuffed doll - have to see about that - I may do it yet.

I took most of my clothes to the cleaners a few moments ago so at any rate I should have plenty of clean clothes over the Holidays. We are doing much better on the crossword puzzles lately and the food situation has improved again. I guess that takes it all in for this one. Be good, people.

Lotsa Love, Frank

December 13, Thursday

Dear Mother, Harry and Mike,

Things have quieted down a bit at the Separation Base today. Schedules are erratic and not nearly as full as they have been for the past 3 or 4 weeks. Thusly, we have had most of the morning off and were sure glad to get it.

I went to Riverside last night and poked around without too much results and was hoping for a letter this morning - oh well, perhaps I'll get it this afternoon.

The Lieut. in charge of our group today told us definitely that this job ends on Friday or Saturday and then of course we await new assignments. He said that many of us who were formerly rated flying personnel would be apt to be returned to that category with a new B-29 Group, which forms here soon. They will also have a couple jet fighter groups here with the bomb group. Of course, how this will affect me, I have no idea. I doubt that I'll be ordered to fly again but I may be assigned as a ground radio mechanic or even assigned to Ground Communications here again, which would be fine with me. That is of course if I am not shipped out of March Field. If you are going to send anything to me for Christmas, I guess it best sent here - if I am ordered to leave, it will follow me. All Separation Base personnel are still frozen. A list of personnel working there in Counseling was sent into 4th Air Force Headquarters over a week ago, so they tell us. Evidently the procedure will be to check over our specialties and then assign us accordingly and we'll have to wait patiently, or not, for new assignment orders to come from higher up.

So that is all the information to date - will be sure to let you know as soon as is possible what the final deal will be, but of course no one has any concrete idea as yet.

I will have to get at my Christmas cards if I get any time off this afternoon - that is one job I must get out of the way as soon as is possible now.

I got back early from town last night. Went in with Jerry and a pal of his who came through Separation yesterday. They had gone to school together and were going to tie one on last night. I left them shortly after we got in town and was back at the base to get to my lil old sac early after a good hot shower. Although we get our 8 hours sleep when we're working nights, it is tiring and too many late nights I figure would make it too much. I don't know whether I work or not tonight - I'll have to find out sometime this afternoon.

Well people, I guess that covers it for this one - Be good.
Lotsa Love, Frank

Well people, I wrote this little missive this morning during some spare time I had and now I just ripped the envelope open in order to enclose a couple adjustments on the aforementioned information. Do not send anything here to March Field unless I wire you by the 17th to go ahead. Information passed on to us later today indicates that in all probability we will not be here on the 25th so that is that. I fully realize this means nothing probably for me at Christmas but I feel it is better that you do not send anything and then we stand less chance of losing it by having it hang around here at March Field. I don't intend to be "mysterious" about this, but I spent some time in the Unit Personnel Office today and I have a couple well informed buddies there and with what information was passed on today by our section head, I've come to that conclusion. I know that makes things a "mell of a Hess" but it will have to go that way unless I wire you by the 17th, which I don't think probable. We are supposed to get some clarification of the situation by Monday but you know how that goes. I'm sorry it is all so vague but you know about all I know now. Be good, people.
Lotsa Love, Frank

Sunday, December 16

Dear Mother, Harry and Mike,

Didn't get to write yesterday because we were working in the morning moving all our section's furniture out of the Separation Base. Yup, it closed up at yesterday noon. I got your letter on the Christmas situation and not a moment too soon either *for I had to spend entire afternoon between Riverside and San Bernardino altering and adjusting my plans and arrangements but I did finish and items are on the way so I do hope they get there in time.*

We worked last night so that took care of that evening. Friday night we worked too. I imagine that job over there at the Soda Fountain will end soon now for there are few officers left here now and little reason for keeping it open. It has served its purpose well!

Gosh Mom, I guess a furlough is in order as you suggest - I should mention it to the C.O. At any rate, we have a meeting scheduled for 8 AM to-morrow morning and that should give us some idea of where we are going to be assigned. My spies tell me that a shipping order of 1,500 men comes out to-morrow so I'll be sure and let you know if I am on it. Don't have any idea of how I'd ever get home if I did get a furlough - the papers here are full of how over 12,000 men are sleeping in Los Angeles stations and trains are so congested that it is terrible. It seems a shame that so many chose to travel when there are so many guys just back who deserve so richly to be home at Holiday time. Just heard over the radio that there is 40 inches of snow in Buffalo - I don't envy you people that, especially when today here is just like a mild day in October. It sure is nice here, particularly so when I think of folks at home shoveling that old snow around.

They got all the people around here worked up with an "Air Show" scheduled for here on the base today. They let the civilians look at all the planes and then were supposed to have a demonstration flying one of the P-80s - new jet plane. Well, at the last minute they didn't put the ship up and many were disappointed. They have at least 6-8 of them on the field here - seems like they could have put one of them up.

Well, I guess that takes in most of it from here. I'll let you know when anything turns up of significance - should have something to report definitely to-morrow. Be good, people.

Lotsa Love, Frank

P.S. - You spoke of not sending anything until the 20th - I hope by now you have decided to wait until I'm sure where I'll be - do not send money here either.
Frank

Monday, December 17

Dear Mother, Harry and Mike,

I fear I have not much information for you this time - we are all sorta hanging on a limb - some of us have heard and the rest of us are still waiting. To begin with, the scheduled meeting this morning did not come off as planned. Of course we were on deck - we poor E.M. have to be, but apparently none of the Wheels got up in time and the awaited for statement of policy did not come off. We don't know what the deal will be, especially as concerns the counselors that remain. Late this afternoon orders came out assigning many of the fellows to a Bomb Group, which starts here soon. Then a large list came out on men who have three years service who are going to be discharged. At least they are going through pre-separation processing here - I happen to know that no orders have come through and that they absolutely have no authority to discharge 3 year men as yet. Also, all men who have clerk, clerk-typist or cooks spec. numbers are frozen so that is that. Then they have frozen all men in finance and still others have to report here and there on the base regarding new assignments. No shipments off the field as yet, I suppose they're waiting and holding us for that deal.

I received a letter from Dan Kelley today and it was very nice. He asked me to be sure to stop by at Christmas time - offered dinner and a place to sleep, all of which was grand and greatly appreciated. Also heard from my lil Frances today - she wants me to come to L.A. and soon - mmm I bet she could love me to death and don't think I couldn't take kindly to that kind of treatment however I don't think I'll be able to make it - nor will I get to Kelley's very soon either.

I guess I can cut out all this old Bull Shit right now eh people. At this moment, I have furlough papers in my pocket for 30 days and 10 days travel time. It starts tomorrow, so the next time you hear from me it should be in the flesh. Hope that's what you wanted for Christmas Tess - it's an expensive proposition - anyway, it is what I wanted. Travel conditions are terrible and it will be one helluva drag believe me, but I have plenty of money to make it and also I probably will not be there in time for Christmas, you can bet I'm on the way one way or another. There is nothing absolutely in the way of any type of reservation, bus or train, available for over a week so just don't hold your breath but know that I'm on my way. Jerry is going too - he's bound for Milwaukee so we start together in the same general direction. We will get off the Field as soon as possible - this deal has been cooking but a little time now, and you'll never know how close we came to not getting it. I probably won't get to write again until I arrive so don't expect to hear. I told Jerry we were lucky because you were sayin that rosary Mom, so he says that if the Irish are still lucky, we should make it O.K.

Enclosed please find numbers of some travelers checks I bought here - save it in case I need it - lose checks or something. Don't spend any extra dough because of my coming, for though I have plenty to get a round trip ticket, I may need a little for cigarettes while at home. Be good now, you lovely people - I'd get there if I had to crawl - Take care of each other cause if you don't I'll raise hell when I arrive - I'll be seein you - time of arrival absolutely unknown.
Lotsa Love, Frank

January 1946
Monday, January 14, 1946 (letter from Jerry)

Dear Frank,

Well, it looks as if that furlough is almost ended for me and I'm already getting nervous about the return trip. I've had a swell time so far but get nervous as hell sitting around the apartment.

I had the same shaft you got when I tried to collect my pay, and just don't care much for this idea of "borrowing" the money. Makes me feel as tho (sic) it's not really mine and my conscience hurts every time I reach for the next buck.

I'm going to leave this week Frank, and would like to make the trip with you but haven't decided yet just exactly where I'm going first or where I'll arrive. This would be so much too early for you to start, especially since you aren't due back until the 27th; at least that is the way I have it figured.

I'm starting on Thursday morning from Chicago Municipal and will take a ride to Washington, DC to check up on my job - and I have definitely decided it would only be the "job" I would check on, if you know what I mean.

Went to Ypsi last week - stayed from Friday evening until Wednesday morning and had a wonderful time. Discovered something new while I was there (get your mind up higher Frank - that's not what I mean. ha).

Had to chase up to Appleton this week end and visit relatives. I hated to make the trip but enjoyed the visit anyway.

Well, Frank, - I have to drop li'l ol' Ginny a letter tonight while I'm in the mood for writing so guess I'll close for now.

If you happen to check-in at Riverside before the 24th you might ask at the U.S.O. and see if I have any belongings registered there. I'll be around until midnight the 24th & maybe we can get together.

Good luck on your return trip, Frank, and take care of yourself. Be seeing you soon.
Jerry

Thursday, January 24

Dear Mother, Harry and Mike,

Well, here we go again doing business at the same old stand. I am fine and I do hope Mother's cold is a has-been and that Harry didn't come down with one. I suppose I'd best start at the beginning and tell you all that has passed since Sunday so that you'll be up to date on it.

Nothing much happened on the train to Cleveland, so there is little there - got me a reclining seat from Cleveland to Dayton and slept most of the way, which proved to be almost the sum total of sleep I got on the trip. Once in Dayton, I got to the bus terminal and bused it to Patterson Field, grabbed a jeep from the gate to Operations and signed in for a ride going west. While in Dayton itself, prior to getting boxes, I had me a big bacon and egg breakfast so by the time I hit Operations I needed only to leave for one cup of Java at the Red X Canteen. I had me an "Ellery Queen Mystery" and returned to Operations to sit out a ride (never did find out who did the killings). I have found out that the plane hitching is just like everything else - the guy who is on deck gets the lift and they don't call the Canteen as often as they should. At 01:15 I got a lift on a C-45, which they told us was going through to Kansas City.

I was in the mood to take anything going west since I figured anything in that direction would cut down on the train fare. A C-45 is a small plane - used for navigator trainers - has 4 passenger seats - Colonel (full) piloted it with an engineer and there were two sailors and a marine on it besides yours truly. We stopped at Scott Field (St. Louis, Mo.) and there found out we were actually bound for Oklahoma City so that was fine. We had coffee and refueled the ship and then started off again to arrive at Tinker Field, Oklahoma City at about 7:30 PM. Accommodations there are good but due to so much traffic, no beds were available at Operations and when we went to the Transient Barracks, no one was on duty to give us bedding so we were out of luck and slept in Operations all night, only I couldn't sleep. We had a quick breakfast for we didn't want to miss any opportunity to get a lift, which did come through at about 9:30 AM on a C-47, which was going right through to Mines Field, Los Angeles. We arrived at about 6 PM with one stop [in] Albuquerque, New Mexico - Not bad, what? We got into L.A. in short order - the other fellows were going on to Frisco - almost went myself but decided again it - thought I might go and see Ja Parker in "Dear Ruth."

Anyway, once in L.A. I got a room at the YMCA and then had me a large meal at Mike Lymans - it was really good. I was very tired and wanted only to hit my sac so I picked up my two bags and went back to the "Y" I checked the brown one and took the other - Musette bag - up with me for my clean clothes were in it and a shower was in order in the morning. I went to sleep readily and awakened in the morning to find the bag had been stolen along with my Parker 51 and my pants pockets rifled of small change. You fellows know what was in the bag, so nuff (sic) said - I was heartsick of course but what is the use of crying over spilt milk - it should have been checked but I was too tired to bother I guess.

I started off at about 10 AM for Riverside hoping to run into Jerry there - took me the usual two hours to make it and when I arrived and asked for any message there was none so I figured he'd had more trouble than I had had and hadn't arrived as yet. I took a shower and was shaving when who should pop in to the shower and shave at the U.S.O. than the boy himself. He was fine - had made record time getting here just as I had and was getting tired of moping around alone I guess. While he was shaving I wrapped up the jacket and sent it home.

I neglected to mention that while in L.A. I had called Frances and found she planned to spend next day in Riverside so I made a date with her for last night. She was working on some Unit Teaching project and was using the Riverside Library. I had expected to be in the dog house but I guess the flowers more than did the trick - they arrived on Christmas morning just when she was very peeved and my personal guess is the family had razzed her to distraction. Anyway all was forgiven with a vengeance last night. I had really wanted to take her to the Mission Inn and dance all evening but when I suggested it I found, or rather I sensed, that she wasn't keen about the idea so I kept pushing it around and finally she admitted she didn't think it would be fun for the floor was small and she said the place was full of smoke and she doesn't drink so that was that and we settled for a show.

I met Jerry at midnight and we thumbed to San Bernardino to sleep at the "Y" there. He had tried the dormitory at Riverside and said it was not good. We slept there - ate late breakfast and came to camp today. Jerry reported - he had choice of mechanic on the line, engineer on B-29s or (he finally told me he could type) a clerk - he chose the last. He had already been assigned to the Very Heavy Bomb Group here. I have been retained in Squadron "L" for the present but am investigating possibilities for "L" is now Casual Squadron and I could be shipped out. Open to me is old D/F job and Ground Station R.O., flying occasionally with Generals on the field or just Ground Station R.O. - no flying, or B-29 R.O. assigned to a crew or perhaps instructor. I'm still snooping around - will let you know what I decide - also I'm eligible for discharge or supposed to be on May 1st - Be good, people.
Lotsa Love, Frank

Saturday, January 26

Dear Mother, Harry and Mike,

I guess I told you that I am scheduled to be eligible for discharge on May 1st - it sounds O.K. and I hope it is not just a lot of malarkey. I started out from the Field early - well, 10 AM yesterday - supposed to have a date with Frances in L.A. yesterday. I met her at the college after her 1st class. Occidental College is in a suburb of L.A. called Eagle Rock and the only way to get there is by street car - 30-45 minute ride if you don't have a car. We took in a show, had dinner and danced at the Biltmore no less. Dinner came to $6.12 and the cover charge and a couple drinks for me and a sandwich and coke for Frances came to $4.68 while dancing after dinner. She didn't want to order anything but she finally ordered a sandwich and a coke - the coke she drank and we wrapped the sandwich up in a handkerchief and put it in her purse. Actually for my money you are much farther ahead to go to a nice place like that for actually you don't spend much, if any, more than if you were horsing around at a bunch of joints or some overrated night club. Anyway, we enjoyed ourselves at what is supposed to be the best and nicest hotel in L.A. and it was worth it. I had to get the gal in at 1 AM back at the college and then sacked myself at the "Y" - must have been about 2 AM. Thumbed back this morning and intend hitting my old sac early for I'm still a bit tired. By the way, see "Leave Her to Heaven" and "Spellbound" if you get a chance - I enjoyed a good deal.

Did I tell you that our old job as soda jerks exists no more? But today, coming in from L.A. - got a ride from Riverside to camp with Father Flaherty - Catholic Chaplain - I find that he thought we'd have an easy time working at the Officers Club - the main one. Guess we'll look into it in a few days once we get rested up from our furloughs.

When I got here I found a whole mess of mail had accumulated. I got letters from Shack and Joe on the crew and one from Mike Grailey and cards from lotsa places so I'll have to get busy soon and answer some of them I guess, as well as write the usual letter home. I feel sure I want to make it tonight, for probably a movie will be the extent of my outing.

Jerry plans to go to L.A. this evening to see an uncle he has never visited. While at home I guess he got old Ned for not having been to see him. Seems the old boy has done rather well by himself but doesn't write the rest of the family so I guess Jerry has been appointed a committee of one to go down and get the latest poop.

I have decided that the old job is the one for me - out at the D/F station. I'd sure like to be drawing flying pay but why should I stick my neck out when I don't have to? I'll report in to-morrow afternoon I guess and interview the officers in communication to-morrow - I mean Monday.

Guess that about does it for today people - Be good.

Lotsa Love, Frank

Wednesday, January 30

Dear Mother, Harry and Mike,

Today is more or less a holiday here on the Post. This morning we marched to the parade grounds where we heard a civilian enumerate the many obstacles that G.I.s were having to run up against in returning to civilian life. After that, squadron C.O.s gave a pep talk on the advantages of re-enlisting - that of course is the purpose of the whole thing - to try to get us signed up - diabolical isn't it?

This afternoon there are 800 cases of free beer and free sandwiches and food for military personnel and any civilians that may have been invited or brought on the Post by G.I.s or officers. This evening Skinny Innis and his band for dancing, as well as some shows, ball games, and tennis matches this afternoon. It is all a big plot of course and I don't think they are getting many fellows. Where they get re-enlistments out here is after the fellows have been out for a while and find out that it is a bit rougher than they expected. It was brought out this morning that the biggest problem has been rated officer personnel who are going to have to step down their standard of living and have had no special skill taught them while in the Army. The housing out here is extremely critical - far worse than at home and it is going from worse to still worse what with G.I.s returning and thousands of others trying to establish residence and go to school. Thank heaven I have no home problem to worry about at least and a job to go to, although I have begun to wonder just how tough it is going to be to be back in school - any school. Had you heard how building materials are or will be tied up? I'm sure whether the law has been enacted or is still pending that contractors cannot build unless the home is expressly for a G.I. An independent non-veteran can build but he must guarantee that either his old home or the new one will go to a veteran. Perhaps that is why Pedrick's don't build. Also all building materials will be put under a ceiling within the year I believe.

Well folks, I guess that is about all the poop for the present. I am fine although getting a bit fed up on doing nothing. I do hope you are both well - haven't heard from you out here as yet but mail room was closed today and I suppose that accounts for it. Be good, people.

Lotsa Love, Frank

February, 1946

Friday, February 1

Dear Mother, Harry and Mike,

I was very very glad to hear from you folks - I was beginning to get a bit worried and had planned calling today if I didn't hear from you. I would have wired you when I reached Oklahoma City Tuesday night but I wasn't sure whether you'd be worried more than ever if I did wire and also facilities were not immediately available.

I'm sorry the back is not feeling so good and certainly hope it will be feeling better by the time this reaches home. I'd give my right arm practically if only I could have you out here in this weather Mom - I'm sure it would do you good and you'd certainly enjoy it - how about it if I send you the fare huh?

Please don't worry too much about my clothes being taken - I think I can manage O.K. since now I think I can sign statement of charges for new shorts and I should be able to pick up a few Tee shirts. Do not get me a pen - I have one I'm using - 85¢ worth. An Esterbrook, which will serve the purpose until I get out of the Army.

What kind of cards did you play at Reid's for money - was it bridge or a little nickel-dime? If all you lost was 32¢ I'd say it was O.K. They had a game going here in the barracks all night and it finally quit at 7:30 this AM. Last night I was sorely tempted to get into it but there were too many playing already so I guess it was just as well when I didn't get into it since it lasted so long.

Speaking of letters, my lil old Frances wrote the other day to tell me what a nice time she had on last Friday and I wrote back telling her I was glad. I kidded her quite a bit in the letter about her roommate and a couple other things and this morning did I ever get a Lulu. I think it was quite the nastiest letter I ever received and boy was I floored. I had planned on seeing her this week-end but will more than keep my distance now. I'm quite grateful in a way for that gets me out of any Valentine obligations and also she had asked me to her graduation on the 16th. I never figure a girl has any right to get P.O.'d unless she has a right to regard you as her own special property and for a gal who stated she'd have none of any kind of a permanent set-up at the out-set I was frankly stunned and then amused and relieved.

I'll have to write Coach and Mrs. Ott - I do hope he will be O.K. - perhaps this is the eye opener they need! There is no particular hurry about the overcoat - send it when you get the chance. I sent the jacket back because it would have been taken off of me if I had attempted to bring it on the field - I had some trouble with it on the way.

I am still doing a sum total of nothing all day - been drawing books from the library and once in a while getting down to writing. All I can do is wait for orders to get through relieving me of doing nothing and putting me at some responsible job somewhere. If nothing turns up by Monday I intend starting my old familiar campaign for a job that will bring me a little additional cash. Jerry and I have been seeing all the movies that come to the Post lately good, bad, or indifferent. I haven't been off the Post since I reported Sunday - just getting lazier and lazier in this man's Army I guess.

Well, that's it for today people - be good.

Lotsa Love, Frank

Sunday, February 3

Dear Mother, Harry and Mike,

I am loath to write for there is so little to write about. As to the weather we are having at present, what is known as the bottom dropping out. It has rained steadily all day here today and at least it is a change.

Yesterday being Saturday we were supposed to have an Inspection but it didn't come off and I went into town in the morning with a chap named Willis. I have written of him before—he's the chap who was in the hospital with rheumatic fever not long ago. He has a 40 Plymouth convertible and tools it in to get it greased and washed. While we were waiting for the job to get done, I shopped about and bought some shorts and T-shirts. I also went in to see about a blanket but they have no more of the extra fine ones and will not get anymore. The 16 dollar jobs are not much better than what you already have and don't look like too much of a buy to me.

Yesterday afternoon and evening was spent playing poker. I didn't do as well as you Mom, for I lost 3.50 - 4.00 bucks, but we had a good time and I enjoy it when I'm playing with fellows I know reasonably well.

I slept a bit late this morning and made 11 o'clock Mass and had my throat blessed since it was the Feast of St. Blaise. Last week-end Jerry went to see his uncle in L.A. but missed him since the daughter and husband live in the old man's old home so he went again this week when daughter and hubby will drive him to Santa Monica I think to see the old man.

I am still casual and getting fat doing nothing but reading, eating, and sleeping. If I don't soon get transferred to Base Communications I think I'll see what can be done about getting in an Army Airways Communications System outfit, which is organizing on the field and is in dire need of men. Guess that's it folks—no news—just getting lazier.

Lotsa love, Frank

Tuesday, February 5

Dear Mother, Harry and Mike,

It is about 10 AM and I am just rightly up. I had some coffee at the PX and have glanced at the AM paper. If all this sounds as though I am in the lap of luxury I guess that is correct only I'm not too elated about it.

A couple of opportunities came up yesterday. I don't know as I should wish for more adventurous nature or not for they are looking for volunteers to ferry planes from the U.S.A to South America. This would be fine with me, in the 1st place I would *be making flying pay–flying in all probability in one of the old big birds, B-17s for those and B-24s are what I think they will send down there. Also you'd make overseas pay and most likely per diem at $6.50 a day. I'm not so terribly hungry for money (much) but it would certainly be a wonderful experience for I'll probably never get another chance in this lifetime to get to South America. I think you have to sign up for 6 months and that is the big catch for me although as it stands at present I am not eligible for discharge until May and the way things are going I won't actually be out until June or July for the men here who were eligible for discharge on Jan 1 are still cooking their butts. If I could get in it for 4 months I'd take it I believe–I'm going to sleep on it another night anyway.*

The other thing is working at the Officer's Club soda fountain as a permanent duty assignment at no hourly rate but for a flat rate of $30 a month extra. Of course the first deal appeals to me no end because my guess is that by the time I got out I wouldn't be able to work at the plant full time more than 2 months at the outside. If only they'd order me to take it it would be O.K. but I don't think I'd ever volunteer for a flying assignment.

Last night Jerry and I went to San Bernardino. His mother had received another housecoat for Christmas and he had returned the one he bought and gotten a due bill. He cashed in the due bill but on some slips and nighties and I picked up a couple pairs of shorts. I have hopes of getting some stockings for you Mom, but I'm not supposed to leave the base before 5 PM so that gives me only tonight in both San Bernardino and Riverside when the stores are open. Please let me know if you need the stockings or if they are becoming available at home for the effort is too big a one to make if you are able to get the stockings.

We had a couple beers and returned shortly after 10 PM. There was a big poker game going on, 25¢ limit and Jerry got in. I was sorely tempted but the smallest bill I had was a 10 and I hated to start in with that. I watched until about 1 AM and then hit the sac. I guess Jerry won–he certainly is lucky and I'm kinda glad now that I didn't get in, although I sure love to play that game. It's too bad someone has to lose and it's generally me.

I'm going to hold this letter open until after 11 AM when I check my mail and see if I have any more to report. Plan on doing a bit of washing this afternoon and a bit of snooping around for a job if I have time. I'm glad money order arrived O.K. and how goes things on the financial front? I have about 60-70 here I can and will ship on in a minute if you need it. I would much rather do that than see any bonds cashed. I am genuinely sincere about this "it's his money and we won't touch it" stuff. It is ours, like everything else, and if you want all or any part of it just say the word.

Well, I left this but nothing new has come up so I guess that is it for today people. Be good.

Lotsa Love, Frank

Wednesday, February 6

Dear Mother, Harry and Mike,

As per usual, doing very much of nothing. I'm glad to hear in Harry's of Sunday that Tess is feeling a bit better and also that the bowling scores are a bit better—they are consistent and that is important. So Alice is getting on to it a little eh? Where did you go bowling—at Facazio's?

One of the boys got me up for breakfast this morning and it was good. There are only about 10 of us upstairs in our barracks and about 4 of us who have no jobs are in a bad rut—like the one I got the Thompson household in when I was home. We get up early and eat—read the paper and then after cleaning up the barracks we return to the sac. It has become a contest as to who can put in the most sac time. We have little reciprocity agreements—"I didn't wake you up last night so you better not wake me up this AM or PM" whatever it happens to be.

I didn't know that I could sleep so much. I don't know whether I'm getting ready for something or catching up on something but I am just about at the end of my rope of doing nothing. I'd better get some action by the first of next week or I'll go over the hill or something.

That deal about ferrying planes to South America closed today at noon. Gosh but that was a temptation—there are only a few men on the field qualified to do the job and I was one of them—as it turned out they wanted only radio operators and instead of 6 months to a year it was from 1-6 months—they got two men from March Field.

Say, I saw a picture this evening I'd recommend highly—nothing terribly outstanding about it but I wish the pair of you would see it—I came out feeling kinda warm inside and maybe you will too. It was "Miss Susie Slagle" with Lillian Gish, Sonny Tufts, and Veronica Lake and very important—Jane Canfield. I guess that sums it up for today people. Be good.

Lotsa Love, Frank

Thursday, February 7—4 PM

Dear Mother, Harry and Mike,

Am at present in metropolis of Riverside and am penning just a bit of a note to let you know that one Valentine is on its way as of to-morrow morning by express so be on the lookout for it.

Let me know immediately upon arrival of its condition for it is insured and is rather fragile. I got off the base this afternoon today but it is not too easy to do. They caught me for a detail (sweeping) before I did manage to get in and as you can well imagine I am very bushed since it is the first 20 minute work I have done in some time.

There is nothing new to report! I believe I'll return to the base now and continue to rot. They made us move to a different barracks today, which was a strain since they woke me out of a sound sleep at about 10 AM.

I guess that is about it for this one folks—I have no idea of what I'll do this evening since I've already seen the movie—maybe I'll come in to a dance here at the U.S.O. Be good, people.

Lotsa Love, Frank

February 8, Friday

Dear Mother, Harry and Mike,

Well, another ol fish day has arrived and the complexion of things certainly has not changed to any extent. I got me three books at the library last night and have settled down to read some more. I have another deal or two cooking and propose to get some the first of next week in some direction or else.

A new show starts this evening at the theatre so I'm set for tonight. I feel I must get into something soon now or go a bit batty. Never since Basic Training have I been so at a loss as to what to do with myself and sorta lonely. Jerry is busy at an office job all day and I see very little of him. All the fellows I knew at all are out now and of those that are left I am not too keen about getting chummy with and as ever I cannot see tearing about or drinking alone.

My present views on this base are as follows. All the lads who were in combat and were in the Army to fight—transmuted civilians—have been discharged. This leaves mostly a conglomeration of fellows who held office jobs and put in all their time in the States and the old Army men and those who have re-enlisted. Of the first group I have little in common, although many of these guys were not all the time in the States because they personally chose it. Of the regular Army men, I have less in common and so I keep to myself. Don't take this personal analysis as bitching on my part or think that I'm horribly discontent for I refuse to get het up about it. The situation is normal actually as the war time Army degenerates into a peace time organization of men who sit around all day and talk about women.

Quotas for men to be discharged are starting to come to this base now after being held up from two to three months. Many of the fellows are due to get out and I'll be glad when they do go for I get fed up on listening to the gripe. Just in passing, remember that I become eligible for discharge in May so leave us not get excited about it.

Well, I guess that is [the] sum total of the report for today so be good, people.

Lotsa Love, Frank

February 11, Monday

Dear Mother, Harry and Mike,

Well, things unfolded a bit today and I hardly think it for the better but for the final result I'll have to wait and see. This morning the 14 of us who came on Saturday reported for interview with the Major. It was short and sweet and I still don't know whether I impressed the guy or whether he just decided that I looked like a sucker and is sticking it to me—counterclockwise.

It seems because of my rank, I have been made a Duty NCO, which is nothing more or less than general overseer of the work that is being done here. All they are doing is sweeping out buildings and tearing out any partitions, which are not permanent, also any temporary fixtures–shelves, etc. My job is to assign the men to the detail and then cruise around all day and keep checking to see that the fellows keep working. This base was constructed early in the war and is very widely dispersed so that is miles between areas–sooo I have a jeep at my disposal all day just to run all over and checkup. Well, you can imagine me taking over the jeep, but thank heavens I had had some driving, and altho (sic) I don't make out well with it I do get there. Do I like the job? Well, I'd say definitely no and if I'd had a choice I wouldn't have taken it–under ordinary conditions I'd refuse it but I don't expect to be here long and I thought it would be some gauge of my leadership ability of which I have always had nothing but doubts. It will be a test all right for the number of men here is small and one in my position is apt to find himself a complete social outsider if he doesn't manage well.

Another thing of course is that I don't know the Post or the job and I'm trying to tell fellows what to do who know more about it than I do, also the ones who have been here any length of time feel any of them should have had the job and all the fellows I came in with are razzing me about being a Wheel. On top of that I step into a bit of organization which existed before my time and all the older fellows are at present eligible for discharge and won't do much (and I hardly blame them)–these fellows are in charge of the 4 different sections which comprise the 30-40 men who are my responsibility. All in all it is a pretty screwed up mess but I'm stuck with it. I talked with the Major this afternoon and he at least appreciates that I'll have my hands full and he termed the job "turkey" (an advanced form of chicken shit).

Another thing–each man here gets 1-2 day pass a month and you can just imagine how the fellows look forward to them–well–part of my job is to punish those who goof off by turning them in and having the pass taken away. Hardly a job for a guy who has tried to mind his own business and keep away from all this stuff, but as I said I want to see how I make out. You cannot get work out of the fellows by ordering because they all expect to be out soon and you can't get it out of them by threatening to fire them as you would in civilian jobs for that is what they want, so you figure it out, as yet haven't been able. I guess that covers most of it and you can gauge what I'm up against. I'll let you know how I make out and figure myself lucky if a mutiny doesn't break out. Wish me luck people.
Lotsa Love, Frank

OVER THERE

Present Day

"Where should we go next?" my cousin Suzanne asked me over one of our "coffee" calls. Since our trip to Paris in 2014, we'd found we were ideal traveling companions, both domestic and abroad. After our successful trip to Sioux Falls, it was time to plan another trip. Needless to say, since I'd been bitten by the travel bug, I'd started a bucket list and the more letters I typed, the more I wanted to visit England.

Suzanne had already been to England, but she was up for another go. That cold Saturday morning, over long-distance coffee, we decided to go to London. Though she'd been before, there were a few sites she'd not yet seen. I, of course, had multiple reasons for wanting to go. First, I'd never been there, then there was the fact that my ancestors on my father's side were from there, add to that the places mentioned in the letters I wanted to visit, and that Suzanne and I both had cousins on our mothers' side living in London, and Plymouth. We started to formulate our plan.

Knowing my primary reason for this trip was somewhat military focused, ever-supportive, Suzanne allowed me to work out the details as long as I incorporated the few destinations she had on her list, conceding she was not opposed to another research adventure. With the destination determined, she shared our plan with her brother Charlie, who also had been to London before, but with his love of history and intrigue with the military, he'd expressed an interest in joining us, and so our twosome became a threesome.

What started out as a simple trip to London in short order, took on a life of its own. By the time we left in August, our trip had truly morphed into anything but coddiwompling. Though both Suzanne and Charlie had been to London previously, neither had been to Brussels, so we added that and a pop over to see my cousins who lived just outside Rotterdam in The Netherlands. It was decided. Three countries in twelve days complete with planes, trains, and automobiles.

Determined to visit as many places as possible that my father had mentioned in his letters, I had some success in London–getting to Covent Garden, the Royal Opera House where the dances were held, and some of the sites including the Tower of London, and a drive-by of the art museum and Madame Tussauds. For me, just knowing that I had been to the same places my father had visited over seventy years before somehow made me feel closer to him. In an odd way, I felt as though we shared something he'd never been able to share with any member of his family, strengthening my connection with him even more.

Once I knew we were definitely going to England, I had contacted my helpers to see if it was possible to meet up. I contacted my friends at the Red Feather Club Museum of the 95th Bomb Group where my father had been stationed, as well as Art & Val Stacey from The Goldfish Club. Both had indicated that if we ever visited the UK, Beverley would be happy to provide us with a tour of the museum, and Art would share with me all things Goldfish. True to their word, they were eager and excited to work with our schedule and we made arrangements to meet Beverley and Linda in Horham, and Art & Val in Stamford. Since our visit did not fall during normal museum hours, our hosts made a special effort to be open and receive us. Upon arrival, we learned that they had also been contacted by two other American families whose parents had been stationed in Horham, so there were actually three different American servicemen's families at the museum that day.

The base was out in the country. How we found it, I'm not sure, but as we approached the turn, in the distance you could clearly see the Nissen huts and the American flag blowing in the breeze. The sign at the turn off read RED FEATHER CLUB 95th BG H. Once we parked, we made our way to the museum entrance. That's when it really hit me. My eyes welled up and I had to choke back the tears. It was very emotional to be standing on the grounds of the distinguished 95th Bomb Group, knowing that the museum was located in the restored NCO club my father had frequented. Beverley had met us at the door and as I stood to collect myself, she put her arm around my shoulders and allowed me the time I needed. "It's quite emotional, I know," she said. "Take all the time you need."

Upon entering the museum, directly opposite where I stood, hung the painting I'd been told about. Measuring six feet by four feet, in vivid color was a beautiful reproduction of Heavy Date, the B-17 bomber my father's crew had left at the bottom of the North Sea.

We spent a little over two hours at the museum, not nearly enough time, but we had made arrangements to carry on to Stamford and meet up with Art and Val Stacey for dinner. Had it not been for the three-hour drive and our prior commitment, we could easily have remained for hours. It was quite obvious that the volunteers had taken great effort to restore the building to its original state, with every square foot filled with the most remarkable collection of items from the WWII soldiers who had been stationed there, many of them having been donated by family members. I knew once I'd started walking through the museum with the volunteers that the two hours we'd allocated was completely inadequate. I knew I would have to return.

As we said goodbye to our new friends at the 95th Bomb Group Heritage Museum, we left with heavy hearts. I cannot remember feeling more welcomed, or more honored—though we were not actual soldiers, as family and friends of soldiers, we received the red carpet treatment. Piling back into the car, we set our course to Stamford to meet Art and Val Stacey. Art and I had been emailing back and forth for several months coordinating our visit. With photos taken, and the navigation set, we were on our way.

Over the past two years, Art and I had communicated on and off whenever I had a question. It was Art I had come to rely upon when I was researching my father's tour in England; he always came through for me. To travel all this way and not meet him was never an option. The way our schedule worked out, we'd agreed to leave Horham and meet for dinner. Prior to our trip, I'd sent Art the accident report of the ditching, and Art was working on reinstating my father and Roger into The Goldfish Club. I was to receive their membership cards when we met.

The drive through the English countryside was winding and beautiful. After about three hours, we exited at Burghley House in Lincolnshire; barely able to see this glorious manor house from the road, we carried on toward the The George Hotel in Stamford. As we approached the town, nestled on the River Welland, we felt as though we were entering a movie set. One of the few remaining towns with seventeenth and eighteenth-century stone buildings and boasting five medieval parish churches, we were entering a living museum. It was breathtaking.

Having never met Art and Val, we were texting and calling one another as we approached our rendezvous point. As with everyone I've met on this journey, we embraced as family, had tea in The George Hotel, took a walk around their beautiful town, and then headed to dinner at an authentic English pub. As I'd promised Roger, I ordered gammon steak with eggs, which was both delicious and voluminous. I couldn't finish. Our time together was non-stop conversation, stories, and laughter, culminating with Art officially welcoming me as an Associate member of The Goldfish Club and presenting me with my very own membership card, complete with Goldfish lapel pin. As we parted in the dark parking lot, I knew in my heart that I would remain friends with Art and Val until the end of my days. It was sad leaving them, not knowing when and if we would meet again, unaware that our next reunion would actually take place in less than a year.

BORING BLYTHE

1946

Return Address:
S/Sgt. F. G. Thompson12107602
420 AAFBU Sqd "E"
Blythe Army Air Base
Blythe, Calif.

February 10, Sunday

Dear Mother, Harry and Mike,

You will note the change of address on the envelope, and believe me it is as much of a surprise to me as it no doubt will be to you. Saturday, after I had written you, we were told that Squadron L was to move to another section of March Field. There was some controversy among the Brass Hats and the result of it was that we had to move Friday night at 7 PM.

Shortly after the announcement, I discover that I was alerted for shipment to Blythe. Friday night we moved to a section of March Field I hadn't known existed. It is about 1 ½ miles from camp proper. Saturday morning we had to report to old area to clean up barracks we had evacuated and I discover that a bus had arrived and was waiting for me to take me to Blythe, so I had the driver return to new area and pick up my bags and by 6 PM yesterday we had arrived at Blythe Air Base. There were originally 20 men on the shipment but two were on pass and 4 could not be found so that left14.

The assignment here is temporary and the job is detail work closing down the Air Base. Does it sound like I got the purple shaft? Well, at least it is better than sitting on my old rusty dusty all day. Total compliment of the base is now 57 men and 22 of these are due to return to March Field since they are eligible to come out on quota for discharge. Blythe is a satellite base of March Field hence we are sent to close up the base, which by now consists mainly of cleaning up barracks and boarding them shut. A Major and a Warrant Officer are the only officers here. The base itself is or was a large one originally housing 10 thousand men or more. And it is dispersed all over the damn desert. You'd better get a big map of Calif. if you are going to look for the place. The town—ten miles from camp—has a population of about 2 thousand, although I'd say it is a progressive little town for all of that. We went in last night and wound up at an American Legion stag party with an excess of free beer and all the liquor you could drink, plus food, etc. Things are pretty lax here and you can wear about anything or almost nothing—no ties, the chow seems O.K., and everyone very chubby. The barracks are exceptionally good since we are using those built for WACs (no urinals) and it seems like a tight little spot.

We went into town this morning to get to 9 o'clock Mass and afterwards stopped for coffee and bought the papers and returned. Only about 7 or 8 went in in a Recon car. To go to town each night you use G.I. transportation–cars or trucks, and you are picked up at 12 midnight and another round is made for drunks at 2:30 AM. I drank some Mexican beer last night–it is 12-14% stuff and did it ever go through me! Like a dose of salts yet.

Well, I guess that gives you most of the poop. The weather is typical Arizona weather–desert weather–for this time of year. It gets very cold along in the early morning–good for sleeping–and it is quite warm in the noon and afternoons. Well, thas (sic) all for this one, be good, people.

Sincerely yours in Blythe

Lotsa Love, Frank

Tuesday, February 13

Dear Mother, Harry and Mike,

Well, things are rolling along here in Blythe. My personal appraisal would be that I am not doing too good but I guess I could be doing a good deal worse - at least the fellows aren't sneaking up behind me with knives and clubs as yet. I have been pretty well chewed out by the Major but I guess I'll absorb a lot of that before this job is over. I drive about in my Jeep like a Wheel, in fact that is what I'm being razzed as "Wheel." Of course, I still dislike the whole business but still am chalking it down as good experience. I'd say the fellows are doing exceptionally well but what is my opinion. I am really learning to drive in that Jeep, getting over 50 miles a day. There is no traffic here on the base so I am having a driving field as far as driving is concerned. As usual in any bunch I have a couple guys who are incorrigible and it is a temptation to leave them alone but you actually don't dare do it for if you don't chase after them the fellows who are doing O.K. feel there is no advantage in doing the job properly. Oh there certainly are lots of angles to it. I got stuck today when my Jeep hung up in second and I couldn't shift any gears at all (as usual my "clutch" was ok) but the Master Sgt. at the motor pool fixed her up for me by welding on a couple pieces in the right place so I'm O.K. now. It sure is a great racket - I almost hate to see the dawn of each day but I reckon I'll get over that. It sure isn't dull anyway.

It is healthy weather out here and fairly decent living almost rigidly scheduled by lack of things to do for it is too expensive and dull to go into town often. We eat, sleep, and work and are out in the fresh air all day - the food certainly could be a lot better but I've eaten much worse and so at this writing I breeze along and hope for the best.

Of course, I haven't heard from you folks in some time and probably won't since mail from March Field is not forwarded as it should be but I hope to hear by next

Monday or Tuesday anyway. I guess I'll be going off now to do a bit of laundry, so be good, people.

Lotsa Love, Frank

February 15, Friday

Dear Mother, Harry and Mike,

It has been a long time since I have been so glad to see a Friday come around. To-morrow I should be able to relax in my duties most of the day and it will be more than a welcome respite to me. I do not enjoy this business of running about checking up on people who are doing a job I care less about. At any rate I have elected to try it and am doing my very best.

Yesterday things went very well and as I expected it was merely the calm before the storm. Today I ran into Personnel trouble with a vengeance. I had three boys just about ready to kill me I think. They were pulling what I might have, and I certainly don't blame them, but they gave me a hard time for a while - it upsets me but I knew it was bound to come. Three of the fellows tried to pull the wool over my eyes and get off early on a 3 day pass - about 18 hours early so I put the kibosh on it. This is known as Chicken Shit in the Army and for myself I certainly don't care if they all take off but I cannot be easy on three while the rest are out in the desert working like hell. That is the whole trouble and there are one or two like that in every outfit who are forever goofing off and won't do a thing.

Nobody here asks anybody to kill themselves with work as long as they put in the time and look busy and accomplish something definite every few days to show some progress. The fellows who don't do anything just throw off those who would and any morale that exists is extinguished. What to do is a problem but I expect it will be ironed out. The orderly room of course backed me up but I hate to be a killjoy and hate worse to be made a fool of. I hope to-morrow will be easier since we are only on a half day and if I can keep the men out of sight until 10:30 we may be able to get off O.K. - I certainly hope so. Practically all the men who have done a lot of this work around here are leaving and they were all on Pass today, which made things kinda rough but I guess it will work out O.K.

To-morrow night is a dance in town so I certainly must go and see what it is all about. They only have one every month or so I guess. There is little new to report - haven't heard a radio or seen a newspaper since I got out here - haven't heard from you folks either, although I didn't expect to until Monday or Tuesday direct and nothing has been forwarded from March Field as yet. I myself am fine and the fresh air is doing me good I guess - face is all windburn from tooling about in ma Jeep. Be good, people.

Lotsa Love, Frank

February 17, Sunday

Dear Mother, Harry and Mike,

Well, yesterday and today I hit the jack-pot on the mail situation and it sho (sic) felt good. I got me a good sized box this morning and also Harry's first letter came direct to Blythe so I expect I can be expecting my usual share of mail now. Only 5 of us went to Mass this morning and when I got back I found my box - I was very glad it came and we all had a pre-dinner snack - wished we'd had it in town with us when we had our after church coffee but it hit the spot well. I have put everything away except the baked goods and we all have been putting them away. There is but one piece of cake left and about 7 or 8 cup cakes. The remainder of the staple candy and nuts will come in fine during the evenings when we are all hanging around with a beer or 5 or 6.

Last night we all went into town to the dance. It was a big splurge for Blythe all right but I certainly didn't feel it was worth the $1.20 they charged us. I had a fair time and a few beers and latched onto one of the best looking blondes in the place but I didn't pursue it too rashly and her mother called for her so that was that. I'm in a rather funny situation out here with this job and I'm not being too conscious of it either. I was a bit afraid she might have been lined up with one of the lads who has been here some time but, as it turned out, she was just in from El Centro over the week-end. The fellows out here treat me fine so far and I certainly don't want to get in any jams over the few available desirable gals around here. I get my mail delivered to my sac and am treated with all respect and deference up to this point. Only a few of the fellows call me by first or last name as yet - it is always "Sgt." If only I can keep things rolling along for a couple more weeks the worst part of the job will be done I believe. I think we have gotten more work done during the past week than has been done before but it is almost too good to last so I'll be holding my breath this week.

I know you'll let me know as soon as possible when that pkg. arrives from Riverside - I am a bit worried about it now but I believe I still have the receipt for it - it was insured.

Among my mail I got forwarded from March yesterday I got a Valentine and an invitation to graduation from lil ol Frances - don't know what to think now but I guess I'll just let the situation be as it is. Boy am I ever the thoughtful one! I haven't written Sally since I've been back and then I forgot Valentine's Day as far as she was concerned - what do I do now - any constructive suggestions will be appreciated. The last bowling scores sure sound good Harry. If you keep that up, I'll not be going bowling with you that's for sure!

We had turkey today of all things and it was really well cooked - about the best turkey I've had in the Army. We got good chow here all right but I often feel that for such a small outfit, it should be better.

Well folks, I guess that is about it for this one. Thanks millions for the box - we are now eating the nuts and they're swell. One of the lads took the curse off some cake for us as the blots on the top of this page will attest. Be good, people.
Lotsa Love, Frank

February 19, Tuesday

Dear Mother, Harry and Mike,

Not a great deal to report from Blythe today although things are rolling along as well as can be expected. According to my estimate we have completed a great deal of work and the lads who have been here some time say that they have never done so much in so short a time. It certainly isn't because I have driven them or bawled them out for I don't believe in that stuff but the important thing is that they have done a great deal and done a good job too.

The Major returned this afternoon and I don't expect I'll get a chance to go over it with him until sometime to-morrow. Last night we had a movie in the dayroom brought here by a roving U.S.O. man and I for one enjoyed it. There is very little to do out here but most of us are tired when we get through our days work and are glad to take a shower and climb in the sac at 8 or 9 PM. It is a good life although I do not like the job I have. At the present time we have accomplished so much that nothing further has been outlined and I suppose the C.O. will lay awake nights thinking up some beautes for us. We have a Warrant Officer who is 2nd in Command here and he asked me very nicely today if I wouldn't drive the Jeep slower and I said "of course." Poor me who has never driven before - it is a wonder I haven't ruined that Jeep - drove it over 100 miles today.

I think we are all going into Blythe to see a basketball game - some of the lads here are in a local league and are leading it so we may go in to see how they make out.

I am sweating out a letter from you people - nothing since Harry's on Sunday with the box, but then we only get one mail call and delivery here.

I guess that takes in most of it for this one people. Be good.

Lotsa Love, Frank

P.S. Hold your breath on next few letters - I'm running out of air mail stamps and can see no way to get anymore - got one more angle to try to-morrow.

F.

February 23, Saturday

Dear Mother, Harry and Mike,

I am late all right with this one. Don't let the stationery fool you although I am at present at March Field. I got me a 3 day pass up there at Blythe and an opportunity came up to ride into Riverside Thursday evening so we took advantage of it. Stayed Thursday night here at March Field and had lunch here and then took off for L.A. and Hollywood. Fooled around there until this afternoon and then returned to March for chow this evening and we may go to a dance in Riverside this evening. We are not well enough healed to have a big time in L.A. but we spooked around and saw a couple broadcasts and a stage show last night. We figured almost anything was better than staying at Blythe if we didn't have to stay. You are allowed a 3 day pass each month there and if we didn't take ours now we just would have stayed around and worked until Sat. noon. One of the lads up there at Blythe with us has a 39 Olds and we came the 175 miles from Blythe to Riverside Thursday night in about 3 1/2 hours. I think the work at Blythe is pretty well cleaned up and they are asking around who wants to stay there. It would be kinda fun and probably better for me in some ways if I were to stay at Blythe being a "Wheel" up there and all but I think it is really better to stay at March if possible with discharge proceedings. It takes a week or so for any news to get up there from March Field.

One reason I wanted to get down here over a week-end was to get to Confession and I expect we can do that right after chow even though we are a bit tired. I am with a chap named Cyril Vasko. He is a Czech - at any rate his people came from there and he has been having a helluva time with the State Dept. over some property he has in the Old Country - left to him by his father and has been cared for by his uncle who is over there. Cy - we call him - lives in Cleveland and gets out about the same time I do I guess. He is one of the boys that was shipped up to Blythe when I was.

I was very sorry to hear about little Alice and will write of course - no doubt you'll let me know how she is getting on in each letter. Was unable to get hold of any nylons in L.A. or Hollywood for you Mom. I saw some saddle shoes there. Do they have em a plenty at home or had I best get some here?

One thing I must get to work on here immediately is establishing a legitimate reason for staying out here and getting discharged at Ft. MacArthur. By doing that I can make myself 100-125 dollars extra on travel pay and also stand a chance of getting out sooner than if I wait to get on a Quota going to Ft. Dix. I plan to get that excuse by applying to one of the colleges in L.A. for entrance. I stand a good chance, I believe, from that angle since I'd be starting on my third year at most engineering schools and not trying to get in with the freshmen.

Gosh people, I guess that about does it for the present moment. We went in all the Auto Showrooms in Hollywood this AM and drooled over the new cars - they are really alright especially a Plymouth Convertible with red leather seats. It is getting about chow time now so guess I'll go feed my face. Be good.
Lotsa Love, Frank

March 1946

March 1, Friday

Dear Mother, Harry and Mike,

I received a couple letters in jig time today. I guess I'm getting very bad on the writing - no question about it. I certainly will try to do better in the future. There seems so little to write about around here - hardly anything that would be of much interest to anyone, even ourselves.

Wednesday we worked very hard here on the base. You see we had finished all the work previously outlined by the Major so we got started on a new tack. Wednesday night I should have written but I was tired and quite sick of the look of this place so we went into town to see a movie. It was "The Great John L" and we enjoyed it all right.

Upon getting back we found out that we were to go to March Field the next day to get paid. That was different at least. Harland Reid, one of the lads here, drove his 39 Olds in so I rode along instead of going the 175 miles in the G.I. bus. I wish we could have come back in it but Reid got a pass and had a deal all cooked up to sell the car so that we came by bus. It was some trip in that buggy but we made it back O.K. Of course we took the curse off it by stopping at each town for a brew or two but there are only three towns along the way so we didn't get too liquored up. I was quite tired and so hit the sac early upon returning. We did manage to get haircuts at March Field for the usual 50¢ - it costs 1 berry for one in Blythe. We got paid and came back and that was about the crux of it.

This morning we did a token job of cleaning barracks and the dayroom and then loafed. They paid off - by check - those of us who did not go on the bus to March Field and now we are off until Monday AM. We are just now wondering what to do with ourselves. We got paid true, but we're not too anxious to start out and shoot the works so soon especially here in Blythe so I reckon we'll go in for a quiet evening and see what develops in the next week or so. I asked the Wheels in the orderly room today for permission to take one of the Jeeps to Indio - about 98 miles from here - but the answer was a big "No" so that was that. There is so little to do in Blythe, save get drunk, that most of us don't deem it worthwhile going unless the movie is worth seeing.

I sure am glad that Mike is home again - is his condition of a temporary nature or will he have to be carefully looked after all the time now? Don't complain about poor values in Real Estate at home - things are terrific out here. It always has been bad around Riverside and all it needed was this shortage in housing to really make things hit the ceiling. I know of places built to sell at 4500 three years ago that are going for 9-12 [thousand] now. It is murder out here!

So Don O'Hara plans on marriage and then school - I wish I had the courage some of these guys seem to have but I still think marriage is a full time job at first and school should be full time at any time. What does Ted Fairchild plan on taking? By the way, how is Bobby making out at school - I hope he is still getting along fine.

I had some trouble with my Jeep when the boys took it last week so the M/Sgt. at the motor pool told me to take the rotor out of the distributor cap so no one could take it. I have been doing that. Today some of them wanted to take it into the desert and I wouldn't give up the missing link. No doubt they thought me very chicken. At any rate the Jeep is gone now although I sure as hell don't know how they got it going but it is gone. Oh I have my little problems no question about that.

Well people, I guess that is about it for today. The target for tonight is Blythe - no women there I'm afraid (or maybe it's good). It is just about time for evening chow and I have just been treated to a big ol Coke and a generous shot of 3 Feathers. Got a big appetite now so I'll be seeing you people.

Lotsa Love, Frank

Sunday, March 3

Dear Mother, Harry and Mike,

Well my dears, today is the Sabbath and our own day. We had yesterday off and most of Friday and have been enjoying, up to the limits of Blythe, our leisure. Mom says in her last that you are having ice and snow at home. Here it is beginning to really get warm. It is very warm just around noon at the present but I look for it to really blaze up in a couple weeks. At present I'm sitting in the barracks in shorts and no shirt. We have filled up the pool out here after cleaning it and went swimming yesterday afternoon. Prior to the swim, four of us took a trip in the Jeep to the base of the mountains about 8-10 miles distant here within the limits of the Post. They are dry and rugged mountains and it was rough on the Jeep going cross country to get there especially with me driving.

Friday night we went into town. I tied on a pretty good one but at no time felt more than fairly high. I stuck to beer all evening, which was the reason. Many of the lads mixed up their drinks and as a result we had quite a few get sick the result of which means I'll have to have my battle jacket cleaned due to a too near miss. It is too bad you can't do much in town aside from drinking but that is fun if you don't go at it rabidly but moderately. Aside from a few of the local punch boards, I have come in contact with no women to speak of at all and I guess I'm better off that way. After having gone to March Field the other day, many of us are inclined to weather the rest of our time here at Blythe - March is not so good anymore as we see it. Not that Blythe is so wonderful, but they keep you busy and military regulations are far less stringent here almost to the point of being non-existent.

While I think of it - I didn't realize I'd done so poorly on the writing. As I have said before there is little or nothing to write from here but I'll try to dream up something to say. You fellows are so good and I can't expect you to stay that way if I don't do a bit better myself.

Last night we planned on getting into town but three of us who were going fell asleep right after chow and didn't get up until 10:20 PM so we were out of luck. The bus goes in at 7 PM - I guess we were pooped from our ride in the desert and swim and then a big meal. Reason for going in last night was to go to Confession. We didn't get there as planned last week at March Field. We went over to the Chapel at 6:30 only to find Confessions were from 7:30-9 PM so then we went to the 6:45 movie and returned at 8:30 and Father Flaherty had left. We were out of luck there and then we slept through the bus last night so next Saturday is a must.

Of all things, I found out yesterday that one of the fellows here is from the Falls. His name is Beckford and he married one of the Buck girls - they (the Bucks) live on Ferry Avenue in Gallagher's old place I guess. Boy isn't that a coincidence! Do you know the Bucks, Mom? - he says his wife knows Bill Reid's mother for Beckford's place is out on LaSalle Avenue.

Well people, I guess that does it for this one. Expect a busy day to-morrow. I plan on basketball after chow and then we have our weekly movie - "George White's Scandals" - Huba Huba.

Of all things - it has just clouded up in the past hour or so and almost looks although we might have rain. Be good, people.

Lotsa Love, Frank

P.S. Sure is good to hear that Mike is home again and seems almost good as new. F.

Tuesday, March 5

Dear Mother, Harry and Mike,

Well, as per usual there is not much to report. We have done little beyond working yesterday and today. Monday it turned chilly here again so we have not been in the pool since Saturday. Sunday we had a great deal of wind and a bit of rain. Last night we had our usual U.S.O. movie and after that the boys went to town to play basketball. They lost their first game last night. It will do them good I think for they were getting just a bit cocky.

Tonight we are going into town to the movie. It is going to be the "Picture of Dorian Gray" which is reputed to be pretty good so I guess we will make that one. As I see it, the work here has been generally caught up and we're just doing small pick-up jobs now. I do not think they intend to ship us back to March Field and that is that. I'm not too anxious to get back myself since I only have a couple months more to go I may just as well weather it here - getting to the point where I had to move about and start all over again a phenomenon which is so characteristic of the Army.

I had a bit of a "run in" with the Major yesterday but aside from he and the Warrant Officer being on my tail all day today I guess nothing will come of it. He pulled an old Army trick on us by having us move some equipment a couple miles one day and bring it back a few days later. I wouldn't have minded if the stuff had been light but I figured someone might get hurt every time we had to handle it so I called him on it and he didn't like it too well. At any rate, he went with me this morning and inspected the last area on the field and it came through with flying colors so that was that.

Well people, I reckon that just about covers it for this one. I'm alive and well and leading a very sterile but healthy life here at God's last outpost - Blythe. Be good. Lotsa Love, Frank

Thursday, March 7

Dear Mother, Harry and Mike,

I guess I'd best toss this one off in a hurry. You see I'm off to town this evening (I think) to play ball with the boys on the Post here against the local High School team. We leave in a few minutes so I'll try to scratch this off in a hurry so I can mail it in town.

Today I received that great big box you fellows sent on the 2nd and also your two cards. I knew you'd remember of course and I was very glad to get your two cards - a day ahead to be sure but I couldn't wait to open the box. The eatables sure have gone over swell - that candy is of the variety I enjoy eating. But what really went over was the shorts and tee shirts - outa this world - what I mean. The handkerchiefs were swell, too, but the underclothes were the cat's meow.

We went into town last night to see the "Picture of Dorian Gray" - it was unusual to say the least and we enjoyed it. We took some time off this afternoon to practice basketball.

Well people, I quit here when they called me in the supply room to throw a suit at me and then we went into town on the bus to play the local high school. Ka-runch but was I ever sad! I wouldn't feel so bad if they'd razz me a bit but no one even had the heart to do that I guess. I didn't get in but for about 4 or 5 minutes but I stunk to profusion and tire easily. I guess my 25 years as of to-morrow are showing in my wind and stamina. Basketball was always one game I felt I could have played had I played more of it. Frankly, the only reason I went out for it was that the other night, when the boys lost their first game, they had only 6 players, so they all had to play almost the whole game. I figured maybe if the other lads weren't going to help out I at least could play well enough to keep the other fellows from scoring while the stars rested. I haven't played, of course, in 7 years or more and can't expect to be much after a couple practice sessions. At any rate, I'll stay with it till they throw me out - Huba Huba. We had a shake after the game and I'm very ready to hit the old sac now.

Thanks a million again people for the swell birthday box - it was grand and greatly appreciated. Be good.

Lotsa Love, Frank

Saturday, March 9 - 10 PM

Dear Mother, Harry and Mike,

Well, here I am on good old Saturday night. There was quite a Hubbub yesterday. It seems that Wing (321st) Inspectors arrived on the field and everyone scurried around to be out of the way and to have things in readiness. The upshot of the whole thing was that we got an "excellent" on the field - the first items they inspected were in such good shape that they gave up trying to find anything wrong and left very shortly after lunch. As a result, the Major gave us today off and we have enjoyed it in a lazy manner.

I got up for chow and spent my morning at ping pong, pool, and swimming myself. This afternoon I finished a book I had hanging fire and then joined everyone else at the swimming pool. I hope I didn't get too much sun - just listen to me gloat - I judge that weather at home is either slushy or cold. It is just beginning to get warm here and I mean really warm. I expect I'll be complaining of the heat in 3-4 weeks.

In answer to Mother's of the 4th about the mail, I did get a couple letters forwarded from March Field but I never realized I had so many coming that I didn't get. I often wonder how you are getting my letters from Blythe since the system on it going out is nondescript to say the least. They have a poor system for getting our letters out and half the time you can't be too sure of that. I very much appreciated the birthday box and to me it was very satisfactory. Thanks a million for laying the ground work for me on the Parker 51. I sure do miss the one I had. Please do not work on it too hard unless you are already committed too far to stop it. I asked you not to get me one because I figured that they might come through the PX one of these days and I'd get one a good deal cheaper than you fellows could. If they don't come through I should be able to get one by the time I get home. I'd hate terribly to have one and then lose it again while I'm in the Army. I want to get the pencil with the next one I get too. The pen I have is plenty good enough until I get home. Please do send the overcoat on to Blythe. What is the latest poop on my watch - I certainly need it and miss it down here. Heaven knows I should write the Otts, but I don't seem to be able to get down to writing here - why it is such a hard chore I don't really understand unless it is because nothing seems to happen here that would be of any interest to anyone who, outside of those who have someone in the Army, care what happens to G.I.s now anyway.

I did go to town for a short while this evening - didn't even have a beer! One of the boys and myself went to Confession and returned early and he is in the sac now and I'm not far behind him. It makes me sad to hear that my boy Mike is becoming aged but that is the trouble with dogs. You lavish so much affection on them and enjoy their company so much and they live so comparably short a span of years. He is such a lover is our Mike - I'm forever showing his pictures and bragging about him.

Well folksies, I guess that is about 30 for this one. Be good.
Lotsa Love, Frank

Tuesday, March 11

Dear Mother, Harry and Mike,

I missed last night because I went to the basketball game. I didn't play but 4-5 minutes but at least I was there if they had needed me. We won again last night but for a while it looked pretty bad for of course since we have lost only one game everybody in town would like to see us get it on the chin including the local referees and umpires. We had a couple beers after the game and then hit the sac. We have been getting up these mornings quite early - that is 5 of us. We get permission from the Major to take a vehicle into town each morning to make 7 o'clock Mass so we have been trying to make it during Lent. We can only go 5 mornings a week in Blythe but we thought it would be O.K. if we could make it then. Most of us are not giving up anything and it seemed logical to try to get to Mass each morning instead. We have a time getting around about breakfast and making our first formation but we manage although it is a chore getting some of the brood up. I made Communion Sunday and yesterday but had some breakfast this morning.

I have been feeling pretty lazy the past couple days and I think it is because of a cold I picked up here - of all things. The boys turned on the air conditioning the *other day and the draft is what did it I'm sure. It is just in my head but darned uncomfortable because of so much dust around.*

We have been working about as per usual and getting more things done which all contributes to the eventual closing of things here at Blythe.

They took all our K.P. boys here for discharge today so that leaves us without and we'll have to do it ourselves from now on. They want to get men to do it as a permanent detail and believe it or not I volunteered. I talked with the 1st Sgt. and the Warrant Officer who is adjutant here but they won't let me take it - say it would never do to have a S/Sgt. on K.P. sooo I took it to the Major and he said he'd think it over so as yet I haven't the final word on it. The reason I want it is because I have discovered there is a good deal in town. They are now packing melons in there and the pay is very good and on K.P. you get a schedule of 2 days on and 2 days off so I would stand a chance of making myself a piece of change. I could sure use it because out here I can't save a nickel and seem to have a time keeping even, so I would have appreciated a chance to pick up something extra. I don't think they are going to let me have it - the stinkers!

Well people, I guess that is about all the poop. Can't think of anything more to-night people so I guess that is all for this one. Be good.
Lotsa Love, Frank

Thursday, March 14

Dear Mother, Harry and Mike,

Well, here I am at it again. Not a great deal to say as per usual. Yesterday we had quite a celebrity here on the base - she blew in on a plane quite similar to those we flew at radio school. It was Jacqueline Cochran who is about the most noted woman flyer in the U.S. today. Amelia Earhart is about the only gal to ever eclipse her fame and I guess she has done far more than Amelia ever did. She and her party were forced down here yesterday afternoon by a rather bad wind storm. She evidently has a good sized estate in Indio about 90 miles from here and asked the Major for a Staff car to take her and her party to Indio. The Major stalled around on the score so she said she'd call General Spaatz in Washington and arrange it and he broke like a rotten limb then and she sure as hell got her car.

The weather here has cooled a great deal and it has been very windy, which makes it darned uncomfortable at times with all the sand and dryness around here.

Mom, you say "things are not too bright." They seem worse now than ever. Personally, I would much rather get at the job now and complete it rather than be called back in a year or so. We will never be in better shape to take on Russia and if we must do it - let's do it now. I have no patience with appeasement - they must see things fairly and renounce this imperialistic trend - we'll never lick 10-20 years from now.

It is a temptation to go to town this evening I'll say that but as usual there is nothing to do there besides drink and maybe get mixed up with some of the local gals and I can't see much future in that but it is beginning to be quite a temptation.

We got to Mass this morning and will be on deck again in the morning. We have quite a system now - we've been eating before going, which is not any good for going to Communion but is much better for our not screwing up the Army routine about here.

I guess that is about it people - will try to write Al but don't know what I'll use for ideas.

Lotsa Love, Frank

P.S. Cold is improving although the dust around doesn't help much.

Sunday, March 17

Dear Mother, Harry and Mike,

And a verra verra (sic) Happy St. Pat's day to you too. Here we are on Sunday and it is a pleasantly lazy day - quite warm but not so much as to be uncomfortable. Last night we all went into town all steamed up for the finest local den of iniquity was opening - "The Tijuana." It is really a very nicely set up place - the Falls has nothing as nice and mind you Blythe has a population of but 2,000. How the hell they expect to keep it open is far beyond me with Phoenix 165 miles one direction and Indio 98 miles the other direction being the two closest communities. We all went down to the place last night but when the "Troops" got there we found there was a $2.40 admission charge to get in so we all turned about and went back to our old 25¢ beer joint. Returned to the base early and hit the sac and made 9 o'clock Mass this AM.

As per usual, not very much is going on here abouts. Came back after Mass and coffee at the drug store and played basketball until chow time and since chow I have been badly beaten at ping pong and now I am writing.

Acccording to Harry's letter of the 13th, which I received this morning, things sure are popping at the Carbo - when do you take over Tony's job Harry?

Gosh people, I don't know what to tell you, no how - may go in swimming this PM and later this evening may try the Tijuana for dancing if the $2.40 charge has ceased to exist. I am fine - having a dull time - no doubt about that, but leading a good healthy Peace Time G.I. existence. Be good, people.

Lotsa Love, Frank

Tuesday, March 19

Dear Mother, Harry and Mike,

I well realize that my last few communiqués have been nothing more than putrid but all I can do is beg off on the fact that not much happens about here. I told you of the opening of the Tijuana so one of the boys - Tom Sheehan (Polish) and I went in Sunday night to have another look. We got hold of a couple of the local belles but didn't dance there because they still wanted $2.40/person to dance. We went to another of the drinkerys. They had no beer there so Tom and I ordered a drink and the girls would have nothing. We no sooner got the drink than the waitress informed us that we would have to hurry with our drinks as the girls were minors (under 21) and could not stay. So then we proceeded to the only other decent bar in town - there is no dancing there but they had beer - they know the girls in there - won't serve them but don't throw them out. We had a beer - Tom and I - and then we had a bite to eat. Thence to where the girls live. This is good!

There are 6 of them who live in a place in Blythe by themselves. Their parents, as near as I can find out, all live in Blythe or in the vicinity but the gals have a place of their own. My guess is that the setup is strictly no good and that the fellows are taking one helluva chance going there for the civilians around here are sure jealous of their women and then (just my guess) I'll bet some of them may be kicking in for the rent and that sure complicates things. Lordy, what a drab outlook they must have here on life - classed as minors in all the local joints, all they talk of is drinking and carousing and the one I was with has been married three months - met the guy one day and married him the next. The one Tom was with has been married and divorced at 19. Cripes, what a mess. I left early and all the lads razzed me for I guess it is a sure thing, but I couldn't see it from any prospective whatsoever and believe me I'm not narrow minded and am as much tempted by a "go at it" as the next one. What an outfit! I don't know where they think their futures will take them or what they look forward to in life.

I guess I didn't tell you that one of our young hopefuls went into town the other night and spent the night in the local cooler with 14 Hispanics, who I hear did not smell too pleasant. He went into town with yours truly. We went to the library and got books. I came home and he stayed. It seems he got pretty well looped but at 12:30 was seen ordering a steak and he ate it. All's well up to this point and the bars (both of them) close at 12 but it seems he had to pass his water and proceeded into the main drag, whipped out the Brute and let her go. The local gendarmerie got him for indecent exposure and Mr. Brown went down in the morning and retrieved the culprit and now he is known as I.E. Warburton.

Last night we practiced basketball and then went to the U.S.O. movie in the day-room. This evening we went to town to play ball but the other team didn't show so they forfeited the game sooo we had a practice scrimmage and a beer later and now we're back at the sac.

I guess that takes in most of it for right now. We go to Midland to-morrow night to play ball - it is 22 miles from Blythe I guess. Be good.
Lotsa Love, Frank

March 21, Thursday

Dear Mother, Harry and Mike,

Well, it seems we have been quite busy at basketball of late. Monday night we practiced, Tuesday we were supposed to play and had only a scrimmage and we did play last night. I played almost a whole half last night and made 1 basket too. You see it was a push-over and we were all having a good time. We go to Midland 22 miles from Blythe to play our last game next week. Then we have only the play-offs left.

I got a swell three pager from Tess today - hers of the 18th. I don't like the sound of that delayed action ankle and I sure hope it is better now. Things like that are not good at all and worry me so be sure to let me know how it is feeling. By the way, don't let this paper worry you - I'm not in the hospital but safe (?) at B.A.A.B. but it is for free and saves me bringing any. Plenty of it around so I may as well be using it I figure.

Actually there is no particular rush about the overcoat - it is a damned bother to me as it must be to you but I'll have to turn it in so I may as well get it and get rid of it.

Speaking of cars, I have an opportunity to get a rather good deal out here with some luck. There have been a great many Air Bases closed down here and there are quite a few Staff cars available according to what my spies tell me. Some of these are still crated, not having been used at all. They are available for from 600-400 dollars - absolutely unused but of course they are painted olive drab. Chevys and Plymouths. You have to prove you will use one in a business to be eligible to buy one even as a G.I. but I think I can manage that easily enough out there since I have developed a connection or two. Tentatively you might let me know what you think of the situation. Even if you don't plan to use it much, you would have a good deal to turn in on a new car as you pointed out Mom.

We have been making Mass O.K. but they didn't have it Monday so we had an extra morning to get that extra hour sleep.

Things must be rough all right at Carbo - it is terrible to have to work under a strain like that - kinda like the old days, what? Some change from a couple years ago!

I'm glad the weather is going fine at home. It makes such a difference there whereas here it is more or less taken for granted, although it has been quite cool here of late.

I guess I told you that my "position" of responsibility is gone and I only have 5 men now. I'm happier that way and still have my Jeep. I work hard with the rest of the boys in the good old sun all day and let them refer their bitches to the orderly room.

No, we don't have any doctor here - only a Medic, but he gave me some sulfa compound - only 2 applications of 2 drops in each nostril and believe me that cold was gone but good. I must find out just what that stuff is - never experienced anything like it in my life.

I plan to get a box ready to ship out to you people to-morrow night. Nothing much in it except stuff I want to get rid of anticipating my coming release - (eligible for discharge in about 40 days you know) so I may as well be getting sorta ready. I don't want a lot of stuff hanging around at the last minute don't ya know.

Well I guess that takes in most of it for this one people - be good.
Lotsa Love, Frank

Sunday, March 24

Dear Mother, Harry and Mike,

Greetings from the Palo Verde Valley. At last I have something to report of a little more definite nature. The Warrant Officer, who is second in command here, has left and in honor of his parting it was decided to throw a bit of a party. This parting co-incided nicely with the delivery here of Squadron Entertainment Funds from March Field. Sooo we had a party with free beer and fried chicken - of that at least we were sure. I went over to the dayroom about 7:30 and it looked like it would be a very dull affair so I started in on the beer with a vengeance. We had moved a piano from the Chapel to the dayroom earlier in the day and one of the boys plays quite well so we had some music. As I say, the aspect was dull - who the hell wants to party with a bunch of men but then the local talent from the town started to arrive and it wasn't bad at all. The gals brought a recording outfit borrowed from Blythe's 5 & 10¢ store - and all of their little selves of course.

I tried a little of a few of them and wound up with a rather luscious blonde. I was fairly well looped and of course had that glint in my eye and what the Scotchman had too. Anyway, I was having a splendid time and then of course it came about time for the gals to go home. They climbed into their Olds but of course I was in no mood to let them go. It just happened (get that one) that I had my Jeep parked in an out of the way place and also that I happened to have a key to the main gate so I let them out and offered to drive little Jeanie home in the Jeep. She accepted with a vengeance so I took her home with more vengeance and me under the influence too. I was mighty sober by that time anyway. It was the first time I ever drove a girl home from a dance and - I like it. It was lucky I didn't get caught with the Jeep off the base - that would have been curtains but good, but I made it back O.K. and hit the sac with a smug satisfied feeling (in my mind only!). It was a good party and was the first time I'd ever been to an Army affair where my rank helped any. Maybe it wasn't that but for some reason the lads left me strictly alone with any of the girls I was with and razzed hell out of me yesterday for not settling down to work on one sooner. The Major and his wife were there. She is considerably younger than he and the lads had her out there cutting a rug with the best of them. It was a good party all right and I think everyone had a good time. The consensus of opinion is now that we should chip in a couple bucks a piece, a couple times a month, and do more of the same more often.

Yesterday one of the boys had a sun stroke out here and it was an abject lesson to all of us. He is a buddy of mine and he sure was a wreck for about 6 hours. He seems O.K. today but is still as weak as a kitten - all 6 feet 2" of him.

We spent most of the afternoon standing by with him - the Medic was in town and could not be found.

Last night I went to Confession and [to] Communion this morning, and stopped in to say hello to aforementioned Blonde. We got back early and hit the sac.

This afternoon a group of the girls are driving out here to have a go at the swim-ming pool so I suppose we'll spend the afternoon at the pool admiring the contours of the Desert Flowers.

The Otts sent me two boxes of Fanny Farmer Candy, which I received yesterday. I suppose I'd best write and thank them today but probably won't get to it until this evening.

Well, I guess that takes in most of it my dears. Oh yes I got a note the other day from lil old Frances in Riverside asking me to call when I next hit Riverside so I guess that is on the fire again. I'll have to see if I ever get back to March again. That's it for this one people. Be good.

Lotsa Love, Frank

March 28, Thursday

Dear Mother, Harry and Mike,

I'll be trying to get this one off during the lunch hour. I received coat yesterday all O.K. - thanks and also received your (Mother's letter of the 25) latest yesterday, which needless to say I was glad to get. If the watch isn't O.K. now, I guess you'd best keep it for since I've not had it this long I guess I can manage O.K. without it for another month or so.

This week has been kinda busy - not so much on the work side but in the evenings. Monday we played ball - I managed to play a half and scored 6 points, which was superb for me. The score was 41-9 in our favor. Our last game is tonight and if we win it, there will be no play-off since we will have won both the 1st and 2nd half of the league. Don't think I'll be playing much tonight because the team we're playing is pretty good and they keep the 1st string in for that.

After Evening Chow

Well, I fear I shall have to hurry this just a bit since we have a ball game in town this evening and also I have discovered I have to take a group of fellows who are about to be discharged to March Field to-morrow at about 8:30 AM so I'll be driving about 4-5 hours to-morrow and don't know whether I'll have to be back to-morrow or not.

The big news broke here today that a group of Chinese Cadets will be here on Monday. After closing the base almost completely we now have to open portions of it up again. They will have to bring planes in as well as communications, weather, and aircraft repair equipment and personnel.

That is really going to bring a lot of changes here and I'm glad I'll only be here about another month - it really ought to be good while it lasts. They will have to open all these places we have closed and get back much of the equipment that has been shipped out - such a business!

Well people, I guess that is about it for today. So lil old Donnette went the way of all flesh. I never did get her out of my system, but I guess it would be a good idea now eh? Felt no earthquake here but we have been having nasty wind storms, which are only dust and sand storms out here. That takes in most of it folksies so, be sure and be good.

Lotsa Love, Frank

Saturday, March 30

Dear Mother, Harry and Mike,

I am writing you with a new Parker 51 I purchased last night for $7.25 at the PX. You never told me that you canceled your order on the one you people were going to get me so I'll rush this missive along immediately. As you can see I got it at a considerable saving as compared to what your fellows would have had to pay - by the time you paid the tax - a little less than half is my guess.

I went to March Field yesterday in the Staff car - I had one of the other fellows drive both ways. We had to take 4 lads down for discharge and then we had quite a few items to take care of for Headquarters here. We were busier than a cat on a tin roof and the whole trip could certainly not be put in the pleasure category. We had to pick up Warrant Officer Brown, who was formerly adjutant here and bring him to Blythe. It was a deal cooked up here so he can get to be with his wife here in Blythe each week-end and that's the way the taxpayer's money goes. I'll say this though - we certainly would have had a time of it with that Plymouth if we had not had to pick up Brown.

After hearing from both of youse guys on the car situation I'll say just this: I'm very glad that both of you feel the way I do about it however, to get the thing will not be easy but I will have a try at it. I do not feel qualified to attempt to buy any car other than a brand new one or one with a couple thousand miles on it. Having been in the Army, I know how these vehicles are treated and anyone would be a fool to take anything other than a new one. I have laid the ground work for proving that I will use a car in my business, which will be an electrical repairman out here. So much for that - I'll write Harry necessary instructions to cover my leaving with the car as soon as I get it but Do Not plan on it. I believe it worth a try and will make one but any little slip can queer the deal so until I wire home for the money. I'll write the necessary letter requesting withdrawal of money when I think things are beginning to break. The whole thing is merely a shot in the dark but it is certainly worth a try.

We lost our big ball game the other night. The M/Sgt. who manages the team was back from furlough and put in our best boys and let them play the whole game. The other 4 of us didn't get in at all, which didn't make me tear my hair, but it was too bad for we were ready to go at any time and while we certainly are not the players the 1st string are we might have held the "Alfalfa Growers" (how about that?) in check a while so that the stars could catch a bit of a rest. As it was, the boys were so tired in the last quarter that when they got the ball they didn't know what the hell to do with it. It was a crying shame. After the game a couple of the local gals, well, three or four of them, took us to a bar and they bought the beers since we were all broke.

I guess that about brings us up to date people. Don't' know for sure whether I'll be going to town tonight or not. Be good, people.

Lotsa Love, Frank

April 1946

April 2, Tuesday

Dear Mother, Harry and Mike,

As per usual, I have not a great deal to report from dear old Blythe. We played ball last night - it was a close, rough game and we lost. It was finally decided by the League members that Army won the tournament so we are Champs but we have lost to one of the teams and play the 2nd in a 2 out of three series tonight - for fun I guess. I'll be glad when it is over, which quite probably will be tonight.

We got paid last evening by check but I didn't cash mine last night. I had a few beers on the returns of what some of the lads owed me and called it a night. We all went in at noon time and cashed the monthly stipend.

Today ground crews arrived by C-47 for the Chinese cadets who as yet have not come. There were only about 25 of them I think - all regular Army and mostly all Tech and Master Sgts. To me they are a pretty crummy looking outfit and I'm glad I don't have to be around in this Man's Army much longer.

I'll be without my Jeep for some time now since it is badly in need of repairs. Also, I have no idea how this new influx of men will affect my having a Jeep at all, as I'm afraid will be the case. It needs a new muffler, spring and radiator. All these things happen to it when the laddy bucks sneak off with it over the week-ends when I'm not driving it. Glad to say none of its trouble is any result of my driving it.

This new mess of men no doubt will make quite a difference in the town situation and I doubt that many of us will journey there quite as often as has been our practice.

Well dears, I guess I have given you all the new poop from here. Have to be getting ready for our last game this evening. Be good, people.
Lotsa Love, Frank

Saturday, April 6

Dear Harry,

I send this to the office for your immediate information in reply to the questions you have asked me and to put you straight on what I expect the coming month to bring.

Foremost and primarily of course is my discharge - God willing - which should come off early in May by virtue of the fact that with overseas service, I enjoy 1st priority before men with dependants who are merely service. I expect to leave Blythe on about the 27th or 28th of this month and report to March Field. If experience of personnel leaving here last month and the month before are any criterion, I should be on orders by the 5th and discharged by the 10th of May. I am applying for discharge at Camp Beale, which is 60-80 miles north of Frisco. The point in this is to collect travel pay at $.03/mile to Camp Beale and also travel pay from Beale to home at $.05 per mile if I'm lucky, which should amount to over 100 dollars. Also, due to the large number of air bases and ground camps here in California, I must stand at least a possibility of getting a car here whereas at home anything that did exist at a base has long since been deactivated and the surpluses disposed of long since.

Bear in mind that discharge must come first before I can move on the car. I have to present my discharge papers to get a certificate of eligibility to buy any surplus property. On top of that, I shall have to prove a definite need in my job in civilian life for a car to get. I have two different fellows lined up who will give me letters stating that I need a car in a job they are offering me. These letters, one of them, should turn the trick but I may have trouble getting the right connections since both these guys have left for discharge and will return to separate businesses here at Blythe and in L.A. One is the electrical line - wiring houses, installing fixtures etc. and the other in L.A. is the installation of window frames and sashes in buildings in L.A. If I actually did work for either, I would need a car in the work not merely as transportation to and from a place of business, which is not considered sufficient need. Either of these two possibilities failing I would apply for a job in L.A. in the selling line somewhere and then get any prospective employer to write a letter that a car was necessary on the job.

Of course, the actual deal would be that I would never work at the job and upon receipt of a telegram from the Falls would have to proceed directly home - with the car.

As you can see there are a lot of hitches involved and if the thing rolls along smoothly, I'd be willing to sacrifice a week or two in starting from California in order to get the car, however if I should run into too much trouble even at the outset, I am not going to fool around out here when I belong home and want to be there especially now. As I said at the outset, the idea was tentative and it looks like about the best automobile deal to me in the country. I don't want you to get too worked up about it. I will do my best and if it goes smoothly we'll have one - I know I could get one out here if I were willing to spend a month fooling with it but I am not and it would be too expensive to live out here anyway without working somewhere and I won't start that! It would be a good idea if you would forward to me some idea of just what kind of letter I would have to write in order to get my money out here through that Power of Attorney. Please let me know immediately on that score. You can be sure I'll do my best at any rate.

Thursday afternoon another fellow and I drove a truck to March Field and returned yesterday afternoon. We split the driving and Thursday evening I took lil old Frances to a movie and we fooled around a while afterward. She is teaching school now - a kindergarten - and likes it. I got back yesterday at 4:30 PM only to find that my job has been changed and I'm now Sgt. of the Guard. It involves 24 hours on and 48 hours off, which is nice but I sure as hell was annoyed when I discovered that I had to start last night. Part of the job is taking the lads to town and picking them up. You should have seen me wheeling that bus in and out of town a couple times last night. I sure as hell couldn't drive when I got out here but it won't be the Army's fault if I can't drive when I leave. I have been quite tired all day and got almost no sleep last night so I doubt that I'll be going into town this evening.

Well Kiddo, I guess that brings us up to date. Be good.

Lotsa Love, Frank

April 9, Tuesday

Dear Mother, Harry and Mike,

Well, how are youse all today? I just got off my 24 hour guard trick and I'm tired. I should have written last night but it is a bit hard to work it in on the job.

Sunday we had a fairly good time. After Mass we had our usual stop for coffee and met a couple of the local gals there who come out to the pool Sundays. They asked us if we wanted to go to Palm Springs to see a Rodeo - the same one that plays Madison Square Garden in N.Y.C. We said of course, of course, and the two gals picked 4 of us up in front of the main gate at about 1 PM. It is about a 150 mile drive and I drove about 100 miles of it on the way down in a '40 Ford - Lotsa Fun! We saw the Rodeo and then stopped for a few drinks and dinner in Palm Springs and returned - it was different anyway.

As per usual, there is not much new around here. Of late, we have had some intruders on the other side of the base. They have been breaking into the buildings and taking out the window sashes and cleaning out the mess halls and hospital units of anything they could move sooo some of the lads will mount guard this evening at 4 hour tricks. I don't envy them.

One of my buddies and I have an invitation to dinner - a home cooked meal tomorrow evening so I suspect we'll be cleaning and pressing & getting ready on the morrow. Also have another invitation for a Sunday chicken dinner next Sunday - Karunch - are we ever a social success in Blythe!

No new poop on discharges people, just that the time draws nearer and it keeps lookin better all the time.

Well folks, I guess that is about it. It is not 7 PM yet but I'll not be long out of the dear old sac. Be good, people.
Lotsa Love, Frank

April 11, Thursday

Dear Mother, Harry and Mike,

Haven't heard from you in a couple days so will not seal this one in the envelope until I check the morning mail at noon time. Things have been popping around here in some respects during the past couple days. It seems that a band of culprits have been entering the base at points out on the desert with a truck and systematically going to work on the barracks and mess halls. They have been getting off with anything that moves, even the window sashes in the buildings. I was scheduled for dinner in town, which put me in a bit of a position because Guard Duty is a very touchy thing if you don't know it and I finally got one of the lads to take it for me for a few hours. We didn't stay long in town - after dinner, took them for a drink and a couple dances and met a truck, which came in to get us at 9:30. I think the girls were sore, but that is tough. Cy had to go on guard under a new setup - armed and in Jeeps trying to catch the thieves when they came in again. A bunch of us had to work in that direction last night and that was the reason we had to leave town so early.

Things really popped when the Sheriff's men informed us that the invading truck had been on base 3 hours at about 12:30. The civilians were guarding possible exits from the camp and we got the rest of the G.I.s out on trucks and covered more of them only to have the report qualified later that truck in question had approached the base but had been scared off by something so that was that and I finally made it to the sac at 3:30 AM - had to get up early of course and I'm tired right now.

Yesterday morning three of us went into town and got ourselves a job - 3 of us who are working this 1 on and 2 off deal - work is for the Irrigation Co. at Blythe so we're going in to-morrow morning to try it - we sure don't have to work if we don't like it. The way they spoke - 3 of us will be working together and one of the guys has a car to lug us back and forth so we shouldn't be too badly off. Might as well do something with that time off. Well people, I guess that about does it for this one. Be good.
Lotsa Love, Frank

Sunday, April 14

Dear Mother, Harry and Mike,

I should have written earlier but didn't so here I am rather late this evening and my sac looks very inviting. I have been a busy boy this past few days to say the least. Three of us started to work for the Palo Verde Irrigation Co. last Friday afternoon. We started out helping one of the Engineers but that was merely to keep us busy. We started to work with a pick and shovel gang Saturday. Only there are no picks in this outfit. They have these large irrigation channels out here to water the desert and they are often bored through - that is the walls - by large rats. This causes a break in the wall, which has to be filled in. And that is what we are doing. Sorta the keepers of the Dikes. We shovel dirt and sand onto a truck all day long and it is really quite a racket. It is not too hard and we make 85¢ per hour, which is what we are after mainly.

Today we had an invitation to a Chicken Roast and we went with a vengeance. I was supposed to be working but I got one of the married lads to guard the phone and I drove the lads down and back on the bus. It was really good - deep pan fried chicken like I've never eaten before. The WE pertains to all the lads who frequent town and they welcomed any of the soldiers who cared to come. I guess there were 12-15 of us. We had a good time all right. The home belonged to the Aunt and Uncle of the only gal who works here on the base and it was down on the farm all right. Later - after the dishes were finished up, we brought the bunch back and went swimming - later the girls bought a couple cases of beer at the PX for all of us. It is hard to understand the women out here, but in a way you can't help but feel for them in some ways. There is a very considerable shortage of available eligible fellows and those who are around are hardly what they want after associating with the varied personalities who have been here at the base for the past 3-4 years. They sure understand us and that we're broke much of the time and they try to make up for the money we spend on them in all sorts of ways and we all have fun. You have to be very careful with them though, because they're all after husbands and that ain't good.

I certainly should have written before about Easter and no doubt this will come too late but if you are not sending anything it is O.K. and just what I asked for. It is getting very warm down here and we have air conditioners going all day so I hope there will be nothing too perishable in a box if you have sent one. I still have the box I was going to send but don't have it quite full as yet - hope to get it off soon. It is just odds and ends I have accumulated while in the service and want to get rid of before I start pulling out. I guess that takes in most of it my dears - have to arise at 5:30 this AM for we work from 7 AM until 3:30. Be good, people.

Lotsa Love, Frank

Wednesday, April 17

Dear Mother, Harry and Mike,

And how are youse guys today? It is getting quite warm out here these days - I judge it will soon be unbearably warm and am glad at the prospects of leaving dear old Blythe in the not too distant future.

We worked for the Irrigation Co. Monday and Tuesday and today we're staying at the base. I guess we'll have another go at it Thursday. I was a tired pup yesterday but got about 10 hours sleep last night and am ready to go again today. Very little has happened around here of late and I hardly know what to write about.

We had two main schools of rumors here as to our discharge. The First Sgt. tells me we will be paid here at Blythe this month but that would make things kind of slow for getting out. The other school has as its promoter one of the boys who went to Classification at March Field and was told that discharges for April were way ahead of schedule and that we would be on our way to the Separation Base by the 1st of May so you can take your choice on that one.

Gosh folks - there is just nothing new to report - I am fine and at last this discharge business is beginning to get under my skin - I'm getting eager to be home and on the go. This working in town has got me adjusted already at least on the boss to worker relationship. It is a shame to waste an airmail stamp on this one but there is just nothing new - be good, people.

Lotsa Love, Frank

Saturday, April 20

Dear Mother, Harry and Mike,

Thanks muchly for the card and I was very glad to get a letter today and two yesterday. I don't write like I should, I know, but I have been busy getting my 8 or 9 hours of sleep each night because after working I get tired. It is good hardy work - this shoveling we're doing and we've had a good deal of fun doing it. We got in 4 days last week and hope to do the same this week.

No, I don't carry a gun except occasionally when we feel trouble is ahead and we've had no actual contact with the thieves as yet nor do I expect we will while I'm here. You'll be glad to hear I have a new buddy. I call her Brownie and she is the saddest hunk of Fox Terrier I've seen in ages. She looks like she had a family a short time ago and she follows me about like Miker only maybe more so. She is very scary and just showed up at the base a few days ago. I finally got close enough to pet her one morning when she followed me out to put up the flag. Of course I fed her and have been feeding her but I figured she was so scary that she'd never have any spunk but she looked so forlorn I just had to be nice to her. That evening when I went to sleep in the Guard Office, she wouldn't let anyone in until I quieted her down. Believe me, no one will sneak up on Francis George while Brownie is around.

Sunday

I stopped here yesterday afternoon. Last night we went to town and had a good time. We went to Confession and made Communion this morning. Yesterday some girls came from town to the swimming pool. Since I was Sgt. of the Guard, I went over and listened to the boys beef because they didn't know who the girls were and then pseudo-officially I gave the girls a hard time - getting their names and telling them that if they were coming out to the pool they would have to be guests of some G.I. - I made each one of them responsible to one of the fellows out here in an effort to get them acquainted. Anyway, we met them in town last evening - they are all home from college on Easter vacation - Blythe's "Culture Vultures." Of course, there is one in particular - Mercedes Mahoney (How's that) "Micky" for short. She is quite a gal - swell personality and that's not all. She's the daughter of (I think) one of the Board of Directors of the Irrigation Co. for which we've been working. She is taking Bacteriology at Mt. St. Mary's in L.A.- she went to Communion this morning too and then a bunch of us went to Rosie's house for breakfast. Father Loftus showed up a bit later. This afternoon they came swimming again and tonight we're having a Hamburger Roast or something out on the desert. We just brought a quarter of beef up from the warehouse and have yet to gut it up and grind it. I don't dare make this session too late this evening because I have to be up bright and early in the morning at my shovel. Well people, I guess that is all the poop for the present - I'll be looking for the box. Thanks a million for sending it.

Lotsa Love, Frank

Wednesday, April 24

Dear Mother, Harry and Mike,

Well dear people, I have been very muchly on the go of late, what with working and putting in my tour here at the base as Sgt. of the Guard. Today I should have worked but took the day off since I was a bit tired and since there are a few things I feel I must take care of here before I leave. We got some second hand poop last night that we'll be on orders to go to March Field by the end of this week so that doesn't leave much time. I don't know how authentic it is but one of the boys who is getting out drove to March yesterday and got the information from Classification. And so I am finally being prodded into finishing up many odds and ends I have let hang fire since I've been here.

I received your box yesterday along with the Otts and everybody was raising hell around here wondering if I'd had a birthday. It sure was a dandy one and there is a large hole in it right now. It all arrived in fine shape except [the] chocolate cake, which was on the bottom and slightly squashed but that sure didn't deter from the flavor - what I mean! The temperature has really been up here and has affected all our appetites but you sure wouldn't think it when my box arrived. I've got so much candy now I don't know what to do with it. That Easter egg was a nice touch people - I always did like to have one around Easter time.

Last night I had a good time doing a bit of dancing and a couple drinks in town. I was with the lads and the gals who were still home from college - they were supposed to have been back today but decided to stay the extra day - why - of course I couldn't say. They did leave this morning and have invited us to their Senior Dance at Mount St. Mary's in L.A. on the 4th but we couldn't really accept for we expect to be on the discharge train by then. If we are still at March Field though, we should be able to make it with little trouble.

We have had a fine time with these girls - it is a shame we didn't get to know them sooner but that's the way it goes. You just really begin to get situated when you're leaving - worse luck. All the kids in town call the girls the "Culture Vultures" for there are few of them in town who have managed to get to college. It's a good thing I'm leaving here I guess because this Micky Mahoney I've been playing around with is really nice people. They have a grand home and she has very nice people. She is as Irish as Paddy's Pig and lots of personality and that's not all. She has a Civil Service appointment to the County Hospital in L.A. in the Lab when she graduates in June. She has about everything I've looked for in a girl to say nothing of two cars in the family.

Well people, I must be getting off now. We are all getting our clothes set to get out of here and I'd best be at it myself. Be good, people and thanks again for the box. Lotsa Love, Frank

April 25, Thursday

Dear Mother, Harry and Mike,

Well, how are you all today? We got the latest poop on discharge today upon the Major's return from March Field. We will not leave here until the 1st or 2nd of May and will be paid here, which brings things a bit later than we had planned but things are rolling no question about that.

Yesterday I shipped home a box by Express - cost me $4.20 - probably the stuff in it is not worth that but there are 4 lbs. of brown sugar in the box - hope it comes in handy. Also, yesterday I applied for a job selling - the product is venetian blinds and the pay is a flat $35/week + commissions - liberal ones they say and the territory is about 1,000 square miles. Of course I must have a car. I have to see the Wheel as yet and I hope he approves of me. I think they are very anxious to get someone to take it.

We have been shipping out beds here, which have been brought by civilians. It seems the truck drivers have been trying to steal various items from hangars - etc. and we caught them. We have been standing armed guard over the vehicles and I don't know what the hell will happen but we'll probably find out around 12 or 1 AM tonight when the manager of the truck co. is due to arrive from L.A. to straighten things out.

I am trying to gradually get myself set for discharge as far as my clothes are concerned. We worked today and intend working only one more day - Saturday.

Been having lots of fun fooling around lately with John Serway who lives in Utica, N.Y. He plays piano quite well and he plays orchestrations and I sing or try to sing them - we have a big time no question about that.

Received letters from Mrs. OH and Al Bealy today - guess those will be the last I'll answer from Blythe. When you get a letter saying I'm leaving Blythe I guess you fellows can stop the splendid job of writing you've been doing for almost 2 1/2 years. I'll be on the move then and I doubt that your letters would catch me. One thing I'll promise you is that I'll write or telegraph each day while I'm on the move to let you know what is cooking and how I'm making out and the telegrams will be sent from places where I'll be staying over long enough to get a reply from you if sent immediately. As ever, I don't want to miss anything. I guess that's it for today people - can't think of anymore poop to pass on to you.
Lotsa Love, Frank

April 2(?), Sunday

Dear Mother, Harry and Mike,

Well, at last I have some definite news to give you. This is what we have all been waiting for. We are on orders to report to Camp Beale for discharge on the 4th of May. We will be paid here Tuesday and go by bus to March Field Wednesday morning at 8 AM. We have to clear the field there and then we'll be all set to proceed to Beale. It may take a day to get cleared of March Field and I estimate "out" about the 7th so after I do some snooping about a car I'll be home as fast as I can get there safely. I think Harry's idea of not writing is O.K. although I do want letters. It would be best not to write. I'll write or telegraph every day so you'll know of my whereabouts. I'll include specific address where you can telegraph me when I'll be at some place where you can telegraph back if there is some necessity. I will not expect telegrams from you just for fun or even for peace of mind but will check all places feasible just prior to leaving any address I send you. I will not be alone. I will be with Cyril (Cy) Vaska a 6 foot 3" Czech who can take care of himself and me too. I will take no chances anywhere. My foremost purpose is to get home to my most loved ones as soon as I can. Cy lives in Cleveland and will be with me till there through any roaming part of the journey home. My money will be in travelers checks and I shall send duplicate numbers to you in case I should lose them. The only delay will be the car business. There has been a big stink here lately because Veterans are not getting any break on war surpluses however I think many are being discouraged from buying and I mean to make an honest try. If it is too much of a time waster I'll let it go and perhaps try in N.Y. State.

Harry - if I wire you at the office that I am inquiring as to Mother's health - have prepared a telegram stating terse concern of Mother's health due to the fact that I have decided to remain and work in "California." Demand that I return home immediately. Don't state any locality out here. You will know then that I have a car - insured, and a full tank of gas and am waiting only your answer to hit the road. Save any telegrams I send you. I have a good many problems yet to take care of concerning clothing transportation to Beale etc. but I don't expect any difficulties there. I shall be sending things home right along now. Since I am here I'll get a chance to keep most of my clothes and they may come in handy in civilian life. I think that covers most of it people. I'll have to do a lot of canoodling on my own but there is no sense in boring you people with it. You can be sure I'll keep in touch with you in any event. I'd almost give my right arm to stop in L.A. on the way to Beale to see Mr. Mahoney's pride and joy where she is in school at Mt. St. Mary's but we won't have time I'm afraid.

I guess that is it for today people. Be good.

Lotsa Love, Frank

May 1946

Wednesday, May 1st

Dear Mother, Harry and Mike,

Huba Huba - here I am in keeping with my general information policy. Last night Cy and I decided we had a bad case of ants in our pants and we would jump the gun on getting to March Field. We started to thumb on the Godforsaken desert road and landed in Riverside at 1 AM after starting at 8:45. Not bad for 2 hitches to go 175 miles eh, what? The first ride was on the back of a truck and very cold since all we had on were Sun Tans so we voluntarily abandoned that ride at the first cafe in the desert 43 miles from camp. We were about five minutes getting another ride, which took us right into Riverside - very good luck I'd say.

We cleared the field today and would have been on our way this evening except that they screwed up on our orders and now we won't be able to get going till probably 9 or 10 AM to-morrow. All day they were going to let us have our records but we haven't got them as yet.

We are going to get to Beale as quickly as possible and waiting to start on the 2nd to be there the 4th is not as good as we had hoped for but we are ahead because the bus that brought the boys down today broke down and the fellows who waited to come on it are a whole day behind us now. We could have ill afforded to lose that extra day planning to thumb as we are. Of course if our luck runs out we can always grab a bus but it would be nice to save the dough for other things if possible. What am I doing in Riverside this evening? As if you didn't know. I've got a final date with lil ol Frances and although she's not "number one" out here anymore, she's very nice people and she wrote she wanted to see me "one more time."

Well folks, I guess that is it for this one. I can't think of any more pertinent poop to tell you in this one so this will have to do it I guess. I expect we'll be held up at Beale over the week-end - it's good for going to church but hell on the time schedule. The next you hear should be from on the road - be good, people.

Lotsa Love, Frank

Telegram: May 4

DEAR FOLKS ARRIVED BEALE YESTERDAY MORNING. EXPECT DISCHARGE MONDAY. IF NECESSARY CAN BE REACHED AT WEST-ERN UNION CAMP BEALE CALIF LOVE = FRANK

Return Address:
S/Sgt. F.G. Thompson
Camp Beale
Separation Center Sect #2
Calif.

Saturday, May 4 D (discharge)-Day minus 2

Dear Harry, Mother and Mike,

Wow - did you notice how I screwed up that salutation - ah well - just a bit excited I guess. I'm going to endeavor to give you an idea of the jaunt so far and then tell you my expectations so I'd best get at it. I just sent a telegram - cost $2.56 - that old stuff will have to cease.

The night I wrote you from Riverside I went out with Frances we had a grand time. We danced a while, then took a ride in some electric boats they have in an artificial lake there. This was really O.K. - they are comfortable and all have radios in them - what a place to get in a little lovin. Later we took in a carnival for an hour or so. I finally arrived at camp at 3:30 AM. Up next morning at 6:30 - coffee'd up and stood in line to get our records. Upon receipt of records still had to clear Finance & Transportation. We thumbed into Riverside had more coffee - got O.D.s pressed and finally started for L.A. Made L.A. in about 3-4 hitches stopping at Ontario for lunch at about 11 AM. Upon hitting L.A. we made our way to Mines Field to try to get a plane to Frisco. They told us they would put us on the next day but we decided it was too much of a chance and this Beale Formation was one we weren't anxious to miss or be late for, so we returned to L.A. proper and took a street car out to main artery, which went through Sacramento and Marysville.

On San Fernando Blvd., it took us 4 hitches to get just outside Glendale and then it was beginning to get dark. We then hit some "shit-house" Irish luck. A fellow just out & his wife were going to Eugene, Oregon and stopped for us in a 41 Ford Club Coupe Convert. Sooo we rode all the way to Marysville with them. Arrived at 4:30 AM yesterday. Had coffee & breakfast in town and then hopped bus to camp. Ate breakfast again here. Had initial clothing check and initial record check yesterday. We have to stand by at barracks for processing lists now to start final processing, which takes about 36 hours. I expect to be a civilian again by Monday morning. The waiting now is just for our turn. Of course you can be turned back for any physical defects such as teeth, eyes, etc., but I think I'm grade A since while at Blythe - the time I took the Staff car down, I was checked at the hospital at my own request with an eye toward this business.

All the Desert Rats from Blythe have arrived and we're together and are sweating it out as well as possible under the circumstances. One of the lads from Berkley, Calif. has a station wagon here and will take Cy and me to Frisco or Sacramento or both on the car deal so that (either place) is next call from here. I'll let you know from day to day by airmail and by telegram when I'll be any place long enough to receive an answer, which I'll look for only in case of necessity on your part. Be good, people. God willing it won't be long now.

Lotsa Love, Frank

May 5, Sunday

Dear Mother, Harry and Mike,

I'd best start this one by stating that we managed to make 8:15 Mass this morning. I finally made a Processing Roster this morning and am about halfway through. I am scheduled to finish to-morrow at 1:30 PM and then I'll be a civilian again. All this of course if I don't get called back and although I don't know what I'd be called back on still you never know. Teeth were class "4," which means no repairs needed.

Three of us "The Desert Rats" leave here to-morrow probably around 6 PM for Berkley. Bob Warburton, who lives there, will drive us down and has invited us to stay overnight with his people there, which is very nice I think. In the morning we go to Frisco to investigate the car situation. At this point with information I can get here it is only honest to tell you people that the outlook is very drab, but I am determined to find out for myself. One thing I didn't know of before is that there is a waiting list for these cars and if this is true it makes the situation impossible from the California standpoint anyway.

If I am completely stumped early it will mean starting home by Wednesday or Thursday whereas if I should accidently get a break on it, I'd feel it worthwhile to wait around a few days.

I guess there is no more poop from this end people. Oh yes - I'll bet you died when that bag arrived. I hope the price was not too staggering for it. I'll reimburse you of course and by all means save the shipping ticket and receipt for I plan on collecting from the government for the shipping costs. There are certainly some big deals around Calif. now but I'm afraid I won't be around to capitalize on them. I'd sure give a lot to spend Mother's Day with you Sweetheart - home for good!

At any rate, it won't be long now people. I have a 7:15 appointment to start the beginning of the end processing to-morrow. Since we are leaving as soon as possible after the 3 of us get discharged (all at different times, Cy, Bob & I) I must shower and shave and get all set this evening. Be good.

Lotsa Love, Frank

May 9, 1946:

Telegram (Hamilton Field, Novato, Calif.) 3:50 AM

DEAR FOLKS CAR DEAL IMPOSSIBLE HERE COMING HOME AS SOON AS POSSIBLE LOVE = FRANK

May 11, 1946:

Telegram (Williams Field, Mesa, Ariz.) 4:59 AM

DEAR FOLKS HUNG UP IN FRISCO THREE DAYS FINALLY ON THE WAY BE HOME SOON LOVE = FRANK

BUCK HOUSE AND BEYOND

Present Day

The feeling I had as I typed the last of my father's letters was similar to that feeling a reader gets when they don't want the story to end. My frequency of typing was reduced and more spread out, delaying as much as I could the end to my personal connection to my father. Eventually, there were no more. It's difficult to express the emotions resulting from severing that connection. I can honestly say that I experienced a level of depression, but once again the Lord provided the cure needed to keep the sadness from taking hold of me and I bounced back quickly.

Art Stacey and I had continued our correspondence since 2015, and I'd sent him a set of my father's letters—those that were written while my father was based in Horham, England. Needless to say, Art relished them and in one of his letters requested permission to send them to The Goldfish Club for possible reproduction in a future newsletter. Of course I granted him permission. Then, in Art's reply, without warning, came the most unexpected, fantastic, invitation I'd ever received:

. . . By the way, how do you, or Roger or both of you, fancy attending a garden party at Buckingham Palace. The Goldfish Club receives a few tickets from the Not Forgotten Association to attend their annual garden party. A member of the Royal family will be there. This year it is on Thursday 7th June between 2 and 5pm and I have a couple of spare tickets left. Lots of people, a few celebrities, music, sandwiches with their crust removed, strawberries and cream and lots of military bands, mainly the Guards in their red tunics and bearskins. It really is a great day out and a tremendous experience. A long way to come for three hours but have a think about it and let me know. Val and I are hoping to be there.

—

Dearest Val and Art,

How exciting about Buckingham Palace. I will check with Roger. How many tickets might you have available? I ask because I would want Gloria, his wife to attend, so even if I couldn't I would escort them to England for the event and then the four of you could go and fill me in on it. He is the actual "goldfish" not me, I'm just the daughter of one. Let me know and in the meantime I'll see if they still travel. He is 94 and she is 92 - not sure if they're done traveling or if this might be something they'd like to attend. I'll let you know what they say.

—

Hi Loretto,

If Roger and Gloria can make it and you are accompanying them then I will get you an invite as well. You can't come all this way and not go to the ball Cinderella . . . !!! No problem. Let me know what they say.

—

Hello my friends,

Well, the verdict is in, Roger and Glo wish they were 10 years younger, but reluctantly decline your invitation. That said, if the invitation is still open to me, I've mentioned it to my brother - Frank's youngest child - who is a 1st Sergeant in the U.S. Army and an Iraq War Veteran. Our father never met him. He was born one month to the day after he died. He has also come to know him through his war letters, which I believe has transformed him as well. If the invitation is still open, and I'm able to bring a guest, Peter and I are seriously considering coming.

Today is my father's birthday. He would have been 97. The day of the garden party is the death anniversary of our step-father (the only father we ever knew) - we're both finding the timing of these communications and the event quite surreal.

Then commenced numerous email communications between Art, Peter, and me, but over the coming months we were able to shore up all the details. Our invitation arrived from the Not Forgotten Association. We were truly going to be guests at a Garden Party at Buckingham Palace, in honor of our father and Roger, and on the anniversary of our step-father's death of all days. It was clear to us that something much bigger was at work here and we knew this entire experience had been arranged for us by both of our fathers.

As our departure date neared, I'd contacted Art to arrange a surprise for Peter.

—

Hi again Loretto,

Apologies. With all the other bits and pieces going on I completely overlooked the most important question you asked me, that of Peter becoming an associate member. Of course we would love to have him join the shoal. If you intend to surprise him with it then perhaps when we have lunch prior to Buck House would be the ideal time. I could present him with his lapel badge and formally welcome him to the shoal. How does that sound?

Perfect!

—

We arrived in London, took our hired car to our hotel, only one block from the RAF Club where we were to meet Art and Val the next day for lunch prior to heading across Green Park for our date at Buck House. Once checked in, we took a tour bus around London as Peter had never been, grabbed a bite, and "hit the sac" early in an effort to sleep off the jet lag.

To say our trip was a whirlwind would be an understatement. In addition to the Garden Party, we had rented a car in order to also visit my friends at the 95th Bomb Group Heritage Museum in Horham—allowing four hours this time—and then onto Stamford for an overnight with Art and Val, a visit to the Cambridge American Cemetery and Memorial, and back to London for our return flight. All of this activity took place between our arrival Wednesday morning and our departure Sunday morning.

The morning of the Garden Party, we took our time getting ready. I chose to wear red, white, and blue in honor of both countries—complete with a red fascinator pre-approved by Val via an emailed photo. Peter wore a suit, one of our father's ties, our father's Matrix shoes, his military medals, and his uniform beret. I have to admit, I think we would have done both of our fathers, and Roger, proud as their representatives.

We met Art and Val at the RAF Club, a museum unto itself. While at lunch in the pub downstairs, we connected with another Goldfish member—Kate Burrows—and together we walked, still very much in disbelief, through Green Park to get into the queue at Buckingham Palace. Once through security, we were met by the most gracious lady. She was greeting all the guests along with another gentleman from the Not Forgotten Association. She asked Peter and me where we were from and we told her the U.S. and that we were with The Goldfish Club. We explained our reason for coming, to which she replied, "How amazing that you've crossed the pond to attend. We're thrilled to have your father represented." We were given programs and continued on to the garden. It's truly quite an experience to have royalty treat you like royalty, and that was very much the case. There were roughly 2,500 in attendance from all branches of the military, from all countries comprising the UK. All were veterans accompanied by their family or friends. We made our way to find a table and then took in all the activity. First up were the bagpipes, then the Beefeaters came from the palace and mingled with the crowd for photos until which time they assembled along the rope in preparation of Princess Anne's arrival.

The buffet was opened under this huge white tent, tea was served (I had iced coffee and Val had lemon squash—delicious). We were in line to get a bite when we realized it was getting close to 3 o'clock, when the Princess Royal, Anne, was due to arrive, so we left the line and moved toward the velvet rope separating us from the veterans who were to be presented to Princess Anne. The Band of the Corps of the Royal Engineers had arrived after the bagpipers and played music in a tent by the lake until 3 o'clock, when they assembled and marched to the steps of the palace from which Princess Anne emerged. The national anthem was played and Her Royal Highness proceeded to greet the veterans and injured military lined up on the lawn.

The amount of time Princess Anne spent with each of these men and women was what impressed me the most. It was clear she had a genuine interest in every single one of them, conversing at least a minute or more with each of the over fifty honorees being presented. In all the photos taken at that event, it is obvious to any observer that she was listening with her heart as she addressed them one by one.

Once our representative, Leslie Stephens, was presented we made our way to the buffet once again. There we found proper finger sandwiches and beautiful cakes with chocolate discs on top imprinted with a gold crown. Of course we had strawberries with clotted cream, which I somehow managed to eat three bowls—mine, my brother's and Kitty's (Leslie's wife). About that time, the band had returned to begin beating retreat and Princess Anne departed. The pomp and circumstance of the event was like nothing I have ever experienced. It was an honor to be there and share in the recognition of so many service men and women.

In typically, efficient British style, we were all led through the palace to exit out the main doors. Outside, we took more photos, and said our good-byes to Leslie and Kitty, who would be returning home to France. Kate, Art, Val, and I made our way back through Green Park with a stop at the Royal Air Force Bomber Command Memorial. It was a fitting way to end the day, paying our respects to the crews that had joined our father and Roger on so many missions all those years ago. Each bomber crew member is represented in bronze with magnificent detail. Much the same crew as the U.S. bombers, we were able to imagine each statue as each member of our father's crew. The memorial was erected in 2012 in honor of the over 55,000 RAF airmen who died serving in World War II.

Crossing the very busy Piccadilly traffic, Val, Kate, and I returned to the RAF Club, while Peter and Art went to pick up our rental car. Once changed into traveling clothes, the three of us returned to the pub downstairs to await Art and Peter. It wasn't long before they joined us; we all raised a pint, talked about our afternoon, and finally said our goodbyes, Kate, returning to the Isle of Man, one of the Channel Islands, and Val and Art, back to Stamford. We would be rejoining Art and Val later the following day after our visit to the The Red Feather Club 95th Bomb Group Heritage Museum in the morning.

I had learned from our last visit to London, the earlier you are able to get out of the city proper, the better. Having never driven in London, it took Peter a bit of time to adjust to being on the right side of the car, and the right side of the road, but eventually we found our rhythm and managed to get out of the city and to our destination without incident; there were a few frayed nerves, but we were otherwise unscathed.

Having been to the museum the previous year, I knew what to expect, and I was so excited to share it with Peter. No doubt it was as emotional for him as it was for me. This visit, we'd allowed four hours and were able to take our time. Once again Beverley Abbott, Alan Johnson, Glenn Miller, and Reg and Scott Bradley rolled out the red carpet. I had brought them a bound copy of the letters our father had written while based in Horham to contribute to the museum, and this time we were able to take our time with the exhibits, tour the other buildings, and enjoy a lovely lunch before we needed to depart for Stamford. As with my visit with my cousins the previous year, when Beverley, Linda, Reg and Alan welcomed us as family, we felt the same sadness at leaving, but knew we would be back someday.

The trip to Stamford was also uneventful, though the jetlag was taking hold. So many long-anticipated events playing out and all filled with a variety of emotions that, once in the car, the long, straight, highways began to lull us to sleep—so much so, we needed to stop and walk around to wake ourselves up. We arrived in Stamford, got settled and sat down to a lovely supper Val had prepared for us. Now, properly full from our meal, combined with our previously identified jetlag, we regrettably needed to retire early in anticipation of a full day of activities on Saturday.

The next morning, after breakfast, we visited Burghley House, walked about the town a bit, stopped at Art and Val's pub, and then headed to Cambridge to see the cemetery. After an emotional visit, we hopped on a bus and went into the city center with the goal of having dinner at The Eagle pub, known as the place where Francis Crick announced that he and fellow scientist James Watson had discovered DNA, the "secret of life." After a feast of fish and chips, we returned to London, where we stayed our last night as new members of the Victory Services Club, before being collected the next morning by our car service and delivered back to the airport. The long flight home provided plenty of time for reflection, and while we were both exhausted physically, our minds and spirits were perfectly sated.

—

As we flew back across the pond, I mentally collected all the experiences I'd been through since the discovery of my father's letters. How, as with any coddiwomple, the travel was purposeful, yet the destination was unknown. When I initially learned of the letters, I was intrigued. The discovery was both exciting and interesting. I had seen photos and movies of my father, and had heard some stories about him, but he was a stranger to me and I could not possibly conceive of the role this dusty box of letters would play in my life. Finding the letters, reading them, taking the time and effort to investigate who and what he was talking about, and then experiencing some of the same things he had, brought me closer to him than I would ever have thought possible. After over fifty years of not knowing him, I feel as though I've known him my entire life. Who would have thought that a box of letters from seventy years past would provide such a profound transformation in a person's life? My entire experience is a true testimony to the value of the written word. In a day when most communication has become digital, the chances of another daughter's life being transformed in such a way is minimal at best. I can honestly say, with all my heart, I am not the same person at the end of my journey that I was at the beginning. My life has been forever changed.

EPILOGUE

May 1946 - Present

When my father returned home from California, he set about on an entirely new mission: To become a medical doctor. What I learned with all my genealogy work, and what he probably never knew, was that his great-great-grandfather was also a medical doctor in London, England, in the 1800s.

My father had some hurdles to overcome, having only completed two years of undergraduate courses–studying part time while working full time - prior to reporting for duty. He was now twenty-five years old and, like many of his comrades who survived the war, he intended to make up for lost time. The standard requirement for entrance into medical school was to have an undergraduate degree in a related field, but it appears my father was not about to take two more years of coursework after giving two and a half years to the Army.

After numerous unfruitful attempts to speak to the chair of the department at University of Buffalo Medical School, apparently my father got in the car and went to the campus. He found out where he would find the chair and waited for him on the steps outside the building until he emerged. The poor guy didn't stand a chance. I don't know exactly what my father said, but at the end of it the chair simply said, "I'll see you in class, Thompson." With that, he was accepted into medical school, without an undergraduate degree. Four years later, he graduated and went to complete his residency at E.J. Meyer Memorial Hospital, in Buffalo (currently Erie County Medical Center), where he remained until 1956, working as an internist.

Dr. Muldoon was mentioned twice in the letters. This is when I learned he was my father's family doctor. What my father didn't know was that another patient of Dr. Muldoon's would become his future wife. Dr. Muldoon was my mother's uncle and also her family's doctor. Throughout my mom's life, she suffered from chronic allergies and made frequent visits to see her Uncle Art Muldoon for care. On one such occasion in 1953, Uncle Art was traveling and another doctor was covering for him. When Mary A. showed up for her appointment, she met Dr. Frank Thompson, who promptly ordered a series of skin tests for her allergies and scheduled a follow up appointment at his office on Main Street in Niagara Falls.

Allergies can be difficult to identify and skin testing, while not pleasant for the patient, was the most accurate means by which to diagnose the specific allergen and establish the most successful method of treatment. Treatment often requires a battery of shots that have been known to result in a variety of side effects, which need to bc closely monitored. Patients receiving allergy shots are often started with smaller doses, having to remain at the doctor's office for a period of time afterwards to ensure they do not exhibit any dangerous side effects. As the patient becomes more tolerant of the shots, the frequency of their visits and the length of time they are required to remain at the office is reduced until eventually they are able to go in for their shot and leave immediately.

This was the process my mother began as Dr. Thompson's patient in 1954. She still has the appointment card. Perhaps she had some sense that this man would not only change the course of her lifetime struggle with allergies, but would also change the course of her entire life. As she would frequent his office for allergy shots, the brief, polite conversation became less brief, and the post-shot time spent in the waiting room was companionably spent with Mrs. Ott, my father's longtime friend, neighbor, and patient. Both Mrs. Ott and my mother were teachers and had much to discuss as they graded their papers to pass the time. It is conceivable that, as Mrs. Ott came to know my mother, she encouraged my father to consider the possibility of dating my mother once she was no longer his patient. After all, my mother possessed numerous qualities of which my father sought in a "dolly." She was educated, working on her master's degree in English, a teacher, a redhead, a Roman Catholic, and eight years his junior.

In the spring of 1955, my father left his practice to return to school to specialize in internal medicine. It was then that he would "just happen" to be driving by my mother at the bus stop on her way to classes at Buffalo State Teachers College. Of course he'd offer her a ride and they would spend the ride getting to know each other better. It had never occurred to my mother that Buffalo State was in the complete opposite direction of the University of Buffalo. This courtship developed over the next few months until he abruptly stopped calling. Etiquette in those days did not permit women to call men, and while she was disappointed and annoyed that he just disappeared without any explanation, she focused on her studies and graduated with her master's degree at the end of the summer. Upon graduation, she received a lovely bouquet of flowers from none other than Little Francis George.

With permission from her mother to call him and thank him for the flowers, my mother intended to learn the reason behind his sudden disappearance. As it turned out, my Uncle Harry had lost his job, which had put the entire financial support of the household on my father. Knowing he could not "take my mother out as he'd like to," being so strapped for funds, he decided it best to just stop calling. Learning this, my mother explained that she "did not need to be wined and dined," that she was perfectly happy going on a picnic, or an afternoon drive. At that, my father was back in the picture and the courtship resumed, part of which included my mother riding along with my father as he made house calls, waiting in the car for him, and then continuing on to the next call, all the while growing closer in their relationship. The timing of the rekindling of their courtship was ideal because a few months later, on October 3, 1955, my father and Uncle Harry would lose the love of their lives, their beloved mother.

In the months that followed, Harry returned to work, and my mother and father returned to dating. At Christmastime, 1955, after countless picnics, dinners, dancing, birthdays, and holidays, my father presented my mother with a gift. Though unable to recall the specific gift, "Your father was always buying me gifts," in keeping with her habit of saving mementos, she kept the card and it read: "The initials aren't put on as yet - cause I expect to change them —F." On November 15, 1956 their engagement announcement appeared in the Niagara Gazette. As an engagement ring, my father had had his medical school class ring sized to fit my mother. She was to wear it until he had paid off her diamond engagement ring, which she still wears today.

Their wedding date was set for February 16, 1957. After returning from their honeymoon, my mother and father moved into the upper flat of the front house on 9th Street. Harry remained in the "little piano box" at 450 1/2 over the garage in the back. This would be their home for the first two years of their marriage, but after the arrival of their first two children, and wanting a large family, it was time to look for a bigger home.

During my father's career as a doctor, he was responsible for office visits, hospital rounds, and house calls. One of my father's patients lived on a quaint residential island in what was previously the village of LaSalle before it became part of the city of Niagara Falls in 1927. While making a house call on Cayuga Island to his patient Charlie Buhr, he may have noticed the house for sale on the same street. When he and my mother went to see it, they decided instantly that it was to be theirs. My mother's Uncle Tom Muldoon, her mother's brother, had joined them for the showing of the house. In order to hold it, a good faith deposit of $50 was required, which would mean a visit to the bank. Today that $50 would equal $455. Uncle Tom, not wanting them to lose the house to another buyer, got on his bike, rode home, got the $50, and returned to West Rivershore Drive. They moved into their new home in November 1959. I was born nine months later.

Between 1959 and 1965 another three children would be born, fulfilling yet another of my father's dreams "to have as many children as the good Lord would send him." My mother once told me that one of my father's favorite spots in which to sit and relax was in the grand living room, directly off the front foyer. It was in that spot that on one random occasion my mother recalls him looking at the large triple window above the couch and telling her, "When I die, I want to be laid out right under that window." At the time, my mother had thought it an odd comment, but when the time came to decide where to have my father's wake, those were exactly my mother's instructions to the funeral director.

———

It's referred to as a widowmaker by medical professionals. It's a heart attack beyond all heart attacks and is rarely survived. Unlike other types of heart attacks resulting from blockages of the arteries in the heart, this particular heart attack results when blood flow to a very specific and important junction in the heart becomes blocked, ultimately shutting down the entire left side of the heart. If the blockage is not removed immediately, the result is sudden death. This is the type of heart attack my father suffered on that lovely spring day in 1965.

True to its name, a widow is precisely what my mother became that day. However, my father didn't ignore the signs; after all, he was a doctor. The chest pains a few days earlier; the sleepless nights during which my mother watched him pace in front of the moonlit window in their bedroom when he thought she was asleep. That very morning he'd had an electrocardiogram (EKG) while at St. Mary's Hospital, making his rounds. This type of test would actually have shown if he was having an active heart attack, or if there were areas of the heart that were not getting enough oxygen. However, according to the results of the test, it didn't show any of this. I learned recently that this conclusion was not acceptable to him, and he intended to show the report to another physician for a second opinion after he'd finished his rounds at Niagara Falls Memorial Hospital. He never got the chance. That morning he had also taken some nitroglycerine, a medicine that opens blood vessels to improve blood flow. Learning of this, it was clear to me that he knew something was very wrong, and he had been systematically trying to figure it out.

Of all places, the attack occurred in a hospital. After completing his rounds at St. Mary's Hospital in Lewiston, N.Y., he called my mother, and then drove to Niagara Falls Memorial Hospital to make his next rounds, the EKG test results lying on the back seat of the car. They'd had a brief conversation, she mentioning that she was taking the boys for haircuts; he mentioning he was heading to Memorial for his rounds. She had no idea this would be the last time she would ever speak to him.

He collapsed shortly after leaving a patient's room. It was a little after noon on Friday, June 25. I can't imagine the bedlam that took place as the medical staff tried to save him, attempting every possible method known at the time. They would bring him back repeatedly, only to lose him again. These efforts went on for three hours. He did not recover. He was pronounced dead at three o'clock. How awful for his colleagues to be unable to save him. The fact that a partner in his practice, Dr. Herman Brezing, participated in the autopsy, which was conducted at 7:10 p.m. that evening, leaves little doubt of his compelling need to know the cause of what killed his partner, colleague, and friend.

From outward appearances, my father was a healthy forty-four year old man, though overworked and a smoker, a habit that would surely have contributed to his condition. The warning by the medical profession of the impact smoking had on people's health was not acted upon by Congress until early 1965, and was just gaining recognition throughout the medical community at the time of his death. The pathology report indicated several blood vessels were affected. While they performed CPR on my father for a very long time, bringing him back only to lose him again and again, the blockages were many and wide-spread; he was a walking time bomb

My entire life I hoped he had not suffered, and after uncovering the pathology report fifty-two years after his death, a surgeon friend of mine confirmed: All that could have been done at that time had been done. She explained that since it was that particular junction of the heart that was blocked; the outcome is usually immediate death. How do you find peace in news like that? Yet, in a strange, uncomfortable way, I actually felt a sense of relief learning that he had not suffered long. Indeed, it would be his family, friends, and colleagues who were to suffer over the years; suffer the loss of so fine a man. A man I hope you have enjoyed meeting.

—

With seven children, his legacy lived on, though none of us really knew it until we were well into our fifties. My mother carried on like a champ. She occupied her life by ensuring we wanted for nothing. Our childhood was filled with swimming, dance, and music lessons. Girl and Boy Scouts, camping, and ice skating. We were loved by her enough for two parents, without a doubt. She raised us for ten years, along with her Aunt Alice, Dr. Muldoon's wife, and our babysitter Missy Buhr, Charlie's wife. The days ran into years and the years into a decade, and then everything changed again.

In 1974, my mother went on a blind date to a church dinner and was introduced to Paul McDonough, a gentleman who had lost his wife and was raising eight children on his own. I can't imagine what their friends were thinking when they introduced them. Perhaps because the two of them shared the same trials and tribulations of single parenthood they figured they had a lot in common. As it turned out, they were right. On July 4th, 1975 we all got married. Combined, I have eleven brothers and three sisters in my family. It was easy to get close to my new siblings. It was like having a bunch of your friends move in with you. The challenge for me was getting close to my new dad after never having had one. That challenge disappeared in the spring of 1980.

After so many years without a father, I found the somewhat sudden addition of one to my family difficult. I was fifteen years old when my parents married.

Teenage years are awkward enough, but to suddenly have a dad at that time in my life released a flood of conflicting emotions. In general, we got along fine and we all seemed to be settling in to our new way of life by the time I left to go away to college in the fall of 1978. I attended Mercyhurst College (now Mercyhurst University) in Erie, Pa. Far enough away to live on campus, but still close enough to get home if I needed, or wanted to. Mercyhurst College had originated as an all-girls college, and while it was co-ed by the time I attended, some of the legacy events were still in place since 1926.

One such legacy event was Father-Daughter Weekend. It was held annually in April. My first year of encountering this event was strange for me. All these years I'd had no father, and now I had one but I wasn't sure I felt close enough to him to ask him to go to this event with me. My mother told me it was up to me and Dad would honor whatever I decided. I decided not to invite him. Instead, I did what I had always done, what I was comfortable doing: I shared all my friends' dads. It was a fun event. The dads were the girls' dates. We had a dinner dance on Saturday, and then a Mass with a breakfast following on Sunday morning. There were lots of questions about why my dad wasn't with me, and all the girls and fathers seemed to understand. Admittedly, I felt a slight tug on my heartstrings about my decision.

The following year when the father-daughter weekend rolled around, I had already decided I would invite my dad. He and my mother drove down together. Her plan was to relax in the hotel while we were at the dinner dance, and then join us for the Mass and breakfast the following day. It was a little weird having my dad as my date. He came to the dorm and someone came to tell me he was there. When I met him at the front desk, he gave me the corsage he'd brought for me. We drove to the dinner dance venue together in an awkward silence. Not knowing him very well, I really didn't know what to talk to him about, but the drive was short and we survived. We sat at a table with a few of my girlfriends and their fathers, and all the dads got along great, laughing, telling stories; it was actually more fun than I'd thought it would be. After dinner, the dean took the lectern to give his keynote speech. The room fell silent.

After some lighthearted comments, he got into the heart of his speech. He said that he was honored to be asked to speak at such a significant event, but that initially he wasn't sure what he'd talk about because he himself did not have a daughter and was unsure of how he would connect with the audience. He went on to explain that he thought the best way would be to speak with several of the young women on the campus and have them share with him what they remembered most about their fathers. It was this decision, made by the dean, which changed everything for me.

The dean started with some stories from different women that were both funny and entertaining. Everyone seemed in a jovial mood, and then he changed it up a bit. He started telling more heartfelt stories the women had shared with him and the room became a bit more somber.

"When I asked this young lady what she remembered most about her father," he began, "She told me that it was the day her father told her that her mother had died."

You could hear a pin drop. I don't know what he said after that because the thought popped into my head that my dad actually had to do that very same thing when his first wife died and left him with eight children. Realizing this, I glanced over to where he was sitting, and I saw him wiping tears from his eyes. It was at that moment that I fell unconditionally in love with him, and we remained close until he joined my father in heaven.

We lost our dad in 2002, which I still cannot talk about. He was the only dad I'd ever known and my love for him cannot be expressed with mere words. I don't recall ever not being together, and though our home had two stories, there were never any "steps," as my oldest brother pointed out in our dad's eulogy. To this day, all fifteen of us could not be any closer, forever one family. But that is a story for another time.

—

In addition to her fifteen children, my mom has twenty-six grandchildren and twenty-four great-grandchildren, with one on the way. At the time of this writing, we will celebrate two weddings that I know of, but you never know with a family this large! Our lives are full of love and laughter, and it is difficult to recall the times in our lives when we were not all together. For the Thompson children, we knew we were blessed when our dad came into our lives, and then to have our father, who we've never really known, come into our lives fifty years after his death, there is no denying we have been doubly blessed. Thank you, Lord. Amen.

NOTES

All letters to or from Frank Thompson, or to or from his family members and friends, are from the Thompson family collection.

All conversations and emails between the author, Art Stacey, Beverley Abbott, Roger Sundin, Jr., and "Big Sundin," are shared with permission and are dated accordingly.

The Mix Up

13   Bell Aerospace was hard at work producing the P-39 Airacobra and eventually the P-63 Kingcobra, which were ultimately sent to the USSR. The chemical warfare plant, while creating harmful gases to be used in warfare simultaneously created harmful gases affecting the environment, and the lives of Niagara Falls residents. Kratts, Michelle Ann, *Niagara Falls in World War II* (Charleston, SC, 2016), p. 113.

14   War news in January of 1943 signaled a change in the British approach to their efforts against Germany following the Casablanca Conference between President Roosevelt and Prime Minister Churchill. The outcome of this conference was the decision to commence 24/7 destruction on Nazi Germany with the Brits continuing their night bombings and the Yanks commencing the controversial daylight bombings. That January the first B-17 Flying Fortresses and B-24 Liberators began arriving in England as part of the U.S. Eighth Air Force. Miller, Donald L., *The Story of World War II* (New York, 2006), p.162.

15   By now it was late July, 1943 and the British military had reluctantly shifted from their previously moral position of dropping only leaflets on German civilians to relentless bombing raids targeted at the German workforce itself. While this was something Churchill had claimed he would never do, they were forced to acknowledge that if the number of factory workers was reduced in addition to damaging or demolishing the factories, production would be severely crippled or eliminated. Two of Germany's cities suffered the worst consequences of this decision. The first being Hamburg, where half of the city was destroyed leaving almost half a million people homeless and over 40,000 dead as a result of non-stop day-night-day raids that created the first "fire storm" of WWII. Ibid, p. 259-262.

Fort Dix, New Jersey

33   *Agnes had skipped a house party on Long Island to be present – darn white of her I'd say.*

This reference to 'darn white' implies that it was good of her to forgo a party to be with him.

The Turning Point

55   In February 1944, the B-17 Flying Fortresses were joined by their "little friends," the P-51 Mustangs. With the help of these long range American fighters, the focus of the air operation shifted to destroying the Luftwaffe. From February 19 through February 26 the exclusive targets were the aircraft factories and oil refineries. Charged with defending these facilities, the Luftwaffe would take the bait resulting in their anticipated obliteration. In the eight days that comprised "Big Week," the Germans lost over 600 fighters to the Americans 226 bombers. Ibid, p. 279.

Just up the road from "the little piano box" that was their home stood the Hooker Electrochemical Company, a veiled contributor to the top-secret Manhattan Project. Much of the damage to the city and its citizens as a result of this contribution would not be known to the fullest extent for decades. Kratts, p. 119-121.

On other fronts, U.S. forces began the assault on the Mariana Islands, and in Burma the ground forces advanced in the north while the long-range air forces were starting to land behind Japanese lines in central Burma. Polmer & Allen, p. 35-36.

Sioux Falls, South Dakota - Part 1

95   *You run the risk of a frigid exterior of a man whose stuff from home you refuse - I had to learn that the hard way. In the barracks you share anything to eat - the guy that doesn't is black.* The reference to being 'black' implies that the soldier is blacklisted or excluded.

109   *Harry speaks of the stink (political) at home. Send me some of the dope, I mean the inside, on the story will you.* The reference to the 'stink (political)' appears to be with regard to the ousting of the City Manager by the City Council. This would be of personal concern to Frank and his family as his uncle Bob (J. Robert Perry) was employed by the City of Niagara Falls. Any change in leadership could potentially impact his position.

111   *No - I didn't know Dick was in England - looks like he'll be flying paratroopers over for the big invasion doesn't it - well he'll be in on the biggest show on earth - in a way I envy him - in a way I don't.* The reference to 'the biggest show on earth' pertains to the D-Day invasion.

Nice to Meet You

114   In the Pacific, April saw the activation of the U.S. Twentieth Air Force under General Henry H. Arnold; his job was to execute strategic bombing operations against Japan. While Allied troops landed in New Guinea, the Soviets took Yalta in mid-April, and by early May, had secured the port city of Sevastopol in the Crimea. Polmar & Allen, World War II; The Encyclopedia of the War Years 1941-1945 (Mineola, New York, 2012), p. 36-37.

Sioux Falls, South Dakota - Part 3

148   As my father moved forward with his training, the war was moving forward on all fronts. Early in the month the B-29s completed their first combat mission in Japan while the U.S. and British airborne troops, with many losses, managed to land behind German lines in preparation for the "Allied Campaign in Europe." Polmar & Allen, *World War II; The Encyclopedia of the War Years 1941-1945* (Mineola, New York, 2012), p. 37.

148   Meanwhile, back in Niagara Falls, the first German prisoners of war (POWs) began arriving at Fort Niagara. By the end of the war, their ranks had grown to just under two-thousand. Through the terms of the Geneva Convention, these POWs were not permitted to undertake any military tasks, and therefore they were put to work on local farms. This was the ideal solution as there was a shortage of men to work the farms, and later harvest the crops. The alliance proved beneficial for my father's loved ones at home; while on the other side of the ocean the invasion that had been planned for the past two years was being set in motion. Kratts, Michelle Ann, *Niagara Falls in World War II* (Charleston, SC, 2016), p. 136-137.

151-152   *Of course the big news of the day is invasion. Oh God may it only be a speedy success. Reports we have had up to this point are of course too general as it is much too early to ascertain any success or failure. I fear this is the answer to Aunt Maime's mail problem too. Dick has probably been a busy boy.* This reference is to the D-Day and that Dick Perry was most likely part of it.

167   *Gee the War news sure sounds good doesn't it? Hope to goodness they can push on successfully and rapidly.* This reference is to successes realized by the Allies the Pacific when the first bomb raid of B-29s on Japan, The Marines landing in Saipan, and the destruction of over 200 Japanese planes in the battle of the Marianas. Polmar & Allen, World War II; The Encyclopedia of the War Years 1941-1945 (Mineola, New York, 2012), p. 37-38.

193   *Say isn't the war news splendid. I eat it up every day – have even taken to reading some of the news in the newspapers for a change.* This mention of the war news references the end of the U.S. "battle of the hedge-rows," near Normandy, France, as well as the liberation of Guam. In addition, the Soviet troops were recapturing cities from the Germans, while British and Canadian troops took hold of Caen, France - considered the "gateway to Paris." Ibid, p. 39.

Sioux Falls - Part 4

197   *I have been reading of the murder in town since I've been getting the Gazette again – certainly don't like it and it worries me with the Big Boy out so much. Thank Heavens we still have de la Shpusie – he is darn good protection as an adequate warning.* The murder mentioned references the case against Robert W. Barnes, who was charged with the August 4, 1944, first-degree murder of Miriam Kennedy.

Yuma, Arizona - Part 1

233   *War news, what we get of it, is great – sure doesn't look like a much longer pull in Europe at any rate.* The reference to the war news most likely is points to the liberation of Paris, Rumania's declaration of war on Germany and the liberations of Brussels and Antwerp by the British. In addition to the British penetration of the "German Gothic Line in Italy," the armistice between the Soviets and Bulgaria, and the German surrender at Toulon and Marsailles all point to the end of the war. Ibid. p. 40.

Yuma, Arizona - Part 2

254   *Say - I'm not too keen about the war news of late - what say you - looks like the stalemate that the Germans are playing for. If a decisive break is not made within the next two or three weeks I fear at least another 6 months before they can clear out the rats.* The war news not being too good may be a reference to Operation Market-Garden, a plan to seize the bridges between Belgium and Holland that failed when the bridge at Arnhem could not be taken due to the attack by German SS troops. Miller, Donald L., *The Story of World War II* (New York, 2006), p.320.

Gulfport, Mississippi - Part 1

325   *The war news is terrible - strangely enough it has a very direct bearing on us. The last class of men to be trained in B-17s arrived here a few days ago - I believe they will work with larger ships - B-32 - Consolidated's new job, or B29s . . . If this goes on much longer I doubt that we will finish*

training here in its entirety I hope they stop them soon! Here, the war news references the Battle of the Bulge, which lasted from December 16, 1944 until January 7, 1945. Ibid, 338.

Connecting the Dots

337   In his December 20 letter, he made a reference to the "bitter pill" of the Germans breaking through, which sent me directly to my WWII encyclopedia to read about what he was referencing. He, of course, was referring to the counterattack in Belgium that had started the Battle of the Bulge. The battle would continue into early January and officially end on the 7th, being declared "an American victory." Years later, Hitler's minister of armaments and war production would admit that the German loss of that battle in Ardennes marked the beginning of the end of the war for Germany. Polmar & Allen, *World War II; The Encyclopedia of the War Years 1941-1945* (Mineola, New York, 2012), p. 99.

Gulfport, Mississippi - Part 2

354   *By the way, can you get me any 828 category film? Here I am asking again. Here is the set up plain and simple. Would like very much to get 828 for John's camera but can use 127, 616, 116, 120, or 620 or Univex 00.* 828 category film was 35mm film without the sprocket holes introduced by Kodak in 1935.

357   *The war news is good – let's pray it stays that way.* The war news references the Soviets taking Warsaw and Lodz, Poland, and the armistice signed between the Allies and Hungary.
    Vincent Shanahan in V-12? Just make sure that that is not the deal where they sign up for 6 years – ugh. The Navy does a better job on educating a man for his job – but these sailors lack something – ask any Gulfport girl. The V-12 Navy College Training Program created to supplement commissioned officers in the United States Navy during World War II.

358   *Somehow – if the Russians keep on we won't see much of anything in Europe I judge. As the intelligence officer put it the other day, "American forces were considerably het up and jubilant when they captured 3 miles of front and St. Milo – they were glad they got there before the Russians."* See previous entry The war news is good . . . page 357.

362   *Ah well, if the Russians keep rushin maybe I'll be there sooner than we think. It will be grand to start living my own life again.* See previous entry The war news is good . . . page 357.

363   *By the way, the Rooshans are only 58 miles from Berlin by the newspaper not bad, what? I'd like to get to England just in time to see it finish.* See previous entry The war news is good . . . page 357.

Savannah, Georgia

409   *With Spring on the way, if those Yanks and Russians keep going as they have, they won't need a lot of crews.* This references the U.S. bomb strikes on Berlin on February 26, 1945. Polmar & Allen, *World War II; The Encyclopedia of the War Years 1941-1945* (Mineola, New York, 2012), p. 45.

Horham, England - Part 1

433   *Biggest News of all I forgot to mention - the death of the President!* References the death of President Franklin D. Roosevelt on April 12, 1945.

437   *The war news is splendid and I suppose you noted Eisenhower's statement that strategic warfare is over. That means our effort is of a strictly tactical and support nature now.* The war news reflects the U.S. arrival at the Elbe River outside Berlin, the Canadian troops reaching the Dutch coast, and the sinking of the German battleship by the RAF. Ibid, p.46.

441   *Try to remember that no news is the very best news you can have. If anything has happened the government will let you know sooner than my airmails could ever get there. Then too if you ever get an M.I.A. (missing in action) don't hope too much but just remember that right now chances are better for getting out of Germany than they have ever been. You must know from the papers that right now things are better for the type of war we fight than it has ever been. We have the best equipment obtainable and we have plenty of fighter support!* This is Frank's way of addressing his families concerns should he be shot down and captured, or killed in action.

Horham, England - Part 2

467   *Thanks for the compliment (S/Sgt.) but we happen to still be a lower class known as "black ass" sergeants or buck. Some of us have "it" and some of us don't. (We don't - none of us.)* This reference implies that John's crew was never promoted to S/Sgt as with Frank's crew.
    No, I never did hear from "Wabbit Twacks" or Kranshaw. These were the two girls from N.O.

Horham, England - Part 3

480   *There is a lot of nasty business going on in London now. The Tommies are returning, there are some shootings! I hope I never get into London in uniform when they all return - there sure will be hell to pay.* More research is required to determine specifically what Frank was referencing.

Horham, England - Part 4

493   *By the way, I'm expecting, by the time you get this or shortly thereafter, to receive a bit of Literature from "Flying" magazine. Please do not send*

it over here to me just keep it - unopened please. Flying magazine was the American Division sponsor of the Goldfish Club.

Sioux Falls, South Dakota - Part 5

499   *What do you fellows think of this Atomic Bomb business? Oh Lord, what have our chemists done for the world in this or should I say what have they done to the world? I'm not particularly the squeamish type but would that this had never come. It is almost as though a world stinking with sin and destruction were preparing to destroy itself. God must be tiring of man's independence and ego and while his mercy is limitless so is his justice. Maybe it doesn't scare the Nips but it sure scares me.* This is a reference to the first Atomic Bomb dropped on Hiroshima, Japan on August 6, 1945 and that the Japanese issues a declaration of war to the Soviets. Ibid, 49.

501   *Well, today has indeed been one for the books! Got up about 6:30 for breakfast and into mess hall in time to hear latest from Japan. It sure sounds good doesn't it? I can't see letting Hirohito returning his so called "Prerogative" anymore than we would have allowed Hitler or Il Duce to remain, even as nominal head of their countries, but then I suppose it is just as well I'm not administering the job. If peace does come in reality our real troubles will just have begun but then we all want to be free at our earliest opportunity to cope with our own specific personal problems as soon as is possible. Not a lot of excitement here we all just hope it will end soon.* This is a reference to the second Atomic Bomb dropped on Nagasaki, Japan on August 9, 1945 and the Japanese decision to make peace with the Allies.

506   *From Stimson's Statement and clarification for it, I read in paper today, it doesn't look to me as though I'd get out for a year or more anyway – well, at least no one will be shooting at me I hope!* References Stimson Doctrine, which is the policy adopted by the U.S. in 1932 indicating the U.S. would not recognize any states that were created as a result of result of aggression, specifically from China and Japan.

507   *Almost looks as though the Japs haven't quit yet doesn't it?* Refers to the attack by the Japanese of two B-32 Dominator bombers that were on a photo mission over Tokyo; the attack took place on August 18th, but Frank wrote about in on August 17th because Japan time is 14 hours ahead of Sioux Falls time. Polmar & Allen, *World War II; The Encyclopedia of the War Years 1941-1945* (Mineola, New York, 2012), p. 49.

Riverside, California - Part 1

527   *No we weren't near the wreck, but I heard about it. Guess it was pretty bad but we were very fortunate – only mishap was cramps which soon disappeared . . . "Alive and well" in telegram was to dismiss worry on your part, not incite it. I wanted you to know just that in least possible words and since I'd heard of train wreck I thought you might be worried.* Referenced the train wreck in Michigan, North Dakota on August 9, 1945, which occurred when two trains, traveling as a pair to the west coast, collided after the first train stopped due to a mechanical failure and the second train was unable to stop before crashing into the first. 237 people were in the first Pullman sleeper car and roughly 650 people were in the second coach cars. Passengers were mostly military personnel, with the balance women and children. Michigan 1945 Train Wreck, https://www.michignnd.com/?SEC=31FFF3FA-49E9-4C7B-900A-B326700E1E44, retrieved October, 2017.

533   *Did I hear correctly yesterday when they said they'd start to discharge 800 thousand/month? Also this two year number whereby all with 2 years in can get out. I hope so for if they take it from time of enlistment I have 3 years in and if they don't I'd just have to go until February of 1946.* Refers to the rapid and massive demobilization of troops from Europe and the Pacific, and the designated point system.

538   *I was very pleased as punch to get my Goldfish - I'm going to sew him on soon - I'm a bit proud of it don't y'know - sorta my only claim to fame.* References Frank's receipt of his Goldfish patch, designating his ditching survival.

Riverside, California - Part 2

577   *We might as well face it - there will be trouble in Asia, and Heaven only knows how that will work out.* This statement references the changes in the occupation of Korea, and the resultant splitting of the country.

Boring Blythe

613   *So lil old Donnette went the way of all flesh. I never did get her out of my system but I guess it would be a good idea now eh?* This references Donnette's engagement. There was a prom-type photo of Frank with Donnette among the few photos we have of him when he was young. It may have been a senior formal dance as his photo resembles his yearbook photo from his senior year.

GLOSSARY

104th Article of War A military justice procedure whereby a commanding officer was given the authority to impose limited disciplinary punishment upon a soldier under their command without resorting to a court martial.

3.2 Beer Beer containing 3.2% alcohol by weight or roughly 4% alcohol by volume.

A.S.T.P. Army Specialized Training Program.

A.T.C. Air Transport Command.

A-1 A style of flight jacket.

A-3 bag A canvas duffle bag.

AEF programs Allied Expeditionary Forces Programme was a BBC (British Broadcasting Corporation) radio station broadcast during WWII.

Aggregation A cluster of things that come together.

Allotment A family allowance; pay for soldiers' dependents.

APO Army Post Office.

AWOL Absent without leave.

B.A.A.B. Blythe Army Air Base.

B.T.C. #10 Basic Training Center #10.

B.U. Base Unit.

B-10 A style of flight jacket.

B-15 A style of flight jacket.

B-4 bag An Army-issued folding suitcase.

Banty Rooster Someone who is small in stature but spirited in nature.

Battle of Malta A military campaign in the Mediterranean Theatre involving the fight for control of the island of Malta, a British colony at the time of WWII; the conflict involved British air and navy forces fighting against the air and navy forces of Italy and Germany.

Berries A slang term for money; when something is considered outstanding.

Bivouac A temporary camp offering no tents or cover.

Blitz Cloth A cleaning cloth designed to clean all metals.

Blouse A waist-length jacket; referred to as an "Ike" jacket in reference to the Commanding General of the European Theatre of Operation, Dwight D. Eisenhower, who had requested a waist-length jacket, similar to the British battle jacket, for his troops.

BTOs Built to order.

C.B.I. China Burma India.

C.O. Commanding Officer.

C'est la guerre The verbal shrugging of shoulders or upturned hands, implying resignation. A popular French phrase used during WWII.

Canoodling Used to reference lazing about; meaning has changed since the 1940s.

Carbines A shorter version of a full-length rifle.

Casablanca Conference A meeting held in 1943 between Franklin D. Roosevelt, President of the U.S. and Winston Churchill, Prime Minister of Britain to plan the Allied strategy in Europe for the next phase of WWII.

Cat's meow A slang term referring to something outstanding.

Cl 2 Chlorine.

Class A's Soldier's dress uniform worn with a long tunic-type dress coat.

Dansant Refers to a tea dance, usually held in the afternoon or early evening.

Dead Reckoning A navigational process of calculating a current position by using a previous position and then moving that position forward based on estimated speed over a period of time.

Dickering A petty argument.

Dope Slang for information.

Dough Slang for money.

Dr. Lyons A brand of tooth powder.

Edgerton A brand of shoes.

El 'Chem A magazine published in Niagara Falls, NY for the employees of the Electrochemicals Department of E. I. du Pont de Nemours & Co, Inc.

EM Enlisted Men.

Emperin compounds Generic name for aspirin.

ERC Enlisted Reserve Corps.

Father Flanigan of Boy's Town Originally an orphanage founded by Monsignor Edward Joseph Flanagan, a Catholic priest, it currently serves as a center for troubled youth.

Feast of St. Blaise A Roman Catholic feast day celebrated on February 3rd whereby Catholics take part in the Blessing of the Throats.

Fieldstrip To take apart a weapon for cleaning purposes.

Fire Storm Refers to firebombing, designed to destroy targets using fire via incendiary devices versus large bombs.

Fitch shampoo A brand of shampoo manufactured by the F.W. Fitch Company.

Flak Term referencing anti-aircraft fire.

Flying (magazine) An aviation magazine that was also the sponsor of the American Division of the Goldfish Club.

Fr. Baker's The Our Lady of Victory Basilica is a Catholic parish church and national shrine in Lackawanna, New York founded by Father Nelson Baker.

FUBAR Seriously damaged beyond repair.

G.I. Bill of Rights Also known as The Servicemen's Readjustment Act of 1944 provided a variety of benefits to the veterans returning from WWII. It was signed into law on June 22, 1944 by President Franklin D. Roosevelt.

Gammon Cured or smoked ham; similar to bacon.

Gazette Refers to the Niagara Falls Gazette, newspaper in Niagara Falls, New York.

Gem Brand of steel, single-edge razor blade.

Het up To be angry or agitated.

Hied To go quickly.

Homburg A gentleman's hat style made of stiff wool felt featuring a single dent running down the center of the crown; worn by Eisenhower and Churchill.

Japs An ethnic slur referring to Japanese people during WWII.

Jeep A nickname for lower ranking soldier such as a Private; a brand of vehicle.

Jiggaloo Humorous reference to a gigolo.

Jitterbug The jitterbug is a fast dance popular in the United States in the 1940s that was performed to swing music.

K of C Knights of Columbus.

K rations Proportioned foods packaged for emergencies; developed for the armed forces in WWII.

K.P. Kitchen Police or Kitchen Patrol.

Kegle/Keggler To bowl; a bowler.

Kiries Young women.

Kirk A church.

Kleinhans A men's department store located in Buffalo, New York.

LaSalle A high school located in Niagara Falls, New York.

Leaflets Printed flyers used as a form of psychological warfare intended to alter the behavior of people in enemy territory; sometimes used in conjunction with air strikes, sometimes used as part of humanitarian air missions.

Left-handers Refers to those practicing any religion other than Roman Catholic.

Liggett's A drug store chain; the predecessor to Rexall.

Lister bag A canvas bag used to supply purified drinking water to military troops.

Little piano box Refers to Frank's home in Niagara Falls, New York, complete with a baby grand piano.

London Dock A brand of pipe tobacco sold at the time.

Longies Long underwear.

Looy Lieutenant.

Lucky Bastards An esteemed, informal group of WWII bomber crews from the Eighth Air Force in the European Theater of Operation who had completed their tour of duty.

Luftwaffe German air force.

Malarkey Without meaning; useless.

Matrix A brand of men's shoes.

Meat wagon An ambulance.

Mess hall A large room where members of the armed forces eat their meals.

Mission (religious) A series of eight consecutive Catholic masses, of which a minimum attendance at 5 are required to receive a Papal Blessing.

Monya A slang word meaning money.

Morpheus The Greek god of sleep.

Mouth organ A harmonica.

Musette bag A small, backpack-style bag used by the American military in WWII to carry extra gear.

N.U. Niagara University.

NCO club Non-commissioned officers club.

Nettleton A brand of men's shoes.

Niffles A humorous reference to the city of Niagara Falls.

Nips An ethnic slur referring to Japanese people during WWII.

Non-coms Non-commissioned officers.

Novena A series of nine successive days of special prayers or services practiced by Roman Catholics.

O.D. Olive drab.

O.T.U. Overseas Training Units.

OCS Officer Candidate School.

P.A.C. Pre-Aviation Cadet.

P.W. or **POW** Prisoner of War.

P-40 The Curtiss P-40 Warhawk is an American single-engine, single-seat, all-metal fighter and ground-attack aircraft that first flew in 1938.

Parade To stand Military Parade is when soldiers are in close formation, which restricts their movement for drilling or marching.

POE Port of Embarkation.

Post Yarns A small booklet distributed by DuPont filled with jokes and short stories intended for entertainment.

PT Physical Training.

Pup tents A small tent with room for up to two men.

Q Signal A type of code signal used in radio communications that combines three letters where the first letter is Q.

Quiz Kids A humorous term used in Technical School to refer to having to take a test.

R.C. Roman Catholic.

R.C.A.F. Royal Canadian Air Force.

R.O. Radio Operator.

R.O.G Radio Operator Gunner.

R.O.M. Radio Operator Mechanic.

R.O.M.G. Radio Operator Mechanic Gunner.

R.O.T.C. Reserve Officer Training Corps.

R.T.U. Replacement Training Unit.

Retreat A ceremony taking place in the unit area at the end of duty for that day that also pays respect to the flag, when taking place on the parade ground, the ceremony is part of the parade ceremony.

Reveille A bugle or trumpet call mostly used to wake military personnel.

Right-handers Refers to those practicing the Roman Catholic religion.

RON Remain overnight.

Ronson fluid A brand of lighter fluid.

Rooshans Reference to the Russians.

Rosary A prayer said by Catholics using a string of beads whereby each bead represents an individual prayer.

Roy Hotel A dancing establishment.

RPM Revolutions per minute.

Sad sacs An inept person based on an American comic book character created during WWII by Sgt. George Baker.

Samoans A slang word meaning money.

Sandhurst A community located on the shores of Lake Ontario in Ontario, Canada.

Sawbuck A slang word meaning money.

Semolians A slang word meaning money.

Shekels A slang word meaning money.

Shelter halves Half of a two-man tent carried by one soldier, when paired with another soldier's shelter half, creates a two-man tent.

Ship Airplanes were referred to as ships in the Army Air Corps during WWII.

Signal Corps A division of the Army responsible for communication.

SNAFU A military acronym meaning "Status Nominal: All Fucked Up."

SPAR Women's branch of the United States Coast Guard Reserve.

Spics An ethnic slur used during WWII referring to So. American people.

Stars & Stripes The U.S. military newspaper.

Stibokes A slang term for money.

Stimson's Statement A statement issued on August 6, 1945 by then Secretary of War Henry Stimson, regarding the atomic bomb and atomic energy.

Strumberries Humorous term for strawberries.

Sulfadiazine Sulfonamide antibiotic.

Suntans Summer uniform.

Ten-in-one rations A food ration used by the U.S. Army that provided one meal for 10 men.

The Ted Roy (The Roy) See Roy Hotel.

Thompson machine gun A submachine gun invented in 1918 by John T. Thompson.

Tommies British soldiers.

U.S.O. (United Service Organization) An American organization that provides entertainment for members of the military.

V-E Day Victory in Europe Day.

Victory Gardens Food gardens planted by private citizens in the U.S, U.K., Canada, and Australia during WWII to help with food production.

V-J Day Victory in Japan Day.

V-mail Refers to Victory Mail, a mail process used by the U.S. soldiers stationed abroad during WWII.

WAC Women's Army Corps branch of the U.S. Army created in 1942 and abolished in 1978.

War Bonds Debt securities designed to remove money from circulation in order to avoid inflation during the war; the bonds were issued by the government in an effort to finance military operations.

WAVE Women Accepted for Volunteer Emergency Service; part of the U.S. Naval Reserve.

Way of the Cross The Stations of the Cross, or the Way of the Cross, also known as the Way of Sorrows or the Via Crucis, refers to a series of images depicting Jesus Christ on the day of his crucifixion and accompanying prayers.

Wheel Nickname for officers.

Whitsuntide Sunday Britain and Ireland use this word to refer to the seventh Sunday of Easter, or Pentecost Sunday, which celebrates when the Holy Spirit descended upon Christ's disciples.

WREN Women's Royal Navy Service.

WWII World War II.

YAAF Yuma Army Air Force.

Yank An American soldier; also a publication.

Yardley's A brand of soap.

Youse 1940s slang for you guys, or you.

MOVIES, BOOKS, AND MUSIC

Movies

*Indicates a film mentioned in a letter that was cut in final editing.

Harvest Moon
Broadway Rhythm
The Unlimited*
Gung Ho!
Pin Up Girl
9 Girls
The Fighting Chetnicks
Trade Winds
Foreign Correspondent
The Story of Dr. Wassell
Bathing Beauty
The Desert Song
The Canterville Ghost
Step Lively
Janie
Summer Storm
Mr. Skeffington*
Home in Indiana
Dragon Seed
Kismet
Till We Meet Again*
Going My Way*
The Princess and The Pirate
The Prisoner of Zenda
How Green Was My Valley
Thirty Seconds over Tokyo
Together Again
To Have and Have Not
Human Wreckage
Music for Millions*

Frenchman's Creek
Practically Yours
A Song to Remember
Buffalo Bill
Laura
George White's Scandals
Miss Susie Slagle
The Great John L.
The Picture of Dorian Gray
Incendiary Blonde
You Came Along
Johnny Angel
State Fair
Mildred Pierce
The House on 92nd Street*
The Spanish Main*
Love Letters
Because of Him*
Objective Burma
Dear Ruth
Leave Her to Heaven
Spellbound
Janie
Wilson
Rhapsody in Blue
Uncertain Glory
Battle of China
Battle of Britain
Battle of France
None but the Lonely Heart
Goin My Way

Books
The Curious Quest
Forever Amber
The Robe
Rome Haul
Botany Bay
Without Armor
Nero Wolfe Mystery
Spy Stories
North West Passage
A Night in Bombay
The Doctors Mayo
King's Row
The Valley of Decision
Ellery Queen Mystery
Wuthering Heights

Music
Del Courtney - playing at the Blue Room in New Orleans
Dinah Shore - I didn't know about you
Fred Waring - Stardust; Time on my hands; the time is now
Wayne King - Josephine
Moonlight Sonata
Overture - The Barber of Seville
G.I. Jive
Kostelanetz - Ferde Grofe's Grand Canyon Suite
Selection from AIDA & Old Man River
T. Dorsey
Les Brown
Al Donahue & his Band

FRANK'S FELLOW SOLDIERS: MAY THEY NEVER BE FORGOTTEN

Frank's Crew:

Roger W. "Big Sundin" - Pilot: Alive and well and 95 years young at the time of publication; living in Maine with his wife Gloria; had two sons, and still attends swimming classes at the "Y" twice a week.

Robert B. "Lips" Turner - Co-Pilot: Hailed from Albany, N.Y.; he enlisted in 1942.

Herb Robinson - Bombardier: Became an accountant after the war.

Wilton H. Shackelford - Navigator: Lived in Tidewater area of lower Virginia.
John Kimpel - Waist Gunner: Unable to locate information.

Sterling Harry Shaffer - Ball Gunner: I learned from Big Sundin that Shaffer joined because his brother was killed in the war; when he was old enough, he signed up. The crew called him "Pop." He enlisted October 8, 1941. He married Nadine, lived in Manchester, Md., and died October 21, 2002.

Joe "Lobs" Ferniza - Engineer: Born in New Mexico, he enlisted in December, 1942; after the war, he lived in the San Francisco, Calif. area until his death in December of 1974, shortly after his 51st birthday. He is buried in Willamette National Cemetery in Portland, Ore.

Dan "Grasshopper" Spencer - Tail Gunner: Lived in Southern California, where he owned and operated a Guardian Fence Company; he only had one daughter, but three grandchildren; Dan died January 23, 1996, a year after organizing a 50th Anniversary Reunion for his crew in Gettysburg, PA. Only Frank and Joe didn't attend.

Frank's Fellows:

Abe Aroni	Jack Stoltz
Al Daher	Jerry Braheny
Beckford	Jerry O'Hara
Ben Baker	Jim Fahl
Bill Hughes	Jim Kucera
Bill Rollo	John Dick
Bill Siebolt	John Serway
Bob Forgit	John Staeger
Bob Walsh	Johnny Kostishack
Bob Warburton	Johnson
Bollard	Kelly
Brownell	Lew Harwick
Claude Pilcher	Mike Grailey
Cofrances	Miller
Cyril (Cy) Vaska	Moals
Daggett Morse	Ned Maloney
Dan Kelley	"Red" Olsen
Demianovitch	Richard "Dick" Perry
Denny O'Sullivan	Ron Zschau
Don O'Hara	Rudy Knitter
Dorothy O'Hara	Tommy Kilcoyn
Duttine	Trombino
Goodliffe	Weicht
Harrison	Witman
J.Robert "Bobby" Perry, Jr	Zona

ACKNOWLEDGEMENTS

Over the past four years of writing and researching, there were many people who came to my aid. I'd like to acknowledge some of them and extend my heartfelt thanks, for without them, I would never have completed this massive project.

To my friends across the pond, Art and Val Stacey from The Goldfish Club, Phil Sampinaro, James Muttons, Linda Woodward, and Beverley Abbott from the 95th Bomb Group Heritage Association, thank you for enduring my non-stop questions. To Roger, Jr. and Geralyn Sundin, thank you for welcoming me into your lives, without you, I'd never have found "Big Sundin." To Gloria and Roger, I am grateful beyond words, and love you with all my heart. Your unwavering love and support is truly what kept me going. To my readers, Lucy Smith, Amy Fischer, Susan Rechin, and Leslie Ackermann, and my preliminary editor (and niece) Joan McDonough, your time and dedication to this project is the greatest gift anyone could receive. I am forever indebted to you all.

Researching a project of this size is daunting enough, but to do it alone would be exhausting. I've been fortunate to have many helpers. To Dr. David Walborn and Bridget Quinn Walborn, RN, thank you for helping me answer all my medical-related questions. To Adam Nyhaug at the Siouxland Heritage Museums, Craig Fuller at AAIR Aviation Archaeological Investigation & Research, Russ Askey from the 95th Bomb Group in the U.S., Courtney Geerhart and her assistant Helga from Niagara Falls Local History, Heather from Gate of Heaven Cemetery, thank you for showing me the way.

Throughout my project, people have popped in and out, all contributing to moving it forward. To my friends at the Lewiston Writers' Group, your feedback was invaluable. To Gil Cohen for granting me permission to use his painting on my cover, and to Kevin Opp for designing a cover that tells my story. I'd like to thank my friend Paul Maurer and his cousin Joseph Maurer for helping me recognize what this story was truly about and Barry McAndrew, my former professor, who echoed realigning my approach. To my friend, Kim Danitz Szetela for introducing me to JuLee Brand at W. Brand Publishing, Erin, my editor, and Heidi, my indexer, without whom my father's story would not have been told.

Finally, to my friends, colleagues, loving family and, most of all, my mother, for encouraging me all these years, I am forever grateful.

SELECTED BIBLIOGRAPHY

BOOKS

Kratts, Michelle Ann, *Niagara Falls in World War II*. Charleston, SC. The History Press, 2016.

Miller, Donald L., *The Story of World War II*. New York. Simon & Schuster Paperbacks, 2006.

Oyos, Lynwood E., *Reveille for Sioux Falls: A World War II Army Air Forces Technical School Changes a South Dakota City*. The Center for Western Studies at Augustana College, 2014.

Polmar, Norman, and Thomas B. Allen, *World War II: The Encyclopedia of the War Years 1941-1945*. New York. Dover Publications, Inc.,2012.

WEBSITES

95th Bomb Group Archives, No date. https://sites.google.com/site/95thbgarchives/ The 95th Bomb Group Memorial Foundation, 2015. http://95thbg.org/ j3migr/

AAIR Aviation Archeology Investigation and Research, 2010. https://www.aviationarchaeology.com/

Air Mobility Command Museum, 2019. https://amcmuseum.org/history/world-war-ii-transport-and-troop-carrier/, https://amcmuseum.org/at-the-museum/aircraft/c-47a-skytrain/, https://amcmuseum.org/history/troop-carrier-d-day-flights/

Airplanes of the Past, 2019. https://www.airplanesofthepast.com/b17-flying-fortress-surviving-aircraft.htm

American Air Museum in Britain, 2019. http://www.americanairmuseum.com/place/25, http://www.americanairmuseum.com/unit/500

Ancestry.com, 2019. https://www.ancestry.com/

East Tennessee Veterans Memorial Association, 2019. https://etvma.org/veterans/kenneth-r-rader-9592/

Eighth Air Force Operations History; Aircraft Groups, 2019. http://www.8thafhs.com/get_one_acgroup.php?acgroup_id=11

Fulton History, 2018. http://www.fultonhistory.com/Fulton.html

The Goldfish Club, 2019. http://www.thegoldfishclub.co.uk/

Horrific WWII Statistics, 2019. http://pippaettore.com/Horrific_WWII_Statistics.html

HyperWar Foundation, The Army Air Forces in WWII, No date on site. https://www.ibiblio.org/hyperwar/AAF/VII/AAF-VII-11.html#fn1

March Field Air Museum, 2019. https://www.marchfield.org/aircraft/bomber/b-17g-flying-fortress-boeing/

Michigan 1945 Train Wreck, Michigan, North Dakota, 2019. https://www.michigannd.com/index.asp?SEC=31FFF3FA-49E9-4C7B-900A-B326700E1E44&Type=B_BASIC

National Archives; Records Relating to D Day, 2018. https://www.archives.gov/research/military/ww2/d-day, https://www.archives.gov/veterans/locate-service-members.html

National Museum of the Mighty Eighth Air Force, 2016. http://www.mightyeighth.org/bigweek/

Old Fulton NY Postcards, retrieved from http://www.fultonhistory.com/Fulton.html. 2014-2019.

Paridon, Seth, The Eighth Air Force vs. The Luftwaffe, The National World War II Museum, New Orleans, 2017. https://www.nationalww2museum.org/war/articles/eighth-air-force-vs-luftwaffe?utm_source=Facebook&utm_medium=social

The Statue of Liberty Ellis Island Foundation, Inc., 2019. https://www.libertyellisfoundation.org/

Sutterfield, Jon M., Major, USAF, AIR COMMAND AND STAFF COLLEGE AIR UNIVERSITY EIGHTH AIR FORCE BOMBING 20-25 FEBRUARY 1944: HOW LOGISTICS ENABLED "BIG WEEK" TO BE "BIG"; A Research Report, Maxwell Air Force Base, Alabama, 2000. http://citeseerx.ist.psu.edu/viewdoc/download?doi=10.1.1.733.100&rep=rep1&type=pdf

U.S. ARMY AIR CORPS RECRUITING TRAILER - WORLD WAR II Charlie Dean Archives / Archival Footage, 2012. https://www.youtube.com/watch?v=CbWKTiS207w

U.S. Army Divisions, 2019. https://www.armydivs.com/european-theater/

WW2 Research Inc., 2019. https://www.ww2research.com/locate-individual-by-army-unit/

Weather Underground, 2019. https://www.wunderground.com/history/daily/us/ny/niagara-falls/KIAG/date/1944-1-27

World War II Foundation, Facts and Figures, 2019. https://www.wwiifoundation.org/students/wwii-facts-figures/

ABOUT THE AUTHOR

Loretto M. Thompson is a marketing professional who has longed to venture beyond writing for "work" to writing for enjoyment. After co-authoring and self-publishing Thompson's Eldercare Source Book in 1997, a reference guide for adult children caring for their aging parents, she knew she was meant to write. The interim years consisted of pursuing her MBA in Marketing and completing her Doctoral coursework, throughout which time she continued her search for a compelling subject for her next writing endeavor. Upon discovering her father's WWII letters, written 70+ years prior, she knew she'd found her second book. Since 2014, she's immersed herself in typing, traveling, and researching for The Unexpected Coddiwomple, wholeheartedly committed to sharing her inspiring, funny, and fascinating story.

Loretto lives in Niagara Falls, New York in a "tiny house" nestled along the Straits of Niagara.

INDEX

Page numbers in **bold** indicate photographs

A

Abbott, Beverley, **389**, 593, 631

Air Cadets: acceptance by Aviation Cadet Examining Board, 26, 27; classification tests for, 39, 41, 42, 44, 45, 46, 48–49, 50, 51–52, 53, 55; disqualification on psycomotive tests and not making air crew, 64–65, 66; disqualification/flunking out, attitude and feelings about, 64–67, 78–79; flunking out for Pilot, refusing Air Crew in event of, 48; flunking out/casualty rate for, 41, 46; ground forces assignments for, 79, 98, 100, 122; Mental exam for, 46, 48; physical for, 42, 43, 52, 53, 58; qualifications for and advice that most will not be accepted, 41–42, 47; qualifying for, counting on, 19–20, 42, 47, 48–49; recruitment of pilots and air crew, 13–14, 42, 95; statement of facts about qualifying but being flunked out, 78–79; washed out Cadets at Sioux Falls, 86–87, 108, 149

air crews: discharge of pilots and co-pilots, 545; disqualification on psycomotive tests and not making air crew, 64–65, 66; eligibility for, 187; Infantry assignments for, 308–9; qualifying for Air Crew and accepting second choice, 62; radio operator as most-schooled man on bomber crew, 221; refusing Air Crew in event of flunking out for Pilot, 48

Air Force, U.S.: aircraft accident reports, website with copies of, 208; assignment to, 420; bombing missions, number in tour for Medium compared to Heavy bombardment, 344; Separation Centers for, 538

Air Medal, **386**, 446, 480

Air Transport Command (A.T.C.), 292, 322, 417, 446, 536, 554, 556

aircraft: accident reports, website with copies of, 208; disappearance of en route to foreign locations, 496; flying getting to your blood, 203; scenic views from, 203; transition from school to plane in radio school, 203

Aircraft Recognition training and checks, 162, 163, 164, 166, 247, 249, 252, 256, 261, 262, 263

allotments: amount of and when they should start, 78, 87; amount of when going overseas, 354, 364; applying for, setting up, and filling out forms for, 69, 71, 77, 87, 132; deduction from pay, 530; letting know when started, 128; sending money to Frank once they start, 125–26; starting to receive, 152; telling mother and Harry to not feel bad about, 90

Anniversary Reunion, 50th, 655

anoxia, 226

APO number, 398, 413, 415, 417, 425

Army Air Corps/Army Air Forces, U.S.: Age of Education, end of and surplus of trained men, 65; age of men in, 170; Air Corps equipment, turning in of, 566; attitude about being in, 78–79, 111–12, 183, 264; attitude of men in, 138; attitude of other services toward Air Corps men, 143–44; Chicken Shit in, 599; civilian pilots, program to make them service or liaison pilots, 88; classification officers, uncertainty expressed by, 65–66; close-combat training and learning to fight dirty, 51; crime of wasting cream of America for lack of incentive, 201; day-to-day outlook instead of worrying and speculating about future, development of in, 78; decisions and activity in, pace of, 202; demobilization and discharges, number of men per month and service years required for, 533, 567; fear of unknown places and associations, killing off through travel with the Army, 217–18; first Day Off since joining, 49; food for men in, quality of, 143; gratitude for being in Air Corps and not Infantry, 66, 308; habits and characteristics developed during service in, 51; hurrying everyone up and then keeping you hanging on, 78; inactivity and old Army game, 200; Infantry, priority of, 118, 309; laziness in, 24, 158, 167, 201, 224–25; lesson about can't have everything you want, 50; maturity gained through service in, 42, 50–51; number of men to be drafted/enlisted this year, 118; peace time schedule in, 524, 528; points needed for discharge, 460, 466, 501, 538, 543, 549, 550, 562, 567; recruitment of pilots and air crew for, 13–14, 42, 95; revelation about getting along so well with other fellows, 78; small units in and development of independence, 143–44; Tech Schools, no rush for men and freezing men in, 192; tests, not passing on own but points added to pass, 227; travel experiences gained through service in, 82, 83; Weather Service meteorologist applications, demand, and mixup with order, 14, 15, 16; wondering what comes next, 78; work in the Army doesn't hurt a damn bit, 220

Army Specialized Training Program (A.S.T.P.), 39, 65

Article of War, 93rd, 186

Article of War, 104th, 166

Asma, Loretto Gertrude Muldoon, 12

Asma, Mary Augusta, 12. *See also* Thompson, Mary (wife)

Augustana University, 106, 516–17

Australia, 10, 288, 315, 394, 395, 396

Aviation Archeological Investigation & Research website, 208, 484

661